ITALIAN MEDIEVAL AND RENAISSANCE STUDIES

3

ITALIAN MEDIEVAL AND RENAISSANCE STUDIES
THE UNIVERSITY OF WESTERN AUSTRALIA

3

ALISON BROWN

THE MEDICI IN FLORENCE

The exercise and language of power

LEO S. OLSCHKI EDITORE
FIRENZE

UNIVERSITY OF W. AUSTRALIA
PRESS. PERTH

In publishing this volume we wish to acknowledge a grant from The Isobel Thornley Bequest to the University of London, and the generous sponsorship by Filippo Fochi S.p.A.

ISBN 88 222 3959 8

TABLE OF CONTENTS

INTRODUCTION

Although the essays in this volume were written at different times and over a wide time-span, they are linked by two interacting themes: the practical exercise of power by the Medici family and the language and ideology of Renaissance Florence. Both involve problems of interpretation. The fascination of fifteenth-century Florence, like Augustan Rome, lies in its lack of clarity. Outwardly still a republic in institutions and ideology, it was behind its republican facade increasingly controlled by the Medici with all the same techniques that were used in late republican Rome: patronage, public shows, financial manipulation and the slow but remorseless transformation of the constitution. The purpose of these essays is to investigate some of these techniques, as well as the interplay between power and political language. Sometimes descriptive, sometimes propaganda and sometimes a constraint, this language is difficult to interpret, like a coin whose value and meaning is often very different from what is inscribed on its surface and needs a variety of skills to interpret – a knowledge of markets and exchange rates as well as of types or genres. The point is worth insisting on, if only because it seems tempting to react against an over-idealised view of Renaissance republicanism and the Golden Age by rejecting the whole tradition as a myth or fantasy.[1] This, I argue, it clearly was not. The ways in which it helped to describe

[1] For a valuable discussion of the problem, see M. M. BULLARD, *The magnificent Lorenzo de' Medici: between myth and history* in *Politics and Culture in Early Modern Europe: Essays in Honour of H. G. Koenigsberger*, ed. P. MACK and M. C. Jacob, Cambridge, Cambridge University Press, 1987, pp. 25-58, as well as Ernst Gombrich, *Renaissance and Golden Age* (1961), repr. in *Norm and Form*, London and New York, Phaidon Press, 1966: "It would not serve our purpose if the somewhat sycophantic tone of court historians, past or recent, provoked the modern historian into an attitude of sceptical debunking" (p. 31).

and mediate power, as well as to constrain it, are some of the themes discussed in these essays.

The fact that they are divided into three sections, separating the Medici from my investigation of more general themes and from review articles, should delude no one into thinking that I am committing the error of separating 'history' from language and concepts, or that because I do not discuss method, I have none. My approach to history was formed long ago by Ernst Gombrich, who taught me healthy scepticism about deterministic models of historical explanation that are divorced from the social and intellectual context, and who above all stimulated my interest in the problematic relationship between genres and representations.[2] Although it is now very fashionable for historians to apply theory to history and argue for a close relationship between texts and contexts, this approach to history has for a long time been taught at the Warburg Institute in London where I was a student, following the example of Aby Warburg and his attempt to discover what it was Renaissance people saw in the antique.[3]

The first two essays, which happen to be my earliest and my most recent writings, discuss these problems in relation to the antique image of Cosimo de' Medici as Pater Patriae. This was the title awarded to him soon after his death and inscribed on the commemorative medal struck at about the same time. Although this might alert us to the propagandistic function of the image, we have for a long time accepted uncritically its portrait of Cosimo as the *civis togatus*, the unarmed citizen. The fact that it was based largely on eulogies imitating classical epideiktic models urges caution. But instead of rejecting the portrait as 'false' or 'sycophantic', the basis of the later myth of Cosimo,[4] I argue on the contrary that the restraint and consisten-

[2] In addition to his two volumes of collected essays, *Norm and Form* (above) and *Symbolic Images*, London and New York, Phaidon Press, 1972, 1978, see E. H. GOMBRICH, *Art and Illusion*, London and New York, Phaidon Press, 1960, esp. pp. 3-30.

[3] See E. H. GOMBRICH, *Aby Warburg. An intellectual biography*, London, The Warburg Institute, 1970. There is discussion of some recent new approaches to history in *The new cultural history*, ed. with an introduction by L. HUNT, Los Angeles and London, University of California Press, 1989, pp. 1-22; L. S. KRAMER, *Literature, Criticism and Historical Imagination* (discussing Hayden White and LaCapra), *ibid.*, pp. 97-128; and J. CULLER, *On Deconstruction*, London, Routledge and Kegan Paul, 1982; cf. R. CHARTIER, *Cultural History*, tr. Oxford, Polity Press, 1988.

[4] According to A. MOLHO's reductive interpretation, *Cosimo de' Medici: Pater Patriae or Padrino?*, «Stanford Italian Review», I, 1979, pp. 5-33, esp. pp. 7-8,33. For a recent account of the importance of the republican tradition as a focus of opposition, see now M. PHILLIPS, *The Memoir of Marco Parenti*, Princeton, Princeton University Press, 1987, London, Heinemann, 1989, esp. the introduction and part. III.

cy with which humanists praised Cosimo accurately reflect contrasting attitudes to the Medici. For whereas the humanists who praised Cosimo as a Roman republican used this ideology to constrain Cosimo and later to justify their opposition to the Medici, the more extravagant eulogists were men of lower status who needed patronage from the Medici; their praise of Cosimo as Augustus or Plato's philosopher-ruler was propaganda to encourage him to play this role.

Exploration of the apparently consensual image of Cosimo reveals how ambiguous it was in being able to conceal behind its classicizing exterior a variety of meanings and intentions. The same is true of another well-established image of Cosimo as a man of wit and "salty replies", which I explore in the second paper. First developed by the bookseller Vespasiano da Bisticci and later popularized by Machiavelli, this image appears to substantiate our received picture of Cosimo as the shrewd but humane man of the people, providing us with a popular counterpart to the serious portrait of Cosimo the statesman painted by the humanists. Investigation of the literary tradition to which these jokes belong, however, raises doubts about their authenticity and value as historical evidence, as with the eulogies. But they should not be rejected any more than the eulogies since they too, I argue, served a variety of purposes. They can be read as messages which diffused his political and social wisdom to all levels of society and at the same time undermined criticism through ridicule and laughter. Thanks to their irony, they were as ambiguous as the utterances of the Delphic oracle and were just as useful in communicating with the people at large.

More light is throw on Cosimo's political behaviour by his relationship with his nephew Pierfrancesco. This and the following paper on the Guelf Party were written as a result of my research into the life of Bartolomeo Scala,[5] but they both relate directly to the wider problem of Medici power. By separating his household from Pierfrancesco's and profiting from his nephew's minority, Cosimo began the process which culminated in the alienation of Pierfrancesco and his sons from the elder branch of the family in the later fifteenth century. By then the extent of the cousins' disagreement was betrayed by their contrasting patterns of patronage, differing alliances and at-

[5] *Bartolomeo Scala, 1430-1497, Chancellor of Florence,* first published in English by Princeton University Press, Princeton, N.J. in 1979, published in a revised edition in Italian by Le Monnier, Florence, 1990.

titudes to law and order, which served as signals of political dissent in a society that lacked formal opposition groups and party programmes.

Underlying their private quarrels about money was the issue of public funding and the Medici's use of their wealth as a form of political control. Despite all that has been written on the political and social history of Renaissance Florence, following the fundamental studies of Nicolai Rubinstein, Gene Brucker, Dale and F. W. Kent and R. C. Trexler,[6] as well as recent work on the public fisc,[7] we still lack a full account of the financial basis of Medici power. Although it may be true that the Medici did not use political power to eliminate business competitors, as Richard Goldthwaite has argued,[8] they clearly did use their banking wealth to bolster their semi-official position in the state. Cosimo's attempts to reduce the wealthy Guelf Party and his use of his family's bank as its treasurer anticipate his grandson Lorenzo's activities in the field of government finance, where the boundary between the public interest and Lorenzo's private interest was becoming very indistinct. As I illustrate in the paper in this section, Lorenzo was able to win special financial favours for himself by manipulating communal institutions, exploiting his ambiguous position in the state to his own advantage.

The transition from commune to principate in Florence was accompanied by new images and ideologies that reflected cultural as well as political change, the theme of papers in the second section. Two of the most powerful of these were the image of the platonic philosopher-ruler and the image of the prophet Moses, both adopted

---

[6] N. Rubinstein, *The Government of Florence under the Medici, 1434-1494*, Oxford, Clarendon Press, 1966; G. Brucker, *The Civic World of Early Renaissance Florence*, Princeton, Princeton University Press, 1977, and *Renaissance Florence*, rev. ed., Berkeley, Los Angeles and London, University of California Press, 1983; Dale Kent, *The Rise of the Medici*, Oxford, Oxford University Press, 1978; F. W. Kent, *Household and Lineage in Renaissance Florence,* Princeton, Princeton University Press, 1977; R. C. Trexler, *Public Life in Renaissance Florence,* New York, Academic Press, 1980, discussed with other recent studies by J. M. Najemy, *Linguaggi storiografici sulla Firenze Rinascimentale,* «Rivista storica italiana», XCVII, 1985, pp. 102-159.

[7] See especially the late E. Conti's *L'imposta diretta a Firenze nel Quattrocento (1427-1494)*, Rome, Istituto Storico Italiano per il Medio Evo, 1984, and his edition of M. Palmieri, *Ricordi Fiscali (1427-1474)*, Rome, Istituto Storico Italiano per il Medio Evo, 1983, reviewed by L. Martines in «The Journal of Modern History», LX, 1988, pp. 300-311; cf. G. Ciappelli, *Il cittadino fiorentino e il fisco alla fine del Trecento e nel corso del Quattrocento: uno studio di due casi,* «Società e storia», XLVI, 1989, pp. 825-872, and Kirshner and Molho's forthcoming study of the Dowry Fund.

[8] *The Medici Bank and the World of Florentine Capitalism*, «Past and Present», CXIV, 1987, pp. 3-31.

in the later fifteenth century to justify the need for a single head of state. The image of platonic philosopher-ruler had been applied to Cosimo before his death by a few humanist eulogists, but it was only after the first translation in Latin and printing of the whole platonic opus in 1484 that it became widely diffused among the people at large to idealize not only Lorenzo's all-powerful and ill-defined position as arbiter and balance but also the growing professionalism of the governing elite. On the fall of the Medici, acknowledging Florence's need for a public head of state, "being accustomed to live with a private one", Savonarola replaced the platonic image with the biblical image of the populist but autocratic Moses, whose toughness and charisma Savonarola hoped but failed to emulate. Its relevance was not lost on Machiavelli, for whom Savonarola's Moses provided a valuable model of the leadership necessary to reconcile the contrasting trends of this transitional period.

The shift from piazza- to court-based culture, as Machiavelli defined it, is illustrated on another level by the humanist Alessandro Cortesi, who moved uneasily between Florence and Rome in search of patronage in the 1480s. His polarized view of the two cities, Florence the home of wit, cash and republicanism, Rome of boredom, pomp and curial service, suggests the emerging courtly culture was a cross-breed of urban and curial values. Far from reverting to old courtly and chivalric life-styles, the society of early modern Italy was something quite new, influenced by the political and cultural 'republicanism' of Medicean Florence as much as by revived aristocratic values.

The theme through all these essays, to which I return in the last paper in this section as well as in the review articles that follow, is the role played by classical ideology in mediating change. This paper was written for a comparative conference on classical and medieval Italian city states, for which we were asked to address the question raised by E. J. Bickerman about the patriciate/plebs relationship and the value of Italian models in explaining classical developments.[9] So

---

[9] E. J. BICKERMAN, *Some reflections on early Roman history*, «Rivista di filologia e di istruzione classica», XCVII, 1969, pp. 393-408, especially his suggestion that in ancient city states, as in medieval Italian city states, the patriciate and the plebs were "correlate terms", the class of plebs or *popolo* being created by the closure of the patriciate of established office-holders; cf. A. MOMIGLIANO, *Osservazioni sulla distinzione fra patrizi e plebei*, in *Les Origines de la République romaine*, Paris, Diffusion, Libraire Klincksieck, (Entretiens sur l'Antiquité Classique, ed. O. Reverdin, vol. XIII).

in it I discussed the late medieval communes' perception of themselves as classical city-states, reflected in their republican ideology and the apparently close parallel between their bicameral system, with separate councils and officials to represent the nobility and the *popolo*, and the Roman Senate and People model.

An initial reading of the evidence – both literary and political – confirms the accepted picture of the Italian communes' close identification with the city mentality and politics of ancient republics. A more critical re-reading of the evidence, however, betrays disquieting signs of alienation on both levels of civic consciousness – fear of urban spaces and disinterest in political participation. Even Machiavelli and Guicciardini's much-vaunted pragmatism and republicanism seem to be contradicted by their talk about role-playing and about life as a confidence game, and by their scepticism about 'so-called' liberty and equality. Alerted by this, we must examine their use of classical models very carefully. While admiring the Roman republican state for its tough laws, patriotism and concept of the public interest, both men in practice turn out to reject its dualism in favour of a tripartite system with a third party or arbiter balancing the conflicting interests of the nobles and the people. The Senate and People model was all right for Rome, Machiavelli thought, where the temporary office of Dictator acted as a third party in times of crisis, but not for factious Italian city-states. So the apparent analogy is misleading. This is partly due to the ambiguity of the republican language but also to the use made of it. Republicanism did not merely – as is sometimes suggested – supply the categories through which politics were experienced but it was also used for comment and criticism. It still had a role to play but the use made of it in the late communal period was more complicated than the usual straightforward reading suggests.

This paper, together with the review articles in the last section discussing the early modern state, Hans Baron's Renaissance and Machiavelli, bring me back to my starting point, the interplay between power and language. The books on Machiavelli discussed in the last paper illustrate the strengths and weaknesses of a purely literary approach to political texts particularly well. Analyzing Machiavelli through literary genres and treating all his writings as equally valuable because they address the same audience, Rebhorn and de Grazia produce a new, multifocused view of Machiavelli which dissolves our old rationally-constructed portrait into new shapes and surfaces.

Without a historical dimension to help us to differentiate the use made of genres or distinguish between authentic and apocryphal texts, this Machiavelli is as impressionistic as the opaque images in Plato's cave, where appearances are all that count. Yet the image usefully reminds us how ambiguous and opaque the world and language of Renaissance politics was. This is true not only of Cosimo's socratic irony and his ambivalent republican image as Pater Patriae, but it is also true of government laws like the one granting financial concessions to Lorenzo, which can be read in opposing ways. If some areas of Medicean Florence described in this volume emerge in a comparatively clear light, there are others – if my interpretation is correct – that must remain as shadowy as they were represented by the men who wrote about them at the time.

I would like to express my gratitude to Professor Vincent Moleta as editor of «Italian Medieval and Renaissance Studies» for his support and encouragement in this project, as well as to the editors of the journals and volumes in which the essays were originally published for generously allowing me to reprint them here. I am indebted to a grant from the late Isobel Thornley's Bequest to the University of London and to sponsorship in Western Australia, which together made publication possible.

THE MEDICI IN FLORENCE

1

THE HUMANIST PORTRAIT OF COSIMO DE' MEDICI, PATER PATRIAE

Honoured by his fellow-citizens as Pater Patriae of Florence and condemned by Pius II as her paramour, the figure of Cosimo de' Medici still remains enigmatic. For although he was eulogized by the humanists as *princeps* of the republic and given the title of Pater Patriae on his death, Florentine chronicles are strangely silent about his political rôle in the city and rarely mention his name after his return from exile in 1434 until his death thirty years later.

No serious attempt was made to appraise his political position in the city until the following century. The histories which were then written, however, in many ways differed little from the panegyrics of the humanists, and Machiavelli, whose description of Cosimo was the source of so much that was later written about him, actually cautioned his readers not to be surprised if in describing Cosimo's life he had "imitated those who write the lives of princes instead of those who write universal histories".[1] Despite Leonardo Bruni's dictum *aliud est historia, aliud laudatio*,[2] it is difficult to draw a clear dividing line between humanist eulogies and histories, and for this reason

This paper was originally published in the «Journal of the Warburg and Courtauld Institutes», XXIV, 1961.

[1] *Istorie fiorentine*, Florence, Le Monnier, 1888, bk. VII, p. 340: «Se io scrivendo le cose fatte da Cosimo ho imitato quelli che scrivono le vite dei principi, non quelli che scrivono le universali istorie, non ne prenda alcuno ammirazione, perché essendo stato uomo raro nella nostra città, io son stato necessitato con modo istraordinario lodarlo».

[2] In a letter to Carlo Malatesta, *Epistolae*, Florence, ed. Mehus, 1741, II, p. 112; cf. Cicero, *De Orat.*, II, XII, 51 - XV, 64.

the writings in which Cosimo was praised during his lifetime, although they made no claim to be histories, are nevertheless important as contemporary evidence of how the Florentines idealized Cosimo and interpreted his role in the republic.

These writings fall into four fairly well defined categories: prefaces to translations dedicated to Cosimo; letters of consolation; orations written for public delivery; and poetic elegies and epigrams. Each one of these types of writing is to be found in the *Collectiones Cosmianae*, a codex of writings in praise of Cosimo in the Biblioteca Laurenziana in Florence upon which this study of the humanist portrait of Cosimo is largely based.[3] It was compiled by Bartolomeo Scala, who lived in the Medici house until Cosimo's death and later became Chancellor of Florence, and was sent to Lorenzo de' Medici some time after the death of Cosimo with the following prefatory note: "I have collected, dearest Lorenzo, many writings and almost all of those I came across in which the name of Cosimo, your grandfather, father of this city, may be read. I have gathered them together in the book which I am now sending to you".[4] The collection contains prefaces and letters of famous humanists which are already well known and other less well-known and mainly unpublished letters, eulogies and poems, all of which, although important in themselves, are given in-

---

[3] MS. plut. 54, 10, a fuller account of which I should like to publish at a later date. My attention was originally drawn to this codex by Professor E. H. Gombrich, who suggested this to me as a subject for research (later submitted as a thesis for an M. A. degree in London University, 1958). I am deeply indebted and grateful to him for the unfailing help and stimulus he has given me throughout, and should like to thank him also for allowing me to read the paper on "Renaissance and Golden Age" which he delivered at the Rome Congress of Historical Sciences in 1955, published in «Journal of the Warburg and Courtauld Institutes», XXIV, 1961, pp. 306-309, now reprinted in *Norm* and *Form*, pp. 29-34. I should also like to express my deep gratitude to Prof. N. R. Rubinstein of Westfield College, London University, for all the help he has so generously given me and for the many helpful suggestions he has made; also my supervisor, Miss M. J. Tooley, Professor C. Dionisotti of Bedford College, London University, and all friends and librarians who have helped me, particularly in Florence. Finally I should like to acknowledge the large debt I owe to the Governors of Bedford College, the Italian Government and the Central Research Fund of London University, for their generous assistance.

[4] *Ibid.*, f. I*v*: "Collegi, Laurenti carissime, Scripta compluria et omnia fere in quae manus inciderunt ubi nomen COSMI Avi tui, patris huius urbis legeretur. Ea redegi in volumen quod mitto nunc ad te" (printed in «Rinascita», a. III, 1940, p. 364, and «Gior. St. Lett. Ital.», L, 1907, pp. 59-60. On Scala, see now my biography, *Bartolomeo Scala, 1430-1497, Chancellor of Florence: The Humanist as Bureaucrat,* Princeton, Princeton University Press, 1979, Italian translation, Le Monnier, Florence, 1991.

creased importance by being brought together into a memorial volume to serve, like a history, as evidence of Cosimo's greatness.[5]

The close relationship of these writings with the fifteenth-century revival of classical literature needs no emphasis, for at this time the Italian humanists were recovering and translating not only models of each of the four types of writing mentioned above, but also classical handbooks on rhetoric, teaching the concept of an epideiktic literature whose sole purpose was to please, which made possible the development of eulogistic writing in Italy.[6] Cosimo was first described in this epideiktic type of literature closely influenced by classical models, and emerged not surprisingly in classical guise, as a statesman of ancient Greece or Rome. What is far more surprising is that although the humanists possessed models of classical panegyrics to imitate (Pliny's *Panegyricon*, for instance, was discovered by Aurispa in 1433),[7] it was not until after the middle of the fifteenth century that any Florentine addressed an open panegyric to Cosimo.

Just as remarkable as their restraint was the consistency with which they praised him, for in his lifetime Cosimo was praised first as a Roman republican statesman whose greatest virtues were practical and patriotic; later as a platonic philosopher-ruler who "governing the Republic attained to philosophy and philosophizing governed the Republic"; [8] and at the same time, though by a different class of men, as a generous Maecenas and Augustan ruler. These three tradi-

---

[5] See Scala's preface, *ibid.*, f. 4: "Nam et haec paucula quae ex infinitissima suarum laudum copia delibavi illuc tetenderunt, ut ostenderem exemplis nostris non iure quidem conqueri nonnullos de vitae brevitate cum videamus aliquos eadem brevitate tot tantaque consecutos ...".

[6] See T. C. BURGESS, *Epideiktic Literature*, «Studies in Classical Philology» III, 1902, pp. 89 sqq., especially p. 139; and in general W. KROLL's article on "Rhetorik" in Pauly-Wissowa, *Real-Encyclopaedie*, Suppl. VII, pp. 1039-1138, and E. R. CURTIUS, *European Literature and the Latin Middle Ages*, New York and Evanston, Harper and Row, 1953 (first publ. Bern, 1948). It is interesting that Cicero should say (*De Orat.*, II, LXXXIV, 341) that the Romans did not use panegyrics as much as the Greeks, who wrote eulogies for reading and entertainment, since it was the recovery of Greek rather than Latin texts which provided the novel element in the fifteenth-century literary revival.

[7] R. SABBADINI, *Le scoperte dei codici latini e greci nei secoli XIV e XV*, Florence, Sansoni, 1905, I, pp. 23, 243. That the humanists were well aware of the "genus dicendi quale postulat laudatio" is shown by Bruni's letter in defence of his *Laudatio Florentinae Urbis*, closely modelled on Aristides' praise of Athens (*Epist.* ed. Mehus, II, p. 111; cf. H. BARON, *The Crisis of the Early Italian Renaissance*, Princeton, Princeton University Press, 1955, I, pp. 164 sqq.

[8] The words are those of ANGELO SEGNI to describe Donato Acciaiuoli (*Vita di D. Acciaiuoli*, ed. T. TONELLI, Florence, 1841, p. 35; see E. GARIN, *Medievo e Rinascimento*, Bari, Laterza, 1954, p. 211).

tions of praise were never confused or merged in Cosimo's lifetime, but were developed independently with notable consistency and, I think, sincerity. So while insisting on its classical and rhetorical origins, it is also necessary to stress the restraint and consistency of the humanists' portrait of Cosimo which make it possible to describe it as it developed in three different, coherent literary traditions.

Cosimo was first praised as a practical republican statesman by famous humanists like Leonardo Bruni and Poggio Bracciolini, *littérateurs* rather than politicians, whose praise of Cosimo was intimately connected with their work of recovering and translating classical texts. The earliest writing in his praise was the preface to a translation, which as a form of writing was inevitably limited both in scope and style. In Bruni's preface to his translation of ps.-Aristotle's *Economics* dealing with the administration of family affairs, which he sent to Cosimo in 1420, Cosimo is described in terms of his wealth, as head of a prosperous merchant family.[9] But by the time of his next preface to Cosimo (in 1427, accompanying his translation of Plato's *Letters*) the emphasis has changed; riches are no longer praised as "both an ornament to those who possess them and a means of practising virtue" [10] but are dismissed as "nec animi neque corporis bona", and Bruni extols instead the virtues of the mind, advising Cosimo to remember Plato's words, "especially those concerning the republic".[11]

Bruni's terms of praise were, of course, largely imposed on him by the subject of the translation he was sending to Cosimo, but one may well wonder whether his change of emphasis from private family virtues to public political virtues does not reflect Cosimo's increasing authority in the city. By the time of the next writings to be addressed to Cosimo some six or more years later, during and after his return

---

[9] MS. plut. 54, 10, f. 22, in H. BARON, *Leonardo Bruni Aretino: Humanistisch-Philosophische Schriften*, Leipzig-Berlin, Teubner, 1928, p. 120; cf. E. GARIN, *Le traduzioni umanistiche di Aristotele nel 15 sec.*, Florence, «E. Ariani» e «l'Arte della Stampa», 1951, p. 11.

[10] *Ibid.*

[11] BARON, *Schriften* cit., p. 135, quoted with abbreviations by E. GARIN in *Ricerche sulle traduzioni di Platone*, in *Medievo e Rinascimento: Studi in onore di B. Nardi*, Florence, 1955, p. 365, also in *Medievo e Rinascimento*, p. 252, n. 48. Compare Bruni's letter to Cosimo sending him Alcibiades' account of Socrates' praise of philosophy (*Epist.* ed. Mehus, II, p. 72, dated 1435 (?) by Baron, *Schriften, p. 211)*: "Sciatis, enim, quia neque pulchritudinem corporis cuiusquam quicquam aestimat neque divitias, neque honores neque cetera quae vulgus admiratur, sed ea cuncta longe spernit ac pro nichilo ducit". For a discussion of the value of wealth in this period, see H. BARON, *Franciscan Poverty and Civic Wealth*, «Speculum» XIII, 1938, p. 20.

from exile, his role as a leading republican statesman in Florence is unambiguously stated. The most important of these are Poggio Bracciolini's letters of consolation and congratulation to Cosimo on his exile and return and the prefaces of Lapo da Castiglionchio and Antonio Pacini to their translations of Plutarch's *Lives of Themistocles* and *Timoleon*, in which the events of 1433-34 in Florence are translated into terms of Greek and Roman history.

In his letter of consolation to Cosimo on his exile in 1433 Poggio likened Cosimo's fate to that of famous Romans like Furius Camillus, Scipio Africanus, Publius Rutilius and Cicero, all of whom had been exiled from their native city,[12] and when Cosimo returned to Florence a year later Poggio sent him a letter of congratulation in which he praised him as unequalled in past or present times for being recalled to his country without any initiative on his own part and, unlike Cicero, for being rewarded on his return with increased dignities: in order to recall him, he said, the supreme magistracy was of one accord; the state took up arms; the people were summoned to a meeting and came; and a plebiscite was formed "de summo imperio creando" (an event which happened only in very important and difficult times), Cosimo and his brother being recalled to Florence on the Roman cry of "pax et otium".[13]

Following closely this interpretation of Cosimo's exile and return, Lapo da Castiglionchio and Antonio Pacini also described Cosimo in a classical role in prefaces to their translation from Plutarch's *Lives*, a work engaging the attention of nearly all the leading humanists of the time, upon whom its influence must have been considerable.[14] Obvious precedents for Cosimo's return were offered by Aristides and Furius Camillus who also survived exile to return in glory to their native cities, and Lapo in his preface to the *Life of Themistocles* praised Cosimo for accepting exile as they had done and like them being recalled by his citizens as a reward for the constancy and wisdom he had shown in exile.[15] Antonio Pacini of Todi, too, praised Cosi-

[12] Laur. MS. plut. 54, 10, ff. 24*v* sqq., P. BRACCIOLINI, *Opera Omnia,* Argentinae, 1513, ff. 118*v* sqq., in English in W. SHEPHERD, *Life of Poggio Bracciolini*, Liverpool, 1802, pp. 242-253.

[13] Laur. MS. plut. 54, 10, ff. 28 sqq., *Opera Omnia,* ff. 128 sqq.

[14] For a list of its translators, see the edition sent by Campano to Francesco Piccolomini, publ. by Gallus, Rome, 1470. Vespasiano da Bisticci's letters provide evidence of the excitement the *Lives* aroused in Florence, see BNF, MS. Magl. VIII, 1390, ff. 49, 102, 103*v* and 104*v*, partly publ. by Garin, *Mcdiocvo c Rinascimento,* p. 220, n. 13.

[15] *Vitae*, Rome, 1470, f. 81*v*, dated 1434-36, by F. P. LUISO, *Studi sul Epistolario e le traduzioni di Lapo*, Florence, 1899. On Lapo see also E. GARIN, *Prosatori Latini del Quattrocen-*

mo in his preface to the *Life of Timoleon* "as if he had been born at Rome or Athens" and described how he returned from exile with the favour of all good citizens and incredible popular support, all those who had acted against him being exiled and the names of those believed to be hostile to him destroyed by the senate and the magistrates.[16]

In all these writings Cosimo was praised for defending the liberty of Florence and suffering exile in the interests of his country, for which he was rewarded by recall and honours greater than any he had previously enjoyed, a portrait of selfless patriotism which recurs in all the other writings addressed to Cosimo in this period. In the year of Poggio's Consolation to Cosimo on his exile, Carlo Marsuppini sent him and his brother Lorenzo a letter of consolation on the death of their mother, Piccarda Bueri.[17] Like the writings already discussed, this letter was also strongly influenced by classical models to which it adhered too closely to have much original literary value,[18] but it provides further evidence of the consistency with which Cosimo was being idealized in the role of a Roman republican statesman, praising him for his "gravity, skill and prudence" in governing the republic and for his patriotism in always acting in its best interests. Ambrogio Traversari, another and very important member of this early circle of Florentine humanists, also praised Cosimo for the same virtues, and in a letter to Niccolò Niccoli after Cosimo had ceased to serve on the magistracy of the Dieci mourned Cosimo's departure as a great public loss to the city, for while he had served them, he had brought nothing but good to Florence: he was generous and helped the fallen, was vigilant and industrious. "Would we had more

---

to, Milan and Naples, Ricciardi, 1952, p. 169, and VESPASIANO DA BISTICCI, *Le Vite,* ed. A. GRECO, Florence, Istituto del Rinascimento, 1970, 1976, I, pp. 581-583.

[16] *Vitae,* cit., f. 196. For Pacini, tutor to Cosimo's children, see R. WEISS, *Humanism in England during the 15th century,* Oxford, Blackwell, 1941, p. 52; V. ROSSI in *Rend. della R. Accad. dei Lincei,* Cl. sc. mor., ser. V, II, 1893, p. 37; A. ZENO, *Dissertazioni Vossiane,* Venice, 1753, I, pp. 358-360.

[17] Laur. MS. plut. 54, 10, f. 33, printed from another MS. in «Rinascita» III, 1940, pp. 389-433.

[18] See P. G. RICCI's introduction to this consolation in «Rinascita» sup. cit., p. 381. For the common literary form of the consolation, see C. FAVEZ, *La Consolation Latine-chrétienne,* Paris, 1937; E. CURTIUS, *Europ. Lit.,* pp. 80-82; also B. CALZAFERRI, *La tecnica adottata dagli umanisti bergamaschi Gasparino e Guinforti Barzizza negli scritti d'indole consolatoria,* in «Convivium», X, 1938, pp. 425-38, for the reference to which I am indebted to Miss A. de la Mare.

such citizens", he concluded, "for never was a republic more happy and prosperous".[19]

At the beginning of the next decade, in 1440, Antonio Pacini's funeral oration on the death of Lorenzo de' Medici praised Cosimo and his brother again as famous Roman statesmen who always acted to defend the liberty of their country. There is little new in Pacini's comparison of Lorenzo's humanity or liberality with that of Scipio or Caesar, but what is novel is his suggestion that if Camillus or Cicero deserved to be called Patres Patriae by the Romans, then why not Lorenzo, who like them had expelled the enemy from the gates of his city at a time of extreme danger.[20] In the very same year a similar idea was expressed by Francesco Filelfo in a letter appealing to Cosimo to recall the exiles to Florence, in which he promised Cosimo that "if you prefer to restore the exiled citizens to their patria instead of awaiting with such determination for them to restore their patria to its ancient liberty and dignity, then you will most certainly, with no opposition, be called princeps of the republic and Pater Patriae, then all will honour you, all admire you".[21] Cosimo did not recall him and so laid himself open to being vilified by Filelfo as a tyrant, upstart and evil-liver,[22] but Filelfo's letter is important because, together with Pacini's oration, it provides evidence that in rhetorical

---

[19] Laur. MS. plut. 54, 10, f. 22, in L. MEHUS, *A. Traversarii Epist. et Vita,* Florence, 1759, bk. VIII, 2 (271): "Ex quo noster Cosmus Decemviratu discessit, deteriore in loco sumus. Is enim perpetuo celebrandus, gratus civibus ita se gessit in eo magistratu ut nihil praetulisse patriae, ne salutem quidam suam, lapides ipsi clamare videantur ... atque utinam tales cives haberemus plures! Nulla umquam fuit Resp. beatior ac felicior ...'" 8 July [1432?]. The *Collectiones Cosmianae* contains many letters by Ambrogio to Cosimo. In general see also G. MERCATI, *Per una nuova edizione delle lettere di A. T.* in *Ultimi contributi alla storia degli Umanisti,* «Studi e Testi», XC, fasc. I, 1939, pp. 56-68.

[20] Florence, Bibl. Riccardiana, MS. 928, f. 4*v*: "Itaque si a romanis Camillus et M. Cicero patres patriae appellari meruerunt: quod alter armis hostes urbe propulsavit; alter consilio libertatem conservavit; quid est quod non eodem nomine Laurentium appellare debeamus qui hostes consilio et facultatibus suis iam libertate huius reip. fere labente ab ipsis portis expulit".

[21] Florence, Bibl. Laurenziana, MS. Strozz. 105, f. 18*v*: "Si malueris patriae exules cives restituere quam id pertinacius expectare ut patriam ipsi pristinae libertati dignitatique restituant, tum eris sane adversantibus nullis in republica princeps, tum pater patriae appellaberis. Tum omnes te colent, omnes admirabuntur".

[22] As in his "Commentationes de Exilio", BNF, MS. II, II, 70, partly publ. by E. GARIN in *Prosatori Latini del Quattroc.,* cit., pp. 494-516; and in *Testi rari ed inediti di Landino e Filelfo,* Florence, Fussi, 1949, pp. 43-47; see also C. ERRERA in «Archivio Storico Italiano», ser. V, V, 1890, pp. 193-227; his "Orazione in Cosmum ad Exules", Milan, Bibl. Ambrosiana, V, 10 *sup.,* see R. SABBADINI in «Giornale storico di letteratura italiana», V, 1885, pp. 162 sqq.; and his *Satyrae,* Milan, 1476, cf. MSS. Reg. lat. 1981, ff. 165-7 in the Bibl. Vaticana, Rome, and BNF, Magl. VII, 628, ff. 221-4; see also *Testi rari ed ined.,* cit., p. 40.

humanist writings Cosimo and his brother were being discussed as Patres Patriae twenty-four years before this title was formally bestowed on Cosimo.

The early humanists' idealization of Cosimo as a Roman statesman is closely related to the first humanist histories of Florence, for they were both inspired by the same patriotism and republican pride.[23] Bruni said his intention in writing his *History of Florence* was to rescue present times from the obscurity in which they lay,[24] and it was with the same cry of "let us celebrate our famous citizens like the Ancients to restore glory to our age" that Benedetto Accolti and Vespasiano da Bisticci later wrote their *Lives* of famous Italians.[25] This is the context in which Cosimo was first praised, and long before he was eulogized in his own right he was being called "another Aristides" or "another Cato" by patriotic Florentines and described as her Pater Patriae at the same time as Bruni was given the role of the Florentine Livy in the literary battle for prestige with the Ancients.[26]

The patriotism of the early humanists was inherited by their successors in Florence. By 1453 the last of this early generation had died

---

[23] See N. Rubinstein, *The beginnings of political thought in Florence*, «Journal of the Warburg and Courtauld Institutes», V, 1942, p. 198; W. K. Ferguson, *The Renaissance in Historical Thought*, Boston, Houghton Mifflin, Riverside Press, 1948, pp. 9 sqq.; and B. L. Ullman, *Leonardo Bruni and Humanist Historiography*, «Medievalia et Humanistica», IV, 1946, pp. 45-61.

[24] *Historiarum Florentini Populi Libri XII*, ed. Muratori, *R. I. S.*, XIX, pt. 3, p. 4 (preface): "... ita dum quisque vel quieti suae indulget, vel existimationi consulit, publica utilitas neglecta est et praestantissimorum virorum rerumque maximarum memoria pene obliterata. Ego autem non aetatis meae solum verum etiam supra quantum habere memoria potest, repetitam huius civitatis historiam scribere constitui". The preface was begun after 1415, see Baron, *Crisis*, pp. 144, 611, n. 14.

[25] B. Accolti, *Dialogus de praestantia virorum sui aevi* in F. Villani, *Liber de civitatis Florentiae famosis civibus*, ed. Galletti, Florence, Sansone Coen, 1847, p. 105 (preface): "Ex quo quidem accadisse ... vetustiora secula magis abundasse praestantibus viris quam aetatem nostram vel superiores proximas, quoniam veterum gesta et mores innumeri rerum Scriptores celebrarunt, ea vero quae longe postea gesta sunt magna ex parte pene interierunt ob Scriptorum inopiam ... parumper otium nactus libellum edidi, qui non solum aevi nostri sed prioris etiam mediocrem defensionem contineret", and Vespasiano da Bisticci, *Vite*, I, pp. 1 sqq. (preface): "Ho io più volte considerato meco medesimo di quanto lume sieno stati gli scrittori appresso degli antichi e de' moderni, per avere illustrate l'opere degli uomini singulari; e di molti uomini degni essere perita la fama per non c'essere chi abbia mandato a memoria delle lettere l'opere loro ... Ha la presente età fiorito in ogni facultà d'uomini singularissimi, se le vite loro fussino mandate a memoria delle lettere, come degli antichi, per esservi stati infiniti iscrittori ... Sendo stato in questa età, e avendo veduti tanti singulari uomini ... ho fatto memoria di tutti gli uomini dotti che ho conosciuti in questa età ...".

[26] See C. Landino's poem, *De Primordiis Urbis Florentinae*, in *Carmina Omnia*, ed. A. Perosa, Florence, Olschki, 1939, pp. 86-91, esp. lines 91-98.

or left Florence with the exception only of Poggio, and the vacuum they created in the Studio threatened the literary primacy which Florence had until then enjoyed in Italy.[27] The seriousness of the situation was appreciated by a small group of young citizens which included men like Donato Acciaiuoli, Alamanno Rinuccini and Andrea Alamanni, who feared the lack not merely of someone to teach them Greek, but of someone to replace the famous humanists who had brought glory to Florence by their writings. In this year Donato Acciaiuoli wrote to Jacopo Ammannati mourning the death of Marsuppini who, he said, had awoken the Latin tongue as though from a long sleep and brought it back to the light of day: "I can't see what hope there is left for young students of letters", he despaired, "for since they have lost their most learned master they have no one left to teach them",[28] and in January 1455 he wrote to his friends encouraging them to bring about a revival of letters, recalling their grief at the death of Bruni and Marsuppini, "not unaware that in their lifetime the study of letters flourished, but with their death they were almost extinguished".[29] Alamanno Rinuccini described to his son sometime later the "quandam disciplinarum perturbationem" into which his generation was thrown by the deaths of the most famous men, Leonardo, Poggio, Giannozzo, Carlo and others who flourished at the time, since there were "extremely few left from whom much could be hoped for",[30] and two years after Marsuppini's death he wrote to Andrea Alamanni exhorting him to use his influence to see that some of the learned and famous men of their day were called to the

---

[27] See A. DELLA TORRE, *Storia dell'Accademia Platonica di Firenze,* Florence, G. Carnesecchi, 1902, pp. 356 sqq. and G. CAMMELLI, *I Dotti Bizantini e le origini dell'umanesimo,* II, "Giovanni Argiropulo", Florence, Le Monnier, 1941, pp. 50 sqq.

[28] CAMMELLI, *op. cit.,* p. 51: "Quid igitur adolescentibus ingenuis et litterarum studiosis amplius sperandum sit, non video; cum amisso peritissimo duce huius disciplinae nemo relinquatur qui eos erudiat".

[29] BNF, MS. Magl. VIII, 1390, f. 92*v*: "Hec eadem nos sepe deflevimus, sepe calamitatem bonarum artium deploravimus, sepe Leonardi et Caroli aretini interitum lacrimis prosequiti sumus non ignari eorum vita vixisse studia litterarum: morte autem una cum illis pene esse extincta. Quare hortamur omnes qui id facere possunt ut ea restituant in pristinum statum et in lucem excitent nobilissimam omnium artium disciplinam iam in summo squalore summaque obscuritate nostrorum hominum constitutam ...".

[30] *Lettere ed Orazioni,* ed. V. R. GIUSTINIANI, Florence, Olschki, 1953, p. 87, dated 15 January 1473: "Nam post clarissimos viros Leonardum, Poggium, Iannoctium, Carolum et alios nonnullos qui ea tempestate floruerunt, paucissimos licet intueri de quibus magnum aliquid sperare detur ... hoc etiam vehementer obesse adolescentibus animadverti quod in quandam disciplinarum perturbationem a praeceptoribus coniecti ...".

Studio in Florence to fill the place left vacant by the death of Marsuppini.[31] When at the beginning of 1455 the Commune decided to appoint a new professor, it did so "as much for the honour as for the utility of the city", considering that "since the whole glory and magnificence of the city consists in having wise, well-lettered and worthy citizens who lead to an increase in the glory and standing of the city, there are now very many young men who would most eagerly wish to study letters if any learned and eloquent men were invited to teach publicly in Florence",[32] an indication, perhaps, of how far the political prestige of Florence was involved in this whole question. Evidently the saying of the humanists that fame and glory are dependent on letters was to some extent true, for the Florentines discovered that the early generation of humanists had indeed brought fame to Florence and on their deaths they were praised for their patriotism in restoring glory to their city.[33]

In this way the patriotic and republican literary tradition of the early humanists was handed down to their successors, and with it their tradition of eulogizing Cosimo; for in this later period Cosimo was praised like Poggio and Bruni as an exemplar of the greatness of Florence. Before Argyropoulos arrived in Florence, Alamanno Rinuccini had written to him in praise of the city to which he was coming as "inferior to none in Italy in beauty and charm",[34] and seven years after his arrival there Donato Acciaiuoli wrote a glowing eulogy of

---

[31] *Op. cit.*, pp. 10-12, dated 31 May 1455.

[32] A. GHERARDI, *Statuti della universita e studio fiorentino;* «R. Deput. di Storia Patria», VII, Florence, 1881, p. 264, no. 167, 25-26 February 1454/5: "Cum omne decus omnisque magnificentia civitatis potissime consistat et sit habere cives sapientes, licteratos ac virtutibus ornatos a quibus postmodum procedit ampliatio glorie et status civitatis prefate; hinc est quod, considerantes ... quod hac in civitate in presentiarum sunt plures ac plures adolescentes qui vehementer exoptarent dare operam litteris ... si hac in civitate conducerentur aliqui viri doctissimi et eloquentissimi qui publice legerent et docerent in facultatibus predictis; ea propter volentes tam pro honore quam etiam utilitate huius civitatis huic operi formam et modum prebere ..."; see also CAMMELLI, *op. cit.*, p. 67.

[33] See POGGIO's oration on the death of Bruni, in E. BALUZE, *Miscellaneorum*, Paris, 1678-83, III, p. 259; MARSUPPINI's "Carmina in Leonardum Aretinum" in Florence, Bibl. Laur. MS. Ashb. 1703, ff. 91-100*v*, and LANDINO's "Eulogium in Carolum Aretinum", *Carmina Omnia*, cit., pp. 103-113. Vespasiano da Bisticci attributed the fame of Florence to the writings of Bruni and Poggio (*Vitae*, cit., II, p. 208), and Pius II gave special praise to the Florentines for choosing humanists like Poggio, Bruni and Marsuppini as their chancellors (*Historia de Europa*, in *Opera*, Basle, 1571, p. 454).

[34] *Lettere ed Orazioni*, cit., p. 14, dated 4 August 1455: "nam et in urbem venies pulchritudine et amenitate italicarum nulli inferiorem", see also GARIN, *Medievo e Rinascimento*, p. 239, n. 35.

his city to Alonso da Palencia on behalf of Vespasiano da Bisticci. In this letter he told Alonso that at no time would Florence give more pleasure than at present, for the study of letters was flourishing under the teaching of Argyropoulos; her young citizens were most learned; and the city was daily made more beautiful by buildings constructed by her citizens. He continued: "Cosimo himself, a most famous man, builds now private homes, now sacred buildings, now monasteries, inside and outside the city, at such expense that they seem to equal the magnificence of ancient kings or emperors".[35] Note that Donato praises Cosimo not in his own right but for his contribution towards embellishing his *patria*, and some years later Alamanno Rinuccini when writing to Federigo of Urbino in praise of Florence included Cosimo in his list of exemplars of men who in his time were "so excellent in the different kinds of arts and disciplines that they can be compared with the ancients".[36]

It was in exactly the same context that Benedetto Accolti praised Cosimo in his *Dialogus de praestantia virorum sui aevi*, written probably about 1460.[37] For although Cosimo was given a place of undoubted supremacy among the protagonists of the *Dialogus* (which was dedicated to him) and praised more extravagantly than in any of the writings so far discussed, yet the context of the praise remains the same and Accolti, who as we have already seen wrote his book in order to defend the glory of present times, bestowed his highest praise on Cosimo by calling him "inter praeclaros veteres togatos cives pari gradu esse annumerandum, et illis forsitan merito anteponendendum".[38]

The title of Pater Patriae which was awarded to Cosimo when he died, in accordance, we are told, with the custom of the ancients

[35] BNF, MS. Magl. VIII, 1390, f. 48, in GARIN, *op. cit.*, pp. 237-238, n. 33: "Cosmus ipse clarissimus vir, nunc privatas domos, nunc sacras edes, nunc monasteria, tum in urbe tum extra urbem tot tantisque sumptibus condit, ut antiquorum vel imperatorum vel regum magnificentiam equare videantur".

[36] *Lettere ed Orazioni*, cit., pp. 104-116, esp. pp. 106, 109, dated 28 April 1473: "Mihi vero contra gloriari interdum libet quod hac aetate nasci contigerit, quae viros pene innumerabiles tulit, ita variis artium et disciplinarum generibus excellentes, ut putem etiam cum veteribus comparandos ...", etc. Cf. also the oration sent to Cosimo on the death of his son Giovanni in 1463 by Andrea Alamanni, friend of Donato Acciaiuoli and Alamanno Rinuccini, which reveals the same patriotism and republican pride (Laur. MS. plut. 54, 10, ff. 86-89), see V. ROSSI, *L'indole e gli studi di Giovanni de' Medici*, *Rend. della R. Accad. dei Lincei,* Cl. sc. mor., ser. V, II, 1893, p. 37.

[37] Dated by A. GASPARY, *Storia della Letteratura Italiana,* 1900, II, I, p. 171, n. 1.

[38] *Dialogus,* ed. Galletti, cit., p. 119.

who similarly rewarded citizens deserving well of their country, is part of exactly the same republican tradition which for the past thirty years had been praising Cosimo as though he were a statesman of Greece or Rome.[39] The orations of Donato Acciaiuoli and Alamanno Rinuccini conferring this title on Cosimo were inspired by the same republicanism as their earlier writings, for in them they praised him for his outstanding services to his *patria* and expressed the hope that in honouring him in this way they would create an exemplar to stimulate future generations to a ready defence of the liberty of Florence.[40]

In form these orations differ little from the oration of Antonio Pacini of Todi written in 1440 on the death of Cosimo's brother, which also praised Cosimo and Lorenzo for their liberality and compared their help to Florence with that for which Cicero and Camillus had been called Patres Patriae; similar, too, to Andrea Alamanni's oration of the previous year, which he wrote to be delivered before the "patres conscripti" of the senate on the death of Cosimo's son Giovanni.[41] Nor was there anything unusual in the custom of honouring Florentine citizens when they died: the deaths of both Bruni and Marsuppini were celebrated publicly by the Commune and both were awarded laurel wreaths "secondo l'antica consuetudine",[42] and other private citizens seem to have been mourned with little less ceremony when they died.[43] Cosimo himself left strict instructions

---

[39] See the opening of Donato Acciaiuoli's oration referred to below: "Quam gratae debeant esse Respublicae ... erga eos cives qui bene de sua Patria meruerunt, ex antiquorum litteris et monumentis facile intelligi licet ... Nam et in Graecia ab Atheniensibus, Thebanis, Lacedemoniis, Rodiis, et in Italia a Romanis hunc morem sic servatum fuisse accepimus, ut frequenter aliis in foro statuas, aliis sepulcra in campis, aliis aliud honoris genus ob bene gestam rem publicam ex Senatus Populique autoritate decernerent ... Vos autem, prudentissimi Cives, qui originem Florentini generis in Romanos refertis, non solum oportet, sed etiam decet in decorandis Civibus vestris, qui bene de re publica meriti sunt, maiorum vestrorum consuetudinem imitari".

[40] D. ACCIAIUOLI's oration in A. FABRONI, *Magni Cosmi Medicei Vita*, Pisa, Alexander Landi, 1789, II, pp. 260-262; E. SANTINI, *Firenze e i suoi oratori nel Quattroc.*, Milan-Palermo, Biblioteca «Saudron», 1922, p. 212; and A. SEGNI, *Vita di D.A.*, cit., p. 49; that of A. RINUCCINI (written but not delivered) in *Lettere ed Orazioni*, pp. 125-126.

[41] See note 36 above.

[42] See VESPASIANO DA BISTICCI, *Le Vite*, I, p. 498 (Life of Giannozzo Manetti); G. CAMBI's "Istorie" in Ildefonso, *Delizie degli Eruditi Toscani*, XX, 1785, pp. 245, 310-311, and D. MARZI, *La Cancelleria della Repubblica Fiorentina*, Rocca S. Casciano, Cappelli, 1910, pp. 197-198, 215-216. This comparison was suggested to me by Prof. Rubinstein.

[43] E.g. Neri Capponi, Matteo Palmieri and Donato Acciaiuoli; see B. FONTIUS, *Annales Suorum Temporum* in F. Villani, *Liber de civitatis Florentiae*, ed. GALLETTI, cit., pp. 154, 157-158.

that his death was to be celebrated with no pomp, and in the previous year he had not allowed his son's death to be celebrated in public,[44] so the decision to confer on him the title of Pater Patriae was made after long discussion in despite of Cosimo's wishes and perhaps in recompense for them.[45] Although this honour is unique in Florentine history as a reward to a private citizen for political greatness, too much importance need not be attributed to it, since it is closely paralleled by the literary honours bestowed on Bruni and Poggio when they died and owes as much as they did to the classical enthusiasm of the humanists; to their tradition of praising Cosimo as a leading republican statesman of ancient Greece or Rome the bestowal of this decree provided a natural and fitting climax.

In idealizing Cosimo as a Pater Patriae, these young *ottimati* were following the literary tradition of the earlier generation of humanists in Florence which was inspired by an ardent republican patriotism. In 1456 an event of considerable importance took place, namely the appointment of Johannes Argyropoulos to the Chair of Greek in Florence. From his lectures on Aristotle stemmed new ways of thought in Florence, and with them a new tradition of praising Cosimo; beside the old tradition of Roman republicanism grew up a new philosophic tradition which praised Cosimo in terms of his learning and wisdom.

Argyropoulos's lectures in the Florentine Studio followed a systematic course: in February 1457 he apparently lectured on the fifth book of Aristotle's *Ethics*, and in the following year on the sixth book; in November 1458 he lectured on the first three books of Aristotle's *Physics*; two years later he delivered two lectures on the *De Anima*

[44] See B. Scala's letter to Lorenzo and Giuliano on the death of Piero reporting Cosimo's dying words (BNF, MS. Magl. VIII, 1439, f. 75*v*): "Mortuum igitur me nulla funebri pompa, nulla inanitate huiusmodi proseguere ... humi non excelso aliquo monumento sepultum decorabis"; B. Coluccio, *De discordiis Florentinorum*, Florence, 1747, p. 7; and Piero de' Medici's "Ricordi" on Cosimo's death in Fabroni, *Mag. Cos. Med. Vita*, cit., II, p. 254. For Cosimo's unwillingness to allow his son's funeral to be publicly celebrated, see A. Alamanni's oration on his death, Laur., MS. plut. 54, 10, f. 89: "Sed nulla preter Pistoriensium atque Prathensium insignia ex illis ut videtis adsunt, quia pater suus Cosmus, seu reipublicae contemplans conditionem et temporum, seu invidiam more bonorum civium declinans, noluit assentiri illis populis".

[45] A Committee of Ten was appointed less than a week after Cosimo's death to discuss how to honour him, although their decision was delayed until the following March, see Florence, Arch. di Stato, (ASF), Provvisioni vol. 155, ff. 104 sqq., 261*v* sqq., partly quoted and summarized in Laur. MS. 54, 10, ff. 165-166*v* and printed in this version by Fabroni, *Mag. Cos. Med. Vita*, II, pp. 257-258. This version attributes the delay to the fear of plague which kept the Florentines outside the city, but this is not mentioned in the Provvisioni.

and by November 1462 he was lecturing on the *Mechanics*.[46] By the time of Cosimo's death, therefore, a large part of the Aristotelian corpus had been systematically expounded and discussed in Florence before a young and enthusiastic audience of her most influential citizens. Its impact on them was immediate, due partly to the novelty of a Greek teaching Greek to a Latin audience,[47] partly to Argyropoulos's new and clearer interpretation of Aristotle based on new standards of textual criticism, but most of all to the extent and comprehensiveness of the material he was expounding, for here was no *pièce d'occasion* merely, but a whole body of material which could influence both the form and content of new ways of thought.[48] It is easy to understand, therefore, why Argyropoulos's teaching influenced the way in which Cosimo's rôle in Florence was interpreted.

Evidence of this new interpretation is contained in Argyropoulos's prefaces to his translations of Aristotle (made at Cosimo's behest and dedicated to him),[49] in which Cosimo is for the first time praised consistently as a learned and virtuous Aristotelian ruler whose task of ruling has a moral rather than a practical purpose. Hitherto Cosimo had been praised for his practical virtues as a statesman and for the outward and visible signs of his political and financial power in the city, but by Argyropoulos he was praised first for his wisdom and his moral responsibility to his citizens, and only secondly for his more material achievements. The traditional ideal of the perfect ruler as a man of arms and letters was somewhat difficult to apply to a merchant banker like Cosimo, but Argyropoulos resolved this difficulty in using Aristotelian terminology to say that material possessions were necessary to achieve ideal ends, that virtues of the body and mind

---

[46] This reconstruction by CAMMELLI (*op. cit.*, pp. 86-87) is based on six surviving prefaces to Argyropoulos's courses in Florence.

[47] See, for instance, A. RINUCCINI's letter to Donato Acciaiuoli, 9 November 1456 (*Lettere ed Orazioni*, p. 18, cf. GARIN, *Medievo e Rinascimento*, p. 235): "De Argyropolo vero nostro, qui tantam lectionum suarum expectationem concitaret, quemque nos tam avide expectabamus audire, ne verbum quidem illum auditur".

[48] For Argyropoulos's translations, see E. GARIN, *Le traduzioni umanistiche di Aristotele*, cit., pp. 28-32; *Medievo e Rinascimento*, cit., p. 248; also L. FRATI, *Le traduzioni aristoteliche di G. Argiropulo*, «La Bibliofilia», XIX, 1917, pp. 1-25.

[49] See Laur. MS. plut. 54, 10, ff. 54, 56, 56*v* and 57*v*, pp. 44-49 below, and his preface In *Libros Physicorum* to Piero de' Medici, Laur. MS. plut, 84, 1, in BANDINI, *Catal. Codic. Lat.* III, 233 (unless this is an example of the "modesty topos" described by CURTIUS, *European Literature*, p. 85). All these prefaces to Cosimo are contained in the *Collectiones Cosmianae* (ff. 51*v*-50*v*, publ. in the Appendix, pp. 41-52 below) where they form a large and important part of all the material in praise of Cosimo.

were both necessary although one was subordinate to the other, in this way praising the material aspects of Cosimo's prosperity within a strictly moral framework.[50] He never forgot to teach, however, that material possessions are no more than means to achieve a moral and intellectual end which is the discovery of truth and enjoyment of happiness.

In these prefaces Cosimo was described for the first time as the undisputed head of Florence and his authority in the city sanctioned by metaphysical arguments. Whereas he had been described as one of the principal citizens of the republic or even its *de facto* leader, he had never been praised in such absolute terms as those used by Argyropoulos, as the philosopher-ruler whom "that divine Plato wished to govern cities and public affairs" and as "the very man in real form whom Aristotle described as perfectly blessed".[51] It is important, perhaps, to recall that Argyropoulos was not a Florentine nor even an Italian by birth, so that his writings do not reflect the same degree of political responsibility as those of the Florentine *ottimati* whom he taught.[52] Although the *ottimati* later idealized Cosimo's learning, they never at this time described his political power in this form.

The only other man to do so, Niccolò Tignosi, was not a Florentine either by birth but came to Florence from Foligno as a doctor. In the eulogy he sent Giovanni de' Medici "De laudibus Cosme Parentis Eius Opusculum" he described Cosimo's position in Florence in natural Aristotelian terminology as Argyropoulos had done,[53] justifying Cosimo's magnificence because it provided "potentiam ad agen-

---

[50] *Ibid.*, ff. 54, 55*v*, pp. 44-46 below. In view of the criticism of Cosimo's wealth, this was a useful argument for his defence which he himself used (see B. SCALA's *Dialogus de Consolatione* in Laur. MS., 54, 10, f. 117*v*); cf. also TIMOTEO MAFFEI's treatise *"In Magnificentiae Cos. Med. Flor. Detractores Libellus"* in LAMI, *Deliciae Eruditorum*, Florence, Gaetano Cambiagi, 1747, XII, pp. 150-168, about which see E. H. GOMBRICH, «The Early Medici as Patrons of Art» in *Italian Renaissance Studies*, ed. E. F. JACOB, London, Faber, 1960, pp. 285 sqq., now reprinted in *Norm and Form*, pp. 35-57.

[51] *Ibid.*, ff. 52, 60, pp. 214, 221 below (prefaces to ARISTOTLE's *Physics* and *Ethics*).

[52] So little did he know of Florentine tradition that when he first arrived he had to be advised by Filelfo not to criticize Bruni but to praise him because he enjoyed great esteem with the Latins; see E. LEGRAND, *Cent-dix lettres grecques de F. Filelfe*, Paris, Ernest Le Roux, 1892, pp. 92-94. Cammelli (*op. cit.*, p. 93) refers to Argyropoulos's praise of Bruni at the end of his first lecture.

[53] Laur. MS. plut. 54, 10, ff. 60*v*-73*v*. For Tignosi, see DELLA TORRE, *op. cit.*, pp. 495-500 and L. THORNDIKE, *Science and Thought in the 15th Century*, New York, Columbia University Press, 1929, pp. 161-179; also GARIN, *Medievo e Rinascimento*, p. 244, n. 39. By 1450 he was sufficiently well known to be included by Poggio as one of the interlocutors in his "Historia Tripartita" with Benedetto Accolti and Marsuppini (P. Bracciolini, *Opera*, cit., ff. 14 sqq.).

dum" and defending his authority in Florence on the analogy of the superiority of mind to matter, since states need to be directed by rulers just as workmen need direction from architects.[54] He praised Cosimo's wisdom and learning and described his intelligence and mental pre-eminence as equally natural to him "as flying is to a bird, leaping to panthers, racing to horses and savageness to lions".[55] Such was Cosimo's extraordinary authority in Florence that he directed and decided everything, "quasi gubernator omnium"; he was consulted before marriages were arranged, before buildings were constructed, before any decision of importance was taken, and was revered and respected not only by his fellow-citizens but by kings, princes and popes.[56]

Tignosi's eulogy is important for its description of the extent of Cosimo's authority in Florence, but even more for its justification of the limited republicanism which this entailed, for although he never described Cosimo as more than leader of the republic ("qui civis solum fuerit, non rex, non divinus, nec imperator"),[57] Tignosi nevertheless justified his extraordinary position there as essential for the well-being and prosperity of the state, and after attributing the

---

[54] *Ibid.*, f. 66*v* ("Manifestant haec [the palaces and temples he built] quidem illa quae antiquitus dicta sunt, scilicet, affuisse potentiam ad agendum"), ff. 61-61*v* ("Quanto quidem anima corporibus interest homoque ceteris et animata metallis, tanto corporeis ipsis sensibilibus et caducis ratio discernitur esse praestantior; hinc nostra mens quibusvis rebus anteponenda est, nam eius agitatio atque solertia suam originem celestem esse demonstrant ... Penitus prudentior sapientiorque cognoscitur qui se nobilioribus operibus iam adheret ... Si quidem res civilis cunctis facultatibus dominatur et presidet, cui honoratissime scientie subacte sunt, quibus omnibus quid agendum, a quove abstinendum mandat et ordinat. Prorsus gubernatores illius etiam ceteris praeponatur, inter quos tamen velut inter architectos et manus artificium sit comparatio. Constat igitur eos veneratione dignissimos, qui pro republica omne studium omnemque operam assidua meditatione posuerunt").

[55] *Ibid.*, ff. 67-67*v* ("Qui naturalibus et moralibus scientiis imbutus refertusque historia, omnique annali, rebus arduis et dignissimis expertus ... Nam sicut avias ad volandum, pardi ad saltum, equi ad cursum, leones ad saevitiam a natura gignuntur, hic huic homini naturalis et propria est mentis agitatio atque solertia, quibus dignissimum est quo ceteris preponatur").

[56] *Ibid.*, f. 67*v* ("Is omnium firmat animum, disponit vitam, dirigit actiones, ut quasi omnium gubernator agenda et omittenda demonstret"), f. 68 ("Nihil sui cives se recti fecisse putant si se tantum hominem non consuluisse cognoscant, vel negocia peragantur, vel aedificia construantur, vel exercitia invadantur alia, in omnibus hic consultus est. Si puelle nubant vel capiantur uxores, hic Ciclopis viri regii gravissimi atque potentissimi doctissimique Athenarum principis persimilis est, quem bicipitem pinxit Antiquitas, quod primus marem et feminam legittimo matrimonio coppularit"), f. 65*v* ("Is etiam solus habetur quem profetissimi reges metuant et venerentur, quem duces et reges patrem appellant, et summi pontifices consulunt et admirantur").

[57] *Ibid*, f. 65*v*.

fall of the Greek and Roman republics to the want of such leadership, declared that a happy republic is one in which "...the greatest and most respected citizen is he who alone (for several can rarely agree) can devote himself sedulously to considering how to increase the state and care for its interests in such a way that the whole republic will benefit by it".[58]

His description of Cosimo as the man "who rules and regulates all your inclinations as God moves the heavens" [59] was not, however, endorsed by Florentine *ottimati*, who although no less influenced by Argyropoulos's teaching, praised Cosimo merely in terms of his learning, attributing to him the wisdom of Plato's philosopher-ruler without his political power. So Donato Acciaiuoli in the preface to his *Exposition* of Argyropoulos's commentaries on the *Ethics* praised Cosimo and his son Piero for their help in bringing Argyropoulos to Florence to resolve the crisis caused by the deaths of all the older generation of Greek scholars.[60] Later, in the preface to his translation of Plutarch's *Life of Hannibal* addressed to Piero de' Medici, he again paid tribute to Cosimo's wisdom and learning, praising his study of letters and calling him the father of learned men, their patron and constant friend and helper.[61] Alamanno Rinuccini, too, largely attributed Argyropoulos's appointment in Florence to the influence of Cosimo, whose desire to encourage ability and "incredible love of letters" moved him to support the project of the young *ottimati*.[62] Yet apart from these prefaces, there seems to be little evi-

---

[58] *Ibid.*, f. 62*v* ("Quas ob res illam rempublicam esse felicem quilibet arbitratur, in qua ... inter cives is maximus est et ho [no] ratissimus qui solus (nam plures plurimum secum dissident) pro augendo servandoque statu fidelius ac santius noverit consultare, cuius animus illuc sedulo omnınoque vertitur, unde civium totiusque reipublicae salus et commodum esse potest et gloria").

[59] *Ibid.*, f. 72*v* ("In hoc uno homine spes vestre site sunt, et velut celum Deo volvitur, sic omnes vestre voluntates ab hoc uno regantur et regulentur").

[60] Venice, 1535, preface: "Verum tibi Cosmae ac Petro filio tuo haec omnia accepta referri debent; quorum opera factum est ut ex uberrimis sermonibus huius summi philosophi, antiquorum more ad cives vestros manaret doctrina", see CAMMELLI, op. cit., p. 73, n. 1.

[61] PLUTARCH, *Vitae*, Romae, Udalricus Gallus, 1470, f. 119: "... non habeo quod tibi reddam pro tantis beneficiis quae non solum a te sed etiam a Cosmo patre tuo optimo ac sapientissimo viro accepi... qui amor erga studia litterarum exercitationesque virtutum? ille erat unus doctorum hominum pater, ille patronus, ille perpetuus fautor et adiutor". This translation was finished by 1467, see GARIN, *Medievo e Rinascimento*, cit., p. 274.

[62] Letter to R. SALVIATI in 1489, *Lettere ed Orazioni*, p. 189: "primi de ipso conducendo cum Cosmo Medice agere coepimus, qui cum ingeniis faveret et incredibili amore litterarum teneretur ... illum ut publice ad philosophiam edocendam publica mercede conduceret operam dedit". Cf. also his preface, "In Vitas Niciae Crassique", to Piero de' Medici, *ibid.*, p. 23.

dence of Cosimo's responsibility for inviting Argyropoulos to Florence. Certainly, Piero as an Official of the Studio at the time was partly responsible for his ultimate appointment, but the delay in making this appointment (more than a year after the decree of the Commune, three years after Marsuppini's death) and the fact that the Medici possibly supported another candidate, Landino, suggest that Cosimo's initial enthusiasm for Argyropoulos was not as great as his promoters imply.[63]

A more vivid picture of Cosimo's learning is contained in Rinuccini's preface to his translation of Plutarch's *Consolation to Apollonius* which he sent to Cosimo after the death of his son in 1463. This preface, which at first appears to contain little original material, leaves the customary form of such writings to describe the occasion when Argyropoulos visited Cosimo and was told of his decision to read Aristotle's *Ethics*; Cosimo, who had been defending the merits of republics with great dexterity against Nicodemo Tranchedini, "quoting from Cicero from memory as if from a book", suddenly recalled the study of philosophy after the example of that wise man Cato, and said he had decided to read Aristotle's *Ethics*.[64] We are told by Vespasiano that in the year before he died Cosimo asked for the *Ethics* and Donato Acciaiuoli's *Commentary* on them to be read to him by Bartolomeo Scala,[65] and it is to Scala that we must turn for a fuller and more detailed description of the picture of Cosimo's learning suggested by Alamanno Rinuccini.

At the beginning of the year following the death of Giovanni de' Medici, Scala sent a letter of consolation to Lorenzo de' Medici describing a long conversation he had with Cosimo shortly after Giovanni's death.[66] Scala lived in the Medici house up to the time of Cosimo's death and as we have seen read to Cosimo at his request, so it is

---

[63] Cf. CAMMELLI, *op. cit.*, p. 73, n. 1, and in general pp. 69 sqq.; also DELLA TORRE, *op. cit.*, pp. 380-381, and R. MARCEL, *Marsile Ficin*, Paris, Societé d'Édition, «Les Belles Lettres», 1958, p. 190. Vespasiano da Bisticci, too, made Cosimo responsible for Argyropoulos's appointment in Florence (*Vite*, II, p. 203: "Meser Giovanni Argiropolo fu cagione Cosimo che venissi a legere in Firenze").

[64] *Lettere ed Orazioni*, pp. 59 sqq., esp. p. 62: "quinetiam, sapientis illius Catonis exemplo philosophiae studia revocans, quibus adolescens multum operae impenderas, Aristotelis *Ethica* legere instituisse dixisti ...".

[65] *Vite*, II, p. 210.

[66] Laur. MS. plut, 54, 10, ff. 104-122*v*, *sup. cit.* Scala's prefatory letter to Lorenzo is dated 1 January 1463/4 in ASF, MS. Strozz. ser. I, CXXXVI, f. 55; my biography (preface, n. 5), pp. 34-41, 268-269 (Italian edition, pp. 22-25, 185).

likely that the conversation he describes actually took place. If so, it provides a fascinating account of Cosimo's conversation and learning which corroborates Vespasiano's description of him as "tanto universale in ogni cosa che con tutti quelli che parlava aveva materia" [67] and reveals him as a man with knowledge of classical, especially Roman, literature and *exempla*, well versed in the arguments of Roman philosophies, yet at heart deeply Christian. Scala said he reported his conversation with Cosimo in order to hand down to posterity this incredible example of "divine fortitude and wisdom",[68] and after Cosimo's death he did all he could to impress his example upon his descendants, particularly Lorenzo as future 'princeps' of the republic; and when he quoted to Lorenzo Plato's words, "beatas republicas futuras cum aut illas philosophi administrunt aut ii a quibus administrantur philosophari ceperint", and urged on him the importance of study,[69] there is little doubt he had in mind the image of Cosimo whom he had begun to idealize even during his lifetime in terms of his wisdom and learning.

The difference between this ideal of the learned ruler and the ideal of the practical republican politician praised by the earlier generation is the measure to a large extent of the influence of Argyropoulos's teaching in Florence. It was he who first idealized Cosimo as the divinely inspired philosopher-ruler of Florence and from his writing and teaching developed the tradition which praised Cosimo rather as a philosopher than as a politician, a tradition summarized by Benedetto Colucci when he described how Cosimo on his deathbed "spoke of divine matters so divinely that those who were present thought of him not as a politician but much rather as a most fertile metaphysician".[70] It did not attain its most exalted form until some years later, in the writings of Ficino, but even during his lifetime Cosimo

[67] *Vite*, III, p. 56.

[68] Laur. MS. plut. 54, 10, f. 105*v*: "nephas esse duxi tantae rei memoriam divinaeque penitus et fortitudinis et sapientiae adeo rarum mirandumque exemplar, quod maxima cum utilitate posteri cognoscerent, quemadmodum quidem possem non mandare litteris".

[69] BNF, MS. Magl. VI, 166, ff. 98*v*-99*v*. The date and occasion of this letter are uncertain for it lacks a beginning and is attached to a letter to Piero de' Medici, "Ducenda ne sit uxor sapienti video" (see BROWN, *Scala*, p. 263, n. 24 (Italian edition, p. 191). See also Scala's praise of Cosimo in his letter to Lorenzo and Giuliano on the death of their father in 1469, MS. Magl. VIII, 1439, f. 73: "Me enim ut vos scitis vehementer amavit atque ego virum illum et colui et sum admiratus. Atque eam virtutem, pietatem, sapientiam semper putavi esse divinam".

[70] *De Discordiis Florentinorum*, cit., p. 8: "Tum sic divine divina commemorasse ut qui aderant non politicum sed penitus metaphysicis illum fertilissimum iudicaverant".

was being praised in a third tradition which was less restrained than either of the two earlier ones.

This tradition originated in the new school of lyric poetry founded in Florence by Carlo Marsuppini and Cristoforo Landino and praised Cosimo as a Maecenas and imperial Augustus. It was inevitable that Landino's lectures on Vergil and Horace in the Studio should have led to the development of a more extravagant form of praise, for Vergil had been the eulogist of imperial Augustus, not of republican Rome, and gradually all the themes of Augustan verse praising the return of a Golden Age, the imperial greatness of a Caesar and the generous patronage of a Maecenas were absorbed into this poetic tradition until Cosimo was praised with less restraint than before. The moment when he emerged in the role of Augustus and Maecenas and was praised for his 'imperialism' was of great significance, for it implied a transition from one ideal of political rule to another.

At first Cosimo was praised in verse as in prose for his patriotism and republicanism: Marsuppini's long poem on the death of Bruni described Cosimo in terms of his patriotism for making his city famous,[71] and Landino in his two poems "De Primordiis Urbis Florentiae" and "Ad Urbem Florentinam" praised him as "another Cato" and "another Aristides" for making Florence as great as Greece and Rome.[72] But it was not long before Landino wrote to the Medici as patrons of learning [73] and announced the arrival of another Maecenas in Tyrrhenian shores whom he encouraged the poets to praise.[74] Not surprisingly they showed little hesitation in doing so, for, as Ugolino Verino told the Medici,[75] Landino had become famous in Florence through the favour shown to him by the Medici, and it was natural for other poets to hope for similar success. Gradually all the themes used by Landino to praise the Medici were imitated by his disciples; his praise of Cosimo's "benigna manus" recurs in poems

---

[71] Florence, Bibl. Laur. MS. Ashb. 1703, f. 100.

[72] *Carmina Omnia*, p. 90, line 97, also p. 71, lines 3-4, 11-12. Cf. Ugolino Verino's poem "De laudibus Poetarum et de felicitate sui saeculi", *Flametta*, ed. Mencaraglia, Florence, Olschki, 1940, pp. 92-97, esp. lines 117-120.

[73] *Ibid.*, p. 1, esp. lines 7-8: "ipse etiam Medicis se Maecenatis in aula / sperat honoratum posse tenere locum".

[74] *Ibid.*, p. 53, lines 45-48.

[75] *Flametta*, cit., p. 44: "At nunc Landini, Medicum, Petrique favore / Cantatur tot nomen in orbe tui".

by Ugolino Verino, Gentile Becchi and Alberto Advogadri; [76] his celebration of the return of a Golden Age under the Medici in poems of Ugolino Verino, Gentile Becchi ("Gratie pro anno aureo") and Naldo Naldi.[77]

At first Cosimo was represented as the *civis togatus* who had helped his country as a private citizen,[78] but soon Naldo Naldi compared his glory to that of Augustus,[79] and his role became increasingly exalted until after his death he was deified and given a divine mission more in keeping with the epic tradition of Dante or Vergil than with the lyrical tradition of pastoral verse.[80]

But the theme underlying all these poems was the search for patronage. Landino eulogized Piero de' Medici as a "Maecenas Tyrrhenis alter in oris / Claris qui favet ingeniis",[81] Naldo Naldi praised him as the Maecenas celebrated by all the ancient poets of Rome; [82] and other aspiring poets like Francesco da Castiglione or Angelo Lapo of Faenza referred to Cosimo's patronage and openly expressed their hope of being rewarded for their verse.[83] Antonio Benevieni's

---

[76] *Carmina Omnia*, p. 117, lines 39-40; U. VERINO, *Flametta*, p. 96, line 131; G. BECCHI, "De laudibus Cosmi", Laur. MS. plut. 54, 10, ff. 135-136*v*; A. ADVOGADRI, *De Religione et Magnificentia Cosmi Medices* in LAMI, *Delizie*, cit., p. 145.

[77] *Carmina Omnia*, p. 135, lines 17-18; *Flametta*, p. 95, lines 109-110; Laur. MS. plut. 54, 10, f. 137*v*; and N. NALDI, *Elegiarum lib. III*, ed. L. Juhasz, Teubner, Leipzig, 1934, p. 71, lines 73-75.

[78] *Carmina Omnia*, p. 118, lines 43-44 ("Magnus erat Caesar sed magnus Caesar in armis / At tu Cosme tua maior in urbe toga es"), cf. G. BECCHI, Laur. MS. plut. 54, 10, f. 135, "Et qua pontificum nec regum nomina tendunt / Quod tu privato nomine Cosmus eas".

[79] *Elegiarum*, cit., p. 74, lines 197-9 ("Sic Medicis partes hinc fusum est nomen in omnes, / Ut Romae fuerat qui princeps optimus olim, / Augusti nusquam celebretur gloria maior").

[80] See A. CORSINI, *Compendium in Vitam Cosmi Medicis*, ed. Juhasz, Leipzig, 1934; U. VERINO, "Paradisus", Laur. MS. plut. 26, 21, publ. Lyons, 1679?; and G. M. FILELFO, "Cosmiados", *ibid.*, MS. plut, 34, 43, which closely resemble vernacular moral allegories like B. FORESI'S *Trionfo di Virtù* (BNF MS. Magl. VII, 816, partly publ. in Ancona, 1883, per le Nozze Pellegrini-Marchesini) and G. M. FILELFO'S poem to Cosimo, "Specchio di virtù e ornamento di questa etate" (Laur. MS. plut. 34, 43, ff. 75 sqq.).

[81] *Carmina Omnia*, p. 52, lines 17-18, dated 1454-1458 by A. Perosa (introduction, p. XLI).

[82] *Elegiarum*, p. 69, lines 113-116 ("Ut Maecenatem cuncti cecinere poetae / Quos tulit antiqui terra beata Remi").

[83] Laur. MS. plut. 54, 10, ff. 154, 155*v* (*Carm. Ill. Poet. Ital.*, III, p. 311-312, VI, pp. 123-125). Francesco of Castiglione, appointed to the Chair of Greek in Florence in 1446 through Medici influence and in 1462 made a Canon of S. Lorenzo (see CIANFOGNI, *Memorie Ist. della R. Basilica di S. Lorenzo*, Florence, Ciardetti, 1804, pp. 274-280; P. O. KRISTELLER, *Supplementum Ficinianum*, Florence, Olschki, 1937, II, p. 340; CINELLI in Florence, Bibl. Naz. MS. Magl. IX, 66, pp. 528-529), sent a consolatory letter to Cosimo on the death of Giovanni in December 1463, also in Laur. MS. plut. 54, 10, ff. 89*v* sqq.

Enkomion Cosmi, written after Cosimo's death in 1464, also adheres closely to the literary tradition of Landino's school, praising Cosimo for bringing glory, peace and quiet to his city as a *civis togatus*, and describing his help to learned men as that of a Maecenas.[84] In order to illustrate Cosimo's patronage, Benevieni cites examples of Florentines who had received help from him, among whom the names of Ficino, Scala and Landino are conspicuous.[85] Until then only famous humanists like Poggio, Bruni or Marsuppini had been cited to illustrate Cosimo's patronage of the arts, all of whom brought credit to their patron in the field of letters; the names of Ficino or Scala, on the contrary, can in these early years have brought no glory to Cosimo and are interesting as evidence of the development of patronage of a new class of men, which was most praised by those who benefited from it most.

One of these men, Marsilio Ficino, as poor and dependent on the support of a Maecenas as any of the poets, described his relationship with Cosimo as that of philosopher and prince[86] and later praised Cosimo in his most exalted form. In its origins, Ficino's idealization of Cosimo's cultural mission in Florence owed much to the ideal of the learned ruler praised by Argyropoulos and his disciples, and in a preface to Piero de' Medici in 1465 he interpreted his work of translation as the continuation of the work which Cosimo had entrusted to Argyropoulos.[87] Twenty-five years after this, however, he reinterpreted this same work as a divine mission with which he had been personally entrusted by Cosimo.[88] In the intervening years he developed his idealized account of Cosimo's patronage to him.[89]

---

84 Ed. R. Piattoli, Florence, Gonnelli e figli, 1949, pp. 30-31 ("quicquid magnificum et laude dignum edidissent, Cosmo non secus ac alteri Mecennati dedicarent"). Benevieni was taught by Landino, whom he calls "praeceptor meus, vir omnium nostre aetatis eruditissimus" (p. 31).

85 *Ibid.*, pp. 31-32.

86 "In Decem Dialogos Platonis" (1464), *Suppl. Fic.*, cit., II, pp. 103-105.

87 "In Xenocratem de Morte Platonis", *Opera Omnia*, Basle, Henricus Petri, 1576, II, p. 1965. See A. Chastel, *Marsile Ficin e l'Art.*, Geneva, E. Droz, and Lille, R. Giard, 1954, pp. 8-9; R. Marcel, *Marsile Ficin*, cit., pp. 149, 190 sqq.; and E. Garin, *Medioevo e Rinascimento*, cit., p. 284, for possible practical and political reasons governing the establishment of a Platonic academy in Florence.

88 "In Plotinum" (1490), *Opera*, II, pp. 1537-38; see D. P. Walker, *Spiritual and Demonic Magic*, London, The Warburg Institute, 1958, p. 62.

89 For the dating of the beginning of their friendship, see P. O. Kristeller, *Per la biografia di M. Ficino*, in «Civiltà Moderna» X, 1938, pp. 277-298, reprinted in *Studies in Renais-*

Cosimo's gift to Ficino in 1462 was a generous one consisting of a house in S. Egidio in Florence, a *poderetto* near Careggi and codices of Plato and Plotinus from which he was to make his translations,[90] and before Cosimo died Ficino was able to send him translations of the *Pimander* of Mercurius Trismegistus and ten *Dialogues* of Plato.[91] After Cosimo's death Ficino continued to dedicate his work to the Medici, first to Piero and then to Lorenzo, whom he praised as "the cultivator of religion and patron of philosophy" by whose help and favour he had been recalled to the great platonic misson for which Cosimo had destined him.[92] Gradually, however, the Valori family were assuming the place of the Medici as Ficino's patrons [93] and from this time Ficino began consistently to idealize the image of Cosimo as a moral exemplar. It is evident from Ficino's letters that Lorenzo's interest in him was beginning to wane and it was natural he should want to urge Lorenzo to imitate the example of the man from whom he had received so much generous help: [94] as a platonist believing in the potency of the visual image,[95] he attempted to do this by recreating the image of Cosimo with all the force of a moral exemplar. Writing to thank Amerigo Benci for his gift of Plato's *Dialogues* he said, "I think you wanted to imitate the great Cosimo in this as in many other things", and went on to explain how "the deeds of heroes inflame men to virtue more ardently and form them more ex-

---

sance Thought and Letters [I], Rome, Edizioni di Storia e Letteratura, 1956, pp. 196 sqq., and R. MARCEL, *op. cit.*, pp. 197 sqq.

[90] L. GALEOTTI, *Vita e Scritti di Ficino* in «Archivio storico italiano», n.s., X, 1859, pt. I, p. 17. DELLA TORRE, *op. cit.*, pp. 541-542; and MARCEL, *op. cit.*, p. p. 251; cf. Ficino's letter and preface to Cosimo, in *Suppl. Fic.*, II, p. 88 and *Opera*, II, p. 1836.

[91] *Opera*, II, p. 1836; *Suppl. Fic.*, II, pp. 103-105.

[92] *Opera*, II, pp 1128-1129 ("In Platonis Commentarium"): "Verum tu et religionis cultor et philosophiae patronus me revocasti".

[93] See his preface to Francesco Valori to his translation of Theophrastus, *Opera*, I, pp. 896-897 (March 1488).

[94] See the fragment of a dialogue in which Ficino pictures himself excluded from Lorenzo's banquet because of his country garb; when asked who he is, he replies "Cosmianus quidam sum, Laurenti" and denies he disturbs the "Cosmiana sacra" since he alone is missing and has been invited by Cosimo's spirit from above (*Suppl. Fic.*, I, pp. 47-48); see also his letters to Piero Leo and Pietro Dovizzi asking for financial help from Lorenzo (*ibid.*, pp. 874-875 and 912-913) and his letter to Filippo Valori defending himself against gossip that while others received much from the Medici he carried little away (*ibid.*, p. 943).

[95] "Sed puto virtutem ipsam (si quando producatur in medium) multo facilius meliusque quam verba hominum ad se cappessendam cunctos adhortaturam", *Opera*, I, p. 807; cf. E. H. GOMBRICH, *Icones Symbolicae*, «Journal of the Warburg and Courtauld Institutes» XI, 1949, pp. 163 sqq.

actly than the words of ancient philosophers disputing about ethics".[96] He told Niccolò Michelozzi that he recognized in Cosimo as an old man "not human, but heroic virtue",[97] and in a letter to Giovanni Cavalcanti said he had experienced in actual fact that philosophers are reborn from the love of heroes.[98]

To Lorenzo, Ficino used Cosimo's image to caution him against wasting time[99] and to encourage him to celebrate the Festival of SS. Cosmas and Damianus in Careggi.[100] But his most impassioned appeal to Lorenzo to imitate Cosimo is contained in a letter extolling the value of moral exemplars: as the example of Christ teaches more than the words of orators and philosophers and the example of Socrates more than the words of Aristotle, he wrote, so Lorenzo should learn from the example of "the great Cosimo, his grandfather". He broke into a glowing eulogy of Cosimo, to whom he confessed he owed as much as to Plato, for Cosimo practised every day that ideal of virtue which Plato once showed him. And emphasizing the amount of time Cosimo used to devote to the study of philosophy and how he died while reading Plato's *De Summo Bono*, he concluded: "Farewell, and just as God formed Cosimo [Cosmas] in the image of the world, so you should model yourself, as you have begun, on the image of Cosimo".[101]

Although Ficino's idealization of Cosimo in this letter owes much both to the optimate ideal of the learned ruler and to the poets' ideal of the generous patron, it alone praises him in the philosophical image of a Platonic Idea and it is in this image that Cosimo's portrait attains its most exalted form.

---

[96] *Opera*, I, p. 609 ("Imitari in hoc, sicut in plerisque aliis magnum Cosmum, ut arbitror, voluisti... Heroum opera ardentius ad virtutem inflammant, exactiusque formant, quam veterum Philosophorum de moribus disputantium verba").

[97] *Ibid.*, p. 622 ("Cognovi in eo sene non humanam virtutem sed heroicam").

[98] *Ibid.*, p. 624 ("Quoniam ut Platoni placet Heroes ex amore Deorum sunt geniti. Ego re ipsa expertus sum philosophos ex heroum amore renasci"); cf. A. CHASTEL, *op. cit.*, p. 180 and n. 5.

[99] *Ibid.*, p. 646.

[100] *Ibid.*, pp. 728, 843.

[101] *Ibid.*, pp. 648-649 ("... Multum equidem Platoni nostro debeo sed Cosmo non minus debere me fateor. Quam enim virtutum ideam Plato semel mihi monstraverat eam quotidie Cosmus agebat... Vale e sicut Deus Cosmum ad ideam mundi formavit ita te ipse quemadmodum coepisti, ad ideam Cosmi figura").

These were the three traditions in which Cosimo was praised during his lifetime and shortly after his death. One thing that emerges clearly from them is that these praises were not merely rhetorical and irresponsible extravagances intended only to flatter, but were serious in intention: if the humanists' dependence on classical literature tended to make them often imitative and insincere, it also widened their scope by teaching them of the practical function of eulogies in encouraging or dissuading certain actions, and there is no doubt that the Florentines praised Cosimo with discernment only for the virtues they liked, "ut crescat laudata virtus".[102] In the writings discussed above, some such intention is suggested both by the restraint and consistency of their portrait of Cosimo and by the extent to which they reflect their authors' own political attitude to him.

First, their restraint and consistency. It is remarkable that Cosimo was praised by three generations in three different literary traditions. The earliest generation of writers were humanists of international repute, more interested in literature than politics, and all well acquainted with the whole field of classical writing. If because of this their praise of Cosimo tended to be rhetorical, they never sent him an open panegyric or wrote his life as they might well have done. Non-Florentine humanists like Filelfo or Panormita who had once sought Cosimo's patronage (as early as 1426 Panormita had praised Cosimo as a Maecenas of poets) settled in the courts of Milan and Naples where they wrote epic praises and lives of their patrons,[103] but in Florence the humanists praised Cosimo with restraint and never as more than the leading citizen of a free republic.

The second generation of writers were socially a more coherent group, for they all belonged to the great optimate families of Flor-

[102] "Est tamen pervetus sententia ut crescat laudata virtus", POGGIO BRACCIOLINI, "Oratio ad Nicolum V", *Opera*, cit., p. 109. For the practical purpose of eulogy, see Aristotle, *Rhetoric*, I, 9, 35; the pseudo-Ciceronian *Rhet. ad Heren.*, III, 4, 7; cf. Ficino's words to Lorenzo (*Opera*, I, p. 655), "hactenus semper te ita laudavi ut admonerem similiter atque exhortarer".

[103] For Panormita, see V. ROSSI, *Il Quattrocento*, Milan, Vallardi, 1956, pp. 128, 267, his poem to Cosimo is in *Carm. Ill. Poet. Ital.*, II, p. 111; for FILELFO's *Sphortiados*, see C. DE ROSMINI, *Vita di F. F.*, Milan, 1808, II, pp. 158 sqq., 175; A. NOVARA, *Un poema latino del Quattroc.: La Sforziade di F. F.*, 1879. In 1454 Filelfo sent Piero de' Medici the first four books of the *Sphortiados* (DELLA TORRE, *op. cit.*, p. 367, n. 4), and later his son wrote a "Cosmiados" and a "Laurenziados" (Laur. MS. plut. 34, 43 and B. L. Harl. MS. 2522, partly printed in *Carm. Ill. Poet. Ital.*, VII, pp. 166-168) to regain Medici favour; cf. Lorenzo de' Medici's letter to Filelfo in 1474, ASF. MS. Strozz. ser. I, CXXXVII, 141, the reference to which I owe to Prof. Rubinstein.

ence who played a pre-eminent part in the political and economic life of the city. The restraint of their praise of Cosimo is perhaps even more remarkable, for at a time when Cosimo's power in the city was undoubtedly greater than it had been in earlier years they praised him still only in terms of his selfless patriotism and republicanism, and although they could, like Argyropoulos and Niccolò Tignosi, have exalted him as the Aristotelian ruler whose power was sanctioned by metaphysical arguments, they never did so and only commended his encouragement of learning in Florence.

The third tradition which eulogized him extravagantly as a Maecenas and Augustus was not developed at all until after 1454, and then not by the *ottimati* but by a different social class of poverty-stricken poets in whose interest it was to extol the political power of the Medici, since it was from them that they received what wealth and position they enjoyed.

This is the second striking feature of the portrait, that far from being detached it was directly affected and influenced by the humanists' own political and social preoccupations in the city – in a word, it was *engagé*. Of the three generations the first was the least involved politically or socially in the Florentine scene and their praise of Cosimo is correspondingly the more detached. Bruni and Poggio were both papal secretaries before settling in Florence and enjoyed fame and standing throughout Europe in the field of letters. Bruni, who became Chancellor of Florence in 1427, addressed only two of his writings to the Medici, for which it is unlikely that he received any special help or protection; most of his early works he sent to Niccolò Niccoli, his later ones to such patrons as Pope Eugenius IV, Alfonso of Aragon, or the Duke of Gloucester. Only to one family did he express devoted service, and as a Papal Secretary and Chancellor of Florence he was in any case able to exercise some small patronage himself in the form of recommendations to offices.[104] Poggio, whose complaints of poverty were constant and who appealed openly for the patronage of men like Alfonso of Aragon, the Marquis of Mantua or Cardinal Beaufort, nevertheless died a rich man and although in debt to the Medici for small sums in 1430-33 appears by 1457 to

---

[104] For his relationship with the Malatesta, see *Epist.* ed. Mehus, I, pp. 82-83, II, pp. 51-52 (cf. *Schriften*, p. 5); there are allusions to his patronage in *Epist.*, ed. Mehus, I, pp. 45, 68-69; II, p. 187, etc.

be in their credit for as much as 2,600 florins.[105] Both Ambrogio Traversari (in 1431 General of the Camaldulensian Order) and Niccolò Niccoli were helped by Cosimo's money, but this probably implied supplying them with ready money to buy books, and although Cosimo was owed 344 florins by Niccolò in 1433 and undertook to pay all his debts on his death, he did so in return for Niccolò's library which was to be placed in S. Marco with a plaque to commemorate the generosity of Cosimo as well as that of its original owner.[106] Probably only Carlo Marsuppini of this generation benefited directly from Medici patronage, and when he died the Medici were privately responsible for having his epitaph written.[107] The help Cosimo was able to give these humanists was that of laying open to them the facilities of his bank with its supplies of ready money, its courier-system between Florence and Rome, and its agents scattered throughout Europe who could help to recover newly discovered manuscripts; [108] his relationship with them was probably that of a friend who shared common literary interests rather than that of a patron.

Their writings were nevertheless involved in Florentine politics to the extent that as Chancellors of Florence, Bruni and Poggio, at least, had to act as her official apologists: [109] from this point of view praise of Cosimo as an exemplar of the present glory of Florence was

---

[105] See letters printed in *Spicilegium Romanum,* X, 1844, pp. 241, 250, 265, 300, 342, etc.; E. WALSER, *Poggius Florentinus: Leben und Werke*, Leipzig-Berlin, Teubner, 1914, pp. 344, 347, 413; cf. VESPASIANO DA BISTICCI (*Le Vite*, I, p. 548), that by the time of Poggio's death "aveva denari contanti non picola somma, possessioni, assai case in Firenze, bellissime masserizie e molti libri et degni, e per questo non aveva bisogno di guadagnare". Poggio sent his translation of XENOPHON's *Cyropaedia* to Alfonso of Aragon in the open hope of reward (Laur. MS. plut. 45, 16, see BANDINI, *Cat. Cod. Lat.*, II, 352 and BALUZE, *Misc.*, III, p. 154 and letters above).

[106] See G. ZIPPEL, *Niccolò Niccoli*, Florence, Fratelli Bocca, 1890, pp. 66-68; for Cosimo's help to Ambrogio in buying books, see letters in *A. T., Epist. et Vita,* ed. Mehus, cit., XI, 17 (383), XIV, 28 (557) and *Epist.*, ed. MARTÈNE AND DURAND, *Vet. Script. et Monum.*, III, 1724, XII, 9.

[107] G. ZIPPEL, *Carlo Marsuppini d'Arezzo*, Trento, 1897, and A. LAZZARI, *Ugolino e Michele Verino*, Turin, C. Clausen, 1897, p. 14, n. 3. For Marsuppini's friendship with the Medici, see also Antonio Aglio's Consolation on the death of Cosimo (Laur. MS. plut. 43, 10, f. 132: "Carolum Aretinum virum egregium in primisque eruditum, quantum hic dilexit quoad etiam provexit Fluentiae nullus ignorat") and Vespasiano, *Le Vite*, I, pp. 591-594.

[108] See Poggio's letters asking for the help of the Medici in sending him CICERO's *Orations* and procuring LIVY's *Decades* in Denmark through their agent Gherardo Bueri (*Epist.*, ed. TONELLI, I, pp. 153, 104; cf. B. L. ULLMAN, *Studies in the Italian Renaissance,* Rome, Edizioni di Storia e Letteratura, 1955, p. 64).

[109] Cf. G. ZIPPEL, *Lorenzo Valla e le origini della storiografia umanistica a Venezia*, «Rinascimento», VII, 1956, pp. 127-128.

entirely consistent with the patriotism their office required of them. Moreover, their praise of Cosimo had more immediate political importance as evidence of their support of the Medici faction during the years of political change from 1433 to 1434. Poggio, before sending Cosimo his letter of consolation on his exile in 1433, wrote to Niccolò Niccoli for his approval, and having received it wrote another letter to Niccolò in which he referred to what must surely be the political situation in Florence in 1433: "You already know", he wrote, "what state our affairs are in, but they could not be worse than they are. Unless you look ahead as quickly as possible, this storm will break upon you, or rather bear you away, for these counsels are the work of him who has always hated peace".[110]

Even before these years it was evident, at least to Filelfo, that Bruni, Poggio and Marsuppini were supporters of the Medici and he attributed his displacement in the Studio by Marsuppini in 1431 to their influence. Marsuppini retreated from Florence with the Medici in 1433 and when he returned in the following year, Filelfo was once more displaced from his Chair and left Florence for good.[111] The fact that he appealed simultaneously to the Signoria of Florence and to Cosimo to be allowed to return from exile in 1440 suggests that there was no doubt in his own mind who was responsible for preventing his return to Florence.[112] In a situation such as this, praise of the prosperous state of Florence and the greatness of Cosimo as a republican statesman indicated approval of the Medici régime as clearly as criticism of Cosimo as a libertine and tyrant suggested opposition to it.[113]

The political significance of the writings of the second generation

---

[110] *Epist.*, ed. TONELLI, II, bk. V, 4, p. 13, 21 January [1433]: "Res nostrae quo in loco sint iam scio notum esse tibi: sed peiore quam sint esse non possunt. Nisi provideritis, quamprimum in vos haec tempestas defluet, vel potius ruet; eius enim artificis haec sunt consilia qui pacem semper odit". His letter asking for Niccolò's approval, *ibid.*, bk. V, 3, pp. 11-12, 9 January.

[111] G. ZIPPEL, *Il Filelfo a Firenze*, Rome, 1899, p. 26 sqq., 40.

[112] Laur. MS. Strozz. 105, cit., f. 4: "Exhortatio ad Florentinos de revocandis in urbem optimatibus exulibus"; f. 15*v*: the same to Cosimo, "qua eumdem ortatur ut et se optimatibusque exulibus reconciliet". For his other numerous appeals to the Medici to be allowed to return, see ROSMINI, *Vita di F. F.* cit., pp. 31, 79-80; A. BENADDUCI, *Bibliografia di F. F.* in «Atti e Memorie d. R. Deputazione di St. Pat. prov. d. Marche», 1901; A. FABRONI, *Mag. Cos. med. Vita*, II, p. 115.

[113] See FILELFO, *Comment. de esilio*, cit., f. 25*v*; cf. Pius II's *Commentarii* (*Memoirs of a Renaissance Pope: The Commentaries of Pius II*, transl. by F. A. GRAGG, Smith College Studies in History, Northampton, Mass., 1960, p. 108, January-May 1459).

is undoubtedly much greater, for their authors were all members of the prosperous, politically responsible optimate class which was closely involved in the political and economic life of Florence and whose attitude to Cosimo would be all-important in determining whether the Medici régime would be established there or not. In 1448 Donato Acciaiuoli had written to a friend in bitter criticism of the government by whom, he said, the citizens were being beguiled and misled,[114] and even twenty years later Lorenzo was apparently still uncertain of his attitude to the régime.[115] Alamanno Rinuccini, like Donato a member of one of the leading optimate families of Florence, in his *Dialogus de Libertate* (composed in 1479) wrote a trenchant criticism of Lorenzo, "who exercises the tyranny *which he inherited from his grandfather* much more savagely and insolently than either his father or grandfather had done" (the italics are mine).[116] So the fact that in the middle years of this period between 1454 and 1464 Cosimo was praised by them as a republican statesman and protector of learning is of considerable importance. Although this evidence is too limited to be considered representative of all the *ottimati*, its consistency and the absence of other evidence to the contrary at least suggests that it was to some extent typical of them and throws interesting light on their attitude to Cosimo in this period of changing power.

Of all the writings in praise of Cosimo the most prejudiced were those of the poets. The practical purpose of their praise of Cosimo's patronage is made all too apparent by the fact that every poet to praise him in this way did in fact seek patronage from the Medici family, and although they were far less involved in Florentine politics than the *ottimati* discussed above, it is surely no coincidence that Cosimo was first praised as an imperial Augustus and Maecenas by men of

[114] BNF, MS. Magl. VII, 1390, f. 98 (6 July 1448), partly printed in C. Gutkind, *Cosimo de' Medici,* Oxford, Clarendon Press, 1938, p. 134, n. 1; cf. E. Garin, *Medievo e Rinascimento,* p. 217, n. 9 ("quis est enim tam rudis ingenii qui iam non modo intelligat sed et manu teneat hos nostros cives qui in republica principatum obtinent moliri semper bella ex bellis et falsa quadam spe futurae concordiae depasci populum florentinum. O miseram patriam...").

[115] See Gentile Becchi's letter to Lorenzo from Rome, 28 March, 1470/1 (ASF, MAP, fil. 61, 28): "Se voi mi dicessi che temi tu del nostro Donato, teme sforzatamente in dimostrarsi et uscendo per boschi incogniti non si smarisca. Più honore credo vi farà che quest'altri".

[116] Printed in «Atti e Memorie dell'Accademia ... La Colombaria», XXII, n.s., VIII, 1957, p. 301: "qui acceptam ab avo tyrannidem acerbius multo quam pater aut avus multoque insolentius exercet".

humble social origin who were entirely dependent on the Medici for wealth and honours.

Landino, who had been the first to eulogize the patronage of the Medici, was one of the first to confess his humble origins and the debt he personally owed to them. His first poems in their praise are closely related to his desire for patronage, for it was during the years 1454-58 when he was hoping for a public lectureship in the Studio that he reorganized the 'Xandra' which he had previously collected for Leon Battista Alberti and sent it instead to Piero de' Medici.[117] Although disappointed in his hope of being appointed to teach philosophy in 1456, he was elected to the Chair of Poetry and Oratory in the Studio in January 1458,[118] but his search for patronage continued and on the death of Poggio in the following May he sent the Medici a long elegy in his praise, which was accompanied by a letter to Piero hinting of his desire to be made a secretary of the Commune.[119] What was implicit in this letter was made explicit by Landino some six or seven years later in a letter to Lorenzo,[120] and although he did not receive the hoped-for appointment his appeal was not entirely in vain, for he was appointed Secretary of the Parte Guelfa in 1467, probably in the place of Bartolomeo Scala when he became Chancellor.[121]

The vacancies in the Chancery in 1465-66 aroused great interest among all those in search of patronage in Florence. Another eulogist of the Medici who applied for a post there was Ugolino Verino, who apparently wrote to Francesco Tranchedini expressing his desire to be elected one of those "qui apud secretarium istiusce reipublicae designandi sunt".[122] Although Francesco begged his father, Nicodemo

---

[117] *Carmina Omnia*, cit., introd. pp. XXXVII-XLIV; as Prof. Dionisotti suggests, this is significant evidence of the changing political power of these two families at this time. See also R. MARCEL, *Marsile Ficin,*, pp. 191-194.

[118] ROSSI, *Il Quattrocento*, p. 334, and in general BANDINI, *Specimen Liter. Flor. sec. XV*, Florence, 1747-51; G. BOTTIGLIONE, *La Lirica latina in Firenze nella 2ª metà del sec. XV*, Pisa, Nistri, 1913, pp. 11-32; MARZI, *La Cancelleria*, pp. 239-41; and E. GARIN, *Testi Ined. e rari*, introduction, pp. 3-11.

[119] *Carmina Omnia*, pp. 123 sqq. and 187-190, letter dated 7 May 1458.

[120] BANDINI, *Collectio Veterum Aliquot Monumentorum*, Arezzo, M. Bellotti, 1752, p. I, dated by Marzi (*op. cit.*, p. 240, n. 3) 1465-1466, not 1475 as Bandini suggests.

[121] MARZI, *op. cit.*, p. 251, and BANDINI, *Specimen*, cit., II, pp. 102-103.

[122] Florence, Bibl. Riccard., MS. 834, f. 179 (14 May 1465): "Cupet is [Ugolino Verino] abs te magnifico et prestantissimo viro Petro Medici commendari et opera vestrum alterum eligi eorum qui apud secretarium istiusce reipublice designandi sunt ut plane indicant eius littere ad me nuper scripte ...".

Tranchedini, to use his influence with Piero and those "by whom these things are decided",[123] Ugolino was unsuccessful in obtaining the desired position and after being employed as a notary in a series of different offices, became Notary of the Otto di Balia in 1481.[124] Two years later he apparently tried in vain to secure another office in the Chancery and wrote bitterly of being neglected by Lorenzo, his patron, who, he said, "Omnibus ... quidem largitur honores / Uni, quod doleo, defuit ille mihi".[125]

Naldo Naldi, too, was a hopeful applicant for an office in the Chancery, and in 1466 after the Chancellor had been appointed Nicodemo Tranchedini wrote to Piero de' Medici on Naldo's behalf asking for him to be sent "into the place as a coadjutor of our messer Bartolomeo or elsewhere as you think best".[126] But Naldo was no more successful than Ugolino Verino had been; in 1476 he was to be found asking Lorenzo to recommend him to the tax-collectors,[127] and two years later appealing for the custodianship of the fortress of Corzana.[128]

Yet another was Peregrino Aglio, a Florentine by birth who returned to his native city in 1463. Even before leaving Ferrara where he had been living he wrote to Ficino asking him to commend him to the Medici,[129] and as soon as he arrived in Florence addressed him appeals for help to the Medici themselves, supporting them with verse in their praise: in October 1463 he wrote to Lorenzo of his

---

[123] *Ibid.*: "... Te obsecro igitur elabores cum apud Petrum Medicem tum apud eos a quibus res ipsa decernenda est itaque efficias ut commendacionem hanc fraternam esse intelligat".

[124] LAZZARI, *Ugolino e Michele Verino*, cit., pp. 79-91; cf. KRISTELLER, *Suppl. Fic.*, II, p. 354.

[125] LAZZARI, *op. cit.*, p. 69.

[126] ASF, MAP, fil. 16, 197 (23 July 1466): "... Me scorday questa matina recomandarvi el vostro o nostro Naldo che ve piacesse inviarlo in palazo per coadiutore del nostro M. Bartolommeo, o altrove como meglio ve paresse".

[127] *Ibid.*, MAP, fil. 33, 150 (27 February 1476), see Della Torre, *op. cit.*, p. 674.

[128] *Ibid.*, MAP, fil. 36, 428: "Tecum coram locutus sum clarissime Laurenti de me corzane arcis custode statuendo. Sed cum tu mihi prudenter ut soles omnia respondisses plures esse qui hoc idem peterent, tamen non fuit consilium supersedere a petendo, cum certo sciam te multo magis ratione quam aut benivolentia aut gratia cuiusquam moveri ... Quare te per patrem per avum tuum quos quidem colimus colemusque semper memoria sempiternas vehementer te rogo ut subvenias huic mee necessitati". In 1484 Naldi became Professor of the Humanities in the Florentine Studio and in 1497 Professor of Rhetoric and Poetry (DELLA TORRE, *op. cit.*, p. 674, and in general, *ibid.*, pp. 668-681; BOTTIGLIONE, *op. cit.*, pp. 45 sqq.; LAZZARI, *op. cit.*, pp. 41-43; and KRISTELLER, *Suppl. Fic.*, II, p. 328).

[129] F. FLAMINI, *Peregrino Allio*, Pisa, 1893 (Nozze Cassin-d'Ancona), p. 17.

devotion to him and his grief at his absence in Pisa,[130] a month later sending him a poem on the death of Giovanni de' Medici; [131] at the beginning of the next year he commended himself to Nicodemo Tranchedini and sent him a poem which ended in praise of Cosimo, "mundi ornamentum"; [132] in April he asked Lorenzo to commend his father's cause to the President in the Mercanzia,[133] and in the following November wrote to him with renewed insistence as the only person who could help him in his necessity, asking him to buy books from him for twenty-five florins.[134] Cosimo's death provided the occasion for a lengthy poem in praise of Piero de' Medici,[135] and in April 1465 he wrote to Piero about the vacancies in the Chancery for which he was yet another hopeful applicant. He told Piero that Lorenzo had already written to him about the substitution of the new Chancellor and his two assistants and had suggested that if he would like one of these offices at 100 florins a year he should write at once to Piero; he expressed his gratitude for their interest in him and said he was most willing to follow their advice and patronage.[136] His gratitude seems to have been premature, for he was not given an office in the Chancery, but by this time he was at the court of Paul II at Rome, where his search for patronage seems to have met with better success.[137] A year later, however, in 1467, he was still appealing to Lorenzo for his favour, nor is there any evidence that he ever received from him the help he sought.[138]

---

[130] ASF, MAP, fil. 20, 107 (29 October 1463), Flamini, *op. cit.*, pp. 18-19; cf. also Florence, Bibl. Riccard., Fond. Moreni, Racc. Frullana, no. 38, letter to Lorenzo dated 24 November 1463.

[131] *Ibid.*, MAP, fil. 21, 6, dated 1 December 1463: "Mitto ad te carmen quod in funere Johannis vestri nescio quo vento impulsus festinato composui". This poem is probably that in *Carm. Ill. Poet. Ital.*, I, pp. 125-127.

[132] Florence, Bibl. Riccard., MS. 834, f. 109; Flamini, *op. cit.*, pp. 37-38; cf. *Carm. Ill. Poet. Ital.*, I, p. 128.

[133] ASF, MAP, fil. 21, 10 (30 April 1464), Della Torre, *op. cit.*, p. 553, n. 1.

[134] Flamini, *op. cit.*, pp. 19-20.

[135] *Carm. Ill. Poet. Ital.*, I, pp. 119-123.

[136] ASF, MAP, fil. 16, 177 (Rome, 20 April 1465): "Lorenzo vostro a questi di me scrisse una lettera sopra la substitutione del nuovo Cancielliere et de due coadiutori, de quali se io volevo essere l'uno con C flor. di salario lanno, me dicievi debba avisare ... Et prima cognosciuto et in altro et in questa faccienda maxime el vostro paterno amore verso di me ringratio quanto posso la benignita vostra che vi sete degnato pensare di me come di figliuolo per aiutare la mia poverta senza aviamento et sono parato sequitare el consiglio et patrocinio vostro"; see Flamini, *op. cit.*, p. 21.

[137] He was given a priorate in the diocese of Siena (Muratori, *R. I. S.*, III, pt. 16, p. 79, line 60 (*Le Vite di Paolo II*).

[138] ASF, MAP, fil. 20, 307 (Rome, 21 April 1467), Flamini, pp. 22-23.

The office of Chancellor for which there had been so much competition was given to Bartolomeo Scala, "benché non degno di tanto honore", as the Rinuccini commented in their *Diario*.[139] It seems probable that his election was a foregone conclusion, for he had been Chancellor of the Parte Guelfa since 1461 and lived in the Medici household; according to the Rinuccini *Diario* he was actually elected on April 24 although he had begun to write letters for the Republic four days earlier,[140] and in the following year his election was confirmed for ten years. Scala had been a eulogist of the Medici, like Landino, and in his poem "Ad Poetas ut canant Cosmum Medicem" had taken up Landino's cry of "Ergo, agite o vates, sublime insurgite versu".[141] His origins, too, were as humble as those of Landino and his dependence on the Medici family as great; the Medici, he proclaimed, had given life to him and fashioned him "ex humili materia et rudi" and the *ottimati* with some reason criticized the appointment of this "son of a miller from Colle" as their Chancellor.[142]

The patronage of the Medici was not confined to political offices but extended to the University and the Church. The re-establishment of the University of Pisa in 1475 besides bringing great glory to Florence also brought the Medici increased powers of patronage. One of the first to be rewarded with a professorship there was Niccolò Tignosi whose "Opusculum de laudibus Cosmi" had already provided convincing evidence of his devotion to the Medici, and he duly expressed his gratitude to Lorenzo in the dedication to him of his translation of Aristotle's *De Anima*.[143] Another teacher to be appointed by Lorenzo in Pisa was Lorenzo Lippi of Colle, who had already dedicated translations to Cosimo and Piero and sent Lorenzo three epigrams in praise of the three generations of the Medici, his patrons.[144]

[139] *Ricordi storici,* ed. Aiazzi, Florence, 1840, p. XCVI.

[140] ASF, Sig. Missive, XLV (20 April 1465 - 15 December 1468), the originals of which are contained in Munich, Staatsbibl., MS. Clm. 10781, ff. 101 sqq.

[141] Laur. MS. plut. 54, 10, f. 135, *Carm. Ill. Poet. Ital.,* VIII, p. 489.

[142] "Me certe ex humili materia et rudi / Informique luto alta arte Promethei" (Laur. MS. plut. 54, 10, f. 164, *Carm. Ill. Poet. Ital.,* VIII, p. 491); see F. GUICCIARDINI, *Storie fiorentine,* Bari, Laterza, 1931, p. 79: "messer Bartolomeo Scala, quale, figliuolo di uno mugnaio da Colle, sendo cancelliere maggiore della signoria, fu fatto gonfaloniere di giustizia con grandissimo scoppio e sdegno di tutti gli uomini da bene").

[143] Laur. MS. plut. 82, 17, published in Florence 1551.

[144] He dedicated his translation of ISOCRATES *Oration* to Cosimo (Laur. MS. plut. 47, 17, f. 100) and PLATO's *Ion* to Piero (see GARIN, *Ricerche sulle traduzioni di Platone*, cit., p. 370; cf. also the dedication of his "Proverbia" to Lorenzo, B.L. Add. MS. 22157. His epi-

The Church provided another potential source of patronage for the Medici family, and although their main concern lay in trying to procure the most important bishoprics in the Florentine *dominio* for their family, they eagerly sought the patronage of smaller benefices for their hungry dependents.[145] One priest to benefit from this was Francesco da Castiglione who was the first person to be appointed to the Aldobrandini prebend in S. Lorenzo in 1462.[146] The influence of the Medici in this appointment seems clear, for in 1462 Francesco wrote to Giovanni di Cosimo de' Medici saying he had heard from Peregrino Aglio that when Giovanni was asked "super canonicatu qui vacaturus putabatur" he replied, "Francesci Castilionensis ratio nobis habenda est"; Francesco then reminded Giovanni that it had been through him that he had received the Chair of Greek in the Studio in 1446 and appealed to him to continue his patronage.[147] As we have seen, Francesco sent his earliest poems to Cosimo appealing to him for help as his "father, master and his patron", and later in the letters of consolation he sent the Medici he consistently praised Cosimo as the man from whom he had received friendship and patronage.[148]

Another priest who benefited directly from the patronage of the Medici in S. Lorenzo was Antonio Aglio, who was the first cleric to be presented to one of the two new prebends with which Giovanni

---

grams to Lorenzo are in BNF, MS. 11, 11, 62; ff. 101-102*v*; cf. his letter to Lorenzo, 18 December 1476, asking for his protection in the Studio, ASF, MAP, fil., 33, 43.

145 See G. B. Picotti, *La Giovinezza di Leo X*, Milan, Hoepli, 1927, pp. 67-159 (Ch. 2, "La Caccia dei Benefizi"). One of the prebends belonging to the Cafaggiuolo branch of the Medici was given to Ficino in 1487 and in 1492 to Matteo Franco, "schiavo et martiro" (Picotti, p. 83; I. Del Lungo, *Florentia: Uomini e cose del 400*, Florence, G. Barbèra, 1897, pp. 440 sqq.; cf. also B.L. Add. MS. 48764 B (Medici Papers), f. 43).

146 Cianfogni, *Memorie Ist.*, cit., p. 274, continued by D. Moreni, 1816, pt. 1, p. 100.

147 ASF, MAP, fil. 8, 438 (8 December 1462): "Ea verba que Peregrino Allio eruditissimo adolescente referente accepi, nam cum quidem te super canonicatu qui vacaturus putabatur rogaret, hec te habuisse verba referebat: Francesci Castilionensis ratio nobis habenda est... Facis quod te decet ut quem semel coeperis beneficio iuvare, perpetuo favore auxilioque non privari studeas, tu prior ex vobis in me beneficium contulisti, priusque fui abs te adiutus auxilio quam cognitus; nam xvi fere annis iam elapsis cum officium gymnasii publici restituendi gereres, tuo suffragio tuaque opera, rogante id Bernardo meo Castilionensis ad lectionem grecam electus fui", partly printed in Della Torre, *op. cit.*, p. 350, n. 3.

148 "Tu pater et dominus simul es mihi, Cosme, patronus" (Laur. MS. plut. 54, 10), f. 154, *Carm. Ill. Poet. Ital.*, III, p. 311). His consolatory letter to Cosimo in Laur. MS. plut. 54. 10, ff. 89*v* sqq.; to Alessandro Gonzaga on the death of Cosimo, MS. plut. 53, 11, ff. 8 sqq.; and to Lorenzo and Giuliano on the death of Piero their father in 1469, printed in C. Müllner, *Reden und Briefe italienischer Humanisten*, Vienna, 1899, p. 214.

de' Medici, Cosimo's father, endowed S. Lorenzo in 1428.[149] Although he enjoyed greater independence than Francesco of Castiglione, being tutor of Paul II before he became a Cardinal and protected by him after he became Pope,[150] he was just as devoted a supporter of the Medici and after Paul II's death became dependent on them again for patronage. As Bishop of Volterra he appealed to Lorenzo for a new house after his old one had been destroyed in the revolt in 1472,[151] and when he sought the Archbishopric of Pisa as a last reward for long service with the Medici, it was to Lorenzo that he wrote, declaring his devotion to the Medici House.[152] But even his devoted service was insufficient to obtain this reward and he died in 1478 still Bishop of Volterra.[153]

The Medici prelate *par excellence* is Gentile Becchi, appointed Bishop of Arezzo in 1473, whose poems in praise of Cosimo have been already mentioned. He himself has left us in no doubt of his absolute dependence on the Medici, in one letter calling Lorenzo more single-handed than Prometheus in "curdling him like a cheese",[154] in another declaring that he obeyed Lorenzo before he could move his eyelid.[155] Becchi's vivid imagery should not make one forget what

---

149 Cianfogni, *Memorie*, cont. by Moreni, cit., pt. 1, pp. 22-24.

150 See Muratori, *R. I. S.*, III, pt. 16, pp. 78-79, n. 3; also Vespasiano, *Vite*, I, pp. 295-297 and Kristeller, *Suppl. Fic.*, II, p. 335.

151 ASF, MAP, fil. 28, 311 (17 July 1472): "Io o ad parlare teco molte cose, ma al presente non ti ramento altro chella casa ... Le masseritie mie che sono rimase nel palazzo del vescovado sio nollene cavo presto mi saranno arse et guaste ... il perche io ti prego et gravo che tu adoperi chio abi una casa conveniente al bisogno et allo honore del vescovo".

152 *Ibid.*, MAP, fil. 30, 902 (25 September 1474): "Michi Laurenti suavissime hodie interriatum est reverendissimum patrem ac dominum meum archiepiscopum pisanum ... Si autem tua opera mihi ecclesia illa p[isana?] conferatur ita deo dante in illa ipse me gerere enitar ut pro me laborasse te demum haudquaquam peniteat, Magna equidem fiducia id a te petere audeo semper enim filius extiti vostre domus Petri genitoris tui ac Iohannis patrui preceptor utique fui. Quanta vero mihi cum felici memoria Cosmi avi tui amicitia fuerit, tu ipsemet nosti ... Obsecro ut tua opera me ad huius ecclesie presulatum promoveri disponas. Beneficia mea scio in manu tua nullo dubio futura sunt".

153 ASF, Sig. Missive, XLVII, 9 February 1477/8: letter to Donato Acciaiuoli: "Scrivemoti a questi di intendendo il R.do Padre Vescovo di Volterra Piovano di S. Maria inpruneta havere agiunto al morbo della vecchiaia...". Cf. C. Eubel, *Hierarchia Catholica Medii Aevii*, Librariae Regensbergiane, II, 1901, p. 105, *d.* 1477.

154 *Ibid.*, MAP, fil. 21, 428 (23 October 1473): "Prometheo non fu si solo quanto voi qui me sicut caseum coagulasti". The letter begins: "Operi manuum tuarum dexterum porrexisti et postomi in luogo che dio voglia si dica tanto di vostra beneficentia quanto del potere. Io sono pure il bronchone vestro schietto dove non ha sua foglia lui proprio non che alcuno altro albero ...".

155 *Lettere a Lorenzo dei Medici*, Florence, 1870 (Nozze Soria-Vitta), p. 5: "... che io sono si acconcio a vostri cenni che innanzi moviate il ciglio vi potrei avere ubbidito".

Lorenzo said about him, that if he had given Becchi all he had of dignity and honour Becchi had given him all he had of virtue,[156] and there was probably much truth in this, for as Lorenzo's tutor and afterwards his trusted emissary he was never just a servile flatterer of the Medici but rather a devoted friend of the family and their régime.[157]

The poets' praise of Cosimo, therefore, was undeniably self-interested, for in glorifying the return of the Golden Age of peace and plenty in which the Muses would flourish under the patronage of the Medici they were attempting to stimulate the Medici to play an imperial rôle in Florence, a rôle which they were in any case only too soon to adopt.

In conclusion, the study of the literary origins of the humanist portrait of Cosimo and its possible political significance help to emphasize the danger of exaggerating Cosimo's power in Florence. A letter written by Angelo Acciaiuoli to his son Jacopo in the year of Cosimo's death in fact suggests that far from being too great, it was at that time insufficient to do what was necessary for the city.[158] Cosimo himself, when asked personally by the Pope in 1463 to use his public and private authority in Florence to grant him a subsidy, replied that he could only do what was possible for a private citizen in a free republic,[159] while to Piero his son he wrote that "I replied to him [Otto Niccolini, Florentine envoy at the Papal Court] that what belongs to my *specieltà* determines and obliges me to do what I have directed him to say, and that I care nothing for his other arguments, nor for them would I spend ten ducats. But what I have said

---

[156] Letter to Jacopo Ammannati, 1477 (Picotti, *op. cit.*, p. 213, n. 31): "quello che è del prefato vescovo et quello che ha di degnità o di honore è tutto fatto da me, come è fatto da lui quello poco di vertù o discretione che io ho".

[157] See Kristeller, *Suppl. Fic.*, II, p. 340; Picotti, *op. cit.*, pp. 167 sqq.; R. Palmarocchi, *Lorenzo de' Medici e la nomina cardinalizia di Giovanni*, «Archivio storico italiano», an. CX, 1952, pp. 38-54; Canestrini-Desjardins, *Négotiations Diplomatiques de la France avec la Toscane,* I, pp. 205, 272 sqq.

[158] ASF, MS. Strozz. ser. 1, CXXXVI, f. 28, June 1464: "Queste nostre cose della terra non potrebbono *essere in più cattivo ordine e peggio governate:* Cosimo e Piero si stanno nelletto e fanno quello che possono: ma e non possono fare quello che bisognerebbe alla citta. Queste sono cose da riservare di parlarne a bocca ..." (the words in italics were originally in code).

[159] Fabroni, *Mag. Cos. Med. Vita*, II, p. 245: "Illud enim ut curem ut auxilium tibi publice decernatur nosti profecto quid in libera et populari Republica possit privatus civis: tamen id ego quantum in me erit quantumque potero, annitar ...".

I will do, I do first for the honour of God, next for the honour of his Beatitude, and lastly in respect of my soul".[160]

Yet such was the power of the humanists' pens that the eulogies they wrote of Cosimo during his lifetime to some extent helped to mould all later portraits of him. Machiavelli, as we have already seen, actually confessed how closely his description of Cosimo resembles a panegyric and his praise of Cosimo's virtues of liberality, magnificence, prudence and modesty conforms quite closely to the classical pattern. Less restrained than Guicciardini, who although praising Cosimo for similar virtues described how he was buried at his own request without ceremony and given all those honours which "a free republic could give to one of its citizens",[161] Machiavelli praised all Cosimo's actions as regal, called him alone 'principe' in Florence, a lover and patron of learned men ("condusse in Firenze lo Argiropolo...Nutrì nelle sue case Marsilio Ficino"), who was accompanied to his grave by all his citizens with the greatest pomp and honoured with the title of Father of his Country.[162] More than a century later the orations delivered in S. Lorenzo on the Feast of SS. Cosmas and Damianus in praise of Cosimo reiterate the same praises. In his oration of 1693, Salvino Salvini, like Poggio, compared Cosimo's exile and return with those of Aristides and Publius Rutilius, his title of Pater Patriae with that given to Cicero; he described his love of letters (fostering Ficino and restoring to light books which had long lain in squalor), and praised especially Cosimo's piety and immortal wisdom which he had attained through the study of philosophy.[163] And scarcely less panegyrical is Angelo Fabroni's *Magni Cosmi Medicei Vita* published in 1789, the first and only fully documented biography of Cosimo to be written, which praised Cosimo with uncritical ad-

---

[160] Florence, Bibl. Riccard., Fond. Moren., Racc. Frullana 1212 (Florence, 24 December 1463): "... Io glo risposto che quello che apartiene alla mia Specielta e confermigli et oblighimili a far quanto glo mandato adire Et che Io non curo dellaltre cose che si sono ragionate ne per tal rispetto spendrei x ducati. Ma che quello ho detto di fare lo fo prima per honore didio, Apresso per honore della sua Beatitudine Et ancora ultimamente per rispetto della anima mia" (autograph).

[161] *Storie Fiorentine*, p. 11: "ma furongli dati tutti quegli onori che può una città libera dare a uno suo cittadino ...".

[162] *Istorie fiorentine*, pp. 335-40. Cf. Piero de' Medici's "Ricordi", cit., in which he says that Cosimo was buried in S. Lorenzo "senza alcuna honoranza o pompa funebre ...", and note 44.

[163] *Orazione in lode di Cosimo, Pater Patriae*, publ. by D. MORENI, Florence, 1814, esp. pp. 51-53, 55-58.

miration for the same virtues, as a moral exemplar worthy of imitation.[164]

Compare this with Angelo Gaddi's summary but no less impressive description of Cosimo on his death as "il principale cittadino di Firenze, huomo di grandissima fama e virtù e ricchezza" [165] and one has some idea of how far the humanists were responsible for the traditional portrait of Cosimo as Pater Patriae, Maecenas and divine philosopher of Florence.

---

[164] See in particular his preface on ff. 1-2 and his praise of Cosimo on ff. 174-177. Note how closely his phrase "Quod vero eius comitas non sine severitate erat neque gravitas sine facilitate" (p. 176) resembles that used of Cosimo by Antonio Aglio in his letter of consolation to Piero (Laur. MS. plut. 54, 10, f. 128*v*): "gravitate comitas comitate gravitas ei condita fuit".

[165] Priorista of ANGELO and FRANCESCO GADDI, ASF, Tratte 62 (new numeration), f. 192, British Library, Egerton MS. 3764, f. 195; cf. G. RUCELLAI's *Zibaldone* (*G. Rucellai ed il suo Zibaldone,* ed. A. PEROSA, London, The Warburg Institute, 1960, I, p. 54).

APPENDIX

Johannes Argyropoulos, prefaces to his translations of Aristotle addressed to Cosimo de' Medici. The text is taken principally from Laur. 54,10 (C) with supplementary readings from Laur. 84,8 (W), 84,13 (X), 71,22 (Y) and 79,1 (Z). When the supplementary reading appears to be the correct one, it is substituted in the text with a reference to the version in C in a footnote; additional readings are included in the text in square brakets. Paragraphs and punctuation have been added, and in order to normalize the spelling the diphthong *ae* has been used throughout: the scribe of C is never consistent in its use and on the whole tends to use the abbreviated *e* cedilla at the end of words, seldom at the beginning.

PRAEFATIO IOHANNIS ARGYROPILI CONSTANTINOPOLITANI IN LIBROS PHISICORUM AD COSMUM

Si qua me unquam tenuit admiratio, si quam rem unquam praeclaram summamve exstimavi, haec una vel maxima fuit profecto, quam explicare tibi brevibus operae pretium esse putavi. Nam cum perrarum esse admodum videatur, hominem unum aut in rebus agendis, aut in prospicienda veritate praestare, tu miro quodam vigore naturae ingenioque praestantissimo hac nostra tempestate solus unus utrunque plane complexus es, atque adeo ut alterum haud ab altero ullo unquam pacto prohibeatur. Tanta est enim rerum agendarum prospiciendaeque veritatis scientiae difficultas, ac tantum utraque circa diversa variaque versatur, ut raro quidem in altero praestare genere virum, ac alterum absque altero, rarissime vero admodum utrunque simul homine in eodem invenias. Auget item difficultatem non solum eorum ordo, qui quidem diverso ex genere virium humanarum exoriri videtur, sed vis ipsius quoque fortunae rerumque omnium affluentia, cuius alterum perinde atque faber indiget instrumenti; alterum non modo non indigere videtur sed impediri etiam ab ea vehementer putatur. Indicat idem, ac eodem accedit, summa etiam difficultas adipiscendae perfectionis omni ex parte prorsus humanae, qua persimilis homo verae causae suae Deusque tandem evadere potest; hinc heroum complures, deorum perpauci admodum homines honores assequi potuerunt; hinc plures respublicas gubernarunt, perplures etiam rerum causas perspexerunt. At quam perpauci exiquoque vehementer in numero utroque studio flagraverunt, genereque in utroque perfecti homines extiterunt. Quid plura? si memoria vetera repetantur, vix fortasse numerum facient, qui studium utrumque complexi sunt ac in utroque genere floruerunt, ita difficile, ita perarduum, ita commune hominum ingenium viresque studium utriusque generis superare videtur.

Quamobrem me haud iniuria, sicuti dixi, non mediocris admiratio tenet, cum te nunc rempublicam regere summa cum prudentia video, perinde ac si in hoc studium solum nullumque [*in* W] aliud doctrinae unquam incubuisses, nunc in percipiendis causis rerum investigandaque veritate summa cum subtilitate versari, atque adeo prompte ut ab ineunte aetate philosophiae solum, omnibus aliis posthabitis neglectisve studiis, incubuisse facile videare. Atque si vera fatenda sunt,[1] livorque atque invidorum hominum stultorumque temeritas nihilpendenda esse videtur, te palam profitendum est talem hominem profecto iam evasisse, qualem divinus ille Plato civitatibus praeesse rebusve publicis voluit. Hoc ipsa res ostendit, hoc experientia rerum declarat, huius denique praeclara ipsa facinora, quae abs[2] te per virtutes assidue peraguntur, testes verissimi sunt, qui vel gratia vel ullo unquam alio pacto corrumpi verumque offendere minime possunt.

Te nanque ex nobilissimo splendidissimoque sanguine natum, honestissimis moribus, praeclarissimis virtutibus, humanitatis ingenuarumque artium ac philosophiae studiis sub praestantissimo patre tuo praeclarissimoque omnium, adeo egregie educatum regieque instructum esse percipimus, ut antiquorum iam licet nemini, si cui praeclara unquam contigit educatio, pace id omnium dicam, primas in hac post te ortum sibi tribuere atque sine iniuria vendicare. Quid enim aliud, aut ullum decuit tam studiosum tam excellentem hominem piumque patrem erga carissimam suam prolem egisse, aut admirabili tuae naturae divinoque ingenio contigisse oportuit, quod adeo aptum idoneumque erat ad finem summum humanum facile admodum assequendum, ut ob id ipsum fato procreatum delapsumque (*esse* W] quasi ab ipso caelo divino quodam consilio videatur? Quapropter id illi nimirum evenisse manifestissime cernitur, quod omnes patres vehementer exoptant, rarissime autem evenire videtur. Sese enim abs te atque [*a* W] solo superatum fuisse vidit.[3] Certoque percepit talem post se ipsum huiusce praeclarae moderatorem gubernatoremque reipublicaeque reliquisse quod quidem apicem fecilitatis suae putavit, ut abs te non solum haec sua carissima patria, sed Italia etiam tota iam gubernari peroptime possit.

---

[1] *fateri oportet* W.

[2] W] *ad* C.

[3] W] *velit* C.

Licet cuivis hominum id ita esse facile admodum intelligere, si partim tuae patriae florentem hunc statum, quem quidem summa cum prudentia conservas et auges, partim aedes sacras intueatur, quae tum religionis tum perornandae urbis causa, complures maximis tuis sumptibus vastae molis extant extructae, partim omnium civitatum omniumque principum erga te amorem, benivolentiam, admirationem, observantiam cultumve sentiat summum, qui te medius fidius patrem omnes communi consensu et existimans et appellant, quod nondum cuiquam principum contigisse percepimus. Et enim cum de te loquuntur (saepe autem id faciunt), patrem te cum veneratione maxima vocitant. Cum dant litteras, hoc idem in ipsis litteris scribunt. Cum aliquid quod aut ad universae Italiae statum, aut ad rem familiarem etiam suam pertineat, quisque nititur agere abs te tanquam a patre summo atque sapientissimo, tum consilium, tum opitulationem, auxilium, opem flagitat, poscit atque expectat. Cum ad sedandas discordias ad pertractandamve pacem nuntios legatosque mittunt, per te tanquam per patrem id ipsum prorsus efficiunt; per te transeant ipsi legati oportet. Cum res postulat necessitasque compellit, te civitatum ipsi praesides, te velut patrem principes adeunt, nonnulli quoque persaepe visundi tui causa [*tantum* W] perinde quasi debitum inde quoddam paternum officiumque suum absolvant, ad te maxima cum aviditate proficiscuntur; licetque saepenumero tuas maximas aedes praeclarissimos homines praesides urbium principesque egredientes ingredientesque prospicere. Ex quibus universis compluribusque aliis, quanta est vis tuae prudentiae, quantum ingenium, quanta sapientia, quanta denique rerum omnium agendarum experientia tua, facile percipi potest. Quae cum ipse cogito, te quidem beatissimum talemque, ut antea dixeram, invenio virum, qualem divinus ille Plato civitatibus praesse rebusque publicis voluit.

Tuam vero praeclarissimam patriam felicissimam omnium esse non iniuria censeo, tum quia virium tantum ac talem tandem potuit procreasse, non modo suum sed totius etiam Italiae decus, tum quia talis hominis tantique sapientia regitur. Accessit eodem et externarum rerum prosperitas affluentiaque fortunae, quae partim amplissimis patrimoniis, partim providentia tua, tibi iuste atque honeste comparata est in tanta sane mensura, quo tantae prudentiae, tantae virtuti, tantae liberalitati, tantae magnificentiae suppeditare subministrareque possit. Ex quo fit ut neque tibi quisquam actus virtutis ullius unquam deficiat modo velis (vis autem semper universis illis conditionibus observatis, quae actionem quanque studiosam efficiunt) neque tuae patriae tempora, occasiones, oportunitates ullae praetereant, quod in civitatibus plerisque saepenumero fieri solet, aut aerario forte iam exhausto, aut oblato tempore pluribus indigente, quam ipsum aerarium potest. Tu nanque praesens confestim succurris ipsi magnificentia tempori, nullamque pateris unquam comoditatem utilitatemque carissimae tuae patriae praeterire. Quibus quid aut ad bene beateque vivendum, aut ad conservandum augendumque patriae statum, comodius unquam inveniri fingique potest?

Quae cum ita sint, si quis tibi ea obtulerit, quae aut ad activam aut ad contemplativam ipsam pertineant vitam, is certe scio rem pergratam tibi peregerit. Non propterea quia nunc illis indigeas, nihil enim profecto deesse tibi videtur, cum utranque fecilitatem adeptus iam sis, perfectusque evaseris; sed quia res huiuscemodi iocundae tibi solum existimentur teque vehementer oblectent. Nam uti musicus concentu sonorisque vocibus ac eleganti cantu delectatur et gaudet, sic haud mediocrem voluptatem delectationemque suscipere solet vir felix, cum ea sibi offerentur eaque videt, quae homini competant optimo, ad beatamque vitam pertineant, praesertim si ad praestantiorem vivendi modum videantur conferre; illaque vel maxime bonorum per ea comparentur ac acquirantur, quae cum interna sint bona, in potestate nostra dumtaxat, sita collocataque esse dicuntur. Atque ob id ipsum, ego cum me tibi vehementer obstrictum convinctumque mirum in modum esse censerem, eo vinculo sane quo se suapte natura ii qui tam virtutes quam scientias amant cum studiosis atque eruditis hominibus vinciunt, cuperemque non mediocriter ut per me tibi gratum iucundumque quippiam fiat, quo simul meum in te officium aliqua ex parte videar exercere vehementemque meum erga te amorem ostendam, librum divinum Aristotelis illum, quem Auditum Naturalem Peripateticis placuit appellare, ex eo quia[4] dignus auditu prae caeteris esse videtur, elegantius ut puto causa tua traductum, offerre tibi decrevi.

Nihil enim ferme gratius, nihil iocundius, nihil suavius hoc tibi libro fore existimavi, cum speculativam tu quidem vitam semper anteponas activae. Perpulchre id quidem, nam tam etsi utraque vita perfectissime vivis ambabusque simul vehementer indulges, alteram tamen ob alteram esse cogniscis. Alteri magis incumbis contemplationemque finem ultimum penitus humanum esse existimas atque ipsi semper primas tribuis partes. Hunc vero non solum ad istam vitam conferre, sed primas etiam obtinere omnium fere librorum Aristotelis partes nonnullis rationibus constet.

Equidem Aristotelem illum divinum hominem, quem certo scio te non modo fama sed experientia quoque scientiaque diligenter iamdiu qualis fuerat percepisse, hoc in egregio suo libro conficiendo, non mediocriter superasse se ipsum inventio. Quod ita esse, quivis homo doctus intelligere potest si omnes eius perleget libros. Nam hunc his omnibus simul, subtilitate inquam scientiarum, ordine atque elegantia praestare caeteris mirum in modum inveniet. Accessit eodem et mea tui causa diligentia, quam non solum in traducendo librum ut latinus evadat, concinnitate verborum quoad potui, materiesque fert ipsa. Non enim, ut scis, in huiuscemodi materiis campus orationi latus conceditur, sed in sententiis etiam dilatandis aperiendisve ubi opus erat necessitasque atque obscuritas compellebat adhibui, quo cognitu faciliores sententiae philosophi totusque suus iste liber reddatur.[5] Quod si

---

[4] W] *qui* C.

[5] W] *redditur* C.

ad interpretem ipsum pertineat, tu te ipse consi[*derabis* W]. Ex quibus omnibus fit ut haud iniucundum, sed suavissimum ferme omnium munerum hoc fore tibi munus existimetur.

Accipe igitur hunc librum, vir praestantissime, perinde atque quasdam primitias studiorum nostrorum a nobis tibi oblatum. Nam ut regibus illae, sic res huiuscemodi praeclarae a nobis tibi offerantur oportet, tibi inquam quem ut caeterorum nobis bonorum sic et studiorum principem esse putamus. Nos tale deinceps operam dabimus, ut nunquam ab huiuscemodi offerendis tibi primitiis desistamus, quando quidem nihil aliud praeter ad genus munerum aut nos tibi offerre, aut te a nobis accipere decet. Vale.

IOANNIS ARGYROPILI PRAEFATIO IN LIBROS DE ANIMA ARISTOTELIS AD COSMUM MEDICEM TRADUCTOS

Hominem, ut te non praeterit, magnifice atque ornatissime Cosma, non sua fortuito causa procreavit, ne[*c* X] frustra viribus muneribusve tam amplis, tam praeclaris, tam admirabilibus perornavit. Primum emin ignorationem sine dubio, secundum stulticiam temeritatemve procreantis nimirum significasset ac indicasset, quibus quid ab omnium praestabilissimo exterminandum magis esse videtur? Quod si neque forte neque frustra fabrum quidem anulum, figulum autem olulam unquam confecisse finxisseque dixerimus, modo mentis integrae sanaeque simus, qui fieri potest, ut iis animadvertendi diiudicandique vis ulla iure tribueretur, qui nec animadversum atque prospectum esse, nec ob finem quenquam confectum hominem ab effectrice rerum omnium causa censuissent. Omitto brevitatis causa caetera, naturae scilicet vim, artis imbecillitatem, primae nobilitatem mentis, infinitasque vires ac opificis huiusce tenuem admodum exiguamque conditionem. Quibus perspicitur eo non fortuito, non frustra magis hominem ortum esse quam anulum, quam olulam, quo tam arti naturae, quam rebus omnibus Deus praeest.

Sed si res eas tantum animadvertere voluerimus, ex quibus homo primo conficitur, facile sane rei quam quaerimus veritas elucescet. Inspiciatur, enim diligenter ipsius corporis humani dispositio constructiove, quam adeo miro natura callidissimoque artificio fabricata est, ut nihil sit omnino quod aut addi aut mutari aut detrahi possit. Excogitetur animo substantia, vires eius praeterea muneraque pervestigentur, quae quidem tum multa, tum varia diversaque sunt, tum ordinem talem inter sese subeunt, ut gradu quodam sineque intervallo aliud excellat aliud ac comitetur. Etenim in homine plures esse variasque vitas ob animi munera viresque complures non dubitamus asserere, quanquam[1] unum id ipsum est, cui talis varietas attribuitur vitae. Nam homo nutritur, incrementa suscipit, procreare potest, sentit, resque sentien-

---

[1] X] *quenquam* C.

do dissimillimas comprehendit, calorem, inquam, saporem, odorem, sonum, colorem. Se ipsum item motu ciet interiore et suo. Quid plura? Ipsa quoque mentis vivit conditione, honestum percipit, rem familiarem constituit, civitatem gubernat, veritatem discernit. Denique rerum omnium suique cognitionem consequitur. Ac tandem omnium ipsum perfectissimum Deum inspicit eiusque cognitionem summa cum subtilitate complectitur. Quae, cum tam multa, tam admirabilia sint ordineque miro conficiantur, quis unquam sane mentis fortuito talem aut frustra dicet hominem natum ortumque fuisse?

Equidem quum haec animadverto (id autem saepenumero facere consuevi), mirari vehementer soleo primae vires atque sapientiam mentis, quae quidem non solum segregatam a corpore mentem, nec vacantem naturam anima procreavit, nec sensum rationis expertem, sed mentem quoque cum ipso sensu corporisque mole coniunxit. Quod sane non modo non fortuito frustrave, sed neque sine prudentia summa viribusque immensis fieri potest. Quorsum igitur haec perguntur, aut cur his affari te oportere continuo duxi? Ut inde statim emergat ac patefiat et eos qui se nimium neglexere lucem hanc mala fortuna frustra vidisse, et te summo studio fatoque felici consecutum esse [2] res omnis eas, ob quas assequendas natura talis oritur homo, et eo iam esse profectum atque deductum ubi tandem natura calcem humani cursus praemiaque collocavit atque constituit.

Nam et utrunque finem hominis es [3] adeptus una cum universis externis bonis, quae quidem cum absint, obfuscare quodam modo beatitudinem soleant, et omnium hominum communi sententia primas inter omnis optines partes atque adeo ut nemo sit homo, cedat modo livor iniquus omnisque temeritas, qui quidem hac aetate posthabita non conferendum te cum his hominibus censet, quorum usque adeo fama celebratur et gloria, ut non bonorum hominum, sed deorum honores consequi non iniuria videantur. Quid enim boni non in te summum intueri licet? Quis [4] actus exercendus virtutis non supremus abs te fieri continueque videtur? Inest tibi profecto summa prudentia, quare cunctis virtutibis tuus animus est imbutus. Adsunt [5] tibi facultates abunde, omnis affluentia prosperitasque fortunae, quare cuncti virtutum actus abs te semper proficiscuntur neque liberalitatis minus magnificentiaeque quicquam efficitur munus. Inest tibi praeterea veri perspiciendi summa vis et facultas, quare pars altera mentis id est adepta profecto, quo rerum contemplator cum libet perspicitque naturas. Finem igitur utrunque complexus es humanae naturae, ob quem homo talis a sua causa sicuti diximus procreatur in lucemque venit.

---

[2] *conservatum* C.

[3] X] *est* C.

[4] X] *Quid* C.

[5] *Assunt* X.

Quamobrem te nunc fortunatum, te nunc felicem, te nunc beatum appellare non immerito sine formidine licet, et si Soloni fortasse non placet, qui quidem sine dubio si nunc adesset teque iam felicitatem humanam hoc pacto consecutum vidisset, mutata statim sententia ter te felicem[6] ante vitam exactam, quater te dixisset beatum. Est enim iniquum eum in vita non felicem esse putare, qui felicitatem est consecutus, summum inquam hominis bonum fixum atque perpetuum, quod quidem nulla vi prorsus nulla temeritate fortunae unquam expirare dissolvique potest; haec cum ita sint constetque felicem perinde atque Deum inter homines esse, quibus te nos, o vir felix, [*tandem honoribus quibus* X] muneribus afficiemus ac prosequemur? Nam et offerenda sint omnino munera tibi, et in offerendis muneribus adhibenda[7] est diligentia, ut honestas, ut decorum, ut dignitas conservetur. Paret igitur atque offerat quisque tibi, quod sibi magis videtur ad conservandum decorum accedere; mihi semper ea tibi sunt offerenda, quae iam pridem accommodata esse dignitati tuae putavi quaeque offerre institui partimque obtuli, genere quorum nihil tibi profecto gratius, nihil carius, nihil iucundius, nihil denique accommodatius esse potest. Quid enim vir animi magni sibi oblatum magnifaciet unquam, praeter res eas quae continuo suapte natura sineque intervallo ad ipsam consequendam humanam ducunt felicitatem, qua quidem nihil omnino praestabilius homini posse contingere putatur?

Post librum itaque Aristotelis Naturalis Auditus elegantius causa tua traductum tibique oblatum, librum nunc eiusdem De Anima traductum identidem offero, praeclarum et ipsum, ut scis, et admirabile opus. Quod quidem eo caeteris operibus naturalibus antecellit quo scientia animae mentisque humanae cognitio omni scientiae naturae cognitione praeest, hinc hominis sane natura perfecte perspicitur; hinc cognitionis lumen humanae notum evadit; hinc scientia naturalis exactius; hinc moralis philosophia tota percipitur; hinc et immortalitas animae demonstratur et mentes a corporibus esse separatae probantur, et philosophia prima suae processionis exordia sumit.

Accipe igitur et hunc librum a me tua traductum ut dixi causa felix, et studio tibi perlege consueto. Invenies saltem ut puto nun[*c* X] faciliores illas omnes sententias cognitu quas perobscuras olim interpretandi modus ille simplex reddebat. Vale, et si quid tibi gratum, si quid iocundum hoc pacto subministramus, id omne vinculo benivolentiae tribuas velim, quod quidem me virtutum amatorem tibi studiosissimo, ut par erat, vehementer coniuxit.

---

[6] X] *felicitatem* C.

[7] X] *offerenda* C.

IOANNIS ARGYROPYLI BIZANTII AD MAGNIFICUM VIRUM COSMAM MEDICEM DE LIBRO POSTERIORUM PRAEFATIO

Iohannes Argyropylus bizantius Magnifico viro Cosme Medici Salutem perpetuamque fecilitatem. Ut tibi semel promisi, ita facio, magnifice Cosma; atque neque munus docendi, neque calamitas generis, neque cura rei familiaris extinctae studium erga te meum diminuere potest, tantum apud me tua virtus ac auctoritas potest.

Post librum igitur Aristotelis eumque Naturalem Auditum appellant, et librum item De Anima tuo nomine tuaque traductos causa, libros nunc eiusdem Posteriorum Resolutiorum eadem ratione traduxi, pergratum et tibi sane, quem res maxime quaeque ad hominem pertinent [1] solum delectant, et universis hominibus non mediocriter utilem atque iucundum, ut puto. Nam est quidem, ut scis, totius logicae finis atque ob id ipsum omnium librorum ipsius praestabilissimus, traditque modum sciendi, sine quo fieri nequit ut quisquam ullam scientiam assequatur. At cum partim suae materiae causa, partim nescio quo stilo vehementer esset obscurus, nec ullo pacto videretur esse latinus, nunc dilucidus, nunc latinus evasit, licetque cuique sententias ipsius praeclares atque subtiles facile summaque cum voluptate percipere. Accedit eodem et explicatio sententiarum per figuras modosque perinde ac philosophus affert, quod quidem ante hoc tempus philosophia latina non vidit.

Quod si liber hic et huius aetatis hominibus et posteritati fuerit gratus, ut consentaneum est rationi, hoc ad te totum non iniuria redigetur ut auctorem, cuius causa liber hoc pacto extructus est. Accidit enim perrecte ut quem aetas nostra perfectissimum hominem ac beatissimum vidit, et a quo profluxere plurima bona, is et rerum earum hominum communitati sit auctor, quae ad ipsum hominem maxime pertinent [2] atque ad bene beateque vivendum. Nam ad talem hominem spectare profecto videtur earum rerum administratio, quibus homines bene recteque vivere ac faciles tandem evadere possunt. Quippe cum id sit ad res gubernandas hominum ipse quod ad universa Deus existit.

Accipe igitur et hunc librum et perlege felix. Invenies et diluciditatis in eo tantum et elegantiae quantum ipse modus et materia poscit. Val perpetuo felix atque beatus.

EIUSDEM EXORDIUM IN LIBROS ETHICORUM

Si ea mihi servanda sunt erga te quae iam olim institui, sapientissime Cosme, ea tantum sunt a me tibi offerenda quae praeclarissime rerum esse

---

[1] *pertinere* Y.

[2] Y] *pertinet* C.

censentur, nec a quibusvis hominum offerri facile possunt. Nam neque tantam virtutem sine ullis muneribus praetereundam esse existimavi, et quicquid obtulero muneris, id omne accommodatum esse virtuti oportere putavi. Nec enim amor virtutis unquam illud sane perferre posset, et cuique pro dignitate semper tribuendum esse videtur iustitiae lege, ad quam omnis res talis omnino est referenda. Quod si maxime omnium ea studioso sunt offerenda quae vehementer ad ipsam virtutem felicitatemque pertinent, atque haec sunt sine controversia philosophorum maxime libri praesertim divini hominis Aristotelis, quem solum omnium ad artes scientiasque tradendas hominum generi, ac modum sciendi munere quodam divino naturaeve natum fuisse nemo est fere qui ignoret. Hi tantum a me tibi profecto sunt offerendi emendatius in latinam linguam elegantiusve traducti, quamquam id ipsum effici non sine labore nimio potest, ut et meo in te amori et dignitati satisfaciam tuae. Non solum ob eam quae dicta est causam, sed ob illud etiam maxime quo tale Aristotelis libri tuis civibus caeterisque hominibus causa tui tradantur, quo quidem nihil gratius, nihil accommodatius, nihil optabilius homini studioso felicive contingere potest. Quapropter hos continuo libros tui traductos causa, Naturalem inquam Auditum, et De Anima, et Posteriores Resolutivos tibi obtuli tuoque nomini dedicavi.

Et nunc librum de Moribus ad Nicomacum praestabilem et ipsum summeque necessarium emendatius elegantiusque traductum tibi similiter offero. Est enim ad humanam vitam, ut scis, non mediocriter utilis, et omnino ad consequendam felicitatem beatemque vitam vehementissime prodest. Hic status hominis duplex gratia cuius oritur ipse atque agit omnia declaratur; hic virtutis conditio naturaque adversantis habitus explicatur; hic ea sane sternitur via, qua recta pergitur ad virtutem strataque demonstratur; hinc, ut omittam caetera, vir ille summe bonus tandem emergit qui dispersos homines passim in unum compellere congregareque locum moenibusque claudere, atque urbem civitatemque constituere; denique mores, leges, religionem omnemque vivendi cum honestate modum tradere atque instituere potest.

Quibus efficitur ut qui libros quidem tibi caeteros obtulisset, hunc vero dumtaxat subtraxisset ac neglexisset, hic neque iustitiae leges hac re profecto servasset et praeter decorum ipsum egisset. Nam ut colores exemplumque pictori, equus atque arma militi instituta rei militaris duci pergratum sunt donum, sic institutiones morum ad bene beateque vivendi iucundissimum donum felici maximeque accomodatum esse videntur, ut non ipse non mediocres inde saltem voluptates summat legendo. Fit enim perinde ac si ageret per virtutem, sed et hominibus res maxime ad beatam vitam accomodata per ipsum, ut par est, universis tradatur. Quod si tale donum tam praeclarum, tam necessarium hominum debeat trad[*i* Z] communitati, qui non per hominem felicem id ipsum egisset cum posset, is aut ignoratione profecto aut livore summum quoddam munus officiumque felicis hominis abstulisset. Quod enim ad gregem est pastor, ad natos parentes, ad universum Deus:

id ad suos cives communitatemque hominum vir felix esse censetur. Atque vel ab his omnibus ad ea quibus praesident omnia cuique accommodata profluunt atque proveniunt [*bona* X], sic et per homines felices atque beatos ea quae ad bene beateque vivendum maxime conferunt, civibus omnibusque hominibus non iniuria tradenda esse videntur.

Accipe igitur et hunc librum, sapientissime Cosma, et perlege felix, ac tuis civibus, qui quidem tibi sunt curae perinde ac filii patri, caeterisque hominibus trade. Placebit et tibi certo scio et caeteris non iniocundus erit. Est[1] enim in ipso et diluciditas summa et elegantiae satis quoad materia poscit; et illud sane non abest quod praeter quam caetera praesertim in talibus exoptatur, quorum omnium te assero auctorem fuisse, non ob eas solum quae dictae sunt causas, sed ob illud quoque potissimum, quod me ad hunc librum traducendum ipse hortatus es maximopere, etsi bis iam ipsum ne dicam pluries lingua traductum vidit latina.

Quod si commentariolis quoque nostris, ut petis, dilucidior evadet cognituque facilior, quis est qui non et huiusmodi te auctorem comoditatis censebit? Sed ego sane propensior quidem sum ad obsequendum praeclaris studiis tuis, nam neque auctoritate quisquam medius fidius apud me neque voluntate plus valere te potest. Angustiis tamen, ut scis, temporis et asperitatibus rerum impedior atque premor. Nam generis me totius occasus excidiumque luctuosissimum patriae ac omnium tam publicarum quam privatarum disturbatio rerum indigna atque acerba spesque sublata funditus ademptaque bonae fortunae distrahit, angit atque perturbat. Non enim

duris genuit non cautibus horrens
Caucasus Hycanaeque admorunt ubera tigres.[2]

Homines et nos et cives fuimus orti. Nec nobis solum nati sumus, ut ait Plato, sed ortus nostri partem carissimam patriam, partem amicos vendicare oportebat. Homines praeterea hominum causa Stoicorum sententia generatos esse percipimus, ut ipsi inter sese aliis alii variis in rebus prodesse possint. Nec ignoramus si hoc loco nos quisquam carpat aegrotis consilia dare. Sed animadvertatur ne fines hoc humanitatis atque cancellos egrediatur, ut aut praestabilioris naturae quam hominis sit, aut cuiusquam stupidae sensuque vacantis naturae, quando quidem ab expertibus rationis animalibus, nisi perperum habeant sensus ut late patet exterminantur. Fit enim ut perinde plus ipse doleat animo qui res huiuscemodi magis discernere potest, atque ipse dolores magis corporis sentit quem natura temperatiore corpore procreavit. Augere praeterea solet dolorem, et si quis suis prodesse potest idque ab ipso non ignoratur, nulla tamen ad hoc agendum datur facultas, sed omnis iniquo

---

[1] Z] *Et* C.

[2] Vergil, *Aen.*, IV, 365-366.

fato penitus aufertur. Sunt insuper et utilitatum varii gradus et item calamitatum, ut si ad summas accesseris cogitatione ille si nequeant profisci, hae si adsint magnis, ne dicam summis, afficiant doloribus animum vehementerque vexent.

Equidem certo scio non mediocribus eum haud immerito doloribus affici, cui beneficentia quidem ac liberalitas adest, facultates autem ad conferenda beneficia desunt, et iustitia quidem inest, nulla tamen distribuendi datur facultas. Fit enim sane perinde ac si quisquam egregiam quidem pulsandi citharam summa industria, summo studio, summisque laboribus tandem adeptus est artem, instrumento autem caret, aut vetatur ut pulset; quod, si ob operationem omnis acquiri soleat habitus, quis est qui frustra comparatum habitum eum non asseruerit esse, a quo nunquam operatio ulla proficiscitur? At enim ut is homo procreatus est sine controversia frustra quem virtus non exornavit, quique nullam virtutem est consecutus, sic et frustra quodam modo virtutem is est adeptus, a quo nulla unquam operatio per illam proficiscetur ac fiet. Nam hoc inter hos homines interesse videtur quod ille magis hic minus distat [3] ab eo quod summum hominis dicimus bonum. Quod quidem ni fiat atque proveniat omnis opera, omne studium, omnis denique labor qui antecessit ob huiuscemodi finem hac sane ratione frustra fuisse videtur. Eodem accedunt et ea quae de felicitate dicuntur operationem ipsam esse vel in operatione consistere atque in vita perfecta et indigere prosperitatis externae bonaeque fortunae, et item ea quae de felice dici percepimus, non differre ipsum a miseris dimidio vitae et percupere vivere doloreque maxime cum discedit e vita, et quae sunt similis generis. Quod si calamitates omnino ferendae sunt atque iniqua fortuna id inquam id quod vulgo dicere consuevimus hominique magnanimi [*atque forti tribuitur. Ferantur ubi placet et fortes homines et magnanimi* Z] esse volumus, hoc tamen profecto ferre ac perpeti esse sine ullo dolore non potest, ut ipsum nomen indicare videtur. Et insuper ea quae boni homines exoptant atque percipiunt agere, et ob quae summo studio summisque laboribus tales ac tantas virtutes tandem sunt consecuti, non sane fient obstante temeritate fortunae, quod quidem [*si* Z] non dolore ullo afficiant animadvertatur. Quid si quispiam complures quidem nescio quos in prosperitate affluentiaque fortunae sentiat collocatos temeritateque eiusdem videat abutentes, se vero neque suis neque sibi soli rebus in necessariis posse subministrare gaudebitne, perferetne, ut ipsum sine ulla perturbatione fiat animi sineque ullo dolore?

Ommitto dignitatem meritaque afferre virtutis et indignationem insuper, quae quidem inde suapte natura nimirum emergere solet. Sed cur id tam pluribus est defendendum, quod aut dissimulare nonnulli [4] homines solent, ut fortitudinis inde munus ut magnanimitatis exercere contemptoresque re-

---

[3] Z] *discat* C.

[4] *nulli* Z.

rum omnium quidam ob excellentiam quasi animi nimiam videantur, aut si penitus absit, stupidam quandam naturam atque insulsam ostendit? Est et hic profecto mediocritas quaedam servanda. Atque haec est aequabilitas ea, quae rebus in adversis perinde ac in secundis est adhibenda. Et laudatur profecto atque fortitudinis et magni est animi munus. At fieri ne potest ut impeditus quisquam quo minus agat ea, quae vehementer expetit, summe exoptat et ob quae tantummodo peragenda vivere cupit, omni dolore penitus vacet? Inquiunt etiam et fortitudinem voluptate vacare. At haus scio si semper illam doloris vacuitas comitetur, praesertim his in rebus, in quibus indolentia humanitati adversatur, neque non carpi merito potest. Ex quibus sane non solum perspicitur animi nostri necessaria conditione temporis perturbatio, sed et tuae quantus est felicitatis status elucet, beatissime Cosma, si tibi virtutibus omnibus praedito perfectissimoque homini summa prudentia, summaque sapientia nihil omnino deest. Sed prosperitas omnis adest fortunae, rerumque omnium affluentia, quo nullum unquam virtutis exercendae tibi munus impediatur nullusque prorsus dolori sic locus, sed semper potius partim ex ante actis, partim ex his quae aguntur, partim etiam ex agendis rebus resultans, non iniuria te comitetur voluptas. Quibus efficitur ut re vera te talem ante oculos habeamus, qualem Aristoteles hoc in libro perfectissimum felicem verbis descripsit.

Sed ut eo redeamus unde digressi sumus, non tamen extra fines huiusce facultatis egressi, asperitas quidem rerum atque iniqua fortuna animum sane perturbat neque vacare studio permittit ut decet. Adest et officium munusque docendi quod fere totum occupare tempus videtur. Conabor tamen ipse atque enitar in hisce vel asperitatibus rerum vel angustiis temporis, honestissimis tuis quoad possum studiis obsequi et voluntati tuae morem gerere atque obtemperare, nullisque in rebus omnino tibi aut hortanti aut roganti deesse. Nihil est enim omnino quod apud me plus valere auctoritate tua voluntateque potest. Verum si id [*quod* Z] percupis, aut tardius quam desideras absolvetur, aut non tam exactum ut affectas a nobis efficietur, cum rei magnitudini, tum occupationibus nostris utrumque assignare atque fortunae debebis: non enim universa quae volumus nostra sub potestate sunt collocata. Vale.

2

COSIMO DE' MEDICI'S WIT AND WISDOM

One of the most consistent, though little studied, characteristics of the opaque figure of Cosimo de' Medici is his wit. Initially, it was the Florentine bookseller Vespasiano de Bisticci who made Cosimo's "salty replies" a theme of his short but authentic biography of Cosimo, written in the late fifteenth century.[1] The theme was then adopted and popularized by Machiavelli in his *Florentine Histories*, completed in 1525, where Cosimo's witticisms occupy a quarter of the space devoted to Cosimo's life.[2] Other witticisms are immortalized in books of jokes or *facetiae*, such as those of the Ferrarese humanist Lodovico Carbone, the *Detti piacevoli* attributed to Angelo Poliziano, a collection of over 400 jokes of which nearly 10 per cent relate to Cosimo, and the *Facezie* collected by Niccolò Angèli da Bùcine.[3] And there are, of course, other jokes told in letters and chronicles, such as Pius II's *Commentaries*.

This paper was delivered at a conference to commemorate the 500th anniversary of Cosimo's birth, held by the Society for Renaissance Studies at the Warburg Institute in May 1989, whose proceedings have been published in the volume *Cosimo 'il Vecchio' de' Medici, 1389-1464,* ed. F. Ames-Lewis, Oxford, Oxford University Press, 1992.

[1] *Le vite,* ed. A. GRECO, II, Florence, Istituto Nazionale di Studi sul Rinascimento, 1976, p. 197: "Tutte le sue risposte erano condite col sale": translated by W. G. & E. WATERS, *Renaissance Princes, Popes, and Prelates. The Vespasiano Memoirs,* New York and London, Harper and Row, 1963. On the probable date of completion, between 1494 and 1496, see GRECO, I, p. VI.

[2] *Istorie fiorentine*, VII, 6 (ed. F. GAETA, Milan, Feltrinelli, 1962), p. 461: "ne' suoi detti e risposte era arguto e grave". On the date of completion, p. 48.

[3] *Facezie di Lodovico Carbone Ferrarese,* ed. ABD-EL-KADER SALZA, Livorno, R. Giusti, 1900, no. XC, pp. 64-65; A. POLIZIANO, *Detti piacevoli,* ed. T. ZANATO, Rome, Istituto d. Enciclopedia italiana, 1983, (= *Detti*), also published by A. WESSELSKI, *A. Polizianos Tagebuch (1477-1479),* Jena, 1929; *Facezie e motti dei secoli XV e XVI,* ed. G. PAPANTI, Bologna, Gaetano Romagnoli, 1874, repr. 1968 (= PAPANTI): 280 jokes, including some of the above, probably collected by

Here Pius relates the joke Cosimo told when unable to bend to kiss the pope's foot because of his gout: he laughed and said, "Two Florentines named Papo and Lupo returning from the country met in the piazza and offered each other their hands and a kiss. But they were both very fat and there was such corporosity (if I may use that word) on both sides that they could touch only their stomachs. Gout now denies me what corpulence refused them". Whereupon the pope "*laughingly* dismissed him".[4]

Although this was not Cosimo's own joke, it reveals him to be jocund and a man of the people – as well as politically shrewd in avoiding a gesture of homage to the pope. His truer feelings about Pius as pope and a native of Siena are revealed by other witticisms. Pius's crusading zeal he said was that of "an old man undertaking the enterprise of young men".[5] When Pius was criticized for being carried around on a litter "and other ambitious things", Cosimo riposted that on the contrary Pius was prudent for, as he wanted everyone to know he was Sienese, to behave so pompously was the best and quickest way to do it. And when the Sienese commented that the Florentines had lost their brains, he retorted: "Indeed, it's not possible for them to lose theirs!".[6]

It is for such pithy one-line replies that Cosimo is best known, thanks largely to the popularity of Machiavelli's *History*. In addition to the joke about Pius as crusader and maxims such as "eight yards

---

Niccolò degli Angeli dal Bùcine, professor of Humanities in the Florentine Studio in 1497, and his son, partly edited in translation by C. SPERONI, *Wit and Wisdom of the Italian Renaissance,* Berkeley and Los Angeles, University of California Press, 1964. Thirty-eight of the *Detti* concern Cosimo (ed. Zanato, nos. 2-4, 7, 16, 20, 22, 45-46, 131-132, 134, 136-139, 141-142, 145-146, 148, 152-153, 157-158, 164, 175-176, 181, 195, 203, 234, 268, 272, 311-312, 331, 339), compared with twenty-one relating to Lorenzo il Magnifico and nine to other members of the Medici family. On their attribution and dating (1477-1482), T. ZANATO, *Sull'attribuzione e la cronologia dei "Detti piacevoli"*, «Cultura neolatina», XLII, 1982, and BARBARA C. BOWEN, *Renaissance Collections of facetiae, 1344-1490: a new listing,* «Renaissance Quarterly», 39, 1986, pp. 1-15, 363-375 (no. 8, pp. 12-12, pointing out that the text now depends on the first part of LODOVICO DOMENICHI's *Facetie et motti arguti,* Florence, 1548, where they are attributed to 'lo Stradino', and that she regards the case for Poliziano's authorship 'not proven'). Here, however, I consistently refer to them as Poliziano's.

[4] *Memoirs of a Renaissance Pope. The Commentaries of Pius II*, translated and edited by F. A. GRAGG and L. C. GABEL, abridged edn., New York, Capricorn, 1962, p. 147, with thanks to Dr. Ruth Rubinstein for the reference. The entire joke, with *laughingly*, was omitted from the expurgated edition attributed to J. GOBELLINUS, Rome, 1584.

[5] MACHIAVELLI, *Ist. fior.*, p. 461: "gli era vecchio e faceva una impresa da giovani". For other replies concerning Pius and the crusade, cf. note 65 below.

[6] POLIZIANO, *Detti,* nos. 157, 158, p. 68.

of rose-coloured cloth make a man reputable", and "states are not held by chanting prayers" ("with paternosters in hand"), Machiavelli quotes other similar quips: to the exiled Rinaldo degli Albizzi who threatened that the hen was brooding, Cosimo replied, "it will brood badly outside its nest"; to the rebels who conveyed to him the message that they were not asleep, that he could well believe it, since he had deprived them of sleep; to the Venetian and Neapolitan ambassadors who complained about the Florentine republic, that their senators' hair would soon be the colour of his – white, in their own words; and to critics who accused him on his return from exile of ruining the city, "a ruined city is better than a lost city".[7]

Cosimo's family provided the context for other witticisms. When Cosimo cried out one day as the chair in which he was being carried was about to hit a doorway and his servant asked what was the matter, "you cry out before anything's happened", Cosimo replied: "What use would it be to cry out afterwards?".[8] Asked by his wife shortly before he died why he was so taciturn, he answered that when she went to their villa, she spent fifteen days preparing to depart: "Since I have to leave this life and go to another, don't you think that I have a lot to think about?".[9] And when a few hours before he died she asked him why he kept his eyes shut, his dry rejoinder was: "To get them used to it".[10]

The same familial setting provides another story (hardly a joke) about Cosimo told by Lodovico Carbone, Ferrarese ambassador to Florence in 1473, which has the air of being well-founded, if not based on Lodovico's own experience. Cosimo was receiving some ambassadors from Lucca in his own house when one of his little grandsons came to him with some reeds and a small knife and asked him to make him a whistle. Cosimo did so, to the anger of the ambassadors, who complained that he had deserted their serious discussion to attend to little children:

---

[7] *Ist. fior,* pp. 461-462: "due canne di panno rosato facevono uno uomo da bene [cf. A. FABRONI, *Magni Cosmi Medicei Vita,* II, p. 222, note 118: 'un cittadino ed un amico']; e che gli stati non si tenevono co' paternostri in mano"; on the latter, S. DE GRAZIA, *Machiavelli in Hell,* Princeton, Princeton University Press, 1989, p. 226; "che la poteva mal covare fuora del nidio" (PAPANTI, no. 6, p. 5), "egli era meglio città guasta che perduta".

[8] POLIZIANO, *Detti,* no. 195, p. 74; PAPANTI, no. 221, p. 122.

[9] VESPASIANO, *Le vite,* II, p. 210: "avendo io a partirmi di questa vita et andare all'altra, non ti pare egli che si sia assai da pensare?".

[10] MACHIAVELLI, *Ist. fior.,* p. 461: "Per avvezzargli".

Laughing and embracing them, Cosimo said: "O my brothers and elders, were you not fathers, too? Didn't you too experience love for children and grandchildren? You're amazed I made a whistle, lucky for you he didn't ask me to play it, since I'd have done that too". And replying to what they had said, he showed them that he had his mind on their affairs.[11]

The story raises several questions about Cosimo's behaviour: were the ambassadors not entitled to feel annoyed by this interruption during their audience in the Medici palace; should Cosimo have been receiving ambassadors there at all; and was he not – as with Pius – using the occasion to gain political advantage? Nevertheless, what it most obviously demonstrates is Cosimo's skill in combining politics and family affairs, the loving *pater familias* as well as *pater patriae*.

At the same time, Cosimo clearly had no use for over-fond parents and stupid children, like the child of Tegghia, taken to Cosimo by his admiring father, who had a high opinion of his son's intelligence. When asked by Cosimo in what he studied, and the child replied "in books", Cosimo riposted: "Make him study, he needs it".[12] He was equally impatient with citizens whom he thought unintelligent, such as Franco Sacchetti, descendant of the poet and novelist, a member of the governing elite and host of literary gatherings. For all this, Sacchetti was cruelly dismissed by Cosimo for consorting with the learned and knowing nothing, "like the kidney, surrounded with fat and always lean".[13] Just as Cosimo dismissed a "learned, but bad and mad" man with the words: "You have too much good wine in such a bad barrel".[14]

---

[11] *Facezie*, XC, pp. 64-65: "Cosmo, ridendo e abraciandogli disse: O fratelli e mazuri miei, non setti anche voi padri? Non sapetti che amor sia quello de' fioli e nipoti? Vi datti maraveglia ch'io habia fatta la piva: bon fo che non disse ch'io sonasse, che averia anche sonato. E replicando ciò che haveano detto, gli fece intendere che avea hauta la mente a' fatti suoi".

[12] POLIZIANO, *Detti*, no. 4, p. 44; PAPANTI, no. 103, pp. 74-75.

[13] *Ibid.*, no. 16, p. 46: "il quale sempre usava co' dotti e non sapeva niente, era come l'arnione, che sta nel grasso e sempre è magro", cf. PAPANTI, no. 109, p. 77; VESPASIANO, *Le vite*, II (Vita di Franco Sacchetti), pp. 218-219: 'Fu molto amato da Cosimo de' Medici, e da Lorenzo suo fratello, da frate Ambruogio degli Agnoli, da meser Lionardo d'Arezo, e da meser Carlo d'Arezo, da Nicolaio Nicoli, da meser Giannozo Manetti, e da tutti gli uomini degni aveva la città nel tempo suo'. On Sacchetti and his villa as "the perfect setting of quattrocento classical republicanism", M. PHILLIPS, *The Memoir of Marco Parenti,* Princeton, Princeton University Press, 1987, pp. 55-56, 59-63.

[14] POLIZIANO, *Detti,* no. 146, p. 66, PAPANTI, no. 207, p. 118: "Tu hai troppo buono vino a sì cattiva botte!"; cf. PAPANTI nos. 66 and 255, pp. 52, 138-139 (Cosimo's sayings about the 'store' of unlearned doctors of law and about impractical students of oratory in Florence).

So intelligence was at a premium, madness always to be avoided, since the mad "always abuse others physically or verbally".[15] Equally, however, Cosimo disliked pretension in any form, intellectual or moral. So he cut down the man who said that although he could no longer see with "corporal eyes" he retained "mental eyes", by replying that it must be doubly distressing to him not to be able to use his corporal eyes and to have to use mental ones.[16] To a sycophant who told him God would take great pity on him for all his good works and pious foundations, Cosimo – 'unusually' – replied at once that God alone knew his (Cosimo's) motives, and if he had sought worldly pomp and glory, he would pay for it, adding that we never followed the course we should and no one in this life should rest on his laurels.[17]

Cosimo similarly resisted the pretensions of people seeking patronage from him – such as the citizen who, wanting to be in the government, commended himself to Cosimo by saying that he had never opposed the regime and always went to Santa Reparata, the cathedral. "So you should do. Stay there – Cosimo advised him – because it's a good place to be, cool in summer and warm in winter".[18]

To Mariotto Baldovinetti, who tried to win Cosimo's favour by reminding him that he had been one of the priors responsible for saving Cosimo's life in 1433, Cosimo replied that if Mariotto had not got him into trouble, it would not have been necessary to get him out of it; [19] which resembles what he said to another citizen who told him, "as a great kindness", that when others put it about that Cosimo was dead [in 1433], he himself was not around and had not been involved: "what I needed – Cosimo replied – was for you to have *been* around!".[20]

In the same vein he criticized rich, pompous clerics and friars, like fra Roberto, an Observantist, who returned from a visit to the

---

[15] *Ibid.*, no. 145, p. 66: "Soleva dire Cosimo che non si vuol mai impacciarsi con pazzi, perché sempre o fanno altrui villania o ne dicono".

[16] VESPASIANO, *Le vite*, II, p. 191.

[17] *Ibid.*: "fuori della sua consuetudine".

[18] *Detti*, no. 155, p. 68: "Così si vuol che tu faccia: stavviti, perché v'è buona stanza, perché di state v'è freddo e di verno caldo".

[19] *Ibid.*, no. 154, p. 67, PAPANTI, no. 211, p. 119.

[20] *Detti*, no. 153: "Il bisogno mio era che tu vi ti trovassi!".

duke of Milan richly dressed in Flemish cloth. Seeing him so pompous, Cosimo asked if it was sack cloth. Roberto replied that the duke had given it to him. "I didn't ask who gave it but if it was sack cloth". So when Roberto asked Cosimo for 200 florins, Cosimo refused because he did not like his change of ways. But – Vespasiano added – his criticism was delivered in such a way "that no one around noticed", and only after the friar left did Cosimo explain that he disliked his changed way of life: "this is how men called wise should live and Cosimo hated those who were the opposite".[21]

Here discretion is the hallmark of Cosimo's wisdom, as it is in another tale told by Vespasiano describing Cosimo's encounter with a leading citizen who, angered with Cosimo, was openly complaining about him. Instead of replying to him publicly, Cosimo went to bare his soul to him in private. Honestly admitting their differences ("You concern yourself with infinite, I with finite affairs. You raise your ladder to the heavens, while I place mine close to the ground lest flying too high I might fall") and his intention of placing his own interests and those of his family first, he suggested they should agree to differ, like two large dogs, "who, when they meet, sniff each other, and because they both have teeth, go their own ways".[22]

This "sniffing dog" image cunningly presents Cosimo (as Mark Phillips has recently suggested) as the realist and "plain-spoken citizen", but the story also serves to justify Cosimo's reticence, as Vespasiano realized in commenting that although Cosimo revealed himself more openly than he had ever done before in order to silence his critic, it had the opposite effect in ensuring the latter's opposition to Cosimo's son after his death. This reticence was the subject of another joke, in which Cosimo quipped "Learn my language" when Neri Capponi asked him to speak clearly so he could be understood.[23]

His language as a merchant banker was also that of the honest broker, who described approvingly a man who was "quick and alert" as someone with a mind "in ready money".[24] A similar pun under-

---

[21] VESPASIANO, *Le vite*, II, pp. 198-199: "Queste sono le conditioni che vogliono avere gli uomini che si chiamano savi et così come Cosimo aveva in odio quegli ch'erano l'oposito".

[22] *Ibid.*, pp. 195-196, quoted by PHILLIPS, *Memoir*, p. 10.

[23] VESPASIANO, *Le vite*, II, p. 199; POLIZIANO, *Detti*, no. 176, p. 71: "Io vorrei che tu mi dicessi le cose chiare, sì che io t'intendessi –, gli rispuose: – Appara il mio linguaggio!"; cf. note 51 below.

[24] POLIZIANO, *Detti*, no. 272, p. 89, PAPANTI, no. 180, p. 105: "Cosimo, di qualche uomo pronto et accorto, soleva dire che egli aveva il cervello in danari contanti".

lies another banking joke, which plays on the double meaning of *fede* as faith and trust. When complimented on his trustworthiness by a papal secretary, amazed to receive money from the Medici bank in Florence from a cheque paid in in Rome, Cosimo replied: "Messer Piero, the treasure of merchants is faith and the greater the faith of the merchant, the richer he is".[25] Playing in the same way on the double meaning of *rendere* as giving back (giving up the ghost) and repayment of interest, Cosimo also 'almost' joked with God when he used to say: "Have patience, o Lord, in me, and I shall return everything to you".[26] And similarly, when someone complained to Cosimo of being too heavily taxed, Cosimo replied "Well then, settle with God" – or "farewell".[27] As a merchant-banker he called the sterile wealth of notaries money which "swells the legs" – by not circulating, like Cosimo's gout.[28]

The same dry humour was also an effective means of communicating with Florence's soldiers and *condottieri*. Antonello da Forlì was a respected constable who had on one occasion broken his contract with Sigismondo Malatesta and made off with his salary; when Astorre Manfredi repeatedly praised him in Cosimo's home for his 'solicitude' and eagerness, Cosimo interjected, "Say no more about that, since he's now demostrated how eager he is by fleeing before it was time".[29] And to a soldier who when fixing his contract demostrated his battered face to Cosimo as evidence that he did not flee, Cosimo replied: "Nor can the man who gave it to you in the face have fled!".[30] When asked why Francesco Sforza had failed to capture the town near which he was encamped, Cosimo replied with dead-pan humour: "Because he is Duke of Milan".[31]

In the absence of any biographies of Cosimo written during his lifetime these jokes and sayings present a remarkably consistent por-

---

[25] *Detti*, no. 175, p. 71: "O Cosimo, *magna est fides tua*! [paraphrasing Matt. 15, 28] – e lui – Messer Piero, el tesoro de' mercatanti è la fede, e quanta più fede ha il mercatante, tant'è più ricco!".

[26] "Eleganter quasi cum Deo iocaretur dicere solebeat: Patientiam domine habe in me et omnia reddam tibi", Modena, Bibl. Estense, MS. Campori App. 1407 [Z. 6. 25], fol. 30*v*, Francesco Paduano, funeral oration on Cosimo's death. I owe this joke to Prof. James Hankins, who discovered and very kindly sent it to me.

[27] Poliziano, *Detti*, no. 312, p. 97: "Beh, fatevi con Dio! – e andossene".

[28] *Ibid.*, no. 331, p. 100: "e danari de' notai facevano infiare le gambe".

[29] *Ibid.*, no. 276, pp. 89-90, Papanti, no. 170, p. 102.

[30] *Detti*, no. 22, p. 47.

[31] *Ibid.*, no. 339, p. 101.

trait of the shrewd but humane man of the people that substantiates what we already know about him, the witty counterpart of the serious *optimus civis* and *pater patriae*. However, there are problems about accepting this evidence at face value. In the first place, there is the question of genres and models. There was a long tradition of *beffe* and Tuscan witticisms to which some of the jokes attributed to Cosimo clearly belong – such as his joke about Franco Sacchetti.[32] According to fra Salimbene of Parma, the Florentines enjoyed a reputation as jokers in the thirteenth century. On one occasion they discouraged the entry of a friar known for his skill in raising the dead, by exclaiming: "For God's sake, don't let him come here, we're already so numerous, that the city can't hold any more". On another, they upheld their reputation by their response to Dietisalvi, a Florentine friar who was himself a "great joker, as is customary with the Florentines". Slipping on the ice in Florence, he was asked if he wanted anything put under him, and when he replied "yes, the wife of him who asked", the Florentines applauded, saying "Good for him, he is one of us".[33] Joking in Italy, as Creighton Gilbert puts it, was "the city man's collective expression, showing his superiority over the country bumpkin",[34] and even before Boccaccio, humour was a necessary accomplishment in Florence in order to be accepted as "one of us".

There was an equally pervasive – though less demotic – classical tradition of jokes and witticisms. The model of the 'magnanimous' man, familiar through Aristotle's *Ethics*, included wit and urbanity as valuable social virtues, provided they toed the middle line between boorishness and buffoonery. As Aristotle put it, "ironical persons, who depreciate their own merits, give an impression of superior refinement" – even if "at times their mock-modesty looks like self-

---

[32] *Formes et significations de la 'Beffa' dans la littérature italienne de la Renaissance*, I and II (Paris, 1972, 1975), Bowen, *Renaissance Collections* (and now *One hundred Renaissance Jokes: an anthology*, Birmingham, Al., 1988); I have also enjoyed and profited from discussions on *beffe* and classical *ironia* with my colleague, Dr. Letizia Panizza, and with Dr. Dilwyn Knox (who suggested the relevance of Aristotle's magnanimous man). On the derivation of some of Cosimo's jokes, see T. Zanato's notes to Poliziano's *Motti*, nos. 16, 142, 148, 158, 311, pp. 124, 145-148, 174.

[33] Salimbene da Adam, *Cronica*, ed. G. Scalia, Bari, Laterza, 1966, I, pp. 117, 111 ("qui more Florentinorum magnus trufator erat ... Benedicatur ipse, quia de nostris est"; cf. p. 109, about Boncompagnus Florentinus, "cum more Florentinorum trufator maximus esset").

[34] C. E. Gilbert, *Italian Art, 1400-1500*, Englewood Cliffs, N.J., Prentice-Hall, 1980, p. 170.

advertisement".[35] For Aristotle, as for Cicero and the Romans, Socrates was the model ironist: fascinating, witty but deceitful, his feigned simplicity offered a useful strategy for social advance.[36] With Cicero and Quintilian as practical guides and Diogenes Laertius' newly – translated *Lives of the Philosophers* as a source-book, used by Panormita in his *De dictis et factis Alphonsi regis Aragonum* and by Machiavelli in his biography of Castruccio Castracani, urbane jokes and ironic witticisms not surprisingly returned to circulation in the course of the fifteenth century.[37] Cosimo's platonizing joke about "the corporal eye" and "the mental eye" clearly derives from Diogenes Laertius' *Life* of Diogenes the Cynic, the joke about the soldier's battered face from Quintilian and Macrobius, while the one about the man whose brain was "in ready money" was attributed by Seneca to Augustus.[38] Since we know that Machiavelli's friends criticized his list of Castruccio Castracani's "detti o sali" in his biography as too derivative – as well as too numerous – we can ill afford to assume that Cosimo's jokes, any more than Castruccio's, are authentic.[39]

Associated with this is the problem of their promiscuity. Jokes attributed to Cosimo by Poliziano reappear later as Lorenzo's jokes, while Rinaldo degli Albizzi is replaced by Palla Strozzi in Giovanni Pontano's version of the egg-hatching joke.[40] The witticism in Polizi-

---

[35] *Nich. Ethics* IV, 7, 14 (1127 b 22-26), transl. J. A. K. THOMSON, *The Ethics of Aristotle*, London, George Allen and Unwin, 1953, p. 116, and on the middle line between boorishness and the "ill-bred buffoon who feels he must be funny come what may", *ibid.*, (IV, 8), pp. 116-118.

[36] ARISTOTLE, above; CICERO, *De orat.* II, LXVII, 270; *De off.* I, 30, 108 and *Acad. prior.* II, V, 15.

[37] The *Lives* were translated for Cosimo by Ambrogio Traversari in the 1420s. On the different Greek and Roman traditions, see G. LUCK, *Vir Facetus: a Renaissance Ideal'*, «Studies in Philology», LV, 1958, pp. 107-121, and now D. KNOX, *Ironia. Medieval and Renaissance Ideas on Irony*, Leyden, Brill, 1989. PANORMITA's biography of Alfonso of Aragon was first printed in Pisa in 1485 (see BOWEN, no. 3. pp. 6-7; cf. J. H. BENTLEY, *Politics and Culture in Renaissance Naples*, Princeton, Princeton University Press, 1987, p. 224, on the influence also of XENOPHON's *Memorabilia* as a model.

[38] *Lives of the philosophers* VI, 53, London and Cambridge, Mass., (Loeb edition, 1965, II, pp. 55-56), repeated in LODOVICO CARBONE's *Facezie*, no. 33, p. 31; POLIZIANO, *Motti*, Zanato's notes for nos. 22, 45 and 272 on pp. 125, 131, 166.

[39] On MACHIAVELLI's *Vita*, see F. GAETA's introduction, *Ist. fior.*, pp. 3-4, referring to Zanobi Buondelmonti's letter to Machiavelli of 6 Sept. 1520, *Lettere*, ed. F. Gaeta, Milan, Feltrinelli, 1961), no. 177, p. 394: "oltre all'essere troppi quegli suoi detti o sali, ve ne è una parte che furono ad altri et antiche et moderni savi attribuiti". According to Machiavelli, Castruccio was "mirabile nel rispondere e mordere, o acutamente o urbanamente" (*Vita*, in *Ist. fior.*, p. 36).

[40] G. PONTANO, *De sermone libri sex*, Verona, Thesauro Mundi, 1954, IV, XI, p. 153.

ano's collection attributing to Cosimo the observation that the Medici villa in Cafaggiuolo had a better view than the Fiesole villa – "because what it saw was theirs, which was not true of Fiesole" – reappears in the slightly later, more ponderous compilation by Niccolò Angèli dal Bùcine. In this version, Cosimo's son Giovanni is forced to justify to his father his expensive construction of a villa on the steep hillside at Fiesole on the grounds of its view; Cosimo counters that there could not be a better view than that from Cafaggiuolo, and when asked how this was possible since Cafaggiuolo was in a valley, Cosimo replies: "Because what you can see from there belongs to you". And in Paolo Cortesi's *De Cardinalatu* the joke becomes one of Lorenzo de' Medici's 'salty' witticisms about refusing to cut down a pine tree in his suburban villa "because he would never deprive himself of his own in order to see another's possessions".[41]

There are also surprising lacunae, in which Cosimo is notable for his absence from contemporary collections of jokes. For example, he does not appear in the *Facetiae* of Poggio Bracciolini, Cosimo's companion at the Council of Constance, which might have been expected to provide fertile soil for witticisms from the observant and critical Cosimo.[42] Nor does he figure in the many Florentine anecdotes of the Piovano Arlotto, the popular Tuscan parish priest who travelled on Florentine galleys to Flanders and was a frequent winer and diner in Florence. The general authenticity of Arlotto's jokes, which F.W. Kent and Amanda Lillie have recently demostrated, makes Cosimo's absence the more surprising.[43]

This raises questions about the value of the jokes as first-hand evidence of Cosimo and his jocundity. As Renaissance humanists realised, a *iocundus homo* was not necessarily a jolly man himself but one who imparted jollity and happiness to others.[44] Is this the sense

---

[41] Poliziano, *Motti*, no. 3, p. 44; Papanti, no. 93, p. 70; P. Cortesi, *De cardinalatu libri tres*, Castro Cortesio, 1510, fol. 88*r*): "numquam esse adimendum suum ut cerni aliena possint"; cf. note 58 below.

[42] *Liber facetiarum* in Poggio Bracciolini, *Opera*, Basle, 1538, repr. Turin, Bottega d'Erasmo, 1964, I, pp. 420-491.

[43] P. Arlotto, (*Motti e Facezie del Piovano Arlotto*, ed. G. Folena, Milan and Naples, Ricciardi, 1953), and on their authenticity, F. W. Kent and A. Lillie, *The Piovano Arlotto: New Documents*, in *Florence and Italy. Renaissance Studies in Honour of Nicolai Rubinstein*, eds. P. Denley and C. Elam, London, Westfield College, 1988, pp. 347-367.

[44] See ASF Acquisti e Doni 82, fol. 66*r*: "Iocundus homo dicitur non qui laetus est sed qui laetitiam alterum affert, unde potest aliquis tristis maestusque esse, tum iocundus nobis. Cicero hanc differentiam exprimit ad Sulpitium consolantem".

in which Cosimo was jocund? In the course of Cosimo's lifetime, reflecting the increasing influence of classical literature as well as changing social conditions, jokes were changing their form and function in Florence. Although the older tradition of puns and *beffe* continued, as we can see from the jokes of Luigi Pulci and Lorenzo's intimates, growing sophistication and courtliness made humanists more selfconscious about models and types of jokes.

In the hands of courtiers like Platina, Pontano or Castiglione, Aesopian fables and apologues were condemned as puerile, while the "sparkling salty witticisms" of Florentines, so much in demand, were transformed into ponderous illustrations of "methods of producing laughter" – as we can see from Pontano's transformation of Cosimo's witticism about the broody hen:

> Palla Strozzi, driven from Florence by the Medici faction, is said to have said in flight, "It is necessary for us to incubate, o men, both our intelligence and our strength, that we may free our patria from domination by one man". When this was related to Cosimo, he replied: "These few words are to be sent back: it is not possible for one who has lost its nest and is deprived of feathers to incubate".[45]

In this version it is difficult to recognise Cosimo's wit, let alone laugh at it. According to Platina, Cosimo thought "urbane wit" of the type favoured by Caesar Augustus was all right for "the best citizen", but the scurrility and obscenity of farces and mimes were definitely not: "totally reject them", he said.[46]

Even without this courtly transformation, it is notable that with one exception (to which I shall return in conclusion), there are no jokes attributed to Cosimo that are at all *risqué* – in an ambience

---

[45] See Paolo Cortesi, *De cardinalatu*, fols. 84*v* ("At maxime inane est et puerile illud quo videmus fabellarum apologorumque genus commentitia ratione texi"), 87*v*; G. Pontano, *De sermone* IV, xi ("Quae servanda sint in risu provocando"), pp. 147-148 and 153, cf. IV, *ibid.*, p. 130, and B. Castiglione, *Il Cortegiano*, ed. V. Cian, Florence, Sansoni, 1947, II, 65 and 78, pp. 240-241, 264. On the demand for Florentine jokes in Rome ("eight or ten of Lorenzo's jokes would be enough", Paolo Cortesi wrote to Francesco di ser Barone on 17 May 1497, provided they were 'sharp'), see ASF Lettere varie 16, 422, quoted in *Between curial Rome and convivial Florence*, pp. 253 below.

[46] B. Platina, *De optimo cive*, ed. F. Battaglia, Bologna, Zanichelli, 1944, p. 210: "Scurras vero, gnathones, mimos, omnino abs te reiice, cum dignitatem optimi civis obscoenitate verborum et turpitudine indecentes motus ac gestus dedecorent". It is interesting that by the end of the sixteenth century, it was found necessary to explain and comment on Cosimo's *Detti* in the Venice (1599) edition of Lodovico Domenichi's *Facetie*.

in which sexual and body jokes were the breath of life. In contrast to ser Filippo Pieruzzi, whom Vespasiano describes as "very merry, it seemed he was always laughing", Cosimo "was very serious, spending his time with serious men who disliked any form of levity, because he hated all buffoons, clowns and those who spend their time ungainfully" and "never delighted in any game whatsoever, except for the game of chess, which he would sometimes play after supper to pass the time – but very seldom".[47]

In a revealing passage in his *Dialogue on Laws and Legal Judgements*, Bartolomeo Scala described how Cosimo used to disagree with Niccolò da Uzzano about the pranks young people played at Carnival time, blocking off roads and demanding payment before allowing people to enter them. Whereas Niccolò da Uzzano thought such games were to be tolerated as a form of letting off steam, Cosimo thought they were "detestable and pernicious", since they set a bad precedent which would corrupt children for the rest of their lives.[48] He would have enjoyed, one feels, the interjection of a Florentine when he saw children throwing stones or heard them making a noise: 'O Herod, where are you now?".[49] Cosimo's platonic view of children's games may also throw light on his socratic irony and attitude to jokes.[50] Is it possible that Cosimo was not humorous at all?

In 1432, just before his exile and triumphant return, a political opponent, Francesco Filelfo, described in a letter how Cosimo, in contrast to his "open and lighthearted" brother Lorenzo "is, I notice, despite appearing devoted to me, the kind of man who feigns and dissembles everything. He is so taciturn that he can scarcely be understood even by his intimates and servants in his family circle".[51]

---

[47] *Le vite*, II (Vita di ser Filippo di ser Ugolino), p. 245: "era molto alegro, sempre pareva che ridessi"; (Vita di Cosimo), p. 169: "Fu molto volto alla gravità et d'usare cor uomini grave alieni da ogni legereza, perché aveva in odio tutti i bufoni, istrioni et tutti quegli che ispendevano il tempo disutilmente"), 195 ("Non si dilettò mai di giuco ignuno, se non del giuoco degli iscacchi, che alle volte per pasare tempo, dopo disinare arebbe giucato uno gioco o dua, ma rade volte").

[48] B. Scala, *Dialogus de legibus et iudiciis*, ed. L. Borghi, «Bibliofilia», XLII, 1940, p. 258: «ea... carnispriviorum licentia... detestari etiam et pernitiosam putare Cosmus Medices pater patriae noster sapientissimus civis consuevit».

[49] Poliziano, *Detti*, no. 50, p. 52: "O Erode, dove se' tu ora?".

[50] On Cosimo's socratic wisdom, see *Platonism in fifteenth-century Florence*, pp. 223-227 below; on socratic irony, D. Knox, *Ironia*, chs. 6-9; cf. note 52 below.

[51] Francesco Filelfo to the Cardinal of Bologna, Niccolò Albergati, *Epistolae* (Milan, 1502), p. 11*r* (b3*r*), 22 Sept. 1432, quoted by W. Roscoe, *The Life of Lorenzo de' Medici*, London, A. Strahan, T. Cadell Jun. and W. Davies in the Strand and J. Edwards in Pall Mall,

As Gutkind has suggested, in this situation Cosimo's use of proverbs and fables served a useful political purpose – in delivering messages "in such a way that no one noticed", as Vespasiano put it. It is notable that in Scala's fables (which were praised for "platonically mixing the sweet with the sour, the serious with jokes"), Cosimo appears as one of the foremost admirers of Wisdom and Truth, with a message "for my people to worship [Wisdom] continually".[52] As unofficial head of an ostensible republic, Cosimo lacked the means to publicize his will and the legal sanctions to make it obeyed. Necessarily he had to act covertly, using 'sayings' (*dicerie*) – like the Delphic oracle – to diffuse his political wisdom to all levels of society.

From this point of view, Cosimo's wit may have served an equally practical purpose. Although Vespasiano professed to admire Cosimo's discreet use of veiled jokes to purvey home truths, there is a less pleasant aspect to his humour. The only occasion on which Cosimo laughs in Vespasiano's memory is when he got his own back on the dishonest overseer of his building works by simply withdrawing his commission from him. News rapidly spread through the city and no one talked of anything else. The man went to Cosimo, in Vespasiano's presence, and told him the whole of Florence was saying that he had stolen from Cosimo and this was why he had been deprived of his position. In reply, Vespasiano reports, Cosimo did not say he had been robbed, as he had been, but he merely asked the overseer what he wanted him to do. The man replied that if asked whether he had stolen from him, Cosimo should deny it.

> Cosimo said: "See that I'm asked and I will say it". Without saying anything, he turned to the people around him and began to laugh and said nothing to them; and no one dared to speak because of his authority.[53]

1796, I, p. 32; C. Gutkind, *Cosimo de' Medici*, Oxford, Clarendon Press, 1938, p. 240: "At Cosmus, quamquam videtur amantissimus mei, eiusmodi tamen virum esse animadverto qui et simulet et dissimulet omnia. Estque usque adeo taciturnus, ut ne intimis quidem familiaribus ac domesticis queat intelligi. At Laurentius huius frater ingenio est et aperto et levi". For one of Cosimo's quips about Filelfo, see Poliziano, *Motti*, n. 181, p. 72.

[52] Alison Brown, *Bartolomeo Scala*, pp. 285-286 and 211 (Italian edition, pp. 201, 143), quoting *Apologi centum*, ed. C. Muellner, Vienna, Verlag des K. K. Staatsgymnasiums im XVII Bezirke von Wien (Hernals), 1896, nos. lxiii and lxv, and Alessandro Farnese's letter to Scala: 'Vero te Platonicum esse dixerim ita congrue dulcia amaris et iocis seria lepidissima quadam permisces').

[53] Vespasiano, *Le vite*, II, p. 209: "Disse Cosimo: fa che io ne sia domandato et dirollo. Sendo alcuni collui, sanza dire nulla si volse loro, et cominciò a ridere et non disse nulla, né ignuno fu che avessi ardimento di parlare per la autorità sua".

Far from illustrating Cosimo's "great patience", as Vespasiano suggests, the story can be read as an example of Cosimo's manipulative behaviour in relying on public opinion and gossip to do what would have been better done by him openly. According to St Benedict, "the mouths of those who uttered witticisms causing laughter should be closed with eternal padlocks" – for the reason, Savonarola tells us, that jokes are the weapons of a tyrant, "who when he wants to put down someone, orders his friends and satellites to ridicule him, while he stands on one side laughing, without it seeming that it was he who was responsible".[54] Savonarola, of course, had Lorenzo de' Medici in mind, not Cosimo, but the story of the contractor suggests that Cosimo may have used jokes in the same way, as a hidden form of political control.

To read Cosimo's witticisms with the benefit of Savonarola's hindsight alters our initial impression of the humane and witty man of the people. Far from speaking plainly, the reverse was obviously true, as Vespasiano admitted in saying that his "replies were brief and somewhat obscure, so they they could be taken in various ways".[55] To investigate these ways, or levels of interpretation, offers an approach to re-assessing Cosimo that I can here only begin to explore.

* * *

The most obvious function of popular proverbs and fables is to offer homely moral lessons condemning avarice, ignorance and greed. Cosimo's saying about not watering envy, his advice to a jealous husband to bury the horn on his head outside the city, and his criticism of fra Roberto's pomposity are all examples of this function.[56] So too is his retort to an employee, who thinking to frighten Cosimo with the balance-sheet of his building expenditure, reported that 7,000 florins had been spent on the Badia at Fiesole and 5,000 florins on San

---

[54] G. SAVONAROLA, *Prediche sopra i Salmi*, ed. V. ROMANO, Rome, Belardetti, 1969, I, p. 139 (8 May 1495) and *Prediche sopra Amos e Zaccaria*, ed. P. GHIGLIERI, Rome, Belardetti, 1971, I, p. 227 (25 Feb. 1496): "Il tiranno si ride sempre del compagno, e quando e' vuole deprimere uno, egli ordina tra gli amici, tra satelliti sua e tra' compagni, che quel tale sia sbeffato, e lui sta da canto e se ne ride, e non pare che sia lui che lo faccia sbeffare".

[55] *Le vite*, II, p. 192: "Le sue risposte erano brieve et alquanto oscure, che si potevano pigliare a' varii sensi".

[56] *Ibid.*, pp. 197-198, 209-210 and note 21 above. On not watering envy, cf. *Detti*, no. 132, p. 63, PAPANTI, no. 78, p. 59.

Lorenzo; to which Cosimo calmly responded that the workers in San Lorenzo should be criticized for not working as hard as those in the Badia. However, although Cosimo's stated intention (according to Vespasiano) was to reprehend the avarice and ignorance of his factor, the story clearly works on more than one level, since it also serves to illustrate Cosimo's generosity, as Vespasiano himself points out. And since Cosimo rapidly related it to visiting friends, it demonstrates, too – like the story of the dishonest overseer – Cosimo's publicity skills.[57] We know from other building jokes, including Cosimo's rebuke to a citizen for overspending on a house he was not capable of completing, how delicate the balance was between legitimate magnificence and extravagance in Renaissance Florence.[58] His sayings clearly helped Cosimo to draw the line to his own advantage.

The stories also operated as lessons in social behaviour and what Elias would call "civilized manners". A good example of this is the tale of Cosimo, the peasant and the pears, in which Cosimo set before a visiting peasant the delicacy of muscatel pears. Being used to fat, wild pears, the peasant said: "Oh, we give them to the pigs"; then Cosimo, turning to a servant, said: "We don't. Take them away".[59] A similar story describes a supper given by Cosimo's father to an alpine peasant with whom he was friendly, at which he asked his wife to recite some sonnets. Asked if he had enjoyed them, the peasant replied "Yes, but he would rather his wife knew how to make a new gown from two old ones that recite these fables".[60] Another similarly contrasts the lives of the rich and poor: "On being urged by Cosimo to draw close to the fire during a period of great cold,

---

57 VESPASIANO, *Le vite,* II, p. 182: "una risposta degna di lui".

58 *Detti*, no. 46, p. 51: when asked by Albizotto degli Albizi for 100 fl. to complete his house, "parendo a Cosimo che non fussi uomo da poterla condurre, rispuose – 'Io son contento di prestartene dugento: ma serbami all'intonacare!' ", PAPANTI, no. 129, p. 87, P. CORTESI, *De cardinalatu*, fol. 87*v*; there are other building jokes in L. DOMENICHI'S *Facetie,* fols. k2*v* ("Dell'edificar sontuosamente", k3*v* ("D'un pazzo"). On problems of building in Florence, A. D. FRASER JENKINS, *Cosimo de' Medici's patronage of architecture and the theory of magnificence,* «Journal of the Warburg and Courtauld Institutes», XXXIII, 1970, pp. 162-170; F. W. KENT, *Più superba de quella de Lorenzo': courtly and family interest in the building of Filippo Strozzi's palace*, «Renaissance Quarterly», XXX, 1977, pp. 311-324, and his *Palaces, politics and society in fifteenth-century Florence*, «I Tatti Studies», II, 1987, pp. 41-70.

59 POLIZIANO, *Detti*, no. 45, p. 51; cf. A. MOLHO, *Cosimo de' Medici, Pater Patriae* or *Padrino?*, «Stanford Italian Review», I, 1979, p. 12, who reads this and the following stories as descriptive accounts of Cosimo's relationship with his peasants and their 'sense of deference, almost of awe' towards their landlord.

60 *Ibid.*, no. 171, pp. 70-71.

the poor peasant replied: 'Cosimo, I don't feel cold' ". And Cosimo: "I wish you would teach me what you do". He replied: "If you put on all your clothes, as I do, you wouldn't feel cold".[61] In this case the story follows a common model about a *dives* and *rusticus*, which Poggio Bracciolini adopted for one of his jokes.[62] In another, a poorly-dressed scholar, blamed by Cosimo for gambling, wittily turns the tables on the moralizing Cosimo (like the pirate's 'witty' rejoinder to Alexander the Great in St Augustine's *City of God*) by attributing Cosimo's wealth solely to the scholar's losses when playing and losing the game of chance: "Delighted, Cosimo re-clothed the scholar and gave him money".[63] In all these stories, our sympathies are intended to lie, in Aesopian tradition, with the underdog. But underlying their outward simplicity is a more devious socratic message enforcing the Medici's superiority – as openhearted and generous patrons (as their biographers have consistently interpreted them to mean), and as models of cultured urbane behaviour to amuse and instruct the circles in which the stories circulated.

The same is true of Cosimo's witticisms at the expense of the clergy. As the earliest Florentine *beffe* demostrate, the clergy had long been the butt of popular humour and their laxity and pretensions provided Cosimo with an easy target. In addition to the story of fra Roberto, there are two involving the saintly archibishop of Florence, Antoninus. When asked by the archbishop to support a law prohibiting priests from gambling, Cosimo replied that the church might begin by setting its own house in order, "so they don't use bad dice"; and when Antoninus's successor, Orlando Bonarli, complained of being unable "to do as Antoninus did", Cosimo's tart response was, "if you want to do as he did, live as he did".[64] On another occasion Cosimo 'wisely' responded to the papal legate's request for money against the Turks with a story about the king of Hungary: after twice imposing heavy taxes and twice being defeated by the Turks, he was told by God, with the consecrated Host in hand ("which, as a consacrated king, he was allowed to touch"): "Do it with your own and you will be victorious". The legate, getting the message, replied:

[61] *Ibid.*, no. 311, p. 97; PAPANTI, no. 191, pp. 111-112.

[62] *Liber facetiarum*, no. 153, p. 461, cf. *Detti*, p. 174, note to no. 311.

[63] POLIZIANO, *Detti*, no. 268, pp. 88-89; ST. AUGUSTINE, *City of God, IV, p. 4;* on Cosimo and Donatello, *ibid.*, no. 234, p. 84.

[64] POLIZIANO, *Detti*, nos. 2 and 131, pp. 44 and 63; PAPANTI, no. 102, p. 74.

"Deservedly, Cosimo, all the world considers you wise" and so came to a satisfactory agreement with him.[65]

This Delphic utterance, like the joke Cosimo told Pius II to excuse himself from kissing the Pope's foot, not only showed his common touch (ensuring wide diffusion), but also enabled Cosimo to assert his secular independence of the Church – by avoiding a gesture of homage and by invoking royal sacral authority (which he himself lacked) to condemn papal taxation of the laity. It was Cosimo's lack of authority as unofficial ruler, or 'paramour' of Florence,[66] that gave his jokes special importance as political utterances. Although he outwardly disclaimed the value of models – "the last thing that man should want to do, or should do, is to behave according to models", he said –,[67] his popular but allusive sayings nevertheless projected his opinions with maximum publicity and minimum responsibility, as the story to the papal legate demonstrates.

On this level, we can interpret his numerous witticisms about his exile and return in 1433-34 as a successful re-writing of this chapter in Florentine history to transform his initial defeat into a critique of his opponents: thus on the 1433 *parlamento* which exiled him: "they have taught us what we have to do to them" and to Palla Strozzi: *Hodie mihi, cras tibi*, "my turn today, yours tomorrow".[68] Although many of the political aphorisms attributed to Cosimo lack originality, they enforce the image of Cosimo's shrewd realism and worldly wisdom – such as his warning to a peasant not to get involved in quarrels. When the peasant said he only had one enemy, Cosimo replied "Ah me, try to make peace with him, for in every big state one enemy is too many and a hundred friends too few"; or his advice to a rich but not very clever friend who asked how to comport himself in the external office he was about to assume: "Dress in red and say little".[69]

---

65 *Detti*, no. 141, pp. 65-66: "perché, essendo re, potea toccarla come quello che è sacrato", "Fa con tuo et avrai vittoria", "Meritamente, Cosimo, tutto il mondo vi stima savio". Cf PAPANTI, no. 62, pp. 48-49 (another oblique *risposta* to Pius, rejecting his demand for a subsidy to the Turks).

66 Pius II, *Commentaries*, p. 108.

67 PAPANTI, no. 98, p. 73: "Cosimo de' Medici usava dire: che l'ultima chosa che l'huomo voleva et doveva fare, era condursi al paragone".

68 POLIZIANO, *Detti*, nos. 164, 148, pp. 69, 67, PAPANTI, no. 215, p. 120; cf. note 7 above on his replies to the exiles.

69 POLIZIANO, *Detti*, no. 142, p. 66; PAPANTI, no. 205, p. 117; B. CASTIGLIONE, *Il Cortegiano* II, 78, p. 264: "Vesti di rosato e parla poco"; cf. *Detti* no. 152, p. 67, PAPANTI, no.

In one story Cosimo's wisdom is contrasted with the madness of two of his fellow members on the war commission of Ten, not only "an audacious artisan" who criticized Cosimo for disregarding the people, but also his friend and rival Angelo Acciaiuoli. Angelo committed the mistake of "misinterpreting the signal" when Cosimo, after this attack, had set before Angelo the silver bowl used for collecting votes. Thinking he was intended to hit the artisan on the head with it, Angelo picked it up – to be restrained by Cosimo's hand on his arm: "there's already one madman among us, it would have been said that there were two!".[70] In another story, by contrast, we see Cosimo cleverly understanding the signal delivered to him by his henchman and political manager, Puccio Pucci, who anticipated political danger in a forthcoming law against a tax dodger and wanted to warn Cosimo during his son's wedding celebrations:

> Unable to have an audience with [Cosimo] as he wanted because of the festivities, [Puccio] said to him: "For God's sake, Cosimo! After the wedding, you can go on holiday! (*in villa*). Immediately understanding what he meant, Cosimo remedied the situation".[71]

In contrast to Angelo (who subsequently proved himself a political opponent by conspiring against Cosimo's son), Cosimo was not only politically shrewd himself but was adept at understanding the signals of others.

Cosimo's wisdom was itself the butt of at least two surviving jokes, showing the extent to which it had become a coin of common currency. One is a joke about the gout of a woman called 'Wisdom' (La Sapienza), which "she began to have from the time of Cosimo". The other more audaciously counters Cosimo's criticism of a political rival. To Cosimo's accusation, "This is too fine a gown for such a small tax assessment", Dietisalvi Nerone 'instantly replied': "And that

---

210, pp. 118-119 ("Diceva Cosimo che si dimenticano prima cento benefici che una iniuria, e chi iniuria non perdona mai"), *Detti* no. 203, p. 75, PAPANTI, no. 225, p. 124 ("Cosimo diceva che quando uno era tornato d'uficio et era domandato dove fussi stato,era buon segno, perché non s'era di lui sentito nulla"). Cf. PAPANTI, no. 237, p. 131 (on suspicion, wind and loyalty as three constants).

[70] POLIZIANO, *Detti*, no. 137, p. 64, PAPANTI, no. 202, pp. 115-116: "Intese ⟨male⟩ messer Agnolo il cenno", "Egl'era qui fra noi un pazzo, e sarebbesi poi detto che e' ve ne fussino stati due!" The artisan was Giuliano di Particino, an *albergatore*, member of the Dieci in 1451-52.

[71] *Ibid.*, no. 134, p. 64: "Beh, a Dio, Cosimo! Fatte le nozze, te ne potrai ire in villa! – il che subito inteso, Cosimo rimediò al pericolo".

is too small a brain for such high political status".[72] In this street dialogue about power, Cosimo (on surviving evidence) emerges as the victor – as two last stories demonstrate particularly well. The first concerns Puccio Pucci again. When urged by Puccio to accept the Gonfalonierate of Justice, a citizen replied he was not wise enough and asked if it would be enough to be as wise as Cosimo.

Half as wise would be enough, Puccio replied, haven't you any wisdom?
A little, he replied.
Do what Cosimo tells you and you'll have all his wisdom; add to it your own little wisdom, and you'll have more, and so be wiser than Cosimo'.

The story neatly combines Plato's unegalitarian idea of 'equality' with the order to obey Cosimo, "do as he tells you": by obeying the wisdom of the ruler, the citizens will, in Plato's words, "all be brother and equals"; and by adding to this his own, the citizen will be even wiser than Cosimo – provided he obeys him.[73]

If Cosimo was to be obeyed because he was wise, the mad – as we saw – were to be avoided, because they "always abused others physically or verbally".[74] As we know from Shakespeare, madmen and fools are wont to deliver home-truths to rulers and tyrants. In Florence, it was the citizen Valore Buondelmonte who enacted this role by feigning madness in the time of the tyrannical duke of Athens. Emptying his shirt of cherries, he went into the piazza and said to the children: "Pluck me, I am the Commune".[75]

This is the context for understanding the one sexual joke attributed to Cosimo, a genre which otherwise, as we have seen, he abhorred:

There was in the time of Cosimo a madman called Uguccione, who, finding himself in the piazza together with one of the Salviati, a prudent man but somewhat infamous for his sodomy, said to him: – "Bugger Cosimo!" – Then, turning round, Cosimo said: "Bugger him, since he enjoys it!";

---

[72] *Detti*, no. 20, p. 47: "Ella le cominciò ad avere sino al tempo di Cosimo!"; PAPANTI, no. 45, pp. 34-35: "Questa è troppo bella cioppa a sì poca gravezza... Et cotesto è troppo poco cervello a sì grande stato".

[73] *Ibid.*, no. 7, p. 45, PAPANTI, no. 105, pp. 75-76; PLATO, *The Republic*, bk. IX, 590. For other stories involving Puccio Pucci's political skills, *Detti*, nos. 124 and 138, pp. 62-65.

[74] See note 15 above.

[75] POLIZIANO, *Detti*, no. 231 (cf. 232), p. 83. For illustrations of the "Comune in Signoria" and the "Comune Pelato" in the Duomo, Arezzo (1223), see C. FRUGONI, *Una lontana città*, Turin, Einaudi, 1983, plates 79, 80.

and he [Salviati] replied: "I must say, Cosimo, you know how to derive pleasure from the wise and from the mad!".[76]

Once again Cosimo wins all the prizes for his performance, showing himself to be one of the people and at the same time diverting public abuse of himself in the piazza – for which, in the time of Lorenzo, the offender might well have been summarily punished for lese-majesty.

Re-read carefully, we can understand better some of "the various ways" in which Cosimo's "brief and somewhat obscure sayings" can be interpreted. It remains difficult to know at what level to approach them. To some extent they evidently represent a later re-working of his image, a popular counterpart to the humanist tradition of eulogising Cosimo as the serious Pater Patriae.[77] That they also served a practical function in Cosimo's own day, in the way I have suggested, is clear from a letter written by Cosimo to his cousin Averardo in 1431. He wrote, he told his cousin, not "to criticize or instruct" him, since that was not his practice nor his profession, but since their opinions clearly differed and each was determined to stick to his own, they should "follow the authority of ser Muccio" by agreeing to differ and making a joke of it.[78] So jokes could also help to defuse tense situations and paper over differences, a useful means of avoiding confrontation without loss of honour in Florence's conflictual and outspoken society. Although it may be argued we should distinguish such *battute* from more serious utterances, it is not always easy to do so, nor helpful if we are to understand their scope. Without committing him to precise statements, thanks to their allusiveness and irony Cosimo's sayings – like those of the Delphic oracle – enabled his wisdom to be diffused among all levels of society at the same time as they undermined criticism through ridicule and laughter. Cosimo remains as wise and shrewd as he is reputed to be but much less jocund than his many witticisms suggest.

---

[76] POLIZIANO, *Detti*, no. 136, p. 64, PAPANTI, no. 46, p. 35: "Cazzo in culo, Cosimo! – Allora, voltosi, Cosimo disse: – Dàllo qua a costui, che se ne diletta! – ; et egli rispose: – Tu sai pur, Cosimo, pigliar piacere de' savi e de' matti!". Cf., PAPANTI, no. 43, pp. 29-30 (Poggio Bracciolini, kept from lunch by a long meeting, said "C... in c... a questo popolo", to which Cosimo "udendo, dixe: *Maledictus puer centum annorum*".

[77] I owe this observation to Mark Phillips.

[78] Florence, Archivio di Stato, MAP IV, 311 (31 Oct. 1431): "Io non dicho per riprendere né per insegnare, che non è mia usanza né mio mestiere; ma più la speranza mi conferma in sull'openione mio e tu veggio ti stai in sul tuo, e a questo modo seghuireno l'autorità di ser Muccio [mucciere = fare beffe]". I owe the reference to this letter and its interpretation to the generosity of Dale Kent, at present working on Cosimo's letters. Cf. the story about the sniffing dog, note 22 above.

3

PIERFRANCESCO DE' MEDICI, 1430-1476

A RADICAL ALTERNATIVE TO ELDER MEDICEAN SUPREMACY?

A man of "a rare and courteous nature",[1] "a bit of a backwoodsman", 'fat' and slow:[2] none of these contemporary descriptions of Cosimo de' Medici's nephew suggests a political activist. Pierfrancesco's character and his role in Florence remain obscure. Was he simply a large, slow-moving country-lover who genuinely preferred to escape the urban pursuits and political responsibilities enjoyed by his more sophisticated cousins? Or did his placid exterior conceal the germs of that resentment which later led his sons to break from the elder branch of the family and survive its downfall in 1494? This political question is also of social and cultural interest, since the division of the family entailed disagreement about patronage and the social bifurcation of a household which had lived in common until the 1450s and made no wills until the 1470s.

Outwardly the family was united until the events of 1494, but in fact the roots of division were formed in Pierfrancesco's lifetime and were nourished by a variety of causes: by the lack of primogeniture in Italy which gave financial advantages to single heirs; by Pierfrancesco's own ambivalent and uncertain attitude towards his cousins, by (according to one observer)[3] the contaminating influence of his

---

This paper was originally published in the «Journal of the Warburg and Courtauld Institute», XLII, 1979.

[1] Nicodemo Tranchedini to Francesco Sforza, 2 December 1454, ed. R. MAGNANI, *Relazioni private tra la Corte Sforzesca di Milano e Casa Medici, 1450-1500,* Milano, 1910, p. IV, doc. 6: "ha l'animo gentile et pelegrino".

[2] Cf. pp. 80 and 91 below.

[3] Cf. pp. 91-92 below.

father-in-law Angelo Acciaiuoli. Above all, the growing authority of Cosimo and his descendants strained family loyalty. As the elder branch advanced, its members became less willing to share power and status in Florence, even with their own cousins. The separate tax returns submitted in 1469 and the separate wills of the next decade were signs of a diverging attitude to authority and the exercise of power in Florence. This culminated in the revolt and exile of Lorenzo and Giovanni di Pierfrancesco in the spring of 1494, and their triumphant return, re-named 'Popolani', after their cousins' downfall in November 1494. The account which follows offers fragmentary but important evidence of this private – and ultimately public – dissension among the Medici.

Pierfrancesco was born in 1430 to Lorenzo di Giovanni di Bicci de' Medici and Ginevra di Giovanni Cavalcanti.[4] As a boy he visited the Val d'Arno with his mother and members of her powerful and old-established family.[5] But when his father died on 23 September 1440, his mother and his maternal grandmother, Costanza Malespini (who came from another old magnate family) renounced their right to guardianship over the ten-year-old Pierfrancesco in favour of his father's brother, Cosimo de' Medici.[6] The brothers had shared a common household in Via Larga and after his father's death Pierfrancesco continued to live on close terms with his cousins. He was evidently loved by the whole Medici family. He is mentioned fondly in their letters and included in family events. In 1443 he asked his cousin Piero to send some bagpipes to him in Trebbio, a fortified residence in the Mugello, to help him entertain "lots of women" who were coming on Sunday.[7] And when he returned from Rome with

---

[4] On Pierfrancesco and his father, G. Pieraccini, *La Stirpe de' Medici di Cafaggiolo, I,* Florence, Vallecchi, 1924, pp. 43-47, 149-155 (who refers to another brother, Francesco, who predeceased his father [p. 149]). Pierfrancesco was born on 15 May 1430, ASF, Libro di età, *Tratte* 443 *bis,* f. 213*r.* Cf. Lorenzo de' Medici's *Ricordi* (ed. A. Fabroni, *Laurentii Medicis Magnifici Vita,* Pisa, Jacopo Gratioli, 1794, II, p. 6).

[5] Contessina to Cosimo de' Medici, 4 March 1438, ASF *MAP* 11, 227, Pieraccini, *La Stirpe,* I, p. 46, translated by J. Ross, *The Lives of the Early Medici,* London, 1910, pp. 10-11 (with the incorrect date '1427-28'): "La Ginevra et Piero Francesco sono in Valdarno et Amerigho Chavalcanti è rimaso chon loro". On the Cavalcanti, L. Martines, *The Social World of the Florentine Humanists, 1390-1460,* London, Routledge and Kegan Paul, 1963, pp. 60, n. 149, 202, *cf.* Giovanni Cavalcanti, *Istorie fiorentine,* Milano, Aldo Martello, 1944, p. 263.

[6] ASF, *MAP* 161, ff. 1*r*-5*v* (2-13 December 1440).

[7] ASF, *MAP* 17, 29 (2 August 1443), G. Baccini, *Le ville Medicee di Cafaggiolo e di Trebbio in Mugello,* Florence 1897, p. 124, Pieraccini, *La stirpe,* I, p. 150: "perochè ci verà domenica di molte done e non se ne truova una [cornamusa] in questo paese".

Piero in 1451 his aunt Contessina asked her other son Giovanni "to greet Pierfrancesco on my behalf and say welcome home, telling him how much I want to see him".[8] On another occasion Pierfrancesco wrote affectionately to this cousin, "the young Giovanni de' Medici", whom he addresses as his "dear brother":

I have heard that you would very much like to come and stay up here and that the only reason you didn't come was to prevent me from catching the pox. There's no need for you to stay away for this reason, since Lorenzo says there's no more danger as it's all dried up. So I beseech you to come at all costs so we can spoil you and you can benefit in other ways.[9]

He was consulted by Cosimo on family marriages,[10] and he provided horses for the "young Lorenzo de' Medici" in 1465.[11]

No dissension between the cousins was as yet apparent, but the seeds of future trouble were already there. Pierfrancesco's father, like his father before him, left no will. On his death his fortune was shared with his brother Cosimo. All business contracts were automatically terminated; and as soon as his maternal relations had renounced their rights on 13 December 1440, Cosimo was appointed Pierfrancesco's guardian.[12] On the same day an inventory was prepared for the Guardians of Wards in Florence which listed only their joint property (including their house in Via Larga "with another house adjacent and next to it" and the fortified houses at Trebbio, Cafaggiolo and Careggi, but excluding their business assets and Monte investments):

---

[8] *VII Lettere di Contessina Bardi de' Medici ai figliuoli Piero e Giovanni,* ed. T. Casini and S. Morpurgo, Florence, 1886 (Nozze Zanichelli-Mariotti), no. VI (5 January 1451), Pieraccini, *La Stirpe,* I, pp. 152-153: "Saluta Pierfrancesco per la mia parte e dìlli che sia il ben tornato, che gran voglia ò di vederlo".

[9] ASF, *MAP* 103, 93, n.d.: «Charo fratello, etc. Ho sentito chome tu ai grande voglia di venire a starsi quassù, ma solo lasci perchè il vaiuolo non mi si appichi. E non bisogna che per questo tu lasci peròche Lorenzo dicie non è più da dubitare conciossiacosachè sia secchato. Sichè io ti priego che tu venga a ogni modo imperochè noi ti faremo vezzi di starne e d'altre cose vantaggiate ... Tuo Pierfrancesco a Trebbio". *Verso:* "giovane Giovanni di ——— de' Medici. In Firenze". Pierfrancesco also addresses his cousin Giovanni di Cosimo as "Iuveni Iohanni de' Medicis Fratri [honora]ndo" in 1445 (ASF, *MAP* 5, 577).

[10] See Cosimo's letter to Pierfrancesco, 26 November 1461, ASF, *MAP* 2, 480 (cf. Pieraccini, *La Stirpe,* I, p. 152), asking for his advice on Nannina's possible marriage to a Rucellai (anticipating her engagement to Bernardo Rucellai which took place that year).

[11] Pierfrancesco de' Medici to "... Iuveni Laurentio ... de Medicis Florentie", 6 April 1465, ASF, *MAP* 137, 140 (cf. Pieraccini, *ibid.*): "Ho avuto una tua lectera ... dove mi chiedi chavagli [the horse he wanted being ill, he sends two others] ... ti priegho potendo lo facci achonciare, et racchomandotegli, se ò altro che ti piaccia, manda per esso».

[12] ASF, *MAP* 161 cit., ff. 5*v*-7*r*.

the said Cosimo... protesting that because of his many public and private commitments and because of the multiplicity of his business operations and uncertainty about [their] debts and credits and possessions and rights, he was incapable of giving or adding any more definite possessions to the said inventory at the moment.[13]

In the course of the next three years Cosimo gradually added details of Monte holdings (totalling some 78,265 florins) and other credits, including the estate of their cousin Francesco di Giuliano di Averardo de' Medici who had died intestate by 1443.[14] On 25 March 1441 Cosimo "changed the books and the names of the companies" of their bank before drawing up, in November 1441, a statement of its total capital value of 73,956 florins.[15] During his tutelage Pierfrancesco's capital was not allowed to be put at risk by participation in the bank's profits and losses; it could merely draw interest at 5% on loan to Cosimo. For administrative reasons, and because Pierfrancesco's share of the profits of the bank would have been more than the interest to which he was restricted, he was later compensated for the financial difference from the time of his father's death until 24 March 1441, when Cosimo closed the accounts and restructured the bank.[16] He was not, however, reimbursed for the same financial

---

[13] *Ibid.*, ff. 8*r*-11*v*: "Protestans dictus Cosma ... quod propter multas occupationes quas habet et publice et privatim, et propter multiplicia eius traffica et propter incertitudinem debitorum et creditorum et bonorum et iurium ... ipse non potest ad presens alia certa bona dicto inventario ponere et seu addere" (f. 11*r*).

[14] *Ibid.*, ff., 11*v*-14*r*. On the inheritance of Francesco di Giuliano di Averardo, R. DE ROOVER, *Il Banco Medici dalle origini al declino, 1397-1494*, Florence, La Nuova Italia, 1970, pp. 58-59, and D. KENT, *I Medici in esilio: una vittoria di famiglia ed una disfatta personale*, Archivio storico italiano, CXXXII, 1974, pp. 62-63.

[15] ASF, *MAP* 161, f. 20*r*: "et cum nobis constet quod dictus Cosma sub die xxquinta mensis martii anni domini mccccquadragesimo primo mutaverit libros et nomina societatum", cf. *MAP* 153, no. 3, f. 1, DE ROOVER, *Banco Medici*, p. 89. Of this sum, roughly two-thirds belonged to Cosimo and Pierfrancesco, *ibid.*, tav. 13, p. 90. According to Lorenzo de' Medici (*Ricordi*, p. 7), however, the total capital worth or *valsente* of Cosimo and his brother in 1440 was 235,137 florins.

[16] ASF, *MAP* 161, ff. 20*r*-21*r*: "laudamus ... quod non obstantibus supra dispositis ... quod dictus Pierfranciscus habeat participare cum dicto Cosma in lucris et comodis factis et obventis occasione trafficorum ... etiam a die mortis et post mortem dicti Laurentii usque ad per totam diem xxquartam mensis Martii de dicto anno mccccquadragesimo ... Et hoc maxime quia rationes trafficorum ... non potuerunt nec poterant comode videri nisi in fine dicti anni et finito dicto anno, et quia comoda et lucra obventa occasione dictorum trafficorum a dicta die mortis dicti Laurentii usque ad per totam diem xxquartam dicti mensis martii mccccxl magis conferunt et maiorem utilitatem faciunt dicto Pierfrancisco quam quod dicto tempore dicte pecunie steterint in depositum penes dictum Cosmam ad rationem quinque pro centinario" (f. 20*v*).

difference between this time and his coming of age ten years later.[17] Since this was a time of expansion for the bank, with new branches founded in Avignon, London, Pisa and Milan, Pierfrancesco must have felt he was being treated unfairly, and this may account for the charges of maladministration which Pierfrancesco's sons later levelled against Cosimo's guardianship of their father, as well as against their own guardian, Cosimo's grandson Lorenzo il Magnifico.[18]

Pierfrancesco emerged from tutelage at the age of twenty-one, and it was then agreed to make a formal division of the Medici estate. Six arbitrators were appointed on 23 March 1451. They were carefully selected from both sides of the family, but of the six only Carlo Marsuppini and Bernardo de' Medici made the final arbitration eight months later.[19] On 17 November 1451 it was decreed that the house in Via Larga was to remain in common between both branches for the next five years (by which time the nearby palace, still under construction, would be ready to receive Cosimo's household and his family).[20] Cafaggiolo and Careggi were given to Cosimo; Trebbio to Pierfrancesco. The entire capital of the family bank was divided equally between both branches; and as Cosimo took this opportunity to retire officially, the share of Pierfrancesco, newly-qualified partner, was in effect double that of his two cousins – 27,000 florins as against their 13,500 florins each.[21] Lorenzo de' Medici, in his *Ricordi*, commented bitterly that this arbitration consigned Pierfrancesco:

---

[17] *Ibid.*, ff. 20*v*-21*r*: "Ita quod in effectu dicta ratio provisionum dictarum pecuniarum dicti Pierfrancisci ad dictam rationem quinque pro centinario pro anno et ad rationem anni de qua et quibus in proximo precedenti capitulo facta est mentio, incipiat et incipere debeat die xxquinta mensis martii anno domini mccccquadragesimo primo et sequi debeat usque ad per totam diem xxquartem mensis martii proximo preteriti [1451]".

[18] ASF, *MAP* 88, no. 392, f. 508 (1499), referring to the "administratione di tutelle di Pierfrancesco nostro padre et nostre, nelle quale pretendiamo essere stati gravati et doversi ritentare molte cose a nostro benifitio che per ancora non se ne trova la via". On the expansion of the bank, DE ROOVER, *Banco Medici*, pp. 89-95.

[19] ASF, *MAP* 161, ff. 19*r*-34*v*. The arbitrators were Marcello Strozzi, Carlo Marsuppini, Alamanno Salviati, Amerigo Cavalcanti, Giovanni Serristori and Bernardo de' Medici. Cf. LORENZO DE' MEDICI's *Ricordi*, cit., n. 4 above, p. 7, PIERACCINI, *La Stirpe*, I, pp. 149-150, C. S. GUTKIND, *Cosimo de' Medici*, pp. 197-199.

[20] See I. HYMAN, *15th century Florentine Studies: the Palazzo Medici and a ledger for the church of San Lorenzo*, New York, esp. pp. 70-79; cf. A. WARBURG, *Der Baubeginn des Palazzo Medici*, «Gesammelte Schriften», I, Leipzig, Teubner, 1932, pp. 167-168, pl. XXIII; W. A. BULST, *Die ursprüngliche innere Aufteilung des Palazzo Medici*, «Mitteilungen des Kunsthistorischen Instituts in Florenz», XIV, 1969-70, pp. 369-392.

[21] DE ROOVER, *Banco Medici*, p. 95, and pl. 14, p. 97.

half of all our possessions, giving him a gross advantage over us and all the best items... and at the same time he carried off a third share as a partner in all our companies, in which he has gained more than us through having fewer expenses.[22]

The arbitrators also specified that Pierfrancesco was to share only the expenses incurred in rebuilding San Lorenzo where his father and grandfather were buried: not Cosimo's expenditure on his palace in Via Larga, no expenses in San Marco (which Pierfrancesco's son Lorenzo later said "we do not want on our backs, because our father never wanted them"), none in Santa Croce, SS. Annunziata, San Miniato al Monte, San Francesco dal Boscho in the Mugello, the Camaldulensian hermitage of Camaldoli, nor the Holy Sepulchre in Jerusalem.[23]

We do not know if this implies that Pierfrancesco wished to disown Cosimo's political and cultural imperialism or merely to escape its cost. San Lorenzo, close to the houses of Cosimo and Pierfrancesco in Via Larga, was a family church and burial place; and there shared expenses were justifiable. San Marco was another matter. Cosimo was entitled to regard the cost of its renovation as shared until his brother's death, since it was begun as a joint project attributed to both Cosimo and Lorenzo in the monastery's chronicle. Moreover, shortly after Lorenzo's death, work was apparently halted on account of the opposition of families owning rights there. On the other hand, as elsewhere, it was Cosimo who received the credit – and the criticism – for his munificence. Despite the terms of the 1451 arbitration, Pierfrancesco's sons were charged as much as 7,776 florins for their inherited share of the building expenses, suggesting that work may in fact have continued after 1442. If so, Pierfrancesco's unwillingness

---

[22] *Ricordi* cit.; "la metà di tutti i nostri beni, grassamente dandoli il vantaggio ed migliori capi ... e nel medesimo tempo lo ritirò compagno per il terzo in tutti i nostri traffici, dove ha avanzato assai più di noi, per aver avuto manco spese".

[23] ASF, *MAP* 161, ff. *22r-v*, and on San Marco, *MAP* 104, no. 48, f. 456*v*: "La spesa della muraglia di san marcho nolla vogliamo adosso, perchè nostro padre nolla volle mai"; on Cosimo's building programme, GUTKIND, p. 198, and E. H. GOMBRICH, *The Early Medici as Patrons of Art*, in *Norm and Form*. pp. 35-57. There is a list of building expenses in San Lorenzo owed by Lorenzo and Giovanni di Pierfrancesco to Lorenzo di Piero de' Medici, 1476-80, in ASF *Notarile* 10200 (new numeration) (ser Simone Grazzini, 1472-94), f. 218*v*, and *MAP* 104, no. 48, f. 455*r*, 469*r*: four sums totalling 3285 florins, representing half of the total expenditure. Lorenzo and Giovanni accepted these sums but complained: "non c'è stato mai mostrato il conto delle spese" and feared that the expenditure since the death of their father was "un residio di denari che s'avevano a spendere in detta muraglia" (*MAP* 104, no. 48, f. 456*v*).

to be saddled with additional expense is understandable.[24] Patronage was a field in which the family was already beginning to be divided.

At this stage of his life Pierfrancesco appeared uninterested in both politics and culture, preferring to spend his days in the wild and beautiful castle of Trebbio. From the summit of its tower overlooking the Apennines it is just possible to see the red rooftop of Cafaggiolo, his uncle's allotted domain, lying strategically below, on the main road to Bologna and a stone's throw from the other main route across the Apennines through Imola.[25] There Cosimo was able to see visitors passing in and out of Florence and entertain them with lavish hospitality. But Pierfrancesco in his eyrie did not share his uncle's enthusiasm for politics, choosing to spend his time hunting and riding, sending game to his friends and family, buying and selling horses and descending to Florence as infrequently as possible.[26]

Left to his own devices Pierfrancesco might have been happy to remain a countryman all his life – but this was not to be. In May 1456 he married Laudomia, daughter of Angelo Acciaiuoli,[27] Cosi-

---

[24] On Cosimo's reputation for munificence, A. D. FRASER JENKINS, *Cosimo de' Medici's patronage of architecture and the theory of magnificence,* «Journal of the Warburg and Courtauld Institutes», XXXIII, 1970, pp. 162-170; and on criticism of his intervention in San Marco, GOMBRICH, *The Early Medici,* p. 42. The chronicle of San Marco is edited by R. MORÇAY in «Archivio Storico Italiano», LXXI (I) (1913), p. 11 (cf. FRASER JENKINS, p. 169), On Medici expenses there, see n. 94 below.

[25] On Trebbio, described in 1440 as "unum casamentum sive fortilitium" (ASF, *MAP* 161, f. *9v),* B. PATZAK, *Die Renaissance-und Barockvilla in Italien,* II (*Palast und Villa in Toscana),* Leipzig, Klinkhardt e Biermann, 1914, pp. 67-75, pls. XXXIV-XXXVII, and BACCINI, *Le Ville Medicee,* cit.

[26] PIERACCINI, *La Stirpe,* I, pp. 151-152.

[27] According to LITTA, *Famiglie celebri italiane,* I, tav. 5, PIERACCINI, *La Stirpe,* I, p. 154, and C. UGURGIERI DELLA BERARDENGA, *Gli Acciaiuoli di Firenze,* Florence, Olschki, 1962, II, p. 532, Laudomia was Angelo Acciaiuoli's sister; but all contemporary evidence suggests she was his daughter: Tranchedini's letter, 2 December 1454 (n. 1 above: Piero Francesco... ha preso per dona la figliuola del nostro Angelo Azaiolo"), the chronicle of Fra Giovanni di Carlo (quoted by R. HATFIELD in *Studies on Machiavelli,* ed. M. P. GILMORE, Florence, Sansoni, 1972, p. 331) referring to the marriage of Angelo's "aliam filiam suam Laudomiam" to Cosimo' de' Medici's nephew; Angelo's letter to Pierfrancesco referring to him as his "figliuolo" (ASF, *MAP* 2, 442, 4 March 1457); and BNF, Magl. XXVI, 146 (del Migliore), recording Pierfrancesco's marriage in 1456 to "Laudominae domini Angeli de Acciaiuolis". On the date of their marriage, see Pierfrancesco's letter to the Priors of San Gimignano (10 May 1456, ed. A. GHERARDI, *Spigolature Sangimignanesi,* «Miscellanea Storica d. Valdelsa», X, 1902, pp. 135-136, doc. VI): "A dì xxiii di questo io meno la donna", and DEL MIGLIORE above. Tranchedini in his letter of December 1454 must refer to their betrothal. On Angelo Acciaiuoli, *Dizionario biografico degli Italiani,* I. *s.v.; Dispatches with Related Documents of Milanese Ambassadors in France and Burgundy, 1450-1483,* ed. P. M. KENDALL and V. ILARDI, I, Athens (Ohio), Ohio University Press, 1970, pp. XLI-XLIII; MARTINES, *Social World,* pp. 335-336, etc.

mo's faithful supporter and now a pre-eminent member of his regime. Angelo was soon worried by his son-in-law's way of life and in September 1456 wrote to him with advice:

Don't be robbed of a moment by saying "we'll do it tomorrow", because the moment never returns. You are of an age when you should be acquiring some talents. It's no use procrastinating. It will bring you honour and profit to adopt the habits of your relations and to begin a new way of life which will lead you from this one. I love you so much and my love is equalled by my sense of responsibility for you, so although I know you mean well, I can't stop continually thinking about you; and thinking about you, I can't write without saying something to you. Please excuse my importunity as a sign of the love that I bear you.[28]

Worse than Pierfrancesco's sloth, however, was his apparent disregard for Cosimo, by then an old man, as Angelo reminded Pierfrancesco a few months later. Nothing pleases old men more, he told him, than to see themselves not only loved, honoured and obeyed by the younger generation, but cherished by them as well:

I know you are a bit of a backwoodsman and hold Cosimo in such respect that you don't cultivate him as I would like, nor do you try to learn from him as you need to do. And so I tell you that while he lives, stay around him as much as you can, for you cannot have a truer nor a better master than him.[29]

Was this true? According to Nicodemo Tranchedini, Cosimo loved Pierfrancesco as much as "any of his sons". Angelo Acciaiuoli himself also assured this somewhat 'unusual' and wayward youth that he loved him "no less than the five sons of my own".[30] But the am-

---

[28] 2 September 1456, ASF, *MAP* 2, 445, ed. Pieraccini, *La Stirpe*, I, p. 150: "non ti lasci furare il tempo con dire 'domane faremo', perchè il tempo non si riaquista; tu se' in età da darti a 'mparare qualche virtù; non volere indugiare. Ad te fia honore et utile seguitare e costume de' tua e dar loco alle conversationi che ti levassino da questa via. Io t'amo tanto e tanto mi pesa il fatto tuo che, benchè io intenda da te l'animo tuo buono, nientedimeno non posso fare che continuamente non vi pensi, e pensandovi non ti posso scrivere che io non te ne dica qualche cosa. Priegoti che tu scusi la mia importunità come amore che io ti porto".

[29] 4 March 1457, ASF, *MAP* 2, 442, partly edited by Pieraccini, *La Stirpe*, I, p. 150: "io so che tu hai un po' del salvaticho et è tanta la reverenza che tu hai a Cosimo che tu non li stai d'atorno come vorrei; nè cerchi da imparare da lui come è il bisogno tuo. Et così ti dico che in mentre che vive, stàlli d'atorno il più che tu puoi, perochè tu non puoi haver nè più vero nè miglior maestro che lui".

[30] N. Tranchedini to Francesco Sforza, 2 December 1454, ed. Magnani, p. v.: "che l'ama como qualunque sia de li figlioli"; Angelo Acciaiuoli to Pierfrancesco de' Medici, 4 March 1457, above: "io non amo meno te ch'e cinque figluoli che io ho".

bivalence Cosimo felt towards his nephew and former ward is revealed in a letter he wrote to him in 1459, which concerns a joust in honour of the young Galeazzo Maria Sforza when he visited Florence in April that year:

Today I have had a letter from you and understand what you write about the business of your horse – having heard of the joust to be held for Count Galeazzo's visit – and how you have had the idea of jousting yourself, if I were agreeable. I never dreamt you were thinking of such a thing, having heard you say more than once that you were not thinking of jousting any more. For this reason we did not believe you needed the horse, and also I did not think we ought to embark on such an expense for you at the present. However, if it would please you, I will be content with what you want.[31]

From Trebbio Pierfrancesco asked his secretary, Bartolomeo Scala, to tell Cosimo that "it's not true what he's been told";[32] and he neither took part in the joust nor joined the banquet given by his cousins for Galeazzo Maria, instead awarding his horse and armour to Guido da Faenza.[33] Since it cost Lorenzo de' Medici's father at least four thousand florins to have him joust in 1469,[34] Cosimo may understandably have been unwilling "to embark on such an expense" for Pierfrancesco, especially as Pierfrancesco had already enjoyed his joust with horses provided by both Borso d'Este and Francesco Sforza.[35] This time, it was true, he had his own horse and armour; but a joust was evidently a privilege – like a coming-out ball – which young Medici could enjoy and win but once. Cosimo may also have

---

[31] 17 March 1459, ASF, *MAP* 2, 452 (cf. PIERACCINI's misinterpretation of this letter, *La Stirpe*, I, p. 151): "Questo dì ho avuto una tua lettera et inteso quanto mi schrivi sopra 'l fatto del tuo chavallo, avendo inteso della giostra si debbe fare per la venuta del chonte Ghaleazzo, et chome aresti il pensiero a volere giostrare se io me ne chontentassi. Io non chredetti tu fussi in tal pensiero, avendoti sentito dire più volte tu non avere pensiero più a giostrare, et per questa chagione non credemo avessi il bisogno del chavallo, et anchora mi pareva non fusse da entrare in questa spesa per te al presente. Pure, se ttu te ne chontentassi, io sarò chontento a quello vorrai tu".

[32] B. Scala to Pierfrancesco de' Medici, 21 March 1459, ASF, *MAP* 4, 377: "ditemi vadi a Cosimo a dire non è il vero di quanto gli è suto detto, che lo farò di subito et aviseròvi della risposta".

[33] PIERACCINI, *La Stirpe*, I, p. 151.

[34] According to Piero de' Medici's catasto it cost fl. 4269.15.4, ASF, *Catasto* 924, cit., f. 311*v*), but according to Lorenzo's *Ricordi* (ed. FABRONI cit., II, p. 40) it cost his father "circa a ducati diecimila".

[35] Tranchedini's letter of 2 December 1454, ed. MAGNANI, p. IV, and I. DEL LUNGO, *Florentia: uomini e cose del Quattrocento*, p. 412.

been deterred by the fact that his grandson Lorenzo was appearing "in a fine display of arms" with eleven young Florentines the following night.[36] However, he was scrupulous to let Pierfrancesco do what he wanted, just as he was willing to let him play his full part in the state when he came of political age.

Pierfrancesco's initiation into politics began in August 1458 when he was elected a member of the Balìa which followed the *parlamento* of 11 August. He was not yet of statutory age for this council and was not among those elected for his district on 14 August.[37] But all his family were represented in it *ex officio*, as were his father-in-law Angelo Acciaiuoli and his maternal uncle Amerigo Cavalcanti; and perhaps as a result of their influence his name was added to complete San Giovanni's quota of representatives.

Political responsibilities followed quickly. In the autumn of 1458 Pierfrancesco was elected one of six ambassadors to congratulate and offer homage to the new Pope, Pius II. Angelo Acciaiuoli was also a member of this embassy; and he must have welcomed the opportunity of initiating his son-in-law into the world of diplomacy and business in Rome.[38] A year later, in November 1459, Pierfrancesco was elected to the Signoria in Florence, although still under age. In this capacity he was asked to do his first political favour for his cousins. Piero di Cosimo, a Monte Official, had already told Pierfrancesco that he wanted to escape "the nuisance" of the Monte, and on 7 December (with one month of Pierfrancesco's office as prior gone, Piero reminded him, and Christmas approaching) he asked Pierfrancesco to effect their "exchanges at the Monte" and to assure everyone of his sincerity "without believing what others say". However, on the 15th Piero and his four co-officials were re-elected for another year, so at least on this occasion Pierfrancesco was unable to grant his cousin's request.[39]

---

[36] CAMBI, *Istorie*, in *Delizie degli eruditi toscani*, ed. I. di SAN LUIGI, XX, Florence 1785, p. 371: "una bella armegiera".

[37] N. RUBINSTEIN, *The Government of Florence under the Medici*, pp. 107, n. 5, and 290. The minimum age was 30.

[38] C. GUASTI, *Due legazioni al sommo pontefice*, «Scritti Storici», Prato, 1894, pp. 85-90; CAMBI, *Istorie, Delizie*, XX, p. 362 (but omitting Angelo Acciaiuoli's name); cf. R. MORÇAY, *St Antonin*, pp. 269-271, and L. PASTOR, *Storia dei Papi*, II, Rome, Desclée & C., 1961, pp. 16-17. This legation, like the one to congratulate the previous Pope Calixtus III in 1455, in which Giovanni de' Medici was included, was headed by S. Antonino, Archbishop of Florence.

[39] ASF, *MAP* 5, 750 (7 December 1459): "Havendovi parlato quanto è el desiderio mio circha al uscire di questa noia del monte, richordo alla S. V. chome voi siate al secondo mese

The following year (1460) Pierfrancesco was elected to another important office, the Otto di Guardia, which had been given absolute authority or *balìa* to deal with political crimes after the discovery of Girolamo Machiavelli's conspiracy against the regime in 1458. Contessina de' Medici told her son, Giovanni, that Cosimo was only too thankful to give up "the burden" of this office and to appoint Pierfrancesco in his place. Yet Cosimo was not a member of the Otto in 1460; and although Giovanni had been elected to it in 1456 (when it lacked *balìa*), his mother's admonition to him to "look now to yourself" suggests that there may have been an element of rivalry between the cousins.[40] Whatever their personal relationship at this time, it is at any rate clear from his offices that Pierfrancesco was approved by the *accoppiatori* and the new Council of One Hundred; and he had now to be taken seriously by other members of the family. He had entered upon the "new way of life" his father-in-law had urged upon him.

This life introduced Pierfrancesco to new acquaintances such as the eminent Cardinal of Rouen, Guillaume d'Éstouteville, whom he met in Rome in 1458. As a client of the Medici Bank, Éstouteville's bonds with Pierfrancesco were mercenary rather than pastoral. But letters written after Pierfrancesco's return to Florence show that Pierfrancesco had succeeded in establishing a personal relationship with the Cardinal, expressed by gifts of wine and sparrow-hawks and offers of hospitality in Florence. Éstouteville professed to be 'amazed' not to have heard from Pierfrancesco since his return and feared he had forgotten the Vernaccia wine: if not yet drinkable, he was to let him

---

del vostro offitio et avicinate alla pasqua che con le feste vi torrà tempo assai. Priegovi che operiate che si faccia gli scambii nostri al monte in favore del quale non potresti fare più utile chosa ... Et fate fede a ciaschuno che quanto io schrivo vengha dall'animo et dal chuore senza dare fede alle parole d'altri". On his office CAMBI, *Delizie*, p. 377 (correcting PIERACCINI, *La Stirpe*, I, p. 153). The minimum age for the Signoria, Colleges and Otto di Guardia was 30 years, for the Gonfaloniership of Justice, 45 years. For Piero di Cosimo's re-election as Officiale del Banco, ASF, *Tratte* 81, fol. 58*r*.

[40] ASF, *Otto di Guardia*, 2723 bis, f. 57*r*, *Tratte* 81, f. 5*r* (Pierfrancesco was elected on 22 August for 4 months from 1 September 1460, cf. f. 3*r* for Giovanni's appointment in March 1455/56). Contessina to Giovanni and Ginevra de' Medici, 28 August 1460, in *VII Lettere di Contessina ne' Bardi*, no. VII: "Cosimo ci à levato via la ricadia d'essere degli Otto e fattone Pierfrancesco in suo scambio, sì che attendete pure a voi", translated by JANET ROSS (*Lives of the Early Medici*, London, Chatto and Windus, 1910), p. 63: "This might also be done for thee", cf. PIERACCINI, *La Stirpe*, I, p. 153. On the Otto, G. ANTONELLI, *La magistratura degli Otto di Guardia a Firenze*, «Archivio storico italiano», CXII, 1954, pp. 3-39, and on its special powers in 1458 and 1460, RUBINSTEIN, *Government of Florence*, pp. 111-112.

know when it would be.[41] Pierfrancesco's apologies secured from Éstouteville confirmation of his promise to stay with him on his way to the Congress of Mantua the following spring, the promise of a cardinal "in this day and age" being "worth more than that of a merchant whosoever he is".[42] Subsequently the Cardinal urged the merchant not to overdo preparations, he was sure his quarters were more than adequate.[43] While attending the chapter of Augustinian Friars in Siena, "free from curial cares",[44] he welcomed as "a great pastime" a gift of sparrow-hawks. When he wished to complain of his treatment at the hands of customs officials at the gates of Montepulciano, "which offends too much the dignity of the [Cardinal's] Hat', it was to Pierfrancesco he wote, enclosing letters for Cosimo, Piero and Giovanni de' Medici and Luca Pitti.[45]

The buying and selling of horses plays a large part in Pierfrancesco's correspondence and it is probable, as Pieraccini has suggested, that he dealt in them commercially and not simply for pleasure.[46] He enjoyed racing, as we know from a poem by his secretary and factotum, Bartolomeo Scala, in praise of his champion, Swallow, as fast as "swift-flowing rivers".[47]

Bartolomeo Scala, subsequently chancellor of the Guelf Party and

---

41 Carlo de' Medici to Pierfrancesco de' Medici, 1 December 1458, ASF, *MAP* 137, 93: "essendo ieri a cena con Monsignor di Roano... ragionando di voi dixe che si maraviglava che poi vi partiste non gli abiate mai scripto nè mandato a dir niente, et che dubitava non vi fusse uscito di mente la vernaccia, che se non è anchor da bere, avisatelo quando [s]ia".

42 The same, 9 December 1458, ASF, *MAP* 137, 86, referring to Pierfrancesco's letter to him of 2 December: "La scusa vostra a Monsignor di Roano feci oggi... Fugli grata et dissemi ch'io vi dovessi scrivere che in ogni modo è disposto di farvi chiaro per effetto che la promessa d'uno cardinale è più da stimare al dì d'oggi che quella di qualunque merchatante che sia, inperochè quello vi promisse, c[i]oè dismontare in casa vostra, vedrete ve la terrà meglio non avete fatto voi della promessa della vernaccia".

43 Éstouteville to Pierfrancesco de' Medici, 11 April 1459, ASF, *MAP* 139, 225, referring to his letter "sopra lo apparechiamento havete fatto de la casa vostra e grande vostra affectione verso di noi" for which he thanked him warmly, "rendendone certi la stantia sia molto più in ordine de quello voriamo, la quale havendo noi acceptate liberamente, haveriamo a caro non ve forzassaste tanto de ornare". The Cardinal of Rouen was one of six cardinals chosen to accompany the Pope to the Congress of Mantua, staying in Florence from 25 April until 6 May 1459, O. Raynaldus, *Annales Ecclesiastici, X*, Lucca, 1753, pp. 180, 196.

44 The same, 30 August 1460, ASF, *MAP* 103, 91: "sichè in questo mezo staremo de qui liberi dale sollicitudini curiali, haveremo bono exercitio in fare e provare essi terzoli, che ne serà uno grande passatempo".

45 The same, 22 November 1462, ASF, *MAP* 139, 223: "contra la dignità del Cardinalato... offende troppo la dignità del Capello".

46 *La Stirpe*, I, p. 152, cf. also de Roover, *Banco Medici*, p. 206.

47 BNF, MS. Conv. Soppr. G. 8. 1438, f. 20*v*: "par cum rapidis currere fluminibus".

then 1st Chancellor of Florence, was appointed in 1457 to work for Pierfrancesco, and his years in Pierfrancesco's service coincided with the latter's initiation into politics.[48] Scala may have been intended to act as tutor as well as political mentor, to encourage his pupil to emulate the cultural interests of his cousins. Scala's classes on Vergil, which the poet Luigi Pulci attended, were conducted in Pierfrancesco's house, and it was while Scala was with him that Pierfrancesco wrote to ask Carlo de' Medici in Rome for some manuscripts, among them an Apicius.[49] Pierfrancesco's artistic patronage was, however, minimal.[50] Since he was a partner in the Medici Bank, much of Scala's work for him must have concerned business matters which had to be dealt with during Pierfrancesco's lengthy absences in Trebbio, chasing debtors, authorizing payments and writing letters.[51]

As long as Giovanni de' Medici was alive there were no open signs of discord between the two branches of the family. As Director General of the Medici Bank Giovanni enjoyed clear authority in business matters and Pierfrancesco collaborated with him as a partner, often through the offices of Scala.[52] Pierfrancesco was elected an Official of the Zecca or Mint for six months from March 1463, to be replaced on 6 June when he went on an embassy to Mantua.[53] But the death of Giovanni in November 1463, followed by Cosimo's death in August

---

48 For Scala's career, see BROWN, *Bartolomeo Scala,* esp. pp. 22-31 (Italian edn. pp. 17-22).

49 See Carlo de' Medici's letter to Pierfrancesco, 9 December 1458, cit., 'De' libri mi scrivete farò ogni diligentia perchè n'abiate copia et maxime di quello Apicio'; PIERACCINI, *La Stirpe,* I, p. 151; *Bartolomeo Scala,* p. 25 (Ital. edn. p. 18). Dr Albinia de la Mare suggests that MS Laur. 30, 2 (a Latin translation of Ptolemy's *Cosmography*) belonged to Pierfrancesco before his son Lorenzo, whose ex-libris it bears, and since it is in the hand of a scribe used by Bartolomeo Scala, Scala may have been responsible for commissioning it on Pierfrancesco's behalf, see *B. Scala's Dealings with Booksellers, Scribes and Illuminators, 1459-63,* «Journal of the Warburg and Courtauld Institutes», XXXIX, 1976, p. 244.

50 A pair of chests and a tondo commissioned for his marriage from Apollonio di Giovanni in 1455 is all that we know of; E. CALLMANN, *Apollonio di Giovanni,* Oxford, Clarendon Press, 1974, pp. 35 and 79 (no. 113); P. SCHUBRING, *Cassoni,* Leipzig, K. W. Hiersemann, 1915, p. 435; E. H. GOMBRICH, "Apollonio di Giovanni", *Norm and Form,* p. 16. But his deficiencies were more than made up for by his sons, who revealed themselves to be more adventurous patrons than their cousins by the end of the century, see pp. 100-101 and n. 108 below.

51 See, for example, Pierfrancesco's one surviving letter to Scala, 19 December 1457, ASF, *MAP* 98, 525, and BROWN, *Bartolomeo Scala,* p. 26 (Ital. edn. p. 18).

52 DE ROOVER does not discuss Pierfrancesco's role in the Medici bank as such, but there are references to his partnership in *Banco Medici,* pp. 127, 338, 359 and 551, cf. the *Inventarii* to the Medici Archives, *esp.* vol. IV (Rome, Ministero dell'Interno. Pubblicazioni degli Archivi di Stato, 1963).

53 ASF, *Tratte* 81 f. 47*r,* cf. PIERACCINI, *La Stirpe,* I, p. 153.

1464, revealed a rift among the leading citizens which had important repercussions on Pierfrancesco's career. His father-in-law no longer attempted to conceal his growing hostility to Piero de' Medici's leadership and the city became deeply divided.

In 1466, as a result of a scrutiny of offices and disagreement over whether to grant a subsidy to the Sforza rulers of Milan, it was considered necessary to make all Florentine citizens over fourteen years old who were *veduti ai Tre Maggiori Uffizi* sign an official oath to agree to keep the peace.[54] But before the month was out another oath was signed by more than four hundred citizens. This unofficial oath was specifically republican, vowing (in breach of the official oath) to uphold "just and popular government by customary means". It was signed by men such as Angelo Acciaiuoli, Luca Pitti, Niccolò Soderini and Dietisalvi Neroni, who later that summer led a conspiracy against the regime. It was also signed by Pierfrancesco, sole Medici representative – and this was the first open sign of political dissent.[55]

Pierfrancesco's equivocal attitude to his cousins at this time is graphically illustrated by an entry in the recently discovered chronicle of Marco Parenti. Describing Piero de' Medici's preparations in the days of crisis preceding the quashing of the conspiracy on 2 September 1466, Parenti relates how Piero sent for his cousin Pierfrancesco, "a very rich man", and asked him for a loan of ten thousand florins:

Having seen how serious the disturbances were, [Pierfrancesco] was unable to refuse what at another time he would not have given him. He at once took this money to his house and showed great generosity in all his financial needs.[56]

---

[54] On 8 May 1466, ed. A. MUNICCHI, *La fazione antimedicea detta del Poggio,* Florence 1911, doc. 4, pp. 116-117; cf. G. PAMPALONI, *Il giuramento pubblico in Palazzo Vecchio a Firenze e un patto giurato degli anti-Medicei, Maggio 1466,* «Miscellanea di studi in memoria di G. Cecchini: Bullettino Senese di Storia Patria», LXXI, 1964, pp. 212-238, *esp.* 224; RUBINSTEIN, *Government of Florence,* p. 156.

[55] The oath of 27 May 1466 is edited by PAMPALONI, above n. 54, pp. 233-238, cf. RUBINSTEIN, pp. 156-158. Pierfrancesco's name is on p. 236.

[56] BNF, MS Magl. XXV, 272, discovered by Professor Mark Phillips, to whom I am indebted for this reference (see M. PHILLIPS, *A Newly Discovered Chronicle by Marco Parenti,* «Renaissance Quarterly», XXXI, 1978, pp. 153-160); "Piero trovandosi in quel tempo male in ordine a denari, mandò per Pier Francesco de' Medici, suo cugino, huomo richissimo, et chiesegli in prestanza fiorini 10,000. Lui, veduto tanto tumulto, non glele seppe negare, che in altro tempo non l'harrebbe servito. Subito glel' portò a casa con questi denari, monstrò gran larghezza in tutti e bisogni dello spendere" (p. 78, see now his *Memoir of Marco Parenti,* pp. 192-193).

Here we can see the conflicting traits of openheartedness and alienation which were to characterize Pierfrancesco's attitude towards his cousins. Faced by a crisis for survival, the family bond still ensured his generous support; but already money as well as politics was affecting the relationship.

After forming part of the Balìa which followed the failure of the Pitti conspiracy in September 1466, Pierfrancesco enjoyed no more political office in Piero's lifetime. Despite his loan to Piero, he was evidently compromised by his relationship to Angelo Acciaiuoli, now exiled from Florence for life, as well as by his political and financial differences with his cousins. Relations with Piero, which remained outwardly friendly, were inwardly detached, as we can see from letters exchanged in 1469. At the suggestion of two friends (both keen supporters of the Medici regime), Pierfrancesco offered to escort Clarice Orsini from Rome for her wedding to Lorenzo de' Medici in June 1469. This was the first time the mercantile Medici had married out of Florence into the Roman aristocracy and the Milanese ambassador in Florence predicted it would give the people – as well as some leading citizens – plenty to talk about.[57] But when Pierfrancesco heard Piero had changed his mind and had, after all, decided to send his son Giuliano to Rome to escort Clarice to Florence, he was quick to retract his offer – deciding (if Piero approved)

> to take the route to fill my barrels, because my company would indeed be superfluous to them. I shall do my best to return as quickly as possible to be in time for the wedding, and I shall leave this responsibility to Giuliano, for it seems to me this would be more honourable for you and for all the family.[58]

Later that year, in August 1469,[59] Piero de' Medici wrote to Pierfrancesco about the forthcoming Catasto, for which the two branches of the family had hitherto submitted a joint return:

---

[57] S. Sacramori to G. M. Sforza (7 December 1468), Milan, Archivio di Stato (ASMi), SPE Fir. 275: "Secondo mi questa cosa darà da dire assay al populazzo et ad altri de quisti principali".

[58] Pierfrancesco to Piero de' Medici, 28 March 1469, ASF, *MAP* 16, 286, Pieraccini, *La Stirpe*, I, p. 153; "Piglierò partito, se vi parrà, seguire il cammino a fornire e miei boti perchè invero la mia compagnia con loro parebbe superflua. Et ingegnieròmi tornare più presto potrò di costà, per essere a tempo alle nozze e lascierò questa cura a Giuliano, che mi pare sia più l'onore vostra e di tucta la casa". The two friends were Giovanni d'Antonio di Salvestro [Serristori], who witnessed Pierfrancesco's will in 1476, and Angelo della Stufa.

[59] ASF, *MAP* 137, 114. Although '1463' is written on the back of the letter and is given as the date in the *Inventario*, the letter is actually subscribed "11 August 1469".

I thought it would have been a good idea for us to have had a good talk together, either here or with you, to discuss your and my affairs – in my opinion, a matter of some importance. You do not think so, and I am willing to accept this patiently and will do by letter what I would have done *viva-voce*. Principally it seems to me we should divide our taxes for reasons you can understand better than me, especially in the present distribution decreed by law; and if it were arbitrary or anything else, do not doubt that as long as I am alive, you would be treated on the same basis as me. And as for pecuniary and honorary offices, I would also do the same for you as for myself, and of this you can rest assured.[60]

He went on to tell Pierfrancesco that Tommaso and Accerito Portinari and all the partners and agents of the Medici companies were foregathering to settle the accounts and do their duty by Pierfrancesco and himself:

For I decided once and for all to know how we stand and in how many feet of water I find myself, in order to be able to navigate according to the disposition of the times.[61]

He was determined, he said, not to labour as in the past, despite understanding "little, as you know"; he was infirm, weighed down by troubles, ill-served by everyone; and such time as was left to him he wished to spend more tranquilly than hitherto.

All these things need careful examination and I would willingly tackle them with you, because they concern you as much as me. But if you do not agree, then nor do I, though this could or should be no reason for renouncing such a task. So what I would dearly like would be for you to change your mind. If not, I shall persevere according to God's guidance and will try to see they do their duty by us both. And you will be informed of the outcome one way or another.[62]

---

[60] *Ibid.*, "Io giudicavo essere stato bene che qui o costì ci fussimo abboccati insieme per conferire de' facti tuoi e miei, che secondo il parere mio importa. Non ti pare, et io resto patiente e contento, e farò per lettera quello che viva voce harei facto. Et principalmente a me pare che per te e per me faccia il dividerci alla gravezza per rispecti che meglo di me puoi intendere, maxime nella presente distributione che è per leggie, e quando fussi arbitraria o per altro modo, non fare dubbio alcuno che vivente io, tu sarai tractato al pari di me et circa l'utile et honore tanto sempre farò per te quanto per me proprio, et di questo vivi sicuro".

[61] *Ibid.*, "perchè io delibero una volta sapere e fatti nostri, et in quanti palmi d'acqua io mi truovo, per navicare poi secondo la dispositione de' tempi".

[62] "Perchè me ne intendo poco, come tu sai"; "Tucte queste cose voglono bona examina, e con te io le praticherei volentieri, perchè ti tocca come a me. Hora se non ti pare, non pare ancora a me, nè per questo si debbe nè può lasciare tale opera adrieto. Il perchè se muterai

Piero's wish to ascertain "how many feet of water" he found himself in is consistent with what we know of his attempt to discover the true state of the Medici bank after the deaths of Giovanni and Cosimo, as a result of which he tried to liquidate some branches and introduce economies in others.[63] As Giovanni's, and subsequently Giuliano's, partner in many contracts of the Medici bank, Pierfrancesco was intimately concerned with its affairs. One should not read too much into the tone of these letters, but Piero's and Cosimo's to Pierfrancesco both suggest that they were dealing patiently but firmly with someone rather intractable whom they could ill afford to alienate. Despite their clear political advantage (with their implied power to influence tax officials) Pierfrancesco was their business equal and would shortly succeed to the position of senior member of the family.

In the event the cousins did present separate tax returns, which provide interesting evidence of their relative wealth. Although Pierfrancesco was described as 'richissimo' in 1466 when he lent money to Piero, in 1469 Piero declared himself to be the richer with some 23,763 florins invested in the Monte as against Pierfrancesco's 17,163 florins, and about 44,649 florins in property as against Pierfrancesco's 30,198. The difference between their taxable assessments was some 21,000 florins, Piero (or rather, by then Lorenzo, his heir) being taxed 332 on 66,452 florins, Pierfrancesco 225 florins on 45,065. Pierfrancesco left it to Piero to give details of their shared business profits, which were agreed in both returns to be 5000 florins, increasing Pierfrancesco's final tax to 244 florins and Piero's to 350 florins.[64] Since Piero's tax was finally reduced (after deductions for alms and household salaries) to 254 florins, whatever the supposed advantage of Pierfrancesco after the 1451 arbitration, it had by then apparently disappeared.

Piero died less than four months after writing to Pierfrancesco, leaving him (after Carlo de' Medici, Cosimo's illegitimate son) doyen of the family. Pierfrancesco and Carlo headed the funeral procession, followed by the young Lorenzo (heir apparent) in the second group

---

proposito, l'harò charo; perseverando, io andrò drieto alla opera secondo che dio m'amaestrerà, e ingegneròmmi che a te e a me sia facto il dovere, et del seguito per uno modo o uno altro harai notitia".

63 DE ROOVER, *Banco Medici,* pp. 519-524.

64 ASF, *Catasto* 924 (S. Giov. Leon d'Oro), ff. 295*r*-313*r* (Piero's return) and 314*r*-326*r* (Pierfrancesco's return), DE ROOVER, *Banco Medici,* p. 39. Their Monte shares were nominally worth about four times their market value.

of mourners and his brother Giuliano in the third. Lorenzo wept copiously on their return and "he and Pierfrancesco made each other many grand gestures" (Marco Parenti reported) "and their friends try to keep them united: we'll see what happens".[65] The day after the funeral Pierfrancesco lent Lorenzo and Giuliano 8166 florins; [66] in return he was appointed to a series of offices. This underlines his virtual exclusion from public life during Piero's lifetime.

On 17 December Pierfrancesco was appointed an Official of the Monte in Piero's place. According to the Milanese ambassador it was a clever move. In this way Lorenzo drew Pierfrancesco to him without any show of having done so, "although he is what your Excellence knows him to be" wrote Sacramori, referring presumably to known differences between the two Medici.[67] The following year Pierfrancesco was appointed a Keeper of the Laws and one of the all-important *accoppiatori* in charge of electing the Signoria.[68] During his term as *accoppiatore*, as we shall see, Pierfrancesco was accused of deviating from the wishes of the Milanese in the election of the Gonfalonier of Justice; and the same year saw an attempt to reform the method of choosing *accoppiatori*, since it was felt they could no longer be relied on.[69] Pierfrancesco was nevertheless elected one of the first forty members of the Balìa created in 1471 to carry out this reform.[70]

At the end of August 1470 Pierfrancesco was sent as ambassador

---

65 Marco Parenti to Filippo Strozzi, 3 December 1469, ed. C. GUASTI in A. MACINGHI NEGLI STROZZI, *Lettere di una gentildonna fiorentina,* Florence, Sansoni, 1877, pp. 608-609, cf. PIERACCINI, *La Stirpe,* I, p. 153: "Lorenzo al tornare dal morto piagneva molto per la via. Lui e Pierfrancesco si sono fatte molto grande proferte, e i loro attendono a tenergli uniti. Vedremo il fine".

66 ASF, *MAP* 148, no. 42, ff. 61-62: receipt to Pierfrancesco signed by Lorenzo and Giuliano de' Medici, 4 December 1469, cf. *MAP* 104, no. 48, f. 460*r* (1485 settlement); cf. LORENZO DE' MEDICI, *Lettere,* I, ed. R. FUBINI, Florence, Giunti Barbèra, 1977, p. 184, note, referring to 30,000 ducats lent by Pierfrancesco on the death of Piero to the Rome branch of the bank.

67 S. Sacramori to G. M. Sforza, 13 December 1469, ASMi SPE Fir. 283, f. 36*v*: "Lorenzo va repezando assay de li mali contenti del Mco. Piero et ad altro non attende. Suo cosino Pierfrancesco, benchè'l sia quale sa la Ex^{tia}. Vostra, l'ha saputo tirarlo a si, et hallò facto fare offitiale del Monte in locho del padre senza dimostratione che esso l'habia facto". Pierfrancesco's election as an Official of the Monte "loco dicti Pieri mortui" is in ASF, *Tratte* 81, f. 58*v*.

68 ASF, *Tratte* 81, f. 42*v* (elected a *Conservator Legum* on 5 February 1470 for 6 months beginning on 25 March 1470) and RUBINSTEIN, *Government of Florence,* p. 240.

69 *Ibid.,* pp. 176-177, FUBINI, ed., LORENZO DE' MEDICI, *Lettere,* I, pp. 206-207, F. GUICCIARDINI, *Storie fiorentine,* p. 24: "Ma cominciando qualche volta nel Cento a variare le elezioni de' disegni dati, Lorenzo e gli amici suoi cominciorono a dubitare che non variassi un tratto negli accopiatori, di che sarebbe facilmente seguita la alterazione dello stato".

70 RUBINSTEIN, *Government of Florence,* p. 303.

with Jacopo Guicciardini to Naples and then Rome to negotiate the general league and peace treaty signed there on 22 December.[71] This Italian league of peace and friendship was intended by the Pope as the prelude to a crusade against the Turks, for which the Milanese were notably less enthusiastic than the more vulnerable southern Italian states. Florence was divided between the pro-Neapolitan peace party, which reflected the popular desire for the treaty, and the Mediceans who supported Milan. After Otto Niccolini's death in the autumn of 1470 the Mediceans gained the upper hand and had a secret clause inserted in their ambassador's mandates to impede the signing of the treaty – which they never subsequently allowed to be ratified in Rome.[72] According to Sacramori, Pierfrancesco was transferred from Naples to Rome, where Niccolini was ambassador, to slow negotiations to walking pace, "being fat as he is"; once there Sacramori assured Galeazzo Maria Sforza that Lorenzo de' Medici was having him watched by Gentile Becchi (Lorenzo's former tutor) "to prevent him fishing to the bottom".[73] Although Pierfrancesco's role in these negotiations is unclear, he must have been suspect to the Milanese on account of his relationship to Angelo Acciaiuoli (then exiled in Naples), and perhaps for this reason he was transferred from Naples to Rome and then kept under Becchi's surveillance.

As an *accoppiatore* in charge of selecting the Signoria in 1470-1, Pierfrancesco was in an even better position to support or damage his cousin. In Sacramori's opinion he did not fail to use his power against the interests of Milan and Lorenzo: "If only messer Angelo Acciaiuoli had not launched him on a bad path!"[74] he exclaimed, as he described how "that piece of meat who sees as little with his brain

---

[71] ASF, *Leg. Comm.* 17, ff. 57*r*-58*v* (election and mandate to Naples, 27 July and 31 August 1470), 60*v*-61*r* (instruction to Rome, 10 October 1470). He was instructed to join Niccoli ni in Rome on 14 September.

[72] On the secret clause, see BROWN, *Bartolomeo Scala*, p. 172 (Ital. edn. p. 118), and on the failure to ratify, GUICCIARDINI, *Storie fiorentine*, pp. 23-24; in general PASTOR, *Storia dei Papi*, II, pp. 401-405, and now LORENZO DE' MEDICI, *Lettere*, I, especially FUBINI's commentary and notes to letters 60, 66, 67, 70, pp. 175-179, 211-224, 230-238 and document I, pp. 251-256.

[73] S. Sacramori to Galeazzo Maria Sforza, 1 September 1470 (ASMi SPE Fir. 280): "[Pierfrancesco de' Medici] ha ad essere compagno al ditto d. Otho [Niccolini], perchè essendo luy grasso come è, vadeno di passo et non di corsa ... et cossì andiamo cum più longa et più copertamente si pò; 12 December 1470: "et Lorenzo c'è ha là uno d. Gentile che tene bene dritto Pierofrancesco perchè'l non pescha el fondo".

[74] *Ibid.*, 22 December 1470: "Salvo se d. Agnolo Azzaiolo non l'havesse messo in mal camino".

as with his eyes" was canvassing for Gonfalonier of Justice his own candidate, Antonio Martelli, instead of the protégé of Sacramori and the Duke of Milan, Angelo della Stufa. Fortunately Lorenzo proved more compliant and agreed to support della Stufa, who was duly elected at the beginning of 1471. He introduced reforms to control the election of *accoppiatori*, evidently to eliminate the risk of uncooperative members, such as Pierfrancesco.[75] Before new *accoppiatori* were elected in the summer, however, Pierfrancesco persistently supported for the Signoria men like "Strozzo degli Strozzi whom Lorenzo did not want" but "whom that beast Pierfrancesco wanted, and he allowed himself to be governed by that harmful Domenico Martelli, who is *illud idem* as Jacomo Pazzi".[76] To Sacramori's annoyance, after being first rejected, both Martelli and Pazzi were appointed to the reforming Balìa created that summer, along with Pierfrancesco himself.[77]

Sacramori's reports are biased by personal antagonism. But we know from the attempts of Pierfrancesco's and Lorenzo's friends to "keep them united" on Piero's death that there were serious differences which encouraged Pierfrancesco to oppose the political policies of his cousin. In linking his name with men known to be hostile to Lorenzo (Jacopo Pazzi, Domenico and Antonio Martelli) Sacramori indicates that Pierfrancesco was in the early 1470s in a position to challenge Lorenzo's primacy. This opposition had no coherent programme to compare with the republicanism of the Pitti conspirators. In 1469 Jacopo Pazzi was accused of currying favour with the people during his office as Gonfalonier of Justice by refusing to discuss money matters, thus causing trouble for his successor. Later that year "questa umbra de d. Jacomo di Pazi" offended the Mediceans by entertaining the Venetian ambassadors in defiance of the official alliance of Florence,

---

[75] *Ibid.*: "Et quel pezzo di carne de Pierofrancesco de' Medici che vede sì pocho col cervello como cum gli occhi, perchè l'è de li accopiatori, scrive a Lorenzo che fazza Confallonero Antonio Martello, et dàgli la sua voce et scrive et prega li compagni che fazano el medesimo". On della Stufa's election, see BROWN, *Bartolomeo Scala,* p. 64 (Ital. edn. p. 46), and RUBINSTEIN, *Government of Florence,* p. 180.

[76] 1 May 1471, ASMi SPE Fir. 281: "Ècce anchora certi de' priori che sonno pocho benivoli d'epso Lorenzo ... Ècce un'altro Strozzo di Strocci che Lorenzo nol voleva et quella bestia de Pierofrancesco de' Medici l'ha voluto, et lassassi governare a quel cativo de d. Domenico Martelli, che è *illud idem* che d. Jacomo [Pazzi]"; cf. his letter of 5 May, *ibid.*, "Quel bestiale de Pierofrancesco è stato in gran parte casone de questo per soe fantasie".

[77] RUBINSTEIN, *Government of Florence,* pp. 183, 303, 308.

Milan and Naples against Venice and the Pope.[78] In 1470 it was adherence to the Aragonese party (with which Pierfrancesco was associated through Angelo Acciaiuoli) which signalled dissent, as did electoral opposition to Medicean candidates. In 1484 the son of Pierfrancesco's unpopular candidate for the Gonfaloniership of Justice, Niccolò di Antonio Martelli, offended Lorenzo de' Medici by belonging to a different electoral pressure group from Lorenzo's without his knowledge.[79] By supporting such varied expressions of political dissent Pierfrancesco helped give them a coherence they otherwise lacked.

Pierfrancesco's own discontent, however, was fed by resentment about family precedence and money. Sacramori says he took it badly that the head of the house was younger than him.[80] For his part, Lorenzo resented what he regarded as Pierfrancesco's unfair share of the family possessions and business. His bitterness towards Pierfrancesco is reflected in conversations reported not only by the biased Sacramori but also by Sacramori's nephew and successor as ambassador in Florence. In January 1473, when the Duke of Milan attempted to recover a loan of ten thousand florins to Lorenzo, he was told that, far from returning his money, Lorenzo was on the point of asking for more, motivated by his trust in Galeazzo Maria and the offer made to him when his father died; without this he would have to withdraw money from the Monte,

> as his cousin Piero Francesco does every day, which is a beastly thing to do and enough to make them lose credit.[81]

When Sacramori's nephew renewed the Duke's request a year later, using every argument he could think of, "opportune and inopportune", Lorenzo blandly replied that he could not believe the Duke really needed the money; and he summoned the General Manager of the Medici bank, Francesco Sassetti, to explain his difficulties. These included the death of the Cardinal of San Sisto, who owed him thou-

---

78 S. Sacramori to Galeazzo Maria Sforza, 7 April 1469 (ASMi SPE Fir. 276); and LORENZO DE' MEDICI, *Lettere*, I, p. 46, n. 3.

79 RUBINSTEIN, *Government of Florence*, p. 217, n. 3.

80 S. Sacramori to Galeazzo Maria Sforza, 1 May 1471 (ASMi SPE Fir. 281): "et anchora *egre fert* che la reputatione de la casa loro sia in più giovane de luy".

81 S. Sacramori to G. M. Sforza, 28 January 1473, ASMi SPE Fir. 283: "de' quali dinari luy faceva concto de uscire delle la Monte che d'epso fa ogni dì Pierofrancesco suo cosino, che sonno bestiale e da farli perdere el credito".

sands of ducats, his credit with the Apostolic Camera, from which he couldn't withdraw a penny:

> and as a final powerful argument he alleged the division of the company of Piero Francesco his cousin, to whom he said he owed dozens and dozens of thousands of ducats, which he had to repay before all else.[82]

At the end of that financial year Pierfrancesco was in fact owed nearly sixty-one thousand florins by Lorenzo and his brother Giuliano, and this debt was inherited by Pierfrancesco's sons to spoil their relationship with Lorenzo.[83]

In February 1474 Pierfrancesco elected Lorenzo his procurator (for that occasion alone) for presentation to the church of St. Thomas in Florence of which he was presumably patron. The case has been compared to Lorenzo's presentation of Marsilio Ficino the following year to the Rinieri family's benefice of St. Christopher which, according to Bernardo Rinieri, "we gave ... to the said messer Marsiglio at the request and instance of Lorenzo di Piero di Chosimo de' Medici".[84] It is likely that Pierfrancesco was similarly requested to relinquish his benefice by Lorenzo, for patronage was another field in which Lorenzo, like Cosimo, extended his influence as he became politically more powerful.

Pierfrancesco died on 19 July 1476 from an abscess or growth on the hip with which he had been ill for about forty days, refusing to have it cut until, "urged by Lorenzo and necessity", it was too late to save his life.[85] On the eve of his death he made his will, the first

---

[82] F. Sacramori to G. M. Sforza, 4 May 1474, ASMi SPE Fir. 286: "Et finalmente per potissima allegò la divisione della compagnia de Pierofrancesco suo cosino, al quale diceva esse debitore de desine et de desine de migliara de ducati, et bisognagli li restituisca ante omnia".

[83] ASF, *MAP* 104, no. 48, ff. 454*v*, 465*v* (cf. *MAP* 104, no. 71, f. 651*v*): Lorenzo and Giuliano owe Lorenzo and Giovanni di Pierofrancesco fl. 60,971 1s. 7d. "per resto del conto de' traffichi et delle compagnie avute con Pierfrancesco nostro padre che finirono insino a dì 24 di marzo 1474[5]". According to the account of Lorenzo di Piero, drawn up at the time of the 1485 settlement (see n. 94 below), he owed his young cousins fl. 56,509 4s. 7d. "per uno saldo facto d'acordo con lui [Pierfrancesco] la buona memoria di Giuliano mio fratello ... in dì 26 di marzo 1475". But this account adds a sum of 6,419 florins owed to the cousins for their share in the banking, silk and wool companies in Florence, which does not appear to be separately itemised in their accounts, ASF, *Notarile 10200*, f. 219*r*, cf. *MAP* 99, no. 8, f. 31.

[84] Ricordi di Bernardo Rinieri, ASF *Conv. Soppr.* 95,212, f. 166*r* (27 October 1475): "E a detto messer Marsiglio la demo a preghiera e stanza di Lorenzo di Piero di Chosimo de' Medici e sopra la sua coscienza se non fussi ben ghovernata". The comparison is made by FUBINI, ed., LORENZO DE' MEDICI, *Lettere*, I, p. 503, n. 3.

[85] ASF, *MAP* 104, no. 48, f. 456*r*: "Il dì della morte di nostro padre che fu a dì 19 di luglio 1476"; F. Sacramori to Galeazzo Maria Sforza, 19 and 23 July 1476 (ASMi SPE

within his family, and among the witnesses was Guglielmo de' Pazzi. He appointed his sons his sole heirs, but if they died intestate and without masculine issue Lorenzo and Giuliano di Piero were to inherit his estate. His mother Ginevra, with Lorenzo and Giuliano, were to be their guardians.[86]

Pierfrancesco's death by neglect contrasts with the more sophisticated care lavished on his valetudinarian cousins and is consistent with the sluggish rusticity which seems to have characterized this rotund countryman. Difficult as it is to see him as the leader of a formal opposition party to his cousins, he evidently harboured more resentment towards them than has hitherto been suggested. Fond though he may have been of them his attitude towards the head of the house was always equivocal, not openly rebellious but non-cooperative: unwilling to be burdened with Cosimo's building costs or to discuss his tax returns with Piero, ready to avoid accompanying Lorenzo's bride from Rome and disinclined to follow his political or financial leadership. By openly supporting political opposition to his cousin's policies – signing the republican oath in 1466, backing rival candidates for the Signoria in 1470-1, showing ambivalence as ambassador to Naples and Rome in 1470 – Pierfrancesco anticipated and must have influenced the behaviour of his sons. Thanks to his wealth and the radical example of his wife's family he sowed the seeds of their later role as supporters of policies other than those of the elder branch of the Medici family.

When Pierfrancesco died his sons Lorenzo and Giovanni were only thirteen and nine years old. The tables were now reversed, in that Lorenzo il Magnifico was the oldest member of the family and – after the murder of his brother Giuliano two years later – was entitled to a whole share of the wealth of his branch of the family in contrast to his cousins' divided patrimony. The situation was uncomfortably reminiscent of Pierfrancesco's childhood in the 1440s: for

---

Fir. 291): "la infermità sua fuo una apostematione in una cossa, de la quale el stete amalato circa de xl. dì".

86 ASF, *MAP* 159, ff. 13*r*-15*v*, drawn up by ser Antonio di ser Battista Bartolomei on 18 July 1476. The witnesses were ser Nerozzo di Antonio da Prato, cathedral chaplain, Giovanni di Antonio Serristori, Francesco di Tommaso Sassetti (Director General of the Medici Bank), Guglielmo di Antonio Pazzi, Fruosino da Panzano, Sandro Pagagnotti (Medici factor and arbitrator between the two branches of the family in 1485) and Lorenzo di Bernardo de' Medici. Pierfrancesco bequeathed £1 piccolo to the Opera of the Florentine Walls and £2 piccoli to the Opera of the Duomo and its new sacristy.

the second time the younger branch of the family fell under the tutelage of the elder branch. At first their relationship seemed friendly enough. In September 1475 Lorenzo il Magnifico invited his young cousin Lorenzo to go to Pisa with him. Although Pierfrancesco refused to allow him to go then, he professed to be pleased for him to go later.[87] Shortly after Pierfrancesco's death his young sons accepted Lorenzo's suggestion that they should buy Angelo della Stufa's farm at Castello because (they wrote to him): "we are certain you would not advise us in any manner contrary to our interests and that you have no reason to harm us".[88] In saying this, however, they (perhaps unwittingly) voiced a fear that gained substance in the years which followed. Lorenzo was in a position to exercise the same control over his young cousins as Cosimo had formerly exercised over their father, and to deprive them – like him – of the free use of their money during their years of tutelage. According to them he did not fail to profit from the opportunity.

Their charges against Lorenzo il Magnifico at the time of the 1485 arbitration are quite specific. They include the following: he failed to pay them interest on the value of their companies, which totalled fl. 130,557; or to repay them money lent since their father's death, totalling fl. 53,643; or their father's loan to Lorenzo of fl. 8166.[89] They claimed that they suffered financially from having to keep several thousands of florins at hand in ready cash (referring to the thirteen bags containing 20,043 florins given to them by Lorenzo on 4 December 1476 after their father's death but retained by Lorenzo in his house and taken back for his own use on 1 May 1478).[90] They alleged that they were deprived of their Mugello possessions and produce which, for want of money, they were forced to sell prematurely. By taking their money Lorenzo prevented them from continuing their policy of buying property at a good price when the opportunity arose (here doubtless referring to the series of forced loans totalling 33,600 florins demanded from them during the Pazzi War in

---

[87] Lorenzo di Pierfrancesco to Lorenzo il Magnifico, 4 September 1475, ASF, *MAP* 32, 541, edited and translated by E. H. Gombrich, *Symbolic Images*, p. 79, no. 1.

[88] ASF, *MAP* 33, 741, 2 September 1476, *ibid.*, p. 80, no. 2.

[89] ASF, *MAP* 104, no. 48, f. 456*r*, cf. n. 66 above.

[90] See following note.

1478-9).[91] For the same reason they were unable to pay their taxes, thereby incurring fines in addition to the taxes – and also, they might have added, loss of office, since in 1484 Lorenzo di Pierfrancesco was one of only two members of the scrutiny council to be disqualified because of tax debts.[92] They also lost their payments from the Monte. As a further inconvenience they were unable to invest in the silk or wool or any other industry, for thanks to Lorenzo they had lost credit and could do nothing without money:

If we had been able to avoid lending him this sum of money, we should happily have done so and not only would we not have lent it to him but we would have got back what he held before. But we were forced to lend it, and if we had not done so he had already told me once in his study that as guardian of our inheritance he would take it. Then we asked him every day and tried to withdraw as much money from the bank as possible, but for the last four years he has prevented us from making withdrawals.[93]

---

[91] ASF, *Notarile 10200,* f. 219*v*, listing two sums of 22,600 and 11,000 florins borrowed on 1 May 1478 and 27 September 1479 respectively (Lorenzo il Magnifico's account, drawn up by ser Simone Grazzini, which formed the basis of the official settlement in 1485; a copy or draft of part of it exists in the hand of Lorenzo's secretary, ser Niccolò Michelozzi, in *MAP* 99, no. 8, ff. 30-31), and *MAP* 104, no. 48, ff. 454*v*, 459*r*, 460*r*, 467*v*, listing five sums of 5000, 8000, 8000, 1600 and 11,000 florins borrowed on 2 May, 20 June, 8 and 13 August 1478 and 27 September 1479 respectively (Lorenzo and Giovanni di Pierfrancesco's accounts, a series of drafts in differing arrangements); cf. *MAP* 137, no. 1004 (a receipt for 33,000 *scudi d'oro* lent to Lorenzo il Magnifico by the Bank of Pierfrancesco de' Medici on 14 August, 1 October and 27 September 1479). This sum is considerably less than that of 53,643 florins quoted by DE ROOVER, *Banco Medici,* p. 532 and note 56, using Lorenzo and Giovanni's accounts, misdating the last payment in 1478) or that of 60,000 ducats quoted by GUICCIARDINI (*Storie fiorentine,* p. 76). The difference is accounted for by the sum of 20,043 florins (listed by DE ROOVER as the first of six loans borrowed on 1 May 1478) which was in fact money held by Lorenzo and Giuliano de' Medici for Lorenzo and Giovanni di Pierfrancesco in 13 bags, given to them after the death of their father on 4 December 1476 and taken back by Lorenzo il Magnifico on 1 May 1478. When this sum figures in Lorenzo and Giovanni di Pierfrancesco's accounts of money owed to them by Lorenzo il Magnifico it is nearly always balanced by an identical sum owed by them to their cousin (*MAP* 104, no. 48, ff. 454*v*-455*r*; 465*v*-466*r*) and where it is not, it is listed separately from the other five sums borrowed in 1478-79 (*ibid.*, ff. 461*r*, 462*r*; cf. 459*r*, 460*r*, 467*v*). While it was doubtless used by Lorenzo il Magnifico for the expenses of the Pazzi War instead of for the needs of his young wards as intended, by common agreement it was not included with the other loans from his cousins in 1478-79.

[92] RUBINSTEIN, *Government of Florence,* p. 212.

[93] ASF, *MAP* 104, no. 48, f. 456*v*: "Se noi avessimo potuto fare di non prestargli questa somma di danari, volentieri l'aremo fatto, et non solamente non glele aremo prestati, ma aremo rivoluti quelli teneva inanzi. Ma fu forza glene prestassimo che se non glene avessimo prestati, mi disse già nello scrittoio suo che chome tutore della redita se gli torrebbe. Di poi glene abbiamo richiesti ogni giorno, et ingiegnatoci di trarre del bancho più danari che sia stato possibile. Ma lui da quattro anni in qua ci à serrato la tratta".

There was disagreement about the total amount of money Lorenzo il Magnifico owed his cousins when Lorenzo di Pierfrancesco came of age, but a settlement was made whereby he gave them his Cafaggiolo estate and some sixty-six farms, mills and houses in the Mugello: amendments in favour of Lorenzo il Magnifico were later made.[94]

Lorenzo di Pierfrancesco pursued the *cursus honorum* in Florence, which – like his father – he entered earlier than he should have done: at the age of seventeen a member of the 1480 Balìa,[95] at the age of twenty an ambassador to France (thanks to the mediation of his father's former secretary, Bartolomeo Scala, by then first chancellor of Florence);[96] in 1484 a member of the scrutiny council (though disqualified for debts, as we have seen), in 1493 drawn Gonfalonier of Justice.[97] Through his mother's family he also associated with the 'republican' opposition group of 1466 which came into its own again after the 1494 revolution. He spoke out in favour of his exiled Acciaiuoli uncles, and after their return from Naples was a close friend

---

[94] See ASF, *Notarile* 10200, ff. 218*r*-225*v* (the arbitration by Domenico Bartoli and Ridolfo Ridolfi on 22 November 1485, cf. *MAP* 159, ff. 49*r*-62*v*, and *MAP* 99, no. 8, ff. 30-31 and n. 91 above) and ASF, *MAP* 104, no. 48, ff. 454*r*-469*r*. It is difficult to compare the two sets of accounts accurately, for not only do they present payments differently, but Lorenzo and Giovanni di Pierfrancesco's consist of a series of differing accounts with no final statement, some including interest due and some not. In general both sets agree over sums of money lent to the sons of Pierfrancesco by the Medici bank for expenses during their tutelage, over building expenses in San Lorenzo (see note 23 above), over money owed to them after the death of their grandfather, half of which Lorenzo il Magnifico retained for the building expenses of San Marco (7776 florins, despite the provisions of the 1451 settlement, see above), over their share of the losses incurred by the London branch of the Bank (22,985 florins) and over their loans to Lorenzo il Magnifico during the Pazzi War (note 91 above). According to the 1485 settlement (based on Lorenzo il Magnifico's accounts, see above note 91), Lorenzo owed his young cousins 110,399 florins, they owed him 48,992 florins; according to them, he owed them 130,557 florins, they owed him 51,396 florins, making his outstanding debt to them some 79,161 florins instead of 61,407 florins according to the adjudicators. On 28 September 1486 Sandro Pagagnotti adjudged that Lorenzo il Magnifico was now owed 2,118 florins by his cousins who were to return four farms to him (ASF *Notarile 10200,* ff. 230*r*-231*v*). On 1 February 1488 they acquired more Mugello property from him worth 5200 florins, which they paid by giving him their credit of 5250 ducats with the Duke of Urbino for jewels sold to him (ASF, *MAP* 104, no. 48, ff. 464*r-v*).

[95] Rubinstein, *Government of Florence,* p. 315.

[96] ASF *Leg. Comm.* 21, ff. 49*v*-52*r*; *MAP* 39, 44 and 51, 265, B. Scala and Lorenzo di Pierfrancesco to Lorenzo il Magnifico, 16 and 17 October 1483, see Brown, *Bartolomeo Scala,* p. 120 (Ital. edn. p. 83).

[97] ASF, *Tratte* 15 (unfoliated): 29 September 1484: "scrutineum arrotorum": elected by 64 votes in favour, 2 against; and 28 August 1493: listed under "veduti vivi" (when he was still too young to exercise the office, however).

of his cousin Zanobi Acciaiuoli.[98] He blamed Lorenzo il Magnifico for failing to support his friends the Vespucci in their affairs.[99] In January 1489 he and his brother Giovanni joined the Milanese and Genoese ambassadors in Florence in asking Lorenzo il Magnifico to pardon a youth who had killed a servant of the hated Otto di Guardia and had then attemped to escape. But after giving them "fair words", Lorenzo il Magnifico instead ordered the youth to be hanged from a window of the Bargello and had four of those who had encouraged his escape tortured, refusing himself to leave the piazza until the crowd was completely quiet.[100]

In April 1494 Lorenzo and Giovanni, because of their close relationship with Charles VIII of France and Lodovico Sforza (no longer friends of Piero de' Medici), were exiled to their estates outside Florence for conspiring against the government. For this disloyalty the Council of Seventy wanted to imprison them for life until dissuaded by Piero di Lorenzo.[101] They remained in the Mugello until October, when they fled to join the French King and Lodovico Sforza outside Milan, returning to Florence on 12 November, three days after their cousin Piero had fled.[102]

It was at this time that the brothers changed their name from Medici to Popolani. Nonetheless it is unlikely that their sympathies were any more populistic than those of their great-uncle Angelo Acciaiuoli, who, while fighting for the cause of 'liberty' in Florence,[103]

---

[98] See his letter to Giovanni Lanfredini in Naples, 28 May 1484, BNF MS II, v. 12, f. 52, recommending "la faccenda di Raffaelo Acciaiuolo mio tio", and on Zanobi, see the *Dizionario biografico degli italiani,* I *s.v.*

[99] See his letter to Sandro Pagagnotti, ASF, *MAP* 84, 104 (undated), edited and translated by GOMBRICH, *Symbolic Images,* pp. 80-81, no. 3.

[100] Described by the Ferrarese ambassador in Florence, 19 January 1489, ed. A. CAPPELLI, *Lettere di Lorenzo de' Medici ... conservate nell'Archivio Palatino di Modena,* «Atti e memorie di R. Deput. di storia patria per le provincie modenesi e parmensi», sez. di Modena, I, 1863, p. 305.

[101] See the "Libro di debitori e creditori e ricordanze" of Tommaso Ginori, ed. J. SCHNITZER, *Quellen und Forschungen zur Geschichte Savonarolas,* I, Munich, J. J. Lentner' schen Buchhandlung, 1902, p. 94. Their decree of exile by the Signoria on 29 May is in ASF *Signori Deliberazioni* 96, f. 95*r.*

[102] *Ricordanze* di TRIBALDO DE' ROSSI, *Delizie,* XXIII, p. 295, LUCA LANDUCCI, *Diario fiorentino,* ed. I DEL BADIA, Florence, Sansoni, 1883, p. 78.

[103] *Delizie,* cit., p. 291: "esere tutta 2 baroni de Re di Francia, o veramente Lorenzino sagretario de Re di Francia e Giovanni suo fratelo barone de Re, chosi si dicie per el popolo". Cf. Jean Matharon's instruction, 11 June 1494, ed. G. CANESTRINI - A DESJARDINS, *Négotiations diplomatiques de la France avec la Toscane,* I, Paris, Imprimerie imperiale, 1859, p. 416, commending Lorenzo and Giovanni, "tum etiam ipsius Regis officiales sunt ordinarii". On

enjoyed a close and courtly relationship with the King of France and the Duke of Milan. Nor did the brothers sustain for long their role of party leaders.[104] They offered an alternative to their cousins' increasingly unitary regime in the years before the revolution, like crown princes adopting policies which contrasted with those of the reigning monarch. In Francesco Guicciardini's *Dialogo del Reggimento di Firenze* the Medicean Bernardo del Nero says that after Giuliano was murdered in 1478 and Lorenzo injured, "we thought, if Lorenzo died, of turning to Lorenzo di Pierfrancesco because he was the nearest", suggesting that Lorenzo di Pierfrancesco was regarded as a viable successor (although in these circumstances not an alternative) to the primacy of the elder Medici.[105]

Options for dissent were limited in late fifteenth-century Florence; but such as they were, Lorenzo di Pierfrancesco took them. In external politics he supported the old French and Milanese entente recently abandoned by Piero di Lorenzo with – as Guicciardini thought – such disastrous consequences for the peace of Italy.[106] At home he let himself be associated (at least in public) with a more humanitarian approach to law and order, sympathizing with the popular hatred of the Otto di Guardia and its arbitrary justice which Lorenzo il Magnifico upheld, and perhaps too with the surprised reaction of visiting ambassadors to Lorenzo's secret methods of investigating crimes.[107]

In the field of patronage Lorenzo di Pierfrancesco disowned the building programme of his cousins and supported a new trend which contrasted with their less adventurous tastes. He was one of Botticelli's principal patrons. It was he who commissioned *Spring, Pallas and*

Angelo Acciaiuoli's relationship with the Dukes of Milan, cf. *Dispatches with related documents,* quoted in note 27 above.

[104] On Lorenzo di Pierfrancesco's role after the revolution, see, for example, S. BERTELLI, *Machiavelli e la politica estera fiorentina,* «Studies on Machiavelli», ed. M. Gilmore, Florence, Sansoni, cit., pp. 31-72.

[105] Ed. R. PALMAROCCHI, Bari, Laterza, 1932, p. 165: "noi che desideravamo uno stato simile, pensamo, in caso che Lorenzo morissi, voltarci a Lorenzo di Pierfrancesco, perchè era el più prossimo".

[106] *Storie fiorentine,* p. 88.

[107] See the comment of the Modenese ambassador on the capture and examination of two men suspected of attempting to murder Lorenzo: "Nondimeno l'esame secretissimo che è stato fatto di loro, come si è inteso, ha dato ammirazione non poca a noi altri ambasciatori che lo abbiamo inteso. Il qual esame è stato fatto per li infrascritti cittadini primarii e congiunti di affinità e stretta amicizia con il M^{co} Lorenzo", ed. A. CAPPELLI, *Lettere di Lorenzo de' Medici,* cit., p. 308 (18 May 1490).

the Centaur, a Bacchic frieze for his house in Florence, and probably Botticelli's illustrations for Landino's *Commentary* on Dante.[108] He was one of Michelangelo's first patrons.[109] He befriended Marsilio Ficino, who asked him to provide for his tomb and in return bequeathed Lorenzo di Pierfrancesco, "for his kindness to him and on account of certain just reasons moving his mind and conscience", his treasured copy of Plato's *Dialogues* in Greek.[110] He was a close friend of the soldier poet Michele Marullo, who dedicated to him his *Epigrams* and paganizing *Hymni naturales*.[111] Marullo admired the atheist Lucretius and his doctrine of pleasure as the highest good, so antipathetic to stoic upholders of public order in the state, and he may have helped to stimulate an interest in this still relatively unknown poet among Lorenzo di Pierfrancesco's circle. Lorenzo di Pierfrancesco was also the friend and business associate of Amerigo Vespucci, and it was to him that Amerigo dedicated his famous *Mundus novus* describing for the first time his discovery of people in southern America without temples or laws, who "live according to nature and can be said to be epicureans rather than stoics".[112] Amerigo Vespucci's family, too, felt they had been badly treated by the elder Medici and it is possible that Lorenzo di Pierfrancesco and his friends found in epicureanism support for their anti-authoritarian views.

Pierfrancesco did not share his son's cultural tastes, but in other ways there were strong resemblances between father and son. Francesco Guicciardini, who must have known Lorenzo, described him as "good natured" compared with his more restless brother Giovan-

---

[108] See R. LIGHTBOWN, *Sandro Botticelli*, London, Paul Elek, 1978, I, pp. 56, 70-73, 82, 92, 99, 148; (2nd edn. New York, Abbeville Press, 1989). GOMBRICH, *Symbolic Images*, pp. 128-129, 40-41, 64-66; and in general on Lorenzo di Pierfrancesco, PIERACCINI, *La Stirpe*, I, pp. 353-357; and bibliographics in P. O. KRISTELLER, *Supplementum ficinianum*, II, pp. 331-332, CANESTRINI-DESJARDINS, *Négotiations*, I, pp. 198-200.

[109] LIGHTBOWN, *Botticelli*, I, p. 129.

[110] Ficino's will, dated 29 September 1499, ed. KRISTELLER, *Supplementum ficinianum*, II, pp. 194, 195; "tamquam de se bene merito et ob certas iustas causas animum et conscientiam suam moventes".

[111] *Carmina*, ed. A. PEROSA, Thesauro Mundi, Verona, 1951, cf. A. PEROSA, *Studi sulla formazione delle raccolte di poesie del Marullo*, «Rinascimento», I, 1950, pp. 133-134.

[112] *Mundus novus*, 1503-1504, facsimile reprinted in *Prime relazioni di navigatori italiani sulla scoperta dell'America. Colombo, Vespucci, Verazzano*, ed. L. FIRPO, Turin, U.T.E.T., 1966, p. 88: "Preterea nullum habent templum, et nullam tenent legem ... Vivunt secundam naturam et epycuri potius dici possunt quam stoici".

ni,[113] recalling Nicodemo Tranchedini's description of the young Pierfrancesco's "rare and courteous nature". But both Pierfrancesco and Lorenzo also harboured strong feelings of resentment beneath their friendliness which queered their pitch with the heads of the family, particularly Pierfrancesco's relationship with the young Lorenzo il Magnifico, his son Lorenzo's with Lorenzo and Piero and then, more reprehensibly, with his brother's young son, Giovanni delle Bande Nere.[114] The family bond kept the two branches outwardly united until 1494, but the seeds of dissent, expressed outwardly by contrasting attitudes to politics, law and patronage, had been sown many years earlier in Pierfrancesco's childhood.

---

[113] *Storie fiorentine,* p. 90: "uomo bonario".

[114] PIERACCINI, *La Stirpe,* I, p. 355, describing Lorenzo di Pierfrancesco's treatment of his nephew and ward: "poco scrupoloso, punto generoso, molto egoista".

4

THE GUELF PARTY IN FIFTEENTH-CENTURY FLORENCE

THE TRANSITION FROM COMMUNAL TO MEDICEAN STATE

In the middle of the fifteenth century the future of the Parte Guelfa was in jeopardy. In 1461 Luigi Guicciardini told a *pratica* of citizens that the Signoria had often discussed with them the question of closing it down as 'superfluous' to the government of Florence:

> since in our time, in the absence of guelf and ghibelline factions in the city – everyone now being guelfs – it completely lacks the purpose for which it was created.[1]

His words epitomise the problem faced by the Parte Guelfa in the fifteenth century. Originating as a military society of nobles to combat the imperial ghibellines in the early thirteenth century, it had enjoyed its period of greatest power in the years 1267-1280 as the instrument through which the papal-Angevin alliance governed Florence after defeating the ghibellines. Although it lost political supremacy after Cardinal Latino's settlement in 1280, it retained financial control in the city by appropriating to itself money and property confiscated from its rivals.[2] Perhaps the Statutes of the Podestà exaggerate

---

This paper was originally published in «Rinascimento», XX, 1980.

[1] ASF, *Cons. Prat.* 56, f. 151*v*, cf. p. 119, n. 57 below: "quoniam etate nostra cessabat causa omnino propter quam illud officium creatum fuit, nullam enim nunc esse factionem in civitate gebellinam et guelfam sed omnes guelfos esse, consultasse iam pluries dominos cum civibus, ut ea domus clauderetur velut superflua regimini civitatis".

[2] On the history of the Parte Guelfa, U. DORINI, *Notizie storiche sull'università di Parte Guelfa in Firenze*, Florence, 1902; F. BONAINI, *Della parte guelfa in Firenze*, «Giornale Storico degli Archivi Toscani», I, 1857, pp. 1-41 (ed. 1335 Statuti); II, 1858, pp. 171-187, 257-289; III, 1859, pp. 77-79, 167-184; G. SALVEMINI, *La dignità cavalleresca nel Comune di Firenze*, M. Ricci, Florence, 1896, esp. pp. 67-70, 75-75.

in describing it in 1325 as "one and the same thing" as the people and commune of Florence, "since the money of the Parte Guelfa is, as it were, the treasury of the people and commune".[3] Nevertheless, the Parte continued to enjoy power in the fourteenth century by acting as financial broker to the government as well as to guilds and to merchant companies in Florence.[4] As we shall see, it was precisely because its monies had been communal monies that later governments wanted them to return to the communal treasury. At the same time, the Parte played the role of guardian of civic orthodoxy by promoting as the commune's ideology its own papal-Angevism and the defence of Florentine liberty.[5]

As broker to the commune and guardian of its ideology the Parte Guelfa survived into the fifteenth century, when it has been almost unanimously dismissed as an anachronism.[6] Yet it is precisely in this century that its position is of crucial importance. A powerful attempt to revive the authority of the Parte in the 1420s was frustrated by the defeat of the Albizzi party by the Mediceans in 1434. But far from leaving it to be transcended or simply to wither away as "superfluous" to the government of Florence, the Mediceans engaged in a vigorous and sustained campaign against the Parte. At first they

---

[3] *Statuti della Repubblica fiorentina*, ed. R. CAGGESE, II (Statuto del Podestà, 1325), Florence, Tipografia Galileiana, 1921, bk. II, ch. 95, p. 166: "Cum pecunia Partis Guelfe de Florentia sit quidam thesaurus populi et Communis Florentine ac Pars, populus et Commune sint unum et idem".

[4] ASF, *Capitani della Parte Guelfa* (= *Capit. P.G.*) 26 rosso lists substantial loans to the Comune raised by the Parte, as well as loans to guilds such as the Beccai and the Calzolai, and to the Pulci, Frescobaldi, Spini, Pazzi, Peruzzi and Acciaiuoli companies, 1318-1329. In 1326 the Parte raised money to pay for German mercenaries at the command of Charles, Duke of Calabria.

[5] See the prologue to the 1335 Parte *Statuti* (ed. BONAINI, cit., I, p. 4): "Ad honore et reverenza ... de la santa Chiesa Romana ... ad exaltatione et gloria del serenissimo principe messere Roberto re di Ierusalem et di Cicilia; a grandezza et buono stato del popolo et del comune di Firenze et de' suoi reggimenti ..."; MATTEO VILLANI, *Cronica*, ed. F. DRAGOMANNI, Florence, II, 1846, bk. VIII, 24, p. 109: "la parte guelfa è fondamento e rocca ferma e stabile della libertà d'Italia e contraria a tutte le tirannie". Its role and significance in the fourteenth century are discussed by G. A. BRUCKER, *Florentine Politics and Society, 1343-1378*, Princeton, Princeton University Press, 1962, pp. 99-104 and *passim*; R. WITT, *A note on Guelfism in late medieval Florence*, «Nuova Rivista Storica», LIII, 1969, pp. 134-145; H. BARON, *The Crisis of the early Italian Renaissance*, rev. edn., Princeton, Princeton University Press, with the Newberry Library, 1966, pp. 20-21 and note 8.

[6] With the exception of Baron (*op. cit.*, above) and C. C. BAYLEY, *War and Society in Renaissance Florence*, Toronto, 1961, pp. 209-210, 369-389, editing Leonardo Bruni's treatise *De Militia*, whose interest does not extend beyond the early years of the fifteenth century. See now, however, DIANE FINIELLO ZERVAS, *The Parte Guelfa, Brunelleschi and Donatello*, «I Tatti Studies», 8, New York, J. J. Augustin, Locust Valley, 1987.

attempted to close it down altogether. Then, faced with opposition to the destruction of "so venerable a monument", they attempted to revivify it. Finally, in 1481 they more or less succeeded in reducing it to the condition in which it survived until the eighteenth century: a department of state, prestigious in name and administratively useful but shorn of independent political and financial power. It is my purpose to describe its fortunes in the fifteenth century for the light they throw on Medicean policy and the transition of Florence from a pluralistic to a unitary state. The Parte Guelfa, like the Sei di Mercanzia and the twenty-one guilds, played an important role in communal politics even in the fifteenth century, and like the Mercanzia and guilds it existed as an independent corporation with its own independent assets. It was the ambition of the Mediceans to deprive the Parte captains, the six councillors of the Mercanzia and the twenty-one Capitudini or consuls of the guilds of their *ex officio* role in government and at the same time to deprive their corporations of their independent assets. Although the Medici were not totally successful in this, their policy towards the Parte Guelfa illustrated how they attempted to centralise and unify the government of Florence and the opposition they encountered in doing so.

The position of the Parte Guelfa reached its nadir at the beginning of the fifteenth century. According to Buonaccorso Pitti it by then had:

> lost much of its accustomed honour and reputation. So low indeed had it fallen that the Captains had difficulty in recruiting citizens to accompany them on their processions to make the customary offerings.[7]

He explains that the reason for this was a social one: the "isdegnio" felt by true guelfs for the newcomers, "molti Ghibellini e nuove gienti e di vile condizioni", to remedy which a new scrutiny or revision of those eligible for office was ordered in November 1413.[8] But

[7] BUONACCORSO PITTI *Cronica*, ed. A. BACCHI DELLA LEGA, Bologna, 1905, p. 184: "molto vilipenduta del suo usato honore e reputazione; e tanto era manchata, che a grande pena trovavano i chapitani cittadini che faciessono loro compagnia per andare a l'oferte ordinate per quella Chasa", *Two Memoirs of Renaissance Florence*, ed. G. BRUCKER, New York, Harper Row, 1967, p. 99; cf. G. BRUCKER, *The Civic World of Early Renaissance Florence,* Princeton, Princeton University Press, 1977, p. 314.

[8] PITTI, *Cronica*, p. 184, listing the scrutineers on pp. 184-189; BRUCKER, *Civic World*, cit., p. 314, describing Rinaldo Gianfigliazzi's complaint in a *pratica* on 16 November 1413 that he and his sons had been excluded from the Parte captaincy which had instead been filled by others whose ancestors were 'ghibellini' and 'comitatini'.

political as well as social motives must have contributed to this decision to purge the Parte offices: those keenest to do so were old-established guelfs like Rinaldo Gianfigliazzi, Gino Capponi and Niccolò da Uzzano who were all identified by Buonaccorso Pitti as belonging to the clique supporting Pope John XXIII, and it was they who were doubtless responsible for signing an unpopular treaty with the pope in November 1413, the very month in which it was decided to hold a new scrutiny of offices.[9] This scrutiny marked a revival of the Parte and its claim to be "on a par" with the Palazzo della Signoria in governing the city.[10]

The outward expression of this revival was the ambitious extension of the Parte palace which was begun in or soon after 1418 and continued steadily until after the fall of the Albizzi regime in 1434, haltingly thereafter.[11] Around 1420 the Parte constructed the most prestigious of all the tabernacles in the oratory of Orsanmichele, striking in its position and its classicizing style, for which it commissioned a glittering bronze St Louis of Toulouse (appropriately, an Angevin saint) by Donatello.[12] At the same time, five years after the communal statutes were revised in 1415, the Parte Guelfa statutes were re-drafted with the help of the famous humanist Leonardo Bruni.[13] That such a galaxy of talent was employed to revive the Parte is in itself eloquent evidence of its standing and aspirations at this time.[14]

The inner inspiration of this new guelfism was revealed in a political meeting held in S. Stefano in 1426 which allegedly demanded a return to the ancient form of government and the rejuvenation of the Parte Guelfa. Underlying these demands was a current of anti-

---

[9] PITTI, *Cronica* cit., p. 171 (*Two Memoirs* cit., p. 91); and on the treaty with John XXIII, BRUCKER, *Civic World* cit., pp. 374-375 and n. 275 (quoting Rinaldo Gianfigliazzi: "Bene deliberatum est ut liga cum domino papa firmetur").

[10] See ASF, *Cons. Prat.* 42, f. 88*r-v* (16 November 1413), extracts translated into English by G. BRUCKER in *The Society of Renaissance Florence*, New York, Harper Row, 1971, pp. 88-89; cf. BRUCKER, *Civic World* cit., chs. 5-8, esp. pp. 410-412, 436, 473-481, 489.

[11] ZERVAS, *The Parte Guelfa;* C. DE FABRICZY, *Il palazzo nuovo della Parte Guelfa,* «Bollettino della Associazione per la difesa di Firenze antica», Florence, Giugno 1904, pp. 39-49, and M. SALMI, *Il Palazzo della Parte Guelfa di Firenze e Filippo Brunelleschi,* «Rinascimento», II, 1951, pp. 3-11. For a description of the palace in 1431, see below, Appendix, edited in full by ZERVAS, App. V, C.

[12] *Ibid.*, chs. 4 and 5.

[13] ASF, *Capit. P.G.* 3 and 4 rosso (in Latin and Italian respectively); their preface is edited by C. GUASTI, *Commissioni di Rinaldo degli Albizzi,* III, Florence, Deputazione di Storia patria della Toscana, 1873, pp. 621-623 and is discussed by BARON, *op. cit.*

[14] I owe this point to Zervas.

popularism and the desire for a revival of the old chivalric order under the leadership of Niccolò da Uzzano and that "nobile milite", Rinaldo degli Albizzi, to whom Bruni had dedicated his treatise on knighthood, *De Militia*, in 1421.[15] Niccolò da Uzzano was accredited with a note attached to the Palazzo Vecchio at this time which shares the same idealism: prophesying doom because of the entry of *gente nuova* into the government, it advised that leadership should be restored to the "rossa gallina col drago verde della fedel Parte", alluding to the Parte's Angevin arms.[16]

Further evidence of renewal is provided by an inventory of Parte Guelfa possessions in 1431, undertaken by its newly-elected *provveditore*, Niccolò di Gentile degli Albizzi. It reveals that the Parte then owned some ninety-six rented properties, with possession also in San Miniato and Pisa, and it enjoyed the patronage of about twenty churches. It possessed fl. 28,185 in Monte stock, which it bought from the sale of property in 1426, and it was owed fl. 1339 in interest payments from the commune.[17]

Three years after this inventory was drawn up, the Albizzi regime fell. Although work on the Guelf Party palace continued, its building programme suffered from the crises of the following years. Work was suspended altogether from 1438 to 1442 because of war expenses, a period coinciding with that of the Balìa or Consiglio Maggiore which controlled taxation and expenditure; and in 1442 it was said that nothing had been done for four years because of the "inormes expensas" with which the Signoria had burdened the Parte.[18] From then until 1458 building continued intermittently as the economic and political situation allowed, slowly during the war years controlled by Balìe, with more encouragement after 1454-5 when the Balìa was abolished.[19] The first overt threat to the Parte Guelfa itself followed

---

[15] This S. Stefano meeting is described by GIOVANNI CAVALCANTI, *Istorie fiorentine*, ed. G. DI PINO, Milan, 1984 bk. III, chs. 1 and 2, pp. 45-54 (cf. bk. XIV, ch. 35, p. 413, for this description of Rinaldo degli Albizzi). On its authenticity and significance, see BRUCKER, *Civic World* cit., pp. 473-481, who concludes: "Though he took liberties with the facts, Cavalcanti did portray quite accurately the political climate in 1426 and specifically the aristocratic point of view" (p. 477). On Bruni's *De Militia*, see note 6 above.

[16] «Archivio Storico Italiano», s. I, IV (1843), pt. 1, pp. 297-300, at p. 299.

[17] ASF, *Capit. P.G.* 27 rosso, "Beni 1431": cf. Appendix below. According to BRUCKER, *Florentine Politics and Society* cit., p. 99, n. 182, the Parte only possessed one palace, 11 houses, 6 shops and some land in 1324 and spent fl. 3360 in acquiring property between 1370 and 1377.

[18] C. DE FABRICZY, *Il palazzo nuovo* cit., p. 41 (6 November 1442).

the creation of the Medicean Council of Cento and their tightening control of government in 1458. Significantly, it was to this new council, in which "are all the leading lights of the city", that it was suggested that the "whole business of the Parte Guelfa" should be referred when it was first proposed to close it down in 1459.[20]

Although the Parte survived this first threat to its existence and a committee was appointed to oversee the building work, the palace was never finished. Antonio Manetti, Brunelleschi's biographer, attributes this to political motives, in claiming that it seemed

> to those who ruled the city that it would be better to deprive this magistracy of some of its authority rather than to increase it, and this is the opinion they have persistently adhered to.[21]

Was he right? In order to understand the Medici's sustained campaign against the Parte which followed their abortive attempt to close it down in 1459, we must first investigate its role in Florence at that time.

* * *

Traditionally the Parte Guelfa was the guardian of chivalry and conservative ceremonial in Florence, "that ancient and greatly revered institution" as it was described in 1459, which provided comfortable refuge for

> men of noble birth accustomed to living off the fruits of their estates, who deservedly succeed to the office which had been ... honoured by their forefathers.[22]

---

[19] *Ibid.*, pp. 41-48. On the political situation of these years, N. RUBINSTEIN, *The Government of Florence*, pp. 18-29.

[20] ASF, *Cons. Prat.* 55, f. 124*v* (Luigi Ridolfi: "Remitti enim totum hoc negotium Partis Guelfe ex provisione illa in consilium centum noviter constitutum in quo sunt ipsa civitatis lumina, civitatis videlicet prestantissimi cives et rempublicam optime regere assueti"). Cf. RUBINSTEIN, *Government of Florence*, ch. 5, esp. pp. 113-116.

[21] *The Life of Brunelleschi*, ed. H. SAALMAN, University Park, Pennsylvania State University Press, 1970, pp. 101-103: "a chi governava la città che a tale magistrato fusse el meglio torre qualche cosa di riputazione che agugniergliene, in su la quale sentenzia s'è poi continovamente perseverato", cf. DE FABRICZY, *Il palazzo nuovo* cit., p. 48, and ZERVAS, *Parte Guelfa*, p. 213.

[22] «signum vetustum et honoratum in civitate», see p. 8, n. 52; and ASF, *Cons. Prat.*, 56 f. 142*v* (Manno Temperani, 3 March 1461): "utpote nobiles homines ex fructibus suorum prediorum vitam agere solitos, qui merito ad illud officium assumi solent quoniam a suis maioribus ... honestatum fuit".

As such, its influence declined in the later fourteenth century with the decline of feudalism. The privileges it was allowed to award knights were restricted and it no longer enjoyed the sole prerogative of granting knighthoods, which had now to be awarded or at least confirmed by the commune. The number of awards consequently dropped from over 150 in the fourteenth century to scarcely 50 in the fifteenth century. But it would be a mistake to underestimate the significance of these awards and to conclude that the Guelf Party no longer served a meaningful social role in the city. The knights appointed in the fifteenth century were all politically important men who received this honour as a reward for service rendered to the state.[23] Bongianni Gianfigliazzi was knighted at the end of his term of office as Gonfalonier of Justice in 1470 "on account of his well-conducted office and services to the republic", at the suggestion (the Milanese ambassador in Florence reported) of Lorenzo de' Medici, "per fare omne honore ch'el pò a li amici soy".[24] The same ambassador also said that in Florence

> they accept this military insignia willingly, because the knights are the most sought after, the most honoured and the first to speak when they summon advisory councils and *pratiche* to discuss the affairs of the day.[25]

This was the case. Speakers in *pratiche* always spoke according to their 'order' or rank, knights and lawyers first, and far from being eroded, this social differentiation became more pronounced in the

---

[23] SALVEMINI, *La dignità cavalleresca,* p. 35. On and after 1450, for example, Luca Pitti, Andrea Pazzi and Bongianni Gianfigliazzi were knighted by the Commune (as well as two non-Florentines) and the following had their knighthoods confirmed by the Commune: Giannozzo Pandolfini, Guglielmo Tanaglia, Orlandino de' Medici, Alessandro Alessandri, Carlo Pandolfini, Giannozzo Manetti, Manno Temperani, Piero Pazzi, Tommaso Soderini, Otto Niccolini, Luigi Guicciardini, Antonio Ridolfi, Dietisalvi Neroni, Piero Vespucci, Angelo della Stufa, Niccolò Martelli, Piero Minerbetti, Antonio Canigiani, Bartolomeo Scala, Piero Alamanni and Tommaso Minerbetti (*ibid.*, pp. 133-137, 146-148). On the role of chivalry in the fifteenth century, see now C. DONATI, *L'idea di nobiltà in Italia nei secoli XIV-XVIII*, Bari, Laterza, 1988.

[24] Niccolò Michelozzi to Alessandro Braccesi (both chancery assistants), s.d., Oxford, Bodleian MS. Auct. F. 2.17, f. 117*r-v*: "ob bene gestum magistratum et eius in rempublicam merita equestri ordine decorasse"; Sacramoro Sacramori to Duke Galeazzo Maria Sforza, 27 December 1470, Milan, Archivio di Stato (ASMi), Sforzesco Potenze Estere (SPE), Firenze 280, "ènne casone Laurenzo".

[25] To the same, 24 February 1469, ASMi SPE Firenze 276: «toggono volontera ... questa insegna de militia, perché li cavalleri sonno li più rechesti, li più honorati et li primi dicitori quando fanno rechesti et pratiche per le cose che occorreno et se consultano quy».

course of the century.[26] In 1471 Lorenzo de' Medici proposed that *accoppiatori* should be chosen by a small group of leading citizens to include "tutti quisti cavalleri principali",[27] and in 1478, as a first riposte to the Pope's letter calling for Lorenzo de' Medici's expulsion from Florence as a tyrant, it was seriously suggested that

> Lorenzo's status should be increased and he should be decorated with the honour of knighthood and called Defender of Liberty.[28]

In fact, Lorenzo de' Medici was distinguished by being almost the only leading citizen in Florence who was not knighted in the later half of the fifteenth century. But since he had all his friends and supporters decorated with knighthoods, his unwillingness to accept this honour himself must have been due to political rather than social motives, to fear of "l'invidia de questi chavalleri" among the people.[29]

The medieval pageant and ritual associated with chivalry also continued unabated in the fifteenth century under the auspices of the Guelf Party. After the communal ceremony of initiation, the Parte conducted its own ceremony in which it awarded the newly-dubbed knight a pennant and shield decorated with the Parte's arms.[30] It also organised jousts, especially on the anniversary of the capture of Pisa, and a *palio* on the Feast of S. Vittore on the twenty-eighth of July.[31] Outdated though such displays of chivalry may have been in

---

[26] ASF, *Cons. Prat.* 60, f. 90*v*. The chancellor Bartolomeo Scala begins to distinguish between *equites* and *iurisconsulti* and to refer to the "ordinem equitum" on and after 5 September 1466, *Cons. Prat.* 58, ff. 184*r*, 188*v*-189*r*. Knights and doctors are also distinguished from other citizens in regulations concerning dress and mourning clothes in 1464 (ed. C. Mazzi, *Due provvisioni suntuarie fiorentine,* Florence, Stabilimento Aldino, 1908, p. 7) and in 1473 (ASF, *SS. Delib. sp. aut.* 34, f. 126*v*).

[27] Rubinstein, *Government of Florence*, p. 178, note 5.

[28] By Angelo della Stufa, supported by Antonio Ridolfi and Giovanni Guicciardini, ASF, *Cons. Prat.* 60, f. 162*v*: "augendam esse dignitatem Laurentio censuit, et ornandum equestri dignitate et defensorem libertatis appellandum", 13 July 1478. The Pope's letter of 7 July is in Florence, Bibl. Riccardiana, MS. 913, ff. 69*r*-71*r* and ASMi SPE Roma 86.

[29] Sacramoro Sacramori to Galeazzo Maria Sforza, 4 October 1470, ASMi SPE Firenze 280, referring to Angelo della Stufa's difficulty in getting his knighthood approved by the Council of the People.

[30] See the *Cronica* of Jacopo Salviati (in *Delizie degli eruditi toscani*, ed. I. di San Luigi, XVIII, Florence, Gaetano Cambiagi, 1784, pp. 224-227; cf. Bayley, *War and Society* cit., p. 213) and Vespasiano da Bisticci, *Vita* di Piero Pazzi, in *Le Vite,* ed. Greco, II, p. 314.

[31] See the *Diario* of Bartolomeo del Corazza, «Archivio Storico Italiano», ser. V, XIV, 1894, pp. 242-296, esp. 242-245, 255, 264, 281. The Parte was responsible for ordering the

fifteenth-century Florence, their élitism appealed to the social ambition of the new knights and their pageantry to the people – as we can see from the diary of the wine merchant Bartolomeo del Corazza, who describes in loving detail the richness of the display and the prizes provided by the Parte Guelfa on such occasions.[32]

As a relic of the days when the Parte's knights provided the military arm of the state, its captains continued to exercise ceremonial functions in the state. These included visiting the Podestà, Captain of the People and Signoria of Florence after their appointment to offer them their support, caring for the chapels of S. Vittore and S. Antonio in the Duomo, and visiting the Duomo and other churches to make offerings on special occasions and feast days.[33] The Parte shared an important ceremonial role with the Signoria during visits of the Pope and other dignitaries to Florence, bestowing on both Martin V and Eugenius IV a richly caparisoned white horse and escorting them to and from the state boundaries to the city gates.[34]

Socially, the Parte Guelfa combined the functions of rich dining-club for nobles and foreign visitors, and dispenser of charity to the poor. Its palace in the Via delle Terme was comfortable and well-furnished. In 1431 the first floor over the vaulted storage chambers on the ground floor was reached by a covered staircase, at the head of which was a portrait of pope Clement IV (attributed by fifteenth-century sources and by Vasari to Giotto). The stairs led into the fourteenth-century council chamber or Sala, "una sala grande dipinta e storiata" (whose frescoes were also attributed to Giotto in the fifteenth century). This was the room where the councils met. A passage or *androne* (overlooking the inner courtyard) led from the Sala to the "nuova cancelleria e udienza" on the right and to the "verone che va agli agiamenti" on the left. This new chancery and audience chamber on the south front of the palace overlooking the Via delle Terme were completed by Brunelleschi, according to his biographer Antonio Manetti, together with the "sala nuova" flanking the palace

---

famous giostra of 1475, *Un documento sconosciuto sulla Giostra di Giuliano de' Medici,* ed. P. O. Kristeller, «La Bibliofilia», XLI, 1939, p. 413: "per edictum ducum Guelfarum partium".

32 See preceding note.

33 *Statuti*, 1420, I, i; Salvemini, *La dignità cavalleresca*, p. 68; Dorini, *Notizie storiche,* p. 39. An "Oratione fatta pe' Capitani della Parte Guelfa nella entrata loro quando andarono a visitare i Signori" (Bibl. Laurenziana, MS. 42.10, f. 24*r*) is edited by E. Santini, *La produzione volgare di L. Bruni Aretino,* «Giornale Storico della Letteratura Italiana», LX, 1912, pp. 338-339.

34 Described by del Corazza, *op. cit.*, pp. 256-258, 266, 271-273, 279, 285-286, 293-295.

to the east. In 1431, however, there is no mention of this grandiose new sala, which must therefore have been begun after this date.[35]

There was a *ringhiera* in the old Sala. It also contained seven new benches in 1431 and tiered benches with "spallieri di legname dipinte" for the captains and colleges. It was presumably here that the five eating tables, "tra grandi e picchole" , were kept for banquets. The Udienza de' Capitani contained a large inlaid desk and a painted desk which was covered with "uno tappetto rosso quando si fa le tratte e s'anoverano le fave" (whereas "uno tap[p]eto verde" was used to cover the table "alla tratta de' capitani"). A *tavoletta* was used to "anoverare le fave quando si facesse squittino". The Udienza also contained two new *panche*, as well as "una panca con una spalliera intarsiata" and another "con spalliera dipinta", which were put by the fireplace "quando i capitani stanno al fuoco". A mosaic tavola of the Virgin in a tabernacle of "lengnio trissto" costing fl. 20 was also intended for the Udienza. The chancery contained "molti libri della Parte a guardia del cancelliere" and possibly the "armario grande in che stanno gli arienti e sopraveste e coverte" of the Parte. On the second floor were *cassoni* containing more books belonging to the Parte. More benches, two wooden chandeliers, two iron chandeliers, table cloths in varying states of decay, silver bowls, knives, *confettieri*, pots, pans and a pair of buckets for the well, "quando e c'era", completed the domestic equipment of the Parte palace in 1431. But these were no mere relics of a social past, for in 1453 the Parte commissioned nine sets of "shining silver cutlery" embossed with its arms and emblems, and more than a decade later it still employed cupbearers whom it was prepared to lend to visiting foreign ambassadors.[36]

Every Saturday the Parte dispensed from two to four pounds of

---

[35] See the 1431 Inventario in ASF, *Capit. P.G.* 27 rosso, partly edited in the Appendix below. There are plans of the palace in E. BATTISTI, *Filippo Brunelleschi*, Milan, Electa, 1976, p. 71, and ZERVAS, *Parte Guelfa*, pl. 42-50. The attributions to Giotto are made in *Il Libro di Antonio Billi*, ed. C. FREY, Berlin, 1892, p. 4; cf. *Il Codice Magliabechiano*, ed. C. FREY, Berlin, 1892, p. 51; G. VASARI, *Le vite de' più eccellenti pittori, scultori ed architetti italiani*, ed. MILANESI, I, Florence, Sansoni, 1878, p. 376. According to Manetti, Brunelleschi finished "l'udienza e sì l'andito che viene dalla sala vecchia, e sì la sala nuova" (*The Life of Brunelleschi* cit., p. 101), see now ZERVAS.

[36] ASF, *Capit, P.G.* 7 rosso, f. 87*v* (26 May 1453): "teneantur et debeant ... facere fieri novem paia cultellinorum fulcitorum argentorum cum signis et armis dicte Partis"; B. Scala, chancellor of the Parte, to Nicodemo Tranchedini, 5 October 1464 (Bibl. Riccardiana, MS. 834, f. 108*v*): "policitus etiam fueram duobus tuis nunciis, qui guelfos a me pincernas tuo nomine afflagitabant. Pincernas quidem habebis quot voles et ubi voles".

money near the steps of its palace in the Via delle Terme and two pounds to the Hospital of S. Maria Nuova or to another hospital. At Easter it gave six pounds to the poor and fifty pounds to city monasteries at Christmas. It also administered the Orbatello, an almshouse for distressed gentlewomen of good birth founded by Niccolò Alberti in 1372, which it acquired on the exile of the Alberti at the end of the fourteenth century.[37] So the Parte's social role in the city was not negligible, even in the fifteenth century, harmoniously balancing as it did its responsibilities to rich and poor. Nor is there any reason to suppose that the Mediceans objected to the Parte for these reasons. On the contrary: they actively encouraged it by granting knighthoods to their supporters and by encouraging jousts and lavish pageants.

Their objections were financial and political rather than social. Although not immensely rich in the fifteenth century, the Parte was rich enough to concern the government. It acquired its wealth as a result of its responsibility for administering the property of political exiles. The money and possessions confiscated in 1267 from the Ghibellines and registered in the infamous Libro del Chiodo were retained by the Parte after it lost its political supremacy in 1280. Although it still claimed to be "the treasury of the commune and the people of Florence" in 1325, by the fifteenth century this money belonged not to the commune but only to the Parte. As an institution not paying taxes, 'non-supportante', it contributed no regular taxes to the commune on its properties in Florence. For the same reason its credits were 'non-conditionati', that is, they were free from the condition of having to be paid out to a third party and could be paid by the Monte to the Parte instead of being given to the Camera as taxation. So the state lost doubly, by not receiving taxes from Parte property and by having to pay out interest on its Monte investments, and it was for this reason that the Mediceans wished to control its wealth. In 1472 it owned some 87 properties in and around Florence which it rented for approximately 1624 florins per annum, representing a

---

[37] *Statuti* (1420), I, I; DORINI, *Notizie storiche* cit., p. 40. On the Orbatello, L. PASSERINI, *Storia degli stabilimenti di beneficenza ... della Città di Firenze,* Florence, Le Monnier, 1853, pp. 639-648, esp. 640-642, and G. RICHA, *Notizie storiche delle chiese fiorentine,* I, Florence, P. Gaetano Viviani, 1754, pp. 292-299 (with plan). It was a large palace in Via della Pergola for 200 «povere femmine», divided into 100 quarters consisting of two bedrooms and a kitchen to be shared by two women.

capital value of 23,200 florins.[38] In addition it owned Monte stock worth 32,494 florins (an increase of 4000 florins in forty years), together making a total capital value of 55,694 florins. This was considerably less than Piero de' Medici's declared capital value of 69,709 florins in 1469, but it was intolerable to the government because it drained money from the commune instead of contributing to it.[39] Moreover, as bankers who became treasurers of the Parte in 1463, the Medici had a personal as well as public interest in their funds, from which they apparently did not fail to profit.[40]

Politically, the Parte Guelfa no longer seriously threatened the government after 1434, although had not the Albizzi been so effectively ousted by the Medici, its sumptuous new palace might have offered an aristocratic alternative to the 'popular' government in the Palazzo della Signoria. Leonardo Bruni in his *Laudatio* of Florence had compared the Parte captains to the aristocratic Areopagus in Athens or the Ephors in Sparta, although in practice they enjoyed no such constitutional role in Florentine government.[41] The fact that knighthoods were awarded to well-deserving citizens who then enjoyed a privileged position in *consulte* suggests that they may have exercised a similar unofficial role in the state – at least until the creation of the permanent council or senate of Seventy in 1480, which eroded their authority by offering an alternative political reward for success-

---

[38] ASF, *Capit. P.G.* 29 rosso. Rents are given in florins and soldi, or in pounds, so I have calculated the total on the basis of 20 soldi to the florin and 3 pounds to the florin. In addition to its own 87 properties, the Parte received a single rent of fl. 38 from one of its 14 listed Orbatello properties, together making a total of fl. 1624 which I have capitalised at 7%. These properties are also listed in ASF, *Capit. P.G.* 9 rosso, ff. 6*r*-7*v*, and 30 rosso, giving revised rents, lettings and sales from 1472, and in 28 rosso, "Locationes 1467-1491". Cf. note 110 below.

[39] ASF, *Capit. P.G.* 29 rosso, f. 24*r* (2nd ser. of numbers.) Piero de' Medici's 1469 catasto is in ASF, *Catasto* 924 (S. Giov. Leon d'Oro), ff. 295*r*-313*r*.

[40] See p. 138 below. The Medici were also interested in Guelf Party benefices and their chapel in the Duomo, see ASF, *Capit. P.G.* 27 rosso, ff. 15*r*-16*v*, listing all the churches which the *provveditore* found to be "censuarie della Parte Guelfa ... e lla Parte n'è padrone", properties numbered 98-117. ASF, MAP 6, 181 (Giovanni Neroni, Bishop of Volterra, to Giovanni di Cosimo de' Medici, 18 November 1453, the reference to which I owe to Dale Kent) reveals the Medici's interest in appointing to a benefice owned by the Parte Guelfa; cf. MAP 17, 415 (B. Scala to Piero di Cosimo de' Medici, 31 May 1464) concerning the appointment of a new Parte chaplain by Piero as an Operaio.

[41] Leonardo Bruni, *Panegirico della città di Firenze,* Florence, La Nuova Italia, 1974, p. 92: "Quod igitur Rome censores, Athenis areopagite, Lacedemonie ephori, hoc sunt in Florentina civitate partium duces, id est, ex his civibus qui bene de re publica sentiunt primarii viri electi ad rem publicam tuendam".

ful Gonfaloniers of Justice at the end of their office. In the fourteenth century the Parte had possessed a powerful political weapon in being able to deprive citizens of office by condemning them as ghibellines, and even in the fifteenth century office-holders had still to be definably "cives florentini populares et guelfi".[42]

Nevertheless, it is difficult to believe that all office-holders were formally members of the Parte Guelfa in the fifteenth century. Knights and probably their descendants were certainly members and were granted fifty florins to pay for the Parte insignia which they were entitled to bear (after 1465 the insignia themselves being substituted for the money as "more honorable and less expensive"); but after 1377 even they had to be scrutinized before being qualified for office in the Parte.[43] Probably membership was associated with office holding rather than with inscription, everyone being potentially guelf who had not been proscribed as ghibelline; for it was possible to qualify for office in the Parte by virtue of having been a member of the communal Signoria or colleges, as well as by having held office in the Parte as a captain, member of the colleges or as chancellor.[44] The problem of purifying the Parte in 1411, when Buonaccorso Pitti thought it had been corrupted by ghibellines and *nouveaux riches*, and again in 1459, when it acquired responsibility for Sea Consuls, nevertheless shows that office holding was not a mere formality but was taken as seriously in the Parte as in the commune.[45]

One reason for this was that its officers still enjoyed important *ex officio* rights in the commune which made them politically important. In structure and function the Parte was a microcosm of the commune with its nine executive captains, its two advisory colleges of fifteen Priori di Pecunia (responsible for finance) and twenty Secretarii della Credenza (its secret or privy council), and its two legislative Councils of Cento and Sessanta. All were made up of varying proportions of members of the major guilds and *scioperati* (together usually enjoying half of all the places), minor guildsmen and *grandi* (usually enjoy-

---

[42] On *ammonizione*, see BRUCKER, *Florentine Politics and Society*, pp. 170-172, 340-342, etc.

[43] SALVEMINI, *La dignità cavalleresca* cit., pp. 67-70; ASF, *Capit. P.G.* 9 rosso, f. 76*r*: «pare è più honore e meno spesa... che si dieno e segni facti et non la valuta».

[44] *Statuti* (1420), II, I.

[45] On the close identification of communal and Parte policies and scrutinies, see below.

ing a quarter each).[46] In this way the Parte provided a useful apprenticeship for young Florentines aspiring to communal office as well as a safety valve for magnates otherwise denied access to government, consoling "molti cittadini co' i suoi magistrati", as Cristoforo Landino put it in 1472, "e quali sanza quegli si stimerebbono forestieri".[47]

More important than this, though, was the role played by Parte captains in the communal constitution. To have held the office of captain of the Parte Guelfa was as great an asset in a communal scrutiny as to have held one of the Tre Maggiori Uffici (membership of the Signoria or Colleges), for it enabled one to be voted on before other less privileged citizens. Moreover, the Parte's nine captains were entitled to partecipate in communal scrutiny councils by virtue of their office. They also belonged *ex officio* to all Balìe until 1466, from when until the fall of the Medici regime in 1494 only the Signoria survived as *ex officio* members of Balìe, suggesting that their disappearance was intentional Medicean policy.[48] The political risk of having nine Parte captains represented in scrutinies and Balìe must have been small (although they included two magnates otherwise excluded from such councils). Nevertheless the presence of these and other *ex officio* representatives of the corporations of the Mercanzia and the guilds conflicted with the Medici policy of handpicking councils and were thus a threat to the centralizing policies of their regime.

Although Guelf idealism had ceased to influence communal policies, the Signoria still had to swear an oath to maintain the Parte and to keep the friendship of France and the Church on entering office – as its chancellor reminded the ambassador of Charles VIII of France in 1494.[49] It may be no more than a coincidence that the first suggestion of closing the Parte down followed the return of the

---

46 Brucker, *Florentine Politics and Society* cit., p. 100; Bonaini's edition of the 1335 Statuti and the revised Statuti of 1420, cit. above.

47 BNF, MS. Magl. VIII, 1299, f. 100*v*, discussed below.

48 Rubinstein, *Government of Florence*, pp. 67, 81, 149, note 2, 152, note 2; and on their participation in balìe, pp. 245, 255, 265, 273, 282, (cf. 106, n. 5); *Statuta Populi Florentiae*, II, Friburgi, 1778, pp. 481, 491, 580-658, *passim* (on the captains' participation in scrutinies of the Tre Maggiori Uffizi and various other less important offices).

49 *Statuta Populi Florentiae* cit., II, p. 502; G. Canestrini and A. Desjardins, *Négotiations diplomatiques de la France avec la Toscane*, I, p. 413 (6 May 1494): "magistratus hic in civitate summus, singulis bimestribus, ad augendum ornandumque sacrosanctum sanguinem Regum Gallorum (ita enim verba sunt antiqui juramenti) obligatur".

Angevins to Italy in 1458, yet it was shortly after an embassy was sent to deter René from fighting Florence for not paying money owed to his son that its future was seriously discussed.[50] Of the many factors involved, finance was probably paramount, since the immediate purpose of the government was to acquire the Parte's income for the expense of sending galleys abroad that summer. But, as we have seen, there were also strong political and administrative reasons to account for the government's determined attempt to close the Parte down, and when that failed, to draw teeth which were still too healthy for the government's comfort.

* * *

The Medici programme to reduce the Parte Guelfa falls into three periods of crisis, each precipitated by a death sentence followed by a remission. Finally in 1481 its life was saved by drastic surgery which enabled it to survive until 1769, honoured and even busy in its old age, but a shadow of its former self: no longer a rich and powerful rival to the commune but its fettered servant, a bureaucratic department of state.

The first period begins with the threat of closure in the summer of 1459, although it did not emerge until later that this was what the government had in mind. At the end of May or beginning of June 1459 it was suggested that the income of the Parte should be used to send galleys abroad. But it was not until a bill delegating the matter to the Cento had been twice defeated by the Council of the People and some of its original supporters had changed their minds about it, that it emerges from discussion in a *pratica* that the initial proposal had been to close the Parte down altogether.[51] The first reason why the people had rejected the bill was because it threatened to remove "an ancient and revered monument" from the city, Matteo Palmieri surmised, and Bernardo Giugni agreed that "since that office enjoyed the highest reputation", the benefit of changing it "with

[50] ASF, *Cons. Prat.* 55, ff. 106*v*-107*r*, 108*v*-109*v* (8 and 13 March 1459).

[51] *Ibid.*, ff. 117*v*-123*r* (31 May to June 1459): "Proposuit D. Vexillifer [Bernardo di Bartolomeo Gherardi] formatum fuisse quandam provisionem super negotiis Partis Guelfe diligenter examinatamque coram ipsis legenda est" (f. 122*r*); *Liber fabarum* 66, ff. 21*v*, 22*r* (7 and 8 June 1459): "provisionem continentem auctoritatem in consilium del Cento capiendam de redditibus domus Partis Guelfe qui convertantur pro expensis navigandi"; "disponendi quod de redditibus domus Partis Guelfe capiatur pars que convertatur in expensis navigandi".

the indignation of the people" would be minimal.[52] The people were also afraid that if Guelf Party money was used for navigation, its captains would be elected in the council, as the Sea Consuls were, instead of being drawn by lot - here expressing their resentment of new methods of government by longer-term, hand-picked officials.[53] Fears were expressed in the *pratica*, too, about the wisdom of possibly damaging the Monte by withdrawing Parte stock from it and of destroying an office of such stature as the Parte Guelfa for so small a sum of money, and it was suggested that the necessary money should be raised instead by taxes, by auction or by the recently-created Canal Officials.[54]

At this juncture Luigi Guicciardini intervened in the debate to suggest that since it was too late to accept the latter course, they should take what could usefully be taken from the Parte without incurring "the hatred of the citizens and the desolation of that ancient and greatly revered institution": two thousand florins he thought would be enough, rather than its whole income.[55] But although later in the debate he added that "it was the intention of no one to destroy the

---

[52] ASF, *Cons. Prat.* 55, f. 125*v* (9 June 1459, Matteo Palmieri): "Intellexisse autem se tria obstare quominus provisio obtineretur. Primum ne signum vetustum et honoratum in civitate auferatur"; f. 127*v* (Bernardo Giugni): "quoniam illud officium reputationem habet maximam et facile potest discerni si id mutaretur cum indignatione populi futurum cum pro modica utilitate que inde caperetur".

[53] *Ibid.*, ff. 125*v*-126*r* (Matteo Palmieri): "secundum, quia per eam viam adhuc navigationi bene fiende non videtur provisum esse ... tertium, ne deinceps ipsi capitanei per consilium eligendi sint et sors extractionis omnino auferatur ... Ideoque arbitrari se melius esse ut quoniam capitanei Partis Guelfe futuri sint Consules Maris, officium Consulum removeretur et inbursarentur cives et ex bursa ipsa sex extraherentur». On Matteo Palmieri, A. MESSERI, *Matteo Palmieri cittadino di Firenze del secolo XV*, «Archivio storico italiano», ser. V, XIII, 1894, pp. 257-340; he was described by the Milanese ambassadors in 1468 as a "bon citadino et non cavilloso, nè scandaloso", "Gentilhomo molto acostumato et pieno de ogni bontate", ASMi SPE Firenze 274, N. Tranchedini and Z. Olduino to Galeazzo Maria Sforza, 27 and 30 June 1468.

[54] *Ibid.*, f. 127*r-v* (Francesco Venturi): «si vero hic rumor in vulgus emanet, agi videlicet consilia et iniri quibus pecunie a Monte auferrantur, nocituram Monti famam hanc vehementissime et diminuenda esse creditorum prestantia in damnum civitatis maximum. Ideoque non esse agitandum quod ab officialibus solvatur aliquid sicut nonnulli dixerunt ... advertendum esse an bonum sit pro tam exiguo introitu officium illud tangere quod maximi ponderis existimant in civitate»; ff. 126*v*-130*r* (Matteo Palmieri): "ex incantis fiendis super navibus», «ex incantis subveniendum, ex quibus tria milia et quadringenti florini haberi possent et super hoc assignamento Officiales Canalis mutuare pecunias posse"; (Francesco Venturi): «ex incantis»; (Bernardo Giugni): "quinque Pisarum ... et pro reliquo de incantis providentur"; (Giannozzo Pitti): "Officialibus Canalis".

[55] ASF, *Cons. Prat.* 55, f. 129*v*: "id a Parte capiendum quod commode fieri potest sine hodio civium et desolatione eius loci antiqui et auctoritatis magne. Satius ergo esse duomilia florenorum ab ea capi quam totum introitum".

honour of the House of the Parte Guelfa but rather to conserve it", it seems clear from what he said two years later that this indeed had been the intention of the regime.[56] Then he openly admitted that the Signoria had often discussed the question of closing the Parte down since it was superfluous to the administration of the city, but that "for certain reasons" it had eventually decided to transfer the conduct of maritime affairs to their captains.[57]

This is in fact what happened, although the process of transferring the work of the Sea Consuls to the Parte captains was long and slow, and of very brief duration. Four days after this discussion a bill was introduced and rejected which proposed using the Parte's Monte Commune credits as if they were credits of the Monte delle Doti to pay for the cost of navigation.[58] Two days later a Parte statute stated that when the present office of the Sea Consuls came to an end the Parte captains were to take over their task of auctioning galleys before each voyage.[59] But in the Council of the People all bills concerning the Parte continued to be rejected until 18 August, when a bill assigning its Monte credits to the Sea Consuls and authorising interest on them to be paid to the Consuls was finally passed.[60] In December 1459 the captains began to play an active part in the affairs of the Sea Consuls.[61] In April 1460 they were made responsible for cargoes of ships, in October they took over the books, papers

[56] *Ibid.*: "dixit nullius fuisse mentem ut honor domus Partis Guelfe subverteretur sed ut conservaretur".

[57] See note 1 above. He continues: "Sed quibusdam de causis tandem melius visum esse ut gubernatio marittimarum rerum ad eos capitaneos deferretur".

[58] ASF, *Liber fabarum* 66, f. 22*v* (13 June 1459): "Provisionem continentem quod credita Partis Guelfe sint illius conditionis cuius sunt credita puellarum, et quod page solvantur pro expensis navigandi: displicuit".

[59] ASF, *Capit. G. P.* 5 rosso, f. 121*v* (15 June 1459): "Idem quod finito officio presentium Consulum Maris civitatis Florentiae, Capitanei Partis Guelforum ... teneantur et debeant incantare galeas eo modo et in iisdem locis ut facere consueverant Consules Maris". According to records of the Consoli del Mare, this was decreed "per triginta cives deputatos super augmento Montis", ASF, *Consoli del Mare* 3, f. 126*r* (15 June 1459). The process of auctioning galleys is described by M. Mallett, *The Florentine Galleys in the 15th century,* Oxford, Clarendon Press, 1967, pp. 40-43. The Captains were auctioning galleys by December 1459, see note 61 below.

[60] It was previously rejected by the Council of the People on 8 and 9 August, ASF, *Liber fabarum* 66, ff. 32*r*-34*r*. Cf. ASF, *Provvisioni* 150, f. 84*r*; *Consoli del Mare* 3, ff. 126*r*-127*v*; M. Mallett, *The Sea Consuls of Florence in the 15th century,* «Papers of the British School at Rome», XXVII, 1959, p. 168.

[61] ASF, *Provvisioni* 150, f. 161*v* (5 December 1459): "Item che i Capitani della Parte Guelfa possino, sieno tenuti e debbino ... fare bandire dette due galee"; f. 204*v* (2 January 1460).

and equipment of the Sea Consuls; in November they were asked to auction galleys to Sicily and Catalonia; and finally on 23 January 1461 they were authorised by the commune to auction galleys and adjudicate maritime lawsuits.[62]

The task of regenerating the elderly Parte Guelfa was considerable, for it meant replacing a comparatively modern magistracy of annually elected specialists, the Sea Consuls, with one composed of hereditary amateurs chosen every two months for office by the luck of the draw from the restricted bags of the Parte. Far from being considered "better able to cope with shipping problems under war conditions", as it has been suggested, such work was quite outside the competence of men "of noble birth living off the fruits of their estates".[63] But having been forced to retain the Parte Guelfa, the Mediceans wanted to be in control of it, and to achieve this and to modernise its structure they introduced as its chancellor a loyal Medicean and efficient administrator, Bartolomeo Scala.[64] His period in office from 1459 to 1465 encapsulates Medicean methods of administration and with his appointment begins the Parte's first period of remission.

Although the Medici had hitherto not been closely associated with the Parte Guelfa, the appointment of Scala coincided with the beginning of their more intimate relationship with it. Scarcely more than a week before Scala's election on 24 October 1459, Angelo della Stufa wrote to Piero de' Medici about "una bella aradinanza alla Parte" to discuss the appointment of a new chancellor, which he said was marred only by the absence of Dietisalvi and Guicciardini at their villas. The names of several candidates were mentioned (including ser Nastagio [Vespucci] towards whom "si sia schoperto invidia assai") but not Scala's. Enclosing a sheet of accounts to put Piero in the picture, Angelo merely asked for his comment, if any, to assist the four citizens delegated to discuss the appointment.[65] It was perhaps

---

62 ASF, *Provvisioni*, 151, ff. 22*r*-23*v* (4 April 1460); 245*v*-247*r* (14 October 1460); 283*r*-284*r* (26 November 1460); and 335*r*-337*r* (21-23 January 1461); *Consoli del Mare* 3, ff. 130*r* (12 April 1460) and 139*r-v* (21-23 January 1461); cf. Mallett, *The Sea Consuls*, p. 159.

63 By M. Mallett, *The Sea Consuls*, p. 159. See note 22 above (and Franco Sacchetti, *Cons. Prat.* 56, f. 146*v*: "quando autem Capitanei Partis creati fuerunt, qui legerunt res veteres intelligunt ad alium finem eos creatos esse").

64 Brown, *Bartolomeo Scala*, pp. 28-34, 163-166 (ital. edn. pp. 19-23, 114-115).

65 ASF, *MAP* 17, 273, 16 October 1459.

at this moment that Piero put forward Scala's name, as he later did for the chancellorship of Florence, since Scala was secretary to his cousin Pierfrancesco de' Medici and was well known to the family; or perhaps his informant did so, Angelo della Stufa, whom the Milanese ambassador in Florence considered chiefly responsible for Scala's rise to power and who may have engineered his election with Piero's support on this occasion.[66]

Scala's appointment was not confirmed by the Parte councils of Cento and Sessanta for nearly a month because "the citizens were too busy or away in the country", but when they finally assembled on 20 and 21 November, they increased Scala's salary from the statutory five florins a month to eight florins on condition that he employed at his own expense a notary to keep the accounts (Scala being as yet neither a notary, nor a Florentine citizen, nor matriculated in the Arte de' Giudici e Notai as the Parte statutes decreed he should have been).[67] Two years later, in January 1462, they added another three florins to his salary, "cumciosiacosa che al Cancelliere è aggiunto faticha assai pell' Uficio de' Sei d'Arezo et de' Consoli del Mare". Although the work of the Sea Consuls was taken from the Parte only five months later, in May 1462, it remained permanently responsible for the Sei d'Arezzo. Scala retained his increased salary (as he once again took the trouble of noting in his own hand in the relevant book), and it was not until he left the Parte that the salary of his successor, Cristoforo Landino, reverted to the five florins it had been before Scala was appointed.[68]

In November 1459 the Parte councils also confirmed a very Medicean body of Ufficiali di Muraglia to complete the still unfinished Parte palace, who held their first meeting in January 1460 in the Medici palace: Piero de' Medici, Luigi Guicciardini, Bernardo Giugni, Scala's old friend Antonio Guidotti, Altobianco Giandonati and Andrea

---

[66] ASMi SPE Firenze 276, Sacramoro Sacramori to Galeazzo Maria Sforza, 24 February 1469: "D. Bartholomeo sia tutto de Agnolo et quasi fatto im parte da luy"; cf. *Bartolomeo Scala,* pp. 53-54 (Ital. edn. p. 36).

[67] ASF, *Capit. P. G.* 9 rosso, f. 55*r*: "«propter civium occupationes ac rusticationes"; *Capit. P. G.* 3 rosso, f. 7*r-v*: "Ad offitium cancellariatus dicte Partis sit et esse debeat im perpetuum unus fidelis notarius stirpe Guelfus et in Arte Iudicum et Notariorum civitatis matriculatus et civis florentinus non minoris etatis triginta annorum".

[68] MALLETT, *The Sea Consuls,* p. 159; ASF, *Capit. P. G.* 9 rosso, ff. 66*r* and 71*r-v*. On the Sei d'Arezzo, *Statuta Populi Florentiae,* III, pp. 70-78, 88. The Parte Guelfa acquired responsibility for it on 27 August 1460, *Provvisioni* 151, ff. 204*v*-205*r*.

Guardi.[69] As chancellor Scala wrote to Piero and his brother Giovanni de' Medici, as well as to his own patron Pierfrancesco de' Medici, about Parte and maritime business; and when Giovanni died in 1463 it was Scala who wrote to tell the young Lorenzo that he had been elected an Operaio of the Brigittine monastery in the Paradiso (part of the sequestered Alberti estate administered, like the Orbatello, by the Parte Guelfa) in place of his uncle.[70] It is clear from Scala's letters, and from the subsequent election of Giovanni and Pierfrancesco as captains of the Parte, that the principal members of the Medici family were drawn closely into Parte business once it acquired responsability for defence and maritime affairs.

The methods used to modernise the Parte Guelfa were those used by the Mediceans, and before them the ottimati, to reform the communal offices: firstly, careful revision of election bags to ensure that reliable officers were appointed; secondly, the selection of important officers instead of sortition by lot; and thirdly, much longer-term appointments.[71] A new scrutiny of captains and colleges had been held in 1458 and could not be repeated so soon. Instead the old ottimate solution of creating a *borsellino* of select names for captains was introduced in 1461, as we shall see. A scrutiny of the important offices of *provveditore* and *camarlingo* was undertaken at the time of Scala's appointment, and his first task was to obtain a quorum for this scrutiny. After that he attempted to get the *provveditore* selected instead of drawn by lot, then to get his office extended. The office of *camarlingo* was replaced 'temporarily' by the services of the Medici bank. Finally a new scrutiny of the councils with far more rigorous criteria for eligibility was undertaken in 1462.

First of these tasks was to secure a quorum for the scrutiny of the offices of *provveditore* and *camarlingo*, which was achieved by creat-

---

69 ASF, *Capit. P. G.* 9 rosso, f. 55*v*. Their first meeting "in domo spectabilis ac generosi viri Petri Cosmi de Medicibus" was on 8 January 1460.

70 Scala had been employed as Pierfrancesco's secretary since 1457 and in that capacity came to know and work intimately with his cousins, Piero and Giovanni, and later their father, see BROWN, *Bartolomeo Scala*, ch. 2 and pp. 84-85 above. Scala's letter to Piero de' Medici about the dismissal of the Parte chaplain is in ASF, *MAP* 17, 415 (31 May 1464), to Giovanni about Parte elections, note 73 below (4 September 1460); to Pierfrancesco about movements of galleys, etc. *MAP* 137, 94; 2, 64; 5, 752; 137, 107 (20 January and 14 May 1460; 18 and 22 November 1461); to Lorenzo on his election in place of Giovanni "ex Operariis Sancte Brigide", ASF, *Strozz.* ser. I, CXXXVI, f. 55 (31 December 1463; on the death of Lorenzo his son replaced him as president of the Operai, ASF, *Capit. P. G.* 9 rosso, f. 11*v*, 10 April 1492).

71 RUBINSTEIN, *Government of Florence.*

ing another forty elected members, or *arroti*, in January 1460.[72] The *provveditore* should have been drawn from the new bags on 10 September 1460, two weeks after the Parte had acquired responsibility for the magistracy in charge of fortifications, the Sei d'Arezzo. Six days before the draw, however, Bartolomeo Scala wrote a letter to Giovanni de' Medici which reveals his strategy for getting this officer selected instead of drawn, as well as his complicity with Giovanni in this matter. In the letter he describes to Giovanni in Bagno a Morbo the recent meeting of the Parte colleges:

> and together with other matters relating to the Parte, we put it to them, as persuasively and effectively as we knew how, that we wanted the proveditor to be elected for a year, showing why this was necessary – especially because now that he has also to be proveditor of the magistracy of the Six [of Arezzo], which by a new law has been given to our office to administer, it is essential he should be selected and not drawn, due to the importance of the thing. He was voted on several times and met with very little success, both in votes and words, except for my own. It would perhaps have gone better if you had been there to warm them up. Now the law obliges us to draw the proveditor by the evening of the 10th of this month. I wanted you to know, so that if you think that I should do one thing rather than another before then you can write to me.[73]

The following year, after the Parte had become fully responsible for maritime affairs, as well as for the Sei d'Arezzo, and the problem of acquiring suitable officers had been discussed in *pratiche*, the *provveditore*, Piero di Niccolò Malegonnelle, was elected instead of being drawn by lot. Giovanni de' Medici acted as his guarantor for the newly-imposed penalty of 500 florins on officials exercising two salaried offices at the same time (suggesting that Piero Malegonnelle was the man whom Scala and Giovanni de' Medici had wanted for the office the

---

[72] ASF, *Capit. P. G.* 9 rosso, f. 58*r-v* (14-15 January 1460).

[73] Forlì, Bibl. Comunale, Autografi Piancastelli (4 September 1460): "Habbiamo havuto per l'onoranza del Capitano e Colleghi et insieme con altre cose circa al bisogno della Casa, messo loro inanzi con miglior parole et modo habbiamo saputo di volere eleggiere il proveditore per uno anno, mostrando così essere il bisogno, spetialmente perché di nuovo havendo a essere ancora proveditore dello uficio de' Sei [d'Arezzo], che per nuova legge è dato il governo di quello magistrato a questo nostro, era necessità fusse huomo scelto et non sortito per la inportanza della cosa. Andò a partito alcuna volta; hebbe pochissimo favore et di fave et di parole se non quante ne feci io. Sarebbe forse ita di miglior voglia se cci fussi suto voi che havessi riscaldato. Hora la legge strigne per tutto dì 10 del presente trarre il proveditore. Ho voluto ne siate avisato acciò che se vi paresse ch'io prima dovessi fare più una cosa che un'altra, me ne scriviate".

previous year), and when he broke the law by drawing an extra three florins a month for his office as Captain of the Sei d'Arezzo, the colleges rapidly absolved him, or rather his sponsor Giovanni de' Medici, from paying his 500 florins' fine.[74] This was in January 1462, and a year later the principle which Scala had unsuccessfully championed in 1460 became legalised:

> because sortition often does not serve our need... as your proveditor is at the end of his office and we must make arrangements, and as we want to arrange for the good order introduced by past proveditors to be preserved, it seems better not to use sortition this time, to avoid the above doubt and to be certain that the House is well cared for and administered after the excellent start that has been made.[75]

A year later the new *provveditore*, Lorenzo Davanzati, also a devoted Medicean, was allowed to be re-elected for another year at the end of his term of office at the beginning of March: and so the principle of longer-term offices became gradually accepted.[76]

The problem of securing suitable officers became acute after the Parte finally acquired responsibility for maritime affairs in January 1461, and it rapidly became the subject for discussion in a *pratica*. Nobles were ignorant of "mercantile affairs"; a new scrutiny of the principal offices had only just been held; and yet to elect instead of draw its officials would be unheard of and most unpopular. What was to be done? The solution proposed was a *borsellino* of select names to ensure that some mercantile specialists should leaven the noble lump. Although Otto Niccolini stated confidently in a *pratica* on 3 March 1461 that there were no laws in the Parte preventing this, "because all those which prevented new provisions have been removed", it was not until 17 March that the Parte councils suspended, "per questa volta sola", the clause which should have prevented such alteration

---

[74] ASF, *Capit. P. G.* 9 rosso, ff. 63*r* (21 July 1461) and 65*r-v* (14-18 January 1462).

[75] *Ibid.*, f. 67*r* (8-9 February 1463): "perchè spesso la sorte non serve secondo il bisogno... essendo il vostro proveditore alla fine dell'ufficio suo, et bisognando provedere; et volendo fare tale provedimento ch'el buono ordine cominciato per la diligentia de' proveditori passati si possi conservare, è paruto di non usare la sorte questa volta, per schifare il sopradecto dubio et havere certeza che la Casa sia bene attesa e governata chome è dato optimo principio".

[76] *Ibid.*, ff. 70*v*-71*r* (10-13 Juanuary 1464). He was elected on 9 February 1463 to begin his office on 1 March 1463, re-elected for another year beginning on 1 March 1464 and subsequently by decree of the captains and colleges only. He was re-elected at yearly intervals until at least 1472, *ibid.*, ff. 76*r*, 78*v*, 1*v*.

of the election bags before the appointed time.[77] Then, acting on the advice of the *pratica*, they proceeded to legislate for the *borsellino* which was to provide four out of nine captains and was to be prepared, with the *borsa generale*, by five of the current *accoppiatori* of the Florentine Signoria. Since these *accoppiatori* were all leading members of the regime who had played a prominent part in the debates about the Parte Guelfa in earlier *pratiche* – including Manno Temperani, Dietisalvi Neroni, Otto Niccolini, Matteo Palmieri and Luigi Guicciardini – it is clear that the government intended to exercise direct influence on its affairs.[78] Immediately afterwards, lists of captains are marked with small crosses beside certain names, doubtless indicating those drawn from the *borsellino*, among whom we will not perhaps be surprised to find for the first time Giovanni and Pierfrancesco de' Medici.[79]

Next an attempt was made to restrict membership of Parte Guelfa councils to the same group of politically reliable citizens from whom the captains, members of the colleges and other executive officers had been chosen in the 1458 scrutiny. Hitherto bags for the councils had been filled with the names of those who had been *veduti* or *seduti* captains and members of the Parte colleges since 1393, but on 18 January 1462 it was decreed that these bags were to be filled only with the names of those who had been *veduti* or *seduti* captains, members of the Parte colleges, Conservatori di Legge and Ufficiali delle Possessioni della Parte since 1458.[80] In that year membership of these Parte offices had been restricted to those eligible for the priorate, with the addition of some drawn from seventeen non-popular

---

[77] ASF, *Cons. Prat.* 56, f. 142*v*: "nec ad hanc fiendam provisionem obstare aliquam legem Partis Guelfe quoniam omnes que impediebant novas provisiones illius domus sublate sunt"; *Capit. P. G.* 9 rosso, f. 59*v* (17-18 March 1461): "Acciò che si possi non contrafaccendo ad alcuna legge della vostra Inclyta Università ... venire alla perfectione di quella distinctione delle borse ... si provede ... che si possi fare che quella legge ... 'Statutum et ordinatum est quod im perpetuum' etc. [1420 Statuti, ii, II] s'intenda per questa volta sola essere et sia suspensa". On the communal *borsellino*, RUBINSTEIN, *Government of Florence*, pp. 45-46.

[78] ASF, *Capit. P. G.* 9 rosso, ff. 59*v*-61*r* (17-20 March 1461) and for the *accoppiatori*, RUBINSTEIN, *Government of Florence*, pp. 237-239.

[79] ASF, *Capit. P. G.* 18 rosso, f. 9*v* and following (to be distinguished from the larger crosses). Giovanni de' Medici was elected a captain for two months on 1 June 1461, Pierfrancesco de' Medici on 1 June 1462, 1 August 1463, 1 October 1464, ff. 9*v*, 10*r*, 11*r* and 12*r*.

[80] ASF, *Capit. P. G.* 9 rosso, ff. 64*v*-65*r*. The motive of the reform was declared to be: "ne' tanti tracti che abondantamente suppliscono a' sopradecti consigli, per levarsi da ogni prolixità et confusione et seguire l'ostile del palagio, come sempre s'è facto in questa vostra gloriosa casa".

or magnate families ("le quali sempre sono sute honorate e meritamente in questa Casa; le quali havessino vinto qui nello squittino del 1453 o 1454 nonobstante che non avessino vinto il priorato"), whose names were to be mixed indiscriminately in the bags with those of the popolani qualified for the priorate.[81] Now membership of the Parte councils was to be restricted to these same popolani and magnati who were qualified by holding Parte office since 1458. In this way it must have been hoped, not only to ensure their political reliability, but to overcome the problem of disinterest and non-attendance which had plagued meetings of the councils and held up legislation for want of a quorum.

Only the office of *camarlingo* remained now to be reformed. On 9 February 1463 it was finally decreed that this office was to be terminated when the present *camarlingo* finished his term, at a saving of 36 florins a year and "grandissimo disagio". His place was to be taken by a bank of merchants, and in order to ensure that a trustworthy and reliable bank was chosen with no pressure applied, it was decided that the bank of Giovanni and Pierfrancesco de' Medici should take over temporarily from the treasurer when his office ended:

> Because it is thought that in this way not only will your money deposited here be secure but you will be offered marvellous benefits and help on every occasion wherever and whenever you might find yourselves in need, as indeed can at any moment happen in the course of the great and worthy enterprises you undertake and have to undertake every day.[82]

But far from feeling "sicuro delle vostre pecunie quivi dipositate", the Parte had every reason for apprehension, for in 1496 the heirs of Lorenzo de' Medici e Compagnia were sued for 2370 florins, "occasione depositarie olim facte per dictos heredes et socios suprascriptos de denariis et pecuniis decte Partis Guelfe".[83]

---

[81] *Ibid.*, f. 65*r*.

[82] *Ibid.*, f. 68*r* (8-9 February 1463): "Perché così si stima solo voi potere essere sicuro delle vostre pecunie quivi dipositate, ma anchora in ogni caso et bisogno che intervenisse, come ogni dì può intervenire nelle imprese grandi et degne che fate et havete a fare ogni dì ... prestarvi maravigliose comodità et aiuti in ogni caso et in ogni luogo secondo che accadesse". Thus Giovanni and Pierfrancesco de' Medici, "dispositari della Partte Guelfa" (after Giovanni's death in November 1463, Pierfrancesco de' Medici and Co.) are responsible for paying Scala's salary into his account with the banker Bernardo Rinieri from 11 October 1463, ASF, *Conv. Soppr.* 95, 212, f. 143*r*.

[83] ASF, *Capit. P. G.* 9 rosso, f. 17*r* (10 May 1496): "Cum publice notum sit, Magnifici ac generosi ... Capitanei venerabilesque College, Partem ... Guelforum fore et esse creditricem de societate que cantat et seu cantabat in heredibus d. Laurentii de' Medicis et Sociis ... de quantitate et summa florenorum duorum milium trecentorum septuaginta larghi ... occasione

In addition to reconstructing the administration of the Parte, a series of other measures was introduced to reform and curtail its expenditure which combined practicality with puritanism. A technique was introduced, heralded as new when later used by the commune, which encouraged the collection of rents by reducing the salaries of ministers if the rents were insufficient to pay them and if in excess profiting the Parte.[84] It was decreed that the Parte *donzelli* were to be given uniform and not money; and in January 1460 oblations made on certain saints' days were cancelled by the Ufficiali di Muraglia.[85] Three accountants were appointed with *balìa* to review all the accounts, "intendendo il disordine grande che molti anni già è stato nel governo et administratione delle cose della gloriosa casa vostra captolica parte guelfa. Et intendendo la confusione delle scripture lasciate pe' ministri et suspicando di molte fraude che si crede essere sute facte in molti modi".[86] Piero de' Medici and Antonio Guidotti were made responsible for valuing the marble tabernacle built in Orsanmichele in 1422 to hold the statue of St. Louis, and then left "così voto et quasi cosa abandonata"after the statue was removed, "perché allora per huomini savi vostri cittadini fu giudicato che la dignità della inclyta et excellentissima parte de' guelfi non degnamente fusse collocata quivi fra le capitudini et al pari d'esse"; and the money raised was to be used solely to complete and decorate the ceiling and windows of the audience chamber of the Parte palace.[87]

The next year the eye of the reformers fell on the Orbatello, the almshouse administered by the Parte, which was found to be "in assai disordine" with men and women of different social standing mixed together in the same house. Slaves and Corsicans were to be evicted since they upset and disturbed such a "luogho pietoso" which was

---

depositarie olim facte per dictos heredes et socios suprascriptos de denariis et pecuniis dicte Partis Guelfe".

[84] *Ibid.*, f. 55*v* (20-21 November 1459): "Quod si non tantum exegerint quantum satis sit ad eorum salaria, id minus accipiant, quod secundum equalitatem unicuique contigerit. Si autem plus fuerit exactum pecuniarum quam ad salaria satis sit, id totum conditioni palatii assignetur".

[85] ASF, *Capit. P. G.* 9 rosso, ff. 55*v*-56*v* (20-21 November, 8 January 1460).

[86] *Ibid.*, ff. 57*v*-58*r* (14-15 January 1460).

[87] *Ibid.*, f. 58*v*; cf. H. W. Janson, *The Sculpture of Donatello,* Princeton, Princeton University Press, 1957, p. 46: "uno tabernaculo di marmo, il quale in orto sancto michele altra volta fu facto, cioè insino nel mccccxxii perchè vi dovesse essere dentro la statua di Sancto Lodovico ... Ch'el decto Tabernaculo si possi vendere ed alienare et che le pecunie che se ne ritraesse in nessuno altro uso o ornamento o alcuna altra cosa convertire si possa se non in ornare et finire il palco della vostra udienza et simile le finestre".

intended not for "quella tanto brutta gente" but for "persone di buona conditione per alcuna mala fortuna divenuti vergognosi miserabili".[88] Benefices owned by the Parte similarly revealed "molti e molto abominevoli mancamenti" but here reform was impeded by "la grande humanità de' prelati et in verità troppo misericordia loro inverso e notorii peccatori".[89] Building books were in 'confusione' and 'disordine', debtors listed who were not debtors and likewise creditors, and the accounts were "tucti inviluppati et senza ordine alcuno", as were the Libri della Età, which revealed "grandissimi difecti".[90]

The spirit of reforming puritanism which pervades this legislation is that of the chancellor Bartolomeo Scala himself, who certainly worked hard to improve the Parte's administration even if he failed to retain for it responsibility for maritime affairs. When he moved to the communal chancery in 1465, the captains paid tribute to his qualities in seeking to replace him with a "huomo dotato di molte et varie virtù" but particularly a man of great prudence, loyalty, tact and discretion, "acciò che nel suo pecto come in luogo inexpugnabile tucti i sacreti che apartengono alla Casa Vostra sieno collocati et fermi".[91]

The man they chose was another loyal Medicean, Cristoforo Landino, a humanist and university teacher of rhetoric who subsequently became a secretary under Scala in the communal chancery.[92] He too could be counted on to be discreet in his office, but he was not a reformer and politician like Scala and the tone of the legislation subtly changes: no more concentrated programmes of reform and imprecations against disorder and inefficiency, but instead a series of random measures introducing new scrutinies and economy cuts couched in flowing and rhetorical phrases (befitting their draftsman) which praise the virtues of liberty, liberality, clemency, love and civil concord.[93]

---

[88] ASF, *Capit. P. G.* 9 rosso, f. 61*r-v* (19-20 March 1461).

[89] *Ibid.*, f. 68*v* (8-9 February 1463).

[90] *Ibid.*, f. 63*r* (14-15 July 1461) and 69*r* (8-9 February 1463).

[91] *Ibid.*, f. 71*r* (10-13 May 1465). On Scala's role as a reformer, see *Bartolomeo Scala,* ch. 7. His hand appears listing Parte officials on at least three occasions, ASF, *Capit. P. G.* 18 rosso, ff. 52*r* (Priores Pecuniae, November 1459), 138*r*-140*r* (Secretarii Credentie, January 1460-September 1462).

[92] On Landino's and Scala's contrapuntal careers, see *Bartolomeo Scala,* and D. Marzi, *La Cancelleria della Repubblica Fiorentina,* pp. 239-241. On his writings, R. Cardini, *La critica del Landino*, Florence, Olschki, 1973.

[93] ASF, *Capit. P. G.* 9 rosso, ff. 72*r*-80*v* (November 1465-July 1471), ff. 1*r*-7*v* (March-June 1472). For examples of his style, see ff. 72*v* (21 November 1465, instituting a new scrutiny of offices) and 77*v* (23 January 1467, enlarging the scrutiny).

Civil concord was a necessary virtue in the years of factionalism following Cosimo de' Medici's death in August 1464. Although the opposition to his son Piero claimed to wish to restore a more open and 'republican' system of government, in fact its leaders were (with the exception of Niccolò Soderini) all knights. Five knights headed the subscription list of the republican oath of 27 May 1466, who were perhaps those later alluded to in Francesco Neroni's confession of his part in the Pitti conspiracy as the "5 cavalieri [che] stringneono insieme", the "ciercheliino".[94] The failure of the conspiracy that summer resulted in the appointment of a Medicean Balìa in which for the first time the Parte Guelfa captains, together with the Sei di Mercanzia and the Capitudini delle Arti, were not included as *ex officio* members; nor were they appointed members of such Balìe or scrutiny councils again until after the fall of the Medici regime in 1494. Perhaps for this reason it was considered safe as well as politic to allow a more liberal scrutiny of Parte offices, and in 1467 the names of those who had won the vote for the captaincy and the colleges but had had their names removed in 1458 were restored to the bags.[95] When Piero de' Medici died in 1469 his son Lorenzo succeeded him as one of the six Ufficiali di Muraglia, but neither his appointment nor that of Gherardo Giandonati (who similarly replaced his father on his death) were confirmed until July 1471, "per non essersi di poi ragunati i consigli della Vostra Casa".[96]

The Parte Guelfa might have been allowed to remain in this condition of apparent obsolescence but for another crisis for the leader-

---

[94] Manno Temperani, Luca Pitti, Angelo Acciaiuoli, Giannozzo Pitti, and Dietisalvi di Nerone, ed. G. PAMPALONI, *Il giuramento pubblico in Palazzo Vecchio a Firenze e un patto giurato degli anti-Medicei, Maggio 1466*, in *Miscellanea di studi in memoria di C. Cecchini* (= «Bullettino Senese di Storia Patria», LXXI [1964]), p. 234. See Francesco Neroni's confession, ed. N. RUBINSTEIN, *La confessione di Francesco Neroni e la congiura antimedicea del 1466*, «Archivio Storico Italiano», CXXVI, 1968, pp. 386, cf. p. 383: "cotesti cavalieri". According to Francesco Neroni, the ambassador of Borso d'Este told him "che una comunità di questa qualità stava male senza cavalli" and he also encouraged the conspirators to support the Angevins in Italy according to traditional Guelf policy, but Neroni comments that this would not have met with Angelo Acciaiuoli's approval as a supporter of Ferrante of Aragon, and there is no evidence that his Angevinism was accepted by other conspirators (*ibid.*, pp. 383-384).

[95] ASF, *Capit. P. G.* 9 rosso, ff. 77*v*-78*r* (23 January 1467): "È paruto che sia degna chosa del magistrato loro che tutti quegli a' quali sono state tolte le polize sue sieno interamente ristituiti". On the 1494 restoration of the Parte Captains' *ex officio* rights, see note 123 below.

[96] *Ibid.*, f. 79*r* (2ª ser.), 18-30 July 1471: "per molti rispecti essere utile et honesto et honorevole all'Università de' Guelfi che dicte due electioni habbino sua perfectione". In fact, although under age, Lorenzo had already been authorised to replace his ailing father on 28 November 1465, *ibid.*, f. 75*v*.

ship of Florence as a result of Piero de' Medici's death. This in turn produced another movement for reform among the Mediceans to strengthen their position, which provoked the Parte's second death sentence and second remission. On 7 August 1470 Sacramori reported to the Duke of Milan an attempt by the 'principali', especially those who had been knighted, to reduce Lorenzo de' Medici's power; and after the Duke had successfully encouraged Lorenzo to introduce reforms to strengthen his regime at the beginning of the following year, Sacramori reported: "Questi cavalleri doveranno gustare quanto questo importi et qual sia a dire essere sempre de li Signori et de li Otto chi vorrà Lorenzo; et gustandolo doveranno pensare a li rimedii".[97]

It was perhaps to anticipate the 'remedii' of the knights that a Balìa or Consiglio Maggiore was appointed in July to consolidate Lorenzo's authority. On 13 September this Balìa introduced the Parte Guelfa's second death sentence by creating a commission of five men:

> who are to enjoy all the authority of the people of Florence to oversee and close down all the possessions of the Guelf Party and the Mercanzia of Florence, and to make a Monte of them, that is, Monte money, in order to reduce the Monte.[98]

One of the five members of this commission with full powers to deprive the Parte Guelfa and Mercanzia of their possessions was Piero di Niccolò Malegonnelle, the Parte's first selected and longer-term *provveditore* in 1461-62, suggesting continuity with the reforms of that period. The legislation is presented as a method of raising the 28,000 florins needed annually for defence by creating a new "Monte de' Castellani e Provigionati", which was to be endowed with money from the sale of Parte and Mercanzia property (excluding, however, their residences).[99] As the preface explains, the extra money needed for

---

[97] S. Sacramori to Galeazzo Maria Sforza, 7 August 1470 (ASMi SPE Firenze 279, quoted by R. Fubini, ed., Lorenzo de' Medici, *Lettere*, I, p. 207) and 9 January 1471 (ASMi SPE Firenze 281, quoted by G. Soranzo, *Lorenzo il Magnifico alla morte del padre e il suo primo balzo verso la Signoria*, «Archivio Storico Italiano», CXI [1953], p. 71). On the measures of 9 January to strengthen the regime, Rubinstein, *Government of Florence*, pp. 180-181.

[98] Lionardo Morelli, *Cronica*, in *Delizie degli eruditi toscani*, ed. I. di San Luigi, XIX, Florence, 1785, p. 188, referring to the appointment for six months of "Quinque officialium super negotiis Partis Guelfae et Domus Mercatantie": che avessino tutta l'alturità del popolo di Firenze a vedere e a finire tutti e beni della Parte Guelfa e della Mercantia di Firenze, e con farne Monte, cioè danari di Monte, per diminuzione del Monte. ASF, *Balìa* 31, ff. 51*v*-53*v*.

[99] ASF, *Balìa* 31, ff. 51*v*-52*v* (13 September 1471): "Examinato ... quante sono le spese del nostro commune ... perchè solo i castellani et i provigionati aggiungono a fl. xxviii mila

defence could not be raised from communal revenues, for these were assigned to the Monte which was already unable to pay its creditors; nor could it be raised from catasti because they brought in too little money, especially since many *beni immobili* had been transferred to "non sopportanti" – like the Parte Guelfa itself and religious houses which were exempted from ordinary taxes.[100] By selling this property to tax-paying citizens (who would doubtless have been required to pay in Monte bonds rather than in cash, as they were in 1481), the government would increase the tax yield and at the same time reduce its expenditure on Monte Commune repayments and interest, making a new Monte "per diminuzione del Monte", as Morelli put it.

The Milanese ambassador in Florence interpreted the legislation as an economy measure to "redrizare certe intrate de la Parte Guelfa et del Officio de la Merchantia, che se mangiavano certi officiali et servi deputati a quelle Case cum pocho profito de Comune".[101] But although he predicted that measures such as this and the attempt to curb the authority of the Otto di Guardia would win for the regime "benivolentia nel popolo", on 29 February 1472 the authority of the five officials to sell the property of the Parte and the Mercanzia was suddenly revoked.[102] Since the Parte palace and the palace of the

l'anno... è necessario ordinare uno nuovo monte, che si chiami Monte de' Chastellani e provigionati et sia come il Monte della Mensa, il quale paga l'anno gia xviii mila di fiorini in circa ... bisognando uno principio almeno di xl o cinquanta migliaia di fiorini contanti ... è necessario venire a tale provvedimento ... et questo è ordinare il governo della Parte Guelfa et della Casa della Merchantia et provedere alle spese vi resteranno necessarie per buono modo, et i loro beni immobili vendere a cittadini sopportanti, di che ne crescierà la graveza et il ritracto convertire in crediti di monte di sopportanti et principiare decto nuovo monte ... Questo expressamente aggiunto ... che ... non si possa chiudere la chasa della Parte Guelfa nè per loro scemare il numero de' Sei della Merchatantia nè la auctorità di decti Sei ... non s'intendendo potere vendere la chasa della residentia de' Capitani et de' Sei et la torre della Parte Guelfa a piè del Ponte Vecchio". Cf. Rinuccini, *Ricordi storici*, cit., p. cxviii. On 18 November 1471 the Balìa legislated to increase the yield of a tax first introduced in 1461 on *botteghe* within 3 miles of Florence to pay for the repair of fortresses, ASF, *Balìa* 31, f. 71*r*.

[100] ASF, *Balìa* 31, f. 51*v*: "perché pel mezzo dell'entrate del commune a questo non si può provedere per essere quelle [catasti et gabelle] assegnate al Monte et non essere tante che si possa pel Monte interamente satisfare a' creditori suoi per le doti et per le paghe ... et atteso il catasto gittar pocho et rischuotersene meno et similmente intervenire della gabella de' soldi due per lira et havere a intervenire d'ogni altra graveza per essere transferiti assai beni immobili in non sopportanti".

[101] Sacramoro Sacramori to Galeazzo Maria Sforza (15 September 1471), ASMi SPE Firenze 282.

[102] ASF, *Balìa* 31, f. 82*v*: "Et più si provede che l'auctorità conceduta a' detti cinque uficiali... circa il vendere tutti e beni della Parte Guelfa et della Mercatantia... s'intenda essere et sia solamente quanto alla parte del vendere de' beni di detti due luoghi, et non nell'altre, rivocata et annullata. Ma siano tenuti et obligati detti uficiali in luogo del fare o far fare dette

Mercanzia had been expressly excluded from the sale, this reversal cannot have been simply due to hostility to the removal of "an ancient and revered monument" from the city as in 1459. It is more likely that the regime was suspected of political motivation, especially since the same five officials had proposed to cut the minor guilds from fourteen to five and to add their possessions to the same Monte: "parve cosa che pretendisse a altro fine più importante a chi lo considerava bene", Alamanno Rinuccini commented. And because of opposition, "niuna delle sopraddette leggi si messe a esecuzione".[103]

Once again failure to reduce the Parte was followed by a period of remission: renewed responsibilities were given to it and internal reforms were introduced. The Parte was given back responsibility for maritime affairs and instead of being deprived of its possessions it was ordered to pay an annual tax, subsequently fixed at fl. 650.[104] But as the Parte was unable to pay the tax, it was decided on 16 April 1472 to commute it into an investment in the Monte: "in nome di decta Parte Guelfa di tanti crediti di Monte ... che provederanno et vorranno da sopportanti, c[i]oè come vulgarmente si dice saranno crediti de' sopportanti".[105] "Crediti de' sopportanti" were 'conditionati', that is to say, were bound to be paid to the Monte Officials for the payment of taxes. And so the Parte Guelfa was transformed from a charitable institution not liable to taxes, "non sopportante", to one of taxpaying status, "sopportante", the *paghe* or annual interest on whose capital must total at least fl. 650, to be paid by the

---

vendite porre all'uno e l'altro luogo, cioè alla parte guelfa et alla mercatantia, quella taxa per ciaschuno tale luogo che a lloro parrà conveniente".

103 *Ricordi storici*, p. CXIX: ASF, *Balìa* 31, f. 82*r*, referring to the September provvisione "che le xiiii minori arti insieme si unissimo": "Et considerato tale provisione essere suta facta per utilità universale et per miglior governo di detti luoghi, et nientedimeno arrechare dispiacere d'animo a' sottoposti di tali luoghi, et giudicando essere conveniente alla repubblica et a' governatori di quella tenere gli animi de' cittadini in ciaschuno membro quanto più honestamente fare si può quieti et ben disposti ... si provede ... l'unione delle xiiii minori arti ... s'intenda essere et sia dissoluta". However, according to M. MALLETT, *Pisa and Florence in the 15th century*, in *Florentine Studies*, p. 433, there was a considerable sale of Pisan land administered by the Parte in the early 1470s.

104 See note 102 above and ASF, *Capit. P. G.* 9 rosso, f. 2*r*; *Balìa* 31, f. 83*r* (29 February 1472): "in Firenze l'uficio de' Consoli più non si tragga, ma intendasi finito l'uficio de' presenti consoli, cioè a dì primo di giugno proximo futuro 1472, transferito tale uficio nell'uficio de' Capitani della Parte Guelfa". On 23 March the nine captains had already been reduced to five (note 107 below) and now they were given the same authority and duties as the five Sea Consuls had had (when they recovered it in 1462, see above).

105 ASF, *Capit. P. G.* 9 rosso, f. 2*r*.

Monte officials into the new Monte de' Castellani e Provigionati.[106] In this way a solution was found to one of the problems posed by the Parte's privileged status. Having failed to sell its tax-free property to tax-paying citizens, the government by making it liable to pay this tax of 650 florins had at least managed to retain for the commune the interest from its Monte investments, thus reducing the Parte to the same position as the citizens who belonged to it.

On 23 March 1472 the five officials decreed that the nine Parte captains should be reduced to five, enjoying office for six instead of two months with a salary of five large florins each a month (the first five, drawn from a bag prepared by the chancellor, being Piero de' Rossi, Francesco and Antonio Dini, Donato Acciaiuoli and Niccolò Cerretani). Cristoforo Landino was reappointed chancellor from 1 April with a salary to be fixed by the five officials, and thereafter he was to be re-elected or dismissed by the captains alone. Ser Giovanni d'Attavante da Colle was elected as his *notaio coadiutore* for a year (dismissed in 1492 for *plura delicta et excessus et derobationes*) and Lorenzo di Piero Davanzati (who replaced Piero Malegonnelle in 1462) was re-elected *provveditore* for one year.[107] On 16 April, "auto notitia della gram dificultà che si vede per experientia essere in avere a ragunare e collegi e i consigli generali e particulari di decta Parte Guelfa", the officials gave the five captains *balìa* during their office to act by a two-thirds majority without their colleges or councils in order to introduce the necessary reforms and raise the tax as quickly as possible.[108] Thus the Parte was transformed from a communal institution, governed by short-term captains acting with their colleges and coun-

---

[106] *Ibid.*, f. 2*r-v*: «le pag[h]e loro saranno ciascuno anno infino alla somma et almeno infino in decta quantità di fl. 650 larghi quanto è data annuaria et così saranno decti crediti o capitale conditionati c[i]oè che le pag[h]e succedano et siano in luogo di decta tassa ordinaria». What the Monte Officials receive as "pag[h]e del credito o capitale di Monte ... si debba convertire pe' decti uficiali del Monte i[n] crediti del Monte pello assegnamento et accrescimento di decto Monte di decti Castellani et Provigionati come fare sono tenuti de' crediti e assegnamenti del Monte della Mensa della Signoria".

[107] ASF, *Capit. P. G.* 9 rosso, f. 1*r* (four captains from the *arti maggiori*, one from the *minori*, aged at least 30 years), 1*v*. Here at least the five officials had retained their *balìa* to reform the Parte (cf. note 102 above).

[108] *Ibid.*, f. 3*r*: «E presenti ... Capitani ... habbino ... durante il loro uficio solamente ogni piena e libera altorità, facultà e balìa e tale e tanta e quale e quanta hanno e sono consueti avere i nove chapitani di decta Parte insieme con loro collegi e consigli ... ensieme». After meeting four times between November 1459 and 20 March 1460, the councils met only about once a year until November 1467, then not at all until 1471.

cils, to a magistracy governed by five officials appointed for half-yearly periods of office (after 1530 for one year).

At the beginning of 1472 a series of reforms was introduced by the five officials to "allegerire la decta Parte con risecare delle spese superflue acc[i]ò che più facilmente si possano le spese necessarie e la tassa decta sopportare". The amount of money to be spent on celebrating various feast days was again reduced, so was the amount spent on alms, on tips and on honouring the tabernacle of S. Maria della Impruneta; *donzelli* were reduced from nine to six, an assessor was to review for the Parte all the *provigionati* and *castellani* of the commune, debtors were to be sent *a specchio* (thereby depriving them of political office) and the rentals of all its properties were to be reviewed.[109] This was the occasion when the several surviving inventories of Parte property were made, listing some 87 different rented properties. But instead of increasing its revenue, this review only served to reduce it from approximately 1624 florins per annum to 1462 florins.[110]

In March when the fate of the Parte still hung in the balance, its chancellor Cristoforo Landino wrote to defend it against the charge of partisanship, arguing like Luigi Guicciardini some ten years earlier that "ne' nostri tempi nessuno per ghibellino è conosciuto, ma tutti nel grembo de' ghuelphi ricevuti di tutte le dignità insieme con quelle partecipano".[111] Florence was indeed a one-party city in 1472 and Landino had to justify the Parte's existence on other grounds: as a political and social asset in the city. It was, he explained, a self-supporting institution which paid for its own officials and also devoted a large part of its income to "pubblici navigii", donating what remained, if anything, to charity. It also supported the city by giving office and honours to many who would otherwise be foreigners and by furthering friendly relations with princes and peoples outside Florence.[112]

---

109 ASF, *Capit. P. G.* 9 rosso, ff. 4*v*-6*r* (2 May-1 June 1472).

110 ASF, *Capit. P. G.* 9 rosso, ff. 6*r*-7*v* ("Item i decti ufficiali desiderando et volendo l'entrate delle pigioni e ficti de' beni inmobili di decta Parte migliorare et acrescere con ogni honesta et buona discretione"); *Capit. P. G.* 28-30 rosso. The rents total fl. 1222, £ 721, approximately fl. 1462 (cf. note 38 above).

111 BNF, MS Magl. VIII, 1299, ff. 96*v*-101*r*: "A Maestro Paolo Guinigi da Lucha ... Marzo 1471[2]", inc.: "Intesi da molti che riprendendo tu nelle tue prediche le secte, le quali nelle città per seditioni et gare di cittadini nascono, etiam la Parte de' Guelfi acerbamente damnasti". I quote from f. 99*v*.

112 *Ibid.*, f. 100*r-v*, cf. above.

But such charitable and public-relations functions combined badly with the practical work of the Sea Consuls, and in the course of another reforming movement in 1477 the Parte Guelfa again lost its responsibility for maritime affairs.[113] In June the office of Captain of the People had been abolished "perché più niente si fa" and the jurisdiction of the Mercanzia was then defined and limited, as was that of the guilds, although their possessions, like those of the Parte, were left untouched.[114] The Pazzi Conspiracy and ensuing war made further reform impracticable in that decade. But the financial crisis and the consolidation of the regime which followed the peace settlement of 1480 made it both imperative and feasible. And so the third and final assault on the Parte was launched as part of another movement for economy and for administrative reform.

The former fortress of liberty in Florence, the Parte Guelfa, fell at last to the new "presidio et roccha firmissima et stabilimento certo della salvatione di tutto il corpo et governo et stato vostro", the Monte Commune.[115] In July 1481 control of the Monte was transferred from the new Council of Seventy to the Cento, who delegated overall control of finances to a temporary commission of seventeen men (including Lorenzo de' Medici), and it was these Seventeen Reformers who assaulted the Parte as part of an extensive programme of reform provoked by "le insopportabili spese della guerra".[116] They succeeded in doing what the five officials had failed to do in 1472: that is, to sell Parte possessions to tax-paying citizens, thereby (as the preface to this legislation explains) achieving the double benefit of reducing interest payments on Monte stock (by making them pay in Monte bonds) and converting the houses themselves into taxable property:

And because the magistracy of the Captains of the Guelf Party, which once used to enjoy the greatest authority in our city, is now reduced to very

---

[113] ASF, *Provvisioni* 168, f. 120*v* (23 October 1477, approved by the Cento only); M. MALLETT, *The Sea Consuls*, p. 160.

[114] ASF, *Cento Deliberazioni* 2, ff. 10*r*-29*v* (7 June-30 July 1477); L. F. MARKS, *The Financial Oligarchy in Florence under Lorenzo*, in *Italian Renaissance Studies*, ed. Jacob, cit., pp. 134-135; L. MARTINES, *Lawyers and Statecraft in Renaissance Florence*, Princeton, Princeton University Press, 1968, p. 137.

[115] As it was described in 1470, ASF, *Provvisioni* 161, f. 168*r*, quoted by MARKS, *The Financial Oligarchy*, p. 127.

[116] ASF, *Provvisioni* 172, ff. 81*v*-84*v* (24-26 July 1481), MARKS, *The Financial Oligarchy*, p. 138. The register of the Seventeen Reformers is ASF, *Miscellanea Repubblicana* 109, see *Lorenzo de' Medici, the Monte and the Seventeen Reformers: public and private interest*, pp. 151-211 below.

lowly status and yet still spends as much or more on salaries as it did when it enjoyed great prestige, consuming all its annual income except for what it pays to the Monte as a tax; and because it is said that selling its possessions and using the money to reduce Monte credits would be very useful, because it would reduce interest payments considerably and in time these possessions would pay taxes, it is thought therefore we should at one and the same time secure profit for the Monte and honour and stability for such a worthy Institution.[117]

And so on 22 August the Seventeen Reformers decided to auction all the Parte possessions except for "la chasa della habitudine de' Capitani... et excepto la chasa che è in sul Ponte Vecchio dove sta la Signoria co' Capitani al corso del palio il dì di San Vettorio". The possessions were to be sold freehold to Florentine citizens paying ordinary taxes in Florence, and both the price and the tax were to be paid completely in Monte bonds and not in money (*de creditis Montis et non de pecunia numerata*) to fund the new Monte de' Castellani e Provigionati. No buyer could be nominated and none could be *non-sopportanti*: if they were, the property would be acquired by the Monte. Any property left unsold was to remain as it was until a further decision could be made.[118]

Yet it proved more difficult to close the Parte Guelfa down than the Mediceans could have anticipated in 1459. In fact only about thirty-six of its eighty-seven properties in and around Florence were sold in 1481 (to citizens who included Piero Buondelmonti, Cosimo Bartoli, Filippo Strozzi, Antonio Ridolfi, Lorenzo de' Medici – who bought property in the Via delle Terme and Por San Maria previously rented to his father – ser Giovanni Guidi, Notary of the Riformagioni, and Bernardo degli Albizzi). Those which remained unsold continued

---

[117] ASF, *Provvisioni* 172, f. 83*v*; "Et perchè el magistrato de' Capitani della Parte Guelfa, che già era in grandissima auctorità nella nostra città, è venuto in gran basseza, et nondimeno v'è quella medesima spesa di ministri o maggiore che quando era in tanta reputazione et consumavisi l'anno tutte l'entrate excepto quella parte che al Monte se ne pagha per taxa; et perchè si dice che vendendosi e beni di detta Parte et convertendo e danari in diminutione di Monte si farebbe grande utilità perchè si leverebbe assai d'interesse, et col tempo tali beni sopporterebbono la graveza, però si giudica doversi a uno tracto provedere all'utile del Monte et allo honore et fermeza di sì degna Casa"; cf. RINUCCINI, *Ricordi storici,* p. CXXXV.

[118] ASF, *Misc. Repub.* 109, ff. 10*v*-11*r* (22 August 1481): "Dicta autem bona vendantur libera, et pretium illorum et gabella per emptorem integre solvenda sit de creditis Montis ... Et non possint vendi nisi solum et duntaxat civibus florentinis onera ordinarie supportantibus in civitate Florentie ... Et bona que aliter venderentur vel alienarentur ipso facto spectarent ad Montem Communis Florentie et cum huiusmodi conditione vendantur" (f. 11*r*); 29*r* (1 December 1481).

to be rented out, at least until the 1490s.[119] On 8 May 1482 it was decided that the Captains were to be drawn from the Parte bags as hitherto but without *divieto*. They were to be paid five florins a month and were to perform the Parte's more important ceremonial functions as they had traditionally done.[120]

Shorn of its Monte investments and half of its property, the Parte was still a problem. A new commission of Seventeen Reformers was appointed which attempted to reform it in 1491, "havendo notitia per varii et diversi raporti che nel governo della Parte Guelfa... sono in ogni menbro varii et diversi disordini dannosi assai charichi a' molti ministri di quella Chasa, a chi di pocha diligentia, a chi di non molta nectezza". Debts were badly collected; fines incurred in the Romagna and elsewhere which were not remitted or were badly spent; the *provveditore* of Arezzo performed his office badly; the Sea Consuls elected by the Parte created problems, especially in the Levant, "il che è d'assai momento et bisognerebbevi huomo el quale con magior diligentia et sollicitudine favorisci e nostri merchatanti". And finally, it was complained, the *borsa generale* and the *borsellino* for the Parte Captains needed renewing, having been unaltered since 1458. The Seventeen Reformers granted the communal *accoppiatori* powers to reform the Parte on 27 July 1491; and in November Niccolò Ridolfi, Angelo Niccolini, Antonio di Piero Malegonnelle and Piero Pandolfini chose as captains (with *balìa* from the Seventeen Reformers for one year) Piero Soderini, Jacopo Salviati, Tommaso di Piero Malegonnelle, Bartolomeo Orlandini and Bernardo Puccini, who quickly deprived of office two officials guilty of debts and peculation.[121] Sixteen months later the income of the Parte had almost doubled, thanks to "la diligentia e l'opere de' capitani", and it was made responsible for administering the fines collected throughout the dominion with which to pay for the repair and maintenance of fortresses, "sanza havere a tocchare altrimenti o spendere del publico".[122]

---

[119] ASF, *Capit. P. G.* 30 rosso.

[120] ASF, *Misc. Repub.*, 109, f. 68*r-v*.

[121] ASF, *Capit. P. G.* 10 rosso, ff. 1*r*-2*r*; *Misc. Repub.* 108; *Capit. P. G.* 9 rosso, f. 11*r*. The former *provveditore* Bernardo Bartolini was deprived of office for "plura latrocinia et furta... derobando pecunias dicte Partis et in suum usum et utilitatem convertendo", the notarial assistant ser Giovanni d'Attavante for "plura delicta et excessus et derobationes ... qui pluries ac pluries pecunias ... falso detraxit et derobavit et in suam utilitatem et usum convertit» (*Capit. P. G.* 9 rosso, f. 15*r*).

[122] ASF, *Capit. P. G.* 10 rosso, f. 16*r* (27-29 March 1493). Cf. Consiglio del Cento, Registro 3, ff. 137*v*-138*v*.

After the fall of the Medici in 1494 the Parte Guelfa, together with the Sei di Mercanzia, the Capitudini delle Arti and other magistracies, recovered the *ex officio* role they had formerly enjoyed in the state by being represented in the Consiglio Maggiore, which now elected all office-holders, including the Parte captains.[123] Two years later the Offitiales Rebellium et Sindici claimed fl. 2370 from the heirs of Lorenzo de' Medici e Compagnia which they said had been taken from the captains and colleges of the Parte during the Medici Bank's period of trusteeship of their funds; lacking the means to repay this sum, the heirs were required to give the Parte property in lieu.[124] When in 1497 the Parte was ordered to acquire the office of the Seal of Weights and Measures in Florence, it was told to pay for it by auctioning "tanti de' beni inmobili di decta Parte che faccino la somma del prezzo el quale sarà necessario per la compera di detto sugello".[125] So neither the attempt of the Medici to deprive the Parte of its property nor its attempt to deprive it of its *ex officio* role in the state had entirely succeeded, although they had reduced its financial independence. The restoration of the Medici in 1512 saw a return to the appointment of Parte captains by a Balìa until a new scrutiny was completed, and then by sortition. Their fall and the republican revival in 1527 saw a return to the captains' election in the Consiglio Maggiore. Under the Medici dukes they were appointed by the dukes and their councillors "pro omni futuro tempore quo placuerit Illustrissimo Domino Duci". Their number remained five and their period of office six months until 1538 when it began to be extended to a year or longer.[126]

* * *

The progressive reduction of the Parte Guelfa from 1459 to 1481 is interesting from several points of view. The determination of the

---

[123] ASF, *Provvisioni* 185, f. 10*r* (22 December 1494). According to Piero Parenti (although not Guicciardini), the Parte captains were one of several magistracies asked to contribute a scheme for a new form of government; N. Rubinstein, *I primi anni del Consiglio Maggiore di Firenze (1494-99)*, «Archivio Storico Italiano», CXII, 1954, p. 153.

[124] See note 83 above and ASF, *Capit. P. G.* 9 rosso, f. 17*v* (listing the property).

[125] ASF, *Capit. P. G.* 10 rosso, f. 30*r* (15-16 February 1497).

[126] ASF, *Capit. P. G.* 18 rosso, ff. 28*v* (25 August 1513), 29*r* (23 and 30 August 1515), 31*v* (13 September 1527), 32*r*-34*r*. In October 1532 the formula is "electi et seu prorogati per M. Ducem Alexandrum de' Medici cum consilio seu balìa del 48 per sex menses" and in December 1533, "electi per illustrissimum ... Ducem et dominos consiliarios pro omni futuro tempore", etc. (f. 32*v*). From 1550 the captains were "partim electi et partim extracti".

Medici regime to bring this about and the resistance they encountered suggest that the Parte still played a significant role in Florence at this time. Far from being negligible in the fifteenth century, the Parte still exercised enough social, financial and political influence to concern the government. Socially, there is little evidence of conflict between members of the Parte and Mediceans, between nobles and *nouveaux riches*. Although some Medicean merchants criticized the idea of allowing mercantile affairs to be decided by nobles living off inherited wealth and stressed the importance of trade in creating stable and prosperous cities – as in Venice –, others recognised the valuable role played by nobles as ambassadors and members of the Dieci di Balìa in time of war.[127] By converting the honour of knighthood into a reward for political services for themselves and their friends, the Mediceans in fact encouraged the élitism associated with chivalry and from this point of view gave the Parte extended life. Since such élitism was disliked by the people,[128] popular opposition to closing the Parte must have sprung from their conservatism and unwillingness to see the destruction of "an ancient and revered monument".

It is more difficult to assess the Parte's political influence in the fifteenth century. During the fourteenth century there had been a real danger that the Parte would constitute a state within a state and its renewal in the 1420s revived this threat, especially at the time of conflict between the Albizzi and Medici parties in the 1430s. The Medicean attempt to close the Parte down in 1459 and then to control it was a direct response to the danger of political dualism and to the opposition of leading knights, who in 1466 and 1470-71 still threatened their regime by combining against it. It is notable how closely the Parte was affected by policies introduced by the Medici regime from 1459. Every serious attempt to reform the Parte followed

---

[127] ASF, *Cons. Prat.* 56, f. 142*v*, 3 March 1461 (Manno Temperani, referring to those "qui minime intelligunt res marittimas, utpote nobiles homines ex fructibus suorum prediorum vitam agere solitos", cf. note 22 above), 146*r*, 4 March (Otto Niccolini, "exercitium enim navigandi non posse satis laudari, nam ultra utilitatem multa mala vitantur, presertim iuvenum, qui inhertia et desidia sublevantur; exemplum patere a Venetis qui ob navigationem omnia alia ornamenta acquiserunt", cf. 142*v* referring to "multos nobiles homines quibus quamquam îndocti sint rerum maritimarum non est fienda verecundia"); 143*v* (Dietisalvi Neroni: "nec esse in hac re fugiendum consortium nobilium ... Nam si in officio gravissimo Decem Balìe, quod tempore belli prestari soles [sic], semper nobiles quidam esse consueverant, equo animo ferendum esse ut etiam ex illius modi officio exercerint ex illis quidam").

[128] See note 29 above.

in the wake of crucial Medicean reforms in the state, that of 1459 following the Balìa of 1458 and the creation of the Council of Cento, which it was hoped would specifically be responsible for reforming the Parte;[129] that of 1471 being introduced by officials appointed by the Balìa of that year which confirmed Lorenzo de' Medici in power; and the final reform of 1481 following the 1480 Balìa which consolidated his position after the Pazzi crisis.[130] Scrutinies in the Parte closely followed the pattern of communal scrutinies, severe when communal scrutinies were severe, lenient when they were lenient.[131] So too did methods of administrative reform. The close identification of government and Parte is illustrated in the debate on the creation of a *borsellino* for the office of Parte captains by Dietisalvi Neroni, who said:

> it doesn't much matter whether this reform is carried out in the Palace [of the Signoria] or in the residence of the Parte Guelfa, for often business concerning the Parte is discussed in the Palace.[132]

Moreover, after the Parte acquired responsibility for maritime affairs, leading members of the Medici family as well as other prominent members of the regime entered the bags of the Parte for the first time via the specially selected *borsellino*, and then played an active role in Parte affairs. Their failure to complete the Parte palace even after Piero and Lorenzo's election as Ufficiali di Muraglia suggests there may have been truth in Antonio Manetti's charge that the regime did not want it finished, since it would be a rival to the communal Palazzo della Signoria which was also being embellished at the time.[133]

Here it is not easy to isolate political from financial and adminis-

---

[129] See note 20 above.

[130] On these communal reforms, RUBINSTEIN, *Government of Florence*.

[131] On the communal scrutinies of 1453, 1458 and 1465, *ibid.*; on the Parte scrutinies of 1453-54, 1458 and 1466-67, see above. On the Parte as a "state within a state" and the commune in the fourteenth century, BRUCKER, *Florentine Politics and Society*, cit., pp. 57-59.

[132] ASF, *Cons. Prat.* 56, f. 143*v*: "nec se multi facere an hec reformatio in palatio fiat an vero in domo Partis Guelfa. Nam sepenumero de pertinentibus ad Partem multa in palatio fieri consueverunt".

[133] See note 21 above. On the Palazzo della Signoria, see A. LENSI, *Palazzo Vecchio*, Milan-Rome, Bestetti & Tumminelli, 1929, pp. 52-60, 64-74. On 18 July 1446 Operai were appointed who consisted of Cosimo de' Medici, Bernardo Gherardi, Giuliano Davanzati and Giovanni Pucci, with 6000 florins to spend on the Palazzo della Signoria, raised by a fine on Jewish moneylenders (pp. 53-55).

trative interests. It is clear from the charges of embezzlement raised against the Medici in 1496 that the family had a direct financial interest in acting as trustees of Parte funds from 1463. From an administrative point of view they also wished to integrate the Parte within a more efficient and centralised system of government and use its funds for communal purposes, as those of other corporations like the Mercanzia and the guilds. In centralising government the Medici both increased their own power and made government more efficient: the two interests cannot be separated. The aim of the Medici was to create a unitary in place of a pluralistic state, in which the Parte Guelfa with its imposing residence and duplicated communal institutions could serve no useful purpose except as a focus for discontent. So ultimately, like the Mercanzia and the guilds, it had to yield its independence because it stood in the way of the centralising policies of the Medicean government.

Once its financial and political teeth had been drawn, the Parte was allowed to survive as a useful department of state with particular responsibility for maritime and military affairs. It retained responsibility for the Sei d'Arezzo and the supervision of fortresses,[134] and from 1481 it enjoyed authority for maritime affairs in Florence, its captains always henceforth bearing the title of Sea Consul.[135] In 1497 it was made responsible for weights and measures[136] and in 1549 it took over the work of the Tower Officials, being then responsible for the upkeep of fortresses, roads, walls, bridges and for the

---

[134] The Parte had long enjoyed the right of assisting the Signoria and Colleges to prepare scrutinies for captains and governors of castles (eg. *Statuta Populi Florentinae*, cit., II, pp. 597, 655 bis, 657-658, etc.), and by 1485 it was made specifically responsible for electing officials for fortresses in Sarzanella, Livorno, Pisa, Cortona, Arezzo, Pietrasanta, Volterra and elsewhere (ASF, *SS. Deliberazioni sp. aut.* 37, ff. 17*v* and following, cf. *Statuta*, cit., II, p. 580-581). The captains were also given increasing authority to "gratiare condennatos", for "gratiando ciascuno secondo la sua possibilità, se ne trarrebbe buona somma di danari, e quali sono necessarii per reparatione delle vostre forteze, le quali hanno pochi altri assegnamenti et le spese sono grandi", *Provvisioni* 174, ff. 174*v*-175*v* (11-13 March 1484), cf. *ibid.*, ff. 44*v*-45*r* (20-22 June 1483), *SS. Deliberazioni sp. aut.* 32, f. 175*v* (18 May 1468), etc.

[135] ASF, *Provvisioni* 172, ff. 83*v*-84*r* (24-26 July 1481): "Et intendasi transferito nell'uficio de' Capitani della parte (el quale per ogni tempo vegghi in nome et in facto) l'uficio de' Consoli del Mare di Firenze con ogni sua auctorità ... con quei ministri solamente che ha l'uficio de' Consoli del Mare di Firenze"; M. MALLETT, *Sea Consuls*, pp. 159-160; A. SAPORI, *I primi viaggi di Levante e di Ponente delle Galere Fiorentine*, «Archivio Storico Italiano», CXIV, 1956, pp. 83-84.

[136] ASF, *Capit. P. G.* 10 rosso, f. 30*r* (15-16 February 1497), cf. 9 rosso, ff. 22*r*-24*r*. It bought mills from the Monte Officials – and also sold them, under duress, at the command of the government, *ibid.*, ff. 24*v*, 27*v*, etc.; F. GUICCIARDINI, *Storie fiorentine*, pp. 231-232.

administration of the goods of rebels.[137] In 1558 its palace became the seat of the Monte with adaptations by Vasari. It was finally suppressed on 22 June 1769.[138]

---

137 ASF, *Capit. P. G.* 10 rosso, in which the captains are described as "ufficiali speciali" with "custodia di costruzione, manutenzione delle fortezze, delle vie, mura pubbliche e ponti, consolato del mare, amministrazione dei beni dei ribelli"; G. CANESTRINI, *Note*, «Archivio Storico Italiano», ser. I, IV, pt. I, 1843, p. 291. On the work of the Parte Guelfa in the 16th century, see A. CERCHIAI e C. QUIRICONI, A. M. GALLERANI e B. GUIDI, *Relazioni e rapporti all'ufficio dei capitani di Parte Guelfa*, pt. I and II, in *Architettura e politica da Cosimo I a Ferdinando I*, ed. G. SPINI, Florence, Olschki, 1976, pp. 187-329.

138 *Indication sommaire des réglemens et loix de Son Altesse Royale l'Archiduc Léopold Grand Duc de Toscane, 1765-1778*, Brussels 1779, p. 60 (*Bandi e Ordini* V, n. CLXII), cf. F. DIAZ, *Francesco Maria Gianni: dalla burocrazia alla politica sotto Pietro Leopoldo di Toscana*, Naples-Milan, Ricciardi, 1966, p. 246.

APPENDIX

Parte Guelfa: Inventario di beni, 1431

ASF, *Capit. P.G.* 27 rosso.

Al nome dello Onipotente Sapiente e Clemente Iddio e della sua gloriosa Madre Madonna Santa Maria e del beato Messer Santo Giovanni Batista e de' preziosi apostoli Messer San Piero e Messer San Paolo e del beato Messer Santo Vettorio e del beato Messer Santo Antonio e del beato Messer Santo Dionisio e del beato Messer Santo Lodovicho e di Messer San Barnaba e di tutti gli altri santi e sante della celestiale chorte del paradiso a' quali umilmente facciamo prieghо che salvino e ghuardino la libertà della città di Firenze et exaltino e mantenghino la Parte Ghuelfa nella città di Firenze, contado e distretto, e generalmente inn ongni parte del mondo.

Quessto libro è de' Mangnifici Singniori Chapitani della Parte Ghuelfa che ssono e che pe' tempi saranno, in sul quale si scriverà tutti i beni mobili e inmobili della Parte Ghuelfa, e a cchi i beni inmobili saranno alloghati chominciato per me Niccolò di Gentile degl'Albizi proveditore tratto di borsa della Parte Ghuelfa per un anno inchominciato a dì xxxi di lulglio 1431.

MCCCCXXXI

Perché i proveditori passati anno tenuto in sul libro grande ongnuno scritte le possessioni della Parte e a me è paruto farne quessto libretto di per se e che sia più chiareza, però l'ò inchominciato e partitamente chome a ppiè dirà. E perché veduti i libri di iiij° proveditori stati inanzi a me, non chomprendo che sia stato riveduta la ragione per ragionieri, e perché degli errori si potrebono esere chommessi, e perché se fusse manchato a porre a conto di persona la pigione e si possa vedere più abilemente, inchomincerò indietro a scrivere tutte le possessioni che lla Parte aveva nel MCCCCXXVI. E questo fo perché di lulglio 1426 uscì proveditore della Parte Ruberto di Bartolo Cortigiani e fu riveduta la sua ragione per ragionieri eletti, ciò fu Bernardo di Tommaso di Soldo delgli Strozi e un compagnio e feciono aconciare detta ragione ed era stato proveditore anni .vi. o circha. E di poi si sono mutati più spesso e non se ne riveduto ragione. E ppiù che dal 1426 in qua si sono vendute molte possessioni della Parte, e non ne truovo una distesa e chiara ragione. Per chiarirla il meglio potrò, ò preso questo modo e pongho loro i numeri per poterle meglio ritrovare.

MCCCCXXXI

Qui da ppiè e innanzi scriverrò masserizie e ornamenti della Parte. Im prima: [a]

2 chonfettiere d'ariento entrovi più smalti coll'armi del Comune e della Parte
1 bacino d'ariento mezzano
2 bossoli d'ariento l'uno grande e l'altro picchol0
1 tagliere d'ariento da ffare le tratte in su che si pone chi è tratto e a divieto
1 bossolo d'ariento per anoverare le fave
1 choperchio d'ariento per lo bossolo
4 saliere d'ariento
40 forchette d'ariento
40 chucchiai d'ariento
8 choltella cholle maniche nere cholle ghiere d'ariento
8 choltellini cholle maniche nere cholle ghiere d'ariento
4 choltella cholla maniche bianche cholle ghiere d'ariento
4 choltellini cholle maniche bianche cholle ghiere d'ariento
Uno pennone di drappo biancho laurato d'ariento e vituchiato. E uno aquilino di rame in terzo che si pone in sull'aste sopra il ghonfalone e nel pennone è l'arme della Parte, il quale si porta a chavallo il dì di San Giovanni.
Una choverta da chavallo chol segnio delle Parte
Una sopravessta da huomo chol segnio della Parte
Uno pennone vecchio chol detto sengnio
2 schudicciuoli di rame smaltati
3 pennoncelgli stracciati e vecchi da trombetti col segnio della Parte

---

[a] This and subsequent numbers are all written in roman numerals.

Una sopravesta da huomo di valescio col segnio della Parte
2 pianete vecchie in stuole, 2 manipoli, una verde vergata, l'altra rossa verghata. Sono vecchie e trisste.
Uno rinvolto di ritagli da drappo
2 pezze di bandinelle di panno lino

Una spalliera azurra seminata di gigli soppanata di panno lino rosso la quale istà nella sala prima dipinta. Tiene tutto il seggio de' capitani
3 pezzi di panchali chuciti insieme che dimosstra un pezzo, a schacchi o verde biancho o rosso seminato di foglie soppanato, che serve al sopradeto segio
Uno palio azurro seminato a gigli soppannato che serve alla ringhiera
4 pezzi di spalliera azurra seminata di gigli chon più compassi choll'armi del Chomune e della Parte e più altre. Servono a tuto il segio de' collegi per spalliera
4 pezzi di panchali a schacchi bianchi verdi e rossi seminati di folglie e chol sengnio della Parte soppannate. Servono al sedere del segio di tutti i collegi
2 pezzi di panchali verdi e neri chon alberi chon ii armi della Parte soppannati da panno lino verde per le panche della sala
2 pezzi di panchali verdi chon alberi e con lettere, sono grossi. Soppanati di panno lino vermiglio. Servono alle panche di sala.
3 pezzi di panchali verdi e azurri soppannati di panno rosso di borghogna tristi e rotti, i quali servono ongnindì le panche della auldienza
1 pezzo di panchale rosso con schudi tristo e rotto. È im palagio de' Signiori nella sala grande del consiglio che sta nel segio de' chapitani. Dicono è spezato e un altro meso in que[l] luogho.
8 pezzi di panchali verdi chon alberi e fiori soppannati di panno rosso di borghongnia. È pocho si chomperorono di nuovo. Pongonsi a le panche di sala e dell'androne
Uno tappeto rosso il quale serve il descho quando si fa le tratte. È nell'udienza. Se ne chuopre il descho dove s'anoverano le fave
Uno tapeto verde el quale si pone in sulla tavola alla tratta de' chapitani
[10 tovaglie, alcuni "chon buchi", "triste e rotte", 2 "di renso", da br. 8 a br. 22
10 guardanappe simili, da br. 12 a br. 19
2 tovaglie "di br. l'una, con buchi, vecchie"
10 tovagluole, br. 3 o br. 4: "le 6 sono nuove e lle 4 sono vecchie"
2 involglie lunghe per asciugare le mani]

Uno piattello di stangnio di lib. 8, vecchio
3 piattegli di stangnio
2 bacini d'ottone grandi
2 bacini d'ottone mezani

3 miscirobe d'ottone grandi
Uno bacino grande con bullette nell orlo da porre in sul piedistallo
1 misciroba con ii bachucci
1 piedistallo di ferro
1 parete di ferro da tenere bicchieri
2 alari di fuocho
1 paletta da fuocho
1 forchetta da ffuocho
1 paletta da fuocho vecchia
1 paia di molli
1 chaldaia mezzana e uno tozzo
1 treppie da ferro grande
1 focholare di ferro grande
1 chandelliere di ferro grande che sta nella sala inanzi a la figura di Nostro Signore
Uno paio di secchie che s'adoperavano al pozzo quando e c'era
Uno desscho di bicchieri
1 padella e una teghia grande di rame
2 alari grandi da chucina
1 chatino di rame e uno chalderotto piccholo
1 stadera trissta

8 panche nuove che nne stanno in sala vii e una nel androne
2 altre panche nuove che sono nel'Udienza
8 panche vecchie che sono nell'androne che va al agiamento
Una panchetta di br. 2 che ssi pone in capo di schala
Una pancha con spalliera intarsiata che ssi pone nell'udienza al chamino quando i capitani stanno al fuocho
Uno descho che fu già dal chancelliere quando la cancelleria era piccola con un pezzo d'asse regolata che già serviva col descho
2 chandellieri di lengnio da torchi quando si fa consiglio
Una pancha di br. 3 o circha con spalliera dipinta. Sta nell'udienza per al camino
Uno descho dipinto in su che il cancelliere anovera le fave. Sta nell' udienza
Uno descho grande intarsiato. Sta nel' udienza inanzi a' chapitani
2 chandellieri di ferro da tenere inanzi a' Capitani co' torchietti
4 chandellieri di ferro da candele o torchietti
In chancelleria molti libri della Parte a guardia del cancelliere
1 armario grande in che stanno gli arienti e sopraveste e coverte
5 tavole da mangiare tra grandi e picchole
3 paia di trespoli dale tavole
1 deschetto da sedere choll' apogiatoio
1 deschetto tondo sanza apogiatoio

1 chassone a 2 serami dove i donzegli tenghono le tovaglie e altra ... [illeggibile]

1 chassone vecchio e ij serami entrovi più libri della Parte – è su di sopra

Una chassapancha a ij serami, sta su di sopra

Uno chassone a i° serame che vi tenghono dentro i panchali

MCCCCXXXI

Una tavola di Nostra Donna di musaicho in uno tabernacolo di lengnio trissto la quale si comperò fl.xx da Girolamo di Chambiozo vaiaio. Debbesi aconciare nella udienza de' capitani

Uno compasso de que' del palcho del' udienza, il quale è ispossto e demesso di colore e d'oro che è nella udienza de' capitani

2 vagli da fave

2 chasette dipinte da fave e più bossoli da ricorre il partito

1 tavoletta di br. 4 o circha con ij tresposi da anoverare le fave quando si facesse squittino

Una pancha cholla spalliera da tenere al fuo[co] nell'udienza intarsiata

Più ferramenti trissti che sono su di sopra a guardia de' donzelgli che tengono le masserizie. Non truovo scrittura di quanti si debbano esere

Nel terreno sotto il palagio sono molte pietre concie e usci e lengniami e molti ferramenti e chatene e paletti e aghutami rotti e bandelle e arpioni. Nonne truovo scrittura di che si sieno o quante

In uno fondachetto della Parte che è nel chiasso che riescie a la piaza della Parte dietro a Porta Rossa, ch'è segnato no. xxvii, v'è dentro molto legniame della Parte che è posto in sul palcho chome se travi, bordoni, piave e travicegli, e giù nel fondacho sono più lati d'uscia delle boteghe che si disfeciono

Nella loggia de' Buondalmonti sono molti lengni d'abete della Parte nuovi e alchuno veccio de que' della chasa si disfece. Nonne truovo scrittura ch'io possa vedere quanti si sono.

In Sampiero Scheragio sono viii lengni d'abete della Parte i quali sono confitti insieme e dipintovi dentro il segnio della Parte e sono ritti

Più chiavi che sono nell armario del proveditore, credo fussino delle boteghe e chasa che ssi disfeciono

Uno descho da scrivere con chiave atornio per lo proveditore

Uno armario confitto e con uscio ch' el serra per lo proveditore con armarietto sotto il desscho e con uno sta nello confitto che s'alza il coperchio
Una tascha da llibri dipinta in detto armario
Molti libri di più ragione e di più proveditori passati e loro quaderni e libri di muralglia e della fighura di San Lodovicho e uno libro con bullette e choverta rossa di carte di cavretto che non v'è scritto su niente

MCCCCXXXI

Qui a ppiè e innanzi per alquante carte scriverrò le possesioni della Parte che ssono in Firenze. Im prima e ognuno arà il suo numero di che fia segniata, cioè quelle che lla Parte aveva nel 1426
.I. Uno palagio tutto in volta il primo palcho con una schala dipinta e coperta chon una sala grande dipinta e storiata con panche a ttre gradi pe' chapitani e a ij gradi pe' chollegi e spalliere di lengniame dipinte intorno a detta sala con ringhiera e più panche da sedere e porta che risponde in sul androne in sul quale è la nuova cancelleria e udienza e un uscio che risponde in sul verone che va agli agiamenti. Nelle quali chose sono più aconcimi e masserizie della Parte che tra lle masserizie si scriveranno.
Ed è segniato questo palagio di numero 1°
(cf. f. 41*r*: ".I. Uno palagio tutto in volta di sotto il primo palcho con sala dipinta e schala che va in su detto palagio cho' i suoi abituri di sopra e il terreno nel quale si raghunano i chapitani e collegi e i loro ghuelfi pe' loro bisongni, e di questo non se ne chava niente di pigione sennone d'alchune botteghe che vi sono sotto, che innanzi si scriveranno, segnato n.° .I.")
. . . .
[seguono altre proprietà in Firenze, nn.ii-lx]

MCCCCXXXI

Qui da ppiè e inanzi per alquante carte scriverrò le possessioni che lla Parte Guelfa a o aveva nel 1426 di quelle che ssono fuori di Firenze apresso a poche miglia [ff. 11*r*-13*v*: nn. lxi-lxxxvi, lxxxxvii]
. . . .

Orbatello MCCCCXXXI

Qui da ppiè e innanzi scriverrò i beni della Parte Guelfa apartenenti alla Limosina d'Orbatello. Im prima cioè:

[no.] lxxxvii [cf. fol. 84*v*]: uno luogho tutto murato intorno intorno chiamato Orbatello possto nel popolo di San Michele Bisdomini nel quale abituro s'entra e escie per una sola porta [fol. 84*v*: che è di rimpetto alla via della pergholal] ed èvi dentro una chiesa chiamata Santa Maria d'Orbatello con abituro per prete con chorte e pozo e orto serrato da llato e in detto luogho a due vie ed èvi xxvii chase in iii lati tutte con terreno e con palcho, le quali si danno a abitare [fol. 84*v*: a povere persone] per l'amore di dio [fol. 84*v*: e niente se n'è di pigione].

. . . .

[no.] lxxxxii: una chasa con ii chasette dietro con un pozzo e uno tiratoio da panni in terreno e in palcho e un tiratoio in terreno di chopertoio choperto chon uno orto murato intorno da iiii lati con alquanti frutti e un truogho al pozzo per inmolare panni posti nel popolo di Sam Piero Magiore di rimpetto al munistero di Cesstello, le quali chase et orto servono al tiratoio e per apigionare

. . . .

MCCCCXXXI

Qui dappiè e innanzi per alquanta carte scriverrò tutte le chiese che Io ò trovato esere censuarie della parte Guelfa e in che debbe dare di censo. E lla Parte n'è padrone [ff. 15*r*-16*v*; nn. lxxxxviii-cxvii, con 3 possessioni nn. cxviii-cxx: 'uno abbergho il quale si chiama l'abergho del chappello posto in Pisa', 'una chasa chon bottegha di sotto a uso di setaiuolo', 'uno bancho posto in merchato nuovo'.

MCCCCXXXII

[Danari che lla Parte ha in sul Monte]

La Parte Ghuelfa è creditore del Chomune di Firenze in nome dei Chapitani della Parte Ghuelfa che ssono e che pe' tempi saranno in fl. ventotto migliaia e cento ottanta cinque soldi dieci denari quattro a oro di monte chomuni de' quali n'è per debitore ridotto in una somma il Chomune di Firenze a libro nero segnato S a c. 112 e i detti danari si sono chomperati da più persone, cioè da ddì 17 di dicembre 1426 per insino a tutto lulglio 1432. E Io Nicchòlò di Gentile feci levare una scritta dagli scrivani del Monte della quantità de' danari e da chi e sarano comperati, perchè trovavo davano le paghe di fl. 26,199 e il Chomune non n'era a debitore in su' libri della Parte sennone di fl. 25,258 s.17 d.7 a oro, e riscontrando trovai vi mancavano a scrivere iiii partite in soma di fl. 940 s.12 d.3 a oro, i quali seranno comperati d'aprile 1429 da ppiù persone. Scrissine debitore il Chomune in iiii partite a libro nero segnato S a c. 40 sichè per tuto luglio 1432 la Parte à al Monte fl. xxviii mila clxxxv s.10 d.4 a oro.

Fra lla detta quantità ve ne fl. 1400 del Monte Novissimo di gennaio 1431 che non sse n'ebe le paghe. Era di magio 1432. Arannosi avere a setembre paghe .vi. di fl. 1400.

E fra lla detta quantità sono fl. 4374 s.16. d.3 a oro da gennaio 1427 innanzi, che hanno di paghe sostenute dal 1423 al 1427, fl. 218 s.14 a oro.

E sono tratti alle 153 mila.

E di poi la Parte aveva in sul Monte a gennaio 1431 fl. 26,785 che a aucci le paghe sostenute da gennaio 1427 al 1431 sono fl. 1339 s.5 a oro, vorrasi sapere alle quante migliaia fieno tratti.

MCCCCXXXIII

Qui apresso faremo richordo di tutte le posesioni che s'alocheranno in quello di Sa' Miniato e nel contado, in prima:

Più terre e pasture poste nel comune, di chollocharli...

. . . .

[ff. 19*r*-40*v* vuoti

[ff. 41*r*-138*r* proprietà in Firenze con aggiunte al 1436, numerate a cxx

[ff. 139*r*-176*r* vuoti].

5

LORENZO, THE MONTE AND THE SEVENTEEN REFORMERS

Public and private interest

Ever since Francesco Guicciardini suggested, in his *Storie fiorentine,* that Lorenzo planned to change the state in the year before he died and "make himself Gonfalonier for life" [1] Lorenzo's status and ambition have been a matter of debate and disagreement. From being the dominant figure in Italian politics and culture, his role has recently been reduced to that of patronage boss or *maestro di bottega.*[2] Like the *civilis princeps* of late republican Rome, his skill lay in successfully combining republican modesty with populist bread-and-circuses techniques to win favour. He sold grain at times of famine at cut-rate prices; he infiltrated local plebeian companies or *potenze*; he acted as marriage-broker and threw elaborate spectacles to amuse the people at large, not only plays and classical triumphs in the city but game-

---

A revised version of the paper published in *Lorenzo de' Medici Studi*, ed. G. C. Garfagnini, Florence, Olschki, 1992.

I would like to acknowledge with gratitude the generous help I have received from Professor Basil Yamy in interpreting the Monte accounts, which has made this study possible and freer of errors that it would otherwise have been; it is to him that I owe Table I on p. 175. I am also indebted to Caroline Elam for contributing the important reference to Lorenzo's account in the Libri Fabarum (note 55 below), to Richard Goldthwaite for valuable advice and help in reading the accounts, and to Nicolai Rubinstein and F. W. Kent for reading and commenting on the typescript. It is thanks to the support and hospitality of the Harvard University Center for Italian Renaissance Studies at the Villa I Tatti, Florence, that I was able to embark on and complete this work.

[1] *Storie fiorentine*, p. 71: "riformare lo stato e crearsi gonfaloniere a vita".

[2] On his political role, Rubinstein, *The Government of Florence* pp. 218-228, cf. *Lorenzo de' Medici: the formation of his statecraft,* London, The British Academy, 1978, and M. Mallett, *Diplomacy and War in later fifteenth-century Italy,* London, The British Academy, 1983, esp. pp. 283-288. On his role as patron, F. W. Kent, introductory essay in *Patronage, Art and Society in Renaissance Italy*, Oxford, Clarendon Press, 1987, esp. pp. 4-5, and *Ties of Neighbourhood and Patronage in Quattrocento Florence, Ibid.*, pp. 79-98.

hunts in the surrounding countryside for "more than 1500 people".[3] Although some citizens professed to be ashamed to participate in these "public shows and theatrical games" – at which "not only Caesar was present, who is considered wise, but all the other leading citizens",[4] – they clearly served to unify the city successfully under Lorenzo's leadership.

Yet Lorenzo's position cannot be explained simply in terms of personal influence and patronage. Although he rightly declared in 1481 that he was not "lord of Florence but a citizen with some authority",[5] his power was expanding into the spheres of justice and administration as well as politics, as the following examples illustrate. In 1481 three men who plotted to murder Lorenzo were summarily hanged by decree of the Otto di Guardia for conspiring against the state of Florence and one of its leading citizens. According to the Modenese ambassadors, writing to Ercole d'Este, the men died illegally since they had committed no crime and did not deserve the death penalty. Nevertheless, because they had plotted against the state, which was governed by means of Lorenzo, the Signoria together with the Council of Seventy had decided that it was the crime of lese-majesty: "and so they expressly declared that he who commits or shall commit an offence against Lorenzo will be guilty of the crime of lese-majesty, which indeed attributes honour and respect to Lorenzo."[6] In

---

[3] See A. WALLACE-HADRILL, *Civilis Princeps: between citizen and king*, «Journal of Roman Studies», LXXII, 1982, pp. 32-48. On Lorenzo as corn-broker, undercutting government prices, *Memorie* of ser GIUSTO D'ANGHIARI, Florence, Biblioteca Nazionale (BNF) II.II.127, ff. 107*r*-112*r* (December 1474-April 1475); on *potenze*, TREXLER, *Public Life in Renaissance Florence*, pp. 399-418; KENT, *Ties of Neighbourhood and Patronage*, p. 95: as marriage-broker, GUICCIARDINI, *Storie fiorentine*, p. 78; N. MICHELOZZI's *Notarile*, ASF, M 530; and N. VALORI's *Ricordanze*, BNF, MS Panc. 134, f. 8*v*; on shows and triumphs, TREXLER, *Public Life*, pp. 444-452, cf. GIUSTO D'ANGHIARI's *Memorie*, ff. 114*r*, 137*r*, describing Lorenzo's "bella caccia alle lepri presso a Firenze a sette miglia" on 12 November 1475, and favours received by Giusto d'Anghiari's son, "per mezzanità di lettere del Magnifico Lorenzo de' Medici", after a hunt provided for Piero de' Medici in 1480.

[4] Florence, Bibl. Riccardiana, MS. 915, ff. 197*v*-198*r*, a letter of Ugolino Verino describing the "spectacula scaenicosque ludos quod magni populi ac senatus frequentia sunt celebrati" on the Feast of San Giovanni in 1491, at which "Nec solum his Caesar interfuit, quod sapiens appellatur, sed omnes affuere proceres civitatis".

[5] Letter to Pierfilippo Pandolfini, 26 Nov. 1481, BNF, Autogr. Palat. VI, 25, LORENZO DE' MEDICI, *Lettere*, VI, ed. M. MALLETT, Florence, Giunti Barbèra, 1990, p. 100: "Io non sono signore di Firenze ma cittadino con qualche auctorità"; cf. the letter quoted by RUBINSTEIN, *Government of Florence*, p. 228, note 2.

[6] "Non poteano de iure morire... E impero la Signoria una cum li 70 determinarono che fosse crimen lesae maiestatis, dicendo che voleano torre la libertà e mutare questo stato, il

1488-89 a Gonfalonier of Justice, Neri Cambi, was deprived of office for life for not consulting Lorenzo before punishing four members of the government for unconstitutional behaviour, "which considerably displeased Lorenzo and the leading citizens of the regime".[7] And in 1491 a special command was issued to the chancery by the foreign affairs magistracy, the Otto di Pratica, that they were not to write abroad – to ambassadors, mandatories or to private citizens – about anything concerning the state, even if it was public, "and these words came from the mouth of Lorenzo the Magnificent".[8]

These examples suggest that Lorenzo was intervening more directly in the legal and constitutional procedures of the commune than is suggested by defining his position in purely patronal terms. As the man "through whom the state was governed", Lorenzo used institutional as well as private means of power to assert his authority, making it difficult to distinguish clearly between public and private interest in this period of transition from commune to principate. It is my purpose here to focus attention on one all-important but little-studied aspect of this problem by studying the work of the Seventeen Reformers. This commission was appointed for two brief periods, from 4 August 1481 to 24 July 1482, and from 15 July 1490 (with renewals) to 31 July 1491, on both occasions including Lorenzo as one of its members.[9] Such a short-term and intermittent body offers no more

---

quale si governava per il mezzo di Lorenzo, e così dichiararono expresse che chi offende Lorenzo, od offenderà, commetterà crimen lesae maiestatis, che pure tribuisce onore e riguardo a Lorenzo ...', Modenese ambassadors to Ercole d'Este, 9 June 1481, ed. A. CAPPELLI, *Lettere di Lorenzo de' Medici*, «Atti e Memorie d. RR. Dept. di storia patria per le province modenesi e parmensi», I, 1863, p. 255. The sentence of the Otto, handing the men over to the Captain of the Platea for arbitrary punishment, is in ASF Otto di Guardia repubb. 58, f. 66*r* (5 June 1481).

[7] TRIBALDO DE' ROSSI, *Ricordanze*, in *Delizie degli eruditi toscani*, ed. I. di SAN LUIGI, XXIII, Florence, 1786, pp. 245-246; cf. GUICCIARDINI, *Storie fiorentine*, pp. 69-70.

[8] ser ANTONIO DA BIBBIENA to ser ANDREA DA FOIANO, 23 July 1491, ed. A. GHERARDI in *Miscellanea fiorentina di erudizione e storia*, ed. I. DEL BADIA, II, 1902, p. 142.

[9] On its terms of appointment, notes 18 and 19 below; on its work, the fullest account remains that of LOUIS MARKS, *The development of the institutions of public finance at Florence during the last sixty years of the Republic, c. 1470-1530*, Oxford D. Phil., 1954, which he kindly allowed me to consult some years ago; cf. his article *The Financial Oligarchy in Florence under Lorenzo* in *Italian Renaissance Studies*, ed. JACOB, pp. 138, 142-145; RUBINSTEIN, *Government of Florence*, pp. 204-206, esp. 218, note 4, *The* «Storie fiorentine» *and the* «Memorie di famiglia» *by Francesco Guicciardini*, «Rinascimento», IV, 1953, pp. 190-192, 222-225 (App.). Both Marks and Rubinstein revise Guicciardini's "erroneous description" by underplaying the Seventeen's importance, in contrast to V. RICCHIONI, *La costituzione politica di Firenze ai tempi di Lorenzo il Magnifico*, Siena, 1913, pp. 79-85, according to whom the deliberations of the Seventeen Reformers reveal "fatti di una certa gravità" (p. 80); cf. E. CONTI, *L'Imposta diretta a Firenze nel Quattrocento (1427-1494)*, pp. 67-69.

than a probe to investigate our problem. Nevertheless it illuminates all-important – and hitherto obscure – areas to do with trade and economic policy, as well as Lorenzo's special financial problems as private unfunded head of state. It has recently been suggested that there is no obvious relationship between the Medici's private role as bankers and their public role as effective rulers of Florence''.[10] The records of the Monte Comune, with those of the Seventeen Reformers, provide the missing evidence of such a relationship. It is true that this evidence shows the Medici using power for political rather than economic ends, to dominate politics rather than the market. Nevertheless it shows that politics were far more closely related to economic issues in this period than has been recognised. So although it would be as anachronistic to call Lorenzo an absolutist ruler or his policies mercantilist as it would be to call him an early capitalist, the Seventeen Reformers suggest that the analogy may be helpful for understanding the direction in which Florence was developing under his control.

* * *

The crisis that brought the commission into being in 1481 was government insolvency in the aftermath of the Pazzi War, which caused a fall in the value of shares and non-payment of dowries, exacerbated by coinage problems and tax frauds, "the licence of citizens in not paying more taxes than they want to and frauds committed". There was nothing new in that, but because the war had been fought to preserve the Medici regime, after the abortive attempt to destroy it in 1478, the Medici were closely implicated in the cost of the war and the need for reparation afterwards. So they were now faced with personal bankruptcy as well as responsibility for the public debt. Private and public interests were also closely entangled in the financial administration of Florence. By the later fifteenth century, communal finances were almost entirely in the hands of the officials who ran the state-funded debt, or Monte Comune. Although these five Monte

---

[10] RICHARD GOLDTHWAITE, *The Medici and the World of Florentine Capitalism,* «Past and Present» CXIV, 1987, pp. 25-26, cf. 21-22. I would agree with Goldthwaite that the Medici do not on present evidence appear to have used power as modern capitalists "to reduce and even eliminate [economic] competition" (p. 3), but the subject needs much more investigation by co-relating Medici Bank and Monte Comune records.

Officials were publicly elected, with responsibility for communal finance and gabelles, they were usually rich merchants like the Medici themselves, chosen for their private wealth and ability to lend the commune large sums of money, which they expected to recover at profit from the Monte.[11]

This confusion of interest underlies the problem of interpreting the work of the Seventeen Reformers. They came into being on 4 August 1481 in response to the financial crisis. On 24-26 July the Signoria, its advisory Colleges (the Twelve Good Men and Sixteen Gonfaloniers) and the Council of Cento had been granted full powers *(pienissima et libera auctorità)* to administer the Monte, taxes and the Sea Consuls for one year. Ten days later they transferred these powers to a new commission of seventeen men, the "Reformers of the Monte and the Gabelles of the Commune of Florence", as they came to be called, consisting of the five Monte Officials plus twelve nominated members. All but two of the Seventeen were members of the Seventy, the new Medicean council, or 'senate', appointed after Lorenzo's triumphant return from Naples in April 1480 with peace in hand. It was, in other words, closely associated with the reassertion of Medici power after the crisis of the Pazzi conspiracy and war. And although the traditional method of appointing the twelve nominated members from the major and minor guilds in the four quarters of the city was adhered to, the proportion of minor guildsmen was reduced from the normal quarter to a sixth of the total.[12]

---

[11] There is no single study of the Monte Comune, but see A. MOLHO, *Florentine Public Finances in the Early Renaissance, 1400-1433,* Cambridge, Mass., Harvard University Press, 1971, and *L'amministrazione del debito pubblico a Firenze nel Quindicesimo secolo,* in *I ceti dirigenti nella Toscana del Quattrocento,* Florence, F. Papafava, 1987, pp. 191-207; Marks and Conti in note 9 above. The Monte bonds, too, confused public and private interest, since they were issued by the government to raise capital and taxes but were also bought and sold for profit on an open, fluctuating market.

[12] The members are listed in Appendix I (I) below. Two-thirds of those belonging to the Seventy were among its select "first thirty members"; the two non-members, Cosimo di Matteo Bartoli (from the quarter of Santa Maria Novella) and Maso di Niccolò degli Alessandri (from San Giovanni), were represented in the Seventy by other members of their families. The original members of the Seventy are listed by RUBINSTEIN, *Government*, pp. 316-317 (the select first 30 members on pp. 309-310), the later coopted members by R. PESMAN COOPER, *The Florentine Ruling Group under the «Governo Popolare», 1494-1512,* «Studies in Medieval and Renaissance History» VII, 1984-1985, p. 179. The office held no *divieto*, but no one could be chosen who had been drawn or elected to an office outside Florence. There were also restrictions preventing more than one member of a *consorteria* from being chosen. On 5 December 1481 the Monte Officials were renewed for a further year from 1 March 1482, *ibid.*, ff. 30*v*-31*r*.

When the commission was re-appointed in 1490, only five of its members had belonged to the earlier commission, four of the nominated members and Lorenzo de' Medici, initially appointed as a Monte Official.[13] One member, Piero Guicciardini, succeeded his father Jacopo who had died two months earlier. The remainder were new to it – although nearly all of them belonged to the Seventy.[14] The only artisan on both commissions was Antonio di Bernardo di Miniato Dini, proveditor of the Monte Officials and as we shall see, a key figure in the financial operations of the 1480s and early 1490s.[15]

Instead of being appointed for a year, the second commission was appointed initially for only seven-and-a-half months, until the end of February 1491, with a possible four-months' prorogation. By then, five of its members would have ended their year of office as Monte Officials. Perhaps they hoped for another exceptional renewal as members of the Seventeen; but if so, they were disappointed, for after two small extensions, they were replaced by five new officials on 1 March. Neither Lorenzo de' Medici nor Pagolantonio Soderini lost their membership of the Seventeen, however, since they exchanged positions with two former nominated members. At the same time the commission itself was renewed until the end of June, and then for

---

[13] Eight of the nominated members were given special responsibility for customs and harbour dues (Maso degli Alessandri and Bernardo del Nero), the salt gabelle (Bernardo Rucellai and Antonio di Miniato Dini), wine and contract gabelles (Niccolò Ridolfi and Piero Guicciardini), the Guelf Party and Sea Consuls (Maso degli Albizzi and Antonio Taddei), obviating the need for the four provisors of customs and gabelles joining their discussions, as they had done in 1481-82, Miscellanea Repubblicana (= Misc. Rep.) 109, f. 3*r*, Consiglio del Cento, Registro 3, f. 50*v*, Balìe 39, f. 9*v*.

[14] The five non-members of the Seventy were all there as Monte officials, see Appendix I (II) and note 16 below. The notary was again Giovanni Guidi. The 12 were "nominati per dominos priores" on 12 August 1490 (with Gianpagolo di Pagolo Lotti as Gonfalonier of Justice and Alamanno di Averardo Salviati one of the priors, G. Cambi, *Istorie*, in *Delizie*, XXI, p. 88). Pierfilippo Pandolfini exchanged places with Piero Alamanni when the latter went to Rome as ambassador in January 1491. Rubinstein points out Francesco Guicciardini's mistake in listing Jacopo as one of its members, since he died on "17 or 18 May 1490" (*Storie fiorentine*, p. 192; 17 May is the date given by Ugolino Verino, note 88 below, and in the records of the Otto di Pratica, ASF Otto di Pratica, Deliberazione 3, f. 30*r*: "Defunctus est magistratus de XVII maii 1490 quia die eadem obiit").

[15] When he was elected one of the Monte Officials on 2 Sept. 1494, Antonio was nevertheless confirmed in his office as proveditor, ASF, Cento Protocol 2, f. 336*r*: "Antonium Bernardi Miniatis Dini, qui tunc erat provisor officialium Montis et per presentem etiam in dicto suo officio confirmatus". Dini had been re-appointed proveditor since 1477, with special prorogations during his office as one of the Seventeen (on 5 Dec. 1481 for 2 years from 1 March 1482; on 31 Dec. 1490 f., "aliquibus in contrarium nonobstantibus", and again on 26 January 1494, Misc. Rep. 109, 31*r*; Cento 3, ff. 3*v*, 23*v*; Tratte 904, f. 131*r*, Tratte 905, f. 70*r*.

one more month, the maximum prorogation allowed when it was appointed in July 1490.[14] The replacement of the Monte Officials and the second prorogation of the commission in June were achieved only by using the special prerogative powers of the Reformers themselves, by-passing all the normal legislative procedures – including discussion by the twelve Procurators and the all-important Council of Seventy – "because it seemed to the leading citizens that it should be discussed according to the procedures for Monte matters and taxes".[17] The careful but indignant note by a chancery scribe recording this by-pass provides its own comment on what he evidently interpreted as the derogation of traditional procedures by the special authority of the Seventeen Reformers.

Although the authority of the Signoria, Colleges and council of Cento remained sovereign and could, if desired, be used to override the Seventeen's decisions, the commission nevertheless enjoyed full powers in its area of competence.[18] Everything it decided within its year of office was valid and had the force of law, "whether in species or genus, tacitly or expressly, in perpetuity or temporarily... even if it was something which it was said should be expressly and specially

---

[16] All the prorogations are carefully listed in Balìe 39, f. 8*r-v*; the special authority given to the Signoria and Cento was prorogued 5 times, initially for 1 year (19 July 1482, 28 June 1483, 31 July 1484), then for 5 years (18 Sept. 1484 and 12 February 1489), *ibid.*, f. 8*r*. When the 5 new Monte officials were elected, Pagolantonio Soderini and Lorenzo de' Medici changed places with two of the 12 nominated members, Niccolò Ridolfi and D. Angelo Niccolini, and Bartolomeo Bartolini, Angelo Miniati and Jacopo Salviati were replaced by Jacobo Pucci, Francesco della Scarfa and Filippo Valori. Maso degli Albizzi died in office as *proposto* in 13 April 1491 (Balìe 39, ff. 8*r-v*, 148*v*; Tratte 83, ff. 3*r*, 198*v*; Cento 3, ff. 2*r*, 3*r-5r*; Cento Prot. 2, ff. 242*r*, 245*r*-246*r*, 249*v*, 250*v*, 265*v*).

[17] Cento Prot. 2, f. 250*v* (31 Dec. 1490): "Nota: Ista provisio [proroguing the election of the Monte Officials until 15 January, 'quod in tam breve tempus dicta electio perfici non potest'] non firmatur per procuratores neque deliberatur per 70 viros, neque firmatur per auditores, neque deliberatur per dominos et collegia per 32 fabas nigras sed per duas partes, quia visum est primis civibus quod deliberetur secundum formam traditam pro deliberationibus ad Montem et conditionibus spectantibus, quarum auctoritas est in consilio del Cento etiam cum auctoritate committendi eam, cuius virtute deputati sunt xvii reformatores cum ea quam habent auctoritate, quamvis alias in huiusmodi, etiam stante dicta auctoritate, fuerit facta deliberatio inter procuratores et 70, et dominos et Collegas per 32 fabas nigras"; f. 264*v* (28 June 1491): "Non fuit deliberata per 12 procuratores neque per lxx cives".

[18] They enjoyed the "pienissima et libera auctorità et podestà" initially given to the Cento, Signoria and Colleges in matters concerning the Monte, Camera del Comune, Gabelles and Sea Consuls, and their decisions enjoyed the force of communal laws, although "rimanga l'auctorità intera ... ne' Signori et Collegi et consiglio del Cento"), Misc. Rep. 109, ff. 1*v*-2*r* (quoting from the law transferring to the Cento the powers now delegated to the Seventeen Reformers in ASF Provvisioni 172, ff. 81*v*-84*v*, 24 July 1481, in CONTI, *L'imposta*, pp. 67-68), 3*v*; Cento 3, ff. 1*v*, 49*r-v*; cf. RUBINSTEIN, *Government of Florence*, p. 204, and note 20 below.

mentioned"; and "to provide a clear record for all time", its deliberations were to be drawn up ('rogated') by the Notary of the Riformagioni or his coadiutors and copied into the ordinary book used for the deliberations of the Cento – as though they were communal laws or statutes "in public books", as it was expressed in 1490.[19] Although this did not happen in 1481-82, when a separate (but incomplete) register was kept, the deliberations of the 1490-91 commission were recorded, as prescribed, in the second half of the appropriate vellum volume of the deliberations of the Cento.[20] Legitimated within the leather covers of the "Liber Tertius Consilii del Cento" it is easy to overlook the fact that these sovereign 'laws' represented the will of a minimum of only twelve men during their one year of office.

Moreover, despite being restricted to fiscal matters, with special responsibility for the Monte and taxes, there were in practice few areas excluded from the purview of the Seventeen. They were empowered to absolve criminals from legal sentences, which often involved the death penalty.[21] They were made responsible for granting the Jews licences to practise usury in certain shops in Florentine territory.[22] In both cases the motive was taxes for the Monte, but the

---

[19] Misc. Rep. 109, f. 2*r*: everything they do within the next year, "in spetie o in genere, tacitamente o expressamente, im perpetuo o a tempo, etiam se fussi tal cosa che si dicessi essersene dovuta fare expressa et spetiale mentione etiam in individuo, la quale insino da hora s'intenda essere et sia per facta, vaglia et tengha et appieno s'observi ... come se tutto fussi suto particularmente et distintamente proveduto, ordinato et diliberato pe' consigli oportuni della città di Firenze observate tutte le debite solemnita ... Et di tutte tali deliberationi sia rogato l'uficiale et notaio delle Riformagioni o suoi coadiutori, et faccine scriptura nel libro ordinario che si tiene in palagio dove si scrivano l'ordinarie deliberationi del Consiglio del Cento, aciòche per ogni tempo se ne possa havere chiara notitia"; cf. Cento 3, ff. 1*v*, 49*v*, that the Seventeen may "liberamente come vorranno ... provvedere, ordinare et deliberare et provisioni, ordini et deliberationi fare ... et tali deliberationi si descrivino alle riformagioni in libri publici".

[20] I.e. Misc. Rep. 109 and Cento 3, ff. 49*r*-137*r*. They voted by a two-thirds' majority, ie. by 12 black beans or 14 when the proveditors were voting with them (Misc. Rep. 109, f. 3*r*; Cento 3, ff. 1*v*, 49*v*).

[21] ASF, Misc. Rep. III.87, a gathering of c. 77 absolutions, now titled "Deliberazioni dei Riformatori del Monte e delle Gabelle del Comune di Firenze", 22 Nov. 1481-18 July 1482, all involving a fine, "per convertendum in Montis diminutionem", with small payments also to the Innocenti, the Duomo and the notary of the Camera; see also Monte Comune 884 (Protocol of the Reformers), ff. 41*r*-42*v*.

[22] E.g. Monte Comune 884, ff. 2*r*, 18*r*, 20*v*, 21*v*, 23*r*-24*r*, 25*r-v*; Misc. Rep. 109, ff. 15*r-v*, 19*v*-20*r*; Cento 3, ff. 64*v*, 136*r*, 139*r*-144*v* (the last, licences and *capitoli* granted on 15 Dec. 1491 by the five Monte Officials after the end of the second commission, concluding with an extract from the letter of the Florentine ambassador in Rome, Piero Alamanni, dated 31 Dec. 1491 (f. 144*v*). This assured the Otto di Pratica of what he had already told them, that "insino del mese d'agosto" last, Innocent VIII had absolved all citizens involved in the new

Reformers found themselves exercising the legal prerogative elsewhere reserved for kings and princes. So although Guicciardini exaggerated their authority in suggesting they replaced the councils altogether, "to escape the difficulty and bore of laws and councils", he correctly perceived how unrestricted their ad-hoc powers were.[23]

This is not the place to discuss the Reformers' work in detail, but some idea of its scope is needed to assess their wider role, especcially in relation to Lorenzo. On one hand, their attempt to combine fiscal and administrative control with trade incentives in an enlarged trading area anticipates some features of state-based economic policies; and the topics they dealt with – funded-debt, coinage, taxes, trade and regional policies – all had an important place on the agendas of early-modern governments. On the other, the time they devoted to favours and special cases, including Lorenzo's, shows how difficult it is to distinguish their economic activities from their equally absorbing and time-consuming labours as "Big Men" and patronal bosses. When public and private interests were so closely intertwined, it is not surprising to find Lorenzo and his banking friends invoking the concept that the ruler's private interest and the public interest of the state were identical.

The immediate problem concerned taxes and the over-expanded Monte.[24] Faced with huge carrying charges on the Monte Comune and the payment of dowries that far outstripped the initial investment, the Reformers' two strategies were to reduce Monte Comune bonds by making citizens use them to pay taxes and to reintroduce the 'radical measure', first introduced in 1478, of paying off dowries

"condocta delli hebrei"; but "ad tollendum scrupulum", Piero had returned for confirmation of the absolution of citizens involved in "consiglare o favorire quocumquemodo la conducta facta delli hebrei", which the pope granted, "vivo vocis oraculo".

[23] *Storie fiorentine*, p. 70: "per fuggire la difficultà ed el tedio delle provisioni e de' consigli ... che potessino disporre di tutte le cose della città tanto quanto poteva tutto el popolo di Firenze"; cf. his *Memorie di famiglia* and *Ricordi autobiografici, Opere inedite*, ed. G. Canestrini, X, Florence, 1867, pp. 54, 62, "plenissima autorità e balia, e quanta ha il popolo di Firenze".

[24] Conti, *L'Estimo*, pp. 66-71: in 1482, with dowry repayments 29 months in arrears and interest payments of fl. 280,000 due, the total anticipated Monte income was fl. 290,000 (p. 68). Cf. Marks *Financial Oligarchy*, pp. 141-145; Molho, *L'amministrazione*; Brown, *The Guelf Party in fifteenth-century Florence*, pp. 135-136 above; and in anticipation of their full-scale study of the Monte delle Doti, A. Molho and J. Kirshner, *The Dowry Fund and the Marriage Market in Early Quattrocento Florence*, «Journal of Modern History», L, 1978, pp. 403-438.

in instalments.[25] Although the Dowry Fund has received more attention than the Monte Comune in these years, it was the tax problem that initially claimed the Reformers' attention and, for reasons that will become apparent, must also claim ours. Deprived of interest payments, many citizens were unable to pay the heavy war-taxes of 1478-80 or the two newly-imposed taxes, the *decima scalata* and the *sesto dispiacente sgravato*.[26]

So after offering a series of inducements to pay tax arrears, the Reformers in September 1481 reduced and consolidated all outstanding Monte interest payments owed since 1478 in a single fund, to be repaid by instalments, one third each year over three years (the *terzi* we shall later encounter in connection with Lorenzo). These payments could only be made to those who had paid all their taxes, and if any one needed to enjoy his credits before the appointed time, he could alienate or 'contract' them (at a price later fixed at 1s per florin).[27]

This fiscal strategy – which doubtless reflected the influence on the committee of the five Monte Officials – was accompanied by an assortment of other measures to increase taxes. Because non-payment of interest credits and dowries was forcing many citizens into debt and political disqualification, the Reformers 'humanely' exempted some citizens whose wealth had been reduced, "both to preserve the citizens of the city and make more taxpayers for the future", as well as some poor men who had inherited "old and complicated" debts.[28] But other tax defaulters were dealt with more severely. Husbands and sons were made responsible for the tax debts of wives and mothers,

---

[25] On the development of the 7%, 4% and 3% Monti delle Doti from 1478 to 1491, see MARKS, *Financial Oligarchy* above and *La crisi finanziaria a Firenze dal 1494 al 1502*, «Archivio storico italiano», CXII, 1954, pp. 60-63. An interesting example of the Reformers' practical and discretionary use of power is their decision that, although there was no law to this effect, the unpaid dowry of a bride who died should go not to her father's family but "either to the commune or to the son-in-law", since it was the husband who had paid the tax, the cost of his wife's illness and her funeral, ASF Monte Comune, 884, f. 16 ter.

[26] See especially L. MARTINES, *Forced Loans: Political and Social Strain in Quattrocento Florence*, «Journal of Modern History» LX, 1988, pp. 300-311, reviewing CONTI, *L'estimo*, who discusses these taxes on pp. 278-293.

[27] ASF, Misc. Rep. 109, ff. 4*r-v*, 12*v*-15*r* (7 August, 13 and 15 Sept. 1481).

[28] Misc. Rep. 109, ff. 4*r* (7 August 1481), 12*v*-13*r* (13 Sept.), 24*r*-25*r* (20 Nov.); Cento 3, ff. 82*r*-84*v* (21 June 1491): "volendo ... humanamente procedere per conservare i cittadini alla città et fare assai poste pagante per l'advenire"; Cento 3, f. 79*r* (16 June 1491): "vecchie, intrigate et aviluppate... in grave danno de' poveri huomini, e quali sono prima gravati che uditi".

and they were prohibited from attempting to reduce their tax assessment and escape political disqualification by declaring their possession in their womenfolk's returns.[29] Notaries were disqualified for failing to report or concealing the "true form of contracts" with "circuitous language and verbosity"; customs officers were disciplined; and to prevent "new and ignoble" men changing their names in tax returns in order to obtain offices, laws insisting on 30 years' tax payment were reinforced, with better alphabetized records.[30]

City taxes were also imposed for the first time on non-citizens living in Florence, people who had been taxed neither in the city nor in the contado, either because they were foreigners by origin or because they had known "how to conceal themselves". Such people, the Reformers declared, as foreigners or because they practised "low manual crafts or worse", or were "civil or guild servants", did not deserve to be granted citizen-rights. An annual tax was to be imposed on them, to be registered in a separate book called the "Libro de Taxati".[31]

Closely related to the fiscal crisis was the problem of coinage. The depreciation of silver against gold coinage and the adulteration of the 'black' coinage, the bronze *quattrini* in everyday use, was the subject of the Reformers' second meeting, held in the Audience Chamber of the Signoria on 8 August 1481. A month later, when Lorenzo and Antonio di Miniato Dini were chairmen or *proposti*, a group of eighteen merchants was invited to discuss the problem, some of whom later joined five Reformers in the Mint, "to provide a remedy".[32] Their

---

[29] Misc. Rep. 109, ff. *5r-6v* (17 August 1481), repeating laws of 1431 and 1435, with exemptions, e.g. ff. *54v*, *64v*, *98r-v*.

[30] Misc. Rep. 109, ff. *54v* (30 Jan. 1482): "quegli palliando, et occultando con diversi ambiti d'orationi et assai parole la vera forma del contracto'; Cento 3, ff. *55v-59r* (13 Jan. 1491) "Doganae plura', cf. ff. *65v-66v* (24 Jan. 1491); Misc. Rep. 109, ff. *93r-95v* (24 July 1482), requiring a "novum librum per quarteria et alphabetum" for attestations; the exception for ser Piero da Bibbiena is discussed below, note 52.

[31] Cento 3, ff. *123v-124r* (27 July 1491): "per havere saputo ochultarsi ... exercitii vili manuali o peggio o famigli d'uficio o d'arte et non è bene siano anumerati tra cittadini fiorentini". They also included inhabitants of the contado who had lived in Florence for more than twenty years and were matriculated in one of the twenty-one guilds, or who had lived there for thirty years without matriculation, or whose father and they together had lived there for more than 20 years and had spent 300 fiorini larghi on a site or building in Florence. If taxed in the city, they were exempt from contado taxes and were to be allowed dowries on marriage as for citizens.

[32] ASF, Misc. Rep. 109, ff. *4v-5r* (8 August), Monte Comune 884, f. *4r-v* (6 Sept. 1481). The *merchatores* whose opinion was sought 'supra monetis', at the suggestion of Giovanni Bonsi*,

attempts at reform – by prohibiting the circulation of foreign coins in the Florentine state and revaluing the *quattrino* in 1481-82, and by introducing a new *quattrino bianchito* in 1491 – incurred great hostility, since they meant a reduction in the value of the old coinage in which citizens paid their taxes, as well as a reduction in salary for many communal officials.[33] So in June 1491 the commission's full powers ("non sola ampla ma amplissima") were invoked to appoint as Conservators of the Mint four of its most prestigious members, among them Lorenzo.[34] But instead of emulating towns in southern Germany and northern Italy by producing new large silver coinage, like the heavy coins bearing ducal portraits that Venice, Milan and Ferrara had been producing since the 1470s, the Conservators chose to retain Florence's three medieval coins, the florin, the *grosso* and the *quattrino* and her old-fashioned monies of account. Far from saving "the pilotless boat from shipwreck" by restoring Florence to her former primacy in money matters through their wisdom, as had been optimistically promised, their habitual compromise between reform and conservatism made the city look distinctly 'demodée' by the end of the century.[35]

---

were the following (in the order of speaking): Agostino Biliotti, Guido Guiducci*, Tanai de' Nerli, Giovanni Lanfredini*, Ugo Martelli, Lionardo Manelli*, Piero Mellini*, Averardo Salviati*, Lorenzo Ricasoli, Lodovico Masi, Bernardo Rinieri, Giovanni de' Bardi, Niccolò de' Nobili*, Francesco della Scarfa, Lorenzo Spini, Francesco Girolami, Piero Capponi* and Antonio Sasso. Of these, 8 (with asterisks) were deputed "a intendere e' remedii della moneta e raghunirsi alla Zeccha", together with Niccolò Martelli, Francesco Sassetti and 4 Reformers (B. Gianfigliazzi, P. Pandolfini, Antonio Taddei and Jacopo Guicciardini), *ibid.*, f. 5*r*, cf. Balìa 39, f. 146*v*. The *proposti* are listed in Appendix I (III) below.

[33] Misc. Rep. 109, ff. 4*v*-5*r* (8 August 1481); 18*r-v* (13 Oct. 1481); 25*v*-26*r* (21 Nov. 1481); Cento 3, ff. 52*r* (8 Sept. 1490); 69*r* (28 Feb. 1491); 69*v*-72*r* (23 Mar. 1491); 103*v* (30 June 1491); 129*r-v* (29 July 1491). Cf. GUICCIARDINI, *Storie fiorentine*, p. 70; M. BERNOCCHI, *Le monete della repubblica fiorentina*, III, Florence, Olschki, 1976, pp. 223-230; MARKS, *Financial Oligarchy*, p. 143; CONTI, *L'Imposta*, p. 363, RICCHIONI, *Costituzione*, pp. 76-79. In 1481 the *grosso* (6s. 8d.) was worth 79% of its 1252 value in *lire*, compared with 78.1% in 1471. In 1490-91 it was revalued at 5s. 6d. instead of 6s. 8d. to the pound; while the new *quattrino bianchito*, (4d.) was worth 75.23% and the old *quattrino nero* (now 3d.) 74.45% of its 1252 value in pounds, compared with 80.84% in 1472 (BERNOCCHI, pp. 222-229). In 1490-91 foreign coins were given fixed values until February 1492 when they were to be assayed and revalued. On Florence's coinage and these reforms, see now also G. MANDICH, *I fiorini di conto a Firenze nel 1465-1531*, «Archivio storico italiano», CXLVIII, 1990, esp. pp. 37-48.

[34] Cento 3, f. 103*v* (cf. RICCHIONI, pp. 78-79), appointing for 5 years (renewable, without salary or *divieto*) Lorenzo de' Medici and Niccolò Ridolfi to represent the Calimala and the Merchants' Guild, Bernardo Rucellai and Piero Guicciardini to represent the Bankers' Guild.

[35] According to C. M. CIPOLLA, *La Moneta a Firenze nel Cinquecento*, Bologna, Il Mulino, 1987, pp. 9-14, Florence had to wait till 1503 before producing a silver coin comparable to that of these other states. On the Conservators, see Cento 3, f. 103*v*: that whereas Florence

Underlying the immediate financial crisis was the wider question of the government's relationship with its subject territories. Although Florentine overlordship is now generally acknowledged to have been less "oppressive and rancorous" to small villages and communes than that of the cities who formerly controlled them, it nevertheless contributed to the growing economic disparity between the capital city and its 'empire'.[36] The Reformers therefore introduced changes in customs and port taxes which attempted to stimulate trade within the territory by breaking down old restrictions.[37] In June 1491 they passed a series of laws to encourage immigration and resettlement in Pisa by granting privileges to settlers and reducing the taxes on merchandise, abolishing them altogether on special products like soap and berets. As Mallett suggests, the policy of encouragement may represent "a move towards a planned economy with certain industries allotted to the subject cities, even at the expense of parallel industries in Florence". But as many of the immigrants were Florentine citizens, like the beret-maker Piero Vaglienti, and the tax reductions also favoured Florentine industries such as cloth-making, it seems likely the reforms worked as much in favour of the capital as the region.[38]

The problem of the contado was less easily resolved. The Reform-

---

was formerly a city of "tanta prudentia et senno et dove siano quelli acuti ingegni e quali in tutte le cose sono consueti, maxime in simili cose di monete, trapassare et di lungo avanzare gli altri", it was now like a "nave ... senza nochiere et che si navichi per perduti", hence its need of "huomini di grande auctorità ... et di molto senno per riparare".

[36] On the use of the word "empire", see Misc. Rep. 109, f. 18*r* (13 Oct.): "la cipta di Firenze et suo imperio"; 55*r* (30 Jan. 1482): "fuori della Città di Firenze et suo imperio infra le Cento miglia"; Cento 3, f. 78*r* (16 June 1491): "fuori de' terreni dello imperio fiorentino", 94*v*, etc. (the word is also used by the 30 Reformers of the Monte in 1458-59, eg. Misc. Rep. 110, ff. 16*v*, 17*r-v*). On the relationship of capitals and subject territories, G. CHITTOLINI, *Ricerche sull'ordinamento territoriale del dominio fiorentino agli inizi del secolo XV*, in *La Formazione dello Stato regionale e le Istituzioni del Contado*, Turin, Einaudi, 1979, pp. 292-352, esp. pp. 310-311; and on their economic disparity, D. HERLIHY and C. KLAPISCH-ZUBER, *Tuscans and their families. A Study of the Florentine Catasto of 1427*, Engl. transl., New Haven and London, Yale University Press, 1985, pp. 93-130; CONTI, *L'Imposta*, pp. 24-30; and on the earlier period, MOLHO, *Florentine Public Finances*.

[37] Cento 3, ff. 58*r* (13 Jan. 1491); 61*v*-63*v* (21 Jan.), 63*v*-64*r* (22 Jan.), 73*v*-74*r* (4 June); 91*v*-92*v* (21 June); cf. 97*r* (28 June). There are also measures relating to Bibbiena, Certaldo, Volterra, Arezzo, etc. on ff. 98*r-v*, 106*r*-108*r* (30 June 1491); 115*r*-116*r* (27 July 1491).

[38] Cento 3, ff. 88*v*-94*v* (21 June 1491), cf. M. MALLETT, *Pisa and Florence in the Fifteenth Century*, in *Florentine Studies*, ed. RUBINSTEIN, pp. 403-441 (with a reference to the Seventeen Reformers on p. 425). There is also legislation concerning Pisa in Monte Comune 884, f. 12*v*, and Misc. Rep. 109, ff. 20*r-v*, 40*v*-51*r*, 70*r* (6-10 Nov. 1481, 8 Jan. & 9 July 1482), Cento 3, ff. 73*r-v* (23 Mar. 1491), 114*r*-115*r* (27 July 1491). PIERO VAGLIENTI's *Storia dei suoi tempi, 1492-1514* is edited by G. BERTI, M. LUZZATI and E. TONGIORGI, Pisa, Nistri-Lischi e Pacini, 1982.

ers' first move was to implement the census of contadini proposed but abandoned in 1480, when the tax officials responsible for collecting the 'enlightened' graduated tax, the *decima scalata*, were ordered to discover property not taxed before, especially belonging to 'comitatini'.[39] The imposition of an estimo in 1487-90 once more highlighted the "vexed and troubled" state of the contado, especially in the Casentino, the Mugello and the Valdarno, where organised brigandage was rampant.[40] This made reform a priority in 1490. Accordingly on 21 June 1491 the new Reformers introduced a series of measures to mitigate life in the countryside, reducing the poll tax, establishing fixed rates for the repayment of debts, and relaxing restrictions on inhabitants of the old contado practising trades or crafts in Florence (excluding notaries and lawyers, and workers in white foreign wool). Police officers were to be deputed by the Otto di Guardia to keep law and order in the troubled areas. At the same time, moved now by humanity and "some pity" towards the peasants they had threatened in 1481 with "atrocious punishment", they decreed that, "except for reason of state", criminals could be pardoned by the officials "or commissaries" of the Estimo, provided they made peace and paid fines.[41] As another gesture of humanity combined with shrewd fis-

[39] E. Conti, *I catasti agrari della repubblica fioreintina e il catasto particellare toscano*, Rome, Istituto storico italiano per il Medio Evo, 1966, p. 75 and n. 8, cf. *L'Imposta*, p. 282, and the preface to the law which contrasts "L'oppinione della nuova graveza" that "ha tanto intenebrato la città" with "il contento universale" which "sarebbe a llume" (p. 281); G. Canestrini, *La scienza e l'arte di stato*, Florence, 1862, pp. 232-233. On the new census, to be prepared by local officials, with two of the oldest and most expert members of each commune, see MC 884, 1*r* (undated but immediately following a heading dated 1481): "Forma lecterarum scribendarum ... pro animalibus habendis", followed on f. 1*v* by the same, "pro habendis bonis immobilibus", requiring now an account of "il vero de' beni immobili" of all inhabitants of the Florentine jurisdiction, citizens, religious and subjects: "Et sopratutto punirai atrocemente que' lavoratori che tali beni lavorassino et il vero non ne dessino"; There are lists of officials to whom letters were sent and who replied on ff. 43*r*-46*v*.

[40] ASF, Cento 2, ff. 105*v*-111*r* (3 Aug. 1487): "Pro catasto sive estimo comitationum", etc. On the 1487 estimo and its attempts to defeat the tax evasion of earlier returns, Conti, *Catasti agrari*, pp. 100-102, 116.

[41] Cento 3, ff. 84*v*-88*r* (21 June 1491): "Estimi Comitatus. Correctio quaedam" beg. "Atteso le doglenze facte universalmente da gran numero di contadini et anchora da cittadini, mossi da compassione di molti errori commessi nella impositione dell'estimo": ff. 99*r*-100*v* (30 June 1491): "Pro Comitatinis", beg. "Atteso quanto sia il contado affannato", f. 104*r*-*v* (30 June): "Et parere pure cosa humana usare qualche volta qualche misericordia ... stringendogli nondimeno a qualche pagamento maxime in favore del publico, accioche al tutto el delicto non resti impunito, et che la pietà et misericordia usata loro, se fusse troppo absoluta et larga non generasse captivvo exemplo ... per queste cagioni et altre ... et maxime per repopolare e' luoghi della jurisdictione ... et liberando [tali subditi] da superflue et assai grande spese, providorono", etc.; "excepto per cagione di stato".

calism, the Reformers – because the Colleges (the Twelve and Sixteen) now "rarely convened for non-urgent business" – allowed the Signoria alone to grant contadini and foreigners passes and licences, to prevent them hanging about Florence and eventually leaving with neither pass nor money, since they had used up what they needed for stamp-duty to keep themselves alive.[42]

Despite the Reformers' attempts to arbitrate fairly between Florence and her empire, it was not always easy to reconcile their conflicting interests, as we can see from the Reformers' intervention in June 1490. In May 1488 a tax had been imposed by the Wool Guild on all wool and cloth entering the Florentine dominion – exempting only wool from England – in order to pay for an ensign for the Sultan of Egypt, "to make him more favourable to Florentine merchants there".[43] This was a cause close to the heart of the export-orientated Wool Guild as well as to Lorenzo's, who had been personally involved in negotiations with the Sultan at this time. Nevertheless, Lorenzo and his company had suffered by being charged taxes on wool imports from England, despite the verbal exemption: and he was clearly the main beneficiary of the Reformers' honourable decision to respect this verbal promise by authorising the repayment of these taxes through the Monte, as well as the repayment of the cost of presents from the Florentine mandatories to the chancellor of England and other lords – which amounted to about 2,500 fiorini larghi, "a good sum of money", as the Reformers commented.[44]

---

[42] Cento 3, f. 97*v* (30 June 1491): "quae non urgentibus negociis raro convocantur ... Quod ultra incommodum privatorum non cedit in honorem summi magistratus et vertitur in detrimentum introituum camere armorum".

[43] Cento 3, f. 54*v* (20 Dec. 1490): "taxa grossoni unius pro quilibet panno garbi", 2 gr. "pro qualibet balla lanae ... preterquam de insula angliae ... pro donando Turcho ... ut redderetur magis propitius mercatoribus florentinis quam tunc esset, quia dicebat se solitum honorari in accessu galearum florentinarum, et se tali honore privatum, cum illuc tales galee non accederent". On Lorenzo's close involvement in the Florentine treaty with the Sultan of Egypt in November 1488, S. M. Stern, *Documents from Islamic Chanceries*, Oxford, Cassirer, 1965, pp. 39-51; F. Babinger, *Lorenzo de' Medici e la Corte Ottomano*, "Archivio storico italiano", CXXI, 1963, pp. 305-361.

[44] Cento 3, f. 55*r-v* (20 Dec. 1490): "et volendo, come cosa conveniente, che la fede data, etiam a parole, da' mandatari fiorentini, sortisca effecto", 62*v* (21 Jan. 1491): "E perchè da due anni in qua s'è tenuto certa praticha in Inghilterra per Tommaso ... Portinari et Christofano ... Spini per commissione della Signoria e di consiglio di buono numero di principali et savi cittadini per fare che le lane d'Inghilterra, delle quali haveva bisognio Italia, se ne faciessi stapula a Pisa, s'è pagato buona somma di danari pel Monte a chi di là ne ha tali mandatarii servito"; they were paid 798 fiorini larghi, £ 9327.10 di grossi in cash on 18 Feb. 1491, ASF Monte Comune 1580, f. 773 left. Cf. Ricchioni, *Costituzione*, pp. 81-88: "tra i rinborsati figu-

It is difficult to describe the Seventeen as hard-line reformers and their overall lack of success suggests their importance should not be exaggerated.[45] Nevertheless, thanks to their wide powers and area of competence, they were able to adopt a discretionary and mediatory role in introducing changes and compromise. They granted many favours and dispensations to individual citizens, including a concession (while Lorenzo was chairman) to the son of one of its members, Francesco di Filippo Valori, which allowed him to reserve his sortition as Podestà of Prato until his return from embassy in Milan, "because it seemed expedient, ... and unfitting for him to suffer hardship for the public interest, when both matters can be settled satisfactorily".[46] This raises the question of the political scope of the Seventeen Reformers and the position among them of Lorenzo himself.

Lorenzo de' Medici's name recurs as a leitmotiv. He was granted favours at Poggio a Caiano in January 1491 by being allowed to acquire, by way of exchange, a certain *casetta* belonging to the commune, "which would be useful to Lorenzo de' Medici without damage

---

ra primo Lorenzo de' Medici e i suoi compagni di banco, che l'avevano regolarmente pagato dal 28 giugno all'8 dicembre 1489". The list of English merchants trading through Lorenzo's company, with amounts of wool imported and taxes paid, is edited by RICCHIONI, pp. 82-84, note 1. The revised treaty with England dated 15 April 1490 (referring to Portinari's and Spini's earlier informal agreement about taxes) is published by G. PAGNINI, *Della decima e delle altre gravezze della moneta e della mercatura de' fiorentini*, II, Lisbon and Lucca, 1765, pp. 288-289.

45 CONTI, *L'Imposta*, p. 68: "Questa commissione prese molti provvedimenti settoriali, senza tuttavia eliminare le cause di fondo del deficit del Monte", quoting the Seventeen Reformers' despairing comments on 23 July 1482 that having come to the end of their office, "i casi del Monte" remained "in chattivo essere", dowry payments 29 months in arrears and their commitments ever increasing; cf. the law reappointing the Seventeen Reformers in 1490 (Cento 3, f. 49*r*, 15 July 1490), which complains of "molti disordini, molte cattive consuetudini, anzi corruptele pessime, molte negligentie vi si usano pe' ministri" concerning the gabelles, so that "l'entrate sono assai diminuite' but the 'uscita del Monte non è sciemata, anzi ... è cresciuta assai". If true, this is in striking contrast to the trends described by Molho in the period 1411-1511 (*L'amministrazione del debito pubblico*, above, pp. 192-193), but the figures he gives for Monte credits and gabelles need substantiating from the Monte Comune "libri grandi".

46 "Quod expediens iudicatur... et non decere eum ex causa publica consequi danna, cum possit utrique rei commode satisfieri", Cento 3, f. 99*r* (30 June 1491). In July-September 1491 Francesco Valori acted as procurator for the Medici company in Pisa and in 1492 as Piero's procurator to elect the Spedalingo del Ceppo di Prato, ASF Notarile antecos. 10200, ff. 326, 332-335, 358. There are other favours to citizens in ASF, Misc. Rep. 109, ff. 25*r*, 26*r-v*, 64*v*-68*r*, 97*r*-99*r*; Cento 3, ff. 67*v*, 92*v*, 97*v*, 108*v*, 110*r*-112*r*, 126*v*, 132*v*-137*r*, including one to the sons of Antonio Martelli, who had never been repaid money owed to their father "per cagione d'inchanti di galee"; transferring to the Monte Comune 1000 florins owed to them by the Sea Consuls, the Reformers now allowed them to use this money to pay half their taxes, Cento 3, ff. 133*v*-134*r* (29 July 1491), Monte Comune 1581, f. 714 left, etc.

to the commune".[47] During the last week of the commission, when Lorenzo was himself chairman with Antonio di Miniato Dini, the Reformers dispensed him from paying any tax on property transferred to him by guilds, hospitals or pious foundations to build a new road [Via Laura] and houses running from SS. Annunziata to the Cestello, since it was done for the "public honour" and the benefit of private citizens.[48] Two days earlier, also during Lorenzo's chairmanship with Dini, it was decided that the terminus for paying the tax on dowry contracts should date from the completion of payment of the dowry, not the consummation of the marriage, with a special dispensation for any citizen promised a dowry "of six thousand florins or more" for his foreign wife who had not been paid the full amount: such a citizen was not in debt, the Reformers declared, and did not have to pay the full tax on it until it was paid. And in case there was any doubt whom this generic privilege benefited, the scribe spelt out in the margin the name of Lorenzo's son: "P⟨ier⟩o de Medici".[49]

Lorenzo was the beneficiary, through his bank, of tax rebates on the import of English wool and the remission of the costs of the verbal diplomacy involved in this transaction. He was appointed one of the four Conservators of the Mint for five years in June 1491. And when the 1490-91 commission came to an end in July, as one of the

---

[47] Cento 3, f. 60*r* (15 Jan. 1491): "Et perchè e s'intende che al Poggio a Chaiano è una certa casetta del comune, la quale potrebbe acomodare a Lorenzo di Piero de' Medici et non arecherebbe alchuno sinistro al chomune, però si provede che e' proveditori della dogana di Firenze pe' tempi existenti gli possino concedere decta casepta ad habendum et tenendum in perpetuum per via di baratto ad ogni sua richiesta qualunche volta epso Lorenzo dopo la richiesta facta ne consegnasse una altra già edificata o da edificarsi per lui in luogo commodo et conveniente et almeno di equale bontà; et questo sanza altra solemnità observare".

[48] Cento 3, ff. 128*v*-129*r* (29 July 1491), *in marg.* "Gabella non solvatur per Laurentium Medicem": "per fornirla di case a honore publico et comodita a universale ... credendo quest'opera ad honore publico et comodita de' privati". See also the provision of 27 July 1491, opening a road "nel cortile dell'entrata d'Orbatello" to create "uno T" with Via Laura, "Et sarà molto honorevole" (f. 117*r*); cf. Ricchioni, *Costitutione*, pp. 80-81. On the Via Laura project. C. Elam, *Lorenzo de' Medici and the Urban Development of Renaissance Florence* "Art History" I, 1978, pp. 44-47, quoting Giovanni Cambi, that the project pleased Lorenzo, the people and the guild, "ch'arebbe auto e' denari per fare e' lasci ... et era adornamento della Ciptà" (p. 59, note 10).

[49] Cento 3, f. 127*v* (29 July 1491): "Et perchè a qualche cittadino è suto promesso per dota di sua donna forestiera et da' parenti forestieri qualche buona somma di danari ... Che qualunche cittadino al quale è stato promesso per sua donna forestiera semila fiorini larghi o più ... Et pare che basti il danno riceve sanza agiugnerli altro peso". Piero was betrothed to Alfonsina Orsini on 24 February 1487 and her dowry of 12000 "ducati di Carlini" was ratified on 24 April 1488, ASF, Notarile antecos. 10200, ff. 299*r*-300*v*, cf. G. B. Picotti, *La Giovinezza di Leone X*, Milan, Hoepli, 1928, pp. 166, 212.

two chairmen he was allowed to decide how much to reward the scribes in addition to their salaried offices, notwithstanding the laws against it.[50] The fact that both of the men they specially favoured, ser Piero da Bibbiena and ser Zanobi del Pace, were singled out for attack when the Medici regime fell in November 1494 – with Antonio di Miniato Dini himself – demostrates their position as Medici intimates.[51] One of them, Lorenzo's secretary Piero da Bibbiena, had been absolved from the normal restrictions on guild membership and was given Florentine citizenship by the Reformers in 1482. In 1491 he was also privileged by being allowed to be taxed in Florence. There, living with his brother "in the home of Lorenzo de' Medici", he acted as Lorenzo's middle-man and go-between with leading citizens during his master's frequent absences from the city.[52]

But of all the favours granted to Lorenzo and his family, undoubtedly the most important were two decrees added painstakingly to the first register of deliberations in July 1482 by the notary's coadiutor, Bartolomeo Dei, "so that everyone may be informed about them". The first, dated 9 July 1482, concerned the transfer to Lorenzo's name of Monte credits worth some 9000 florins in cash, which he could order to be paid to him whenever he wanted, by word of mouth alone. These credits, nominally worth 53,335 florins, had belonged to Castello Quaratesi. Castello was already indebted to Cosimo and to the Medici bank in 1458 over the building of the Franciscan convent of San Salvatore al Monte.[53] When Castello died in 1466, his credits were bought in by the Monte Officials for 13,333 florins and resold to

---

[50] Cento 3, f. 132*r* (29 July 1491): "atteso alla fatica durata pe' loro ministri di corpo (et in alcuni di corpo et di animo) ... et che ogni faticha merita premio et non meno la diligentia et fede usata". On 26 October 80 florins were paid out, "per istanziamento fatto pel magnifico Lorenzo de' Medici e Antonio di Bernardo di Miniato", Monte Comune 1581, f. 742 left.

[51] See note 83 below.

[52] Misc. Rep. 109, ff. 92*r*-93*v* (24 July 1482); Cento 3, f. 77*r* (8 June 1491). For ser Piero's confidential letters to Lorenzo as his secretary, see notes 93, 94 below.

[53] According to his 1458 Catasto return (ASF, Catasto 785, SS. Scala, ff. 77*r*-80*r*), Castello owned fl. 63,117 in Monte credits (valued at fl. 12607, s.16), fl. 991 owed in interest payments (= fl. 594, 12s.) and fl. 1423 (= fl. 113, s.18) 'Monta del 1463'. He was owed fl. 6850 by Luigi and Giovanni di Giovanni Quaratesi, part of which he repaid to Giovanni di Cosimo and Pierfrancesco de' Medici and Co., to whom they owed fl. 1276: "paghato per me e a mia istanza alla muraglia si fa a' frati dell'Oservanza da Saminiato, che chosì remasi d'achordo chon Chosimo, che detto lavorio innanzi si chominciassi che ne faciessi alloghagione a' maestri a mia petizione, perchè se ne intende meglio di me e fè chom più vantaggio mio". The figure fl. 53, 335 is quoted by the Calimala in their petition of 10 May 1513, note 60 below. According to De Roover, *Il Banco Medici*, p. 44, he was the fourth richest contributor to this catasto.

Piero de' Medici on 30 January 1467 on condition that Piero paid off Castello's debt of some 2000 florins to the Monte and spent the remaining credits on building "a beautiful hotel" in Florence for the use of foreigners, to be owned by the Calimala or Merchants' Guild, Castello's residuary legatee, to whom he also bequeathed all his Monte credits.[54]

According to the Reformers, Piero failed to build the hotel because the money had never been paid out to him; so they decided, as the end of their first office approached, that it would be 'honest' for the Commune to pay off this debt. In fact, however, Lorenzo had been trying in vain to obtain this money as early as 1470, when a bill asking the Monte to disburse 6000 florins to Lorenzo, "to buy two hospices for the Merchants' Guild", was repeatedly defeated in the Council of the People.[55] So we know that the special powers of the Reformers were being used to obtain what he had been denied by normal constitutional procedures.

On 9 July 1482 – acting retrospectively – they authorised Tegghiaio da 'Montebuoni' (Buondelmonte), a Monte scribe, to transfer the debt from the 1471 register [Monte Comune 2054] to the current 1482 register [Monte Comune 1572]; thereafter, "without any other formality, deliberation or assignment by the Monte Officials" but only at the request of Lorenzo or his legal mandatory, Tegghiaio was to see that the payment was made through his pay-slip to the Monte treasurers, signed by one of the present Monte Officials, "even if the present Officials are no longer in office and after the appointed time, backdating the payment if necessary to make the payment more easily".[56]

---

[54] In his will of 25 April 1465, Notarile antecos. 1743, ff. 280*r*-282*v*, Castello left, among other bequests, fl. 8,600 to complete "opus inceptum" at S. Salvatore (including the dormitory, refectory, infirmary, library, kitchen and cloister); and to the "Artem Mercatorum", "ut tanquam filius eam delexit, et volens in ... testamento et etiam post mortem intelligi eius dilectionem tanquam de optima matre" he bequeathed three farms, and to the "Artem et Universitatem Chalismalae de Florentia", all his remaining possessions and Monte credits as his heirs and "protectorem et gubernatorem sopradictae operis" (f. 281*v*). On his patronage, M. WACKERNAGEL, *The World of the Florentine Renaissance Artist*, tr. A. Luchs, Princeton, Princeton University Press, 1981, pp. 212-213, 224-225. On the conditions of the transfer, Monte Comune 1690, f. 678 right, and Appendix 2 below. Cf. ASF, MAP 96, no. 475: declaring an end to claims concerning Castello's inheritance, 3 March 1466.

[55] ASF Libri fabarum 69, ff. 54*r*-57*r*: bills defeated by the Council of the People on 28 September, 3, 4, and 5 October 1470: "pro Arte mercatorum provisione ut officiales Montis solvant de quodam crediti Castelli fl. 6000 Laurentio Pieri de Medicis pro duobus hospitiis emendis et pro taxis faciendis pro dictis hospitiis: displicuit" (3 Oct., f. 55*r*).

[56] Misc. Rep. 109, f. 72*v*, Appendix 2 below.

Two weeks later the Reformers made another special concession to Lorenzo, which was also scrupulously added to their book of deliberations by Bartolomeo Dei. Lorenzo and his cousins already owed the Monte some 6000 florins in tax debts and now they were faced with new demands based on old assessments that no longer reflected their true financial position (the *sesto* with the *dispiacente*, which was imposed together with the progressive *decima scalata* in 1482).[57] Normally tax dispensations were granted by a petition to the councils, but if Lorenzo had publicized his true state of affairs, which demoted him from his position as the richest tax-payer in the city – the Reformers declared – the prosperity of the city and the government would be threatened, as well as his own well-being, since the former depended both "in reality and in appearance" on Lorenzo's survival. As a healthy Monte – and the prosperity of all its creditors – depended in turn on a stable government, it was clear that nothing would be more useful to the Monte than to prevent this last upheaval by reducing Lorenzo's taxes more than what seemed usual, as much to serve the public interest as to preserve Lorenzo, "since one cannot be done without the other". As this result could best be achieved, not by (by not?) giving him more than a quarter of his *sesto sgravato* and not demanding from him the *decima scalata*, but by allowing him to pay such taxes with interest payments through their special powers and for the evident benefit of the Monte, they decided to allow him to pay these taxes with his reduced interest payments (the *terzi* described above) and with other ordinary Monte interest credits due to him or included in his tax return, as well as with those of others "in any way relating to him".[58]

Despite the perhaps intentional grammatical ambiguity of this passage and what follows, it seems clear that the Reformers' special concession did not, outwardly, reduce his taxes but allowed him to pay them with interest credits, provided he had first paid all taxes owed to the commune, as was the case with credits that were *condizionati*

[57] Lorenzo failed to declare any Monte investments or "traffichi" in his 1480 Catasto return, although he said he was ready to do so verbally or through an employee; there was, he said "gran diferenzia" between his father's time and now, "et per avere ricievuto molti danni in diversi miei traffichi, come ch'è noto non solamente alle Signorie Vostre ma a tutto il mondo". His total *valsente* was 57930 florins 7s., 4d., with reductions making his *decima a scala* fl. 517 10s. 8d., ASF, Catasto 1016, ff. 475*r*, 477*v*.

[58] *Ibid*, f. 80*r-v*, Appendix 2 below; cf. Brown, *Bartolomeo Scala*, pp. 333-334 (Ital. edn. p. 237). On the 1482 taxes, Conti, *L'imposta*, pp. 281-287.

(or 'encumbered', acquired with conditions attached). With this proviso, the Monte treasurer was "to do the will of the said Lorenzo de' Medici or other commissioned by him". Once his own credits had been used up, he could use those of others without paying any gabelle, but such credits could only be used for paying his taxes (including his tax debt of 3000 florins and that of his cousins for the same amount) and could not be paid out in cash if in excess of his taxes. All this, the Reformers carefully explained, was to compensate Lorenzo for what he suffered four years earlier in paying a sixth more in taxes than he should have done, using up his cash in forced loans as well as his Monte credits, "and for other good reasons".

Since one of the Reformers' objectives from the beginning of their office had been to encourage the payment of taxes by means of Monte credits and to restore the long-suspended payment of such credits, there was nothing inconsistent with this policy in their tax concession to Lorenzo. Technically speaking, Lorenzo was being allowed only the privilege of time to pay his taxes "slowly and without any penalty", instead of being disqualified financially from interest payments and politically from communal office by his large outstanding debts. Yet the language of the decree, the special phrases, "to do the will of Lorenzo", "without any formality", "solely at Lorenzo's request", the emphasis placed on why Lorenzo had earned this special treatment, the care taken to validate it, and not least the fact that it was initially omitted from the Reformers' book of legislation: all this suggests that, whatever its literal meaning, its intention was to provide Lorenzo with a means of access to Monte cash.

This, at any rate, is what the decision succeeded in doing, as entries in the Monte registers demonstrate. They also demonstrate that Lorenzo anticipated the decree of 9 July 1482 by some four months, drawing out the sum of 9205 florins from the treasurer of the Monte on 28 February 1482.[59] Although the payments were made "to make a hotel to belong to the Arte de' Mercatanti", Lorenzo never built such a hotel, nor – the Calimala much later complained – did he ever have any intention of doing so. They said that if he had wanted to, he could easily have built the hotel in this time; and in view of the fact he had spent far more of his own money on buildings in various places during this period, he could easily have afforded to

[59] Monte Comune 1569 (1481-82), f. 826 left, Appendix 3 below.

pay for it himself instead of using other people's money paid out in cash; but despite surviving for at least ten years after drawing out this money, he never built nor began to build it. This was the Calimala's case in 1513 for recovering the money it was owed from the Tower Officials.[60]

In addition to receiving this large cash payment at a time of great financial stringency, Lorenzo also drew increasingly large sums of money from the Monte, "by virtue of the law in his favour without any formalities".[61] These were the interest payments due on his own Monte holdings, as well as on those of others "in any way relating to him", as the decree of 22 July allowed, although the payments must soon have far outstripped the amount he and his cousins owed in taxes and were in marked contrast to the heavily-reduced interest payments allowed to his fellow citizens. As Table I demonstrates, by the time of his death in 1492 Lorenzo had received over 50,000 florins from the Monte treasurers. Although in 1482-83 and 1485-86 he kept within the limits of his entitlement, he overdrew his account in the remaining years, initially by small sums but, as the table shows, by increasingly large amounts from 1488-89 onwards, until by 1493 he owed the Monte as much as 22,377 florins.[62]

Most of this money Lorenzo received from Filippo da Gagliano, "with his permission" *(licenzia)* and "per vigore di legie". Filippo's role in these transactions is not as yet clear. The son of "an unknown artisan" who had declared unreserved loyalty to Cosimo de' Medici

---

[60] See the petition of the Arte de' Mercatanti di Calimala before the Tower Officials on 10 May 1513, ed. P. FOSTER, *I primi Medici e un "albergo magno" per Firenze*, "Archivio storico italiano", CXXIX, 1971, pp. 519-525, esp. 522-523 (the reference to which I owe to F. W. Kent). In 1498 the Calimala had been finally awarded two farms, an inn and a house from the Medici estate, valued at only fl. 2583 10s. 8d., in lieu of the fl. 9205 £4, 19s., 8d., they claimed for the hotel the Medici never built for them. This evidence is contained in the guild's lengthy petition before the Tower Officials which rejected the latter's attempt to reclaim this property for the Medici in 1513.

[61] "Per vigore di legie in suo favore sanza altra solennità", Monte Comune 1572 (1482-83), f. 884 right, etc.

[62] Appendix 3 below. The last sum recorded (fl. 22377 for 1492-93) was reduced by the "ritenzione di 6d. per £". One of these payments was subsequently erased from the extraordinary expenditure account of the Camera del Comune, Append. III, 1492-93. With the exception of some repayments in gold florins to Lorenzo as a Monte Official (n. 69 below), the cash payments were made in silver fiorini larghi di grossi, at the rate of £5. 7s. 0d. per florin unless otherwise specified. On the distinction between gold and silver florins, see P. SPUFFORD, *Handbook of Medieval Exchange*, London, The Royal Historical Society, 1986, pp. 27-28.

TABLE I *[1]

	1482-83	1483-84	1484-85	1485-86	1486-87	1487-88	1488-89	1489-90	1490-91	1491-92	1492-93
Credits to Lorenzo's account, i.e. amounts becoming due to him	5762	725	4630	2733	2831	4215	2194	1932	2326	1670	1470
Debits to Lorenzo's account, i.e. payments made to him	5500	2920	2958	1888	3864	6642	10513	3857	8079	4896	1747
Balance of account at end of period	261	1936	261	584	450	2878	11197	13122	18875	22100	22377[2]
CR = owing to Lor. DR = owing by Lor.	CR	DR	DR	CR	DR	DR	DR	DR	DR	DR	DR

* This is a revised version of the table printed in error in *Lorenzo de Medici Studi*, p. 127. I apologize to Professor Basil Yamey for this mistake and thank him again for his help in interpreting this account.

[1] The table ignores all entries for 1482/83 preceding account number 884. It also ignores the special account in 1488/89 (no. 743) for 'Lor de' Medici, uno de prexente ufficiali del Monte', which is self-balancing [see note 69]. Amounts are in fiorini larghi d'oro in oro, converting silver currency at the rate of £5.7s per florin. All the figures in the table are taken from entries in the accounts (Appendix III), and are rounded to the nearest florin.

[2] The corresponding balance appears in the ledger account as 21977 florins. The difference of 400 florins is due to an apparent error in the account. A closing debit balance of 19933 florins £4.10.5 in the 1491/92 account is entered as 19533 florins £4.0.5. in the opening entry in the 1492/93 account.

in 1434,[63] he was closely involved in the financial and business affairs of the Medici family and the regime as a partner in the Bartolini bank.[64] Thanks to the support "of some good friend", he was elected treasurer of the newly-appointed Dieci di Balìa in September 1482 – with a salary that was far from normal, he wrote to Lorenzo's secretary, Niccolò Michelozzi, being "chome si voglia".[65] From then on, as a Medicean supporter, intimate friend of Michelozzi and the banker Bartolomeo Bartolini, he evidently played an active role in the all-important but little-studied world of public and private finance.[66] The money which Filippo paid Lorenzo was derived from a series of reduced interest payments owed to Monte investors (the *terzi,* which had perhaps been contracted to him), according to a formula that rapidly becomes familiar. Consisting in any one year of as many as 20-40 small sums totalling amounts ranging from 757 to 3320 florins, they were "to be taken from the account of several and diverse persons for the interest-payments account of the present year ... by the authority conceded to us by virtue of law, to accredit them to Lorenzo and pay them to him without any further deliberation or formality, by virtue of the law in his favour, as above".[67] The

---

[63] See DALE KENT, *The Rise of the Medici: Faction in Florence 1426-1434*, Oxford, Oxford University Press, 1978, p. 86: "Never have I wished for anything more in life than to take shelter under the wing of your power and authority", 31 July 1434.

[64] See Archivio Bartolini, 224 and 225, which I was allowed to consult by the kindness and generosity of Dott. Arch. Lorenzo Bartolini Salimbene. De Roover says he was probably vice-director of the Medici bank in 1490, in 1491 investing in a wool company with Lorenzo (*Banco Medici*, pp. 536, 242; cfr. ASF Strozz. ser. I, 10, ff. 186-89). Cf. letters in BNF Ginori Conti, 29, 69 (22 August 1479), ASF MAP 48, 260 and MAP 39, 91 (11 Sept. 1484, 23 February 1485, references I owe to the Kindness of Humphrey Butters).

[65] BNF, Ginori Conti 29, 69 (13 September 1482): "imediante la grazia di qualche buono amicho ... benché la elezione non sia secondo el consueto circha al salario ordinario ma ssia chome si voglia". I owe my knowledge of this collection of Filippo's letters, 1478-1495, to F. W. Kent. ASF Dieci, Entrate & Uscite 8, f. 6*r*, records Filippo's accounts from 5 Sept. 1482 to 30 June 1485, when income exceeded expenditure. On 16 May 1481 he received one-fifth of his wife's dowry, Monte Comune 1132, f. 58 left. He is also the subject of one of the *Detti piacevoli* attributed to Angelo Poliziano, ed. Zanato, no. 273, p. 89; see also n. 94 below.

[66] See his letters in Ginori Conti 29, 69 above; as treasurer of the Dieci, he was responsible for making payments to Bartolini's bank, ASF Dieci di Balia, Entrate & Uscita 9, ff. 104-105.

[67] Monte Comune 1572, f. 878 right (1482-83): "Filipo di Piero di Filipo de avere per più denari lo faremo creditore levati dal chonto di più e diverse perssone pel conto dele pag⟨h⟩e del anno 1481 e 1482 tutto per a⟨u⟩turità chonciedutaci per vigore di leggie e ordine degli Uficiali del Monte per farnne creditore Lorenzo de' Medici e a lui pagargli sanza altra deliberazione o solennità per vigore di legie in suo favore" (40 payments, carried over on to 878 left, totalling fl. 2734 £176 8s. 2d.). This initial formula is repeated with slight variants in subsequent entries (usually omitting the phrase "e ordine degli Uficiali del Monte").

phrase "di sua licienzia" which appears in the formula from 1488 onwards suggests that since Filippo's permission was needed, he was not simply acting as Lorenzo's private broker. Although there is no evidence that he continued these payments to Piero after Lorenzo's death, he was involved in the transfer of a sum of 21,760 florins of Monte credits from Piero to his cousins seven months after Lorenzo's death, which may represent an attempt to dispose of this special account. After Piero's fall and exile, Filippo was described (with the Mellini) as one of the Medici's creditors who, as dependents of the commune, were to be repaid after private creditors and before the commune itself, raising again the possibility that these payments were made from communal rather than private funds.[68]

From 1488 until March 1491 Lorenzo was himself one of the five Monte Officials. In 1488-89, he was paid as an official, "for the restitution of money lent to the commune", two sums totalling 4000 large gold florins and 26,197 florins in silver grossi, which were granted "during his office for the benefit of the commune, to serve his needs and by virtue of the law".[69] In addition to his role as papal depositary, with responsibility for collecting and paying to the commune 30,000 florins in grossi from the Papal Tenth in 1488-1490,[70] Lorenzo and his bank became involved in other ways with public funding operations. It was during Lorenzo's first year's office as an Operaio del Palagio (the government palace board-of-works) that his bank was appointed their depositary, with responsibility for funding a total of

---

[68] ASF Notarile antecos. 10200, ff. 362*v*-363*r* (6 November 1492), whereby Piero created Lorenzo and Giovanni his procurators "ad permutandum et permutari faciendum in eos vel aliis usque ad summam florenorum 21, 760 5s. 7d. de creditis montis montis communis Florentie ... volens dictam summam permutandam fieri in una vel pluribus vicibus prout dicet Filippus de Ghaglano"; Filippo decided on 24 December 1492 that 8000 florins should be transferred initially and the remainder on 25 January 1493 (*ibid*); ASF Provvisioni 186, f. 150*r* (26 Nov. 1495): "di poi si satisfacci a ccreditori di decti rebelli o Medici dependenti dal comune come sono e' Mellini et Filippo da Gagliano et simili". For charges concerning Piero Mellini as treasurer of the Dieci (like Filippo), see below (note 77).

[69] Monte Comune 1638, ff. 743, 747. He was repaid a total of 4814 gold florins and 30438 silver florins in grossi, compared with sums to fellow Monte officials of 824 gold and 36939 silver (Pagolantonio Soderini), 3967 gold and 83865 silver (Giuliano Salviati), 36978 silver (Bartolomeo Bartolini), 2457 gold and 54172 silver florins (Antonio di Miniato Dini, proveditore) (*ibid.*, ff. 740-748). However, in the previous year, Dini had been repaid 8871 gold florins, compared with sums of 1893, 716, 1733 and 3165 gold florins to the five Monte Officials, MC 1575, ff. 739-746.

[70] ASF, Monte Comune 1580, f. 773 right: sums owed by Lorenzo de' Medici & Co. and paid in by Bartolomeo Bartolini & Co. in 1490: 16,000 fiorini larghi di grossi for 1488, 8,000 for 1489 and 6,000 for 1490.

5000 florins and £40,000 in grossi for a series of fortresses in the Florentine state.[71] Although it was not depositary of the powerful foreign-affairs magistracy, the Otto di Pratica, which helped to pay for these fortresses through the bank of Bartolomeo Bartolini & Co, Lorenzo's close relationship with Dini and Bartolini in their interrelated public and private activities encouraged the charges of peculation later levied against him.[72]

Many charges were levied against Lorenzo by his contemporaries after his death. Some concerned his private banking affairs, others money purloined from magistracies like the Otto di Pratica, from which his bank was said to have received "about 135,000 florins".[73] Most vociferous were the charges concerning his misuse of public credit funds, the Monte delle Doti and – what concerns us here – the Monte Comune, from which it was claimed he had prevented citizens from receiving interest payments while profiting from it himself.[74] According to Alamanno Rinuccini, Lorenzo tried to destroy the Monte Comune in order to devote all the public revenues to himself, once

---

71 ASF, Operai del Palagio 4, f. 8*v* (15 Nov. 1488, reference owed to F. W. Kent): "absente Laurentio de Medicis ... eligerunt et deputaverunt in depositarium dicti officii Laurentium Pieri Cosme de Medicis et sociorum". Unlike the previous annual appointments, Lorenzo and Dini, with Bernardo del Nero, Giovanni Serristori and Bernardo Rucellai, remained in office until 1492. Lorenzo's bank was subsequently repaid the following sums: Monte Comune 1664, f. 728 left. cf. 1578, f. 587 right (11 Jan. 1490: £10,000 for the castle of Firenzuola); Monte Comune 1580, f. 774 left (11 Jan. 1491: £10,000; 28 Febr. 1491: £8795 3s. 0d. "per la ghuardia de la cittadele e forteze di Pixa"; Monte Comune 1536, f. 575 right, cf. 1517, f. 75 left (31 Oct. 1492: £6048 moneta vecchia to the 'Rede di Lorenzo de' Medici' for the same); Monte Comune 1639, f. 738 left (28 Feb. 1493: 5000 fiorini larghi in quattrini to the same "per le spese e opere del porticciolo di Livornno"), f. 449 left (15 Dec. 1493: £6048 moneta vecchia for the new citadel of Pisa e for "38 provigionati per la guardia di quella"); cf. Operai del Palagio, ff. 27*r*, 31*r*. Lorenzo's bank was also repaid fl. 9980 for the cost of saltpetre for the fortress at Sarzana on 28 Febr. 1488 (cf. ASF Otto di Pratica, Ricordanze, 1, ff. 20*v*, 23*v*) and £1105.10.0 for 221 "coraze de galee" on 28 April 1490, Dieci di Balìa, Debitori Creditori 24, 1487-88, f. 133 left; Monte Comune, 1580, f. 767 left.

72 The three men were all Monte Officials in 1488-90, Dini as their depositary selling large amounts of coinage for reminting to Bartolini as Maestro di Zecca in 1491-92, Monte Comune 1580, f. 791, 1581, f. 715, 5136, f. 609, etc. In addition to his offices as proveditore of the Monte and Operaio del Palagio, Dini was also closely involved in the finances of the Otto di Pratica when Bartolini was their banker, ASF Otto di Pratica, Ricordanze 1.

73 ASF, Monte Comune 1584, f. 761 left: "Rede di Lorenzo de' Medici & Co, banchieri di Firenze ... deono dare a dì 30 di gennaio 9448 fiorini larghi di oro in oro e £261400 di grossi nuovi e £36500 in quattrini nuovi ... dissono ... erono per parte di 135 mila fiorini in circha paghati per ordine degli Otto della Praticha passati".

74 The evidence is assembled by CONTI, *L'Imposta*, pp. 70-71; cf. RICCHIONI, *Costituzione*, pp. 79-80, and DE ROOVER, *Banco Medici*, p. 533, that in January 1495 the government demanded the repayment of 74, 948 fiorini larghi which it claimed had been illicitly drawn from the Monte Comune.

it no longer had to pay out interest and dowries.[75] Francesco Guicciardini also accused Lorenzo of profiting from public funds to save himself from bankruptcy.[76] Piero Parenti was even more precise. He wrote in his chronicle that an audit of communal accounts revealed that Lorenzo and his son Piero availed themselves of 23,000 florins from a fictitious Monte account, with the compliance of the Monte official Tegghiaio Buondelmonti. Referring to another account of 35,000 ducats received from Piero Mellini, treasurer of the Dieci di Balìa, and to sums of more than 100,000 ducats made available for getting his son made a cardinal, Parenti concludes, "Thus many other communal funds were highjacked at different times and in different ways, as the above amply demonstrate".[77]

Despite the danger of exaggerating Lorenzo's personal influence in Monte affairs, many of the charges levelled against him and his colleagues are substantiated by the records of the Seventeen Reformers and the Monte Comune. It was Tegghiaio Buondelmonte, named by Piero Parenti as implicated in Lorenzo's Monte deals, who was responsible for implementing the decision of the Reformers in 1482. Whether or not this account was the one referred to by Parenti, it is clear that Lorenzo could only have contributed to the problems of the Monte by receiving large cash repayments, at a time when other investors were allowed only a small part of the interest they were owed.[78] The tax concessions awarded to Lorenzo in 1482, to the loss of public revenues, were intended to save Lorenzo from bankruptcy and disqualification from political office. And even Rinuccini's sweeping

---

[75] *Ricordi storici*, ed. G. Aiazzi, Florence, 1840, pp. cxlvii, cxlviii-ix.

[76] *Storie fiorentine*, p. 77.

[77] *Storia fiorentina*, BNF, MS II, iii, 169, f. 128*v* (March 1495), quoted by Conti, p. 70: "Così molti altri denari del Comune si usurporono con vari et diversi tempi, dei quali e' predetti a sufficientia sieno notificati". Giovanni Cambi quotes a figure of 50,000 scudi from communal funds to make Giovanni a cardinal, *Istorie* in *Delizie*, XXI, pp. 54-55, Rinuccini 200,000 florins, note 75 above and Conti, p. 70.

[78] In addition to his special concessions, for instance, he was also paid on 23 February 1482 £55,500 "per fine per lui fatta dal comune di Firenze", of fl. 73, 171 of Monte penale at 13 2/3%, "ch'e presenti Uficiali del Monte diminuano da più e diverse persone"; at the same time two much smaller exceptional payments were made to Antonio Pucci of £824 and £682, Monte Comune 1569, f. 865 left, Monte Comune 2220, f. 623 left. Antonio Dini, as Proveditor of the Monte, was also paid large sums, eg. in February 1488 fl. 42, 260 "per lui servito el comune più tempo fa per suoi bixongni" and fl. 2893 "per dischrezione e interesse", Monte Comune 1575, ff. 744 left and 746 left. These payments need to be studied in the wider context of government finance; here I have limited myself to pursuing the exceptional payments to him "per vigore di legie" of July 1482.

charge was true to the extent that the regime's policy was to reduce Monte holdings to save interest and dowry payments. Disbursements of large sums of Monte money to Lorenzo in the years 1488-1491, when Lorenzo was himself a Monte Official, also coincided with Lorenzo's heavy loans to the Papacy preceding Giovanni's cardinalate in 1488-89.[79] After the revolution in 1494, the government attempted to reclaim not only money from the heirs of Piero Mellini, "as part of a larger sum" owed by him as treasurer of the Dieci, but also very much larger sums from the Medici bank, which it said had been paid out by Antonio Dini.[80]

It is likely that Antonio di Miniato Dini was the master-mind behind these financial operations, not Lorenzo. His position as provveditor of the Monte throughout this period, combined with other offices, gave him power to manipulate communal funds, as later communal officials were to do for the Medici in the sixteenth century.[81] Although his activities have still to be fully explored, it is clear that the Seventeen Reformers' most intensive periods of work were when Dini and Lorenzo were chairmen together, and the same is true of their collaboration as Operai del Palagio.[82] In the public eye, as well as that of informed politicians like Francesco Gaddi, Dini was guilty of "failing to act with that trust and integrity which his office demand-

[79] See above. For Lorenzo's loans to the Papacy, BROWN, *Bartolomeo Scala*, pp. 108-109, n. 137 (Ital. edn. p. 78), cf. note 77 above.

[80] ASF, Monte Comune 1782, ff. 751 right (570 florins "per parte di maggior somma" claimed by the 5 syndics of the commune from Pietro Mellini's heirs) and 758 right-841 right, *passim*, (well over 15,366 gold florins and 42,946 in silver grossi in payments owed to citizens lending money to the commune or from the Medici, claimed from the heirs of the Medici bank). The government also paid Cardinal Guillaume Briconnet a total of 17,500 gold florins debited to the Medici Bank in Bruges, which apparently owed him this money, Monte Comune 1584, f. 756 left, 1782, f. 774 left.

[81] See M. BULLARD, *Filippo Strozzi and the Medici: Favour and Finance in Sixteenth-century Florence and Rome*, Cambridge, Cambridge University Press, 1980, pp. 40-43, 132-140, etc. on the importance of the office of depositor of the Signoria in channelling communal money to the Medici in Rome.

[82] Listed in "liber seu quaternus" and the "quadernuccio" of the Seventeen's deliberations in Balìe 39, ff. 9*r*-132*r*, 145*r*-149*r*, Appendix I (III) below. Lorenzo was *proposto* for 7 instead of the average 6 weekly periods, twice with Antonio di Miniato Dini (below) and only once without legislating (11 Oct. 1490). Piero Guicciardini legislated during five out of his six periods as chairman, Dini during four out of six, and Pagolantonio Soderini during three out of five periods. On two occasions when Dini was a *proposto*, the scribe (Dei?) unusually notes that he was drawn last from the bag, Appendix I (III) below (his prorogation as provisor for another year from 1 March 1494 is also marked by a hand in Cento 3, f. 23*v*); on his position, cf. notes 15, 69, 71-72 above.

ed and of having agreed to many extraordinary payments and large sums of money to Lorenzo and Piero de' Medici and others", for which he was condemned to death after the 1494 revolution and ignominiously hanged from the windows of the Bargello.[83]

Lorenzo, of course, had died two years before the revolution, leaving his heirs responsible for repaying the money the government claimed had been paid to his bank by Dini. But the chroniclers and historians who accused him of highjacking communal funds were themselves as Monte treasurers better informed than anyone else about Lorenzo's special position, since it was they who dispensed his cash payments on demand. It was Francesco Guicciardini's grandfather Jacopo who paid out Lorenzo's first tax concession of 3000 florins in grossi on 10 September 1482, to be followed by a series of treasurers from other leading families.[84] And it was Piero Parenti who proposed the bill preventing any further such concessions "to private people" to the Council of the People in July 1482.[85] They had good grounds for accusing Lorenzo of using communal money for his own purpose, despite the argument that he represented the public interest.

* * *

The question remains of how to characterize Lorenzo's role and status in Florence. Was he simply a party-boss, using all the influence at his command – including the commission of the Seventeen Reformers – to win favours for himself and his supporters, or did he play a more limited and constitutional role within the commission, whose powers derived directly from the state itself? Unsuccessful though the Reformers were in resolving Florence's financial problems,[86] they were in some ways forward-looking and provide interesting evidence of the direction in which late fifteenth-century government was moving, away from the strict guild-and-quarter-based system of office-

[83] Gaddi Priorista, ASF, Tratte 62, f. 232*v*: "non si era usato quella fede e integrità che allo officio suo s'appartende (*sic*) e havea consentito a molti pagamenti extrasordinari (*sic*) e di grosse somme a Lorenzo e a Piero de' Medici e ad altri" (cfr. BROWN, *Bartolomeo Scala*, p. 117 and n. 10, Ital. edn. pp. 81-82, 89).

[84] The names of the Monte *camarlinghi* making payments to Lorenzo appear in the accounts in Appendix III below.

[85] See note 91 below. Parenti was one of the priors at the time.

[86] See note 45 above.

holding towards a more fluid and arbitrary choice of members from an approved pool of experts and regime supporters. They also broke new ground in enjoying the status of a legislative council whose decisions had the force of law. Lacking *balìa* and limited in scope, their authority was as much a 'subterfuge' as that of the Council of Seventy when it was created in 1480.[87] Nevertheless, it was a subterfuge that worked. Although Guicciardini was wrong in assuming that the commission enjoyed full sovereignty, ("una plenissima autorità e balìa, e quanta ha il popolo di Firenze"), his view doubtless reflected the impression of contemporaries, especially that of his father, who was a member of the commission and "the first man in Florence after Lorenzo".[88] Its ability in 1491 to by-pass the Seventy, "the pivot of the Medici regime", shows how powerful it was.[89]

The commission did not, however, exceed its brief as a short-term magistracy with wide discretionary powers. Ever since 1434, the Medici regime had favoured the use of small committees to introduce 'arbitrary' tax assessments in place of uniform, 'enlightened' taxes approved by the councils.[90] The appointment of the Seventeen Reformers continued the same policy of using a small body of arbiters with absolute powers to override traditional laws and restrictions. But the commission never became permanent, and when the Signoria and Cento had their special powers renewed on 13 July 1482, they were specifically prevented from legislating in future for "private persons and their profit but must concern themselves solely with matters relating to the public advantage and which principally concern the commune of Florence and not individual people" – effectively preventing

---

[87] J. STEPHENS, *The fall of the Florentine Republic, 1512-1530,* Oxford, Clarendon Press, 1983, pp. 21-22.

[88] According to his grandson, FRANCESCO GUICCIARDINI, *Ricordi autobiografici*, p. 54; on Jacopo, cfr. note 93 below. Ugolino Verino regretted his death on 17 May 1490 as "dannosa non solo a' parenti et amici sua ma ancora a tutta la patria fiorentina ... ancora era utile ad governo della republica". He also commented that "benchè chi è de' primi del governo sia in gran pericolo della salute dell'anima", he believed, "ma certo non sono, che lui sia no⟨n⟩ in cattivo luogho", Riccardiana, MS 2621, f. 154*r*.

[89] RUBINSTEIN, *Government of Florence,* p. 203. When renewed in 1489, it lost its right to appoint the Signoria on the grounds of lack of secrecy, which was evidently becoming a major preoccupation of the regime, Cento 2, f. 146*v* (12 Feb. 1489): "maxime pel difecto del secreto ... essere bene a tal caso pensare in modo che la sicurtà dello stato si mantengha", cf. RUBINSTEIN, p. 209 and note 8 above.

[90] Another similar commission was the Trenta Riformatori del Monte, appointed in 1459, ASF Misc. Rep. 110, CONTI, *L'Imposta,* pp. 42, 51-52.

the grant of any further special privileges to Lorenzo.[91] Moreover, although two of the new elected members in 1490 (Piero Alamanni and Bernardo Del Nero) were on Francesco Guicciardini's list of Medici creations, nine of its members were on the law-reform commission created in July 1494, whose work, although not implemented until 1502, already represented a critical approach to Medici policies.[92]

As a member of both commissions of Seventeen Reformers, Lorenzo was of course fully involved in all their decisions and bound by them. The care taken to insert the concession granted to him in 1482 and the prohibition against any further such concessions demonstrate the constraints that still limited the growth of absolutism in Florence. For all this, the principal beneficiary of the commissions' special powers was Lorenzo and his banking friends. Whatever the reaction after Lorenzo's death, these men as members of the Seventeen and as Monte treasurers helped to ensure his control of Florence rather than limit it. Because they participated in all the decisions that were taken, they accepted the subterfuges involved. And during Lorenzo's frequent absences from the city, they even took it upon themselves to offer Lorenzo advice, summoning his secretary Piero Bibbiena on one occasion to suggest he should "begin to give" his son Piero "reputation, for the public good".[93]

As one of the Seventeen Reformers Lorenzo was able to claim genuine expertise, thanks not only to his trading interests but also

---

[91] Provvisioni 173, f. 73*v* (13 July 1482): "Quod dicta auctoritas non extendatur in tempore huius prorogationis ad privatas personas et ipsorum commoda sed solum versetur in rebus ad publicam utilitatem spectantibus et quae principaliter ad communem Florentiae et non ad singulares personas pertinerent".

[92] GUICCIARDINI, *Storie fiorentine*, pp. 78-79: "che fussino di qualità che sanza lo appoggio suo non avessino seguito". The 23 members of the law-reform commission are listed in Cento 3, f. 30*r*, including the nine Reformers Bernardo del Nero, Antonio Dini, Piero Guicciardini, Angelo Niccolini, Niccolò Ridolfi, Bernardo Rucellai, Giovanni Serristori, Paoloantonio Soderini and Antonio Taddei, plus the son of Filippo Valori. Four Reformers were elected as members of the 20 Accoppiatori in December 1494, Rucellai, Salviati, della Scarfa and Valori. On the law, passed in August 1494 and put into effect only in April 1502, see. L. MARTINES, *Lawyers and Statecraft in Renaissance Florence*, pp. 140-142; M. ASCHERI, *Repubblica, Principato e Crisi del Diritto Comune a Firenze*, "Annali della Facoltà di Lettere e Filosofia" (University of Siena), VI, 1985, pp. 117-140; and now A. ZORZI, *L'amministrazione della giustizia penale nella Repubblica fiorentina. Aspetti e problemi*, Florence, Olschki, 1988, pp. 97-104.

[93] Ser Piero da Bibbiena to Lorenzo, 23 July 1489: "Stamani fui chiamato in piaza da Iacopo Guicciardini et Pier Filippo [Pandolfini] et mi parlarono in questo effecto ... parrebbe loro sommamente necessario et utile alla Città, a Piero, et a loro medesimi per la salute publica et loro per fare Piero bene sufficiente che voi cominciassi a darli reputatione ...", ed. RICCHIONI, *Costituzione*, p. 198, doc. ix.

to his special interest in metals and minerals. The Medici were closely involved in marketing alum from the papal mine in Tolfa and iron ore from Elba, and in 1489 alum was a topic for discussion between Lorenzo's secretary Piero da Bibbiena, Filippo da Gagliano and members of the bank.[94] In 1472 Lorenzo had himself been appointed legal arbitrator to mediate between Florence and Volterra in the dispute about the latter's alum; and in 1490 he was shown a sample of copper by a citizen, who after much thought decided "not to trust anyone else but to put myself entirely in his hands alone".[95] The fact that public force was used to put down the revolt in Volterra following Lorenzo's arbitration, for which Lorenzo was later held personally responsible, shows the extent to which public and private interests were already enmeshed in the early years of Lorenzo's dominance. Afterwards, as we have seen, they became increasingly so.

The conflict between Lorenzo's public and private interests nevertheless created the problem for his contemporaries – as well as ourselves – of how to define his role in the state. As I have argued elsewhere, it was the image of arbiter and wise platonic guardian of the ship of state that proved most persuasive, and we have seen how it was used to justify his appointment as one of the Conservators of the Mint, to prevent Florence from "sailing to its destruction without a helmsman".[96] Although this idealisation was another subterfuge or mystification, like that of the *balìa* of the Seventeen, it was so widespread by the 1490s that it became a new way of perceiving the relationship between Lorenzo and his fellow-citizens. So when Florentine aristocrats like the Guicciardini and the Corsini collaborated and intermarried with the Medici, the marriages were described

---

[94] GOLDTHWAITE, *Medici Bank*, p. 28; Piero da Bibbiena's letter to Lorenzo of 23 July 1489, cit., p. 196: "Mostrai a Filippo da Gaglano quella di Nofri, et stamani questi del bancho gli hanno scripto in oportuna forma circa gli allumi". According to Pius II, Cosimo invested 75,000 ducats in the Tolfa alum mines discovered by Giovanni da Castro, *Memoirs of a Renaissance Pope. The Commentaries of Pius II*, ed. GRAGG and GABEL, bk. VII (Oct. 1461-Apr. 1462), pp. 233-234. On the Medici Bank's involvement in alum and iron ore, see DE ROOVER *Banco Medici*, pp. 218-239.

[95] E. FIUMI, *L'impresa di Lorenzo de' Medici contro Volterra, 1472*, Florence, Olschki, 1948; *Lettere di Lorenzo de' Medici*, I, ed. FUBINI, Excursus II, pp. 547-553; TRIBALDO DE' ROSSI, *Ricordanze*, p. 259.

[96] Quoted in note 35 above. On this idealisation, see my *Platonism in fifteenth-century Florence and its contribution to early modern political thought*, pp. 215-245 below; cf. M. BULLARD, *The magnificent Lorenzo de' Medici: between myth and history*, in *Politics and Culture in Early Modern Europe: Essays in Honour of H. G. Koenigsberger*, ed. P. MACK and M. C. JACOB, Cambridge, Cambridge University Press, 1987, pp. 42-52.

as the 'balancing' of riches and nobility with Medici splendour to create an 'equal' relationship.[97] It was as arbiter and helmsman that both Francesco Guicciardini and Machiavelli assessed Lorenzo's position in Florence after his death; and Machiavelli, shrewdly, was also one of the first writers to articulate the need of an 'arbiter' or 'third man' to create political stability, as Lorenzo had so successfully done during his lifetime.[98]

In this period of transition between the commune and the principate in Florence, Lorenzo presents many of the paradoxes of early court society – in the contrast between his public and private behaviour, his closeness and distance from his colleagues, and the mixed admiration and resentment he aroused.[99] But, as this account of Lorenzo's dealings with the Monte demonstrates, it was by means of communal institutions like the Seventeen Reformers that Lorenzo was partially able to resolve one of the main problems confronting him as unofficial head of state, that of funding. Thanks to them Lorenzo was able "in reality and appearance" to lay the basis for the early-modern principate.[100]

---

[97] According to Ugolino Verino, commenting on the betrothal of Bartolomeo Corsini to Lorenzo's daughter, "ch'el parentado ... sia pari; et se lo splendore della casa de' Medici è maggiore, considerando et le richeze et la nobiltà de' Corsini ... parmi che ognuno nel grado suo debba essere contento", Riccardiana, MS 2621, 147*v*.

[98] "Perchè manchava di chi stesse a timone, chome stava sufficientemente Lorenzo de' Medici", according to the confession of Giovanni Folchi in March 1513, J. STEPHENS and H. BUTTERS, *New Light on Machiavelli,* "English Historical Review" XCVII, 1982, pp. 58-59, 67; on "the third man" in Machiavelli, see *City and citizen: changing perceptions in the fifteenth and sixteenth centuries,* pp. 300-302 below.

[99] See NORBERT ELIAS, *The Court Society*, Engl. transl., Oxford, Blackwell, 1983, and the critique of CHARTIER, *Cultural History,* ch. 3, esp. pp. 81-91.

[100] On the use of communal institutions by the later Medici princes, see now C. B. MENNING, *Loans and Favors, Kin and Clients. Cosimo de' Medici and the Monte di Pietà*, "Journal of Modern History", LXI, 1989, pp. 487-511. I owe to Giorgio Chittolini the suggestion about the importance of communal institutions as foundations of stable principates.

Appendix I

THE SEVENTEEN REFORMERS: MEMBERS AND MEETINGS

In alphabetical order, with quarters, membership of the Council of Seventy (70 + = one of the first thirty members; 70c = a coopted member; UM = Ufficiale di Monte).

I. 1481-82 (ASF, *Misc. Rep.* 109, ff. *3v*, *50r*, MC 884, fl. *7v*-*8r*)

Alessandri, Maso di Niccolò, SG
Bartoli, Cosimo di Matteo, SMN
Bonsi, Giovanni di Raffaello, SS; 70; UM
Capponi, Niccolò di Giovanni, SS; 70 +
Davanzati, Tommaso di Piero, SMN; 70 + ; UM
Delle Colombe, Michele di Corsi, SS; 70 + (artisan)
Dini, Antonio di Bernardo di Miniato, S + ; 70 + (artisan)
Dini, Francesco di Piero; S + ; 70
Gianfigliazzi, M. Bongianni di Bongianni, SMN; 70 +
Guicciardini, Jacopo di Piero, SS; 70 +
Lioni, Roberto di Francesco, S + ; 70 +
Medici, Lorenzo di Piero, SG; 70 +
Niccolini, Lapo di Lorenzo, S + ; 70; UM
Pandolfini, Pierfilippo di M. Giannozzo, SG, 70, UM
Pieri, Piero di Giovanni, SS, 70; UM (artisan)
Pucci, Antonio di Puccio, SG; 70 +
Taddei, Antonio di Taddeo, SG; 70 +

II. 1490-91 (Cento 3, ff. *2r*, *50r*, Balìa 39, f. *9r*)

Alamanni, D. Piero di Francesco (until embassy in Rome, Jan. 1491), SS; 70c
Albizzi, Maso di Luca degli (until death, 13 Apr. 91, f. 148*v*), SG, 70
Alessandri, Maso di Nicolai, SG; 70c

Bartolini, Bartolomeo di Lionardo, SMN; UM (until 1 March 1491)
Del Nero, Bernardo di Nero, SS, 70 +
Dini, Antonio di Bernardo di Miniato, S + ; 70 + 'Antonio di Bernardo'
Dini, Francesco di Piero, S + ; 70
Guicciardini, Piero di Jacopo, SS; 70
Medici, Lorenzo di Piero, SG, 70 + ; UM (until 1 March, then nominated member)
Miniati, Angelo di Francesco, S + ; UM (until 1 March)
Niccolini, M. Angelo di D. Otto, S + ; 70 (nominated until 1 March, then UM)
Pandolfini, Pierfilippo di M. Giannozzo (exchanging with Alamanni) SG; 70
Pucci, Jacopo di Salvestro, SG; UM (after 1 March 1491)
Ridolfi, Niccolò di Luigi, SS; 70; (nominated until 1 March, then UM)
Rucellai, Bernardo di Giovanni, SMN; 70
Salviati, Giuliano di Francesco, S + ; 70; UM (until 1 March 1491)
Scarfa, Francesco di Martino dello, SMN, UM (from 1 March 1491)
Serristori, Giovanni di Antonio, S + ; 70 +
Soderini, Pagolantonio di D. Tommaso, SS; 70c, UM (until 1 March, then nominated member)
Taddei, Antonio di Taddeo, SG; 70 +
Valori, Filippo di Bartolomeo, SG; UM (from 1 March 1491)

III. 1490-91, Meetings when legislation was introduced and approved, with the names of the two chairmen (*proposti*) for that week. Throughout the period two different chairmen were elected every Monday (with two exceptions, noted below). (Balìe 39, ff. 9*r*-89*v*, 146*r*-149*r*)

Aug. 16 1490[1]	Dini (Fr.), Miniati	Gabelles and finance
Sept. 6	Medici, Dini (Ant.)	Customs and coinage
8 (Wed)	—	Meeting of merchants on coinage
Nov. 29	Soderini, Guicciardini	
Dec. 1 (Wed)	—	Dowries
Dec. 20	Bartolini, del Nero[2]	Gabelles on English wool in Pisa
Jan. 3 1491	Miniati, Ridolfi	
5 (Wed)	—	"Congregati sunt no. xii et legerunt multa pro dogana, nihil deliberando"

[1] "de sero".
[2] "in audientia Otto Practice".

Jan. 10	Taddei, Dini (Ant.)	
13 (Thurs)	—	"Deliberaverunt multa pro dogana"
15 (Sat)	—	"Plura etiam pro dogana and pro Monte"
Jan. 17	Soderini, Guicciardini	
21 (Fri)	—	ditto, "and gabelle Petresante and assignamente canalis"
22 (Sat)	—	"Plura pro hebreo Pisarum; pro notaro exitus, pro ser Tucci, et pro passi Buggia"
Jan. 24[3]	Alessandri, Medici	Salt and wine gabelles, etc.
26 (Wed)	—	Dowries, cloth and contract gabelles
27 (Thurs)	—	ditto
Feb. 28	Taddei, Guicciardini	New coinage: introduction deferred
Mar. 18 (Fri)[4]	Medici, Soderini	
Mar. 20	—	
23 (Wed)	—	Coinage, building and trading concessions in Florence and Pisa, dowries
April 4	Taddei, Dini (Ant.)[5]	
April 11	Albizzi,[6] Soderini	
May 2	Niccolini, Dini (Ant.)	
5 (Thurs)	—	Tax collection
May 30	Medici, Guicciardini	
4 (Sat)	—	Pistoiese taxes, roads
June 6	Rucellai, Valori	
7 (Tues)	—	"Reforma Montis"
8 (Wed)	—	Privilege to Piero Bibbiena
June 13	del Nero, Alessandri	
16 (Fri)	—	Gabelles
June 20	Scarfa, Guicciardini	
21 (Tues)	—	Tax favours; contado; estimo; Pisa

[3] Jan. 23 (Sunday): "cras init.".

[4] March 19 (Sat): "proposti per iii diebus di ieri".

[5] Taddei "primus", Dini "ultimus".

[6] Obiit Masus die 13 eiusdem".

June 27	Pandolfini, Medici	
28 (Tues)	—	Favours, etc.
30 (Thurs)	—	"Pro comitatinis"; coinage (deputing 4 citizens incl. Lor.); estimo; favours; Volterra, etc.
July 25	Dini (Ant.), Medici[7]	
27 (Wed)	—	Estimo, Pisa, Arezzo, Guelf Party, customs, etc.
29 (Fri)	—	Favours, etc. (cf. notes 49, 50)

[7] Lorenzo "primus", Dini "ultimus ex pisside extracti fuerunt propositi pro vii diebus ultimis officii".

Appendix II

CONCESSIONS TO LORENZO DE' MEDICI BY THE SEVENTEEN REFORMERS

9 and 22 July 1482

(ASF Miscellanea Repubblica 109, ff. 72*v*, 80*r-v*)

Two insertions in the register of deliberations in the hand of Bartolomeo Dei (coadiutor of the Notary of the Riformagioni Giovanni Guidi), who explains on f. 80*v* that he copied these deliberations on available space from the "public copy by Giovanni Guidi" so that "everyone might know about them" (see below). The date and introduction of the first entry are written by the scribe of the deliberations, who also writes the marginal note for both entries.

⟨f. 72*v*⟩ *in marg.* "Laurentius de' Medicis fiat creditor de quodam monte cum conditione'

Die 9 Julii 1482

I sopradecti Riformatori veduto la infrascripta vulgare scripta della quale questo è il tenore, cioè: Piero di Cosimo de' Medici e compagni deono havere in dì primo di Marzo 1470 fiorini undicimila quaranta septe di suggello soldi xi piccoli per tanti ci furono consegnati per creditori al libro 0/12 del Monte 1470 c. 678 [ASF Monte Commune = MC 1690] per resto della fine che si fè del credito di Castello Quaratesi, e quali denari si dovevano pagare nel modo et forma et in que' tempi et con quelli pacti et conditioni come distinctamente si dice alla levata debitori detto libro in q⟨uest⟩o a c. 533. Vagliono fiorini novemila dugento cinque larghi lire quattro soldi 19 denari 8 – fl. 9, 205.4.19.8. Et che benchè decto Piero di Cosimo e compagnia sieno così creditori nondimeno non s'è facto il pagamento et però non si può adempiere la conditione apposta al decto credito di fare in Firenze un bello a⟨l⟩bergo. Et pure essendo honesto che il Comune paghi tal debito et che il Monte faccia dopo tanti anni il dovere a chi s'appartiene, vorrebbono quelli a' quali attiene si provedessi:

Che per vigore d'una deliberazione de' Riformatori del Monte et delle Gabelle, Teghiaio da Montebuoni, scrivano al campione del Monte, sanza altra solennità observare et sanza suo preiudicio fussi tenuto et obligato spegnere et cancellare dal libro 0/13 dell'anno 1471 a c. 702 [MC 2054] el sopradicto Piero di Cosimo & Compagnia dove restono creditori di fl. 9205 £4 s.19 d.8 per resto della fine del Monte di Castello Quaratesi, et quella tale partita transferire dovessi al campione 0/24 dell'anno presente 1482 [MC 1572, f. 865 left and right]; et quivi di tanta quantità accendere et fare creditore Lorenzo di Piero di Cosimo de' Medici, et di poi tale quantità di fl. 9205 larghi £4 s.19 d.8, sanza altra solennità, deliberatione o stantiamento degli Ufficiali del Monte o d'altri, ma solo a richiesta di decto Lorenzo de' Medici o di suo legitimo mandatario, decto Teghiaio per sua polizia soscripta di mano d'uno de' presenti Ufficiali del Monte ne facessi fare el pagamento da quelli camarlinghi del Monte, etiam che hora habbino finito l'uficio, et da loro mettergli a uscita etiam in dì sostenuti et inanzi al presente dì come gli paressi, et fussi di bisogno per poter fare tal pagamento più commodamente. Et con questa conditione expressa che il sopradecto Lorenzo de' Medici di tal quantità quando et come potrà commodamente debbe far fare uno a⟨l⟩bergo magno et degno nella città di Firenze et in quello tutta spenderla per poter più facilmente acceptarvi gran numero di forestieri come è conveniente allo honore della città. El quale a⟨l⟩bergo facto che sarà appartenga et sia liberamente dell'Arte de' Mercatanti della città di Firenze; et questo perché così era obligato Piero suo padre e Compagnia, nel luogho dove erano et furono da principio facti creditori, come di sopra è narrato. Veduta addunque la sopradecta scriptura et petitione i sopradecti riformatori, et quella diligentemente examinata, sì per le cagioni in quella expresse, sì ancora per molte altri più efficaci et di più utilità, et per lo honore publico, per vigore della loro auctorità obtenuto il partito per tutte le fave nere de' presenti ragunati in numero sufficiente, quella in ogni sua parte approvorono et confermorono, et a cautela ciò che in epsa si contiene deliberorono et vollono havere effecto in tutto et per tutto, come di sopra è scripto et narrato.

⟨f. 80*r*⟩ *in marg.* Laurentii de Medicis et al⟨iorum⟩ onera quaedam solvantur de pagis

Die xxii Julii 1482

Item. I sopradecti reformatori, atteso alla gran somma nella quale Lorenzo di Piero di Cosimo de' Medici si truova descripto nel Sexto accozato col Dispiacente, in sul quale al presente si fa lo sgravo, et cognoscendo che a volerlo ridurre in quella quantità la quale meritano le sue substantie bisognerebbe sgravarlo tanta somma che qualche altro cittadino resterebbe in maggiore graveza di lui et harebbe bisogno della approvatione de' Signori et Collegi, il che harebbe a essere publico et non sarebbe sanza admiratione, et nondimeno resterebbe, quando nel Sexto s'achonciassi bene la sua posta, in tanta graveza della Decima per scala che non potrebbe pagarla sanza gratia, et sarebbe assai di charico non pagando, et fargli gratia pe' consigli o per altre vie sarebbe molto dannoso alla città et al presente stato, perchè si dimostrerrebbe el suo malo essere et assai si perderebbe di reputatione; et pendendo la salute del presente stato in gran parte dalla preservatione di decto Lorenzo et in facti et in dimonstratione; et dalla conservatione dello stato pendendo el buono essere del Monte et da quello havendo ad risultare ogni commodo et ogni bene ad ciascheduno membro di decto Monte; et giudicando non si potere fare per una cosa più utile al Monte che procurare in modo non habbia questo ultimo travaglio diminuendosi le graveze di decto Lorenzo più che paia sia l'ordinario per tanto per fare el bisogno publico con la preservatione di decto Lorenzo, che l'uno sanza l'altro stare non può; credendo questo effecto dovere seguire non gli dando di sgravo [di sgravo *s.l. add.*] più ch'el quarto et non tochandogli la decima per scala ma habilitandolo a pagare tali graveze di paghe per vigore di loro auctorità et per evidente utilità del Monte, facto tra lloro el partito et obtenuto per tutte le fave nere de' presenti, absente solo Messer Bongianni Gianfigliazi et absente decto Lorenzo de' Medici del numero di decti Riformatori, providono, ordinarono et deliberorono:

Che tutte le graveze poste et che si porranno in sulla distributione la quale al presente veghia della Decima per scala et in sul Sexto col Dispiacente, sgravato o no, o in su alchune di quelle o in su altre graveze, la quale dipendessi da alchuna di decte o in su quelle o alchune d'epse fussi fondata, le quali tochassino a Lorenzo de' Medici predecto o alle sue poste et non l'altre, si possino per lui pagare o far pagare non solo di contanti ma ancora de' suoi dua terzi di paghe, de' quali l'uno questo et l'altro quest' altro anno [do *del. post*] si debbono restituire, et ancora di qualunque altre paghe ordinarie così insino a qui guadagnate, come di quelle che per l'advenire si guadagneranno, purchè sieno guadagnate quando le graveze s'achonceranno et non solo delle paghe de' sua proprii crediti o d'altri nella sua posta compresi ma ancora di quelle d'altri a llui in alcuno modo appartenenti, et basti solo che a Teghiaio Buondelmonti o ad altri che in suo luogo tenessi el campione del Monte a boccha si dia licentia che delle sua paghe, satisfacto prima al comune del debito delle sua graveze, come è consueto farsi quando le paghe si conditionano, se ne faccia la voluntà di decto Lorenzo de' Medici o d'altri a chi lui havessi commesso. Potendo questo tale et altri farlo creditore di tali paghe solo per questo effecto; et di poi di tale suo credito achonciare le sopradecte graveze di Lorenzo de' Medici et le infrascripte appartenenti a Lorenzo et a Giovanni di Pierfrancesco insino alla quantità intera [*s.l. ex* infrascripta] et non più nè altrimenti. Dichiarando che ⟨f. 80*v*⟩ decto Lorenzo di Piero [*ex* poi *corr.*] prima faccia achonciare tutte le sua paghe et de' terzi et l'altre di tempo in tempo quando saranno venuti e' termini che rendere si possino tali terzi, et che tali altre paghe sieno guadagnate di poi possa usare quelle d'altri, et per questo fare non s'habbia a pagare alcuna gabella o taxa. Ma non possa le paghe le quali aquistassi da altri sanza pagare la gabella ordinaria rihavere in contanti quando glie n'avanzasse, sì che solo per la sua graveze et degli infrascripti usare le possa et sempre fiorino per fiorino. Potendo ancora di queste et simili paghe cancellare uno debito ha da poco tempo in qua contracto col Monte per le sua graveze, le quali gli Uficiali del Monte gli hanno fatte far buone al Camarlingo delle prestanze che si dice tal debito montare circa a fl. 3000 larghi; et ancora, come di sopra s'accenna, possa con simili paghe pagare il debito hanno per le loro graveze insino a qui corse et non pagate Lorenzo et Giovanni di Pierfrancesco de' Medici solo per insino alla somma di fl. 3000 larghi pure a fiorino per fiorino, che così faccendo questo beneficio torna in decto Lorenzo di Piero di Cosimo de' Medici; et questo si fa in compenso maxime di parte del danno ha decto Lorenzo ricevuto già sono quattro anni in pagare l'un sei di graveza più che non meritava, per havere consumato i contanti dove haveva l'arbitrio della graveza, et havere consumato gran parte del Monte, et per altri buoni rispetti. Et per executione de' sopradecti effecti possa et debba Teghiaio Buondelmonte, et qualunche a decto Teghiaio et altri in suo luogho altro pe' tempi exercitassi al Monte quello uficio el quale lui exercita, sanza alcuna solennita o deliberatione d'Uficiali del Monte o d'altri et alla pena a decto Teghiaio et altri in suo luogho di fl. 100 larghi per qualunche volta a pieno quanto di sopra è decto non observassi, et si ène sottoposto a' Conservatori delle Leggi et il quarto guadagni el notificatore, achonciare le paghe a decto Lorenzo di Piero di Cosimo in alcuno de' sopranominati modi a llui al presente o pe' tempi appartenenti al conto delle sopradette graveze lentamente et sanza alcuna pena; et se bisognasse per via di mettere tali paghe a uscita pel Camarlingo del Monte achonciare tali scripture lo faccia decto camarlingo ad richiesta di decto Teghiaio o d'altri in suo luogo et alla pena decta, et pel Camarlingo delle Prestanze quando poliza gli fusse mandata da decto Teghiaio o altri in suo luogo, o dal [*ex* del *corr.*] Camarlingo del Monte per decti effecti s'accepti et achonci le scripture in buona forma; et a llui tali polize per contanti sieno acceptate nelle sue rimessioni; et per questi effecti si faccia per ciascuni uficiali, et per qualunque ministro del Monte o delle Prestanze al quale appartenesse alcuna cosa fare quanto fusse di bisogno, lecitamente et sanza alcuna pena per obligo del suo uficio, et alla pena sopradecta, ciaschuna cosa intendendo a puro et recto senso et sanza alcuna mala interpretatione, ogni et qualunche cavillatione cessante, et observisi quanto è decto, nonobstante ordine insino a qui facto o che per l'advenire si facessi el quale volessi o disponessi che di contanti o altrimenti tali pagamenti di graveze si facessino, et nonobstante provisione o leggie altrimenti disponente; nè si possa nè s'intenda mai derogato al presente beneficio et commodità di pagare decte graveze et debito di Lorenzo et altri come di sopra, se non se ne farà speciale et expressa mentione, et quello che in contrario o altrimenti si facessi non vaglia et sia per non facto et nessuna executione meriti, et nondimeno le sopradecte cose sortischino a pieno i loro effecti ne' modi sopradetti et observinsi per chi apparterrà, come di sopra è decto et alla pena decta.

Copia [*in margine* in Bartolomeo Dei's hand]

Ego Iohannis ser Bartholomei de Guidis, officialis et notarius reformationum consiliorum civitatis Florentiae de supradectis duabus provisionibus et seu deliberationibus reformatorum Montis et Gabellarum communis Florentiae, una sub die nona mensis Iulii anni 1482 altera sub die xxii dicti eiusdem mensis Iulii deliberatis, rogatus in fidem me subscripsi.

Ego vero Bartholomeus Miliani de Deis coadiutor officialis reformationum praedictas duas deliberationes de quibus in dicta subscriptione ser Iohanni fit mentio, et de quibus una est supra in hoc. c. 72 et altera supra in presenti carta sumpsi et copiavi in hoc libro in quo spatia suo loco [suo loco *s.l. add.*] fuerant relicta, ex publica copia manu dicti ser Iohannis, et ut supra subscripta, ut de predictis ab omnibus notitia haberi posset, et ideo in fidem me subscripsi.

Appendix III

SPECIAL PAYMENTS TO LORENZO DE' MEDICI BY THE MONTE OFFICIALS, 1482-1492

The payments in silver (*fiorini larghi di suggello in grossoni*) as opposed to gold (*fiorini larghi d'oro in oro*) at the rate of £5.7s per fiorino unless otherwise specified)

1470-71 (MC 1670, f. 678 left)	FLORINS	£	s	d
Piero di Coximo de' Medici & Co deono dare adì 7 di magio ... per loro per deliberazione degli Ufic⟨ial⟩i a Chastelo di Piero Quaratesi e sue Rede e beni e per loro a Bartolomeo di Niccholo Martteli, Camarlingho ale prestanze perché n'acchonci dal 5 al 12 dodecimo e da la prima a la 13 ventina, le quali in detto dì detto Castelo e sue Erede sono debitori e detta deliberazione fu per mano di ser Simone Grazini sotto detto dì posto Barttolommeo Martteli debe avere c. 527	2175	490	12	0
E de dare posto debi avere al libro xiii del 1471 c. 702 e creditore e lib. c. 608	11047		11	0

fl. 13222 £491 3s. 0d.

The figures in *italic* type refer to the year, in *normal* type to ASF, Monte Comune, left = Monte debit, right = Monte credit

1470-71 (MC 1690, f. 678 right)	FLORINS	£	s	d
Piero di Coximo de' Medici & Co devono avere in dì primo di marzo 1469 [= 70]... Sono per tantti che ci fu consengniato per creditore dal libro xi° del anno 1469, c. 689. Sono per la fine che si fè del credito di Castelo Quaratesi, e quali si dovevano pagare nel modo e forma e in quei tenpi e patti e condizioni che di sotto si dicie posto dato libro detto debi dare	13333	2	5	0
Dovevansi pagare i sopradecti denari per gli uficiali del Monte in questi tenpi, cioè f. 700 a dì 15 di Marzo 1466 e poi ongni mese f. 700 e per tutto el mese di giennaio 1467 avere pagato interamente ongni resto sino ala soma sopradetta pagato prima tutte le graveze de la posta di detto Castelo in modo ch'el Comune sia conservato sanza dano con questa condizione che pasato el sopradetto mese di giennaio 1467 poi infra 8 mesi prosimi aventie, il sopradetto Piero debi avere conperato uno sito idonio per fare un mangno abergo per onore de la città come parrà al detto Piero, el quale abergo sia del arte de' Mercchatanti e così apare per parttito degli uficiali del Monte per ser Lodovicho di ser Angelo da Teranuova loro cancieliere sotto dì 30 giennaio 1466.				

14

1471-72 (MC 2054, f. 702 left)	FLORINS	£	s	d
[*added in 1482*] Piero di Coximo de' Medici & Co deono dare posto Lorenzo ... de' Medici debe avere al libro 24 1482 ... tutto per vigore di legie degli spettabili huomini S. Riformatori del Monte e dele gabele de la città di Firenze rogato ser Giovanni ... [Guidi] ... sotto dì – di luglio 1482, la quale provixione in efetto contiene ch'el contraschritto credito si debe trasferire i' luogo di detto Piero & Co... per pagargli al detto Lorenzo a sua Richiesta sanza alchuna solennità di stanziamento degli uficiali del Monte pure che la soschrizione d'uno degli uficiali del Monte aparischa in su la poliza che si farà del detto pagamento eziandio richiedendo la detta poliza si trasse ad alchuno camarlingo del Monte in dì sostenuto che aparissi inanza a la deta legie posto debito libro 24, f. 702 debe avere	11047		11	0
Per fare uno abergo che sia del artte de' merchatanti				

[fl. 11047 £— 11s. 0d.]

1471-72 (MC 2054, f. 702 right)	FLORINS	£	s	d
Piero di Coximo de' Medici e Co. deono avere in dì primo di Marzo 1470 ... Sono per ttanti ci fu conxengniato per credito da libro 12 del 1470, c. 678 per resto de la fine che ssi fè del credito di Castelo Quaratesi e quindi si dovevano pagare nel modo e forma e in quei tenpi patti & condizioni che distintamente si dicie a la levata debitore c. 533	11047	0	11	0
Dovevansi pagare come si dice al libro 12, c. 678 per fare uno abergo per acietto de' forestieri per onore de la città el quale sia del Artte de Mercchatanti. Di poi per la riforma del Monte di novembre 1470 per quela si dispone ch'e pagamenti espressi e penali ch'e presenti uficiali e quegli che per tenpi saranno durante la decta riforma de 5 anni sono tenuti e ubrigati e de questo non vi si ragiona alchuna coxa. [*added in 1482*] Di poi del mexe di luglio 1482 per vigore di legie [*as on f. 702 left*] per pagargli inmediate al decto Lorenzo sanza altra solennità di stanziamento degli uficiali solo a richesta di decto Lorenzo de' Medici con la soschrizione d'uno de prexenti uficiali del Monte e per farnne uno albergo mangno [etc.] e puosi fare pagare ne dì sostenuti ... libro 24 del anno 1482 de avere' ... per resto conxengniato al detto per vigore di legie dagli spettabili huomini S. Riformatori del Monte e dele gabele de la citta di Firenze sotto di – di luglio 1482.				
Piero de Coximo de' Medici e Co. conxengnato al libro 24 1482 in quello c. 702 a Lorenzo suo figliuolo posto Piero e Comp. debono dare	11047		11	0
	[fl. 11047	£—	11s.	0d.]

1481-82 (MC 1569, f. 826 left)	FLORINS	£	s	d
Lorenzo di Piero di Coximo de' Medici de' dare ... in grossi. Sono per la valuta di fl. 9205 larghi ... Portò lui detto contante per vighore di leggie in suo favore ottenuta da M. Singnori Riformatori del Monte e delle Gabelle del Comune di Firenze per virtù della quale el detto paghamento fare si può a mettere a uscita a chamarlinghi del Monte ne' dì sostenuti sanza altra solenità di stanziamento ho deliberazione degli uficiali pure che in effetto la poliza nostra sia soscritta per mano d'uno de' soprascritti uficiali e per farne quegli effetti che e chome e quanto apare al libro 24 del anno 1482, c. 865 dove detto Lorenzo è creditore per vighore di detta leggie. Paghò Ghuido di ser Giovanni Ghuiducci camarlingho al Monte creditore c. 624		49251	18	6

[fl. — £49251 18s. 6d]

1481-82 (MC 1569, f. 826 right)	FLORINS	£	s	d
Lorenzo di Piero di Coximo de' Medici de' avere ... per deliberazione al libro 24 dell'anno 1482, c. 865		49251	18	6

[fl. — £49251 18s. 6d.]

1482-3 (MC 1572, f. 865 left)	FLORINS	£	s	d
Lorenzo.. de' Medici de' dare per ttanti che Ghuido Ghuiduci camarlingho da Monte pagò per vigore di nostra poliza per auturita conciedutaci com'al dirimpeto più parttichularmente si narra per vigore di legie [etc] da doverssi e poterssi fare il detto pagamento da camarlinghi del Monte ne' dì sostenuti innanzi ala detta legie. E ongni schrittura oporttuna in su libri del monte indricto per ritrovare per ongni tenpo il vero sanza alchuna solennità o stanziamento degli uficiali del Monte solo sia abastanza la soschrizione di uno degli uficiali del Monte. Apare el detto pagamento fatto per Ghuido Ghuiduci al libro 23 1481, c. 826 posto detto debi avere c. 859		49251	18	6
A dì 28 di febraio 1481				

[fl. — £49251 18s. 6d.]

Lorenzo ... de' Medici levato d'accatto di Piero di Coximo de' Medici e Co ... posto Lorenzo debi avere	7205	5	3	6

[fl. 7025 £5 3s. 6d.]

(c. 884) Lorenzo ... de Medici de' dare a dì 10 di settembre f. tre mila larghi. Ebe lui dato contante per vigore di legie in suo favore del mese di luglio e per ordine degli uficiali del Monte da Jachopo di Piero Ghuicciardini, camarlingho al Monte. Posto dato camarlingho debe avere c. 634		16050		
E a dì 28 febraio f. dumila cinquanta larghi. Ebe lui dato contante per vigore come di sopra in grossi ... da Barttolomeo di Branchazio Dini, camarlingo al Monte creditore, c. 668		13375		
E de dare posto debi avere al libro 25 del anno 1483 per resto di questo conto, c. 809	223	206	0	9

[fl. 223 £29632 0s. 9d.]

1482-83 (MC 1572, f. 865)	FLORINS	£	s	d
Lorenzo ... de' Medici de' avere in dì 9 di luglio 1482 f. nove mila dugiento cinque larghi £5 3s. 6d. Sono per altretanti che cci abiamo fatto debitore al libro 13 del anno 1471 Piero di Coximo de' Medici e Co. c. 702 di f. 11047 di sugielo ... per vigore di legie ... sotto dì 9 di luglio 1482. La quale in efetto contiene che si facci creditore i'luogo di Piero ... e Co. el prexente Lorenzo ... in sul prexente campione del Monte e di poi inmediata a sua richiesta sanza altra solennità di stanziamento ... per nostra poliza gli facciamo pagare e sopradetti denari pure chom detta poliza aparischa la soschrizione d'uno degli uficiali del Monte et con queste condizioni che detti denari detto Lorenzo sia ubrigato a farnne fabrichare una caxa mangna ne la città di Firenze a uxo d'abergo che onorevolmente vi si possi racciettare e forestieri per onore de la detta città el quale albergo di poi el dominio perpetualmente sia del artte de Merchatanti come originalmente el detto credito era ubrigato farssi per resto del fine del monte de Castelo Quaratexi. Con questo anchora dichiarato che bixongnando farssi el detto pagamento da camarlinghi del monte in dì sostenuto inanzi ala prexente legie questo far ssi possa sanza alchuno procciuda⟨mento?⟩. Posto debitore libro 13 1471 debi dare, c. 865	9205	5	3	6
[fl. 9205 £5 3s. 6d.]				
(c. 884) Lorenzo ... de' Medici de avere per resto delle paghe del anno 1481 e 1482 di più crediti di Monte a lui aparttenenti e quali per vigore di legie in suo favore sanza altra solennità questi pagare si posono e debino a ongni sua richiesta. Posto detto Lorenzo debe dare al conto ordinario dele paghe '81 e '82	2989	29	12	7
E de avere per tantti abiamo fatto debitore Filipo di Piero di Filipo per la monta di quello conto e per le paghe '81 e '82 per vigore come di sopra	2734	176	8	2
[fl. 5723 £206 0s. 9d.]				

1483-84 (MC 2349, f. 809 left)	FLORINS	£	s	d
Lorenzo ... de' Medici de' dare a dì 31 d'ottobre 1483 ... Portò contante in grossi ... Paghò Piero di Charlo Chanigiani, camarlingho al Monte, ebe £11523.8.0, c. 579	2153	4	15	0
E a dì 29 di febbraio ... ebbe lui detto contante da Giovanni di Tomaxo Buxini, camarlingho al Monte creditore c. 613	767	3	4	4

fl. 2920 £7 19s. 4d.

1484-85 (MC 1487, f. 761 left)	FLORINS	£	s	d
Lorenzo ... de' Medici de' dare a dì 30 di giugno ... Ebbe contante lui detto da Giovanni di Giuliano Gondi, camarlingho al Monte, in grossi ... creditore di £5804.15.0 di grossi, c. 542	1085			
E de dare per tanti restò debitore a lib. 25 del anno 1483 in quello c. 809	1935	4	2	7
E a dì 28 di febbraio ... Ebbe contante lui detto da Tommaxo di Bernardo Antinori, camarlingho al Monte, di grossi ... creditore detto Tomaxo ... di £10005.5.0 di grossi, c. 602	1870	0	15	0

fl. 4890 £4 17s. 7d.

1485-86 (MC 1574, f. 772 left)	FLORINS	£	s	d
Lorenzo ... de' Medici de' dare a dì 30 d'ottobre ... Portò contante in grossi ... Paghò Piero Boninsengna, camarlingho al Monte creditore c. 575 di £10100 16.0 di grossi	1888			
E de dare per ttanti ci fu consengniato per debitore dal libro del anno 1484, c. 761	261	2	1	5
E de dare posto debbe avere al libro 28, 1486, c. 753, per resto di posto conto in quello, c. 753	562	117	9	2

fl. 2711 £119 10s. 7d.

1483-84 (MC 2349, f. 809 right)	FLORINS	£	s	d
Lorenzo ... de' Medici de' avere a dì primo di marzo 1482 ... sono per ttanti restò creditore al libro 24 del 1482, c. 884, per resto delle paghe '81 & '82 posto debitore c. 781 debe dare	223	206	0	9
E de avere per ttanti abiamo fatto debitore Filipo di Piero di Filippo per la monta del conto delle paghe del 1483 per vigore di legie. Posto debe dare c. 807	714	57	16	0
E de avere posto debe dare al libro 26 del anno 1484	1935	4	2	7

fl. 2873 £267 19s. 4d.

1484-85 (MC 1487, f. 761 right)				
Lorenzo ... de' Medici de' avere dì primo di marzo 1484 ... Sono per altrettanti l'abiamo fatto debitore, c. 243	1542	25	16	1
E de avere ... per lui da Filipo di Piero di Filipo per la monta dele paghe del anno 1484 per vigore di legie in favore di detto Lorenzo posto detto Filipo debe dare, c. 760	3057	139	10	1

fl. 4599 £165 6s. 2d.

E de avere ... posto debi dare al libro 1485, c. 772	261	2	1	5

fl. 4860 £167 7s. 7d.

1485-86 (MC 1574, f. 772 right)				
Lorenzo ... de' Medici de' avere dì 28 de febraio 1485 ... sono per conto dele sue paghe del anno deto per vigore di leggie. Posto debe dare, c. 105	868	10	10	5
E de avere per tante abbiano fatto debitore Filipo di Piero da Ghagliano per la monta delle paghe dell'anno 1485 per vighore di legie, c. 773	1843	109	0	2

fl. 2711 £119 10s. 7d.

1486-87 (MC 1889, f. 753 left)	FLORINS	£	s	d
Lorenzo ... de' Medici de' dare a dì 30 d'ottobre ... Portò contante in grossi a £5.11.0. per fiorino. Paghonsi per vighore di leggie. Paghò Zanobi del Zacharia camarlingho al Monte in £10675.10.0, c. 574	3865	3	2	0

1487-88 (MC 1575, f. 728 left)

Lorenzo ... de' Medici de' dare a dì 30 giugno ... ebbe contante da Iacopo di Francesco Monti, camarlingho al Monte, in grossi, creditore c. 531	1888			
E de dare per ttanti ci fu conxenghiato per debitore dal libro 28, 1486, per resto di quel conto com'apare ala levata in quello, c. 753	450	1	1	10

fl. 2338 £1 1s. 10d.

E a dì 29 febbraio ... Portò contante in grossi ... da messer Guidantonio Vespucci, camarlingho al Monte, creditore di £25433 11.0. di grossi	4753	5	0	0

fl. 7091 £6 1s. 10d.

1486-87 (1889, f. 753 right)

	FLORINS	£	s	d
Lorenzo ... de' Medici de' avere per tanti ci fu consengniato per creditore dal libro 27, 1485, c. 772	562	117	9	2
E de avere ... per lui da Filippo di Piero di Filippo da Ghagliano. Posto debbi dare per vighore di leggie in favore di detto Lorenzo, c. 754	358	19	18	7
E dì 28 di febbraio 1486 ... per lui da Filipo ... da Gagliano. Posto debi dare per vigore di legie come di sopra c. 754	1526	75	10	9
E da avere dì detto ... per ttanti l'abiamo fatto debitore per la monta delle paghe di più creditori a lui apartenenti per l'anno prexente 1486 debitore c. 32	925	22	0	0

fl. 3371 £234 18s. 6d.

E de avere per ttanti l'abiamo conxengniato per debitore per resto di questo conto al libro 29 1487, c. 728	450	1	1	10

fl. 3821 £236 0s. 4d.

1487-88 (MC 1575, f. 728 right)

Lorenzo ... de' Medici de' avere a dì 29 di febraio 1487 per ttanti l'abiamo fatto debitore per la monta delle paghe del prexente anno di più e diversi crediti de' paghe de' quali a lui aparttengono, debitore c. 51	876	25	16	8
E de avere dì 28 di febbraio 1487 ... per lui da Filipo ... da Gagliano. Posto debe dare, c. 725	3320	73	4	1
E de avere per ttanti l'abiamo conxengniato per debitore al libro 30, 1488, a c. 737, per resto di questo conto	2877	4	11	1

fl. 7073 £103 11s. 10d.

1488-89 (MC 1638, f. 737 left)	FLORINS	£	s	d
Lorenzo ... de' Medici de' dare a dì 30 di giugno ... Portò e detto contante in grossi ... per vighore di leggie. Paghò Bertoldo di Bartolomeo Chorsini, camarlingho al Monte creditore di £11893 di grossi, c. 528	2223			
E a dì 31 d'ottobre ... Portò contante ... in grossi. Paghò Nerozzo di Piero del Nero, camarlingho al Monte, creditore di £12739. 14.4 di grossi, c. 576	2381	1	7	4
E a dì detto ... Portò contante in grossi ... per vighore di leggie. Paghò Nerozzo di Piero del Nero, camarlingho al Monte creditore di £5647.11.0 di grossi, c. 576	1055	3	6	0
E a dì 21 di febbraio ... Portò contante in grossi ... Paghò Girolamo di Bernardo Chorbinegli, camarlingo al Monte, creditore di £16722.4.0 di grossi, c. 614	3125	3	19	0
E de dare per ttanti ci fu conxengniato per debito dal libro 29 1487 per resto di quella ragione, c. 728	2877	4	11	1
E a dì 23 di febbraio ... larghi a £1.1.0. Porttò contante in grossi a £5.7.0 piccoli. Pagò Girolamo di Bernardo Corbineli, camarlingho al Monte, in grossi £9240.10.0. creditore, c. 615	1727	1	1	0

fl. 13388 £14 4s. 5d.

1489-90 (MC 1664, f. 738 left)				
Lorenzo ... de' Medici de' dare a dì 30 di giugno ... Porttò e detto in contante in grossi ... Pagò Lionardo Beni camarlingho per virtù di nostra poliza per vigore di legie in £8494.5.0. di grosso posto debi avere, c. 527	1587	3	16	0
E de dare per ttanti restò debitore al libro 30 del 1488 ... conxengniato in questo posto debi dare in quello, c. 737	11197	1	8	4
E a dì 28 di febraio ... Porttò contante in grossi... Pagò Braccio di messer Domenico Martegli, camarlingho al Monte, per virtù di nostra poliza e per virtù di legie in £12140.14.8 di grossi. Posto debe avere, c. 589	2269	1	11	8

fl. 15053 £6 16s. 0d.

1488-89 (MC 1638, f. 737 right)	FLORINS	£	s	d
Lorenzo ... de' Medici de' avere ... per ttanti l'abiamo fatto debitore per la monta delle paghe 1488, c. 51	846	23	17	11
E de avere per ttanti abiamo fatto debitore Filipo ... da Gagliano di sua licienza per vigore di legie per la monta del credito suo, come parttitamente apare, c. 738	1329	75	11	6
fl. 2175 £99 9s. 5d.				
E de avere ... posto gli debi dare al libro 31, 1489, per resto di questo conto, c. 738	11197	1	8	4
fl. 13372 £100 17s. 9d.				

1489-90 (MC 1664, f. 738 right)				
Lorenzo ... de' Medici de' avere a dì 28 di febbraio per ttanti l'abiamo fatto debitore per la monta delle paghe del anno prexente di tutti e crediti del monte a llui aparttenenti per successione eredità paternna e maternna come parttichularmente a suo conto si può vedere, c. 41	846	23	17	11
E de avere ... per lui da Filippo ... da Gagliano di sua licienza e per virtù di leggie debitore, c. 739	1066	85	2	3
fl. 1912 £109 0s. 2d.				
E de avere ... sono per tantti che si fa debitore in questo conto e aconxengniati per debitore al libro 32 del 1490, c. 770	13122	0	14	2
fl. 15034 £109 14s. 4d.				

1490-91 (1580, f. 770 left)	FLORINS	£	s	d
Lorenzo ... de' Medici de' dare dì 25 di marzo 1490 ... Sono per ttanti restò debitore al libro 31 del anno 1489. E conxengniato in questo posto debe avere in quello, c. 738	13122	0	14	2
E dì 30 di giungno ... Portò e detto contante da Nicholò di Tommaso Ghuidetti, camarlingho al Monte, in grossi ... Valsono £8432 7,9. di grossi. Posto debe avere c. 559	1576	0	15	9
E dì 31 d'ottobre ... Porttò e detto contante da Giovanni d'Antonio Serristori, camarlingho al Monte. Valsono £12122 8.0 di grossi. Posto detto cam°. debi avere, c. 584	2275	3	18	4
E dì 25 di febbraio 1490 ... per ttanti ci fu conxengniato per debitore dal libro 30 (2°) del 89 e del 90 in quello c. 354 per ttanti gli faciemo pagare a Bernardo di Pazzino, camarlingho al Monte. E in conto del libro, c. 770	4211	84	3	2

fl. 21184 £89 11s. 5d.

1491-92 (MC 1581, f. 750 left)				
Lorenzo ... de' Medici de' dare dì 6 di maggio 1491 ... per ttanti ci fu conxengniato per deliberazione del libro 32 del anno 1490 per resto di quel conto in quello, c. 770	18874	4	19	3
A monte vecchie a £5.8.4 per fiorino in quattrini vecchi gigliati.				
E dì 31 d'ottobre 1491 ... Porttò detto contante in grossi vecchi a £5.7.0 per fl. Pagò Angnolo di Lorenzo Carduci camarlingho al Monte in £14600 grossi ⟨vecch⟩hi. Posto debe avere, c. 578	2729	0	7	0

fl. 21603 £5 6s. 3d.

E dì 29 di febbraio 1491 ... Pagò Luigi di messer Angelo dela Stufa camarlingo al monte in grossi a £5.7.0 per fiorino a grossi 3 per £. Montorono £11591.11.0. Pagò Luigi dela Stufa camarlingo avere c. 603	2166	3	9	0

[fl. 23769 £8 15s. 3d.]

1490-91 (MC 1580, f. 660 right)	FLORINS	£	s	d
Lorenzo ... de' Medici de' avere ... per la monta de le sua paghe del prexente anno, c. 59	734	24	0	0
E de avere in dì 6 di magio 1491 per ttanti abiamo fatto debitore Filipo ... da Gagliano di moneta vecchia, c. 771	1562	136	8	10
fl. 2296 £160 8s. 10d.				
E de avere per ttanti l'abiamo fatto debitore per resto di questo conto al libro 33 del anno 1491 in quattrini vecchi, c. 750	18874	4	19	3
fl. 21170 £165 8s. 1d.				
Saldati a fl. larghi a £5.8.4. per fl. Libro 30 (2°) del 89 & 90 de avere per più debiti in quello de conxengniati in questo come di sotto: Lorenzo ... de' Medici al detto, c. 354, è debitore, c. 770	4211	84	3	2

1491-92 (1581, f. 750 right)				
Lorenzo ... de' Medici de' avere dì 29 di febraio 1491 ... per lui da Filipo ... da Gagliano per la monta dele paghe del prexente anno debitore, c. 771	757	22	1	6
E de avere dì detto ... per tanti l'abiamo fatto debitore per la monta dele sue paghe del anno 1491, c. 62	905	22	1	0
fl. 1662 £44 2s. 6d.				
E de avere dì primo di marzo 1491 ... posto debe dare al libro 34 del anno 1492 per resto di questo conto, c. 743	19933	4	10	5
fl. 21595 £48 12s. 11d.				
E de avere dì primo di marzo 1491 ... posto debe dare al libro 34 del anno 1492 per resto di questo conto, c. 743	2166	3	9	0
[fl. 23761 £52 1s. 11d.]				

1492-93 (MC 1714 f. 743 left)	FLORINS	£	s	d
Lorenzo ... de' Medici de dare per tanti ci fu consengniato per debitore dal libro 33 1491, c. 750 (moneta vecchia)	19533	4	10	5
E de dare in dì primo di marzo 1491. Sono per ttanti ci fu consengniato per debitore dal libro 33 1491, c. 750 (moneta vecchia)	2166	3	9	0
E dì 30 di giungno 1492. Pagò Mauro Fantoni camarlingho al Monte in grossi co'la rintenzione conxueta, a uscita £3603 4.0. in grossi a gr. 3 per £, c. 546 (moneta vecchia)	663	2	13	0
E dì 31 d'ottobre 1492 in grossi a £4.11.4. per fiorino con ritenzione di d.6 per £. Pagò Angniolo Pandolfini camarlingho al monte in grossi £3034.9.4 a quattrini 5.4.6 l'uno di grosso, creditore, c. 575 (moneta nuova)	664	2	4	0
[cf. c. 737 right: 31 Oct. 1492 (Camera del Comune, conto dello straordinario: 'Lorenzo ... de Medici fl. 664 larghi 9s. 3d. (?) a £4.11.4. con ritenzione di d.6 per £. Debitore c. 000: 3031 grossi nuovi 9s. 4d., with 'h' in margin and sum eradicated and scored across].				
E a dì 28 di febbraio 1492 in grossi a £4.11.4. per fiorino a s.5 il grosso con ritenzione di d.6 per £. Paghò Piero Vettori camarlingho al monte in £1914.5.4. di grossi a moneta nuova, creditore, c. 610	419	—	16	8

fl. 23445 £13 13s. 1d.

1492-93 (MC 1714, f. 743 right)	FLORINS	£	s	d
Lorenzo ... de' Medici de' avere a dì 28 febraio di quattrini nuovi posto Filipo ... da Gagliano debi dare c. 744	318	21	9	8
E de avere a dì detto. Sono per la monta delle sue page come pare c. 54 (quattrini nuovi)	1148	1	6	0
E da avere ... Posto gli debi dare al libro 35 (2°) del anno 1493 per resto di questo conto, c. 24 (f. larghi)	21977 *			

fl. 23443 £22 15s. 8d.

* This figure should be 22377 florins, in view of the error in transcribing 19933 florins as 19533 florins in the debit balance opposite, see Table I, note 2, on p. 173 above.

CHANGING LANGUAGE AND IMAGES

6

PLATONISM IN FIFTEENTH-CENTURY FLORENCE

AND ITS CONTRIBUTION TO EARLY MODERN POLITICAL THOUGHT

Platonism played a more important role in the development of early modern political thinking than has previously been suggested. We can see its contribution clearly if we look in detail at what happened in Florence in the fifteenth century. The rise to power of the Medici family both coincided with and encouraged the first translation into Latin and printing of all Plato's dialogues between 1463 and 1484. This created a widespread vogue for platonic ideas. In the field of politics the importance of Platonism was not simply that it may have helped to discourage political activity, as suggested both at the time and later: "When cities are well governed" – Marsilio Ficino is reputed to have taught – "my Plato said good men should flee as far as possible from involvement in government".[1] Nor was

---

This paper was originally published in the «Journal of Modern History», LVIII, 1986. It was first presented to a colloquium on political theory held by the Society for Renaissance Studies in London in 1981. Since then, it has benefited from the comments and suggestions of many friends in Britain and in America, where I enjoyed three months as a British Academy exchange fellow at the Newberry Library in Chicago in 1982. I would especially like to thank Julius Kirshner and John Tedeschi for their help and hospitality in Chicago, and the British Academy and the Newberry Library for making this visit possible. Translations from Italian to English are mine unless otherwise stated.

[1] According to FRANCESCO GUICCIARDINI in *Dialogo e discorsi del reggimento di Firenze*, p.53; cf. A. RINUCCINI's *De libertate*, in F. ADORNO, ed. «Atti e memorie dell'accademia toscana di scienze e lettere La Colombaria», XXII, 1957 pp. 297-298. Although Eugenio Garin stresses Cosimo de' Medici's practical interest in Platonism as "il tiranno dell'italica Atene", he draws a sharp contrast between republican interest in Plato in the first half of the fifteenth century and the neoplatonic mysticism of the second in *L'umanesimo italiano*, Bari, Laterza, 1952, p. 110; *Medioevo e Rinascimento*, Bari, Laterza, 1954, p. 215, and *Platone nel quattrocento italiano*, Naples, Morano, 1969, pp. 283-284. He and now Cesare Vasoli also describe the role of platonism in the time of Lorenzo as that of encouraging a utopian model of enlightened rule; see the previously mentioned *Platone nel quattrocento italiano*, p. 284, *La cultura filosofica fiorentina*

it simply utopian.[2] More positively, Platonism played a crucial role in helping to legitimize the position of the Medici in Florence. It also offered justification of the increasing professionalism of government and the attendant changes in social structure that Florence experienced at this time. It was not, of course, the only current of political thinking at the time, but unless we isolate it as an independent tradition, we may fail to detect its influence. What was more explicit in Florence was less clear elsewhere. But because other European states underwent some of the same changes as Florence, its experience may throw light on the difficult question of Plato's political influence as his ideas became diffused throughout early modern Europe.

Florence faced a double problem of legitimization in the fifteenth century, one inherited, one new. Externally, the city still owed allegiance to the emperor. Although this was no longer a practical problem in that the emperor rarely came to Italy, it nevertheless prevented Florence from enjoying the full legal and diplomatic status of sovereign states like Naples, the Papacy, or Venice. The new problem was that, internally, Florence came to be ruled by a family that enjoyed no legal or diplomatic standing in the city at all. The Medici alone, of all the "new tyrants", as Philip Jones has said, lacked the status in power of nobles, landed gentry, or even *condottieri*.[3] They were merchants. "A simple merchant" is what Sixtus IV called Lorenzo de' Medici in 1478. "Those whom we call merchants should rather

---

nell'età medicea, «*Idee, istituzioni, scienze ed arti nella Firenze dei Medici*, ed. C. VASOLI, Florence, Giunti Martello, 1980, pp. 84-99; C. VASOLI, *Riflessioni sugli umanisti e il principe: Il modello platonico dell'ottimo governante*, in *Per Federigo Chabod (1901-1960)*, ed. S. BERTELLI, «Annali della facoltà di scienze politiche», XVII, 1980-81, vol. I, pp. 158-162; cf. J. G. A. POCOCK, *The Machiavellian Moment*, Princeton, N.J., Princeton University Press, 1975, pp. 63-65. On its wider influence in Florence, see P. O. KRISTELLER, *Lay Religious Traditions and Florentine Platonism*, in his *Studies in Renaissance Thought and Letters*, (I), pp. 99-122. Only Felix Gilbert and Edgar Wind assess the impact of Plato's political realism in this period; and although Wind in my opinion exaggerates Ficino's political involvement in his interpretation of *Platonic Tyranny and the Renaissance Fortuna: On Ficino's Reading* of *Laws IV. 709 A-712 A* in *De Artibus Opuscula, Essays in Honor of E. Panofsky*, New York, New York University Press, 1961, I, pp. 491-496, Gilbert's article, *The Humanist Concept of the Prince and The Prince of Machiavelli*, «Journal of Modern History», XI, 1939, pp. 449-483, offers the most suggestive and surprisingly neglected interpretation of Plato's contribution to modern absolutism in his theory of law and the unrestrained lawgiver.

[2] For contemporary charges of utopianism, see below and n. 64; for current utopian interpretations of Plato, see GARIN and VASOLI; POCOCK, pp. 20-22; M. GOLDIE, *Obligations, Utopias and their Historical Context*, «Historical Journal» XXVI, 1983, p. 740.

[3] P. JONES, *Economia e società nell'Italia medievale: La leggenda della borghesia*, «Storia d'Italia: Annali», Turin, Einaudi, 1978, pp. 344-345.

be called 'circumventors and oppressors' ", a Domenican preacher at Santa Maria Novella said at about the same time.[4] Plato ranked merchants as third-class citizens, and, in the eyes of some of their contemporaries, this was the class to which the Medici belonged; for they had acquired political power not through noble lineage but through wealth, in particular thanks to their large usurious loans to popes and princes.

Both Florence and the Medici lacked the traditional sanctions of religious or inherited authority. Though on occasion the Signoria of Florence and the Medici were described in religious terms as "like God" or as "God's vicar",[5] as non-consecrated heads of state they could not easily be legitimized within the Christian tradition. Their authority was not hereditary. Nor could they be validated by civil lawyers working within the *Corpus iuris civilis*, which accepted the ultimate authority of the emperor. For, although men like Bartolus or Baldus could give limited authority to self-governing communes, they could not justify their ultimate sovereignty – and even less that of the Medici.[6]

Much better adapted to justifying the sovereignty of city-states were the arguments of classical writers like Aristotle and Cicero. Not only did they expect states to enjoy *summum imperium*, or sovereignty,

---

[4] E. Oldovino, letter to Bona Sforza, September 1, 1478 (Milan, AS, SPE, Roma 86); "uno semplice merchadante"; S. I. CAMPOREALE, *Giovanni Caroli e le "Vitae Fratrum S. M. Novellae»*, «Memorie domenicane», n.s., XII, 1981, pp. 256: «Circumventores nunc aut oppressores magis vocandi sunt hii, quos iniquo vocabulo mercatores appellamus».

[5] See DALE KENT, *The Florentine Reggimento in the Fifteenth Century*, «Renaissance Quarterly», XXVIII, 1975, p. 580: "ut unus Deus est adorandus, sic vos Domini Priores venerandi estis ab omnibus civibus", etc.; on the Medici, see BROWN, *Bartolomeo Scala*, p. 39 (Ital. ed. p. 24).

[6] For example, ANGELO DEGLI UBALDI of Perugia, *Consilia*, Frankfurt, 1575, f. 135*v*: "civitas Florentiae auctoritate Caesarea omnia habeat regalia et omnia iura fiscalia"; FRANCESCO ACCOLTI, *Consilia*, Venice, 1573, f. 175*r*: «civitas florentina subest imperio, non summo Pontifici» (dated 1478). On imperial rights, see W. ULLMAN, *The Development of the Medieval Idea of Sovereignty*, «English Historical Review», LXIV, 1949, pp. 1-33, and in general, F. CALASSO, *I glossatori e la teoria della sovranità*, Milan, Giuffrè, 1957; L. MARTINES, *Lawyers and Statecraft in Renaissance Florence*, pp. 410-448; J. KIRSHNER, *Pursuing Honor While Avoiding Sin: The Monte delli doti of Florence*, «Quaderni di studi senesi», XLI, 1978, pp. 46-47, note 141 (who refers to Florence's de facto usurpation of imperial *jurisdictio* and the *facultas legem condendi*). Even in the sixteenth century the emperor claimed that the title of ambassador should be restricted to representatives of crowned heads and Venice alone, while a treatise on *lesae-maiestatis* in 1557 debated whether this crime could be committed by subjects of an "inferioris Principis recognoscentis superiorem a quo habet plena regalia, ut est Dux Florentiae, Dux Ferrariae, Dux Urbini, Dux Mantuae", (R. DE MATTEI, *La concezione monocratica negli scrittori politici italiani del seicento*, «Studi storici in onore di G. Volpe», Florence, 1958, p. 339, note 1; p. 340, note 3).

but, as they predated the Lex Regia that transferred power from the people to the emperor, they also did not recognize imperial overlordship. Aristotle and Cicero had been well known since the thirteenth century and remained popular throughout the fifteenth century. What was new in Florence in the fifteenth century was the practical application of Roman republican procedures, learnt especially from Livy, to Florentine political and diplomatic practice following the creation of a new council of One Hundred and a new council or 'senate' of Seventy in 1480.[7] So classical republicanism contributed a practical solution to the first problem of Florence's legal and diplomatic status in Italy.

But Cicero and Aristotle were becoming irrelevant to the more serious problem faced by Florence in the fifteenth century: the growing power of the Medici in the city and their threat to its political and judicial institutions. The dual offices of Podestà and Captain of the People that had originally represented the different interests of the noble and popular parties were united into a single office in the fifteenth century, and at the same time the dual legislative councils of the Commune and the People were effectively bypassed by a single council of One Hundred.[8] These changes were accompanied by the growth of executive law administered by ordinary citizens without legal training – such as the Eight of Ward, which gave summary judgments in matters concerning public security, or the Merchants' Court of six laymen dealing with commercial disputes according to their own discretion or 'will', both of which were known to be susceptible to Medici influence.[9] The shift from statutory or Roman law

---

[7] See BROWN, *Bartolomeo Scala* 148-149, note 38; pp. 173-176 (Ital. edn. pp. 108, 118-119), also my review, *Florence, Renaissance and Early-Modern State*, pp. 322-326 below.

[8] The office of Captain of the People was finally abolished in 1477 after earlier reductions in judicial offices; the Council of Cento, created in 1458, substituted the older councils in all important matters in 1471, and its authority was confirmed in 1480 when the Council of Seventy was created (BROWN, *Bartolomeo Scala*, pp. 336-337 (ital. ed. pp. 238-239); MARTINES, pp. 136-137; RUBINSTEIN, *The Government of Florence*, pp. 111-112, note 5; 184, 200-201).

[9] On the Otto di Guardia, see G. ANTONELLI, *La magistratura degli Otto di Guardia a Firenze*, «Archivo storico italiano», CXII, 1954, pp.3-39, esp. p. 26; on the Mercanzia, see G. BONOLIS, *La giurisdizione della mercanzia in Firenze nel secolo XIV*, Florence, 1901, and on Lorenzo's influence, see M. FOSCARI's, *Relazion*, «Relazioni degli ambassadori Veneti al senato», ed. A. SEGARIZZI, Bari, Laterza, 1912-16; reprint ed. A. Ventura, Rome and Bari, Laterza, 1976, vol. I, p. 121; BROWN, *Bartolomeo Scala*, esp. pp. 337-338 (Ital. ed. p. 239), and *Pierfrancesco de' Medici*, referring to Lorenzo's intervention in justice (p. 99 above). Compare with JUDITH HOOK's posthumous article, *Justice and the Ancien Regime in Italy*, «Transactions of the Royal Historical Society» 5th ser., XXXIV, 1984, pp. 71-89.

to executive law that this involved is reflected in contemporary debate by the antithesis between reason, *ragione*, and will, *arbitrium*. These become key words at this time to distinguish rational statute or written law from executive 'will' and Medicean 'arbitration' and also, in the field of administration, the rational assessment, called the *catasto* from forced or arbitrary taxation, the *arbitrio*.[10]

It was over the question of whether the ruler or the laws should be sovereign and whether the state should be specialized or multi-functional that Aristotle differed most clearly from Plato. The change from statutory law to executive 'will' and the transference of power to a professional Medicean elite from a larger and more mixed class of citizens – landed gentry, merchants, and artisans ruling for brief periods and being ruled in turn, as Aristotle had prescribed – made writers like Aristotle and Cicero, with their preference for the rule of law and pluralism, increasingly outmoded.[11] Although Cicero did contain some images (largely drawn from Plato) that would justify the Medici's predominant position in the republic, on the whole both he and Aristotle now served as constraints in allowing the Medici no more than the position of *primi inter pares* within a constitutional republic.[12]

---

[10] The Mercanzia received some of the work of the Captain of the People in 1477: "Perchè il giudicio non in ragione bisogna si fondi, ma puossi dare volontario et nessuno rimedio rimane» (BROWN, *Bartolomeo Scala*, p. 337, note 27, Ital. ed. p. 243). Discussion in 1456-57 of whether to reintroduce the *catasto*, based on written statements according to legislated formula, or to retain arbitrary assessments made the same contrast between *arbitrium* and reason/enlightenment: "aut per arbitrium aut per legem", "de duobus modis datis, unum est arbitrarium, alius est cum aliquo lumine", "puto cum lumine fient onera, arbitratio nunquam" (ASF, Cons. Prat. 53, f. 225*r*; 54, ff. 16*v*, 141*v*; I owe these references to Gene Brucker). Compare *Giovanni Rucellai e il suo Zibaldone*, I, p. 9: "Et spesso si raconciano o vero mutano le gravezze, quando al buio per oppenione et quando a lume con catasti et valsenti", cited in D. HERLIHY and C. KLAPISCH-ZUBER, *Les Toscans et leurs familles*, Paris, 1978, p. 47.

[11] The contribution of Aristotle and Roman republicanism to modern thinking is the central theme of J. POCOCK'S *The Machiavellian Moment* (note 1 above), which, in his article *The Machiavellian Moment Revisited*, «Journal of Modern History» LIII, 1981, pp. 49-72, he now interprets as a reaction to "the specialization of function" that had developed around 1500. See also I. KRAMNICK, *Republican Revisionism Revisited*, «American Historical Review», LXXXVII, 1982, pp. 629-664, commenting that this later Aristotle was not a republican radical but a "theorist of hierarchy and privilege" (p. 653); and now, on intellectual interest in Aristotle, see C. B. SCHMITT, *Aristotle and the Renaissance*, Cambridge, Mass., Harvard University Press, 1983. On political changes after 1380, see J. NAJEMY, *Corporatism and Consensus in Florentine Electoral Politics, 1280-1400*, Chapel Hill, N.C., University of North Carolina Press, 1982, esp. chaps. 8 and 9, describing the two faces of the regime that expanded the class of potential office holders as it limited the inner ruling group (cf. p. 276 and p. 311 below).

[12] On Cosimo's republican position, see *The Humanist portrait of Cosimo de' Medici*, pp. 6-15 above. Relevant republican images were Scipio Africanus (in CICERO's *De republica* 6.13,

Paradoxically, it was Plato who was more relevant to the new situation in Florence, despite being a stern critic of riches and the rule of the appetitive class. He offered three vital arguments to defend the secular power of new-rich rulers like the Medici and the social changes that accompanied their rise to power: that power is justified when combined with knowledge, that rule by a good man or judge is preferable to rigid law codes or entrenched customs, and that functions should be distributed according to ability rather than to hereditary caste or guild status. From the 1460s on, public orations and writings contributed to a widespread diffusion of platonic concepts that served to justify the political developments of the time.

Public oratory was an important form of political control in Florence. Every two months, on the induction of the new government, shops were closed, and an oration on justice was delivered in the vernacular in front of the government palace (or in the loggia if raining) to instil civic virtues into the incoming priors as well as their audience.[13] Similarly, lengthy orations were delivered in public when Florence's military captains received their baton of command or when foreign ambassadors visited the city. All these occasions offered the chance of influencing public opinion, as did church ceremonies. Sermons and addresses to lay confraternities were often political in content and so were the popular religious plays that were enacted before large audiences in front of churches. In each of these media, Plato's influence is betrayed by exhortations to see the government in terms of its wisdom and flexibility, whereby men of ability would rule and allow others to protect the city and produce the necessaries of life. The "philosopher-ruler" who combines "power with wisdom", the "good man or judge" who acts as mediator, the division of labour according to *genus* (reverting to the original Greek word) or natural type: these are the three platonic concepts that gained currency in the language of active politics in Florence in the later fifteenth century.

In Florence the platonic revival in the second half of the fifteenth-

---

reproducing PLATO's argument in *The Phaedrus;* cf. BROWN, *Bartolomeo Scala,* p. 38, Ital. ed. p. 24) and Plato's ship's captain, who controls the whole city through his knowledge (CICERO *De officiis* 1.25, from PLATO's *Republic*).

[13] E. SANTINI, *La "Protestatio de Iustitia" nella Firenze Medicea del sec. XV,* «Rinascimento», ser. 1, X, 1959, pp. 48-54; *Statuta Populi et Communis Florentiae,* Fribourg, Kluck, 1778, II, p. 502; cf. Bartolomeo Scala's description of the function of these orations in his *Dialogus de legibus et iudiciis,* ed. L. BORGHI, «La Bibliofilia», XLII, 1940, p. 277. On the role of public ceremony in Florence, see Trexler, *Public Life in Renaissance Florence.*

century was therefore much more than simply a hermetic and mystical movement. Even Plato's condemnation as an idealist after 1494 by a process of seemingly deliberate mystification suggests close involvement with, not detachment from, Medicean politics. His key ideas about power, law, and class division in fact remained relevant to the elitism and increasing professionalism of government, not only in Florence but also wherever the need for legal and administrative reform encouraged the demand for 'freer', more absolutist powers, and more effective government. Feudal aristocracies as well as guild-based communes were experiencing the rise of an administrative class of intendants and secretaries that made Plato's functionalism as topical as his absolutism. His ideas were widely available in Europe after the repeated printing after 1484 of his works in Latin: [14] the problem is how to evaluate their influence.

We do not know what made Cosimo decide to commission the translation of Plato's opus. In 1427 he had received the dedication of Leonardo Bruni's translation of Plato's *Letters* that urged him to take Plato's precepts about the republic to heart; but although Bruni translated the *Phaedo* and the *Phaedrus*, the *Republic* (which Bruni disapproved of) and the *Laws* were first translated by humanists in Milan and Venice.[15] According to Ficino, writing before Cosimo's death as well as much later, it was Cosimo's meeting with Gemistus Pletho at the Council of Florence in 1439 that was decisive: then, as Ficino picturesquely puts it, "the spirit of Plato living in his writings left Byzantium for Florence... and flew to Cosimo de' Medici".[16] As court philosopher and political apologist for the Palaeologi

---

[14] The Florence 1484-85 edition was followed by Venetian editions in 1491, 1517, and 1581, Basel editions in 1546, 1551, and 1561, and a Lyons edition in 1550; cf. C. B. SCHMITT, *Platon dans les universités du xvi siècle,* «XVI collòque international de Tours: Platon et Aristote à la Renaissance», Paris, 1976, pp. 95-96. Important, too, was the revival of the dialogue form at this time, encouraging open debate and relativity. See D. MARSH, *The Classical Tradition and Humanist Innovation,* Cambridge, Mass., Harvard University Press, 1980, esp. pp. 11-15.

[15] See GARIN, *Medioevo e Rinascimento,* p. 252, note 48, where he suggests Leonardo Bruni may possibly have translated a single book of *The Republic.* Bruni found in it "multa ... abhorrentia a moribus nostris", *Epistolarum Libri VIII,* ed. L. MEHUS, Florence, B. Paperini, 1741, II, p. 148. On Uberto and Pier Candido Decembrio's translation of *The Republic* in 1400 and 1447 and George of Trebizond's translation of *The Laws,* see F. ADORNO in *Studi in onore di Antonio Corsano,* Manduria, Lacaita, 1970, pp. 7-17; E. GARIN, *Ricerche sulle traduzioni di Platone nella prima metà del sec. XV,* in *Medioevo e Rinascimento, studi in onore di B. Nardi,* I, pp. 339-374.

[16] In the preface to his 1464 translation of ten platonic dialogues, dedicated to Cosimo (ed. P. O. KRISTELLER, *Supplementum Ficinianum,* II, p. 105), Ficino said, "E Bizantia Florentiam spiritus eius ipsis in licteris vivens ... ad Cosmum Medicem advolavit"; cf. his more ideal-

in Mistra, Gemistus Pletho's practical approach to politics is reflected in the *Mémoires* he wrote for the young prince Theodore Palaeologus. He also wrote and expounded to his friends in Florence a treatise *On Laws*, in which he argued that, amid great diversity and disparity of laws throughout the world, those standing out as identical represented eternal principles of reason or platonic ideas.[17] This inductive approach contrasted with the deductive basis of Christian natural law and it would have appealed not only to the empirical and much-travelled Florentine merchants, anxious for a common standard for their protection abroad, but doubtless also to Cosimo, busy as he then was transforming the Florentine constitution. Of all Plato's dialogues, it was in fact the *Laws* that Cosimo first wanted Ficino to translate.[18] So although we can only speculate on the reasons for Cosimo's interest in Plato, it was probably more practical than Ficino's account of his platonic mission might lead us to believe.

Cosimo's interest in law is well documented. As Gonfalonier of Justice in 1445, Cosimo commissioned eight citizens to review all the laws, "to be able to arrange the government to please himself ... in order to lead the city slowly to his tyranny", a later hostile chronicler commented.[19] And in 1463 Cosimo was to be found discussing with Giovanni Argyropoulos, a pupil of Pletho's, and Otto Niccolini, a leading Medicean lawyer, the question of whether "the laws of jurisconsults are according to moral philosophy or to which philosophy are they subject?". When Argyropoulos replied that they were "not of the essence of philosophy", the lawyer "got very angry" and wanted them to be a part of and not subject to moral philosophy. Cosimo enjoyed such intellectual debates, we are told, and although he knew laws were subject to moral philosophy, he wanted to see Niccolini's argument since it was difficult to argue that they were not.[20] Here

---

ized account of his platonic mission, "In Plotinum", 1490, in *Opera omnia,* Basel, 1576; reprint Turin, 1962, II, pp. 1537-1538.

[17] On Pletho, see F. MASAI, *Pléthon et le Platonisme de Mistra,* Paris, Societé d'Edition «Les Belles Lettres», 1956. His *De rebus Peloponnesiacis Oratio II* to Prince Theodore is edited in *Patrologia graeca* CLX, cols. 841-866; his incomplete *Traité des Lois* is edited by C. ALEXANDRE and A. PELLISSIER, Paris, 1858 repr. A. M. Hakkert, Amsterdam, 1966. On Cosimo and Pletho, cf. BROWN, *Bartolomeo Scala,* pp. 259-260, 341 (Ital. ed. 182, 240-241).

[18] FICINO, *Opera omnia,* I, p. 611 (641); P. O. KRISTELLER, *Marsilio Ficino as a Beginning Student of Plato,* «Scriptorium», XX, 1966, p. 45.

[19] G. CAMBI, *Istorie,* ed. I. di SAN LUIGI, *Delizie degli eruditi toscani,* XX, p. 250: "Per potere achonciare lo stato a suo modo ... per condurre la ciptà a poco a poco a la tiranida sua".

[20] Described by VESPASIANO DA BISTICCI in his life of Cosimo, *Le Vite,* ed. A. GRECO, II, pp. 203-204.

Cosimo is disassociated from Niccolini's attempt to free law from moral restraints. Nevertheless, it is interesting, and perhaps not coincidental, to find a revived interest in platonic law accompanied by discussion of the very topic that was to exercise lawyers and politicians alike in early modern Europe: was law an aspect of truth to be discovered freely by the philosopher-ruler, or was it subject to moral restraints imposed by the church and customary law? [21] As we have seen, it was Plato's dialogue *On Laws* that Cosimo first wanted translated, and although Ficino was unable to translate it before Cosimo's death, he translated instead the pseudo-platonic dialogue the *Minos* that later formed the basis of the chancellor Bartolomeo Scala's practical discussion of law in Florence in 1483.

Whatever the basis of Cosimo's own interest in Plato, it helped to bring about a changed climate of opinion. Thanks to the university teaching of one of Cosimo's closest friends and confidants, Carlo Marsuppini, these ideas were transmitted to later generations. Marsuppini was himself a great admirer of Pletho, and as a popular teacher as well as a lawyer and subsequently chancellor of Florence (from 1444 to 1453), he was a man of considerable influence.[22] In view of Plato's attitude to law and functionalism, it seems likely that growing interest in Plato coincided with changing political as well as cultural attitudes in Florence. At any rate, by the time Cosimo died the climate had been created that allowed the Medici to be projected as philosopher-rulers whose claim to govern and modify the laws was justified by their power and ability alone. Most striking, initially, was the change in the Medici's political image, but it was accompanied by a more subtle transformation of political values that proved equally important.

The transformation of Cosimo's political image from republican statesman to philosopher-ruler began before his death and continued afterwards, especially during the life of his grandson Lorenzo, who in turn became heir to it. The one essential qualification apart from power was, of course, wisdom, and although in 1427 Bruni had thought

---

[21] See D. R. KELLEY, *Civic Science in the Renaissance: Jurisprudence Italian style,* «Historical Journal», XXII, 1979, pp. 777-794; his *The Beginning of Ideology* Cambridge, Cambridge University Press, 1981, pp. 193-194; J. FRANKLIN, *Jean Bodin and the Rise of Absolutist Theory,* Cambridge, Cambridge University Press, 1973; and, in general, H. CAIRNS, *Legal Philosophy from Plato to Hegel,* Baltimore, 1967, esp. chaps. 6 and 7.

[22] On Marsuppini, see BROWN, *Bartolomeo Scala,* pp. 10-11, 258-260 (Ital. ed. pp. 5, 181-182).

Cosimo richer in gold than wisdom, by the time he died, Cosimo had successfully demonstrated his wisdom both by his political acumen and by his learning. Florentines and foreign ambassadors alike referred to him as "a very wise man" who "behaves very wisely", and even before he died he was described as "the very man whom the divine Plato wanted to govern cities and public affairs".[23] Soon afterwards his image as the all-competent and learned ruler was secure:

He read, he heard, he saw everything. Nothing happened that he did not know about. No one was sharper in debate, no one discovered the truth more easily or expressed it more aptly. It is amazing how many excellent men of every kind were drawn to him (for his house was veritably a gymnasium of the liberal arts), it is amazing, I say, that no one, whatever his special ability, left Cosimo without declaring himself to be wiser than when he arrived. For if the topic concerned the obscurities of nature, such was his understanding of every problem that you'd think he always had Thales, Pythagoras, Plato, Aristotle, Zeno, Democritus and the other philosophers in his hand. If it concerned religion and divinity, good God, what extraordinary, what novel, what unheard of wisdom did he not reveal? And if it happened to concern morals, what law did he not know, what regulation did he overlook? [24]

The language is eulogistic, coming as it does from the preface to Bartolomeo Scala's collection of writings in praise of Cosimo, the *Collectiones Cosmianae*. But the image is pressed home in many other genres, not least in Scala's own pithy, ironic *Apologues* that were greatly admired and read in diplomatic and papal circles in the 1480s, where he praises Cosimo for being in the front ranks of the worshippers of Wisdom and Truth, among kings, emperors, princes, and rulers of people; or in his platonizing *Dialogue on Laws and Legal Judgments* on the nature of law, where Cosimo combines Socrates' wisdom with the mellifluous style of Plato, "that great man and philosopher of clearly divinely-inspired intelligence", whose writings Cosimo was responsible for acquiring and having translated "for his citizens to

[23] See n. 15 above; RUBINSTEIN, *Government of Florence*, p. 102, notes 2, 5: "viro sapientissimo", "Cosimo se ne porti molto saviamento"; see the *The Humanist portrait*, pp. 16-17 above, quoting Argyropoulos's preface, dedicated to Cosimo, to his translation of Aristotle's *Physics:* "te palam ... talem hominem ... qualem divinus ille Plato civitatibus praeesse rebusve publicis voluit"; cf. E. GARIN, *Studi sul platonismo medievale*, Florence, Le Monnier, 1958, p. 189.

[24] Bartolomeo Scala, preface to the Collectiones Cosmianae, Florence, Biblioteca Laurenziana, MS. plut. 54, 10, f. 3*r*, to be printed in my forthcoming edition of Scala's humanistic and political writings.

read and admire".[25] This is also the image of Cosimo that Ficino records, "sharp in discussion as he was wise and strong in government", who died after reading Plato's *Parmenides* and *Philebus* with Ficino: "Certainly", Ficino wrote to Lorenzo, "I owe much to our Plato, but I confess I owe no less to Cosimo. For Plato showed me the concept of the virtues but once; Cosimo put them into practice every day".[26]

Among many other examples, two in particular encapsulate the platonic image of Cosimo in differing ways as it emerges from the private into the public arena. Bartolomeo Platina's *On the Best Citizen* is the work of a non-Florentine that nevertheless reflects Florentine values. Platina had been educated in Florence, and he dedicated his treatise to Lorenzo de' Medici around 1474 as a republican counterpart to his *De principe*, dedicated to the princely Gonzaga family in Mantua. It shows how effectively Plato provides the necessary argument for reconciling autocracy with republicanism. Cosimo is one of the interlocutors, "the wisest of men", "redolent of socratic gravity". In it he plays the part of Socrates in propounding to his grandson Lorenzo crucial platonic doctrines about the state, such as the need for philosophers to rule the ship of state or for rulers to philosophize, the need to rule for the benefit of the state as a whole and not its parts (an argument used to practical and partisan effect by the Mediceans in 1476, as we shall see), and the need sometimes to allow "the best statesman" as tutor "to be preferred to the laws". Despite conforming to traditional advice books for cities and princes, it is original in subtly equating the Medici with rulers like Moses and David the king, as well as with republican heroes, great legislators like Lycurgus and Solon, and Caesar Augustus, to whom we are told the citizens preferred to defer power rather than suffer civil war.[27]

---

[25] BARTOLOMEO SCALA, *Apologi centum*, ed. C. MUELLNER, Vienna, 1896, nos. 63, 65, *Sapientia* and *Veritas*, pp. 27-28, *Dialogus de legibus et iudiciis*, pp. 273-276; compare Scala's letter to Lorenzo and Giuliano de' Medici on the death of their father in 1469, referring to Cosimo's "virtutem, pietatem, sapientiam" that Scala "semper putavi esse divinam" MS Magl. VIII, 1439, f. 73*r*; all to be printed in the above edition.

[26] FICINO, *Opera Omnia*, I, p. 649 (679), in *The Letters of Marsilio Ficino*, London, Shepheard Walwyn, 1975, I, p. 136; cf. BROWN, p. 26, note 101 above.

[27] B. PLATINA, *De optimo cive*, ed. BATTAGLIA, esp. pp. 183, 204-205, 212, 220, 236; cf. PLATINA'S *De principe*, ed. G. FERRAÙ, Univ. di Messina, 1979. On *De optimo cive* and its relationship with *De principe*, see N. RUBINSTEIN, *Il "De optimo cive" del Platina*, in *Bartolomeo Sacchi il Platina*, ed. A. CAMPANA and P. MEDIOLI MASOTTI, Padua, Antenore, 1986, pp. 137-144. On models of advice books, see Q. SKINNER, *The Foundations of Modern Political Thought*, Cambridge, 1978, I, pp. 33-35, 116-118.

The political relevance of Platina's dialogue was immediately commented on in Florence by Mediceans like Bartolomeo Scala (chancellor from 1465 to 1497) and Donato Acciaiuoli. On first reading the dialogue, Scala at once wrote to praise Platina for making Cosimo his model of the best citizen, "as the best citizen, the light and glory of all civil wisdom", with whom he hoped Lorenzo would identify, so that everyone would declare "another Cosimo has returned to our city". At the same time, Scala also wrote to Lorenzo urging him to take the dialogue seriously, in which he "hung on the words of his grandfather, drinking his wisdom as an infant drinks from the breast of his mother".[28]

The other example is Cristoforo Landino's preface to his *Commentary on Dante's Commedia*, which received great public acclaim when printed in 1481. The edition was honoured at a public ceremony at which Landino delivered an oration praising "the divine Plato" as the most outstanding political philosopher, whose precept about republics only being happy when philosophers rule or rulers philosophize justified the education he had given young Florentines for the past thirty-seven years. As university teacher since 1458, as well as public orator and chancery secretary, Landino exercised considerable influence on public life in Florence. Although on this occasion he declined to discuss Plato's and Aristotle's differing views about the structure and division of labour in cities (the chancellor Bartolomeo Scala taking it up two months later on another public occasion), he had in fact adopted Plato's class structure as the framework in his preface for extensive eulogy of outstanding Florentines. Here Cosimo emerges as leader of the guardians or "consultori", whom Landino distinguishes from the platonic second class of soldiers or auxiliaries, the "militi e propugnatori", by implication giving him the role of principal

---

[28] Bartolomeo Scala, draft letters to B. Platina ("Probo etiam tuum consilium qui Cosmum disputantem de civis optimi officio feceris optimum civem lumenque et decus totius civilis sapientiae. Recognoscet sese Laurentius in dictis avi ... ut iam redditum urbi nostrae alterum Cosmum omnes fateantur") and Lorenzo de' Medici ("Te autem pendentem ab ore avi eiusque sapientiam haurientem tanquam ab matris ubere infantem"), April 1474, Archivio Borromeo, Isola Bella, Fondo Autografi S 6, f. *2r-v, Supplementum Festivum. Studies in honor of Paul Oskar Kristeller,* ed. J. HANKINS, J. MONFASANI and F. PURNELL, Binghamton, N.Y., Medieval and Renaissance Texts and Studies, 1987, pp. 327-331. Donato Acciaiuoli wrote to praise its "precepta" on May 5, 1474, saying Lorenzo was very delighted with it; see RUBINSTEIN, *Il "De optimo cive" del Platina.*

philosopher-ruler.[29] Thus by 1481 the Medici have subtly made the leap from Plato's third mercantile and productive class to the top class of guardians.

The quality necessary to transform the power of wealth into a political asset was wisdom, as we have seen. Although the young Lorenzo de' Medici conspicuously lacked this asset at the time of his father's death in 1469, when his notorious love affairs were neither platonic nor wise, his friends and advisers worked hard to transform him in the early 1470s. Bartolomeo Scala in his letters, Cristoforo Landino in his *Camaldulensian Disputations*, and Marsilio Ficino in the preface to his *Platonic Theology* all encouraged Lorenzo to combine philosophy with supreme public authority – as Ficino put it, "as Plato above all wanted to happen in great men".[30] *Sapientia: potentia*, wisdom combined with power, became again the crucial formula to justify Lorenzo's status in Florence. Usually those who hold supreme power lack intelligence, Naldo Naldi writes in an epigram to Lorenzo, but now the fates have united power with wisdom: "As you know everything, o Medici, thus you are all-powerful" ("Sic sapis, o Medices, omnia sicque potes").[31] "You alone of the whole universe of men both rule the republic wisely and recall philosophy home from long

---

[29] Both CRISTOFORO LANDINO's *Proemio al commento Dantesco* and *Oratio* before the Signoria are edited by R. CARDINI in *Scritti critici e teorici,* Rome, Bulzoni, 1974, I, pp. 100-164, 169-174. Compare LANDINO's *Proemio ad commento Virgiliano,* also in CARDINI, ed., pp. 217-218, in which he praises Cosimo's "incredibilis ... sapientia ... ut quaecunque ille diceret, ea non ab humano ore profecta sed a divino oraculo decantata viderentur".

[30] See note 28 above. MARSILIO FICINO's *Theologia platonica,* dedicated to Lorenzo in 1474, is in his *Opera omnia,* I, p. 78 (106): "Quod ille in magnis quondam viris potissimum exoptat, ipse philosophiam una cum summa in rebus publicis auctoritate coniunxeris". On the formula, cf. his preface dedicated to Cosimo in 1464, p. 104 (note 16 above) and his "Apologus: Potentia sine sapientia non regnat", *Opera omnia,* I, p. 848 (878). On the influence of Ficino's platonism on Lorenzo, see P. O. KRISTELLER, *Lorenzo de' Medici Platonico*, in his *Studies in Renaissance Thought and Letters,* (I), pp. 213-219. LANDINO's *Disputationes Camaldulenses,* probably written toward the end of 1473, is edited by P. LOHE, Florence, Olschki, 1980; see esp. p. 11, where Landino quotes the precept he had much earlier described in a letter to Lorenzo, 1463 (BNF, MS Magl. VI, 166, ff. 98*v*, 99*r*-99*v*): "Divinissimo enim consilio multa apud Platonem scripta reperies, sed hoc in primis: Tunc denique beatas respublicas futuras cum aut illas philosophi administrabunt aut ii a quibus administrantur philosophari ceperint". Compare also BENEDETTO COLUCCI's *Declamationum liber,* written in 1474, describing his admiration for Lorenzo, who "inter tanta negotia otium philosophiae suppeditare ... Siquidem apud Platonem lectitastis, quales principes, tales reliquos cives esse solere", in *Scritti inediti di Benedetto Colucci da Pistoia,* ed. A. FRUGONI, Florence, Olschki, 1939, p. 19.

[31] NALDO NALDI, *Epigrammaton liber,* ed. A. PEROSA, Budapest, K. M. Egyetmi Nyonda, 1943, p. 18, no. 49.

exile", Angelo Poliziano told Lorenzo in the preface to his translation of Plato's *Charmides*.[32]

Power with wisdom was also the formula used to praise Lorenzo by the Dominican theologian and regent of the *studium* of Santa Maria Novella, Niccolò Mirabile. After hosting and joining in a discussion on original sin between Mirabile and the Franciscan regent of Santa Croce, Giorgio Benigno Salviati, Lorenzo was described by Mirabile as "the prince and author of our gathering and of our disputation, in whom, according to Plato, God has joined power with wisdom".[33] Salviati, for his part, admired in Lorenzo's sonnets "the intelligence and wisdom of the highest of theologians".[34] The Augustinian Hermit Fra Mariano da Genazzano inscribed above the door of the monastery Lorenzo had built for him, "a marianesque concoction in capital letters, with great charm" (Ercole d'Este's secretary reported): "WISDOM BUILT THIS PLACE FOR HERSELF".[35] And although all too few of Fra Mariano's fashionable sermons have survived, we can imagine that they, too, helped to idealize Lorenzo's spiritual wisdom at the time when "up here in the pulpits one says and quotes nothing

---

[32] POLIZIANO, *Opera,* Basel, 1553; reprint, Turin, Bottega d'Erasmo, 1971, I, p. 448: "Quapropter cum te unum, magnanime Laurenti Medices ... ex universa hominum multitudine existere intelligat qui et rempublicam sapienter geras et philosophiam omnium bonarum artium parentem longo iam tempore exulantem ... in patriam revoces".

[33] NICCOLÒ MIRABILE, *Disputatio nuper facta in domo Magnifici Laurentii Medices... ad Mag. Laurentium Medicem.* The *disputatio* was held on June 30, 1489, and an account of it was printed in Florence by Francesco Dini, July 27, 1489, and reprinted with G. B. Salviati's argument by F. VILMOS and A. JENO in Budapest in 1886: "Ad te unum omnia referre tanquam ad principem et auctorem tam convivii quam disputationis nostrae in quo deus iuxta Platonem potentiam simul cum sapientia coniunxit" (f. a1*v*, Budapest ed., p. 353). Lorenzo, with his friends Ficino, Poliziano, and Pico della Mirandola, intervened in the discussion that continued an earlier debate held in the cathedral. Niccolò Mirabile was a doctor in theology and regent of the studium of Florence in Santa Maria Novella.

[34] On Salviati, a platonizing Scotist appointed by Lorenzo to teach his son Piero philosophy, see C. VASOLI, *Profezia e ragione,* Naples, A. Morano, 1974, pp. 17-120: "l'ingegno e sapienza di altissimo teologo" (p. 41).

[35] Francesco Castelli's letter to Ercole d'Este, describing a visit to San Gallo, is quoted by D. A. PERINI, *Un emulo di Fra Girolamo Savonarola: Fra Mariano da Genazzano,* Rome, 1917, p. 42: "Cum una soscriptione sopra la porta facta in lectere maiuscole de farina marianesca: Sapientia hedificavit sibi locum, cum tanta gratia" (quoting Solomon, Prov. 9:1). On Lorenzo and Fra Mariano, see p. 30; on Fra Mariano's sermons, see D. GUTIÉRREZ, *Testi e note su Mariano da Genazzano,* «Analecta augustiniana», XXXII, 1969, pp. 117-204; and Z. ZAFARANA, *Per la storia religiosa di Firenze nel quattrocento,* «Studi medievali», IX, 1968, pp. 1017-1113. Referring to Lorenzo, NICCOLÒ VALORI, in his *Vita del Magnifico Lorenzo de' Medici,* Florence, Giunti, 1568, wrote: "Soleva dire el prefato Mariano mai havere conosciuto huomo alcuno posto in degnità nel quale fusse tanta pietà et religione et che con più reverenza parlasse delle cose divine, et che sequendo l'oppenion' de' Platonici et molto più de' Christiani, affermava altra vita doversi sperare" (f. e3*r*).

but Aristotle and Plato and a thousand nonsenses", Girolamo Savonarola fulminated. "These days up here one says nothing but: Plato, that divine man. I tell you, one should sooner be in the house of the Devil".[36] Niccolò Valori's biography of Lorenzo later recalled how Lorenzo 'penetrated' the intimate meanings of Plato under the guidance of Ficino, according to whom "Lorenzo used to say that without platonism one could neither be a political citizen nor easily follow the Christian doctrine".[37] So religion served to add another dimension to Lorenzo's reputation for wisdom.

Finally, Lorenzo emerges in the 1490s as the man whose knowledge of music and the universe enables him to predict and "more prudently than the stars" moderate and control Florence's fortune, as writings and orations at this time suggest: by implication the platonic ruler whose knowledge places him "above the laws and the stars".[38] Nor was his reputation limited to Florence by then. The coppersmith Bartolomeo Masi commented that when Lorenzo died "he was considered one of the wisest men in Italy".[39] In Bologna, Lorenzo had the reputation in 1491 of being "wise and powerful", "the wisest of men"

---

[36] GIROLAMO SAVONAROLA, *Prediche sopra i Salmi,* ed. ROMANO, I, pp. 255-256, May 31, 1495: "Che quassù ne' pergami non si dice e non si allega più se non Aristotile e Platone e mille zacchere ... Vedi, che oggidì, quassù, non si dice se non Platone, quello uomo divino. Io ti dico che e' debbe essere più presto a casa del diavolo". On the pervasion of both Fra Mariano da Genazzano's and Savonarola's sermons by platonic concepts, cf. Fra Mariano's sermon: "El Padre à la potenza, el Figiuolo à la sapienza e lo Spirito Santa à la bontà" (ed. GUTIÉRREZ, p. 170), and Savonarola, trust "in Dio, non in sapienza, in Dio, non in potenzia" (ed. ROMANO, II, p. 45, June 9, 1495).

[37] VALORI, f. a4*v*: "Afferma Lorenzo esser solito dire senza la dottrina Platonica ne Politico cittadino potersi essere ne facilmente conseguire la doctrina Christiana". On the dating of the life, see M. MARTELLI, *Le due redazioni della 'Laurentii Medicei Vita' di N. Valori,* «Bibliofilia», LXVI, 1964, pp. 235-253, in which he argues that the Italian version may in fact be taken from an earlier Latin draft written toward the end of 1494. Compare the confraternity sermons of Giovanni Nesi, a platonizing Medicean before later becoming a follower of Savonarola, whose "De moribus" of 1484 (Florence, Bibl. Laur. MS plut. 77, 24, ff. 1*r*, 3*v* sqq.) to Piero di Lorenzo de' Medici eulogizes the Medici for their wisdom and learning; C. VASOLI, *Giov. Nesi tra Donato Acciaiuoli e Girolamo Savonarola,* «Memorie Domenicane», n.s., IV, 1973, pp. 103-179.

[38] See FILIPPO REDDITI's *Exhortatio ad Petrum Medicem in magnanimum sui parentis imitatione,* BNF, MS Palatino 648, f. 7*v* "In Musicis tantopere emicuit ut Musicorum nemini aetate nostra cedere videatur", speaking not about ordinary music but about that "quae proxime ad celestem accedit armoniam, de qua Plato Pithagorasque multa conscripsere ... Nec frustra Plato civili viro ... necessariam musicem credidit", written ca. 1492-94); and Pandolfo Collenuccio's poem "Florentia", delivered by him as podestà in November 1490 on the induction of a new Signoria; see A. SAVIOTTI, ed., *Operette morali, poesie latine e volgari,* Bari, Laterza, 1929, II, p. 109.

[39] *Ricordanze di Bartolomeo Masi calderaio fiorentino dal 1478 al 1526,* ed. G. O. CORAZZINI, Florence, Sansoni, 1906, pp. 17-18: "Uno de' più savi uomini che fussi in tutta Italia".

("savio e potente", "sapientissimo"). "You have wisdom, you have power, you can do what you want in Italy", Pandolfo Collenuccio wrote to Lorenzo, wittily adding biblical weight to his platonic imagery by telling Lorenzo that if he did what the Bolognese wanted, they would sing praises solemnly in Florence "to the wisdom of their Wise Man".[40] In Rome, Paolo Cortesi in his book *On the cardinalate* called Lorenzo wise "by the consent of the whole of Italy".[41] And outside Italy the historian and diplomat Filippe de Commynes described "the lately deceased" Lorenzo as "one of the wisest men of his time".[42] He died, according to Poliziano's description of his last days, as he had lived, torn between his desire to spend the rest of his life philosophizing with his humanist friends and the need to give his citizens the benefit of his authority and counsel: the incarnation of Plato's philosopher-ruler who combines, unhappily, power with wisdom even unto death.[43]

This idealization of Cosimo and Lorenzo de' Medici reveals an important transformation of political ideas. Bartolomeo Fonzio's modish oration on 'Wisdom' or Leon Battista Alberti's *De Iciarchia*, praising the wise prince, "that is, the supreme magistrate" , as the best form of government, show the way things were going.[44] But it was in the field of public oratory that the impact of platonic ideas was most evi-

---

[40] From letters to Lorenzo dated February 8 and 10, and March 13, 1491, in Saviotti, ed., II, pp. 287, 290-294, esp. 291: "Nondimeno V. M. è sapientissima; sia sempre fata la voluntà vostra, la qual, quant'è per mi, ho per summa ragione"; and p. 294: "prometteranno e cantarranno *solemniter* lì in Fiorenza, o dove vorranno, al senno del loro Savio".

[41] Paolo Cortesi, *De cardinalatu libri tres,* In Castra Cortesio, 1510, f. xiii*r*: "Laurentius Medices, qui est totius Italiae consensu iudicatus mentis habitu, litterataque expolitione sapiens".

[42] Filippe de Commynes, Mémoires, ed. B. de Mandrot, Paris, A. Picard, 1903, II, p. 40: "des plus saiges hommes de son temps".

[43] See Poliziano's letter to Jacopo Antiquario in his *Opera,* p. 49; cf. his *Miscellania Centum, Opera,* p. 301 (chap. 90): "Medices Laurentium, Florentiae reipublicae columen, cuius cum iudicium illud circunspectissimum et naturalem quandam mentis altitudinem, maxime quaeque in actum rerum vel civitates experiuntur vel principes, tum eundem in literis et humanitatis ac sapientiae studiis, ei denique non admirantur qui non penitus ut ipsi, qui non introrsus inspexerunt".

[44] See B. Fontius, *Oratio de Sapientia,* in *Orationes*, Florence, n.d., dedicated to Lorenzo de' Medici, f. d1*v*: having previously celebrated all the arts, "novam tandem inveni dicendi viam". L. B. Alberti, *De Iciarchia,* in his *Opere volgari,* ed. C. Grayson, Bari, Laterza, 1966, II, p. 195: "Il principe, cioè il summo magistrato"; cf. Vasoli, *Riflessioni,* p. 293. As one of the interlocutors in Landino's *Disputationes Camaldulenses*, p. 169, Alberti refers to the "supremus magistratus" in a "bene instituta republica ... cuius arbitrio etsi omnia gerantur, alii tamen assunt minores magistratus ... ita totius vitae imperium in mente consistit".

dent. Florentine government had always emphasized the role in the state of the wise man of mature experience as a *savio*, or adviser.[45] What is novel now is the growth of the idea of the wise man who enjoys supreme moral and judicial, as well as political, authority on the basis of his understanding of the laws of the universe. Although no one openly claimed such godlike powers for Lorenzo, he was nevertheless gradually associated with the platonic concept of sovereignty in the writings and orations of a small group of Medicean politicians and chancery secretaries who helped to popularize a different form of government in Florence: no longer government by a fairly wide, multi-ability group ruling 'rationally' according to written statutes administered by impartial outsiders, but, instead, government by a few specialists who acted both as rulers and judges in freely interpreting and modifying the law according to their will, or *arbitrium*.

Plato's paternalistic and holistic concept of justice is first alluded to in public in an oration before the government palace on July 13, 1475, on the occasion of the induction of a new Signoria. Before the assembled crowds, Pierfilippo Pandolfini proclaimed that true justice "is when inferior and less worthy powers obey the superior powers; ... this platonic justice is a true union and peace", for according to "the divine Plato ... the governors of republics should behave like good tutors and do everything for the benefit of the governed, not themselves".[46] The same concept of justice was enunciated more strikingly eighteen months later in the preface to a law that reveals the political implications of this paternalism. According to Plato, as Ficino reminded his fellow citizens, prefaces to laws should serve to persuade citizens "freely, like sons" instead of forcing them tyrannically to obey, and so the partisan law by which the Medici deprived the Pazzi family of their Borromeo inheritance persuasively begins: "One of the precepts of Plato, prince of philosophers, to those who rule republics is this, that they should care for the whole body of the republic, lest by caring only for part of it they desert the rest".[47]

---

[45] On the *savi*, see the 1415 *Statuta* in *Statuta Populi et Communis Florentiae*, II, pp. 622-623; G. GUIDI, *Il governo della città-repubblica di Firenze del primo quattrocento*, Florence, Olschki, 1981, II, p. 37.

[46] *See* E. SANTINI, ed., pp. 68, 74.

[47] "Inter Platonis philosophorum principis praecepta ad eos qui reipublicae praesunt, hoc habetur ut totum corpus reipublicae curent, ne dum aliquam partem tuteantur reliqua deserant", ASF, Statuti 29, f. 416*v* (March 18-20, 1477); FICINO's *Opera omnia*, II, p. 1488 (488): "Libenter parere velint, ac sponte, velut filii legum illis obtemperent"; cf. PLATO's *Laws*, IV,

Underlying this emphasis on unity and holism was the idea that the state itself was more important than the parts or interests that went to make it up. It was a member of the chancery, Filippo Redditi, Scala's personal assistant, who later praised Lorenzo not only for the special knowledge of music that Plato thought essential for the statesman, or *politikos*, but also for "precisely observing that divine opinion of Plato's, that we are born first for God, then for our country, and after that for our parents, relations, and other mortals" – an argument that would have given useful support to the Medici's attempts to weaken the bonds of kin and neighbourhood which competed with the claims of central government.[48]

Closely associated with this theory of platonic justice was Plato's theory of the sovereignty of "the good man or judge" whose knowledge entitles him to interpret the laws or to rule above them. The concept of the ruler as the *lex animata* was of course an old one. Now, however, it is discussed in relation not to the emperor or to kings but to any wise man, as in the 1481 dialogue *On Laws and Legal Judgments* of the chancellor of Florence, Bartolomeo Scala. Influenced by Gemistus Pletho's view of law as well as by Ficino's commentary on the *Minos*, the dialogue discusses whether law should be unchanging and eternal or adjustable to changing situations and circumstances. Praising the equitable justice administered by the six lay members of the Merchants' Court in Florence, "chosen not as experts in law but because they are naturally shrewd and good men", Scala's own opinion was that it is "better to live according to the direction of a good man and a good judge under the guidance of nature" than according to codified laws, which he described as "that necessity which men imposed on themselves".[49] The dialogue form makes its argument allu-

---

723A, BROWN, *Bartolomeo Scala*, p. 339, (Ital. ed. p. 244), notes 37, 38. On this law, see F. GUICCIARDINI, *Storie fiorentine*, pp. 31-32, and *Memorie di famiglia*, in *Scritti autobiografici e rari*, *Opere*, ed. R. PALMAROCCHI, Bari, Laterza, 1936, IX, p. 35.

[48] REDDITI, *Exhortatio*, f. 4*v*: "Quod sententiam Platonis servavit". Ad unguem mihi videtur genitor tuus divinam illam Platonis sententiam custodisse, qua ille nos primum Deo, deinde Patriae, demum parentibus et cognatis ceterisque mortalibus procreatus esse censuit". On Redditi, see D. MARZI, *La cancelleria della repubblica fiorentina*, p. 270; cf. his letter to Lorenzo praising him for his "divino consilio" and control of the ship of Italy (A. M. BANDINI, ed., *Collectio*, p. 93). On the holistic view of the state, cf. FICINO's letter to Piero del Nero, in *Opera Omnia*, I, p. 643 (673); *The Letters of M. Ficino*, I, p. 124; and on kin and neighbourhood values in Florence, see D. V. KENT and F. W. KENT, *Neighbours and Neighbourhood in Renaissance Florence*, New York, J. J. Augustin, Locust Valley, 1982.

[49] SCALA, *Dialogus de legibus et iudiciis*, esp. p. 268: "Sex viros non iuris expertos illos quidem, sed natura scitos et bonos deligunt"; and p. 269: "Quanto igitur ... vivi potuit melius

sive and Lorenzo is not mentioned openly. But its implications are later made explicit by a peripatetic humanist official, Pandolfo Collenuccio, whose story criticizing forensic justice Scala quotes approvingly in the dialogue.[50]

It was in November 1490, on the induction of a new Signoria, that Collenuccio as Podestà of Florence recited before a large audience first a poem in praise of the city and then another exhorting the Signoria to justice. In both, his platonic framework is obvious: his poem praising Florence not only describes the platonic revival there but also refers to Lorenzo as a prophet who "more prudently than the stars" can justly control and improve Florence's lot; while the poem to the Signoria compares the city to man's soul, in which reason reigns as sovereign over the lowly passions.[51]

Only three months later Lorenzo de' Medici produced a play for the entry of his son Giuliano into the religious company of the Evangelist, the *Rappresentazione di SS. Giovanni e Paolo.* In it his son's namesake, the emperor Julian, is made to say: "The king and the wise man are above the stars, whence I am beyond this vain law... I will follow, shepherd of this flock". In fact, the apostate emperor's death, according to the predictions of the astrologers, proved he could not control his fate. Nevertheless, his account of the responsibilities and duties of the true ruler who governs for the benefit of the whole state and helps the people with money and food would have helped to iden-

---

ad boni viri bonique iudicis arbitrium duce natura ... quam eam sibi imposuisse homines necessitatem"; BROWN, *Bartolomeo Scala,* pp. 288-296 (Ital. ed. pp. 202-206). On the *lex animata,* see W. ULLMAN, *Law and Politics in the Middle Ages,* London, The Sources of History, 1975, pp. 60-61, 92; F. DVORNIK, *Early Christian and Byzantine Political Philosophy,* Washington, D. C. Dumbarton Oaks, 1966, II, pp. 622-624. Compare ULLMAN, *The Development of the Medieval Idea of Sovereignty,* p. 3 sqq.

[50] On Collenuccio, see A. SAVIOTTI, *Pandolfo Collenuccio, umanista pesarese;* Pisa, Nistri, 1888, and the bibliography of C. VARESE in *Prosatori volgari del quattrocento,* Milan and Naples, Ricciardi, 1955, pp. 593-595. His story of the lawyer who, after an initial payment, showed his client three rows of books, each giving respectively a favourable verdict, an unfavourable one, and a suspended sentence, and therefore "showing the whole outcome lay in his hands", is in Scala's *Dialogus de legibus et iudiciis,* p. 267.

[51] The poems are edited by SAVIOTTI, *Operette morali,* II, pp. 103-112, 119-122, esp. 108-109 ("sed quae venturi casus oracula, certis / designata modis, praesago nuntiet ore, / quaeque minas trepidae sortis, prudentior astris, / in melius iusto semper moderamine vertat. / Vive diu, Laurus, patriae tutela beatae"), pp. 120-121. The ceremony is described by Poliziano in a letter to E. Barbaro: "Praetor urbanus carmen pro nostris, ineunte summo magistratu, pronunciavit. Materia, laudes urbis ... Omnes enim plane confluxerant, qui sic ab ore dicentis pendebant ut ad unum putares litteratos" (cited by A. SAVIOTTI, *Pandolfo Collenuccio,* pp. 52-53). According to Saviotti, the verses in praise of Lorenzo in BNF MS Magl. VIII, 47 have been deleted; see *Pandolfo Collenuccio,* p. 57, note 1.

tify him, however subliminally, with Lorenzo in the eyes of the popular audience, by whom the play was enthusiastically received.[52] Nor was the propaganda value of such publicity lost on the people, since Machiavelli, possibly one of the audience, later quoted from the play the emperor Constantine's line as Lorenzo's own: "What a prince says today, the people will say tomorrow". Through it, Lorenzo had successfully identified himself as the ruler who acts as model for his people and diffused this image to be recorded, years later, by Machiavelli.[53]

Discussion of platonic justice and the rule of the wise man was accompanied by growing interest in the differences between Plato's and Aristotle's views about political participation and class structure. Here Plato's opinion that "any plurality of functions or shifting from one order to another is not merely utterly harmful but...the extreme of wrongdoing" was directly criticized by Aristotle on the grounds that "the state is a plurality" and that good citizens ought to be capable of "both ruling and being ruled".[54] Although it took time for their differences to be fully appreciated, public orations in the 1480s show the topic was beginning to arouse interest. It was Cristoforo Landino who first raised it at the ceremony held by the government on the occasion of the publication of his *Commentary on Dante* on August 30, 1481. Landino had in fact adopted Plato's class division in his printed preface to the commentary, but there he apparently identified

---

[52] LORENZO DE' MEDICI, *Rappresentazione di SS. Giovanni e Paolo,* in his *Opere,* ed. A. SIMIONI, Bari, Laterza, 1914, II, p. 114: "Il re e 'l savio son sopra le stelle, / ond'io son fuor di questa vana legge / ... io seguirò, pastor di questa gregge"; and on the role of "i signori veri" who "rappresentano il tutto", see p. 111 (cited by GILBERT, *The Humanist Concept of the Prince,* p. 476). It was first performed on February 17, 1491; on its reception, see the *Ricordanze di B. Masi,* ed. CORAZZINI, p. 16: "Eravi a vedere detta festa Lorenzo de' Medici... E di molti altri uomini da bene, e tanto popolo che era una cosa maravigliosa".

[53] N. MACHIAVELLI, *Discorsi,* ed. S. BERTELLI, Milan, Feltrinelli, 1973, bk. 3, ch. 29, p. 465: "E Lorenzo de' Medici, a confermazione di questa sentenza, dice: E quel che fa 'l signor poi molti, / che nel signor son tutti gli occhi volti", quoting the emperor Constantine's lines beginning "perchè lo esemplo al popol molto vale", *Rappresentazione,* II, p. 100. Lorenzo also refers to the ruler's role in "pari la bilancia ben tenere ", p. 101. Compare n. 30 above and A. VERDE, *Lo studio fiorentino,* «Memorie Domenicane», 1977, III, 2, p. 688, no. 60, for other references to this "Platonis preceptum ... quod principum mores populus imitetur".

[54] PLATO, *Republic,* IV, p. 434, ARISTOTLE, *Politics 1263b, 1277b.* On classes, see J. LE GOFF, *Notes sur societé tripartite,* in *L'Europe du IX au XI siècle, ed.* T. MANTEUFFEL and A. GIEYSZTOR, Warsaw, 1968, J. BATANY, *Des "Trois Fonctions" aux "Trois états"?* in «Annales-economies, societés, civilisations», XVIII, 1963, pp. 933-938; G. DUBY, *Les trois ordres ou l'imaginaire du feodalisme,* Paris, Gallimard, 1978.

it with Aristotle's. In his oration before the Signoria he raised the topic only to drop it at once, telling his audience it was not his job and they were too busy to discuss the differences between Plato and Aristotle: "Nor will I be prolix in narrating into how many parts they divide a well-instructed republic, nor to how many different men at different times according to different conditions they attribute different offices".[55]

Thus titillated, Landino's audience had to wait only two months before the theme was taken up again, this time by the chancellor of Florence. On October 4, 1481, Bartolomeo Scala delivered a "very learned and long" but popular oration on the occasion of Costanzo Sforza's appointment as Captain General of Florence, which was greeted with a shout of "Long live Messer Bartolomeo"! taken up by "all the people, in a loud voice".[56] In it, Scala, too, said nothing to suggest there was any practical difference between Plato's and Aristotle's ruling class of guardians and military auxiliaries (tactfully, perhaps, in view of the occasion, since Plato excluded soldiers from his ruling class whereas Aristotle included them); but he did not shirk a detailed and accurate analysis of the differences between Hippodamus's and Plato's three-class division, and Aristotle's sixfold division that distinguished between citizens and non-citizens, using Plato's word *genus* for class or natural type.[57] It was, in fact, during the Savonarolan republic that Scala finally rejected Aristotle's division for Plato's, arguing in his 1496 *Apologia* that the function of ruling and consultation (*publicum consilium*) should be restricted to "senators" alone, who thus come to play the role of Plato's first class, to be distinguished from "the people" comprising soldiers and workers, who "can fill the civil offices".[58]

[55] LANDINO, *Orazione dedicatoria*, August 30, 1481, in *Scritti critici e teorici*, I, p. 170. Compare note 28 above.

[56] SCALA's *Oratio pro imperatoriis militaribus signis dandis Constantio Sfortie Imperatori* was printed in Florence in 1481; on its reception, see BROWN, *Bartolomeo Scala*, p. 99, (Ital. ed. p. 75), note 107: "Viva Messer Bartolomeo! Tutto il populo seguitandolo ad alta voce disse l'istesso", and p. 154, note 51.

[57] SCALA, *Oratio*, f. 2*r-v*: "Tria enim genera quibus constarent urbes posuit Hippodamus apud Aristotelem". This is also the word used by LANDINO in his *Disputationes Camaldulenses*, p. 153: "diversis sive ordinibus sive generibus distinguit"; cf. Ficino's translation of PLATO's *Republic*, in *Platonis Opera*, Lyons, 1588, p. 394: "tria hominum genera"; cf. pp. 375-396.

[58] BARTOLOMEO SCALA, *Apologia contra vituperatores civitatis Florentiae*, Florence, Antonio Miscomini 1496, f. b1*r-v*: Neque rempublicam appellare convenit ubi senatus auctoritas non sit, idest, ubi publicum consilium desideretur (id enim senatus est) aut desit populus, qui civilibus muneribus possit sufficere". The influence of Plato even after the fall of the Medici

The fall of the Medici in 1494 led to an immediate reaction against platonism. The fact that it was Savonarola, the Medici's political opponent, who initiated this attack provides the best evidence of the extent to which Plato had been associated with the Medici in popular opinion. For, as a friend of many platonists and as a philosopher who on his own admission had been very influenced by Plato, Savonarola's sustained attack on Plato and "the wise men of the world" from the pulpit must be explained principally by political motives.[59] He can be quite explicit, as in criticizing "those brains who ruled before, they fell at the first wave, their wisdom didn't help them... Look at Italy, where is the brain that knows how to steer this boat in Italy"? (and the trained ear will of course pick up the allusion to waves and boats as a reference to the platonic captain whose knowledge entitles him alone to control the ship of state); or in his ridicule of the so-called wisdom of the tyrant: "See how wise he is, especially when he wants to propose something in the council that is known to him and concealed from the others; he calls a meeting of many *savi* to discuss the topic they know nothing about, then he speaks as someone who knows a lot about it, and helps them, and makes them look stupid in the sight of everyone and he acquires praise".[60] He can be allusive in contrasting pagan "wisdom and power" with Christian "simplicity", "stupidity", and "madness": "So I speak to you this morning as a madman, *un pazzo*... It's necessary sometimes to become *pazzo*". "Tell me, *savio*, what do you know or think about the stupidity or wisdom of Christ"? "You have so much wisdom, it stinks over all the world". "Let Plato be Plato and Aristotle Aristotle" , he declaimed in March 1498, "and not Christians, because they are not".[61]

---

is demonstrated by Mario Salamonio's orations as Captain of the People in 1498-99, in which he describes Florence according to Plato's tripartite division of society into magistrates, soldiers, and producers as "more perfect" than the others, based as it was on natural qualities of the soul (M. D'ADDIO, ed., *De principatu libros septem nec non Orationes ad priores florentinos,* Milan, Giuffrè, 1955, pp. 89-90).

[59] D. P. WALKER, *The Ancient Theology,* London, Duckworth, 1972, ch. 2, pp. 42-62; E. GARIN, *Ricerche sugli scritti filosofici di Savonarola,* in *La cultura filosofica del Rinascimento italiano,* Florence, Sansoni, 1961, p. 203.

[60] SAVONAROLA, *Prediche sopra Amos e Zaccaria,* ed. GHIGLIERI, I, pp. 152-153 (February 21, 1496), p. 227 (February 24, 1496).

[61] SAVONAROLA, *Prediche sopra i Salmi,* II, p. 211 (October 18, 1495), *Prediche sopra Giobbe,* ed. R. RIDOLFI, Rome, A. Belardetti, 1957, II, p. 291 (April 13, 1495), *Prediche sopra Ruth e Michea,* ed. V. ROMANO, Rome, Belardetti, 1962, I, p. 133 (May 20, 1496), *Prediche*

The combined effect of Savonarola's sermons, the political incompetence of Lorenzo's son and heir, and the changed foreign situation that destroyed Florence's independence all served to undermine the platonic argument. "Certainly, any one wise enough to understand the times and the order of things and who adapts himself to them would always have good fortune... and it would come to be true that the wise man would rule the stars and the fates", Machiavelli wrote in 1506. "But because there never are such wise men... it follows that fortune changes and commands men and holds them under her yoke".[62] His friend Francesco Vettori agreed with him: "I do not want to discuss things rationally any longer because often I have found myself deluded"; "It often seems to me things do not proceed according to reason".[63] So platonic idealism became unfashionable. "I mean to write something useful... searching for the real truth of the matter rather than for its imagined one. Many have dreamed up republics and principalities that have never been seen or known to exist in reality", Machiavelli wrote in *The Prince*. "We do not have to look for an imaginary government and one that is easier to find in books than in practice, as perhaps Plato's *Republic* was", Francesco Guicciardini makes the Medicean protagonist of his *Dialogue on the Government of Florence* say, and again Francesco Vettori agreed in rejecting those republics written and dreamed about by Plato or found in the Englishman Thomas More's *Utopia* in order to speak about "things as they really are".[64] It is this new realism that is regarded as typi-

---

sopra Esodo, ed. P. G. Ricci, Rome, Belardetti, 1956, II, p. 291 (March 18, 1498), cited by Walker, p. 46: "Si vuol fare che Platone sia Platone, Aristotile Aristotile, e non che siano cristiani, perchè non sono».

62 Machiavelli, Letter to Giovan Battista Soderini, *Lettere,* ed. F. Gaeta, Milan, Feltrinelli, 1961, p. 231. It is redated 1506 instead of 1512 by R. Ridolfi and P. Ghiglieri, *I Ghiribizzi al Soderini,* «La Bibliofilia», LXXII, 1970, pp. 53-74 (I owe this reference to Quentin Skinner). It is attributed to Giovan Battista instead of Piero Soderini by M. Martelli, *"I 'Ghiribizzi' ",* «Rinascimento», IX, 1969, pp. 147-180.

63 Francesco Vettori to Machiavelli, in *Lettere,* p. 237 (March 30, 1513): "Io non voglio andare più discorrendo con ragione, perchè spesso mi son trovato ingannato", and p. 267 (July 12, 1513): "Mi paia spesso che le cose non procedino con ragione".

64 Machiavelli, *Il principe,* ed. S. Bertelli, Milan, Feltrinelli, 1973, ch. 15, p. 65; Guicciardini, *Dialogo e discorsi,* p. 99; Francesco Vettori, *Sommario,* in *Scritti storici e politici,* ed. E. Niccolini, Bari, Laterza, 1972, p. 145. This is also the attitude of Matteo Palmieri in his *Vita civile,* ed. G. Belloni, Florence, Sansoni, 1982, p. 7, which was written in the 1430s before Gemistus Pletho's arrival, and its references to Plato come mainly from Cicero's *De officiis,* e.g., pp. 132, 192, 199-200; on Palmieri's later and heretical platonism, see R. J. Palermino, *Palmieri's Città di Vita: More Evidence of Renaissance Platonism,* «Bibliothèque d'Humanisme e Renaissance», XLIV, 1982, pp. 601-604.

cal of 'modern' political thinking, not Plato's idealism. Hence the latter's apparent irrelevance to sixteenth-century developments.

Yet far from being the spent force that these men suggest, Plato remained relevant to the growing elitism and centralization of government. In fact the revival of republicanism after 1494 did not mean a return to the dualism, short-term offices, and multi-ability polity of the medieval commune.[65] Instead it continued the trend of all post-1380 governments towards the concentration of power in a single council (the Great Council replacing the earlier dual councils of the Commune and the People as the ultimate legislative authority), a "senate" of eighty men consisting – as recent analysis demostrates – of the same professional elite as in the Medicean period, and, after 1502, by a permanent head of state, who was also to serve "as head of justice ... to propose what seems to him just and reasonable in every decision, judgment or criminal sentence".[66] It was this regime that Scala described in platonic terms, in that the function of ruling and consultation (*publicum consilium*) was limited to senators alone within an extended citizen body that included labourers (peasants and artisans) as well as fighters.[67] Even Savonarola recognized that Florence needed a platonic arbiter and public head to replace the Medici, "being accustomed as it was to living with a private one".[68] And so did the Florentine merchant Piero Vaglienti, who wrote in his diary in 1499 that it was better to know whom one had to obey "than

---

[65] On "the virtual liquidation of the magnates as a genuine social category in the acts of the Balìa of 1434", see D. KENT, *The Rise of the Medici*, p. 346. Although the Medici did not succeed in abolishing the importance of guild status in Signorie, etc., through their attempt to reduce the number of minor guilds from fourteen to seven in 1472, they did remove them and some other corporations from ex officio membership of *balìe* and scrutiny councils after 1466; see *The Guelf Party in fifteenth-century Florence*, pp. 129-132 above.

[66] "Come capo della giustitia et proporre quello gli paressi giusto e rag[i]onevole in ogni partito, giudicio e sententia criminale" (ASF, Provvisioni 193, f. 50, August 26, 1502), see R. PESMAN COOPER, *L'elezione di Pier Soderini a gonfaloniere a vita*, «Archivio storico italiano», CXXV, 1967, p. 160. Roslyn Pesman Cooper's analysis of the Florentine ruling class from 1494 to 1512 is in «Studies in Medieval and Renaissance History». VII, 1984, pp. 71-181; cf. also her discussion with N. Rubinstein, *Oligarchy and Democracy in Florence*, in *Florence and Venice: Comparisons and Relations*, I, Florence, La Nuova Italia, 1979, pp. 99-115.

[67] See note 58 above.

[68] PIERO PARENTI, "Già suto questo disegno di frate Hyeronimo, il quale volea dare a questa città capo pubblico, sendo assueta a vivere con capo privato", quoted by S. BERTELLI in *Petrus Soderinus patriae parens*, «Bibliothèque d'Humanisme et Renaissance», XXXI, 1969, p. 98.

to have to serve the bunch of lords and cackle of ducks that comprise the government of our city of Florence today".[69]

Political realists and republicans like Machiavelli and Guicciardini also recognized the need for "someone to stand at the rudder, as Lorenzo de' Medici had effectively done", in Machiavelli's reported words.[70] In the blueprint of government he offered Cardinal Giulio de' Medici in 1520, Machiavelli combined republicanism with monarchism by retaining the Great Council but giving Giulio effective sovereignty during his lifetime since "you command the army, you command the criminal judges, you have the laws in your breast".[71] Guicciardini, too, recognized that the Great Council must be retained to give popular consent but thought it should be controlled by a strong and effective government. In the *Dialogue on the Government of Florence* (1523), he argued through Bernardo de Nero that the Medici's "knowing favouritism" was preferable to "popular ignorance", and in 1537 he replied to the exiles that Alessandro de' Medici's absolutism was justified, because once established, a state has unlimited power.[72]

Underlying both Machiavelli's and Guicciardini's recognition of de facto power is in fact a familiar argument for government needing to be dispassionate, based on ability and the division of function – as we can see from Guicciardini's intimate and revealing reflection about the rule of a prince being better and more equitable "to all" than republican government, justice being more effective when quick and based on "living reason" than on dead precedent, and about mixing jobs being not only disfunctional but morally wrong. For just as the people can commit the crime of *lesae-maiestatis* by doing what belongs

---

[69] Ed. BERTI, LUZZATI, TONGIORGI, *Storia dei suoi tempi, 1492-1514*, p. 84: "Meglio sapere a chi l'uomo ha' ubbidire che avere a servire a un mazzo di signori a un tratto e a un guazzabuglio d'anitre come è al dì d'oggi questo governo di questa nostra città di Firenze".

[70] "Perchè manchava di chi stesse a timone, chome stava sufficientemente Lorenzo de' Medici", according to the confession of Giovanni Folchi in March 1513; see J. STEPHENS and H. BUTTERS, *New Light on Machiavelli*, «English Historical Review, XCVII, 1982, pp. 58-59, 67.

[71] MACHIAVELLI, *Discursus florentinarum rerum*, in *Arte di guerra e scritti politici minori*, ed. S. BERTELLI, Milan, Feltrinelli, 1961, pp. 274-275: without Cardinal Giulio, the state would be a republic; with him, "una monarchia, perche voi comandate all'armi, comandate a' giudici criminali, avete le leggi in petto".

[72] *Dialogo e discorsi*, p. 46: Medici favouritism "si far studiosamente, suole avere peso e misura, ma la ignoranza è cieca, confusa e sanza termine e regola". His reply to the exiles in 1537 is discussed in an important article to which I was directed by Julius Kirshner: D. MARRARA, *Il problema della tirannide nel pensiero di Francesco Guicciardini e di Francesco Vettori*, «Rivista storica del diritto», XXXIX, 1966, pp. 99-154.

to the prince, he reflects, so the prince can commit the crime of *lesae-populi* by engaging in trade and "doing what belongs to the people to do".[73] Despite their attack on Plato's idealism and impracticality, they seem to have remained more indebted to him than perhaps they realized or liked to admit.

Jean Bodin made a penetrating comment on these changes in stating that Florence in the time of Lorenzo de' Medici resembled Athens in the time of Pericles; for then, as in Athens, "the commonwealth in shew was popular but in effect a mere Tyranny, for that Laurence governed all alone". Bodin also helps to show why Plato was so relevant to fifteenth-century Florence when he says that Plato thought the best kind of state is "a mixture of a Monarchie and Democratie" in contrast to the aristocracy preferred by Aristotle – and himself.[74] Hobbes, too, noted that Thucydides preferred Athens under the rule of Peisistratus or when "it was democratical in name, but in effect monarchical under Pericles", to the period when it was "mixed of *the few* and *the many*".[75] This combination of monarchy and democracy has no place in Aristotle's popular classification of constitutions, but it in fact provides the model for our "early modern state" that concentrates power in "one man or assembly of men" ruling with the "consent" of all the rest.

---

[73] GUICCCIARDINI, *Ricordi,* ed. R. SPONGANO, Florence, Sansoni, 1951, ser. C, no. 107, p. 118 (Engl. tr. M. Domandi, *Maxims and Reflections,* Philadelphia, University of Pennsylvania Press, 1972, p. 68); see P. ROSSI, *Guicciardini criminalista,* Milan, 1943, referring to *Ricordi* ser. C, nos. 208, p. 220) (94) ("qualche viva ragione" against "l'autorità di uno dottore") and 209, p. 221 (95) (preferring as a lesser evil Turkish sentences "le quali si expediscono presto e quasi a caso" to the delays of Christian justice), and ser. C, no. 93, p. 104 (64) ("quello che appartiene a fare al popolo e a' privati"). In GUICCIARDINI's discussion, *Del modo di eleggere gli uffici nel consiglio grande,* he presents as the counterargument to hereditary aristocracy the fact that "spesso e' figliuoli sono el contrario de' padri e che le virtù ed el cervello non vanno per eredità", *Dialogo e discorsi,* p. 191. There are other analyses of the threefold division of society in the *Discorsi* of LODOVICO ALAMANNI and NICCOLÒ GUICCIARDINI, ed. R. VON ALBERTINI, *Firenze dalla repubblica al principato,* Turin, Einaudi, 1970, pp. 381-383, 391-392.

[74] J. BODIN, *The Six Bookes of a Commonweale,* facsimile reproduction of R. KNOLLE's 1606 translation, Cambridge, Mass., Harvard University Press, 1962, bk. 6, pt. 4, p. 706; cf. p. 721 on Cosimo de' Medici, "whome the banished men of Florence called a tyrant although he were esteemed of many others to be a good and wise prince"; bk. 2, ch. 1, p. 184: "But when Plato said, the best kind of a Commonweale to be composed of the mixture of a Monarchie and Democratie, he was therefore forthwith reprehended by his scholler Aristotle"; bk. 4, ch. 1, p. 407: "As when in our time the Florentine popular estate was changed into a Monarchie".

[75] THOMAS HOBBES, preface to his translation of THUCYDIDES, *English Works,* ed. W. MOLESWORTH, London, Longman, Brown, Green and Longmans, 1843, VIII, p. XVII; cf. L. STRAUSS, *The Political Philosophy, of Hobbes,* Chicago, University of Chicago Press, 1973, pp. 59-60.

The paradox whereby Plato helped to justify post-1494 republicanism is a clue to understanding his role in early modern Europe: outwardly rejected as he had been in Florence for his idealism, his ideas nevertheless remained relevant as an intellectual underpinning to the growing elitism and professionalism of government.[76] For although the specific situation of Florence in the fifteenth century was not repeated elsewhere, other states experienced similar political and administrative problems and similar social unrest. This was also the period when Plato's writings became more familiar thanks to the numerous editons of his works in Latin that followed the Florence *editio princeps* of 1484-85. Here the Florentine experience may be useful in suggesting an approach to the problem of evaluating his political influence in the early modern period.

In ducal courts in Milan, Mantua, Ferrara, or Urbino, Plato served to legitimize the power of their newly-stabilized *condottieri* rulers in terms of their wisdom and culture rather than their military prowess.[77] Elsewhere in Europe the rise of academies and the "Gargantuan appetite for books" that accompanied the cult of "the learned prince" reveal the continuing influence of the platonic image of the philosopher-ruler who combines power with wisdom.[78] Although the

---

[76] On his rejection in France, see J. CEARD, *'République' de Platon et Pensée Politique,* in *XVIe collòque international de Tours,* pp. 177-179; N. O. KEOHANE, *Philosophy and the State in France,* Princeton, N.J., Princeton University Press, 1980, p. 315. In England, see FRANCIS BACON, *The Advancement of Learning,* II.VII.4, in *Works,* London, W. Ball, 1837, III, p. 355. The only reference to Plato in R. DE MATTEI's essay, *La concezione monocratica negli scrittori politici italiani del seicento,* is to G. B. PIGNA's *Il principe,* Venice, 1561, in which Pigna "platonizzi più che aristotelizzi" in describing the prince's authority as that of a hero and father of his family (pp. 324-325).

[77] See B. CASTIGLIONE, *Il libro del cortegiano,* ed. V. CIAN, Florence, Sansoni, 1974, bk. 4, ch. 17, p. 425; ch. 21, pp. 431-432; ch. 47, p. 466, where Ottaviano Fregoso argues that it is better to be ruled by a wise and temperate prince than by a man of courage. In contrast to this political realism is Bembo's more famous disquisition on platonic love, bk. 4, chs. 51-70. As elsewhere, Plato is dismissed in *Il cortegiano* as an idealist, bk. 4, ch. 42, p. 460; cf. J. R. WOODHOUSE, *B. Castiglione: A Reassessment of "The Courtier",* Edinburgh, 1978, pp. 137, 163-181.

[78] On Francis I, see J. BODIN, *Method for the Easy Comprehension of History,* pp. 288-289: "As soon as [Francis I] began to love literature, from which his ancestors had always turned away, immediately the nobility followed suit"; cf. J. BODIN, *Discourse, Oeuvres philosophiques,* Paris, 1951, V, p. 3; R. J. KNECHT, *Francis I,* Cambridge, Cambridge University Press, 1982, pp. 270-273, FRANCES YATES, *The French Academies of the 16th Century,* London, The Warburg Institute, 1947, esp. pp. 124-125; and the useful summary of I. D. MCFARLANE, in *The Age of the Renaissance,* ed. D. HAY, London, Thames and Hudson, 1967, pp. 181-192, esp. p. 186. On the theatre in England that was both "platonic and Machiavellian", see S. ORGEL, *The Illusion of Power: Political Theater in the English Renaissance,* Berkeley and Los Angeles, University of California Press, 1975, p. 40; FRANCIS BACON, *The Advancement of Learning,* I.VIII.3, in *Works,* III, p. 302, quoting from Plato's *Republic,* V.473: "Then should people and estates be happy, when either kings were philosophers or philosophers kings".

Medici dukes themselves had less need of legitimization than their forebears, the institutionalization of the Florentine Academy in 1542 helped to perpetuate their reputation for the learning that was becoming so widely popular, as the orations of someone like Bernardo Davanzati demonstrate.[79]

Accompanying the growth in royal power that fed these images was a changed attitude to law and class structure. Criticism of the law's delays and the venality of lawyers was widespread. It encouraged both a more relativist and a more positivist approach to law, to which Plato was again entirely relevant. So we find his philosophical view of law being discussed by jurists in France and England as it had been by Cosimo de' Medici in Florence in the fifteenth century.[80] In both France and England the changing balance of power was reflected in widespread discussion of social organization as a new administrative class of legally trained bureaucrats gradually gained power at the expense of the nobility and clergy.[81] These are the men Mon-

---

[79] See CLAUDIA BAREGGI, *In nota alla politica culturale di Cosimo I: L'accademia fiorentina,* «Quaderni storici», XXIII, 1973, pp. 527-574, describes the academy as an "efficace strumento per tenere saldamente in pugno la classe intellettuale fiorentina"; cf. P. O. KRISTELLER, *Francesco Cattani da Diacceto and Florentine Platonism in the 16th century,* in *Studies in Renaissance Thought and Letters,* (I), pp. 287-336, referring (p. 303) to Francesco Diacceto's funeral oration on the death of Lorenzo, Duke of Urbino, in 1519, published in *Opera omnia,* Basel, 1563, pp. 368-370. The first university course on Plato alone was in Pisa, where Francesco Verino taught from 1576 to 1588 (SCHMITT, *Platon dans les universités,* pp. 99-100, KRISTELLER, *Francesco Cattani,* pp. 291-292). Bernardo Davanzati's *Lezioni di monete,* referring to Plato's natural functionalism and the role of the prince as "padre di tutti" in controlling currency, and his oration on the death of Cosimo I in 1572 are in his *Opere,* ed. E. BINDI, Florence, 1853, esp. II, pp. 440, 444, 446, 453, 464 sqq.; cf. the *Oratio* of L. SALVIATI, Florence, Paris, 1574.

[80] See LOUIS LE CARON, *Les Dialogues,* Paris, Sertenas, 1556, D. R. KELLEY, *Louis Le Caron philosophe,* in *Philosophy and Humanism: Renaissance Essays in Honor of P. O. Kristeller,* ed. E. P. MAHONEY, Leiden, Brill, 1976, pp. 30-49, his *Beginning of Ideology,* pp. 191-193, 203; and JEAN BODIN, *Method for the Easy Comprehension of History,* p. 2, suggesting lawgivers should study Plato. In England, see Sir THOMAS MORE's criticism of law in *The Complete Works,* ed. L. L. MARTZ and F. MANLEY, New Haven, Con., Yale University Press, 1976, XII, p. 225; CHRISTOPHER ST. GERMAN, *Doctor and Student,* London, Seldon Society, 1974, esp. p. 97; cf. J. A. GUY, *The Public Career of Sir Thomas More,* Brighton, Harvester Press, 1980, pp. 88, 93: ROBERT MASON, *Reason's Monarchie,* London, 1602, and *Reason's Academy,* London, 1609; THOMAS HOBBES, *Dialogue between a Philosopher and Student of the Common Laws of England,* ed. J. CROPSEY, Chicago and London, University of Chicago Press, 1971; and see below.

[81] For example, see C. DE SEYSELL, *The Monarchy of France* of 1515, tr. J. H. HEXTER, New Haven, Conn., Yale University Press, 1981, chs. 15, 17, pp. 60-63; G. BUDÉ, *De l'institution du prince,* Paris, Maistre Nicole, 1547, which refers to Hesiod's threefold division of types; LOUIS LE CARON's *Dialogue de la vraie sagesse,* in his *Dialogues,* f. 43*r*, distinguishing the three estates according to a platonic analogy of body, senses, and reason; CHARLES LOYSEAU, *Traité des ordres et simples dignitez,* Paris, 1613, p. 46, referring to a new class of "honourable hommes"

taigne defined as a new "fourth estate". "In charge of the laws" and also possessing "the sovereign authority of goods and lives", this estate is not only separate from the nobility but also enjoys a different ethos from them, being motivated, Montaigne says, by "justice" instead of "honor".[82]

Divorced though the empirical Hobbes seems to be from the platonic tradition, in fact *Leviathan* incorporates these same ideas. The sovereign, as Kenneth Minogue has already argued, is "a figure performing the same function as a Platonic philosopher-king" in supplying what is defective in the rationality of ordinary men, controlling and civilizing through his knowledge of the certain rules, in which "the skill of making and maintaining commonwealths consisteth... as doth arithmetic and geometry".[83] Law is based on the will or command of this sovereign, who interprets it as "arbitrator or judge" through men he appoints as judges in his name for their "right understanding of the principal law of nature called equity".[84] For, as he later makes the philosopher in his *Dialogue between a Philosopher and a Student of the Common Law in England* say, flexible rule by free reason or equity administered through a court of chancery under the king as judge is preferable to the rule of custom and statutory law.[85] In *Leviathan*, moreover, the men of passion are distinguished from

---

or "honestes personnes" (cf. G. HUPPERT, *Les bourgeois gentilhommes: An Essay on the Definition of Elites in Renaissance France,* Chicago and London, University of Chicago Press, 1977, p. 12; "this nameless class"). In England, Sir THOMAS SMITH's *De republica Anglorum,* written in the 1560s, Cambridge, Cambridge University Press, 1982, p. 76, refers to "the fourth sort or classe" of labourers, or proletarians, "which do not rule", WILLIAM HARRISON, *Description of Britain,* written in 1577, London, 1959, p. 41.

82 M. MONTAIGNE, *Essais,* ed. M. RAT, Paris, 1963, bk. 1, ch. 23, p. 124.

83 T. HOBBES, *Leviathan,* ed. M. OAKESHOTT, Oxford, B. Blackwell, 1946, ch. 20, p. 136, ch. 29, p. 210. Hobbes described *Leviathan* as "Iustitiae mensura atque ambitionis elenchus" in *Opera philosophica,* London, 1839, I, p. XCIV, cited by L. STRAUSS, *The Political Philosophy of Hobbes,* p. 13; cf. K. R. MINOGUE, *Hobbes and the Just Man,* in *Hobbes and Rousseau,* ed. M. CRANSTON and R. S. PETERS, New York, Doubleday, 1972, pp. 66-84, esp. p. 78.

84 On Hobbes and law, his "design being not to show what is law here, and there; but what is law; as Plato, Aristotle, Cicero and divers others have done", *Leviathan,* ch. 26, esp. pp. 173, 180, 184; ch. 6, pp. 32-33 on the role of the sovereign or "an arbitrator or judge" in creating a common standard of good and evil; ch. 15, pp. 104-105, on law as command; and ch. 18, pp. 117-118, on the rights of sovereignty.

85 JOSEPH CROPSEY (ed. HOBBES, *Dialogue between a Philosopher and a Student of the Common Law*), comments in the introduction, pp. 10-11: "Rather generally, there is a correspondence between Hobbes's familiar teachings and the sayings of the Philosopher, while the Lawyer occasionally introduces the doctrines of [Sir Edward] Coke as being authoritative ... This *Dialogue* is to some extent a polemic against Coke". The *Dialogue* was first published two years after Hobbes's death in 1681.

the men of reason, Hobbes preferring government by monarchs advised by wise counsellors "who have learned the art of government" to government by assemblies that are "versed more in the acquisition of wealth than of knowledge".[86]

Florentine political thinkers in the fifteenth and early sixteenth centuries would have agreed with Hobbes. It was then that the city achieved a consensus for a government ruling in the interest of the whole city (as it was generally agreed the Medici did), leaving merchants free to do their business or, as they liked to idealize it, "to philosophize in the country", whereby they agreed or, in Hobbesian language, 'contracted' to opt out.[87] Those who did not freely accept this government were coerced by the arbitrary "will" of summary magistracies and their unofficial head to act "for the good state of the regime". For it was better, as Plato and Hobbes also agreed, to be controlled by one's own reason, if possible, and failing that, to have it imposed from outside. Trust in the ability of the rulers to act in one's interests was essential.[88]

It was not a large step from the view of the ruler and his relation to law that developed during the platonic revival in Florence to the 'revolutionary' view that denied relevance to the old Christian-Aristotelian distinction between monarchy and tyranny and, more generally, between good and bad government. That step was soon taken. It was the popular republic of 1527-30, when the Great Council was described as "the true prince", that caused Francesco Vettori

---

[86] HOBBES, *Leviathan,* ch. 19, p. 123; cf. ch. 25, p. 171, on "the motley orations, made of the divers coloured threads, or shreds of authors" in "an assembly of many", reiterating that "the ability of counselling proceedeth from experience and long study ... When for the doing of any thing, there be infallible rules, as in engines and edifices, the rules of geometry, all the experience of the world cannot equal his counsel, that has learnt, or found out the rule" (pp. 169-170).

[87] On the identification of the "health of the regime" with the preservation of Lorenzo de' Medici in 1482, see BROWN, *Bartolomeo Scala,* p. 333 (Ital. ed. p. 237) and *Lorenzo, the Monte and the Seventeen Reformers,* p. 170 above; on Lorenzo's participation in the profit of commercial companies, see TREXLER, *Public Life,* pp. 429, 447-448; quoting from Savonarola, Nardi, and Tribaldo de' Rossi, see esp. ROSSI's memoirs, *Delizie degli eruditi toscani,* XXIII, pp. 258-269: "Pensai ... di manifestarlo [a sample of copper] solamente a Lorenzo de' Medici e di non mi fidare d'anima nata d'altri e solo in lui rimettermi nele sue mani liberamente" (p. 259).

[88] So although it is Robert Filmer, Hobbes's critic, who is regarded as more platonic on account of his paternalism, in fact, as we have seen, this plays relatively little part in the platonic revival as we have traced it; see G. J. SCHOCHET, *Patriarchalism and Political Thought,* Oxford, Blackwell, 1975, esp. pp. 20-21; J. DALY, *Sir Robert Filmer and English Political Thought,* Toronto, University of Toronto Press, 1979 (but see pp. 152-154).

to comment that he found himself able to make "little distinction between that government which many call tyrannical and the one which at present many call popular or rather a republic".[89] A year or two later he expanded this in his *Summary of the History of Italy* to a condemnation of "all governments" as tyrannical – French and Venetian as well as Florentine, an opinion with which both Machiavelli and Guicciardini agreed.[90] So too did Bodin, who refused to distinguish between governments on moral grounds; "for whether a prince is unjust or worthy, nevertheless the state is still a monarchy. The same thing must be said about oligarchy and the rule of the people".[91] And so did both Robert Filmer and Hobbes, who called tyranny not another form of government but the same "misliked", "For they that are discontented under monarchy call it tyranny".[92] Such political realism is usually contrasted with platonic idealism. But, as we have seen, there was more to the platonic tradition than idealism. The Florentine example shows, on the contrary, how important it was in preparing the ground for distinctively modern ways of thinking about the state.

---

[89] FRANCESCO VETTORI, *Sacco di Roma*, in *Scritti storici*, pp. 277-278, quoted by STEPHENS, *The Fall of the Florentine Republic*, p. 253, who refers to "the revolution" underlying "this simple statement"; on the Great Council as "the true prince", p. 210, from the preface to a law passed in August 1528. Compare MACHIAVELLI, *Discursus florentinarum rerum*, p. 261: in Florence "non è stato mai nè repubblica nè principato ... perchè non si può chiamar quel principato stabile dove le cose si fanno secondo che vuole uno e si deliberano con il consenso di molti", cited by NAJEMY, *Corporatism and Consensus*, p. 316; P. CORTESI, *De cardinalatu*, f. 111*v*, describing Florence as an "agglutinatione" of "optimorum et perpetuae Dictaturae" (in the margin: "Quomodo republica florentina est bene ordinata dictatura florentina").

[90] FRANCESCO VETTORI, *Sommario*, pp. 145-146; cf. STEPHENS, *The Fall of the Florentine Republic*, pp. 253-254; MACHIAVELLI, *Discorsi*, bk. 1, ch. 25, p. 193: "una podestà assoluta, la quale dagli autori è chiamata tirannide"; GUICCIARDINI, *Ricordi*, ser. B, no. 95, ed. SPONGANO, p. 57, M. DOMANDI, *Maxims and Reflections*, Philadelphia, University of Pennsylvania Press, 1965, p. 119.

[91] BODIN, *Method for the Easy Comprehension of History*, p. 179.

[92] ROBERT FILMER, *Observations upon Aristotle's Politics touching forms of government*, in *Patriarcha ... and Other Political Writings*, ed. P. LASLETT, Oxford, Blackwell, 1949, p. 204; HOBBES, *Leviathan*, ch. 19, p. 121.

7

BETWEEN CURIAL ROME AND CONVIVIAL FLORENCE

Literary patronage in the 1480s

Courts, Machiavelli and others believed,[1] were fuller of lies and spies than piazzas and called for different modes of behaviour. The slow progression from piazza- to court-based culture in Italy, with the changing values and behaviour it entailed, can be briefly – but revealingly – glimpsed in the correspondence between the aspiring humanist, Alessandro Cortesi and the Florentine secretary, ser Francesco di ser Barone. The eldest of three sons of a curialist father and a Florentine mother, resident in Rome and Tuscany, Alessandro had, as he put it, dual citizenship, Roman by law, Florentine by habitation, "in matters concerning religion and sacred rites, Roman, in pomp and glory, Florentine".[2] Less grandiloquently, Rome he typified as a place of work and worry, Florence of culture; Rome a source of boredom, Florence a source of pleasure, with its banquets, jokes and laughter in the homes of friends.[3] Does he exaggerate the differences between Florence and Rome, or does his polarizing attitude represent a real dialectic of change and conflicting ideals as he perceived them? Emphasis on the continuity of courtly culture and patronage struc-

---

This paper was originally published in "Renaissance Studies", II, 1988.

[1] Machiavelli, *Legazioni e commissarie,* ed. S. Bertelli, Milan, Feltrinelli, 1964, III, p. 1187, from Mantua, 20 Nov. 1509; Alessandro Cortesi [= A.C.] to ser Francesco di ser Barone [= F.B.], ASF Lettere varie 16 [= LV], f. 354, 28 Jan. [1487]: "habeo exploratores qui referunt quae facit ipse Laurentius, et quae tu paras". Cf. F. Guicciardini, *Ricordi,* series C, no. 94, ed. Spongano, p. 105.

[2] ASF, MAP 102, 130, ed. Pintor (note 5 below), 18, to F.B., 20 Apr. 1487.

[3] LV, f. 359, 10 Feb. [1486], ed. Rossi (note 5 below), p. 600, doc. I: "Iam tedet me urbis Romae et sordent gaudia illa tot mixta sollicitudinibus. O qui me iterum ad vos reducat! Illud cubiculum convivae, ioci, risus non sine ingenua gravitate semper mihi versantur ante oculos".

tures in Italy throughout the late medieval period has tended to blur the distinction we (and Renaissance writers) used to make between courts and cities, raising new questions about the nature of these societies and their values.[4] Thanks to his position, Cortesi was well qualified to comment on changing places and styles of cultural patronage. So although his correspondence has long been familiar to scholars, it can usefully be re-examined for the light it throws on these problems.[5]

Originating from Pavia, Alessandro Cortesi's father Antonio combined work in the Roman curia as a referendary and later a papal abbreviator with residence and citizenship in San Gemignano, where Alessandro was born around 1460. The family were already self-professed Mediceans in this period, "ready and willing to obey your commands", as Antonio wrote to Giovanni di Cosimo de' Medici in 1462; [6] and Alessandro later claimed that he had been "nourished and honoured beneath the shade" of Lorenzo de' Medici since he was a little boy.[7] Despite his largely Roman upbringing and his office of apostolic scriptor, acquired some time after his father's death in 1474, he maintained contact with the Medici when he attended the new university at Pisa promoted by Lorenzo de' Medici in 1477-79. While he was there, he and his mother successfully invited Lorenzo's mother, Lucrezia Tornabuoni, to visit them in San Gemignano.[8] It was probably during this period that Alessandro, "a well-educated

---

[4] See especially the introduction to the recent volume of essays. *Patronage, Art and Society in Renaissance Italy,* Oxford, Clarendon Press, 1987, ed. F. W. KENT and Patricia SIMONS (pp. 1-21) and Ronald WEISSMAN, *Taking patronage seriously: Mediterranean values and Renaissance society, ibid.*, pp. 24-45, suggesting a distinction between classical/renaissance urban patronage networks and feudal, rural hierarchies.

[5] Following FORTUNATO PINTOR's basic study, *Da lettere inedite di due fratelli umanisti (Alessandro e Paolo Cortesi)*,Perugia, Unione Tipografica Cooperativa, 1907; P. PASCHINI, *Una famiglia di curiali nella Roma del Quattrocento: i Cortesi*, «Rivista storica di Chiesa in Italia», 11, 1957, pp. 1-48; F. BANFI, *Alessandro Tommaso Cortese, glorificatore di Mattia Corvino Re d'Ungheria*, «Arch. Stor. per la Dalmatia», XII, 1937, pp. 535-560; A. VERDE, *Lo Studio fiorentino, 1473-1500,* III, I, pp. 20-30; LIBIA C. ROSSI, *La scapigliatura fiorentina*, in *Ecumenismo della cultura,* ed. G. TARUGI, Florence, Olschki, III, 1981, pp. 53-63; cf. *Dizionario biografico d. Italiani* [= DBI], s.v.; J. F. D'AMICO, *Renaissance Humanism in Papal Rome: Humanists and Churchmen on the Eve of the Reformation,* Baltimore, Md, Johns Hopkins University Press, 1983, pp. 72-81.

[6] ASF, MAP 10, 463, 8 Dec. 1462, PINTOR, p. 15, PASCHINI, p. 4.

[7] LV, f. 367, 31 Dec. [1488]: "per infin da putto nutrito et honorato sotto l'ombra della Mtia. sua".

[8] ASF, MAP 35, 513, Bagno a Morbo, 9 June 1477, VERDE, p. 21: "et perchè l'è donna et vedova, m'è stato forza sanza altro tuo sì prometergli".

young man", visited Angelo Poliziano at the Medici villa of Cafaggiolo, where Poliziano was tutor to Lorenzo's children.[9] It was also while he was in Pisa that Alessandro wrote his first surviving letter to ser Francesco di ser Barone, then acting as secretary to the Florentine ambassador in Lucca, Piero Capponi, the beginning of a correspondence that continued till Alessandro's death in 1490.[10]

It is clear from this and Alessandro's subsequent letter to Francesco from Pisa in February 1479 [11] that the pattern of their friendship was established in these university days when Alessandro was a 19-year-old student and Francesco a 29-year-old notary just embarking on his successful political career. Smitten by affecting pangs of love for Francesco, Alessandro combined protestations of devotion with the demand for favours: commendation to Francesco's patron Piero Capponi and help with the return of his books, insisting – with Cicero – that such duties form part of the nature of true friendship.[12] Duty and friendship: this Roman antithesis was quickly adopted by Cortesi to define his relationship with the egregious ser Francesco. As go-between for those hoping for access to Medici patronage as well as the centre of a wide circle of friends of his own making – politicians, writers, gamblers and homosexuals – ser Francesco was well placed to provide both the sodality and the patronage that Alessandro apparently craved.[13]

After completing his studies in Pisa, Alessandro returned to Rome, on 27 March 1479 borrowing Seneca's tragedies from Platina, librarian of the Vatican Library, and two years later Poggio Bracciolini's

---

[9] Ode 'Ad Alexandrum Curtesium adolescentem bene literatum qui ut Politianum videret Florentiam petierat, cum ille se commodum in Cafasolanum contulisset', ed. I. Del Lungo, *Prose volgari inedite e poesie latine e greche edite ed inedite*, Florence, G. Barbèra, 1867, pp. 266-267, cf. Paschini, pp. 5-6, 24-25. Poliziano was already an intimate friend of the Cortesi family, "iam ab ineunte adolescentia in vestram familiam a clarissimo parente vestro sum cooptatus", as he told Alessandro's younger brother Lattanzio, *ibid.*, note 21.

[10] LV, ff. 332-373, at 357 (22 [Jan. 1479?]), Verde, pp. 21-22; cf. MAP 102, 130 and 131, with letters in both vols. also to F. B. from Alessandro's brothers Lattanzio and Paolo (on whom, *DBI*, s.v., Paschini, pp. 5-7, 26-48 and Pintor). They have been listed by G. Ristori, *Il Carteggio di ser Francesco di ser Barone Baroni*, «Rinascimento», XVII, 1977, pp. 279-303.

[11] LV f. 357, cit., and 341 (12 Feb. 1479), Verde, pp. 22-23.

[12] Ed. Verde, p. 23: "officium enim voco quicquid in amicum agimus"; cf. Cicero, *De amic.*, qu. P. A. Brunt, *'Amicitia' in the Late Roman Republic*, in *The Crisis of the Roman Republic*, ed. R. Seager, Cambridge, Cambridge University Press, 1969, p. 199.

[13] On ser Francesco, see G. Ristori, *F. B. e il suo servizio nella cancelleria della Repubblica fiorentina (1480-1494)*, «Archivio Storico Italiano, CXXXIV, 1976, pp. 231-280, esp. 274-275, and R. Ristori in *DBI:* Ceccone di ser Barone (Francesco).

translation of Xenophon's *Cyropaedia*, for which he left as a deposit his own Thuycidides.[14] He was taught Greek in Rome by "a certain little Greek" called Harmonius, then visiting Rome as ambassador for the Turks, on account of whom (as we shall see) he was briefly imprisoned in the Castel S. Angelo. It was thanks to Alessandro's experiences suffered then that he was later able to help his brother Paolo to obtain Platina's position as apostolic scriptor on the latter's death in October 1481.[15] In addition to Platina, the two brothers also knew the humanist called Fosforo, bishop of Segni, and Pomponio Leto, "prince of literary sodality, that most learned of men", who was one of Paolo's teachers.[16]

In this milieu the "modest and erudite" young Alessandro delivered a sermon in the Vatican palace on the eve of the Epiphany in 1483, which is a fascinating mixture of Florentine and Roman culture, Florentine in its interest in wandering stars and the role of the Magi as prophets, Roman in its setting and emphasis on ceremony.[17] Like his other literary productions, it was printed almost at once, for as he told ser Francesco, "all books in my possession, however many they are, are printed".[18] Afterwards his career appeared to progress smoothly. In 1487 he was appointed to the office of master of the register of supplications, worth 1,200 ducats, which he held in addition to the offices of apostolic scriptor, worth 1,700 ducats, and solicitor of papal letters or 'janissary', worth at least 700 ducats.[19] That

---

[14] E. Muntz and P. Fabre, *La bibliothèque du Vatican au XVe siècle*, Paris, 1887, p. 282, Paschini, p. 8.

[15] Paschini, pp. 8-9, 27 and below.

[16] Paschini, pp. 10-11, 26: *Il diario romano di Jacopo Gherardi da Volterra*, ed. E. Carusi, *RIS*, n.s., XXIII, 3, Città di Castello, Lapi, 1904, p. 98: "princeps sodalitatis litterariae, vir doctissimus"; Paolo Cortesi, *De cardinalatu libri tres*; I quote also the 16th *cent* arabic foliation in BL 4.M.6), f. 104*v* (130*v*). Other humanists known to Alessandro in Rome included Giovanni Lorenzi and Alessandro Farnese, Paschini, p. 12, and *Carteggio umanistico di A. Farnese*, ed. A. Frugoni, Florence, Olschki, 1950, p. 30.

[17] *Oratio habita in aede d. Petri in Epiphania*, Rome [aft. 25 i.1483], *Indice generale d. Incunaboli d. Biblioteche d'Italia*, Rome, Libreria dello Stato, 1948, 126, nos. 3238, 3239, referred to by Gherardi, above, p. 113: "modestus et eruditus iuvenis", Paschini, p. 9. I am grateful to Dr. David D'Avray for references to other Epiphany sermons for comparison.

[18] LV, f. 355 (5 July [1488]): "scias omnes libellos penes me esse quotcunque impressi sunt".

[19] LV, f. 371, 10 Apr. [1489?] (cf. f. 364): "L'officii dell'abbreviatorie [which he hoped to buy] vaglano a vendere due mila CCC o ver CCCC duc⟨ati⟩... La Scriptoria vale mille settecento; el Jannizero passa ben settecento. Dell'officio delli Abbreviatori ne sono dodeci", Pintor, p. 30, cf. Paschini, p. 17, Verde, p. 28, D'Amico, p. 74 (but wrongly quoting 2,000 for the abbreviatorship).

year he visited France and in November entertained in Rome one of his Florentine *sodales*, Jacopo Salviati, taking him and Piero de' Medici to visit various cardinals.[20] The following year he went to Naples in the company of Cardinal Pierre de Foix, confident by then of his good standing with the Medici and the prospect of patronage from them in Naples.[21] Publications continued apace, in tandem with his travels, a *Poem in praise of Matthias Corvinus* and a *Silva heroica* celebrating the Spanish conquests against the Moors in Granada (plus ancient epigrams collected at Lorenzo's behest and poems in praise of Louis XI, neither printed at the time).[22] He was unable to preach on Ascension Day 1489 because of illness; and in January 1490 he declined to deliver a funeral oration for Giovanni Lanfredini, Florentine ambassador in Rome, on the grounds that it was not his practice "to emerge unprepared", especially in Italian, not being good at "extemporaneous eloquence".[23] Three months later he was absent from the office of supplications and died shortly afterwards.[24]

Alessandro's career suggests there was nothing remarkable about his moderate success in rising from the provinces. Superficially, his polarized view of life in Florence and Rome seems to represent no more than the contrast between student and workaday life, couched in the classical language of friendship and conviviality. This is one of the important themes of Alessandro's letters and it provides the first level on which we can interpret his divided outlook. In a series of letters to ser Francesco in 1486, Alessandro summons up a vivid picture of the convivial life in Florence.[25] Writing from San Gemig-

---

[20] A. C. to G. Pico della Mirandola, ed. L. DOREZ and L. THUASNE, *Pic de la Mirandole en France* (1485-1488), Paris, Leroux, 1897, pp. 106-108, PASCHINI, p. 11; Jacobo Salviati to F. B., 18 Nov. 1487, ASF MAP 61, 24, see below.

[21] LV, ff. 343-344, 347 (15 and 31 July 1488, PINTOR, p. 27 and n. 3), 356, 363 (8 Aug. and 22 Nov. 1488, PINTOR, p. 28, PASCHINI, p. 18 and below).

[22] *De laudibus Matthiae Corvini poemation,* Rome [aft. I.vi.1485; *Indice* 2:126, no. 3237], ed. J. FOGEL, Leipzig, Teubner, 1934, see BANFI, pp. 146-160; *Silva de triumphata Bassa, Almeria, Granata,* Rome [aft. 5.i.1492; *Indice,* II: p. 126, no. 3240]. His poems in praise of Louis XI, *Ad Christianissimum Ludovicum Francorum Regem,* have recently been edited by D. CORTESE, Padua, Centro Studi Antoniani, 1976. On his epigrams collected and copied for Lorenzo in 1488, see below.

[23] J. BURCHARDI, *Liber Notarum*, *RIS,* n.s. XXXII, I, Città di Castello, Lapi, 1906, p. 267: "quia... ad hoc ordinatus, infirmus erat"; LV, f. 368, 10 Jan. [1490], PINTOR, p. 36.

[24] BURCHARDUS, pp. 302, 267, note 3; PASCHINI, p. 23.

[25] LV ff. 359, 349, 373, 346 (10 Feb., 26 Mar., 31 May and 1 July 1486), ed. ROSSI, DOCS I-IV.

nano in February he recalled "that evening when we dined together" – though dinner was hardly the word for a meal consisting of so many delicacies. There he met "the leading lights not only of Tuscany but the whole of Italy", above all Lorenzo, who inflamed his heart, Jacobo, Giovanni and Accio: referring evidently not to Lorenzo il Magnifico (whom he already knew) but to his young cousin, Lorenzo di Pierfrancesco and his brother Giovanni, then aged 23 and 19, Jacobo Salviati and Zanobi Acciaiuoli.[26] A letter received from ser Francesco while Alessandro was sick with fever in Rome six weeks later filled him again with nostalgia for his Florentine friends.[27] Asking to be remembered to his dining mates, *sodales*, as well as to the humanists to whom he later sent his writings for approval – Poliziano, Pico della Mirandola and Marsilio Ficino, "the honour of our century" – he contrasted, in this and the following letter, the peace of Florence with the clash of arms in Rome, where the "mitre" had been exchanged for the "helmet" as the papacy prepared for war against the Orsini.[28] Suspecting that the marvellous banquet must have begun with drugged wines, so ardently did he continue to burn with love for Lorenzo – "you know which Lorenzo I mean", he wrote at the beginning of July [29] – he asked for kisses as well as embraces to be delivered to him and his other friends, as well as toasts "in the gallic mode" with glasses brimming with Trebbiano.[30]

How seriously to take all this is difficult to know. "I joke, as you know, in my own fashion", he told ser Francesco on one occasion, and on another, when he was afraid his jokes about his friend's love affairs had given offence and was anxious not to lose "this liberty of jesting", he hastened to reassure ser Francesco he was "lascivious in verse" but chaste in mind – as Hadrian had said about a certain poet: what better witness of Francesco's continence than himself, for if Francesco had loved him for his beauty rather than for his intelligence when he was a young and quite striking youth, Francesco's love

---

[26] 10 Feb., Rossi, 1, p. 60 (Ital. tr. pp. 53-54). On Lorenzo and Giovanni di Pierfrancesco's patronage group, see *Pierfrancesco de' Medici*, above. Jacobo Salviati was ser Francesco's close friend and confidant, to whom Alessandro played host in Rome in 1487.

[27] 26 Mar. 1486, Rossi, II, pp. 61-62, tr. 54-55; cf. Verde, p. 24.

[28] 26 Mar. and 13 Apr. (MAP 102, 131, ed. Pintor, *Rappresentazioni romane di Seneca e Plauto*, Perugia, 1906, extr. Verde, p. 24, tr. Rossi, p. 56; cf. 31 May, LV, f. 373, Rossi, III, p. 62, cf. Verde, pp. 24-25).

[29] 1 July, LV, f. 346, Rossi, IV, p. 63 (tr. pp. 58-59): "scis quem Laurentium dicam".

[30] 13 Apr. and 31 May.

should have declined as Alessandro grew older (whereas, we take it, it did not).[31] What is clear is that jokes and music contributed to Alessandro's image of conviviality in Florence and were missed by him when he returned to Rome. On one occasion he asked for the lyre he had been promised to assuage his secret fire with song.[32] On another, failing to understand ser Francesco's joke to do with Pico della Mirandola's 'Paris and Helen' love affair, he asked for lessons in his 'slang' to refresh his memory, since such witticisms would go down well in Rome, especially if thought to be Laurentian[33] – just as his brother Paolo once asked ser Francesco to send him some of the witticisms he thought indispensable for court life, 'eight or ten' would be enough provided they were 'sharp'.[34] Alessandro relished ser Francesco's letters, he said, for their shining and sharp Etruscan 'salt' from Volterran salt mines, in contrast to the sordid and polluted salt of the Roman court: "but you too know the stomach of courtiers".[35]

Rome did not lack wit or conviviality, as we see from Alessandro's letters and his description of carnival time there, or from his brother Paolo's description of the banquets they attended in princely houses; these were amazing, Paolo recalled, not so much for the number of courses consumed as for the greed of the diners: "and when I asked with childish curiosity why they didn't touch the bread, those gourmands replied at once that it wasn't the custom".[36] There was also gaming in Rome as in Florence, and although there is no evidence that Alessandro partecipated in this vice of ser Francesco's, we know his brother played with Florentines, including "Pier de' Medi-

---

[31] 1 July, ROSSI, p. 63: "Iocor ut scis more meo", and 23 Mar. [1487], LV, f. 372, VERDE, p. 26. "hanc inter nos iocandi libertatem".

[32] LV, f. 350, n.d.: "Lyram, quam pollicitus es mitte ... Occultum cupio solari cantibus ignem".

[33] LV, f. 346 (1 July 1486), ROSSI, p. 63, VERDE, p. 25 (but '*Non* [not *Nam*] sum interpretatus el vostro giergo, oblitus explanationis totius'; on the affair, see F.B. to Lorenzo de' Medici, 11 May 1486, MAP 39, 489, ed. M. DEL PIAZZO, *Nuovi documenti sull'incidente del Pico*, «Rassegna d. Archivi di Stato», XXII, 1963, p. 278.

[34] 17 May 1497, LV, f. 422: [his factor is not to leave him] "se non li date octo o dieci di quelli vostri Dicterii e non più. Mi basta questo numero pur che siano acuti", cf. *De cardinalatu*, ff. 87*v*-88*r* [107*v*-108*r*], quoting some of Cosimo and Lorenzo de' Medici's witticisms.

[35] LV, f. 361, 5 Jan. [1487]: "leguntur a me litterae tuae summa voluptate ... tum quod habent ethruscos sales et volaterranis salinis, quae in Italiae salsissimae candidissimaeque sunt. Nos, ut scis, in urbe sordidum salem edimus et ob colluviem non facile purum habemus. Sed nosti etiam tu stomachum aulicorum".

[36] *De cardinalatu*, ff. 190*v*-191*r* [167*v*-168*r*], PASCHINI, p. 26.

ci and... those other good players... for 25 or 30 ducats".[37] But whereas Florentine feasting and jokes were pleasurable and "salty", Rome was boring, her feasts excessive and her jokes stale ("ha, ha, he", Fosforo once wrote somewhat heavily to Alessandro after a pun on Pompey and Pomponio Leto, "how I would like to laugh and joke with you in our letters!"), life there being played out self-consciously and competitively "before these eyes of the Court", "this blessed Court" as Alessandro called it.[38] Clearly, we cannot take Alessandro's polarization too seriously when so much social life was shared in common. Yet his persistency in contrasting the two cities suggests the convivial façade may conceal more serious differences. To investigate the "gall" as well as the "honey" in his jokes,[39] we must look beneath the surface pleasures of life in Rome to its deeper undercurrents.

There is a clue to this lower level in Jacobo Salviati's letter describing his visit to Rome in November 1487. In it he tells ser Francesco that the companionship of Alessandro Cortesi and Cosimo de' Pazzi would have been very enjoyable when they went on their round of cardinals, had not Piero de' Medici got annoyed because he had been told to avoid companions who might give people something to talk about.[40] Seven years after the end of the Pazzi War such scruples might seem excessive but for an incident that Alessandro had described to ser Francesco earlier that year. It must have been in late 1479 or the early 1480s, "when Count Girolamo [Riario] was in control" of Rome, that Alessandro was imprisoned by Sixtus IV for "taking

---

[37] LV, f. 424 [10 Sept., s.a.): "Io giucai l'altro dì qui con Lorenzo Alamanni. Li haviamo im promesso venire per ogni modo costì a giucar 25 o 30 ducati alla corda con Pier de' Medici et con cotesti altri buon giucatori". On ser Francesco's vice of gambling, cf. Jacobo Salviati's letter of 11 Nov. 1490 (MAP 102, 42).

[38] Fosforo to A. C. printed with his Epiphany sermon, f. a7*v*, 25 Jan. 1483; A. C. to F. B. 22 Nov. [1488], LV, f. 363: "tanta è la multitudine delli competitori in questa benedecto corte... in questi occhi della Corte ove son vixo sempre assai bene", cf. 5 Jan. [1488] (LV, f. 361) and 10 Feb. 1486 (note 3 above).

[39] 5 July [1488] (LV, f. 355): "Adde his ioca quibus et mellis et fellis plurimum inest".

[40] 18 Nov. 1487, note 20 above: "Io fui eri con M. Alexandro Cortese, il quale è più vostro che non è suo, et ve n'andò qui a vicitare Piero, gli feci una buona et grata compagnia... & non dubitate che si partì benissimo sodisfatto se già non gli havessi dato noia che andando noi a vicitare cardinali, ci volle tenere compagnia et lui et M. Cosimo de' Pazi, e Piero non se ne contentò, havendo in commessione da L⟨orenz⟩o che non meni secho brigata di che gli potete fare un motto commodamente, & io di bocha suplirò a quello si fussi manchato come la vego".

Lorenzo de' Medici's side" too ardently and conspiring with him against Sixtus. He had been inculpated by his Greek teacher, Harmonius, who was then being tortured in the Castel San Angelo for raping a boy and wanted to take revenge on Lorenzo de' Medici for once expelling him from Florence. "Imagine my state of mind, dearest Baroni", Alessandro wrote to his friend, "hearing the screams of the tortured man and knowing that shortly afterwards I was to suffer a similar fate if he persisted in his accusation".[41] Fortunately for Alessandro, Harmonius retracted his story of conspiracy; and after seeing Alessandro for the first time, Sixtus confessed to being ashamed of imprisoning him, saying that if only he had seen him before, he would have realized Alessandro posed him no threat.[42] But why all this, as Alessandro pertinently asked?

The political tension between his Roman and Florentine patrons in the early 1480s evidently affected Alessandro's attitude to his career prospects. With growing realism Florence was transformed in his eyes from a home of academe and sodality to one of trade and utility: Rome by contrast was no longer boring but a source of offices and honour. For whereas the pope, to compensate for Alessandro's tribulations (and the poems Alessandro wrote in his praise), remitted the 300 golden ducats owed by the Cortesi for the office of apostolic scriptor given to Paolo on Platina's death, and also granted Alessandro's request for the reversion to the Abbey of San Giusto in Volterra,[43] Lorenzo failed utterly to repay Alessandro's loyalty. Not only did he refuse to mediate for him with pope Innocent VIII, he even deprived Alessandro of the reversion to San Giusto by giving it instead to his son Giovanni.[44] When the abbot renounced San Giusto in favour of Lorenzo's son, Alessandro said nothing but protested later to ser Francesco: "it was mine by right and I could have litigated, were it right to fight heedlessly with a prince so well-deserving toward me". But after Giovanni de' Medici also obtained the benefice of Montecassino, Alessandro could remain silent no longer and told

---

[41] 20 Apr. 1487 (MAP 102, 130), PINTOR, p. 19, cf. PASCHINI, pp. 8-9.

[42] *Idem*, PINTOR, p. 19, PASCHINI, p. 9.

[43] *Idem*, PINTOR, p. 20. The presumed verses in praise of Sixtus have been edited by D. CORTESE, *A. Cortese (1459-1490). Carmen in laudem Pontificatus Sixti IV (1475)*, Padua, Centro Studi Antoniani, 1971.

[44] MAP 102, 130, LV, ff. 362, 372, 363-364, 348, etc. (20 Apr., 17 and 23 Mar. 1487, 22 Nov. 1488, 18 Dec. 1489), PINTOR, pp. 20, 16-17, 28, 33, note 4; cf. PASCHINI, pp. 16-17, G. B. PICOTTI, *La Giovinezza di Leone X*, p. 87.

ser Francesco that he wanted to show Lorenzo, "without any embarrassment", why he deserved Sixtus's favour and why Lorenzo, for the same reason, owed him something. Without seeking – or daring to seek – the abbacy of San Giusto, he wanted Lorenzo to understand why he was entitled to some reward: "so that, even if he was ignorant of my dangers and rewards some time ago, now that he is fully aware of them, he should not willingly snatch from me what I achieved thanks to his ignorance".[45]

Florence was also the source of cheap money as well as patronage. Finding himself in debt going to Naples in July 1488, he asked ser Francesco to arrange for him a one year's loan of 200 or 300 ducats at 10 or 12 per cent – or "as little as possible" – since he heard from friends that the interest rate was much lower in Florence than Rome.[46] After failing to acquire a benefice in Naples,[47] he realistically reassessed his position: two ways were open to him to improve his position a little: one was to enter the service of a lord – which he would not have minded doing, had one materialized; the other was to acquire a bishopric, which would exalt all his family. It was here that Lorenzo could be all-powerful if he wanted to, but this he had to leave to him – Alessandro wrote to ser Francesco – and the more he could do so, the more honourable and useful it would be. He had nothing more to say about his father's office, because it was pecuniary, but he would take a secretaryship if he could have one with profit:

> one or the other, which ever is quicker...if you know for certain what Lorenzo's wishes are, tell me and I'll write more openly. In short, a church that came from his favour would exalt me greatly and be no small honour – and I would do him honour, I promise you. No more for now, and if I am too calculating, forgive me, I'm simply stating my case.[48]

Alessandro's diffidence about sounding too calculating or 'reasoning' (according to merchants' use of *ragione* for 'account') and his desire for Lorenzo to act as broker for him, "because I cannot and don't

---

[45] 20 Apr. 1487, PINTOR, p. 20.

[46] LV, f. 343*v*, 15 July 1488, partly ed. VERDE, p. 27: "ob varias enim temporum difficultates rerumque omnium angustias, incidi in aes alienum".

[47] 22 Nov. [1488], LV, f. 363, partly ed. PINTOR, p. 28, summarized in VERDE, p. 27.

[48] 31 Dec. [1488], LV, f. 367, PINTOR, p. 29: "et se son troppo ragionevole, perdonami, che dico el facto mio".

know how to play the merchant myself",[49] belies his shrewd grasp of the job market and the openings available to him. He had, he wrote as a postscript, been hesitant to put himself forward for his father's office, since it would have been arrogant to propose himself for the church; but if Lorenzo proposed him, wanting as he did one of his supporters as secretary, it would be put down to Alessandro's ambition (and not, one understands, Lorenzo's): "Talk to whom you think and especially to him in person, telling him from your position that if the commission was given here to one of his men, I would have it with honour and cheaply".[50] The paternal office that Alessandro hoped to acquire was the abbreviatorship *de parco maiori* valued at 2,300 to 2,400 ducats (less if acquired from the pope).[51] By April the following year he had ruled out a bishopric as "very often fallacious" (doubtless because Lorenzo had failed to support him for one); but as "he loses status who stays in one place", he would have to sell two of his three offices (the scriptorship and the janissaryship totalling 1,400 ducats) in order to acquire his father's abbreviatorship. With his father's books and his own experience, he would take it at once to succeed to the "kingdom" in which his father had been so outstanding.[52]

In fact Alessandro misjudged the market by failing to take political conditions into account – Lorenzo's growing influence with pope Innocent VIII (to whom he was now related by marriage) at the expense of his former close friendship with the king of Naples: "You can accuse me either of imprudence or ignorance: imprudence for not considering the place or time, especially since his wife had died only a few days before; ignorance for not knowing that the Magnificent Lorenzo had much greater authority with the pope, who is the fount of such dignities, than the king". But competition "in this blessed court" was so intense that without Lorenzo's enthusiastic support he would fail to stand out from the herd, "in these eyes of the court

[49] LV, f. 364 [Apr. 1489?]: "Vorrei essere aiutato, perchè non so nè posso mercatantare".

[50] LV, f. 369, partly ed. PINTOR, p. 31: "credo che non mi habbiate inteso bene circa l'officio paterno ... Parlatene con chi vi pare, maxime con esso proprio et diteli da vostra posta che dando tal commissione qui a un delli sui, io lo haverei con honor et a buon mercato".

[51] See note 19 above.

[52] 10 Apr. [1489], LV f. 371, PINTOR, p. 30, cf. VERDE, p. 28, quoting Vergil, *Aen* III, 121; cf. LV, f. 364 (n.d., probably written at the same time), PINTOR, p. 30, note 2, and note 19 above.

where I have always lived".[53] Still believing in February 1490, shortly before he died, that "the fire to burn my wood here" would have to be kindled in Florence, he declared again that Lorenzo alone was the man to "change his status", since having been favoured by Lorenzo in his early adolescence, he had never "thrown himself into the service of, nor was obliged to, anyone".[54]

On this practical level the mercantile language of 'interest' and 'profit' replaces the classical language of friendship and conviviality that dominated Alessandro's earlier correspondence with ser Francesco: "utility and honour", not "friendship and duty", are the antitheses now used to distinguish mercantile Florence from curial Rome. Although Alessandro claimed independence as a man of letters, living 'honourably' at home in his 'academy of letters' in Rome,[55] he would only too readily have sacrificed his freedom to serve the Medici by acting as Lorenzo's man in Rome. As a humanist, he was well qualified to offer the 'official praises' as well as 'the hospitality' expected of a provincial client by his patron.[56] In his Epiphany oration in the Vatican palace, he invoked the pope as "the light of letters and wisdom, the founder of peace and quiet, the divine source and star of all virtues"; and he dedicated the edition printed soon afterwards to Sixtus as his "first-fruits in oratory", having some time earlier celebrated the pope's deeds 'in poetry'.[57] His attempts to procure patronage

[53] 22 Nov. [1488], LV. f. 363: "Posses me accusare vel imprudentie vel inscitie. Imprudentie che non servassi nè loco nè tempo, maxime essendo pochi dì poi morta la [*bis*] moglera. Inscitie che non sapessi la Mtia. di Lorenzo haver molto maior auctorita apresso al pontifice, che è fonte di tal dignità, che del re. A questo ve rispondo che tanta è la multitudine delli competitori in questa benedecto [*sic*] corte che bisognerebbe bene che la Mtia. di Lorenzo la pigliassi calda a farmi uscir di schiera. Et in questi occhi della Corte ove son vixo semper assai bene bisognerebbe che venisse dallo intimo dell'animo di Lorenzo a volermi dare tal cosa che mi potessi mantener chome lo vixo".

[54] 25 Feb. [1490], LV, f. 365: [after expressing his pleasure at the decision taken, to be executed by the new Florentine ambassador in Rome, Pierfilippo Pandolfini, who, he heard, "è homo savio et prudente"]: "bisogna che costì sia appicciato el foco per voler ardere qui, che le mie legne non basterebbeno ad infiammarlo se da costì non venga acceso ... Delli mei desiderii che vi ho scripti, so' certo che intendete chome tutti dependeno da una fonte, cioè di voler mutare horamai stato, la qual cosa non lo vorrei fare senza la introductione del Mco. Lorenzo, dal quale già una volta da principio della mia adulescentia fu cominciato el favore, et io nescio quo meo fato non mi so' mai buttato a servitii di alcuno, nè obligato".

[55] 31 Dec. [1488], LV, f. 367, PINTOR, p. 29: "Vivo et ho viss⟨ut⟩o in casa mia honoratamente, et è stata et è una achademia di letterati".

[56] WEISSMAN, *Taking patronage seriously*, p. 35. On his hospitality in S. Gemignano and Rome, notes 8 and 40 above and LV, f. 354 (28 Jan. [1487]), PINTOR, p. 16, VERDE, p. 26.

[57] *Oratio*, cit., ff. a6*v*, a1*r*. His supposed poems praising Sixtus, under whose principate "è tornato a fiorire quel tempo che dicon fosse sotto il re Saturno", are edited by D. CORTESE (note 43 above), p. 9.

from the kings of France and Naples were accompanied by eulogistic verse, and he would presumably have expected to praise Lorenzo de' Medici in the same way. Yet it was exactly here that the traditions of republican Florence and courtly Rome were most antithetical, suggesting a third level on which his view of the two cities must also be interpreted.

Although Alessandro was fully involved in the Florentine literary scene, sending his writings for the criticism of scholars he valued more highly than those in Rome,[58] he wrote nothing for the Medici to compare with his long poem in praise of Matthias Corvinus or his *Selva heroica* celebrating the conquests of Spanish monarchs. Instead he sent Lorenzo only a consolatory letter on the death of his wife and the ancient inscriptions he had collected at Lorenzo de' Medici's suggestion, "a great and most beautiful work", which – in contrast to his eulogy of Matthias Corvinus that was already in print when circulated in Florence for approval – was 'slowly and sluggishly' being copied by hand to be shown in Naples to fra Giocondo, 'prince of antiquarians'.[59] Despite his hopes of "doing myself honour and pleasing Lorenzo", it was fra Giocondo who dedicated and presented the inscriptions to Lorenzo the following year (though acknowledging Alessandro's help), and when a second edition was produced in 1498, after Alessandro's and Lorenzo's deaths, Alessandro's name (like Lorenzo's) had disappeared entirely from the dedicatory page.[60]

The failure of Alessandro to produce a eulogy of the Medici brings us to the heart of the problem concerning "patronage and the production of history", as it has recently been called.[61] The fact that no biography was written of Cosimo (apart from Vespasiano da Bisticci's brief life) or of Lorenzo during his lifetime to compare with Panormita's and Valla's lives of Ferrante of Naples, or Giovanni Simonetta's life of Francesco Sforza, suggests that Medici clients were faced with a difficult problem. So it is all the more interesting to discover from

---

[58] See esp. LV, f. 355 (5 July 1488: "Istis qui Romae sunt nonnullis perlectum est, sed ego volo etiam iudicium illorum maxime, ne quid erroris insit"), 343-344 (15 July 1488), 367 (31 Dec. [1488], 348 (18 Dec. [1489], ed. FERRAÙ, note 67 below, pp. 95-96), 368 (10 Jan. [1490]), 365 (25 Feb. [1490]), PINTOR, pp. 24, 27, 31-35, VERDE, pp. 26-29, cf. PASCHINI, pp. 19-22.

[59] LV. f. 355 (5 July 1488), PINTOR, p. 25 and VERDE, p. 26.

[60] LV, f. 343 (15 July 1488), PINTOR, p. 26 and note 3, 27, cf. VERDE, p. 27.

[61] GARY IANZITI in *Patronage, Art and Society*, pp. 299-311.

Alessandro's correspondence with ser Francesco that both men were in fact working on historical projects to do with the Medici.

It was at the beginning of 1487 that Alessandro asked ser Francesco to send him some of his commentary on the war of Ferrara, as well as a life of Cosimo de' Medici, "however it is written", "for it seems to me – as I heard from our elders – he is no less worthy of comparison with the ancients than king Alfonso or Francesco Sforza, and I love hearing not only what he did but also his sayings and expressions".[62] In return, ser Francesco wanted a copy of Sixtus IV's interdict against Florence, which was clearly related to another historical project of the chancery secretary, possibly related to the Pazzi War.[63] Although ser Francesco received the interdict safely, Alessandro was still waiting for the outline of Cosimo's life that "he needed" nearly two months later; "and if it has not been written by others, write it yourself", he urged his friend on 23 March.[64] The fact that he also tried to borrow Pico della Mirandola's *Panegyric* of Lorenzo in 1487 [65] suggests he was planning a life or eulogy of the Medici family at this time – which never, however, materialized. Instead, the best he could do was to praise Lorenzo as leader of an expanding republic, taking "incredible pleasure" whenever he saw "the S.P.Q.F. and Lorenzo, leader of the Senate, prospering economically and politically, increasing their authority and reputation in victories and triumphs"; for whereas Rome, his legal patria, had surrendered its empire and authority to the priesthood, Florence, his adoptive patria, was "powerful in war and peace, on land and at sea, filling with dread not only neighbouring towns but almost the whole of Europe, towering over other cities as a cypress over other trees".[66] It was left to his brother Paolo to do his duty by the Medici in the dedication to Lorenzo of his *Dialogus de hominibus doctis* and by his many laudato-

---

[62] LV, f. 354 (28 Jan. [1487], PINTOR, p. 16, VERDE, p. 26.

[63] LV, f. 372 (23 Mar. [1487], describing ser Francesco as: "ingentis facultatis summaeque rerum historiarumque cognitionis hominem, rebus publicis ac privatis expertum, bellis innutritum consiliisque sapientissimorum reipublicae principium atque auribus assuetum"; see also the preceding letter of 17 March, below.

[64] LV, f. 362 (17 Mar. [1487]), PINTOR, pp. 16-17, and 23 Mar. (above): "Vitam Cosmi Medice ut perquiras, etsi ab aliis scripta non est, ipse perscribas oro obtestorque te".

[65] Letter to Pico, ed. L. DOREZ and L. THUASNE, pp. 107-108, PASCHINI, p. 14.

[66] ASF, MAP 102, 130 (20 Apr. 1487), PINTOR, p. 18, quoting Vergil, *Bucol.* I, pp. 25-26.

ry references to Cosimo and Lorenzo in his book *On the Cardinalate*.[67]

So the contrast between republicanism and court culture adds another dimension to Alessandro's view of Rome and Florence. Far from being merely rhetorical, his antitheses – as we have seen – closely reflect his own experiences as a student, client and courtier. By distinguishing clearly between the two cities, he enables us to see the contribution each made to the new culture that was emerging. This was not simply a return to an aristocratic or bastard-feudal culture, as is sometimes suggested, but a crossbreed of old and new: patrons who followed urban Roman, not familial, patterns: courtiers who were not knights and aristocrats but merchants, 'calculating' men like Alessandro himself, who adopted classical learning as a passport to success. Most has been written on Alessandro's literary activities as a humanist,[68] but his position as a Medici client and curialist is equally interesting for the light it throws on changing patronage patterns and the new courtly life-style.

Whatever the Cortesi's initial relationship with the Medici (through their Florentine mother), by the 1480s – as non-residents in Florence – they clearly did not form part of the Medici's neighbourhood or political patronage group. When they needed urban favours, they used the services of the omnicompetent ser Francesco as their literary agent, financial broker, medical supplier and recoverer of stolen horses.[69] It was not in Florence but in Rome that they most needed Medici help in the form of sponsors, introductions and money for their careers, in return for 'official praises' and 'hospitality'. And this was the source of Alessandro's discontent, for although later Medici were able to play the role of "provincial senator" who supports the

---

67 The *Dialogus* is ed. G. FERRAÙ, Palermo, «Il Vespro», 1979, with a dedicatory letter to Lorenzo, 'huius gloriae praeclarus amplificator' (pp. 101-104) and letters from Paolo and Alessandro Cortesi to ser Francesco, 12 and 18 Dec. 1489 (pp. 94-96, LV, ff. 418, 348), in which Alessandro thanks ser Francesco for receiving his brothers in his house and presenting the *Dialogus*: "di tutto vi ringratio sommamente, che so senza vostra intercessione non s'è facto niente"; *De cardinalatu*, e.g. ff. 13*r*, 53*v* [57*r*], 87*v*-88*r* [107*v*-108*r*], 104*r* [130*r*], 110*r-v* [139*r-v*].

68 See esp. PINTOR, VERDE, D'AMICO and recently, R. BLACK, *The new laws of history*, «Renaissance Studies», I, 1987, pp. 126-156, discussing the contribution of Alessandro and especially his brother Paolo to a new approach to history, without however using their correspondence with ser Francesco for the light it throws on history writing.

69 See LV, 353, 355, 382, 383, 403, 404, etc., and notes 46, 50, 64.

interests of local men in the capital city, it was difficult for Lorenzo il Magnifico to adopt it with success, lacking as he still did a patronage base in Rome.[70] Alessandro's letters thus illustrate an interesting moment of transition as the Medici moved out of neighbourhood and family-based networks in Florence into a wider 'imperial' network that embraced Rome and the kingdom of Naples.

It was also an important moment of transition from a republican to a more courtly ethos, represented by new-style courtiers.[71] It is these courtiers and not their masters – as Carlo Dionisotti has already pointed out [72] – who play the title role in the two books that describe this new culture, Castiglione's *Courtier* and its companion piece by Alessandro's brother Paolo, based on their common experiences, *On the Cardinalate*. In its chapters "On friendship" and "On wit and jokes"; its discussion of "Income" and its vignettes of the Florentines as a nation "who measure the passage of time by utility"; and its republicanism ("How republics and the Florentine republic are well ordered"), we can identify Alessandro's contribution to the new composite culture that was emerging.[73] His polarized view of life in Florence and Rome enables us to understand better the transition from Bartolomeo Scala's condemnation of courtiers as sycophants in his apologue *Flattery* in the mid 1480s to Francesco Guicciardini's maxim some forty years later, which realistically accepted that the courtly arts he used to despise as a boy "open the way to the favour of princes" and lead to profit and honour, "for the world and princes are no longer made as they should be, but as they are".[74]

---

[70] Cf. note 56 above.

[71] On Rome as a "forte polo d'attrazione per gli uomini di lettere" and the Florentine ruling elite's gradual loss of "pregiudizi ideologici contro lo stile di vita cortegiana", without however losing "il senso dell'autonomia dello stato e delle sue prerogative", R. BIZZOCCHI, *Chiesa e aristocrazia nel Firenze del Quattrocento*, «Archivio storico italiano», CXLII, 1984, pp. 271, 244, and now his *Chiesa e potere nella Toscana del Quattrocento*, Bologna, Il Mulino, 1987, pp. 351-352.

[72] *Chierici e laici nella letteratura italiana del primo Cinquecento*, in *Problemi di vita religiosa in Italia nel cinquecento*, Padua, Antenore, 1960; esp. pp. 180-181; cf. D'AMICO, pp. 226-237; and on *Il Cortegiano*, J. GUIDI, *Baldassar Castiglione et le pouvoir politique*, in *Les écrivains et le pouvoir en Italie à l'époque de la Renaissance*, II, Paris, Université de la Sorbonne Nouvelle, 1973, p. 243-278.

[73] *De cardinalatu*, ff. 55*v* [60*v*]: "Florentinorum natio cum temporis curriculum utilitate metiatur"; a3*r-v*, a5*r*, a6*r* (bks II, chs 1, 4 and 9; III, ch. 1).

[74] B. SCALA, *Assentatio*, describing harpies being fed by the hand of a prince as they circle around his magnificent palace, to the bland applause of his tame birds, *Apologorum liber secundus*, Florence, Bibl. Moreniana, MS Bigazzi 302, f.47*v*, to be published in my forthcoming edition of Scala's writings; GUICCIARDINI, *Ricordi*, ed. SPONGANO, series C, no. 179, p. 191.

8

SAVONAROLA, MACHIAVELLI AND MOSES

A CHANGING MODEL

Moses is all things to all men: holy prophet and warrior chieftain to popes and kings, constitutional head of a mixed government to Thomist theologians, ancient magus to Renaissance philosophers and a contractual sovereign to Hobbes. So chameleon a character must be approached with caution: an unstable model for imitation but a useful index of changing attitudes and values.[1] From this point of view, the Savonarolan period in Florence is important as a moment of change, an unexpected cataract in the slow meanderings of the Mosaic tradition, from which the holy man re-emerges as a tough and all-powerful ruler prepared to murder "infinite numbers of men" to impose his laws. How did this happen?

This paper was originally published in *Florence and Italy. Renaissance Studies in Honour of Nicolai Rubinstein*, ed. P. DENLEY and C. ELAM, London, Westfield Publications in Medieval Studies, 1988.

[1] In the apparent absence of a single treatment of the subject, see, *inter alia*, L. D. ETTLINGER, *The Sistine Chapel before Michelangelo*, Oxford, Clarendon Press, 1965, ch. 6, pp. 104-119, summarising changing attitudes to Moses and his renewed importance in the fifteenth century, P. WORMALD, *Lex Scripta and Verbum Regis: Legislation and Germanic Kingship, from Euric to Cnut*, in *Early Medieval Kingship*, ed. R. H. SAWYER and I. N. WOOD, Leeds, School of History, University of Leeds, 1979, pp. 131-132; B. TIERNEY, *Religion, law and the growth of constitutional thought, 1150-1650*, Cambridge, Cambridge University Press, 1982, pp. 88-91, 95: "the Mosaic model of a mixed constitution", quoting AQUINAS, *Summa theologiae*, I, 2a, 97.3; I 2a, 105.1; 2.2a, 183.2, J. GERSON, *De potestate ecclesiastica, Oeuvres*, Paris, 1960-73, VI, p. 225; D. P. WALKER, *The Ancient Theology*, pp. 1-2, 19, 49-50, etc., quoting P. CRINITO, *De honesta disciplina*, III, 2, ed. A. ANGELERI, Rome, Bocca, 1955, pp. 104-105; cf. C. LANDINO, *Praefatio in Virgilio* (1462), *Scritti critici e teorici*, ed. R. CARDINI, I, p. 23, etc., M. FICINO, *De christiana religione*, ch. 26, letter to Braccio Martelli, "Concordia Mosis et Platonis", *Opera omnia*, Basel, 1576, repr. Turin, Bottega d'Erasmo, 1962, pp. 29 (59), 866 (869), G. PICO DELLA MIRANDOLA, *Heptaplus*, tr. J. B. MCGAW, New York, Philosophical Library, 1977, preface, pp. 15-21); for Hobbes, note 53 below. Savonarola as the new Moses is mentioned in passing by M. REEVES, *Joachim of Fiore and the Prophetic Future*, London, S.P.C.K., 1976, p. 88.

Despite the underlying continuity of government in the post-Medicean period,[2] the four years of Savonarola's predominance in Florence from 1494 to 1498 presented the city with a quite new situation: the replacement of the Medici as the guiding influence on politics by a Dominican friar, who not only lacked political rights as a foreigner but, because of his religious status, was excluded from direct participation in government altogether. As he said in 1496: "I am a friar and I never saw arms; but if I were allowed to, I would show you reasons to prevent you being so afraid... I wish I could (I say could, that is, that I were allowed to) put on a *cappuccio* and also a *lucco* [the magistrate's hood and gown]".[3] In fact, this did not prevent Savonarola from playing a leading political role. He was sent as one of several ambassadors to the king of France in November 1494 and again, on his own, the following year. He was invited into the government palace in January 1495 to advise the citizens on reform. And he preached regularly at Lent and Advent by invitation of the government, sometimes also at times of political crisis.[4] As a preacher he was able to address a far wider audience than he would have been able to as a politician in the council chamber. Because of his charismatic hold over an entirely new group of adherents – not the members of territorially-based clans and *consorterie* who provided the traditional structure of politics but, thanks to his special appeal to women and children, a wide social and geographical cross-section

---

[2] See H. BUTTERS, *Governors and Government in early sixteenth-century Florence, 1502-1519,* Oxford, Clarendon Press, 1985; R. PESMAN COOPER, *The Florentine Ruling Group under the "Governo Popolare", 1494-1512,* «Studies in Medieval and Renaissance History», VII, 1984-85, pp. 71-181: "The constitutional reforms of December 1494 led to little change in the composition of the Florentine political class or in its inner circles of position and influence" (p. 71).

[3] *Prediche sopra Ruth e Michea,* ed. ROMANO, I, p. 436 (26 June 1496): "Io sono frate, e non vidi mai arme, e, se mi fussi lecito, ti monstrrerei punti, che tu non hai da dubitare tanto ... Io vorrei così potere (dico potere, cioè che mi fusse lecito) questa mattina mettermi uno cappuccio, e ancora uno lucco: io ti monstrrerei punti e rationi che tu non ai bisogno di avere tanta paura".

[4] R. RIDOLFI, *The Life of Girolamo Savonarola,* London, 1959, pp. 82-83, 123-125, 175; D. WEINSTEIN, *Savonarola and Florence.* pp. 115-116, 279, cf. *Prediche sopra i Salmi,* ed. ROMANO, II, p. 71 (21 June 1495: "Io sono stato là in campo", cf. p. 229, 25 October 1495); I, p. 9 (6 January 1495): "Io fui in Palazzo il dì di santo Silvestro per concludere questa pace universale, e dissiti ..."; *Prediche sopra Giobbe,* ed. RIDOLFI, Rome, Belardetti, 1957, II, p. 15 (27 March 1495): "Dissiti ancora, qui e in palazzo, quando tu mi facesti venire lassù"; *Ruth e Michea,* II, p. 320 (28 October 1496): "Come ti ho detto, sono venuto questa mattina quassù per ubidire alla Magnifica Signoria, richiesto che io predicasse, e, benché io non sia sottoposto al foro seculare, ho voluto venire e ubidire".

of the community – he has been likened to a modern party leader.[5] Although there were precedents for religious men intervening in Florentine politics, as he told his audience, citing St Dominic, Peter Martyr, Cardinal Latini, Catherine of Siena and archbishop Antoninus – Savonarola's role was exceptional, as everyone knew, and he drew increasing criticism for "getting mixed up in affairs of state".[6]

Underlying this was the more serious problem of filling the political vacuum created by the fall of the Medici – "our political revolution" as Savonarola called it.[7] Savonarola had been quick to condemn the Medici for behaving as tyrannical heads of a free republic in December 1494 and he continued to hammer the message home in his sermons. "You are frightened by no one now, but when you had a head or tyrant, you know that the law of the tyrant is his will ... that's how the tyrant is: every time he thinks you've done the slightest thing he doesn't like, he doesn't want to see you any more". "In future no more tyrants can arise in our city, because having been given the Great Council and holding firm to it, be certain of this, there will be no more heads in Florence". "In the other regime, you didn't have to dare to speak before you were punished". "You citizens of the other regime, you were subjected to it, and you couldn't have a shop and you had no freedom to marry your daughter".[8] Yet the achievement of the Medici had been to overcome factionalism by their firm control of the republic and Savonarola was the first to admit

---

[5] S. Bertelli, *Embrioni di partiti alle soglie dell'età moderna,* in *Per Federigo Chabod (1901-1960),* ed. S. Bertelli, «Annali della Facoltà di Scienze politiche», Rimini, Maggioli, 1980-81, XVII, I, pp. 17-35.

[6] *Salmi,* I, pp. 107-108 (20 January 1495); on criticism, Weinstein, pp. 238-239, and the doctoral thesis of L. Polizzotto, *The Piagnoni and Religious Reform, 1494-1530,* London University, 1975 (to be published), ch. 1, pp. 15-47. Cf. *Salmi,* I, p. 94 (18 January 1495): "Ma tu dirai: – tu, frate, perché t'impicci tu dello stato?; *Prediche sopra Amos e Zaccaria,* ed. Ghiglieri, II, p. 42 (6 March, 1496): "Tu di' ancora che io mi impaccio dello stato", etc.

[7] *Giobbe,* II, p. 309 (14 April 1495): "Tu sai che innanzi alla revoluzione nostra del stato".

[8] *Prediche italiane ai fiorentini,* ed. F. Cognasso, Perugia and Venice, 1930, I, pp. 195, 215-216, 219 (14 and 16 December 1494), *Amos e Zaccaria,* I, p. 152 (21 February 1496): "tu non hai ora paura di persona, ma quando el ci fussi capo o tiranno, tu sai che la legge del tiranno è la sua volontà ... Così fa il tiranno: ogni volta che gli pare che tu gli abbi fatto una minima cosuzza che non gli piacci, non ti vuole più vedere" (cf. esp. pp. 216-231, 24 February 1496, for an extended account of Medicean tyranny); *Salmi* II, p. 191 (11 October 1495); *Ruth e Michea,* I, p. 358 (19 June 1496): "Tu che stavi subietto all'altro stato, e non potevi fare una bottega, e non avevi libertà di potere maritare la tua figliuola"; cf. Trexler, *Public Life in Renaissance Florence,* pp. 448-450, notes 164, 165, 169.

after their fall that Florence needed "a public head, being accustomed as it was to living with a private one". So he found himself in a paradoxical position: needing the arguments developed by the Medici to justify their arbitrary power as platonic 'wise' and 'good' men, yet forced to denounce them on behalf of the popular republicanism he publicly espoused.[9] Trexler has demostrated how Savonarola solved this problem on an institutional and behavioural level by adopting Medici ceremonies and ritual to "assume the Lorenzan heritage" while condemning their tyranny.[10] It remained necessary, as Savonarola realised, to resolve it in the more explicit language of politics used "in the Palace and in the piazzas" where Florentines conducted so much of their busy lives.[11]

Initially Savonarola pre-empted the old Medici basis of authority by claiming power, wisdom and goodness for God, and kingship – or 'captaincy' – for his Son. "I see you want some one to be your head", he said on 27 December 1494, four days after the Great Council had been created:

One can't deny that those states that are governed by one head alone are best but he must be perfect ... So what would you like, Florence, what head, what king can we give you to keep you quiet? I've told you before that it's not better everywhere, nor in every country, for one head to rule, and St Thomas says, too, that in Italy princes become tyrants – come on, Florence, God wants to satisfy you and give you one head and one king to govern you. And this is Christ ... take Christ for your king and stay under his law and with it he will govern you ... Let Christ be your Captain ... be with Christ and don't seek another head.[12]

---

[9] See *Platonism in fifteenth-century Florence*, esp. pp. 236-239 above; on Savonarola's relationship with Florentine Platonists, WALKER, above, ch. 2, pp. 42-62; and on his republicanism, WEINSTEIN, ch. 9, "Savonarola, Theorist of Republican Liberty", pp. 289-316; Q. SKINNER, *The Foundations of Modern Political Thought*, Cambridge, Cambridge University Press, 1978, I (The Renaissance), pp. 145-148 ("The Survival of Republican Values"); N. RUBINSTEIN, *Politics and Constitution in Florence at the end of the Fifteenth Century*, in *Italian Renaissance Studies*, ed. JACOB, pp. 159-164, and J. H. WHITFIELD, *Discourses on Machiavelli*, Cambridge, Heffer, 1969, ch. 6, "Savonarola and the purpose of the *Prince*", pp. 87-110, all arguing mainly from SAVONAROLA's *Trattato circa il Reggimento e Governo della Città di Firenze*, 1498, repr. Turin, Bottega d'Erasmo, 1963.

[10] *Public Life*, pp. 468-469, 482-484, cf. his article, *Lorenzo de' Medici and Savonarola, Martyrs for Florence*, «Renaissance Quarterly», XXXI, 1978, pp. 293-308.

[11] Cf. *Salmi*, II, p. 208 (18 October 1495): "Molti di voi dicano: Io ero in Palazzo, io ero in piazza, io feci, io dissi, io ho liberato questo stato — e quasi dica: Questo stato è mio".

[12] *Prediche italiane*, I, pp. 362-363 (27 December 1494): "Non si può negare che quelli governi che si reducano ad uno capo solo non siano ei migliori, ma bisogna che quel capo sia

Returning to the theme in June, he asked whether the Florentines would not surely trust a great lord who promised to help them, especially if they saw he had the power to do so: "Everyone knows that God is powerful and wise and good".[13]

Four months later Savonarola skilfully took over two more Medicean images of authority, the naturalistic image of every 'genus' controlled by one leader – the army by a captain, the city by a single magistrate – and the imperial Golden Age image of Caesar Augustus which the Medici had been increasingly assimilating to themselves. "Consider the order of the universe, which provides a leader in every 'genus'... the army isn't well governed without a captain... nor is the city unless it is under one magistrate. You, Florence, have Christ for your king, whom God wanted to demonstrate the fact he was king and dominate right from the moment of his birth... and He wanted him to be born at the time when all the world was under a prince, Octavian, to demonstrate that all the world had to be under him".[14] This subsequently became the image of authority propagated to the children who formed so important a part of Savonarola's following. When Domenico da Pescia printed a letter to "the children of Florence" in September 1497, he sent it in the name of "God the lord and Jesus Christ our king", whom he also called "your emperor" and his mother "your empress".[15]

---

perfetto ... Orsu, Firenze, che vorresti tu, che capo, che re ti si può dare, che tu stia quieta? Io t'ho detto altra volta che non ad ogni luogo, nè ogni paese, gli è meglio un capo solo che governi, e Santo Tomaso lo dice, che in Italia e principi diventano tiranni ... Orsu, Firenze, Iddio ti vuol contentare e darti uno capo ed uno re che ti governi. E questo è Cristo ... piglia Cristo per tuo re e sta sotto la sua legge e con quella ti governa ... Cristo sia tuo Capitano ... Sta con Cristo, Firenze, e non cercare altro capo".

[13] *Salmi,* I, pp. 267-268 (3 June 1495): "se fussi qua uno gran signore, Firenze, che ti dicesse d'aiutarti, tu ti confideresti in lui, non è vero? E se tu vedessi che lui avessi potenzia d'aiutarti, tu ti confideresti molto in lui ... Ognuno sa che Dio è potente e savio e buono"; cf. *Platonism in fifteenth-century Florence,* pp. 227-230 above.

[14] *Salmi,* II, pp. 189-190 (11 October 1495): "Considera l'ordine dello universo, *quod in omni genere est dare unum primum* ... Lo esercito non è bene ordinato senza capitano ... Così la città non è bene ordinata, se non si riduce al sommo magistrato. Tu, Firenze, hai Cristo per tuo Re, il quale Iddio volse che si dimonstrassi essere Re e a dominare insino al principio della sua natività ... e e' volse nascere in quello tempo che tutto il mondo era sotto un principe, Ottaviano, per dimonstrare che tutto il mondo avessi ad essere sotto di lui", cf. *Amos e Zaccaria* I, pp. 215-216 (24 February 1496).

[15] *Epistola ... mandata a' fanciulli fiorentini,* Florence, dated 3 September 1497, f. a1*r*: "A tucti voi fanciulli ... Gratia, pace, salute et opportuno adempimento di tucte le presente et future felicità promesse spetialmente a voi da Dio signore et Re nostro Iesu Christo ... et per e' meriti della passione del suo figliuolo, vostro imperatore, et per le intercessione della gloriosa vostra imperatrice, madre del nostro Salvatore".

Since neither God nor Christ were heads of state, they were replaced for practical purposes by "the people" as lord of Florence. In August 1495 the law abolishing *parlamenti*, to prevent anyone daring "to rise up as Head and make himself dominator and tyrant", declared that such plebiscites were unnecessary now that "government is in the hands of the people, which is the true and legitimate Lord of our city".[16] In October 1495 Savonarola asked his audience, in a new political catechism: "Who is our Lord? – Christ is. – Who holds the place of Christ? – Not the Signoria, but the people are the Lord; and therefore I say to you, keep your eye on the Lord, that is, on the Council".[17] Piero Parenti relates in his chronicle how Savonarola urged the people, "since they were lord, to get to their feet if the Signoria refused, when asked, to execute a just law and say: we want it', which was something extremely important".[18] "The people", as Savonarola said, in effect meant the new Great Council, the sovereign legislature consisting of some three and a half thousand citizens, who themselves, or whose parents, grandparents, or great-grandparents, had held one of the three major offices in the state.[19] This was the body described by Savonarola in February 1496 as "like a prince and lord... this is your king, Florence, this is your Lord". And for this reason, he continued, to attempt to murder the council would incur the same capital penalty as someone who murdered a king or prince, the penalty for treason or *lèse-majesté*.[20]

A council of over three thousand members was an uncharismatic and unwieldy head of state, however. Moreover, since Savonarola was

---

[16] Printed in Florence, 13 August 1495, "in consilio generali", f. a1*r*: "essendo venuto el governo in mano del popolo, el quale è vero e legiptimo Signore della nostra Ciptà".

[17] *Salmi*, II, pp. 217-218 (18 October 1495): "Quale è il nostro Signore? – Egli è Christo – Chi tiene il luogo di Christo? – La Signoria no, ma il populo è signore; e però io ti dico: Fa' di avere l'occhio al signore, cioè al Consiglio".

[18] Ed. SCHNITZER, *Quellen*, IV (Leipzig, 1910), p. 124: "et confortò el popolo poi, da che lui era Signore, che quando con debita reverenza la Signoria rischiesta mettere in opera non volesse la provisione iusta, lui si levasse in pie et dicesse, noi la vogliamo, la qual parola importantissima fu".

[19] PESMAN COOPER, above, pp. 73-79.

[20] *Amos e Zaccaria*, I, p. 151 (21 February 1496): 'Quale è la potestà ordinata a te, populo fiorentino? Ell'è il Consiglio grande, perchè quello come principe e signore fa tutti li offiziali. Questo è il tuo re, Firenze; questo è il tuo signore. Or dimmi: che pena merita colui che amazza uno re o uno signore d'una città? – Oh, merita grandissimo punizione, *quia est crimen lesae maiestatis*. – Che meriteria adunque uno che andassi tentando d'amazzare e guastare questo Consiglio? – Certo meriteria quella medesima pena che merita colui che amazza il re o il principe".

not a member of it, he could not even claim to speak on its behalf, as he could speak for God and Christ as their prophet – or "ambassador", as he more diplomatically called himself in 1498.[21] There was one figure of authority that Savonarola could appropriate for himself to replace the Medicean philosopher-ruler as head of a free republic, and that of course was Moses. He had to be careful not to make the analogy too explicit because of the danger of claiming to be a prophet of Moses's stature – "I am not worthy to be compared to Moses", he said disarmingly in January 1495[22] – which is perhaps why it has been largely unnoticed by Savonarolan scholars. Nor was Moses the only prophet Savonarola used to justify his authority in Florence. As prophet, legislator and stern leader of a democratic tribe, however, Moses perfectly, and economically, fitted the bill.

Savonarola drew many comparisons between himself and Moses. He like Moses had broken tablets of stone and the golden calf, he too experienced popular disillusionment in the desert after crossing the Red Sea, he too recommended "severe justice" like Moses, who had someone killed for gathering wood on the Sabbath, in contrast to the Florentines' "cruel compassion".[23] But among them, it was Moses's role as legislator and harsh disciplinarian that assumed greatest importance. As a lawgiver, Savonarola is better known for his introductory Ten Commandments – the creation of the Great Council, the law of amnesty and appeal, and the abolition of *parlamenti* – than for what followed; but like Moses he too followed up his initial re-

---

[21] See his sermon of 11 October 1495 (note 14 above), in which he goes on to say that God wanted "uno frate e forastiero, che non se intende niente di stato" to act for Christ as head, "acciò che la laude sia sola di Dio e non di omo" (p. 191). For the ambassador image, *Salmi*, I, p. 236-267 (28 May 1495) comparing God's use of an angelic messenger to announce his intentions with a king's use of secretaries and ambassadors acting on his commission, which he applied to himself in the last year of his life, *Prediche sopra Esodo*, ed. RICCI, I, p. 309 (7 March 1498): "io sono imbasciadore, qua, mandato da Dio. Gli imbasciadori possono dire", cf. II, p. 305 (18 March 1498): "lo imbasciadore può parlare in persona sua e in persona del suo signore che lo mandò".

[22] *Salmi*, I, p. 123 (25 January 1495); "Io non sono degno d'essere comparato a Moisè".

[23] *Giobbe*, I, pp. 289-295 (18 March 1495): "O Firenze ... ho spezzato ancora io le tavole come fece Moisè ... E come Moisè destrusse il vitello dell'oro degl'Israeliti, così io ho distrutta e sbeffata la tua sapienza humana" (p. 293); *Salmi*, II, pp. 147-148 (12 July 1495): "Nelli principii della legge bisogna sempre una severa iustizia ... Vedi Moisè nel principio della legge fece morire uno solamente perche coglieva le legne el sabbato ... Voi siate pietosi e non vi accorgerete che la vostra è pietà crudele"; cf. *Salmi*, I, p. 25 (11 January 1495), *Giobbe*, II, pp. 30-35 (28 March 1495, eliding Moses with the prophet Gideon), "sì come e' fece a Moisè e qui a Gedeone"; *Salmi*, I, pp. 202-214 (24 May 1495), II, pp. 64-67 and 195-196 (14 June and 11 October 1495).

forms with a Levitican programme of civil as well as moral legislation for his people.[24] In a sermon delivered in the cathedral before the Signoria and magistrates on the Feast of St Victor on 28 July 1495 he summarized it as follows: fear of God, the common good, peace and reform, "that is, the Council". Of these, it was reform that dominated his sermon that day, in which he proposed laws on sodomy, poetry, prostitutes, games, blasphemers (with St Louis as his model, for cauterising the lips of a blasphemer), balls, taverns, closed shops on feast days, clothes, electoral procedure, the creation of peacemakers, abolition of parties, the need for letters and news to be secret, the completion of the council chamber to be a priority ("quickly, not slow, slowly like the ox"), the abolition of *parlamenti*, the appointment of the Signoria for a year instead of two months in time of plague, silence in the council chamber, petitions to the council to be stuck up in public a day in advance so they could be read and understood in advance, and prayers to be said before deliberations and elections.[25]

The popular republicanism which underlay these reforms was reinforced by a sermon delivered on the day a new Signoria was to be elected in June 1496, when he delivered a long homily on the importance of popular participation in discussion and voting. "This morning a new Signoria has to be chosen and I'm not sure whether I should preach or not – and whether or not I should embark on our text for the day [Mica 5], which is long". He then proceeded to advise his popular supporters to let the leading citizens have their say without protesting:

Don't be bothered by what they say. Hold firm to the Council. Votes count more than fine words. When someone gives his reasons, let him talk away enthusiastically and if you don't like it, go up yourself then, don't complain, don't criticize, but do as those fine fellows do and say: the reasons given are good, but it seems to me there are other reasons to consider – and then give your reasons forcefully. and at the end say: So it seems to me, with due respect to opinions better that mine –. And in this way you will

[24] Exodus 21-23 and Leviticus; for Savonarola, see U. MAZZONE, *"El buon governo". Un progetto di riforma generale nella Firenze savonaroliana,* Florence, Olschki, 1978, and on his introductory reforms, WEINSTEIN, esp. ch. 8, pp. 247-288, and N. RUBINSTEIN, *Politics and Constitution,* esp. pp. 155-165.

[25] *Salmi,* II, pp. 168-176 (28 July 1495): "e che vada presto, non come il bue, che va pian, piano".

find the truth and what is best for you. Don't believe all they say, however.[26]

He also tried to strengthen popular government by indoctrination: getting parents to teach the new legislation to their children, particularly the phrase from the law against *parlamenti* which they should learn by heart: "he who wants to summon a *parlamento* wants to take government from the hands of the people".[27]

For this reason we cannot doubt Savonarola's sincerity as a republican. The problem was, as Rousseau later put it succinctly,[28] the people are willing but uneducated and need a legislator to introduce reforms for them. By identifying himself with the judge and prophet through whom the people of Israel were counselled by God what to do, as he did in an important sermon on Ruth 1:1 in May 1496, Savonarola was able to give himself undisputed authority as God's mouthpiece: for "when I tell you to do justice, He has made me say it and if He errs, I too err. But He cannot err, therefore I do not err either in telling you what God says".[29] Comparing Florence to the people of Israel, who "already ruled and governed, as our Florentine people do now, that is, without a king or temporal prince, because they didn't

---

[26] *Ruth e Michea,* I, pp. 420, 435-436 (26 June 1496, cf. n. 3 above): "Questa mattina ... s'ha a fare la Signoria e per questo io sto in dubitazione, se ho a predicare o no, e se entro nel capitolo del nostro profeta o no. El capitulo è lungo ... Lascia parlare alli valenti omini quello che vogliono e non mormorare. Non ti dia noia a te quello che si parli. Tieni pure saldo el Consiglio; le fave sono poi quelle che hanno a giudicare che ha detto bene omo. Quando uno dice le ragioni sue, lascialo dire arditamente, e se non ti piacciono, va' su poi tu e non mormorare, non biasimare. Ma fa come fanno e valenti omini e di': le ragioni che sono state dette sono buone, ma a me pare che ci sia altre ragioni – e di' le ragioni tue vivamente, e alla fine, di': Così pare a me, salvo ogni migliore iudicio – E a questo modo tu troverrai la verità e li modi che ti sieno più salute. Non credere però che sieno tante cose quante si dicono".

[27] *Salmi,* II, p. 196 (11 October 1495): "Dillo a' tua figliuoli, acciò che lo tenghino a mente e insegnali quello verso che 'chi vuole fare parlamento, vuole torre delle mane al populo il regimento'".

[28] *The Social Contract,* II, chs. 6 and 7, London, Dent, 1973, pp. 193, 196: "Of itself the people wills always the good, but of itself it by no means always sees it ... This makes a legislator necessary", "This is what has, in all ages, compelled the fathers of nations to have recourse to divine intervention" (quoting MACHIAVELLI's *Discorsi,* cf. note 52 below).

[29] *Ruth e Michea* I, p. 27 (8 May 1496): "e' me l'ha fatto dire Lui; e se Lui erra, erro ancora io. Ma Lui non può errare: adunque non erro ancora io a dirti quello che dice Dio'; see the repeated criticism by FRANCESCO ALTOVITI in his treatise *In defensione de' Magistrati et delle leggi et antiche cerimonie al culto divino della città di Firenze contro alle invettive et offensione di Fra Girolamo,* f. a6*v*: "tu me l'ai detto tu, se io mento, tu menti", etc.; PIERO VAGLIENTI, *Storie dei suoi tempi, 1492-1514,* p. 31.

then have a king", Savonarola was also able to appropriate for himself the regal role in Florence's mixed government, as the Medici had done before him:

Your government then, Florence, is like that of a judge of the Israelites. I have distinguished government into three types [royal, optimate and popular]...and I have with reasons shown you that this government of the people is more natural and proper to you than all the others. So I want to tell you that although the government of the Hebrews was popular because the people ruled and the judge didn't command but advised, yet it could be called royal because it depended on the mouth of one person, that is God's, because God was the one who ruled them, because through the mouth of the judge and prophet they were counselled by God what they had to do, and so it was royal; and it was also optimate because God allowed the best to advance and be elected and govern. So, Florence, your time will come if you do what I have said. You will find good government and do well. God will always send someone to enlighten you and you will not be able to do badly.[30]

As the royal figure in Florence's popular government, Savonarola was thus able to justify his otherwise quite unwarranted intervention in legislation. To enforce his laws he urged severity upon the clement and "cruelly compassionate" Florentines in a series of forceful paradoxes. Emulating Moses, who used the death sentence for civil offences, he said he wanted to see three fires in the piazza. "Oh, friar, you are cruel" – "It's you who are cruel who, for one pathetic man, put at risk the whole city".[31] In two repeated sermons in June 1495 and May 1496, he assumed the voice of the prophet Micah to preach against forgiveness, telling the Florentines that the clement Ahab who

---

[30] *Ruth e Michea,* I, pp. 106-108, 121 (18 May 1496): "El tuo reggimento dunque, Firenze, è simile a quello di uno iudice delli Israelliti. Io ti ho distinto el reggimento in tre parti e dettoti che ogni governo o è di uno e chiamasi regale, o è di più nobili e chiamasi di ottimati, o è universale, e chiamasi populare. E hotti monstro con ragione che questo governo del populo ti è più naturale e più proprio che tutti gli altri. E anche ti voglio dire che questo reggimento e governo delli Ebrei, benché fussi populare, perché il populo reggeva e il giudice non comandava, ma consigliava, *tamen* era ancora e potevasi chiamare governo regale – perché dependeva dalla bocca di uno, cioè di Dio, perché Dio era quello che li reggeva, perché per la bocca del iudice e del profeta erano consigliati da Dio quello che dovevano fare ... Era adunque quello reggimento regale, e era anche di ottimati, perché Dio permetteva che gli migliori fussino tirati su, e fussino eletti e governassino. Sicchè, Firenze, sarà ancora el tempo tuo, ché se farai quello che ti ho detto, tu troverrai el vado e il governo buono, e farai bene. Dio ti manderà sempre chi ti illuminerà, e non potrai fare male".

[31] *Salmi,* II, p. 147 (12 July 1495): "Io vorrei pure vedere tre fuochi in piazza. – Oh, tu se' crudele, frate – Crudele sei tu che per uno tristo vuoi pericolare una città".

forgave the tyrant Ben-hadad had "changed that 'c' and 'l' into a 'd', for it was dementia and madness to forgive him". So too, he warned, the Florentines would have to pay the penalty of death for their tolerance of sodomites and evildoers: "Yours is not clementia but dementia", not true piety but cruel piety. "You people don't want to do it. You must get involved: you are the Lord".[32] The Florentines were worse than pagans, for Brutus killed his sons for the sake of his country, "and he was a pagan and you are Christians".[33] And driving home the paradox, he later told his Christian audience that, unlike them, the infidel Moslems were stable because they "defended themselves with the sword".[34]

It was in July 1496 that Savonarola recounted the story of the rebellion of Corah as a warning against disobedience. Comparing the discontented Israelites with the Florentines who wanted Pisa to be restored to them, he described how Corah and his followers had been consumed by God because of Moses' anger with them: "Where is the Promised Land? Is this the land of milk and honey you told us about?...O brother, where is Pisa that we have to have back"? Telling them that Moses got the Lord to destroy the rebels, he ordered them to "stay and listen to this last word and then I'll send you home". With the fate of the Jewish rebels before them, the Florentines were urged yet again to be severe, to pass good laws with no favouritism and to do justice by creating a court of appeal or Rota, with a good man invited to be Judge of Appeals and another Judge of the Mercanzia.[35]

Increasingly under attack and on the defensive, Savonarola also used Moses as a useful reminder to the "grumbling" Florentines that not everything went well, even for Moses, who failed to lead his people to the Promised Land because of a moment of doubt he suffered

---

[32] *Salmi,* I, p. 285 (3 June 1495): "la tua non è clemenzia ma demenzia", and *Ruth e Michea,* I, p. 29 (8 May 1496): "In questa clemenza di Acab fu mutato quel 'c' e 'l' in 'd', cioè fu demenzia e pazzia la sua a perdonarli", both sermons expounding I Kings 20. For a later account of this sermon, see note 42 below.

[33] *Salmi,* II, pp. 196-197 (11 October 1495): "Bruto fece ammazzare il proprio figliuolo per la patria e era pagano, e voi siate cristiani".

[34] *Prediche sopra Ezechiele,* ed. Ridolfi, II, p. 156 (9 March 1497): "tu dirai che quello [fede] di Macometto sia stabile. Sa' tu perché? Perché la si difende colla spada".

[35] *Ruth e Michea,* II, pp. 66-67 (3 July 1496): "Dove è la terra di promissione? E questa la terra che tu dicevi, che ci aveva a dare latte e mèle? ... O frate, dove è Pisa che noi avamo a riavere? ... Stammi a udire questa ultima parola e manderottene a casa", describing necessary reforms on pp. 67-70.

when striking the rock for water. "He died and did not see his work through to the end. I am a very great sinner and I have committed worse sins by far, yet God ... has not wanted to waste his work...You look to yourself, too, Florence. What have you done to boast about?" [36]. The Florentines, he told them in March 1497, were like those grumbling people, the *mormoratori*, who all day long grumbled against Moses – "I don't say against me, but against God".[37]

It was a year later, in March 1498, that Savonarola went furthest in arguing for tough justice and the use of force with the story of Moses killing the Egyptian. Excommunicated and interdicted, he had decided to transfer his Lenten sermons from the cathedral to San Marco on the election of a new, more hostile Signoria at the end of February 1498, and it was there that Machiavelli heard his two sermons on Exodus 1,12: "But the more they affected them, the more they multiplied and grew"; and 2,11-12, with its emotive killing of the Egyptian: "Take this stab, Egyptian...and here's another...Do you know what it means to say 'interdict, interdict, interdict'? It means 'tyrant, tyrant, tyrant'".[38] Summarizing them for the Florentine ambassador in Rome, Machiavelli reported that it was at the end of the first sermon that Savonarola, "digressing, as is his wont, in order to debilitate his enemies as well as to provide a bridge to his next sermon", threatened that factionalism in Florence would encourage a tyrant to rise up and ruin their homes and destroy the land:

> And the next morning, expounding Exodus and coming to that part where it says that Moses killed an Egyptian, he said that the Egyptian represented the captives and Moses the preacher who killed them by revealing their vices. And he said: "O Egyptian, I want to give you a thrust of my sword" and at this point he began to dismember your books, o priests, and to treat them in such a way that dogs wouldn't have eaten them. And then he added – and this was what he was trying to get at all along – that he wanted to give the Egyptian another greater wound, and he said that God had told

---

[36] *Ibid.*, II, pp. 408-409 (27 November 1496): "Morì e non condusse l'opera al fine. Io sono peccatore grandissimo e ho fatto maggiori peccati assai senza comparazione, *tamen* Dio, per sua misericordia e non guardando alli nostri peccati, non ha voluto guastare l'opera sua ... Guarda ancora tu dalla parte tua, Firenze, che hai tu fatto di che tu t'abbi a gloriare?"; cf. *Ezechiele*, I, p. 58 (11 December 1496).

[37] *Ezechiele*, II, p. 265 (16 March 1497): "Tu, Firenze, sei come quello populo mormoratore, che tutto el dì mormorava contro Moyses; non dico io contr'a me, ma contro a Dio".

[38] *Esodo*, I, pp. 146-203, nos. 6 (2 March 1498) and 7 (3 March): "Or, togli, Egizio, questa coltellata ... Ecco ancora un'altra coltellata... Sai tu che vuol dire interdetto, interdetto, interdetto? Vuol dire tiranno, tiranno, tiranno".

him that there was one in Florence who sought to make himself a tyrant and held meetings and plotted to bring this about.

Savonarola went on so much about this that people spent the day publicly speculating about whom he could have meant. He was a man – Machiavelli continued, evidently referring to Francesco Valori – "who is about as close to becoming a tyrant as you are to reaching heaven". But having achieved his purpose of unifying his supporters, Savonarola stopped mentioning tyranny and concentrated his energies instead on attacking the pope: "and so, in my opinion, he keeps changing with the times and colouring his lies to suit them".[39]

Machiavelli was not alone in understanding Savonarola's self-identification with Moses, which to judge from contemporary comment was well understood by his supporters as well as his critics. In his 1496 *Defence* of Savonarola, the chancellor Bartolomeo Scala had argued that a religious leader was necessary even in a republic – as could be seen from Israel, which divided into twelve tribes, "as though into a republic" at God's suggestion acting through Moses, "that very wise and successful leader";[40] while the hostile Francesco Altoviti condemned Savonarola for trying to "control arms and the government like a dictator, in order to be able to give his laws to this city and then to the whole world like Moses".[41] By the middle of the

---

[39] MACHIAVELLI, *Lettere,* 9 March 1498, ed. GAETA: "Dixe di poi, entrato in vari dischorsi, come è suo costume, per debilitare più gli adversarii, volendosi fare un ponte alla seguente predicha ... L'altra mattina poi expondendo pure lo Exodo et venendo a quella parte, dove dice che Moyses amazò un Egiptio, dixe che lo Egiptio erono gli huomini captivi, et Moyses il predicatore che gli amazava, scoprendo e' vitii loro; et dixe: O Egiptio, io ti vo' dare una coltellata; et qui cominciò a squadernare e' libri vostri, o preti, e tractarvi in modo che non n'harebbero mangiato e' cani; dipoi soggiunse, et qui lui voleva capitare, che volea dare all'Egiptio un'altra ferita et grande, et dixe che Dio gli haveva detto, ch'egli era uno in Firenze che cercava di farsi tyranno, et teneva pratiche et modi perché gli riescissi ... che è tanto presso al tyranno, quanto voi al cielo ... et così, secondo il mio iudicio, viene secondando e' tempi et le sua bugie colorendo" (pp. 32-33).

[40] *Apologia contra vituperatores civitatis Florentiae,* 1496, f. b3*r*: "in duodecim tribus ... omnis Israelis populus tanquam in unam rempublicam divisus est, auctore etiam ipso et commonstratore Deo, Moyse autem sapientissimo illo duce atque felicissimo perficiente" (going on to defend Savonarola's role in suggesting legislation and prophesying); cf. BARTOLOMEO REDDITI, *Breve Compendio e Sommario della verità predicata e profetata de R. P. Fra Girolamo da Ferrara,* ed. SCHNITZER, *Quellen,* I, p. 38: "mandò loro un huomo profeta, come fece di Moise al popolo d'Israel".

[41] *Defensione,* f. a3*v*: "Così li pare dovere tenere lo stato et l'arme come dictatore per poter dare le sue leggi a questa città et poi a tutto 'l mondo come Moise"; cf. f. a5*v*: "nessuno altro giamai più se non solo Moise potè udire la gran voce dell'alto Idio", with several references to Savonarola's usurpation of the "cathedra di Moise" (ff. a6*v*, a8*v*: "come perfido Mahometto latrendo nella cathedra di Moise"; a9*r*: "et nella cathedra di Moise gridare arme et

sixteenth century Savonarola's sermon about Ahab and Ben-hadad was being used as evidence that Florence "should have a Head and Ruler – and even as we hope a king, like Samaria – as the friar mentioned several times".[42]

But it was the perceptive Machiavelli who understood Savonarola's political language most clearly. Although he professed not to have heard a fiery sermon by a Franciscan preacher in Florence, because he had "no truck with such affairs",[43] we know he heard at least Savonarola's two March sermons in 1498 and probably – if only at second hand – others. It is partly his sensitivity to language that gives this away: the picking up and reworking of paradoxes like "cruel piety" or "wise madness", and the disjunctive "peace, peace... war, war... you say 'peace, peace', and I tell you 'there is no peace'".[44] At a deeper level it is revealed by the role played by Moses in Machiavelli's political thought. This was not, I think, due to Machiavelli's religiosity (as I have recently heard it said) but to his understanding of Moses's importance to Savonarola and hence his practical relevance to Florentine politics.

---

iustitia, che non voleva altro dire se non sangue et vendetta"). On Altoviti, WEINSTEIN, pp. 230, 238-239.

[42] "Discorso sopra una figura proposta da Frate Girolamo Savonarola per il reggimento e stato di Firenze in una Predica da lui fatto il dì viii di maggio sopra Michae", in a volume dedicated to duke Cosimo de' Medici, 2 August 1562, BNF MS Magl. 25.266, f. 20*v*: "Et principalmente per la città di Summaria intenderemo Firenze nostra, dove si vede ... che Firenze havere doveva in questa sua Repubblica un Capo et Reggitore, et anche come speriamo Re, come Samaria haveva, il quale Reggitore anche è stato più volte dal Frate accennato, et infra le altre nella Predica de xii di giugno sopra l'istesso profeta". Giovannini also describes how Savonarola inveighed about badly-executed justice, defining it not (in Aristotelian terms) "tanto in dar a ciascheduno quello che si gli conviene quanto defendere e rimovere le ingiurie" (f. 28*v*).

[43] *Lettere*, p. 309 (19 December 1493): "La predica io non la udii, perché non uso simili pratiche, ma la ho sentita recitare così da tutto Firenze".

[44] *Il Principe*, ch. 17 "De crudelitate et pietate", ed. Bertelli, pp. 68-69: "Era tenuto Cesare Borgia crudele, non di manco quella sua crudeltà aveva racconcia la Romagna... Il che... si vedrà quello essere stato molto più pietoso che il populo fiorentino, il quale, per fuggire il nome di crudele, lasciò destruggere Pistoia"; *Discorsi*, I, 58: "un principe che può fare ciò ch'ei vuole è pazzo; un popolo che può fare ciò che vuole non è savio", for Savonarola's use of these paradoxes, note 31 above and *Platonism in fifteenth-century Florence*, p. 236 above; *Ezechiele*, II, pp. 46, 112, 173 (3, 7 and 10 March 1497): "Voi dite pur *Pax Pax* e io vi dico: non est *pax*, e' non è pace"; "Tu di' *pax, pax*. E la vigna grida guerra, guerra", in MACHIAVELLI's *Lettere*, p. 292 (26 August 1513): "io credo al frate che diceva *Pax, Pax, et non erit pax*". Cf. also "li uomini sdimenticano più presto la morte del padre che la perdita del patrimonio" (*Il Principe* 17, ed. Bertelli, p. 70), reversing, perhaps, a sermon of fra Mariano da Gennazzano's, "tu vorresti più tosto perdere la roba che uno tuo figliuolo e lui [Iddio] vole più tosto torti el figliuolo", ed. Z. ZAFARANA, *Per la storia religiosa di Firenze nel Quattrocento*, «Studi medievali», 3rd. ser. IX, 1968, p. 1077 (16 March 1489).

The occasions on which Machiavelli refers to Moses and Savonarola are well-known but need to be quickly rehearsed. Both men enjoyed extraordinary authority because they talked – or were believed to talk – with God.[45] They demonstrate that arms are necessary for success; for whereas Moses and other armed prophets were victorious, Savonarola failed because he was unarmed and lost control of his followers after they ceased to believe in him.[46] Moses, we are reminded in *The Discourses*, was also successful because he was the only one in authority; and since "to found a republic it is necessary to be alone", murder and violence to achieve this is 'excused', as it was with Romulus and "infinite examples of other founders, such as Moses". Moses, we are told elsewhere, necessarily acted violently in taking over and renaming lands of others.[47] The lesson of violence and the need for arms is nowhere clearer than in *The Discourses*, III,30, where Moses is again associated with Savonarola:

And any one who reads the Bible judiciously will see that, in order to get his laws and orders adopted, Moses was forced to murder infinite numbers of men who opposed his designs, moved by nothing more than envy. Exactly the same problem was experienced by fra Girolamo Savonarola ... [He] couldn't overcome it through lack of authority ... and because he was not properly understood by his followers who would have had authority. It was not his fault this did not happen, and his sermons are full of accusations and invectives against the wise men of the world.[48]

Although Machiavelli attributed his new insights to a "judicious" reading of the Bible, we can see how much Savonarola himself must also have contributed to them, with his talk about arms and severe justice, his paradoxes about "pagan piety" and "Moslem stability", and his claim to divine sanction as a prophet. Even the hypocrisy and opportunism that Machiavelli condemned in Savonarola – espe-

---

[45] *Il Principe*, ch. 6, p. 31, and *Discorsi*, I, 11, p. 163.

[46] *Il Principe*, ch. 6, p. 32; cf. ch. 19, pp. 83-84, that the "securità e la fortezza" of the Turks depends on arms, unlike other states, and Savonarola, n. 34 above.

[47] *Discorsi*, I, 9, pp. 154-155; II, 8, pp. 298-299.

[48] *Ibid.*, III, 30, p. 468: "È chi legge la Bibbia sensatamente vedrà Moisè essere stato forzato, a volere che le sue leggi e che li suoi ordini andassero innanzi, ad ammazzare infiniti uomini, i quali non mossi da altro che dalla invidia si opponevano a' disegni suoi. Questa necessità conosceva benissimo frate Girolamo Savonarola ... non potette vincerla per non avere autorità a poterlo fare ... e per non essere inteso bene da coloro che lo seguitavano, che ne arebbero avuto autorità. Nonpertanto per lui non rimase, e le sue prediche sono piene di accuse de' savi del mondo e d'invettive contro a loro"; cf. L. STRAUSS, *Thoughts on Machiavelli*, Seattle and London, University of Washington Press, 1969, p. 114.

cially for failing to observe the laws he himself introduced – became an essential feature of his successful leader who changes with the times and is prepared to "do evil" if necessary.[49] Far from it being the constitutional or the reforming millenarian Savonarola that influenced Machiavelli, as has been suggested,[50] it was instead the tough Savonarola with his disturbingly anti-Christian paradoxes that impressed Machiavelli and made his work original and iconoclastic: one has to be prepared to kill in order to establish one's laws, as Moses did and Savonarola was unable to do, such crimes being "excused" provided the end is good; laws once passed must be executed rigorously, which pagans and heretics are much better at doing than Christians: "how it is necessary ... to murder the sons of Brutus", as Savonarola had said;[51] and how, to be effective, laws should be given divine sanction, for "in truth, there has never been any lawgiver who has not had recourse to God when giving extraordinary laws to the people, because otherwise they would not be accepted".[52] This early restatement of the sceptical attitude to law provides perhaps the best evidence of the extent of Savonarola's influence.

Transformed by Savonarola and Machiavelli, Moses begins to look recognisably 'modern' – no longer a holy prophet or magus but a civic lawgiver and popular demogogue, forerunner of Hobbesian Moses, who ruled by popular contract according to a civil decalogue that had to be learnt by children and people alike.[53] Savonarola, too, had rea-

---

[49] For Savonarola's hypocrisy, *Discorsi,* I, 45, pp. 233-234, and Machiavelli's letter of 9 March 1498, note 39 above; cf. *Il Principe,* chs. 18, 25, *Discorsi,* III, 9, etc.

[50] See, for example, Whitfield, "Savonarola and the purpose of the Prince", note 9 above (though agreeing with him that "some of the credit ... given to Machiavelli as innovator needs to go to Savonarola, who plainly showed the way", p. 96), and D. WEINSTEIN, *Machiavelli and Savonarola,* in *Studies on Machiavelli,* ed. GILMORE, pp. 251-264, who uses most of the texts quoted above and provides a very full discussion though with somewhat different conclusions.

[51] *Discorsi,* III, 3 (title), p. 386: "Come egli è necessario, a volere mantenere una libertà acquistata di nuovo, ammazzare i figliuoli di Bruto", cf. Savonarola's sermon on 11 October 1495, note 33 above.

[52] *Discorsi,* I, 9, pp. 163, 161: "E veramente mai fu alcuno ordinatore di leggi straordinarie in uno popolo che non ricorresse a Dio, perché altrimenti non sarebbero accettate"; cf. HOBBES, *Leviathan,* ch. 12, ed. OAKESHOTT; pp. 75-76; ROUSSEAU, *The Social Contract,* note 28 above.

[53] *Leviathan,* ed. OAKESHOTT, ch. 20, p. 134 ("This is absolute obedience to Moses"), 26, p. 178 ("he biddeth them to teach it their children, by discoursing of it both at home, and upon the way; at going to bed, and at rising from bed; and to write it upon the posts, and doors of their houses; and to assemble the people, man, woman and child, to hear it read"); ch. 27, p. 188 ("At Mount Sinai Moses only went up to God; the people were forbidden to

lised the importance of publicity and indoctrination – publicizing laws in advance, teaching children to learn them by heart, engaging in pamphlet warfare – in order to influence and control a newly-defined public. For Savonarola, "the people" no longer meant a restricted class of eligible citizens but the populace at large, women and children as well as men, whom he harangued in emotive sermons and organised into pressure groups for reform.[54] To judge from the notorious "burning of vanities" and from the swift rise in anonymous denunciations of the crimes he inveighed against,[55] his impact on what we can begin to call "public opinion" was impressive – and this, too, clearly impressed Machiavelli, as one of the earliest writers to discuss the political power of popular opinion or "imagination".[56] Supporting the Great Council and recognizing, as he did, the people as the ultimate judge of successful politics, Machiavelli was as 'republican' as Savonarola and as authoritarian. For both, the populist but autocratic Moses provided an invaluable model for reconciling the apparently contradictory trends of late fifteenth-century Florence.

---

approach on pain of death; yet they were bound to obey all that Moses declared to them for God's law. Upon what ground, but on this submission of their own ..."), ch. 40, pp. 308-309, etc.

[54] Trexler, *Public Life*, pp. 474-482; Bertelli, note 5 above, pp. 28-29; F. W. Kent, *A Proposal by Savonarola for the Self-Reform of Florentine Women (March 1496)*, «Memorie Domenicane», n.s., XIV, 1983, pp. 335-341; Polizzotto, *The Piagnoni*, note 6 above, ch. 1, "The Beginnings of a Movement: The Pamphlet War", pp. 15-47; for his sermons, cf. notes 38, 39 above.

[55] In anticipation of Michael Rocke's statistical analysis of *tamburazioni*, a very rough count of denunciations in ASF, Ufficiali di Notte, 25-27 suggests a seven-fold increase from *c.* 100 p. a. in 1489 and 1490 to *c.* 766 in 1491-92, when Savonarola began preaching on the Apocalypse. Savonarola's influence can also be detected in the language of the denunciations, which, because they are anonymous, offer the nearest approach to a medieval public opinion poll.

[56] *Discorsi*, I, 11, p. 163. On the importance of the people, *Il Principe*, chs. 18, 19, pp. 74, 83, *Ghiribizi*, in *Lettere*, p. 229.

9

CHANGING PERCEPTIONS OF CITY AND CITIZEN

IN LATE MEDIEVAL ITALY

Nothing serves better to conjure up images of one's beloved city than absence from it. "I love generally all our city's men, the laws, the customs, the walls, the houses, the streets, the churches and the countryside", Francesco Vettori wrote to Machiavelli from Rome in 1513. "Nor would I have greater displeasure than to think this city had to be tormented and these things ... go in ruins".[1] Leon Battista Alberti, born an exile from Florence, thought that the greatest of all pleasures for a civilized man was to "wander through cities and provinces" and gaze on "the temples, the theatres, buildings of every kind made pleasurable to look at by man and nature".[2] For Machiavelli, it was the hustle and bustle, the changeability and vice of urban life that distinguished "big cities" like Florence, Rome and Athens from "these deserts of Arabia" in provincial Carpi;[3] and the same qualities also made Florence – or "as it might be Rome or Pisa"

This paper was delivered at a conference held in Brown University, Providence, Rhode Island, in May 1989, whose proceedings are published by Steiner Verlag, Stuttgart, and by The University of Michigan Press, Ann Arbor, with the title *City-states in classical antiquity and medieval Italy*, 1991. For discussion of its context and scope, see my introduction on pp. XI-XII above.

[1] 20 Aug. 1513, N. MACHIAVELLI, *Lettere*, ed. GAETA, p. 285: "Amo generalmente tutti gli huomini di quella [la città nostra], le leggi, i costumi, le mura, le case, le vie, le chiese et il contado, né posso havere il maggior dispiacere che pensare quella havere a tribolare et quelle cose... havere andare in ruina".

[2] *De commodis litterarum atque incommodis*, ed L. G. CAROTTI, Rome, Marzorati, 1976, p. 50: "Etenim voluptatum prestantissima et libero homine digna una illa est per urbes provinciasque vagari, multa et templa et theatra, menia atque omnium generum edificia spectare, locaque ambire, que tum natura amenissima, grata, munitissima, tum manu et ingenio hominum fuerint ad conspectum pulcra".

[3] As he told a friar disillusioned with the fickleness of prostitutes in Florence, letter to F. Guicciardini, 18 May 1521, *Lettere*, pp. 409-410.

– the natural setting for comedy, another of the attractions of city life.[4]

These Florentines provide clues to the analogy between ancient and medieval city states at one level of civic consciousness, as a shared memory of city life. It was their size, their buildings, their laws and their customs that enabled cities like Rome, Venice or Florence to identify with Rome and Athens and feel "homely confidence" in ancient literature.[5] We clearly should not exaggerate the importance of specifically classical ingredients in this generalized love of city, indeed it is difficult to isolate them. Nearly all Italian towns were built on classical foundations, cathedrals rising from pagan basilicas, marketplaces located on ancient forums. In the fifteenth century, as earlier, classical and Christian elements were merged to form a cohesive whole.[6] The locus of philosophical discussions in Alberti's dialogues is not the academy but the cathedral, which provided not only a meeting ground for citizens but "shadow enough to cover the entire Tuscan population", in his imaginative image.[7] More than the walls, the cathedral thus served to unite the whole Florentine dominion in the fifteenth century. And what was true of Florence was even more true of Venice, whose basilica of San Marco became the potent centre of civic ritual.[8]

Nor was there any conflict between citizens' patriotism or *campan-*

---

[4] *La Mandragola*, in *Il Teatro e tutti gli scritti letterari*, ed. F. GAETA, Milan, Feltrinelli, 1977, p. 56: "Questa è Firenze vostra; un'altra volta sarà Roma o Pisa", cited by H. LEVIN, "Notes towards a definition of City Comedy", *Renaissance Genres*, ed. B. K. LEWALSKI, Cambridge, Mass., Harvard University Press, 1986, p. 131.

[5] G. BILLANOVICH, explaining Landolfo Colonna's "constant references to matters and places most familiar" to him in his Livy, *Petrarch and the Textual Tradition of Livy*, «Journal of the Warburg and Courtauld Institutes», XIV, 1951, p. 167.

[6] See J. LE GOFF, *L'immaginario urbano nell'Italia medievale (sec.* V-XV) in *Storia d'Italia. Annali*, V, Turin, Einaudi, 1982, pp. 5-43; C. FRUGONI, *Una lontana città*, Turin, Einaudi, 1983, A. I. GALLETTI, *Modelli urbani nell'età comunale: Gerusalemme* in *Modelli nella storia del Pensiero Politico*, ed. V. I. COMPARATO, Florence, Olschki, 1987, pp. 89-101.

[7] *De pictura*, preface dedicated to Brunelleschi, architect of the dome, ed. C. GRAYSON, London, Phaidon, 1972, pp. 32-33; "ampla da coprire con sua ombra tutti e' popoli toscani"; cf. *Profugiorum ab aerumna, Opere volgari*, ed. G. GRAYSON, II, Bari, Laterza, 1966, esp. pp. 107-109. In the *Novella del Grasso legnaiuolo* attributed to Brunelleschi, it was in the Duomo, on a working day, that the master carpenter met Brunelleschi and Donatello, "che s'andavano ragionando insieme, come era di loro usanza", ed. C. VARESE, *Prosatori volgari del Quattrocento*, p. 790, repr. *Novellieri del Quattrocento*, Turin, Einaudi, 1977, p. 70.

[8] E. MUIR, *Civic Ritual in Renaissance Venice*, Princeton, Princeton University Press, 1981, and on the Saint Mark legend, PATRICIA BROWN, *The Self-Definition of the Venetian Republic*, in *City-States in classical antiquity and medieval Italy*, ed. MOLHO, RAAFLAUB and EMDEN, pp. 511-548.

ilismo, love of their city's bell-tower, and their loyalty to the Church. Giovanni Rucellai combined pleasure in being born in Florence, "which is considered the worthiest and most beautiful *patria* not only in Christendom but the whole world", with satisfaction that he was also born "in the middle of the faith, that is, near to Rome, the residence of our most holy lord pope and his honourable brothers, the cardinals, who represent Christ with the apostles".[9] Patriotism continued in this period to underpin religion as a bond to cement the antagonistic classes of these mobile and socially diversified cities. Remigio de' Girolami, as the member of an old aristocratic Florentine family and a Dominican teacher, does not perhaps illustrate 'popular' sentiment, but his sermons on patriotism, with his well-known depiction of the citizen of a destroyed city as "a painted image or a form of stone", succeeded by the fifteenth century in creating widely-shared civic pride.[10] What better evidence of this than the behaviour of Florentines in January 1409, who emerged after a memorable four days' snowfall spontaneously to construct not snowmen but the civic insignia: "a great quantity of lions – beautiful, too – on almost every corner and in the loggias"; and on the piazza of San Michele Berteldi a "six-foot Hercules."[11] By the mid-fifteenth century this patriotism was widely diffused among the citizen class, who now modelled themselves closely on classical precedent. One man who claimed "not to be very clever and to have no grasp of the important matters under discussion" repeatedly intervened in policy discussions in Florence in the 1450s, quoting Sallust and using analogies drawn from 'ancient examples' and 'the fall of Rome' to urge the need for sacrifice and

---

[9] *Giovanni Rucellai e il suo Zibaldone*, ed. Perosa, p. 117, cf. pp. 65-78, listing the beauties of Florence and Rome.

[10] "Unde destructa civitate remanet civis lapideus aut depictus, quia scilicet caret virtute et operatione quam prius habebat", *De bono comuni*, ed. M. C. De Matteis, *La 'Teologia politica e comunale' di Remigio de' Girolami*, Bologna, Patron, 1977, p. 18; cf. C. T. Davis, *An early Florentine Political Theorist: fra Remigio de' Girolami*, in *Dante's Italy*, Philadelphia, University of Pennsylvania Press, 1984, pp. 198-223.

[11] Bartolomeo del Corazza, *Diario fiorentino*, «Archivio storico italiano», ser. 5, XIV, 1894, p. 246: "Fecionsi per Firenze grande quantità di lioni e begli: quasi in sun ogni canto ne era uno; e alle loggie, grandi e begli: e fessi in sulla piazza di San Michele Berteldi uno Hercole lungo ii braccia, e stette bene". Since Savonarola imprecated against "quelli Erculi e quelle cose vane" erected by children who "vorriano fare qualche festa", instead of crucifixes, it was clearly a custom that continued, *Prediche sopra Ezechiele*, ed. Ridolfi, II, p. 208 (12 March 1497). Hercules had been represented on the communal seal since at least 1281, Marzi, *La Cancelleria della Repubblica fiorentina*, p. 377-385.

unity.[12] In other debates, citizens cited Aristotle to argue for humanity in administering the republic and the use of the middle way, "Aristotelico more"; while one citizen – in a confused but pleasing transference of gender roles – stood up to argue that one's *patria* is like a *materfamilias* who, having brought up and educated her children, needs protection by them in their adulthood.[13]

It was at the level of politics that the analogy between classical and medieval Italian city-states was felt most keenly. As Pocock reminds us, the theory of the polis is essentially "political theory in its purest form", and it offered a valuable paradigm to Italian communes about how to govern cities with the mixed and changeable populations described by Machiavelli: "a city composed of interacting persons rather than of universal norms and traditional institutions".[14] The message of the popular Aristotle was participation by all for the sake of the common good – a high-risk commitment, as Pocock says, because unless everyone loved his country more than his soul, corruption and despotism would result: "once justice ... was identified with the distributive justice of the polis, salvation became in some degree social, in some degree dependent upon others".

Greater familiarity with classical texts as they were rediscovered and translated encouraged more detailed comparisons with the structure and constitutions of ancient cities.[15] Bruni's 1403 *Laudatio* of Florence, modelled on Aristides' *Panathenaica*, set the pace, to be in turn imitated by Pier Candido Decembrio's *De laudibus Mediolanensium Urbis in comparationem Florentiae panegyricus* in 1436, and, "in

---

[12] Donato Cocchi, ASF Cons. Prat. 55, ff. 25*v*, 31*r-v*, 38*v* (2-4 July 1458): "cum parvi ingenii sit, res magnas quemadmodum haec sunt se non intelligere dixit", "veteribus exemplis" (38*v*), "excidii plurimarum urbium imprimis Romanae urbis" (31*v*); cf. Coluccio Salutati's letters arguing that "sicut Grecie civitates inter se de imperio dimicantes omnes imperio caruerunt, sic nos in defensionem discordes optatissima, quod cum dolore precogitamus, carebimus libertate", Missive la Cancelleria, 15, f. 16*v*, quoted by R. G. Witt, *Coluccio Salutati and his Public Letters*, Geneva, Droz, 1976, p. 50.

[13] ASF Cons. Prat. 60, ff. 14*v* (Domenico Martelli): "laudavit summum magistratum & decemviros Aristotelis auctoritate qui civilem administrationem humanam et clementem esse iubet et tyrannidis contraria⟨m⟩; 13*v* (Franco Sacchetti): "Patriam matrem fa⟨milias⟩ dixit ... Itaque succurrendum esse matri censuit e proprie et ab omni iniuria et ignominiam vindicandam" (Jan. 1468); 137*r* (*idem*): "In ea ergo medium si inveniri possit perquirendum Aristotelico more" (March 1472).

[14] J. G. A. Pocock, *The Machiavellian Moment*, pp. 74-75.

[15] A. Grafton and L. Jardine, *From Humanism to the Humanities*, London, Duckworth, 1986, esp. pp. 58-98, for an account of the detailed investigation of classical institutions encouraged by new teaching methods in the fifteenth century.

a kind of turning inside-out" of Bruni, Poggio Bracciolini's 1459 *Oratio in laudem Rei Publicae Venetorum.*[16] Underlying their obvious rhetoric and imitation was a serious attempt to analyze the political and legal, as well as the physical, structure of Italian cities in terms of ancient republics – culminating in Machiavelli's prolonged reflections on Roman republicanism in his *Discourses on the first Decade of Livy.*

Thus for Bruni, Florence's liberty consisted in its short-term offices and absence of a single head, as well as in the legislative sovereignty of its two councils; equality consisted in the subjection of all citizens to communal laws and the special protection afforded to commoners from assaults by the nobles – under the control of the Guelf Party, which he compared to the Roman censors, Spartan Ephors and the Athenian Areopagus. When he analyzed the constitution again in 1439, for the benefit of Greek visitors to the Council of Florence, he explained it in terms of Aristotle's polity or middling-constitution that excluded both the highest and the lowest classes from government.[17]

In Venice, by contrast, the best analogy for its mixed constitution of Doge, Senate and Great Council (all drawn, after 1297, from a closed nobility) was provided by Plato's *Laws.* Plato was not initially popular as a model for republican communes, though providing, through Cicero's *De officiis*, an early argument for patriotism and unity. The first translation of *The Republic*, for the duke of Milan in the early fifteenth century, served only to make a familiar moral point about how easily republics decline into tyrannies.[18] It was not until the middle of the century that George of Trebizond's translation of *The Laws* was used to provide a model of mixed government for Venice, to be developed in greater detail in Contarini's *De magistratibus.*[19] In Florence Plato was adopted as a model only in the second half of the fifteenth century, encouraged – as I have argued above – by the growing power of the Medici as unofficial rulers of the city. Then

[16] F. KRANTZ, *Between Bruni and Machiavelli: History, Law and Historicism in Poggio Bracciolini* in *Politics and Culture in Early Modern Europe*, ed P. MACK and M. C. JACOB, Cambridge, Cambridge University Press, 1987, p. 131, the reference to which I owe to Julius Kirshner.

[17] BRUNI'S *Laudatio* is translated in *The Earthly Republic*, ed B. G. KOHL and R. G. WITT, Manchester, Manchester University Press, 1978, pp. 135-175, esp. 168-174; his 1439 *On the Constitution of the Florentines* in *The Renaissance* ed. E. COCHRANE and J. KIRSHNER, Chicago, University of Chicago Press, 1986, pp. 140-144.

[18] F. ADORNO, *Uberti Decembris prologus in Platone 'De republica'* in *Studi in onore di Antonio Corsano*, Manduria, Lacaita, 1970, p. 10.

[19] *Ibid.*, pp. 14-17; F. GILBERT, *The Venetian Constitution in Florentine Political Thought* in *Florentine Studies,* ed. RUBINSTEIN, pp. 468-470.

the revival of the platonic corpus helped to project the Medici as philosopher rulers,[20] who combined power with wisdom by using all the tricks of the ancient trade: bread, circuses, triumphs, exile and penal taxation together with art, culture and a philosophical academy.

Above all, however, it was republican Rome which provided the most appropriate – and easily accessible – analogy for Italian communes. Most obviously it was the polarity of the senate and the people that offered comparison with the commune's dual councils of the Commune and the People, the popular captain acting, like the tribune in Rome, as protector of commoners against the nobles. According to Machiavelli, following Livy, it was the clash of interests between the nobility and people that preserved Rome's freedom, hence the value of the Roman model to Italian city-states. Yet not every one interpreted the analogy in this way, as we can see from the Milanese chronicler, to whom the ideogram 'S.P.Q.F.', inscribed in Roman letters on a shield in Florence's communal palace, immediately signified Florence's propagandistic claim to be Rome's political heir: "as though Florence had been left heir to Roman liberty!" he expostulated.[21]

Within Florence in the later fifteenth century, reflecting the move towards greater elitism, the contrast between Senate and People was used not to distinguish nobility from commoners as two balanced poles in the constitution, but a senate of qualified office-holders from the rest of the populace – a significant shift from a polarized power structure towards a more unitary one.[22] At the same time republican ter-

---

[20] BROWN, *Platonism in fifteenth-century Florence*, pp. 220-235 above. In BARTOLOMEO PLATINA'S *De optimo cive* (ed. BATTAGLIA, p. 183), Lorenzo revealingly asks the question, "Qui de republica scripsere, probaruntne ludos? An haec consuetudo ut alia permulta irrepsit vimque legis in civitatibus cepit?" to which Platina replies that games did not replace laws in republics, since Cosimo not only liberated his city from external enemies but provided it with laws and institutions.

[21] A. BIGLIA, *Historiae patriae libri novem*, ed. L. A. MURATORI, *RIS*, XIX (1723), col. 33, cited by DIANA WEBB in her doctoral thesis, *Tuscan historiography, c. 1400-c. 1460, and the problem of Florentine hegemony in Tuscany* (University of London, 1977), p. 33: "Romanis literis inscriptum S.P.Q.F. tanquam florentino nomini relicta esset romanae libertatis haereditas". On this claim, which gave Florence as heir to Roman republicanism "by hereditary right, dominion over the entire world", see Bruni's *Laudatio*, pp. 149-552.

[22] On the use of *senate* for the Signoria and Colleges, see P. RAJNA in «Archivio storico italiano», ser. vii, XIII, 1930, pp. 189-206; on its use for the Council of Seventy, BROWN, *Bartolomeo Scala*, p. 262 (Ital. edn., p. 183), and for the Council of Eighty, J. NARDI, *Istorie di Firenze*, ed. A. GELLI, Florence, Le Monnier, 1858, I, p. 431: "[E]l senato, cioè il consiglio degli ottanta". Scala uses the formula 'senatus populusque' in letters and orations from 1466 (for example, ASF, Missive la. Canc. 45, f. 106*r*, letter to Ferrante of Naples, 23 Sept. 1466)

minology was used to legitimize changed procedures increasing the power of the government – 'rogation' to legitimize the use of non-notarial 'secretaries' to draft laws and subscribe letters and *'e republica'* to legitimize the granting of unrestricted prerogative powers to individuals for the public interest.[23] Other admired Roman republican practices included methods of election to office, exile "for the sake of one's country", censuses, and the system of rewards and punishments for patriotic and treacherous citizens.[24]

Where circumstances did not encourage active republican government, as in Rome or Milan, its ethos was kept alive by other means. The conspiracy of Stefano Porcari and the Academy of Pomponio Leto served as focuses of republicanism in Rome, where traditions of ancient games, bull hunts and pasquinades were consciously developed as a counter-culture to clericalism.[25] In Milan, the assassination of the duke in 1476 (masterminded by Cola Montano, an alienated academic) was immediately compared to the deed of Scaevola the Roman, "a worthy, virile and praiseworthy undertaking", carried out in imi-

---

and restricts the function of governing to the senate in his 1496 *Apologia, Platonism in fifteenth-century Florence,* p. 235 above. Cf. L. CARBONE's speech in Florence in 1473: "Invero mi parse vedere una similitudine del Senato romano", cit. E. GARIN, *Motivi di cultura filosofica ferrarese nel Rinascimento* in *La cultura filosofica del rinascimento italiano*, p. 403.

[23] Cf. BROWN, *Bartolomeo Scala*, pp. 173-192 (Ital. ed., pp. 118-127), R. FUBINI, *Classe dirigente ed esercizio della diplomazia nella Firenze quattrocentesca*, in *I ceti dirigenti nella Toscana del Quattrocento*, esp. pp. 178-182.

[24] L. BRUNI, *Historiarum Florentini populi*, ed. E. Santini, *RRII* XIX (3), Città di Castello, 1926, bk. V (1323), p. 122: that the Roman system of election to office is better than the Florentine system of lot; Platina, *De optimo cive*, p. 193: "Civitas enim nostra Atheniensium morem imitata, dominatum affectantes, aut in exilium mittit aut ad tempus relegat"; BARTOLOMEO FONZIO's Dictionary, Biblioteca Riccardiana, Florence, MS. 152, f. 100*r*: 'cui quidem persimilis census noster est, quem nos catastum appellamus'; ASF Cons. Prat. 60, f. 159*v*, etc., that Lorenzo was prepared to suffer exile for the sake of his patria; F. GUICCIARDINI, *Dialogo del Reggimento di Firenze*, ed. PALMAROCCHI, p. 136: 'gli antichi savi che ordinarono le republiche... ordinarono el premio e la pena, dicendo saviamente che erano el fundamento delle città'. The public funerals and tombs of Bruni and Marsuppini and the title Pater Patriae awarded to Cosimo de' Medici followed this tradition, as Marsuppini explained in a letter to the Bolognese on 1 July 1445, ASF Missive la Canc. 36, f. 115*v*): 'Solebant antiqui eos qui patriam ex servitute in libertatem vendicassent, non solum amplissimis honoribus ornare et honestare, verum etiam statuis publicisque monumentis decorare'. Cf. the speech of M. Salamonio de Alberteschi as Captain of the People in Florence in 1498 comparing Florence's social structures to those of Athens, *De principatu libros septem nec non orationes ad priores florentinos,*, ed. M. D'ADDIO, p. 101.

[25] C. L. Stinger, *The Renaissance in Rome*, Bloomington, Indiana, Indiana University Press, 1985, pp. 71-72; A. REYNOLDS, *The Classical Continuum in Roman humanism: the Festival of Pasquino, the Robigalia and Satire*, «Bibl. d'Humanisme et Renaissance», XLIX, 1987, pp. 289-307; M. BOITEUX, *Chasse aux taureaux et jeux romains de la Renaissance* in *Les Jeux à la Renaissance*, ed. P. ARIES and J.-C. MARGOLIN, Paris, Vrin, 1982, pp. 33-35.

tation of Catiline by students "who wanted to copy those ancient Romans and be liberators of their country".[26]

* * *

Influenced by all this, there was general recognition of the common ground shared by ancient and medieval city states. This seems to suggest that the analogy between classical and Italian city-states was based on shared – if eclectic and unclearly defined – political ideals as well as on a shared experience of city life. But there are problems with this analogy on both the levels I have discussed. However warm and all-embracing Italian cities were, with their protective walls, patron saints and sociability, it is clear from stories like that of Grasso Legnaiuolo, who was persuaded by Brunelleschi and his friends that he was someone else, that cities also encourage alienation and loss of identity.[27]

Machiavelli illustrates this other face of urban life in his strange poem *The Golden Ass*, which escapes from all traditional models to present an original and disturbing view of city life. By contrasting the angst of city dwellers with the happier existence of Circe's 'beastly' animals in the harsh countryside, Machiavelli most obviously challenges the Florentine proverb, "honour does not dwell in the woods... worthy men are made in cities", which was quoted approvingly by Gino Capponi to his sons in the early fifteenth century.[28] But the poem also offers an alternative reading of Florence's much-vaunted urbanism in the fantasizing story of the running boy with which it opens, in which, far from civilizing him, the sight of via Larga, the Michigan Avenue of Florence, opening out "so straight and spacious" before him, awakens the boy's old malady: his hair

---

[26] *Storia di Milano*, VII, Milan, Fondazione Treccani degli Alfieri, 1956, p. 307; quoting from LUCA LANDUCCI'S *Diario*, ed. I. DEL BADIA, Florence, Sansoni, 1883, pp. 14-15; A. RINUCCINI, *Ricordi storici*, ed. G. AIAZZI, Florence, 1840, p. CXXV; E. CASANOVA, *L'uccisione di G. M. Sforza e alcuni documenti fiorentini*, «Archivio storico lombardo», ser. III, XII, 1899, pp. 306-307: 'E studiavano el Chatilinario'; cf. MACHIAVELLI, *Discorsi*, bk. III, ch. 6 (ed. BERTELLI, to which all subsequent page numbers refer), p. 407.

[27] *La novella del Grasso legnaiuolo*, pp. 47-82.

[28] Cited by F. W. KENT, *Household and Lineage in Renaissance Florence*, Princeton, Princeton University Press, 1977, pp. 250-251.

beginning to rise, he scarcely reaches the top of the street before he casts off his cloak and runs away for ever.[29]

Nor did Renaissance cities themselves represent the civic modesty and republicanism they were once believed to represent. Re-reading Florentine palace through the eyes of contemporaries, as F.W. Kent is encouraging us to do, we find they are as dominating and imperious as the medieval towers and castles they replaced. A student from Padua was stupefied by their immensity and "massive protruding stoniness", like Valhalla "fit for Jupiter and the gods". To someone else, Luca Pitti's palace suggested Caesar's Rome, while Giovanni Rucellai's, in his own eyes, was evidently analogous to that of a Roman citizen who had received "great honour ... on account of his building a most beautiful palace ... on the Palatine Hill". And far from being reticent and utilitarian, as used to be suggested, the scale and bossy surface of the Medici palace in Via Larga in fact carried scarcely concealed messages of imperialism and grandeur, "setting the stylistic terms within which most other Florentine palace builders were to work for the rest of the fifteenth century".[30]

The political language of the later communal period carried similar messages of alienation and growing autocracy beneath its apparent egalitarianism and republicanism.[31] The few republics that survived into the fifteenth century did so by transforming their constitutions. The dualism that had initially protected the people now only served to perpetuate factionalism, and measures were taken almost everywhere to close the political class, unify the legislative councils, and create tough police magistracies with summary powers of justice. Belied by the triumphal republicanism of their architects, the political alienation of this later period provides evidence of changes that are otherwise difficult to document.

---

[29] *Dell'asino d'oro, Il Teatro*, pp. 229-302, esp. 270-271. The same story, located now in Ferrara ("in quella bella, lunga et larga strada, la qual nel vero è la più bella di Ferrara"), was repeated in 1546 in a letter from G. Guarnaschello to S. Magrini in Florence, ed. G. PAPANTI, *Due lettere curiose e facete del Guarneschello non mai stampate*, Livorno, 1872, pp. 7-8.

[30] F. W. KENT, *Palaces, Politics and Society in Fifteenth-Century Florence*, «I Tatti Studies», II, 1987, esp. pp. 51-52, 67. For an earlier interpretation, see GUTKIND, *Cosimo de' Medici*, pp. 220-221, alluding to Vasari's life of Brunelleschi.

[31] Referring to the inequality of a city that has become corrupt (like Thebes, and Italian cities of his own day), Machiavelli said that to restore equality, it was necessary "to take steps which are by no means normal", *Discorsi*, I, XVII, 179: "e necessario usare grandissimi straordinari".

The elitism of medieval communes has been a theme of revisionist historiography for some years now. What is new in the fifteenth century is evidence of passivity and reduced participation, even within inner elites. John Najemy has already identified the beginning of these changes in Goro Dati's willingness to leave politics to others, once he knew he was part of this elite: "I have resolved and sworn to myself that I shall not henceforth invoke the aid of any or attempt to get myself elected to public office or to have my name included in new purses. Rather, I shall let things take their course without interfering".[32] By 1472 someone in a consultative meeting apologized for speaking before his turn, "because having been called on again and again, no one else would give his opinion".[33] In 1490 the Medici had difficulty in finding a representative citizen to join a literary banquet for a visiting scholar.[34] And even after the revolution of 1494 and the establishment of the popular Great Council of some 3,000 citizens, Savonarola found it difficult to get its new members to participate. He had to tell them that votes were more important than rhetoric: having let the leading citizens have their say, he advised, they should, if they disagreed, go to the rostrum and say "the reasons given are good, but it seems to me there are other reasons to consider" – and then give their reasons forcefully and say at the end, "So it seems to me, with due respect to opinions better than mine" – but they should not believe all they were told, however.[35]

His warning provides supporting evidence of growing awareness of the limitations of communal government in the late fifteenth century and the difficulty faced by ordinary people who tried to participate in the political debate. By the early sixteenth century both Guicciardini and Donato Giannotti commented on the same problem. "In our times, and especially in our city", Giannotti wrote "there are very few brave enough to speak before a large crowd", the greatest

---

[32] *Two Memoirs of Renaissance Florence*, ed. G. BRUCKER, New York, Harper and Row, 1967, p. 125, referred to by NAJEMY, *Corporatism and Consensus in Florentine Electoral Politics*, pp. 301-303, 309.

[33] ASF Cons. Prat. 60, f. 137*r* (Franco Sacchetti, 5 March 1472): "cum nemo iterum atque iterum vocatus sententiam diceret, precatus veniam quod ante locum suum diceret". On Sacchetti, see now PHILLIPS, *The Memoir of Marco Parenti*, pp. 59-61.

[34] Piero to Lorenzo de' Medici, 10 May 1490, ed. ROSCOE, *The Life of Lorenzo de' Medici*, II, App. LXXXI, pp. 96-97: "per torre un cittadino, et non uscire di parente et letterato, togliemmo Bernardo Rucellai", cited by TREXLER, *Public Life in Renaissance Florence*, pp. 446-447.

[35] See BROWN, *Savonarola, Machiavelli and Moses: a changing model*, pp. 270-271 above.

problem being "to get people to speak up, so unused were they to speaking before a large audience". To overcome their diffidence, Guicciardini suggested that the Gonfalonier should invite people to go up to the rostrum to give their opinions, "to make them accustomed to this way of speaking and discussion". Not long after this, he confided to his intimate memoirs the danger of being ruled by unskilled leaders and his acerbic view of the populace at large: "a mad animal gorged with a thousand and one errors and confusions, devoid of taste, of pleasure, of stability".[36]

* * *

The distance between political reality and republican ideology in this later period suggests we must investigate the function of this ideology carefully. It has generally been assumed – as it was by E. J. Bickerman [37] – that there was a close resemblance between the political structure of ancient city-states and Italian communes. The republican features both shared were open access to citizenship (controlled in Rome by the censors, in the communes by the councils on the basis of residence and tax-paying), a temporary elective headship (the consuls, soon superceded in Italy by elected external judicial officials, the Podestà and the Captain of the People, with a very short-term, elected head-of-state,) and ultimate control by two citizen councils chosen by differing combinations of locality and wealth (the Councils of the Commune and of the People in Italian communes, both chosen by a combination of locality and wealth, in contrast to Rome, where the *comitia tributa* was based on locality and the *comitia centuriata* on wealth; the later *comitia* or *consilium plebis* alone resembled the Council of the People in excluding the nobility). But whereas in Rome office-holding was restricted to members of the senate, who were men of equestrian standing, this was true only of Venice after 1297, not of other communes where offices were open to all citizens. As we

[36] D. GIANNOTTI, *Della repubblica fiorentina, Opere politiche e letterarie*, Florence, Le Monnier, 1850, pp. 216-217; GUICCIARDINI, *Dialogo del reggimento*, p. 122; *Ricordi*, ser. C, nos. 137, 140, ed. SPONGANO, pp. 149, 152; translated by DOMANDI, *Maxims and Reflections*, pp. 75-76.

[37] E. J. BICKERMAN, *Some Reflections on Early Roman History*, esp. pp. 404-408, the starting-point for this study, see the preface, p. XI, and note 9, above.

have seen, however, this was a feature of the Roman model that increasingly appealed to late fifteenth-century Florentines.

And although nobility and people (or plebs) may be correlate terms, it is not true that the political role of the *popolo* in Italian communes developed only in response to the closure of the patriciate, as Bickerman suggests, since the *societates populi* anticipated the 1297 Serrata in Venice, as well as the much later closing of the ruling group in Florence in 1494. In contrast to Rome, where the plebs were early on incorporated into the ruling group, or nobility, in Italian communes (with the exception of Venice) the *popolo* played an independent role in government as members of guilds. In Florence, according to the Ordinances of Justice in 1293, they even managed to deprive the magnates (defined as families possessing two knights) of a direct role in government altogether. Because medieval Italian cities, unlike ancient cities, were preeminently centres of trade and commerce, the merchant class played a more dominant role in them than in ancient cities – without being able to monopolize power, however, due to the continued residence there of the nobility.

The Senate and People model would seem to have obvious appeal to Italian communes attempting to integrate these two divergent social groups. But now that the myth of the Roman city-state has been dispelled by Cornell as an "artificial construct, the product not of history so much as ideology",[38] we need to examine very carefully its function in the later medieval communes. This is not just because of the obvious economic, social and religious – as well as political – differences between ancient city-states and medieval communes. Interestingly Venice, the city-state that most closely resembled Rome with its closed patriciate and powerful senate, was late in developing an interest in Roman republicanism as a political model.[39] The analogy between classical and medieval city-states is not straighforward for other reasons. Although the recovery of ancient models helped to create a genuine stock of shared experience by enabling communes

---

[38] "Rome: the history of an anachronism", *City-states in classical antiquity and medieval Italy,* pp. 53-69.

[39] PHILIP JONES, *Economia e società nell'Italia medievale: la leggenda della borghesia* in *Storia d'Italia, Annali* I, Turin, Einaudi, 1978, pp. 187-372; cf. LE GOFF, *L'immaginario urbano,* pp. 8-9. On Venice, R. FINLAY, *Politics in Renaissance Venice,* London, Ernest Benn, 1980, F. GILBERT, *The Venetian Constitution in Florentine Political Thought* in *Florentine Studies,* ed. RUBINSTEIN, pp. 463-500.

to conceptualize and organize their history, it also encouraged artificial comparisons through the need to make the newly-discovered material relevant to patrons and audiences. Moreover, use of models was very eclectic, as we have seen. To distinguish false from genuine analogies is not so easy, especially in the later period, when republicanism carried contradictory messages about city life and its political character. Did it offer a descriptive or a prescriptive model or did it simply serve to disguise and conceal?[40]

To attempt to answer these questions, we must turn to the two shrewdest and most incisive commentators in the later period, Machiavelli and Guicciardini. Although both men are usually defined as republicans in arguing for political liberty and popular participation in government, they mark a complete break with the past. In the first place, they firmly denounced as platonic idealism the Medici's attempts to project themselves as republican philosopher-rulers, rejecting this mystification in the name of the new political realism, the investigation "of the real truth of the matter, not what it is imagined to be".[41] More radically, they went on to undermine the foundations on which republican ideology had rested, belief in historical continuity and tradition. It was Guicciardini who declared that "the ancient days of the Romans and the Greeks exist no longer" and that it was wrong to cite the Romans all the time.[42] And Machiavelli equally incisively cut off the present from the past by declaring the fallibility of memory. Not only are people's memories fallible about their own experience in that they exaggerate the past to the detriment of the present, he wrote in *The Discourses*, but all records are prejudiced because they represent the views only of the conquerors.[43]

They also undermined commonly-shared assumptions about historical continuity by describing the world 'as a confidence game' and

---

[40] V. I. COMPARATO, introduction, *Modelli*, p. 9: 'funzione conoscitiva e funzione prescrittiva'. Cf. L. BERTELLI, *Paradigmi platonici, ibid.*, pp. 49-87; L. CANFORA, *Analogia e storia. L'uso politico dei paradigmi storici*, Milan, Il Saggiatore, 1982.

[41] MACHIAVELLI, *Il Principe*, ch. 15, p. 65, GUICCIARDINI, *Dialogo del Reggimento*, p. 99; cf. *Platonism in fifteenth-century Florence*, pp. 237-238 above.

[42] *Del modo di assicurare lo stato ai Medici*, ed. PALMAROCCHI in *Dialogo e discorsi del Reggimento di Firenze*, p. 274: "Non sono più e' tempi antichi de' romani e de' greci"; cf. Ricordo C, no. 110, ed. Spongano, p. 121, tr. Domandi, p. 69: "Quanto si ingannono color che a ogni parola allegano e' Romani". When Bruni had earlier declared the Romans long dead and buried, it was to support Florence's claim to be Rome's heir in face of Valla's criticism, H. BARON, *In Search of Florentine Civic Humanism*, Princeton, Princeton University Press, 1988, I, p. 49.

[43] *Discorsi*, bk. II, preface and ch. 5, pp. 271-272, 292-293.

our activities as 'role-playing', which should not be judged by the role but only but 'the quality of the performance', as Guicciardini put it.[44] This systematic rejection of the basis of republican ideology by two of its leading practitioners poses the question of its function and relationship to social reality. Why do Guicciardini and Machiavelli attempt to demythologize the values they apparently espouse so warmly? Re-reading them on the lines they themselves suggest, we should look very carefully at their words and images rather than at the traditions to which their language belonged. Faced with this seeming paradox, I can do no more than suggest some ways in which Guicciardini and Machiavelli reappropriated the language they had apparently rejected in order to describe the changing political and social values of their day.

The first has to do with religion. Christianity was here to stay, as Machiavelli acknowledged, and bodies exiled in classical and early Christian times to burial outside the city walls were back inside the city for good.[45] Devout citizens, like Giovanni Rucellai and Matteo Palmieri, could still, in the mid-fifteenth century, reconcile the demands of their dual citizenship as members of "the republic in which one is a citizen" and "the universal republic of all Christians".[46] But this dualism was already creating problems for city-states, especially after the papacy's return from Avignon and reassertion of its temporal and spiritual rights in Italy. Gradually in the writings of Machiavelli and Guicciardini we find the Duomo displaced from the centre of the stage. Instead of meeting and talking in its cool shade, they and their friends encounter each other on the Ponte Vecchio, or on benches of family palaces at the corners of streets, and they hold their discussions in the gardens of the Rucellai or outside the

---

[44] *Ricordi*, ser. C, no. 216, ed. SPONGANO, p. 228; tr. DOMANDI, p. 97. On Machiavelli's view of the world, see W. A. REBHORN, *Foxes and Lions. Machiavelli's Confidence Men*, Ithaca and London, Cornell University Press, 1988, quoting Francesco Vettori on p. 12: "in effetto tutto il mondo è ciurmeria".

[45] *Discorsi*, bk. II, ch. 2, p. 282: "avendoci la nostra religione mostro la verità e la vera via", etc.; LE GOFF, *L'immaginario urbano*, p. 9: "l'inurbamento dei morti", after earlier burial outside the walls; PETER BROWN, *The Cult of the Saints*, Chicago, University of Chicago Press, 1981, pp. 40-42, quoting Saint Jerome: "movetur urbs sedibus suis".

[46] Note 9 above and ASF Cons. Prat. 56, f. 60*r-v* (18 March 1460), quoted by R. BLACK, *Benedetto Accolti and the Florentine Renaissance*, Cambridge, Cambridge University Press, 1985, p. 159, n. 108: "duas esse respublicas: unam particularem, id est, eam civitatem in qua quis origine vel constitutione sit civis ... alteram vero esse rem publicam universalem Christianorum omnium".

city altogether, an outward sign of changing attitudes to the church and its role in the state.

Early evidence of this can be seen in Gino Capponi's memoir of 1420, that members of the war magistracy should "love their country more than their soul", and Cosimo de' Medici's dictum, "states are not ruled by paternosters".[47] In the mid-fifteenth century the chancellor Poggio Bracciolini argued that early legislators used religion for political ends, and by the early sixteenth century it was axiomatic to Machiavelli and Guicciardini that political values were autonomous.[48] Both men condoned murder and cruelty for the sake of state interest. "It is impossible to control governments and states according to the precepts of Christian law if one wants to hold them as they are held today", Guicciardini said, and Machiavelli agreed with him, arguing that religion should be used, as the Greeks and Romans used it, "to be an instrument to maintain a civilized state"; but it should always be subordinate to politics and never dominant, as it was for the ancients, who "when reason told them that a thing had to be done, did it even if the auspices were adverse".[49]

Machiavelli and Guicciardini understood, as ancient historians and the Trexlers of the Renaissance world now understand, the importance of religion and ceremony in underpinning political regimes. They also understood (as we are now experiencing) the 'extraordinary authority' of religious states and their leaders, due not simply to their close contact with God but to the permanence of the Church, which – unlike republics – 'never dies'.[50] Their thoughts were prompted not only by the growing power of the Papal States but also by the transformation of Florence into a major territorial state or 'empire'.[51] In

---

[47] G. TOGNETTI, *Amare la patria più che l'anima. Contributo circa la genesi di un atteggiamento religioso* in *Studi sul medioevo cristiano offerti a R. Morghen*, II, Rome, Istituto Storico Italiano per il Medio Evo, 1974, pp. 1011-1026.

[48] KRANTZ, *Between Bruni and Machiavelli*, p. 147.

[49] GUICCIARDINI, *Dialogo del Reggimento*, pp. 162-163, etc.: MACHIAVELLI, *Discorsi*, bk. I, chs. 11-14, esp. pp. 160-170: "quando la ragione mostrava loro una cosa doversi fare, non obstante che gli auspicii fossero avversi, la facevano in ogni modo"; bk. II, ch. 2, pp. 279-285.

[50] GUICCIARDINI, *Dialogo del Reggimento*, p. 160: "la reverenzia ed autorità di chi [la Chiesa] non muore mai"; cf. *Ricordi*, ser. C, no. 29: "hanno di poi la Chiesa vicina, che è potente e non muore mai"; cf. C, no. 48 (ed. SPONGANO, pp. 34, 57, tr. DOMANDI, pp. 49-54); MACHIAVELLI, *Il principe*, ch. 11, *Discorsi*, bk. I, ch. 11, pp. 50-51, 162-163; cf. NICCOLO GUICCIARDINI on republics' need of a "regola perpetua" to compensate for their lack of permanence, *Discursus*, ed R. VON ALBERTINI, *Firenze dalla repubblica al principato*, p. 396.

[51] See especially G. CHITTOLINI, *La formazione dello stato regionale e le istituzioni del contado*, Turin, Einaudi, 1979; FUBINI, *Classe dirigente*.

contrast to the medieval city-states, which were governed according to agreed religious and legal norms, as the Lorenzetti frescoes of Good Government demonstrate so well,[52] these enlarged territorial states were governed by political laws imposed by the will or command of the central government according to new political norms.[53] To governments faced with the problem of overriding local rights and privileges, Greek and Roman city-states again offered a useful analogy, with their confident imperialism and concept of "public interest" – well illustrated by the sextet of Roman heroes painted by Ghirlandaio in the public reception room of the government palace in Florence.

Public interest, for Machiavelli, can mean many things: the right of the state to claim and redistribute booty won in wars (as the Romans wisely did,) its right to minerals mined on public land, as well as its claim on a citizen's loyalty and life.[54] It can also mean that it is excusable to kill and override the laws 'for the public good' and for 'public utility', as the Romans did in killing whole legions and in decimation (killing every tenth man) and as Brutus did in murdering his own sons for the sake of his country; even the Roman people, when invoked as judges, were prepared to use the death sentence – in contrast to Florence's head of state, Piero Soderini, who thereby, in Machiavelli's opinion, ensured the destruction of the republic.[55]

---

[52] On the frescoes, N. RUBINSTEIN, *Political Ideas in Sienese Art*, «Journal of the Warburg and Courtauld Institutes», XXI, 1958, pp. 179-207; Q. SKINNER, *Ambrogio Lorenzetti: the Artist as Political Philosopher'*, London, British Academy, 1986; FRUGONI, *Una lontana città*, ch. 6; and R. STARN, *The Republican Regime of the 'Rome of Peace' in Siena, 1338-40'*, «Representations» XVIII, 1987, pp. 1-32.

[53] On the abortive attempt to modernize Florence's statutes in 1409 in conformity with its new status, 'public utility' now taking precedence over the demands of criminal justice, see FUBINI, *Classe dirigente*, pp. 158-163. The statutes are in Florence, AS, Statuti 23. The 1415 statutes restored the old system, which gave precedence to jurisdictional matters (*Statuta Populi et Communis Florentiae*, 'Friburgi' [Florence], 1778-1783, analysed by G. GUIDI, *Il Governo della Città Repubblica di Firenze*, 3 vols, Florence, Olschki, 1981.

[54] *Arte della Guerra*, ed. Bertelli, p. 455: "I Romani ... provvidero all'uno e all'altro di questi inconvenienti, ordinando che tutta la preda appartenesse al publico e che il publico poi la dispensasse come gli paresse"; *Istorie fiorentine*, ed. GAETA, bks. VI, ch. 1 and VII, ch. 29, pp. 387, 495-496: "Solevano le antiche e ben ordinate republiche nelle vittorie loro riempiere d'oro e d'ariento lo erario, distribuire doni nel popolo, rimettere a' sudditi i tributi e con giuochi e con solenni feste festeggiarli", whereas in Volterra, as citizens complained, "una industria trovata ne' terreni publici in privata utilità si converta"; *Discorsi* bk. II, ch. 2, p. 283, *Arte della Guerra*, p. 326: 'in quale uomo debbe ricercare la patria maggiore fede, che in colui che le ha a promettere di morire per lei?' and *Discorsus florentinarum rerum, ibid.*, p. 275: "credo che il maggiore bene che si faccia, e il più grato a Dio, sia quello che si fa alla sua patria".

[55] *Discorsi*, bk. III, chs. 3, 49 and 30, pp. 386, 504-505, 467-468; *Arte della Guerra*, p. 478. Cf. Guicciardini's defence of the death penalty against conspirators in Florence in 1497, "perché principalmente questo è delitto contro alla patria, alla quale siamo più obbligati che

Through Machiavelli's reiterated use of the public-private antithesis, we can see its important role in his political outlook. Hitherto Florence's standing, like that of other medieval communes, had rested primarily on commercial and industrial wealth, a system based on workshop *(bottega)* or market values. Its transformation into a major political power in Italy implied a change from workshop to state values. Aristotle had declared in *The Politics* that office-holding should "not be a source of wealth", or as the Florentines put it, one should not "make a *bottega* out of the *stato*".[56] In Machiavelli's writings, the contrast between public or state interest and private ambition and factionalism represents one of the main problems faced by the late medieval commune.

This in turn was closely related to changing ideas about social status and the political ruling class. It was the distinction between *bottega* and *stato* that led Guicciardini to criticize the enlarged Great Council for facilitating the entry of men representing Florence's trades and 'workshops' into "the state and the government".[57] No one thought he was a Florentine unless he had been a member of the Signoria at least once, Guicciardini complained in 1512.[58] By then, though, many city-dwellers were beginning to agree with Aristotle that what they resented was not so much being debarred from office, "indeed they are glad to be allowed time to get on with their own affairs, but they do not like to think that officials are stealing public money".[59] For this reason Machiavelli proposed in his 1520 *Discourse on Florentine Affairs after the death of Lorenzo de' Medici Junior* that the sixteen Gonfaloniers in Florence should be deprived of all executive power and instead reside in turn with the government 'as a witness' of its actions.[60] This new passive role for the people marks a

a' parenti, che al padre, che a noi medesimi", 'Accuse', *Opere inedite*, ed. G. Canestrini, Florence, 1857-1867, X, p. 200.

56 Aristotle, *The Politics*, V, viii, 1308 b; Domenico Cecchi, *Riforma sancta et pretiosa*, Florence, 1496, ed. Mazzone, *'El buon governo'*, p. 187: "hanno facto bottega dello stato"; cf. Savonarola, *Prediche sopra Giobbe*, Rome, Belardetti, 1957, II, p. 446 (9 April 1495): "fatto bottega della chiesa".

57 Guicciardini, *Dialogo del Reggimento*, p. 43: "essendo el corso della città fondato ... in sugli esercizi e in sulle botteghe, non sarà col consiglio poca scala allo stato ed al governo ...".

58 *Del modo di ordinare il governo popolare*, '27 Agosto 1512 in Logrogno', in *Dialogo del reggimento*, p. 234, "è diventato uno pasto universale".

59 *Politics*, note 56 above.

60 Machiavelli, *Discursus* in *Arte della Guerra*, pp. 272-273: "non avessi a rendere partito, ma solo essere testimone delle azioni loro".

decisive shift from the guild-based populism of the early communes to the elitist professionalism of the later period.

Symptomatic of future developments was the new title 'priors of liberty' given to the Signoria in 1459 to replace their old name, 'priors of the guilds', which, according to the decree, suggested that "humble and abject people, the lowest of the low" had "worked their way" into government; the old title was all right in the old days, it declared, when the city was small and had no, or a very small, empire – but no longer.[61] So the workshop image was out, republican liberty in.

Underlying the rhetoric more fundamental changes were taking place. Even before the 1494 revolution and creation of the Great Council, political rights were beginning to be disassociated from tax-paying. In 1491 the Seventeen Reformers instituted an innovation when for the first time they imposed taxation on certain categories of city dwellers who did not merit citizen rights, "because they are for a good part foreigners, or practise humble manual crafts or worse, or work for the government or guilds as menial servants"; nor should they aspire to citizenship unless they had first proved themselves by their 'honest trade, ability or upright behaviour".[62] And afterwards, when the political class had been effectively closed, continuing attempts were made to limit government to a qualified elite. Like the early Council of Seventy, the new Council of Eighty became in effect a life office or senate, while the Great Council was limited to approving general laws and choosing office-holders. In their practical reform schemes of 1512 and 1520, both Guicciardini and Machiavelli specifically proposed the creation of a life senate of about two hundred members, "as one sees in ancient republics, in Rome, in Carthage, in Athens and Sparta, in the council they call the senate, where many participated; like the two hundred in Venice, or rather the Pregadi, which is the same".[63]

---

[61] ASF, Balìe 29, ff. 118*v*-119*r* (30 Jan. 1459): "Quoniam dignitati amplitudini ac decori Florentine civitatis eiusque status et regiminis minime decus esse videtur, titulus dominationis ipsius qui Dominos artium priores appellat, quasi humilibus abiectisque personis atque infimis negotiis presidere eos insinuet", cf. Fubini, *Classe dirigente*, p. 181.

[62] ASF Cento 3, ff. 123*v*-124*r* (Seventeen Reformers, 27 July 1491): "perché sono buona parte forestieri o fanno exercitii vili manuali o peggio, o famigli d'uficio o d'arte, et non è bene siano anumerati tra cittadini fiorentini, fra quali non pare conveniente alcuno se ne tiri se non è prima tirato da suo exercitio honesto, virtù o buoni costumi". They were to be taxed separately in a 'Libro de' Taxati'; on changes in the definition of the ruling class, see *Platonism in fifteenth-century Florence*, pp. 234-235 above.

[63] *Del modo di ordinare il governo popolare*, p. 241: "uno numero di dugento *vel circa*.

Guicciardini's attempt at mixing up and 're-forming' the state into new shapes, "like those who make things to eat from pasta", increased the power of a small elite at the expense of the people, whose role in government was reduced.[64] Following 'ancient republics' like Rome, whose grant of *ius suffragii* allowed citizens to appoint magistrates without being eligible for office themselves, he proposed allowing the popular Great Council the same restricted role in order to encourage less self-interested elections.[65] By the time he wrote his *Dialogue of the Government of Florence* in 1521-1523, he had retreated even farther from the polarized model of republican Rome. By creating two separate orders, patricians and plebs, and giving all offices and honours to the former, the Romans, he said, had effectively created a ruling and a servile class.[66] In the dialogue, through the mouth of the Medicean speaker Bernardo del Nero, Guicciardini strongly criticized the patrician-plebs model as divisive, arguing that the kings were better protectors of the people than either the patricians or the tribunate: not only were their taxes fairer to all, but they encouraged social mobility by helping the pleb leaders to enter the patriciate. After royal power had been transferred to the patriciate, the plebs lost their protectors as well as all hope of entering the political class, and the creation of tribunes only created further dissention. It would have been far better, he concluded, if Rome had been united 'in one single body' with no "distinction between patricians and plebs". As it was, the republic was saved from disaster only by its tradition of harsh military discipline.[67]

Guicciardini's argument seems far removed from Machiavelli's admiration for the conflictual politics of Roman republicanism, which ensured its long survival. But in fact the two men shared much com-

---

Così si vede nelle antiche repubbliche, in Roma, in Cartagine, in Atene e Lacedemone, in questo consiglio che loro proprio chiamavano senato, essere intervenuti molti; a Vinegia sono dugento o meglio quelli che e' chiamono pregati, che è questo medesimo".

[64] *Ibid.*, p. 219: "a uso di chi fa cose da mangiare di pasta".

[65] *Ibid.*, pp. 224-225: "si legge tralli altri che e' romani davano a molti la città *cum iure suffragii*, che a giudicio mio non era altro che ammetterli alla creazione de' magistrati, ma non ve li fare capaci".

[66] *Dialogo del Reggimento*, p. 150: "the divisions of the Romans were caused 'da essere distinti gli ordini della città: una parte patrizi, l'altra plebei ... donde si poteva dire che una parte della città fussi in dominio, l'altra in servitù'."

[67] *Ibid.*, pp. 150-156: 'Però el modo vero sarebbe stato che la città fussi tutta di uno medesimo corpo, e quanto al participare del governo non fussi distinzione da' patrizi a' plebei, così sarebbono stati uniti' (153).

mon ground, not only in their political realism and tough view of the state, but also in their view of man's ambitious nature and the need to create an upwardly mobile society, in which the plebs should qualify themselves for rule by their ability and not by protected guild status.[68] Here the image of the classical centaur provided Machiavelli with a new male model. Half-man, half-animal, he served as tutor to "Achilles and many other of those Greek princes" to teach that a prince must be crafty and cunning as well as humane, a political lesson that further weakened the communitarian ethos of the earlier period.[69]

Meditating in *The Discourses* on Roman republicanism, Machiavelli acknowledged how dependent the people were on leaders and wise men to restrain them.[70] He also commented approvingly on the fact that, given the right to elect themselves to the tribunate, the plebs showed their 'wisdom' in electing nobles to this office.[71] And in an undated *ricordo* he noted that artisans did not know how to command when in office because they had always been used to serving, so the magistrates should be men who had served kings or laws, that is, those who lived off their investments.[72] In practice, then, he shared the same attitude to the plebs as Guicciardini, and for the same reasons thought that Roman dualism was not practicable in the faction-ridden Italy of his own day.

Emphasis on the polarity of Machiavelli's political thinking, the conflict between nobles and people, has distracted attention from the importance of the third force that he believed was needed both to initiate new laws and to balance and stabilize existing constitutions. In Rome, it was the consuls who enjoyed 'royal power' or "the power of *arbitrium*", and in times of war, the dictator;[73] in France it was

---

68 GUICCIARDINI, *Del modo di ordinare il governo popolare*, p. 222: "Non è altro lo stato e lo imperio che una violenzia sopra e' sudditi", cf. p. 219; *Dialogo del Reggimento*, p. 152; MACHIAVELLI, *Discorsi*, bk. II, chs. 23 and 2, pp. 346, 283-284.

69 *Il principe*, ch. 18, p. 72.

70 *Discorsi*, bk. I, chs. 3-6, 44, 54, pp. 135-146, 232, 252-254.

71 *Ibid.*, bk. I, ch. 47, pp. 237-240.

72 *Sentenze diverse* in *Il Teatro*, p. 223: "Li uomini che nelle republiche servono alle arti meccaniche non possono sapere comandare come prìncipi quando sono preposti a' magistrati, avendo imparato sempre a servire. E però si vuole tòrre per comandare di quelli che non hanno mai ubidito se non a' re e alle leggi, come sono quelli che vivono delle entrate loro".

73 *Discorsi*, bk. I, ch. 2, bk. II, ch. 33, pp. 134, 377.

the *parlement* which acted as 'third judge' between the nobles and the people;[74] and in Switzerland, the emperor was the 'middle man' or *mezzano*.[75] In Milan it was the absence of a 'potestà regia' or 'living voice' to enforce laws that made the nobility uncontrollable, as in other 'corrupt states' where men need to be constrained by "una podestà quasi regia".[76]

It is important to Machiavelli's argument that the powers of such a third force were not absolutist or 'tyrannous', because they were balanced or controlled within a constitutional system. This was true even in the case of the exceptional powers of the temporary dictator in Rome, as we can understand from the contrast he draws between the dictator's powers, which he admired, and those of the Decemvirate, which he did not. For whereas the Decemvirate replaced the Senate and the People and in time became tyrannical, the dictator was given only executive freedom to take decisions without conciliar approval and with no appeal, but he did not replace the Senate and the People and was appointed for a limited period of time.[77]

In Florence, the earlier Medici and Piero Soderini were seen as potential third forces to balance the permanent nobility-people conflict.[78] But it was in his 1520 blueprint of government that Machiavelli openly conferred the 'majesty' of state on a single all-powerful body, the Medici during their lifetimes and when they died an inner elite of sixty-four citizens, who would govern in turn with a Gonfalonier of Justice as the third force between a select council, or senate of two hundred, and the people, the bottom class or *ultimi*.[79] The People and the Senate are still there, but the dual or, as Bickermann calls it, bicameral system of republican Rome has been transformed into a pyramidal structure, at the summit an all-powerful executive, supported in the middle by a non-noble life-senate or service elite, and at the base a largely silent body of popular voters and

---

[74] *Il principe*, ch. 9, pp. 77-78.

[75] *Discorsi*, bk. II, ch. 19, pp. 335-336.

[76] *Discursus*, p. 267; *Discorsi* bk. I, ch. 18, p. 182.

[77] *Discorsi*, bk. I, chs. 34-35, pp. 209-213; and on absolute power, bk. I, ch. 25, p. 193: "una potestà assoluta, la quale dagli autori è chiamata tirannide".

[78] *Discorsi*, bk. I, ch. 52, pp. 246-247; cf. bk. III, ch. 1, pp. 381-382.

[79] *Discorsus*, pp. 261-277, esp. 274-275: "considerato ... come republica e senza la vostra autorità ... non le manchi cosa alcuna ... ma se si considera vivente la Santità Vostra e monsignore reverendissimo, ella è una monarchia; perché voi comandate all'armi, comandate a' giudici criminali, avete le leggi in petto".

approvers. For Machiavelli and Guicciardini, as for the later Romans, the city-state had become an ideal rather than a practical reality.

* * *

I began by describing the continuity between the earlier and later medieval periods in shared perceptions of corporate city life and political participation which integrated religious and civic experience. Yet at the very moment when republican ideology seemed to have permeated the citizen classes, suggesting a close analogy between ancient and medieval city-states, there is disquieting evidence of alienation and the distancing of city-dwellers on both levels from the civic ideals of the earlier period. This alienation eroded the vitality of the concept of republicanism and prepared the way for Machiavelli and Guicciardini. It was in this context that these two men came to question the assumptions on which the old ideology was based, demystifying its idealism at the same time as they re-deployed its terminology. So we have to examine carefully their use of classical analogies to understand their role in describing and justifying developments in the late communal period. As anachronistic by then as it was to the late Roman republic, the idealized model of the popular or bicameral city-state was replaced by the model familiar to us all today, that of elitist and patrician Rome in which the people, though important, play a much less active role.

By emphasizing their own novelty and role as demystifiers, Machiavelli and Guicciardini themselves encourage us to see how much had changed inside the walls of Italian cities. People still met in piazzas and voted in council chambers. Outwardly city life went on in the same spirit of civic pride and awareness as in the earlier period. Yet behind their urbane republican facades, the old communal spirit of Italian cities had been slowly but surely eroded. The guild regimes had been replaced by new political structures and values, effectively devaluing the republican concepts of equality and what Guicciardini called "this name of liberty".[80] Liberty already seemed as ambigu-

---

[80] *Dialogo del Reggimento*, esp. pp. 37-40: "questo nome della libertà; *Del modo di ordinare*, p. 223: 'non è altro la libertà che uno prevalere le legge ed ordini publici allo appetito delli uomini particulari'."

ous a concept to Italian city-dwellers as it did to Thomas Hobbes, when he reflected on "The word LIBERTAS" "written on the Turrets of the city of Luca in great characters" in the seventeenth century: [81] a last sobering image of Italian cities with which to conclude.

---

[81] *The Leviathan*, ed. OAKSHOTT, ch. 21, p. 140: "There is written on the Turrets of the city of Luca in great characters at this day, the word LIBERTAS; yet no man can thence inferre that a particular man has more Libertie, or Immunite from the service of the Commonwealth there, than in Constantinople. Whether a Commonwealth be Monarchicall, or Popular, the Freedome is still the same".

REAPPRAISING THE RENAISSANCE

FLORENCE, RENAISSANCE AND EARLY MODERN STATE

Reappraisals

Four more books on the history of late medieval Florence: an analytical account of the Florentine electoral system from 1280 to 1400, two biographies of Coluccio Salutati, chancellor from 1375 to 1406, and a transcript of the consultative meetings of Florentine citizens during one year of Salutati's chancellorship, 1401, a key moment for Hans Baron's interpretation of the Renaissance. All are fundamental reading for historians of Florence and the late medieval commune, scrupulously researched and authoritatively presented, but how do they relate to the wider world? Following recent loss of confidence in the much-vaunted 'liberty', 'republicanism', and 'modernity' of the Italian Renaissance, Florence too is somewhat demoded. Here as elsewhere elitism, ritualism, and *longue durée* have taken their toll, leaving Florence no longer precocious but a retarded case of the 'aristocratization' or 'rearistocratization' of society that took place throughout Italy in the late medieval period – or so it is argued.[1]

Nevertheless, Florence enjoyed one of the most developed city economies in the late Middle Ages, with a complex society that included

---

This paper was originally published in the «Journal of Modern History», LVI, 1984. The following works are reviewed in it: *Corporatism and Consensus in Florentine Electoral Politics, 1280-1400.* By John M. Najemy. Chapel Hill, The University of North Carolina Press, 1982. *Le "Consulte" e "Pratiche" della Repubblica fiorentina nel Quattrocento.* Edited by Elio Conti. Volume 1: 1401. Florence, Università di Firenze, 1981. *Coluccio Salutati: Il cancelliere e il pensatore politico.* By Daniela De Rosa. Florence, La Nuova Italia, 1980. *Hercules at the Crossroads. The Life, Works and Thought of Coluccio Salutati.* By Ronald Witt. Durham, N. Carolina, Duke University Press, 1983.

[1] Philip Jones, *Storia d'Italia, Annali,* Turin, Einaudi, 1978: "Economia e società nell'Italia medievale: La leggenda della borghesia"; pp. 187-372: "Aristocratizzazione o di rearistocratizzazione"; p. 343 (cf. p. 355): "Dal punto di vista sociale, 'Rinascimento' è stato l'equivalente di aristocraticizzazione"; p. 371: "È tempo di ridare alla nobiltà il suo posto".

a land-based aristocracy, an advanced commercial class thinking in terms of profit and loss, a large administration, and an industrial proletariat. It developed from a pluralistic guild-based commune towards a more unitary and centralized state in the fifteenth century and at the same time became the centre of a classical revival that had a wide impact on the rest of Europe – from being famous as 'the source of gold', 'the fifth essence' in 1300, Florence was praised by the German reformer Melanchthon in 1526 as the home of the new Western culture.[2] These achievements may be unrelated. Following Armando Petrucci's warning about the dangers of relating politics and culture too closely because of the analogy between liberty and democratic government in Italian city-states, few historians would want to claim too much for civic humanism, preferring with Brian Tierney to interpret it as an "alternative rhetorical strategy" through which "the communal ethos of the middle ages was transmitted to the early modern period".[3] The problem of the relationship between economic development, politics and culture in Florence in these two centuries continues to nag us, however, and can't simply be dispelled with formulas of 'disengagement' and 'coexistence'. Baron's thesis stressing a close relationship between politics and society still enjoys respect as well as criticism, and from a wider perspective Florence remains relevant to the theses of Immanuel Wallerstein and Perry Anderson about the absolutist state as either the underpinning of a new proto-capitalist world system or the 'carapace' of the feudal aristocracy.[4]

---

[2] DINO COMPAGNI, *Cronica,* ed. I. del Lungo, rev. G. Luzzatto, 2:25, Turin, Einaudi, 1968, p. 106; C. LANDINO, *Proemio al commento, scritti critici e teorici,* ed. CARDINI, I, p. 122; MELANCHTHON, *Werke,* Gütersloh, 1961, pp. 167-168. On Florence's economy, F. MELIS, *Firenze,* in *Città, mercanti, dottrine nell'economia europea dal iv al xviii secolo,* Milan, Giuffrè, 1964, pp. 107-150; M. DEL TREPPO, *Federigo Melis and the Renaissance Economy,* «Journal of European Economic History», X, 1981, pp. 725-742; G. DE' ROSSI, *Sviluppo economico e agricoltura,* in *Un'altra Firenze. L'epoca di Cosimo il Vecchio,* Florence, Vallecchi, 1971, pp. 61-104; R. GOLDTHWAITE, *The Building of Renaissance Florence,* Baltimore and London, John Hopkins University Press, 1980, pp. 31-66.

[3] A. PETRUCCI, *Coluccio Salutati,* Rome, Istituto dell'Enciclopedia italiana, 1972, pp. 7-8; B. TIERNEY, *Religion, Law and the Growth of Constitutional Thought 1150-1650,* Cambridge, Cambridge University Press, 1982, p. 87, cf. p. 12. Conciliarism is the other strategy Tierney refers to.

[4] H. BARON, *The Crisis of the Early Italian Renaissance,* I. WALLERSTEIN, *The Modern World-System,* New York, Academic Press, 1974, p. 133 (cf. pp. 37-52, 171-173); P. ANDERSON, *Lineages of the Absolutist State,* London, 1974, p. 18.

Although none of our writers discusses economics or attempts to relate political or cultural developments to them, their books are relevant to these problems. Najemy's account of the genesis and early development of a 'consensus' society in Florence, which is supported in differing ways by our other books, describes a transitional phase between the guild-structured commune and the revamped aristocracies of preindustrial Europe that is identical with neither. Looking backwards to the classical city-state and forwards to a restructured society that paradoxically combined elitism with egalitarianism – like Hobbes's sceptre-bearing *Leviathan* composed of the bodies of all the people – this 'consensus' society throws new light on the Renaissance and early modern Europe.

* * *

The paradox of the two-faced regime that developed in Florence after 1382 is the subject of John Najemy's *Corporatism and Consensus in Florentine Electoral Politics*. This regime developed from a clash between two dialectically opposed ideologies or "contrasting visions of republicanism" that coexisted in Florence in the preceding hundred years from the establishment of the priorate in 1282. These ideologies he defines as 'corporatism' and 'consensus' politics, one egalitarian and corporatist in conceiving of the commune as a federation of equal and autonomous corporations, represented mainly by the lesser guildsmen of shopkeepers and artisans, the other elitist in being based on the 'consensus' of wise and prudent citizens ruling for the benefit of the whole, the view of members of the top five guilds of international merchants. The balance between them was held by the rank and file of the major guilds, "caught between professional ties to their corporate world and patronage and business ties to the oligarchy". Synthesis was achieved between these poles, according to Najemy, by the establishment after 1382 of a widely based class of eligible citizens, many of whom were called but few were chosen. Many were openly nominated in scrutiny councils for office but few were voted eligible (secretly, since their names were not revealed at the time) and even fewer of these were finally chosen, thanks to controls like the *borsellino* and the *accoppiatori* who hand-picked some offices. Thus the paradox was achieved of "an enormous expansion" of the ruling class and a progressive reduction of the ruling caucus or elite, who could nevertheless control those ever hopeful of office by arguments of civic humanism and patriotism, urging rule by the wise and good for the sake of the whole.

Najemy's interpretation is based on a careful analysis of the constantly changing Florentine electoral system as it evolved from 1280 to 1400, from which three topics of special interest emerge: the strength of the popular movement, despite its practical limitations; the development of a new political class through scrutinies and its paradoxical role in post-1382 electoral politics; and the relevance to this class of classical ideology.

Genuinely radical arguments led to institutional change and a democratization of the constitution on three occasions. The first was in the period 1280-1295 when the guilds started to play an important role in politics. Debates in these years centre on who should be eligible for the priorate and on whether nominations for the priorate should be made by localities (more elitist) or by guilds (more popular: in 1282 the 'startling proposal' and 'the astounding suggestion' was made that as many as thirty-two guilds should nominate to the Office of Fourteen. The eventual settlement, the 'revolutionary' Ordinances of Justice of 1293, excluded knights from office and anyone not continuously exercising a profession, a clause not undermined until 1314. The second popular moment was in 1343 after the expulsion of the Duke of Athens, which saw "an unprecedented democratization within the office-holding class" in giving one-third of the places to minor guildsmen. The third was in 1378 following the Ciompi revolution, when equal status was briefly granted to the three groups of major, minor, and new guilds. Although Philip Jones would say these are only 'intermezzi' between two phases of aristocratic or monarchical government, the last gasps of medieval corporatism rather than forward-looking 'democratic' movements, Najemy nevertheless reminds us that before the days of universal suffrage, the interest of the artisans was best expressed by the argument for guild equality and that although artisans made their voices felt very infrequently, they did have an institutionalized voice through the guilds and an ideology that survived to influence Savonarola and even Machiavelli.[5]

In fact, the future lay not with the guild radicals but with a new

---

[5] Discussed by NAJEMY in his article *Arti and Ordini in Machiavelli's "Istorie Fiorentine"*, in *Essays Presented to Myron P. Gilmore*, ed. S. BERTELLI and G. RAMAKUS, Florence, La Nuova Italia, 1978, I, pp. 161-191.

political group that owed loyalty neither to the old Guelf or Ghibelline parties nor to the guilds but which favoured consensus government to avoid party faction. It was not a party with a programme in the traditional sense of the word. According to Najemy it was created and given coherence through the scrutiny councils, which were experimented with before 1328 but afterwards became a permanent feature of the electoral system. These created a 'politically responsible group' who knew they had been nominated and were hopeful of office without knowing whether they had been approved until their names were drawn from the bags. In itself the scrutiny system favoured neither elitism nor populism; initially it created a very limited elite, who were "practically synonymous with the city's dominant banking and commercial interests" and ruled from 1328 to 1339; but in the general reaction against this elite, whom Giovanni Villani condemned as "lords of the republic, elected for life", nominations were made by a far wider group of people and name tickets were no longer replaced in the bags after office but destroyed, thus creating a much wider political class.

It was this class of nominees that vastly expanded after 1382, from 5,350 nominations in 1382 to 6,310 nominations in 1391 and over 8,000 nominations in 1484. These figures have always presented difficulties to those who have seen this period and the Medicean period following it as ones of oligarchic reaction against the more open regime of the period from 1343 to 1382 (see the work of Molho, Dale Kent, Witt, and Brucker referred to by Najemy on pp. 263-264, note 2, on which he builds). But Najemy explains how the scrutiny system encouraged loyalty without direct participation in office, since out of 5,350 nominations in 1382, only about 875 citizens were actually elected for office, 575 of these from the major guilds, while in 1391 only 677 citizens were elected out of 6,310 nominations, 535 of these from the major guilds (in his appendices Najemy also lists distribution of posts in the Signoria according to families, new families, families appearing ten and twenty times).

Yet instead of feeling excluded, these citizens evidently felt privileged to be eligible for office – writing, as Gregorio Dati did when his name was finally drawn, "I feel that I have received a very great favour" and "in order not to appear ungrateful... I have decided and resolved that from now on I must never implore the favours of anyone to secure the offices of communal government for which scrutinies are held. I will instead leave such matters to those who will have authority over them". We don't know if he kept this vow any better than his resolve to keep Friday a day of total chastity, over which he evidently anticipated difficulties (offering 20 *soldi* to the poor each time he broke it, "through forgetfulness"). But although far more needs to be known about attitudes to elections, there is certainly support for Dati's attitude in the Medicean period, when in 1458 Carlo Gondi thanked Piero de' Medici warmly for his election, to be told brusquely: "we have done it more for our benefit than for yours, but you will also benefit from it".[6]

The Medici were heirs to this consensus government in developing the concept of a "leadership elite" qualified to rule by its superior wisdom and experience, a concept that accorded well with Greek and Roman ideas of a strong state composed of more or less equal citizens (excluding the proletariat and foreigners) and presided over by a wise elite. In an interesting last chapter Najemy relates this concept of government to the development of civic humanism in Florence in the fifteenth century, showing how Leonardo Bruni used classical ideology to describe and justify a strong united state of equal citizens freely accepting the control of the Medici (the magnate class was virtually abolished after 1434), the old distinctions between the Council of the People and the Council of the Commune, one popular, the other including nobles, being eventually destroyed by the creation of a single council of One Hundred and a senate of Seventy, in whom real power was vested. Dissent or conflict became not simply crimes of lese majesty against the state, as Najemy describes them, but by the later fifteenth century crimes against the person of Lorenzo de' Medici himself.

In general Najemy's argument is convincing, although in practice his two ideologies were less polarized than he suggests. His use of the word corporatism (in the Roman law sense of the state as a legal person) can be misleading when used to distinguish the corporate state as "a sum of autonomous parts" from the consensus state seen as "an organic harmonious whole". Similarly his use of the currently fashionable word 'consensus', now usually implying the tacit consent of a silent majority, can be equally misleading as a translation of 'consenso'. For although civil lawyers distinguished between active and

[6] G. DATI, *Il libro segreto*, quoted by NAJEMY, p. 302 (cf. *Two Memoirs of Renaissance Florence*, ed. G. BRUCKER, New York, Harper and Row, p. 125); and on his "intention" of chastity, *ibid.*, pp. 124-125. On Carlo Gondi, RUBINSTEIN, *The Government of Florence*, pp. 138-139.

tacit consent, the former being statute law passed with popular approval, the latter custom, Florentine political writers usually use it in the former sense – even though the procedure of popular consent was by then becoming largely formal, as Machiavelli implies in the passage quoted by Najemy (amending Judith Rawson's less tendentious translation of 'consenso' as 'agreement' in Machiavelli's 1520 *Discursus* to 'consensus'). Moreover, it is likely that Najemy's projected second volume will considerably modify his picture of guild government as a federation of equal and autonomous guilds by stressing instead its elitism, since the Mercanzia and major guilds exercised a strong and paternalistic control over the lesser guilds that Najemy defines as typical of 'consensus' government. Nevertheless, it is important to be reminded of the differences between these two traditions that kept political debate open for some two hundred years. In Florence corporatism and consensus government were not simply two "alternative rhetorical strategies" for transmitting "the communal ethos to the early modern period" but represented two very different historical traditions and ideologies that kept the political debate open for so long. Although the *intermezzi* of popular rule were short, their influence was greater than present revisionism allows.

Najemy's analysis helps us to distinguish between the popular republicanism of guild government and the republican face of Florentine politics after 1382, suggesting a fresh approach to the problem of evaluating republican rhetoric and the classical revival in the later fourteenth century. Salutati's defence of Florentine republicanism need not be dismissed as mere rhetoric (as by Seigal and Herde) if there is a real sense in which the regime was open, yet at the same time his republicanism did also serve the interests of the governing elite in encouraging support for its policies in the name of patriotism and concord.

The problem of evaluating this two-faced regime is put very well by Salutati's reply to the Sienese, who accused Florence in 1391 of being ruled by thirty tyrants: "as you know, not only do thirty men not tyrannize our people, they don't even rule them... There are thousands of men who administer our republic". Strictly speaking, he was right, there were thousands of paid and unpaid administrative offices open to Florentine citizens.[7] Yet as we now know from the volume

---

[7] Salutati's reply is quoted in *Le "Consulte"* p. XXXV, R. G. WITT, *Coluccio Salutati and his Public Letters*, Geneva, Droz, 1976, p. 62, DE ROSA, pp. 124-125, translating rather freely.

Le 'Consulte' e 'Pratiche' della Repubblica fiorentina nel Quattrocento, edited by Elio Conti, the consultative meetings of citizens which Salutati attended were dominated by almost exactly thirty citizens, "the dominate elite", "a restricted circle of notables", Elio Conti calls them in his preface. They were themselves both popular (in representing a wide range of opinion, openly expressed) and elitist (in being dominated by this inner core of important and fluent speakers) and they provide valuable evidence of the workings and the ideology of the post-1382 regime.

The *'Consulte e Pratiche'* records in the State Archives in Florence survive in two series, 1349-1480 and 1496-1530, describing three different types of consultative meetings: the restricted meetings of the Signoria and its two advisory colleges (sometimes also with the Otto di Guardia and the Dieci di Balìa), the large 'Consigli de' Richiesti', to which a variable number of citizens, including magnates, was invited to discuss particular problems, and the collective reports of special commissions or 'pratiche'. They are an invaluable source for Florentine history, as has long been recognized. In 1896-98 A. Gherardi published a two-volume edition of the early *Libri fabarum,* voting registers with speeches included (*Le Consulte della Repubblica fiorentina dall'anno MCCLXXX al MCCXCVII*), continued in much more abbreviated form by B. Barbadoro (*Consigli della Repubblica fiorentina* [1301-1315, 2 vols., 1921]). Although the *'Consulte e Pratiche'* volumes have been used extensively by Gene Brucker in his two analyses of Florentine politics from 1343 to 1430, by Guido Pampaloni for the mid-fifteenth century, and by Felix Gilbert for the republican period,[8] the volume under review is the first full edition of these debates and as such is an important addition to the small but growing volumes of primary sources for Florentine history.

Transcribed and annotated by different équipes, it is the first to emerge of an extensive project by two seminars in Florence University to publish all the *'Consulte e Pratiche'* registers from 1382 to 1411.

There is a printed list of all the Florentine offices "di onore ed utile" in Florence, Bibl. Naz. E.63.38.

[8] G. BRUCKER, *Florentine Politics and Society, 1343-1378,* Princeton, Princeton University Press, 1962; *The Civic World of Early Renaissance Florence,* Princeton, Princeton University Press, 1977, G. PAMPALONI, *Fermenti di riforme democratiche nella Firenze medicea del Quattrocento,* «Archivio storico italiano», CXIX, 1961, pp. 9-62, 241-281, and CXX, 1962, pp. 521-585; F. GILBERT, *Florentine Political Assumptions in the Period of Savonarola and Soderini,* «Journal of the Warburg and Courtauld Institutes, XX, 1957, pp. 187-214.

It is edited by Elio Conti (who wrote the preface) and Daniela De Rosa, providing us in all with 364 pages of prefaces, text and notes, together with a glossary of terms and a profile index of participations, listing their offices, tax assessments, and participants. The volume is inevitably fragmentary in the topics it discusses, which mainly concern foreign policy and taxes; but by quoting fully from relevant letters and laws the text is converted into rich polyphony from plainsong chant – or "sonnet-form" as Salutati on one occasion wittily described the repetitious process of assent ("et cetera sicut alii, et unum sonettum").

The year 1401 was not a cultural turning point in Florence, as we know already from Gene Brucker, who has found a new historical awareness emerging in these debates only after 1410. No classical authors are quoted in this volume: only Aesop appears fleetingly in a footnote for having been cited "in many councils". There are not many references to Florentine liberty and Milanese tyranny. The threat from Milan is reflected mainly in increasingly agonized negotiations with the newly-elected emperor Robert of Bavaria, "our natural lord", whose retreat across the Alps without fighting, after receiving Florence's second payment, provided Machiavelli with that familiar maxim, 'never trust a foreigner'. Its principal interest lies, rather, in the statistical breakdown Elio Conti provides of the membership of the consultative meetings and in the evidence in the debates themselves of 'consensus government', whereby agreement is reached from a welter of different opinions.

Numbers and statistical tables demonstrate that of 170 citizens summoned to the *consulte*, 108 or 63.5 percent spoke only once or twice to register agreement or make very brief comments, whereas 18 men (10.6 percent of the total) spoke more than ten times, monopolizing 45.6 percent of the interventions and 58.1 percent of the speeches, those who spoke most often also (a familiar phenomenon) speaking for longest. These eighteen are reduced to thirteen when ex officio members of the colleges are excluded, and on pages xxxvi-xliii are given the names and brief biographies of these thirteen members of the inner circle ("la ristretta cerchia") who consist of six knights, three doctors of law, one medical doctor, and three others. Of the 170, 141 members (82.9 percent) had already held one of the Three Major Offices (the Signoria and Colleges) and "to accentuate the elitism of the advisors", only eleven are members of the minor guilds. An analysis of membership for the period 1401-1405 reveals that new members slowly drop from 41.8 percent of the total to 26.1 percent in 1403, 16.5 percent in 1404 and (a slight rise) to 19.1 percent in 1405, supporting other evidence of "a drastic reduction of political mobility" by 1400.

Although these figures demonstrate that the meetings were dominated by relatively few citizens, the debates themselves reveal differences of opinion that gradually resolve themselves into agreement after discussion – as in December 1401 when a report or *pratica* related that there were initially differences, some wanting one thing, some another: "But at last everyone agreed that..." ("Sed tandem omnes consenserunt quod"). This is government by consensus, not conflict, as Najemy defines it, but agreement is reached by active discussion and usually by voting too. A request for money from Bologna reveals varying opinions: no, not yet (but we mustn't lose her support); yes, it should be lent to her; it should be lent to her with interest deducted in advance. A conspiracy involving citizens in Pistoia shows a similar spectrum of opinion, ranging from softliners who urge kindness, to hardliners who want its parties removed, its revenue sequestered, and its election bags filled in Florence, and realists who argue "it is useful that there should be sects there" ("utile est quod ibi sint secte"). A Florentine magistrate implicated in a conspiracy evokes a similar response, and although the citizens who take a tough line remind their audience that "the foreign judges, not the citizens, are deputed to condemn citizens", in this case the judgment was a political one: the Alberti were condemned to exile by the citizens, not the judge, following a scrupulous procedure that nevertheless bestowed wide discretionary powers on very few men.

Here is Najemy's two-faced regime at work, a small elite taking important decisions with the participation and agreement of a wide number of officials and citizens. Dale Kent has already suggested that these consultative meetings provided a crucial link between politicians and the rich oligarch-magnate class who attended the meetings without participating fully in government, and this volume with its index listing tax assessments of speakers should have evidence for her approach.[9] As Lorenzo de' Medici later said, "the rich live badly in Florence outside the political regime", yet the rich could ill afford the time to live within it; the *consulte* offered one solution to this

[9] Dale Kent, *The Florentine "Reggimento" in the Fifteenth Century*, «Renaissance Quarterly», XXVIII, 1975, esp. pp. 596-608.

problem by enabling them to contribute advice without full-time commitment to politics.

As chancellor during the Ciompi period as well as during the oligarchy that followed it, Salutati played an important role in transmitting communal ideas to the early modern period, using classical republicanism both to justify a strong state controlled by the wise as well as to argue for a 'free' and 'egalitarian' society. He has become a crucial figure in the Renaissance Debate, the link between politics and culture, interpreted either as committed civic humanist or cynical mouthpiece of the elite.[10] Aware as we now are of the elitism as well as of the traditionalism of Florentine society, it is easy to dismiss such ideals as rhetorical; but in fact our books under review help us to define the role of classical republicanism in post-1382 Florence by showing how it served a dual purpose, both educating the wider populace and providing the elite with a means of political control through their appeal to arguments of patriotism, concord, and consent. As one of the editors of the *Consulte* volume, Daniela De Rosa is well qualified to relate Salutati's political career and his writings in her brief but extremely well-integrated biography *Coluccio Salutati: il cancelliere e il pensatore politico.*

In this biography De Rosa uses Salutati's public and private writings to show how Salutati uses republican ideas to encourage a less status- and family-bound society than then existed. Florence was free and equal in the Roman republican sense that laws made by the people in the Councils of the People and Commune were supreme, equal in that they applied equally to all, lords being subject to the same jurisdiction as commoners, in contrast to more feudalized societies that still offered different justice to different estates. And in his letters Salutati argues that families should not be imprisoned for crimes committed by individual members; Jews should be treated like other Florentine subjects, despite "not having as yet recognized the evangelical faith but remain in the observance of the Old Testament"; merchants are all-important as "a most honest breed of men, whose activity beautifies cities and makes nature's local products available and accessible to everyone everywhere", and so are dentists, "to whom God concedes the faculty of knowing how to treat bad teeth which can be saved or pull out those which are already lost". So although

[10] See the summary of these differing interpretations in WITT, *Coluccio Salutati and his Public Letters,* p. 73, note 1.

it may be difficult, as Jones has said, "to demonstrate that government in Florence was more equal and the ruling group more free from the duties and bonds of family party and perhaps also of corporation" than elsewhere, De Rosa helps to do so in her picture drawn from Salutati's letters of an open and multifarious city emerging from a kin society of vendettas and corporate guilt. Of course his letters are often prescriptive rather than descriptive, but the ideal society they extolled of equal citizens "ruling and being ruled in turn" (as Aristotle recommended) doubtless had effect on the public assemblies to which they were read out for approval. The class of potential interchangeable rulers nearly doubled, as we have seen, and although ties of family and corporation remained, clan conflict did weaken within an increasingly homogeneous ruling class once magnate status had been abolished, as did the political influence of corporations. Insofar as this process was encouraged by the ruling elite, they can be said to have used classical ideology for their own interests to encourage consent, as both Najemy and De Rosa have suggested, but at the same time these ideals helped to influence the process of change.

To see how this happened we have to look to the fifteenth century, after the death of Salutati. And this raises the contentious question of Salutati's own position as propagandist of republicanism and his responsibility for fifteenth-century developments. De Rosa on the whole attempts to integrate his public life as chancellor, mediating between the people and the ruling elite, and his humanism. She finds his position as political relativist "more coherent" than Ronald Witt in his earlier *Coluccio Salutati and his Public Letters,* despite sharing Witt's interpretation of Salutati as "neither a republican nor a monarchist", medieval rather than modern (Witt's book came out before hers, as she acknowledges in the preface, but after she had reached many of the same conclusions). Now Witt has produced a new book, *Hercules at the Crossroads*, which is the first full-length biography of Salutati, as he says, and will long remain the definitive account of Salutati's life and writings. Salutati has suffered from being defined, as Petrarch put it, by "one or two well-formulated phrases" and Witt would agree with Petrarch that "he who wants to be safe in praising the entire man must see and examine and estimate the entire man".[11] The entire man certainly defies easy formulation as he

[11] PETRARCH, *De sui ipsius et multorum ignorantia, Prose,* ed. G. MARTELLOTTI, Milan - Naples, Ricciardi, 1955, p. 728, cited by W. BOUWSMA, *The Two Faces of Humanism* in *Itinerarium Italicum,* ed. OBERMAN, Leyden, E. J. Brill, 1975, p. 53.

emerges, convincingly full of ambiguities and contradictions, from these pages. Coherence is to be found if at all, Witt argues, not in his public career and his humanism but in his growing religiosity after reaching the crossroads in his life in 1381-1382. It is one of the merits of this book to turn our attention from Salutati's public life to his private thought, to follow "this Christian conception of the human predicament in Salutati's thought and its effects on his humanism", even if its account of his "genuine development" is not totally convincing.

In Witt's account, Salutati's greatest contribution to Florence was to make her "the leading centre of humanism in Italy" by the fifteenth century. Classical scholarship was Salutati's passport to status and respect. Described by Petrarch as a friend, though not accepted by him as a correspondent, Salutati was nevertheless Petrarch's heir in his meticulous textual criticism and his love of manuscripts (he himself possessed well over 600 MSS: 111 are listed by B.L. Ullman in *The Humanism of Coluccio Salutati,* 1963, one more being identified since then), and he was largely responsible for "the institutionalization" of culture in Florence after Petrarch died – as Fubini puts it [12] – by encouraging the development of public libraries and by founding the Chair of Greek in Florence. The rationalizing classicism of his early education in Bologna and his position as a new man whose closest friends – apart from a few leading humanists – seem to have been "fellow provincials" like himself combined to make him an ideal public servant or bureaucrat after he became chancellor of Florence in 1375. Although Witt prudently warns us that "the term can only be used with qualification" – since as we all know it originated much later – Salutati enjoyed some of the characteristics of later 'bureaucrats' in the chancery in his tenure, salary, and structured conditions of work, though remaining a notary by training and profession.[13]

In contrast to this public and rationalizing Salutati was Salutati the philosopher and thinker, who was as influenced by theologians and natural philosophers as by classical rhetoricians and who (as Charles

---

[12] In his review of Ullman in «Rivista storica italiana», LXXVII, 1965, p. 968.

[13] Following MAX WEBER's definition in his essay "Bureaucracy", *Essays in Sociology,* ed. H. H. GERTH and C. WRIGHT MILLS, London, Routledge and Kegan Paul, 1948, no. VIII, pp. 196-204; but cf. WITT's brief note on the subject, pp. 112-113, note 7.

Trinkaus has already demonstrated)[14] emphasized the will at the expense of reason. This Salutati was influenced by men like Marsilio di Santa Sophia, Biagio Pelacani, and Jacopo da Forlì, who encouraged him to take an interest in new developments in logic and natural science as well as in Dominican and Franciscan theology. In his discussion of Salutati's concepts of time, history, and language Witt shows how open Salutati was to ideas that look forward to fifteenth-century developments ("both an ancient and a modern") while remaining firmly "a man of the middle ages" – as in his controversial *De tyranno,* always a worry to the republican interpreters of Salutati, which Witt credibly argues was "essentially a literary work designed as a defence of the immortal Dante's reputation", Salutati's defence of monarchy – not of tyranny – in no way conflicting with Florence's position "as a *provincia* or *civitas* within the *respublica* of the Holy Roman Empire".

There are different ways of intepretating Salutati's ambiguities and inconsistencies, as we have seen. They can be viewed as aspects of his electicism and relativism, or as constant ambivalence between the two irreconcilable poles of humanist thought identified by William Bouwsma; for as Salutati himself said, "to harmonize Aristotle with Cicero and Seneca, that is, the Peripatetics with the Stoics, is a great deal more difficult than you think".[15] Witt's account suggests detachment between Salutati's growing religiosity after 1368 and his continuing "exuberant faith" in pagan humanism until 1396. Why, then, Hercules at the Crossroads? The title is deliberately paradoxical in that what Salutati apparently discovered when working on his *Labours of Hercules* was that he was unable to make Hercules's choice between virtue and vice on the threshold of manhood. Yet Witt talks as though Salutati did make a definitive decision about his life in 1381-1382, even though as a fifty-year-old man at the time it would surely have been more of a Dantesque climacteric "at midpoint of the journey of our life" than a Herculean choice of a life's career. The Story of Hercules as revived by Petrarch from Prodicus and retold by Salutati has become a paradigm of Renaissance free choice and enlightenment, and by using it in the title, even paradoxically, Witt suggests Salutati as a frontiersman, choosing definitively between vir-

---

[14] C. TRINKAUS, *In our Image and Likeness,* London, Constable, 1970, I, pp. 51-102.

[15] BOUWSMA, *The Two Faces,* pp. 53-54.

tue and vice, Christianity and paganism, even – we might infer – between medievalism and modernity.

Salutati crossed no frontiers: everyone seems agreed about that. Witt's account of Salutati's public role is not in fact inconsistent with De Rosa's, though different in emphasis. What emerges from his biography is that Salutati's main contribution as a scholar to the early modern world was his critical approach to historical sources and his desire to return *ad fontes*: by collecting, reading and making his books available to others, Salutati helped to create a historical awareness of classical republicanism that had its impact on the generation of his successor Leonardo Bruni. As Baron long ago argued, it is in the fifteenth century that the classical revival becomes politically important, although to understand why, we have to go back to 1382.

* * *

The argument of the books reviewed is detailed but not restricted in scope. For it seems to me that in different but supporting ways they contribute a new approach to the much wider problem of the Renaissance in Florence and in early modern Europe. Contemporary criticism disassociates politics and culture, arguing that there is no direct analogy between classical ideology and either the chivalric or the guild ethos of medieval Florence, and that when it was adopted, it was in response to the general "re-aristocratization" of Italian society: the classical revival was better developed outside Florence before the fifteenth century and in any case it was irrelevant to the commercial revolution that was her primary achievement. Now by redefining political change, we can also redefine the role played by the classical revival in Florence. For between the medieval commune and rearistocratized Grand Ducal Florence there was a transitional phase during which political power was held by a small 'professional' elite drawn from a much wider class of men chosen for their political loyalty alone. Although this class became the basis of a new aristocracy of merit, until 1494 it was still fluid and open, as was its leadership, posing problems of legitimization avoided by status-based aristocracies and guild-communes, or by closed merchant-patriciates like Venice. The ruling elite combined a strong concept of the state and the public interest with a proto-mercantilist involvement in finance and trade. Identical neither with landowning aristocracies nor with trade-based communes, it looked back to the classical *polis* and forward to early modern mercantile states. By providing legitimization as well as a practical model of consensus government, classical republicanism was far more relevant to this transitional or proto-mercantilist state than to the regimes that preceded and followed it.

If this is so, we can look for the influence of classical republicanism not simply in the fields of politics and administration, where it is most obvious, but also in social structure and in economic policy. For example, Plato's functional three-class society of professional rulers, soldiers, and producers provided a useful analogy for the restructured society of early modern Europe which increasingly gave the work of government to career bureaucrats, releasing knights, clergy and merchants to engage in their own professional and business activities. As Marvin Becker and Federigo Melis have pointed out, one of the most original features of the Florentine economy was the reliance it placed on sureties taken on trust and on non-notarialized merchant agreements.[16] The post-1382 consensus government relied implicitly on the same trust being placed by the community in its leaders' political and business acumen, and despite lacking an immediate analogy in classical society, the idea of trust – later so important in political theory – became idealized in Florence as willing obedience to a wise platonic ruler.

We can only speak tentatively about the hitherto-neglected field of fifteenth-century fiscal policies which Julius Kirshner and Anthony Molho are now illuminating with their work on the Florentine Dowry Fund.[17] Here too, however, classical ideology may be more relevant than might at first appear in justifying increased government interventionism in trade and finance. Taking control from the Mercanzia and guilds, governments began to intervene in trade and at the same time increased their influence over localities and corporations through the new centralized tax system introduced in 1427 and through their state-funded debt. Florentines saw a direct analogy between the Ro-

---

[16] M. B. Becker, *Medieval Italy,* Bloomington, Indiana University Press, 1981, p. 1-2; F. Melis, *Firenze,* pp. 110-111. On Florentine "protomercantilism" and "consensus" at the end of the fourteenth century, see Becker, *Florence in Transition,* Baltimore, Johns Hopkins Press, II, 1968, pp. 213-219.

[17] They will soon be publishing their analysis of Florentine investment in the Monte delle doti, which they have computerized; cf. their article, *The Dowry Fund and the Marriage Market in early Quattrocento Florence,* cit.; J. Kirshner, *Pursuing Honor While Avoiding Sin: The Monte delle doti of Florence,* «Studi Senesi», LXXXVII, 1977, pp. 175-256; and Molho, *Florentine Public Finances in the Early Renaissance.*

man census described in Livy and Eusebius and "our census, which we call the catasto"; and at the moment of its introduction in 1427 republican arguments of equality, liberty, patriotism, and 'enlightenment' were used to promote it, one citizen quoting the example of Caesar Augustus who "had prepared a uniform and universal system for the collection of tribute, which clearly shows the value of the catasto".[18] By removing tax assessment from the hands of local panels of neighbours and putting it into the hands of state officials using individual returns, the new system was not only fairer to more citizens than the old one, anticipating mercantilist conceptions of wealth by differentiating between the means of production and the surplus, but it was also more uniform and centralized, increasing the power of the state.

Similarly the state-funded debt, or Monte Comune, as well as the state Dowry Fund, appealed to both faces of Florentine society by combining private with public interest. They were welcomed by many citizens who invested in them as a source of profit and speculation (only the Ciompi wanted the Monte Comune destroyed in 1378) and at the same time they increased the power of the state over their investors, who were dependent on the prosperity of the state for their own prosperity.[19] Patriotism became a matter of personal as well as public interest when so much was invested in the state. So although classical ideology was undeniably remote from the merchant en-

---

[18] B. FONZIO in Florence, MS Riccard. 152, f. 100*r*: "Cui quidem persimilis census noster est, quem nos catastum appellamus"; G. BERTI, *Documenti intorno al Catasto*, «Giornale storico degli Archivi toscani», IV, 1860, pp. 40-57: "et Cesar, ut tributa haberet, unite machinam universam describere fecit; et per hoc clare apparet utilem esse via Catasti" (p. 51; cf. BRUCKER, *Civic World*, p. 483, note 47). And on the catasto, D. Herlihy and C. Klapisch-Zuber, *Les Toscans et leurs familles. Une Étude du Cataste florentin de 1427*, Paris, Editions de l'École des Hautes Études en Science Sociales, 1978, Engl. transl. *Tuscans and their Families. A study of the Florentine Catasto of 1427*, New Haven and London, Yale University Press, 1985, CONTI, *I catasti agrari della Repubblica fiorentina*, 1966; D. V. and F. W. Kent, *Neighbours and Neighbourhood in Renaissance Florence*, pp. 24-37 (making the important point that *gonfaloni* did not really lose power until the reintroduction of the catasto in 1458, p. 174).

[19] KIRSHNER and MOLHO, *The Dowry Fund*, esp. p. 436; and on the Monte Comune in the fifteenth century as "the heart of this body we call city ... the guardian fortress, immovable rock and enduring certainty of the salvation of the whole body and government of your State", L. F. MARKS, *The Financial Oligarchy in Florence under Lorenzo*, pp. 123-147 at 127. Cf. R. BARDUCCI, *Politica e speculazione finanziaria a Firenze dopo la crisi del primo Trecento (1343-1358)*, «Archivio storico italiano» CXXXVII, 1979, pp. 177-219; J. KIRSHNER, *Reading Bernardino's sermon on the public debt*, in *Atti del Simposio internazionale Cateriniano-Bernardiniano*, ed. D. MAFFEI and P. NARDI, Siena, Accademia Senese degli Intronati, 1982, esp. pp. 571-584.

trepreneurial spirit that had made Florence rich, it was used to justify the increased interventionism of fifteenth-century governments.

Its influence in the fields of politics and administration is far more striking, as we can see from the fate of three words restored to their original republican meaning by painstaking humanists in the late fourteenth and fifteenth centuries. In the late medieval commune 'the people' had represented one political group in a pluralistic society, sharing legislative power with 'the Commune' unless temporarily replaced by the extraordinary authority of a Balìa, as in 1382. By the fifteenth century, however, 'the people' represent the whole community, as they do in Leonardo Bruni's influential *History of the Florentine People* (1416-1439), following the analogy of the Roman people. Subsequently the phrase 'the Commune and the People of Florence' is replaced by 'the Florentine People' in legal and diplomatic documents to represent the new centralized authority of the council of One Hundred and 'the senate' of Seventy, together constituting the 'SPQF' in the revealing ideogram painted in the Florentine government palace.[20]

Within the chancery a similar reform separated the spheres of public and private authority that had been confused during the Middle Ages. 'Rogation' was transformed from its late-Roman and medieval usage to describe the notarial authentification of private documents and later the public acts of Italian cities to its correct republican usage as the process of public consent to state legislation. At the same time the office of chancellor was changed from a notarial office to a public office of state, with its own protocol, hierarchy, and independent status.[21]

A third concept to change was that of *maiestas*, which in the course of the fifteenth century reverted to its original republican meaning of "the sovereignty of the people". During the Middle Ages "this majesty of the people... was cast upon the emperor", in John Selden's words, and when Coluccio Salutati used the word he still applied it to the emperor, Florence being free because she lived under her own

[20] In January 1459, the name of the Signoria was also changed from "Priores Artium ... Populi et Communis Florentiae" to "Priores Libertatis ... Populi florentini", see now p. 298, note 61 above). On S.P.Q.F., p. 286, n. 21 above and now N. RUBINSTEIN, *Classical themes in the Decoration of the Palazzo Vecchio in Florence*, «Journal of the Warburg and Courtauld Institutes», L, 1987, p. 43 and pl. 13 c.

[21] See BROWN, *Bartolomeo Scala*, pp. 173-192 (Ital. tr. pp. 118-127).

laws, "by the indulgence of imperial majesty". But by the fifteenth century *maiestas* recovers its original meaning and is now applied to the Florentine people, the crime of *lesae-maiestatis* being used to justify summary jurisdiction in crimes against the state, as well as in crimes against its unofficial head, Lorenzo de' Medici.[22] As Jean Bodin and Selden later commented, 'majesty' is synonymous with 'sovereignty' and its use spread thoughout early modern Europe to justify the new absolute powers claimed by its monarchs: "before the time of Henry", Bodin wrote "it is true we never used the word 'Majesty' in addressing the king".[23]

Contemporary studies on civic and court ceremony would interpret the use of this title as a form of ritual rather than as an aspect of the classical revival. As Richard Trexler has shown, Lorenzo de' Medici used ceremony and religion to increase his political authority in Florence, gaining 'majesty' by associating himself with the Three Kings as well as with the Roman Aemilius Paulus.[24] Clearly, there were several strategies available to jusify the political and economic changes of the early modern period, even within Florence. But that should not distract us from recognizing the paramount importance of classical republicanism in offering not simply an ideology but also an institutional model for the early modern state that was particularly effective because – unlike conciliarism, Tierney's alternative model – it specifically excluded the church as well as other corporative interests. As Bodin's and Selden's interest in *maiestas* suggests, this model was influential outside Italy wherever power was being transferred from an established hierarchy to a new professional elite governing an enlarged 'consensus group' by appealing to their self-interest. There

---

[22] See CAPPELLI, *Lettere di Lorenzo de' Medici,* cit. pp. 152-153, note 6 above; cf. G. CAROLI, *In Vitas... Fratrum,* ed. S. I. CAMPOREALE, «Memorie domenicane» n.s. XII, 1981, p. 244; VERDE, *Lo studio fiorentino 1473-1503,* III, p. 142; G. SAVONAROLA, *Prediche sopra Amos e Zaccaria,* I, p. 151; *Prediche sopra i Salmi,* II, p. 191.

[23] J. SELDEN, *Titles of honour, Opera omnia,* London, 1726, III, pp. 221-224; J. BODIN, *Method for the Easy Comprehension of History,* p. 258; *The Six Bookes of a Commonweale,* I, ch. 10, pp. 157-158; cf. M. SBRICCIOLI, *Crimen Laesae Maiestatis,* Milan, 1974, p. 11.

[24] R. C. TREXLER, *Public Life in Renaissance Florence,* pp. 401-452; see also R. HATFIELD, *The Compagnia de' Magi,* «Journal of the Warburg and Courtauld Institutes» XXXIII, 1970, pp. 107-161; R. WEISSMAN, *Ritual Brotherhood in Renaissance Florence,* New York, Academic Press, 1982, suggests that confraternities offered another such strategy, being modelled on the commune and "during the final decades of the century" confraternities were viewed "less as threats to civic order than as potential sources of political support for the Medici regime" (pp. 107, 134, 164-170, etc).

is close similarity between Hobbes's sceptre-bearing *Leviathan* composed of all the people and Florence's paradoxical two-faced consensus society consisting of a roughly equal group of potential officeholders controlled by wise and majestic rulers. Thanks to the books under review, we can understand much better the origins and birth of this new transitional society and its relationship with the classical revival.

11

HANS BARON'S RENAISSANCE

I

Because Hans Baron died in the month in which these two volumes were published, they inevitably become memorial volumes and this review a form of obituary. Yet in some ways it is the wrong moment to assess Baron's achievement, since we are still too close to him and to the reaction which his famous and controversial *Crisis of the early Italian renaissance* provoked. It came out in 1955 just after Eugenio Garin's *L'umanesimo italiano* and *Medievo e Rinascimento*.[1] Together these books created the world of Florentine civic humanism I entered as a 'beginning student', in which citizens "governing the republic applied themselves to philosophy and philosophizing governed the republic".[2] I subsequently read Baron's 1930s essays on Cicero and Franciscan poverty, which provided the hard core for his later constructions and the revisions that went on until his death. To read them again in these two volumes is to follow the development of one of the leading renaissance scholars in this century.

The problem for all renaissance historians *post* Burckhardt lies in defending their field from encroachment by medievalists and early modernists and from wholesale destruction by *longue-durée* hedge-slashers. Jacob Burckhardt's *Civilization of the Renaissance in Italy* was

---

This paper was originally published in the «Historical Journal», XXXIII, 1990, reviewing HANS BARON, *In Search of Florentine Civic Humanism. Essays on the Transition from Medieval to Modern Thought*, 2 vols, Princeton, Princeton University Press, 1988.

[1] Bari, Laterza, 1952 and 1954. *L'umanesimo italiano* was first published in German, *Der italienische Humanismus*, in 1947.

[2] ANGELO SEGNI's *Vita di Donato Acciaiuoli*, quoted by GARIN, *Medievo e Rinascimento*, p. 211.

itself quickly attacked by medievalists for its apparent prejudice against the middle ages, dreaming under their veil of superstition ("as if during the Middle Ages all cultural life had been sound asleep", Burckhardt himself said, when apologizing to his students in Zürich for using the fashionable term 'renaissance' "for want of something better").[3] And since then it has been systematically modified by socio-economic historians of the Weber/Sombart school and by comparative '*Annalistes*' – like Peter Burke, according to his self-definition, whose recent account of early-modern Italian culture has been able to dispense with the concept of renaissance altogether.[4]

From this perspective, Hans Baron's painstaking attempts to distinguish medieval from modern, his whiggish concern for "civic humanism" and his 'crisis' theory of a renaissance which began neatly "around 1400", after Giangaleazzo Visconti's attack on Florence, appear out-of-date and misguided. Since to understand all is to forgive all, it is now explained that he was "a scholar who grew up during the Weimar Republic and remains committed to republican values", the "great appeal for democratic and liberal opinion" of his civic humanism and his "moving picture" of Florence's lone stand against Visconti tyranny in 1402 being due to our identification with Florence as "a precursor to Britain's defiance of Hitler in 1940".[5] His engaged and unfashionable liberalism is nevertheless enough to condemn him today in Anglo-Saxon historical circles.

So to follow Baron "In search of Florentine civic humanism" creates initial ennui: do we need so many articles on 'civic spirit', 'civic wealth', 'civic humanism' and 'the active life'? Is it a good idea to give a face-lift to old articles by cladding their sound but old-fashioned structures with smart post-modernist facades? And don't some of the

---

[3] Quoted by BARON, *Burckhardt after a century*, vol. II, p. 157, from W. KAEGI's 1956 biography of Burckhardt.

[4] PETER BURKE, *The historical anthropology of early modern Italy. Essays on perception and communication*, Cambridge, Cambridge University Press, 1987, defining his own position in *The Italian renaissance*, Oxford, Polity Press, 1986, p. 4; cf. also Sir ERNST GOMBRICH's attack on 'Burckhardt's Hegelianism', *In search of cultural history*, Oxford, Clarendon Press, 1969, pp. 14-25.

[5] BURKE, *The Italian renaissance*, p. 38, added to this recently revised version of his 1972 *Culture and society in renaissance Italy, 1420-1450*, London, Batsford, where Baron is explained instead merely as a pupil of Walter Goetz (p. 18); D. HAY and J. LAW, *Italy in the age of the renaissance, 1380-1530*, London, Longmans, 1989, p. 238. Cf. W. K. FERGUSON, *The interpretation of Italian humanism: the contribution of Hans Baron*, 1956, reprinted in his *Renaissance Studies*, New York, Harper Row, 1970, pp. 111-121.

changes of date and style create a feeling of insecurity rather than confidence? ("Two years earlier" changed to "A few years earlier", "probably about 1360" to "Not long after 1360", and the terse "Would this scholastic equilibrium endure, if the pendulum were to swing back to the humanistic enthusiasm of the twelfth century?" to the ponderous "But gradualism did not endure when the pendulum swung back to a strong enthusiasm for Antiquity, an enthusiasm comparable to that which the twelfth-century renaissance had shown for certain ancient authors". Valuable though it is to have updated bibliographies and new additional material, might this information not have been better confined to notes or appendices, leaving the articles to speak with their original force and clarity?

But whatever our first misgivings may be, the total impact of these collected writings is triumphantly to vindicate Baron's importance as the catalyst of a new approach to the renaissance. Most interesting from this point of view are the last three autobiographical essays, his centenary assessment of Burckhardt in 1960, his account of his own development, delivered in 1965 when he was awarded the Galileo Galilei prize for work in Italian history, and his 1970 'defence' of his *Crisis*. His criticism of Burckhardt in the first enables us to understand his own position within the renaissance historiographical tradition. Defending Burckhardt from charges of underestimating medieval achievements and the importance of religion, he nevertheless accuses him of "one-sided emphasis on the 'individualism' of the Renaissance" to the exclusion of earlier enlightenment and romanticist understanding of "the crucial role of city-state life" – due, Baron suggests, to his retreat "with abhorrence from the rising democratic trend" in the 1840s. This withdrawal (combined with Burckhardt's sympathy for Caesar, revealed in his lectures) prevented him from understanding the contrast between the Tre- and Quattrocento, whose novelty according to Baron was due not to the despots or isolated individualists, as Burckhardt thought, but to men who "were deeply involved in the political struggles and public life of their age": "one is amazed to find that the great master of objective historicism was unable to recognize that two ages and *Weltanshauungen* had clashed". Here, in a nutshell, are Baron's key ideas: changing attitudes as a definition of renaissance modernity, and the importance of 'civic life' in encouraging these changes, thanks to the "delicate balance between unusual stimulation and unusual violation of privacy" that it provided.

Baron, we learn from the second essay, was influenced as a student at Leipzig by the medievalist Walter Goetz, who taught him "that history should be a study of both politics and culture", as well as by the better known Wilhelm Dilthey and Ernst Troeltsch. Arriving in Italy in 1925 to study the impact of Florentine neoplatonism on northern humanists, he quite quickly changed direction. Giving his platonic material to P. O. Kristeller (who included it in his *Supplementum ficinianum*, Florence, Olschki, 1937, see there, vol. I, p. ii), he turned instead to work on Leonardo Bruni, publishing his *Humanistisch-philosophische Schriften* in 1928. He was already attracted by what he identified as Bruni's new economic and political attitudes, and his new-look Bruni helped to set the trend – which I among others followed – towards revaluing the work of Florentine chancellors. So it is perhaps ironic that because Baron died before completing his projected biography of Bruni, Bruni the innovator is now almost the only renaissance chancellor still without a biography.[6]

By 1932 Baron had extended his interest to Machiavelli, arguing in a paper in the *Historische Zeitschrift* on *New historical and psychological ways of thinking: from Petrarch to Bruni and Machiavelli*, that it was the early years of the fifteenth century which were crucial for the development of new attitudes to fortune and virtue. Three years later he published in «Civiltà Moderna» *La Rinascita dell'etica statale romana*, which was quoted by Delio Cantimori in his influential article *Rhetoric and politics in Italian humanism* published in the opening issue of the «Journal of the Warburg and Courtauld Institutes» in 1937. And in the following year he published in England and America the two articles that remain fundamental to renaissance studies, *Cicero and the Roman civic spirit in the middle ages and early renaissance* and *Franciscan poverty and civic wealth as factors in the rise of humanistic wealth* (the first in the «Bulletin of the John Rylands Library», now revised, the second in «Speculum», now expanded into three articles. Also in 1938, Baron published an article in «History»

---

[6] See E. GARIN, *I cancellieri umanisti della Repubblica fiorentina da Coluccio Salutati a Bartolomeo Scala*, first published in the «Rivista storica italiana», LXXXI, 1959, pp. 185-208, and R. BLACK's review article in «The Historical Journal», XXIX, 1986, pp. 991-1003, describing the turning from interest in Bruni in the 1960s to his mentor Coluccio Salutati (discussing, among others, R. G. WITT's biography of Salutati, *Hercules at the Crossroads,*, 1983, and my biography of *Bartolomeo Scala*, 1979; BLACK's own biography of Scala's predecessor, *Benedetto Accolti*, was published by Cambridge University Press in 1985. Baron refers to his planned biography, *The life and literary work of Leonardo Bruni*, in vol. II, p. 211.

on *The background of the early Florentine renaissance*, which was translated and published in the same year in «La Rinascita» (the opening number of the journal of the Istituto Nazionale di Studi sul Rinascimento in Florence, now called «Rinascimento»).

Quoting this article in the same journal three years later, in 1941, Eugenio Garin referred to Baron's repeated insistence on the idea that, in the renaissance, "the citizen could only free himself from his medieval past by adhering closely to classical ideas of citizenship".[7] The diaspora of Jewish scholars from Nazi Germany directly encouraged the diaspora of Baron's ideas, as we can see. But it would be a mistake to attribute the latter's success to political events alone. Already as Privatdozent in the university of Berlin, Baron had aroused the interest of one student, Nicolai Rubinstein, in the renaissance through the stimulus of his ideas; and in the course of the 1930s these ideas made their mark on other scholars – Cantimori, Garin, Kristeller, who like Rubinstein later became leaders in the field – and through them on the opening issues of two new (and still vital) renaissance journals.

So when the *Crisis* (with its companion, *Humanistic and political literature in Florence and Venice at the beginning of the Quattrocento*) emerged in 1955, it gave birth to a thesis that had had a long gestation.[8] Because it presents a mainly political explanation for the renaissance, drawing a direct analogy to Nazi Germany (as well as to Mussolini's Italy, invoked in a note subsequently expunged from the 1966 reprint), it is easy to dismiss it nowadays as unfashionable and biased, forgetting that Baron's influence on pre-war historians was wider and less easily defined – what Garin later called "an orientation which had not yet fixed its results in definite interpretations", based as much on sociology as politics.[9] More influential than the

---

[7] *Noterelle di filosofia del Rinascimento*, «La Rinascita», vol. IV, 1941, p. 409, which begins: 'Hans Baron ha insistito più volte sul concetto che, nel Rinascimento, il cittadino non si potè liberare dal passato medievale si non stringendosi strettamente alle idee classiche del civismo'.

[8] *The crisis of the early Italian renaissance. Civic humanism and republican liberty in a age of classicism and tyranny*, 2 vols., Princeton, Princeton University Press, 1955, reprinted in a single revised volume in 1966; *Humanistic and political literature* was published by Harvard University Press, Cambridge, Mass., 1955.

[9] See GARIN's appreciation in *Renaissance studies in honor of Hans Baron*, ed. A. MOLHO and J. A. TEDESCHI, Florence, Sansoni, 1971, p. LXI: "l'efficacia di un orientamento che non aveva ancora fissato i suoi risultati in interpretazioni definite". Also influential in this period was ALFRED VON MARTIN's pioneering *Soziologie der Renaissance*, 1932, English translation Ke-

Crisis on innovative books like Lauro Martines' *The social world of the Florentine humanists, 1390-1460* (1963) was Baron's declaration in America in 1939: "the sociological direction of historical research has profoundly changed the perspectives of the Renaissance period".[10]

II

So how have the perspectives of the renaissance period been changed by Baron? Criticism of his argument that 1400 was a *tournant* between the medieval and modern periods has ranged from the general to the specific, from rejecting the interdependence of events and ideas to refuting the detailed chronology on which it depends. Baron's crisis theory was itself a reaction to earlier gradualist explanations of the renaissance – "growing knowledge of ancient literature or of a gradual unfolding of *Trecento* ideas" and Burckhardt's growing individual 'autonomy' within tyrant-states. So now, as the wheel turns full circle, gradualism and progressive literary revival are back in favour at the expense of cataclysms and crises; and so too is what Baron has called "distrust of *quattrocento* republicanism".[11]

By demanding a clean break between the Tre- and Quattrocento, Baron has also exposed himself to charges of ignoring earlier republican literature. As Quentin Skinner puts it with inimitable clarity: "The first major difficulty with Baron's thesis about 'civic humanism' can be expressed at its simplest by saying that it underestimates the extent to which the Florentine writers of the early *quattrocento* were following in the footsteps of the medieval *dictatores*"; and elsewhere he questions Baron's contrast between Franciscan condemnation of riches and Florentine admiration for them as evidence of a medieval/modern divide, since riches were an ancient bone of contention between Stoics and Peripatetics and – as Alexander Murray has also demonstrated – were admired by medieval men as much as by

---

gan Paul, Trench, Trubner & Co, London, 1944, see FERGUSON's introduction to the Harper and Row Torchbook edition, New York, 1963. Baron's reference to Mussolini is in *Crisis*, 1955; II, p. 504, n. 38.

[10] Baron refers to Martines' *Social world* complementing *The crisis* "in all matters concerning the socio-economic structure and political role of Florentine Humanism', in vol. II, p. 18, p. 199, note.

[11] In *From Petrarch to Leonardo Bruni*, Chicago, Chicago University Press, 1968, p. 109.

'modern' Florentines.[12] Although Baron has responded to the criticism of medieval scholars like Charles Davis by discussing more fully the writings of Ptolemy of Lucca and Remigio Girolami and the question of poverty, it remains a dangerous enterprise to typify periods, as he does, on the basis of a few exceptional texts.[13]

Underlying these criticisms is the question of literary models and rhetoric. Crucial to Baron's argument that it was the political crisis of 1400-1402 that transformed "a classicism unconnected with the citizen's active life to civic humanism" is his redating of Bruni's *Dialogi* and *Laudatio*. By separating the first dialogue (which must have been written in mid-1401) from the second (which refers to the *Laudatio*), Baron re-dated the *Laudatio* and the second *Dialogo* more coherently to post-1402 and claimed them both as products of the new confident republicanism after Giangaleazzo Visconti's death. For Baron, part of the problem was to explain the apparent discrepancy between the unpatriotic utterances of the Florentine wool-merchant and humanist, Niccolò Niccoli, in the first dialogue (in attacking the heroic Trecento triad Dante, Petrarch and Boccaccio) with his recantation in the second. But as one of Baron's leading critics, Jerrold Seigal, pointed out, such discrepancies were the essence of literary dialogues and should not be taken seriously, that in fact throughout Niccoli was being used to disprove by his eloquence his perversely bourgeois argument about the uselessness of literary discussions.[14] Baron, in other words, was being much too serious about politics and too ignorant of literary matters. Recently it has been persuasively argued by David Quint that although Baron was probably wrong in contrasting the dialogues, he was right in regarding them as evidence of Bruni's republicanism, since despite this apparent recantation, Niccoli in fact retained "a staunchly republican and classicizing" position throughout.[15]

---

[12] *The foundations of modern political thought*, vol. I, pp. 43, 71; cf. A. MURRAY, *Reason and society in the middle ages*, Oxford, Clarendon Press, 1978, esp. ch. 4, and N. RUBINSTEIN, *Political theories in the renaissance*, in *The Renaissance. Essays in interpretation*, London and New York, Methuen, 1982, pp. 153-158.

[13] Vol. I, 8, pp. 114-115, 199-210, and C. T. DAVIS, *Brunetto Latini and Dante*, now reprinted in *Dante's Italy and other essays*, Philadelphia, University of Pennsylvania Press, 1984, esp. pp. 172-173, *Ptolemy of Lucca and the Roman Republic*, *ibid.*, pp. 254-289.

[14] *Civic humanism or Ciceronian rhetoric? The culture of Petrarch and Bruni*, «Past and Present», XXXIV, 1966, pp. 3-48, to which Baron replied in the same journal, vol. XXXVI, 1967, pp. 21-37. Baron summarized his redating in *From Petrarch to Leonardo Bruni*, pp. 102-137, with his final 'Defence' in vol. II, p. 18, pp. 194-211.

[15] *Humanism and modernity: a reconsideration of Bruni's Dialogues*, «Renaissance Quarterly», vol. XXXVIII, 1985, pp. 423-445.

To the uninitiated, this will reek of *odium theologicum* – definitely not an incitement to pursue renaissance history. But of course it has wider implications for us all. Dating does matter, since historical truth or falsehood can hang on it, and we must admire Baron's attention to dates and insistence on their importance. On the other hand, his evidence is often subjective and the chronological gap he creates between the two halves of the literary argument in *Dialogi* I and II is now too long to be convincing. What is surely important about his argument is its demonstration of the impact of professional humanists and propagandists on citizens like Niccoli and Gregorio Dati, a modest silk merchant who wrote a history which, according to Baron, demonstrates the new civic thinking. It was this that made the *Quattrocento* renaissance different from the earlier proto-renaissance. For what Baron's thesis successfully explains is not the revival of classical ideas (which were never lost) but its social basis in cities like Florence, as Baron initially proposed but lost sight of, through over-identifying with Florence's battle against 'tyranny' in 1400-1402.

III

Without wanting to revive Baron's thesis, we can see how fruitful it has been in offering new approaches to the problems he formulated. The economic underpinning of civic humanism has been explored by Lauro Martines to reveal a closer relationship between wealth and civic commitment than Baron proposed. Far from being "adversity's noblemen", in Charles Trinkaus' formulation, Florentine humanists – Martines argues – all belonged to the upper and upper-middle classes. Even low-born scholars from the provinces, like Bruni and Poggio, rapidly became rich and entered these classes through their profession, suggesting that humanism had a social function in facilitating the rise of new men.

The connection between wealth and civic humanism is even clearer in the case of Matteo Palmieri, owner of a drugs-and-spices shop and active statesman, whom Baron described as the Florentine "who brought Bruni's train of thought on *divitiae* to a climax". Not only has Palmieri's book on civic life, the *Vita civile*, been published since Baron wrote about it, but so too have Palmieri's *Ricordi fiscali*. This "obsessively detailed record" of taxes over nearly half a century, from 1427 to 1474, reveals that thanks to his vigilant bookkeeping (the recording instinct that also encouraged precocious Florentine history-writing), Palmieri was amazingly able to weather massive taxes to emerge with a profit over the entire period.[16] The contrast between Palmieri's confident civic spirit and the alienation of impoverished aristocrats "on the run" or sculking at home to escape imprisonment for debt (as Martines describes them) seems amply to vindicate, though with greater refinement, the argument of "Franciscan Poverty and Civic Wealth".

Another approach encouraged by Baron concerns the development of a new historical as well as political outlook from the events of the early Quattrocento. It was not only the famous 1402 crisis that was the catalyst here but also the growth of Florence's territorial state and overseas interests after acquiring Pisa and Livorno in 1406 and 1421, as Baron originally suggested in 1939 and repeated in 1970. Strange though it is to read that "the maturation of the new thought could not occur until Florence had annexed the Tuscan coast", Baron is entirely right to stress the importance of Florence's new empire in transforming old values and making the public language of Roman statism relevant, as debates in advisory meetings and diplomatic documents demonstrate.[17]

Baron also ascribed the growth of comparative and secular history-writing to the balanced states-system – or "equilibrium between regional states" – that developed in fifteenth-century Italy. Despite the 'weaknesses' of this balance-of-power idea in practice, we know from Mark Phillips's recent account of the "ordinary bourgeois" Marco Parenti's *Memoir* that it did play a part in his outlook and rational explanation of events: describing the space between Florence, Venice

---

[16] See MARTINES' recent article, *Forced loans: political and social strain in quattrocento Florence,* «Journal of Modern History», vol. LX, 1988, pp. 300-311, reviewing ELIO CONTI's edition of PALMIERI's *Ricordi fiscali, 1427-1474,* as well as his *L'Imposta diretta a Firenze,* and a new biography of Palmieri, whose *Vita civile* is edited by G. BELLONI, Florence, Sansoni, 1982. *Adversity's noblemen,* first printed in 1940, was reissued by Trinkhaus in 1965 with a preface defining his position on Baron's 'civic humanism'.

[17] Applying the 'Baron thesis' to *Consulte e Pratiche* debates, Gene Brucker finds evidence of a changed outlook among citizens after the later war of 1413-14, *Humanism, politics and the social order in early renaissance Florence,* in *Florence and Venice: comparisons and relations,* I, pp. 3-11; on changes in public and diplomatic language, R. FUBINI, *Osservazioni sugli "Historiarum Florentini Populi libri XX" di L. Bruni,* in *Studi di storia medievale e moderna per E. Sestan,* Florence, Olschki, 1980, I, esp. pp. 417-429; *Classe dirigente ed esercizio della diplomazia nella Firenze quattrocentesca,* in *I ceti dirigenti nella Toscana del Quattrocento,* esp. pp. 178-181; BROWN, *Bartolomeo Scala,* pp. 173-178 (Ital. ed. pp. 118-120) and *City and citizen,* pp. 295-296 above.

and Milan, as "quasi-equidistant in the form of a triangle", Parenti put forward the argument that Milan should be encouraged to become free like Florence and Venice, in order "to keep the peace of Italy strong, the third one always counterbalancing the other two if they wished to clash".[18] This view of Italian politics was in effect delusive, but as Phillips argues, the *Memoir* marks an important step on the way towards the new historical outlook of Machiavelli and Guicciardini, fitting neither the vernacular-chronicle nor the classical paradigm but progressively clarifying "the boundaries between private and public spheres that resulted in the modern conception of an impersonal and sovereign state".[19]

The republican experience was crucial to this process, since Parenti wrote his *Memoir* as a citizen, to record the overthrow of liberty by Medici tyranny in 1466. Because similar ideas underlie Baron's interpretation of Florentine historiography – and especially his analysis of Machiavelli, in which he neatly (though not to me convincingly) severs the pamphleteering *Prince* from the mature fruits of Florentine *Quattrocento* republicanism in the *Discourses* – we could say that here, too, Baron's insights have been vindicated by new evidence and interpretations. Although Florence remains at the centre of these studies, as in Baron's formulation, it is increasingly recognized as a model or 'pattern' of what happened in other cities, which Baron predicted would provide the basis for "a comparative phenomenology" of humanistic views on man and society.

Yet there is a gulf between Baron and contemporary approaches to the renaissance which we bridge at our peril. Whereas Baron is unilinear, talking of events being necessary for ideas to develop and decisive breaks ("now that chivalry had ceased to be the determining factor in Italian medieval life" the ideal of Franciscan poverty "began a victorious procession through all ranks of society"), historians now are multi-dimensional. Chivalry, courtly kow-towing and princely absolutism coexist with republicanism in the worlds of Marco Parenti and Machiavelli, and language is not always to be taken at face-value;

---

[18] *The Memoir of Marco Parenti*, p. 231; cf. p. 190: "In these times a large part of Italy was in a sense renewed by the succession of new princes after the deaths of their predecessors". For recent criticism of the balance-of-power idea, M. MALLET, *Diplomacy and war in later fifteenth-century Italy*, London, British Academy, 1983, pp. 267-270; H. C. BUTTERS, *Politics and diplomacy in late Quattrocento Italy: the case of the Barons' war (1485-86)*, in *Florence and Italy. Renaissance studies in honour of Nicolai Rubinstein*, pp. 13-14.

[19] *Memoir*, p. 273.

sometimes it is propaganda, sometimes description and sometimes, as Machiavelli and his friends knew so well, simply a game.[20] Here too the wheel has come full circle, for just as anti-republicanism is back in fashion after Baron's attempts to rescue the renaissance from its pre-war clutches, so too is rhetoric and philology. Although when he wrote the *Crisis*, he hoped to be able to expand renaissance humanism "beyond its 'rhetorical' and 'philological' dimension into a more complex phenomenon", it is Baron's political interpretations that now appear simplistic in the light of current de-constructed readings of renaissance texts.

Nevertheless, for those of us who believe that outlooks and values do change – even though "much more slowly than most men imagine"[21] – Baron is indispensable as a guide, even if we are less certain than he was of where the middle ages ended and the modern period began. We should be grateful to Princeton University Press for providing us with this beautifully-produced and footnoted edition of his reflections on change in history: a worthy *Memoir* in the best renaissance tradition.

---

20 MACHIAVELLI, *Lettere,* ed. GAETA, p. 374.

21 F. GUICCIARDINI, *Ricordi,* ser. C, 71, cf. B, 140, ed. SPONGANO, p. 82.

12

CHANGING VIEWS OF MACHIAVELLI

Writing in the Sixties, Sheldon Wolin evocatively described Machiavelli's world as one of permanent residence in Plato's Cave, a world of "fleeting sense impressions and phenomenal flux".[1] Inappropriate though this image seemed for the clear bright light of Machiavelli's republican Florence, with its open councils and piazza life-style, it is powerfully re-evoked by these three recent accounts of Machiavelli, the irreverent trickster, who relocated hell "as a suburb of paradise" and founded an arcane "mystery of state". If every writer mirrors his age, Wolin was clearly ahead of his time in anticipating the new direction that Machiavelli studies have taken. Instead of the "proto-political scientist and realist", we are now presented with a literary and fantasizing Machiavelli who expresses himself most revealingly through poems, plays, and 'whimsies' *(ghiribizzi)*.

There is in itself nothing new in this approach. We have for some time been scrutinizing Machiavelli's plays and poems for fresh insight into his world, encouraged by structuralist and post-structuralist attempts to decipher and offer alternative readings of his dichotomous political treatises. Despite the obvious dangers of relying on literature to write history, Machiavelli's imagination paradoxically affords better access to the political world in which he lived than the 'realistic' *Prince* – at least as interpreted in de Grazia's vivid and exciting *Machiavelli in Hell* and in Rebhorn's more thematic *Foxes and Lions.*

A review in the «Journal of Modern History», LXIII, 1991, pp. 407-412, of W. A. REBHORN *Foxes and Lions: Machiavelli's Confidence Men,* Ithaca, N. Y, Cornell University Press, 1988; S. DE GRAZIA, *Machiavelli in Hell,* Princeton, Princeton University Press, 1989, and D. S. DONALDSON, *Machiavelli and the Mystery of State*, New York, Cambridge University Press, 1988.

[1] *Politics and Vision. Continuity and Innovation in Western Political Thought,* Boston, Little, Brown, 1960, pp. 211-212.

By contrast, Donaldson's *Machiavelli and the Mystery of State* is concerned not with Machiavelli but with the way in which his political writings were later interpreted in England and France, but his story repeats the same pattern. The question we must ask is how they enrich our understanding of Machiavelli and help to resolve the old problems.

Confronted with the contrast between the Straussian promoter of despotism and the republican patriot – whose constant preoccupation was, as Quentin Skinner reminds us, political liberty – various strategies are possible to explain these inconsistencies.[2] The most obvious is to explain Machiavelli as a flexible relativist acting according to 'reason of state', as Friedrich Meinecke originally proposed.[3] Another is to integrate Machiavelli's two faces as progressive phases of his development – as he moved either from republicanism to acceptance of the need for princely rule (in *Discorsi*, bk. I, ch. 18), according to Federico Chabod's still widely accepted argument; or, according to Hans Baron's recent revision, from *The Prince*, which epitomized his practical thinking from 1498 to 1512, to the mature historical 'realism' of the three introductory prefaces in the republican *Discourses*.[4]

By turning the tables and reading Machiavelli's works not as political texts but "from the opposite direction", Rebhorn, writing as a professor of English literature, succeeds in demonstrating the importance of literary genres as vehicles for Machiavelli's expression. For too long historians have limited themselves to analyzing his writings within the classical republican tradition; if we are going to use his literary texts for political purposes, we must learn their language and models. Whether we can go beyond this to argue, as Rebhorn does, that these genres did not simply influence Machiavelli's writing but also his perception of reality, is where historians might take issue with this genre-tinted view of the world and prefer the more biographi-

---

[2] L. STRAUSS, *Thoughts on Machiavelli*, Seattle and London, University of Washington Press, 1958; Q. SKINNER, *The Foundations of Modern Political Thought*, I, esp. pp. 157-158, 170-171, 180-182.

[3] *Die Idee der Staatsrason*, Munich, Oldenbourg, 1924, tr. D. SCOTT, *Machiavellism: the Doctrine of Raison d'État*, New Haven, Conn., Yale University Press, 1957.

[4] F. CHABOD, *Machiavelli and the Renaissance*, London, Bowes and Bowes, 1958; H. BARON, *Machiavelli the Republican Citizen and Author of The Prince*, in *In Search of Florentine Civic Humanism*, II, pp. 101-151.

cal approach of de Grazia – although that too, as we shall see, has its weaknesses.

Rebhorn's main thesis is the importance in Machiavelli's writings of the role of the confidence-man or trickster, the *beffatore* or *ingannatore*. Free, amoral, egocentric, energy-charged, this figure not only encapsulates renaissance ideals but also provides Machiavelli with an ideal princely type – such as Cesare Borgia, who controlled his state by deception and public display, unexpectedly murdering his henchman Ramirro de Orco and leaving his body in two pieces on the piazza to "satisfy and amaze" the people.

It was Machiavelli's friend, Francesco Vettori, who declared "all the world is a confidence game" – from the religious to "lawyers, doctors, astrologers, the temporal princes and those around them". The implications of this idea, in terms of political manipulation and control, are explored by Rebhorn in the third chapter, where we enter the opaque world of Plato's cave in which appearances are all that count. Hence the importance of spectacles like Ramirro's body in the piazza, of public image-making to impress the crowd, "since men judge more by their eyes than by their hands, because all can see but few can feel", and – because the crowd is moved more by 'shadows' and fantasies than by the truth – of foxy guile or 'Machiavellian' deviousness.

Machiavelli's awareness of the importance of ritual and ceremony in political control made him not only original in his own day but also topical in ours, as this chapter "Spectacles of Violence and the Memory of Fear", demonstrates. The genre of the confidence-man provides a useful lens through which to focus on this view of the world, enabling us to spot the surprising number of references to *inganno* in Machiavelli's writings. Nevertheless, to use it as our only pair of reading-glasses for Machiavelli provides a biased and, overall, distorted view of his world, as becomes evident when we learn that Francesco Sforza, Cosimo and Lorenzo de' Medici, Henry IV and Prince Hal – as well as Machiavelli himself – are all confidence men. And by the time we reach *The Prince*, Rebhorn is forced to call on the help of another literary model or lens, the heroic warrior of ancient epics, in order to make sense of "this striking deformation" of the confidence man in Machiavelli's political and historical works.

Rebhorn's apparent unwillingness to admit the influence of history on this work, which Machiavelli famously claimed was based on the fruits of his hard-won experience, raises the question of the role of genre models in Machiavelli and the legitimacy of this way of reading his political writings. Do genres simply provide a useful vehicle or language in which to describe shared experience? Do they, rather, enjoy a political, manipulative role in demystifying new rulers through satire, serving as "encoded ideologies" in the way described by Annabel Patterson's discussion of Vergil's *Eclogues* and *Georgics*?[5] Or do they more profoundly mediate experience by providing the categories through which we perceive reality? Rebhorn suggests all three without distingishing clearly between them, unlike Machiavelli, who in a letter to Francesco Vettori drew a clear distinction between his serious talk and his jokes – though recognising that anyone reading his letters might find these changing modes difficult to understand.[6]

The same problem is posed in a different way by Sebastian de Grazia, who makes indiscriminate use of all Machiavelli's writings, stating – logically – that because they employ the same language whether they are light or serious works, they address the same audience. De Grazia's achievement is to present a totally comprehensive view of Machiavelli (I can think of scarcely a relevant text or saying not referred to) mediated entirely through Machiavelli's own language, which like a multi-focus lens constantly shifts and adapts to change. Quoting Machiavelli's letter to Vettori about "the mixture of levity and seriousness" in their correspondence, de Grazia describes this two-sidedness not only as a feature of Machiavelli's perception of people in general but also as typical of Machiavelli's own thought, "which changes with thought" according to "what he reads and with whom he talks". This is the quality that has made Machiavelli notoriously difficult to elucidate; but instead of forcing him into a particular tradition or mould (christian-pagan, republican-absolutist), de Grazia through a kaleidoscope of visual and well as verbal images succeeds in demonstrating his contradictions as well as his originality. For the first time we have a biography that is vivid, credible and readable.

Proceeding at first chronologically and, as it seems, inductively, we are gradually introduced to bigger topics: God, Love (in practice

---

[5] *Pastoral versus Georgic: The Politics of Virgilian Quotation*, in *Renaissance Genres*, ed. B. K. LEWALSKI, Cambridge, Mass. and London, Harvard University Press, 1986, pp. 241-267.

[6] Letter to Francesco Vettori, 31 Jan. 1515, *Lettere*, ed. GAETA, p. 374, quoted by DE GRAZIA, pp. 335-336.

and theory), and Politics. It soon becomes clear that far from simply reconstructing Machiavelli's life as it happens, we are in fact engaged in the pursuit of big teleological prey which we approach in ever-narrowing circles. The prey – as the title suggests, and the index reveals, 27 entries under 'God', 10 under 'Hell' ('congenial', 'lack of real suffering in', 'for men only', 'as suburb of paradise') – is Machiavelli's morality. The trail is Machiavelli's love of country ("the greatest good that one can do and the most pleasing to God, is that which one does for one's country", "I love my country more than my soul"). The clues are phrases and words like 'pleasing to God' (what is it to be a "friend of God's"?), love (what is the alchemy of love of country, is the patriot a dragon-slayer like St. George?) and country (is country the state, and "what is the point of it all?").

In an excellent section discussing the point of the state, de Grazia rightly highlights one passage in book II, chapter 2 of the *Discourses* which I would agree is unique in expressing Machiavelli's ideal of 'a free way of life': a state in which personal freedom to marry and to breed and educate offspring in the expectation of access to elective offices leads to economic and political freedom, which in turn generates greater wealth and prosperity. These views, together with an inherited ragbag of classical-christian ideas about providence, fortune and free will, provide Machiavelli with an everyday conceptual framework that makes him a republican. Combining these ideas with realistic pessimism about men's nature "as rational brutes hell-bent for ruin", Machiavelli is original – we are told – in insisting they must nevertheless "move towards the common good of the state or they are lost". Hence the need for a prince and for Machiavelli's moral novelties, 'The Ungolden Rule' ('do unto others what you expect they will do unto you'), 'First Blush Vice' (the licence permitted to 'the prince new' or *nuovo principe*, here consciously using Machiavelli's inverted word-order to suggest the novelty of his ideas), and 'the reform of Hell' into a patriots' club to prevent it from deterring the prince new from doing what is necessary for his country.

The sting has been removed not only from death but also from the dualisms that have bedevilled Machiavellian exegesis. Or has it? Although we may not dissent from de Grazia's conclusions, his methods of reaching them and his scholarly apparatus are open to criticism. Like Plato, whose discovery of justice in *The Republic* is misleadingly inductive ("Talley-ho, we are on the track ... we have been extremely stupid, the thing has been under our very noses from the start and we never saw it!"),[7] the painstaking trail to Machiavelli's novelty has in fact been under our noses for five years, ever since de Grazia wrote about Machiavelli's "underworld raids" in 1982.[8] His argument, repeated in this book, is that Machiavelli's discussions with the ancients are analogous to the *descensus ad inferos* of Socrates and other ancients, which effectively reduces hell for Machiavelli to no more than reading ancient books. Yet the analogy is achieved almost by sleight of hand, a quick transition from references to hell in the play *Belfagor* and to Circe's cave in *The Golden Ass* to "the story about Niccolò's going to otherworld and back himself" in his famous 1513 letter to Francesco Vettori ("I enter the courts of the ancient men of antiquity"), and thence to a posthumous and undocumented story about Machiavelli, according to which, when asked whether he would prefer to go to paradise with the blessed poor or to hell with the ancients, he replied that he would rather talk about the state with latter and go to hell.

Though translated in full on page 341, we are given neither the original text of this story nor any reference to its source, so it is easy to overlook the fact that apart from a passing reference to Machiavelli's 'famous dream' in 1549, there is no other evidence to support it before the seventeenth-century version in French used by de Grazia (which Villari cites in his full discussion of this anecdote).[9] This introduces my other criticism of de Grazia's book – its total lack of notes or scholarly apparatus other than quotations from Machiavelli himself. Initially this seems a daringly refreshing attempt to unclog the text of gratuitous notes, but when doubts arise about stories so central to the argument as the above, it becomes instead a severe limitation. How much better from a scholarly point of view is Rebhorn's reassuring apparatus, containing full quotations in both Italian and English in the text, easily accessible references in footnotes beneath and a full bibliography at the end.

So there are serious weaknesses in de Grazia's argument and methodology. In addition to reservations about his definition of hell, he

---

[7] *The Republic* IV, 432*d*, quoted by K. R. POPPER, *The Open Society and its Enemies*, London, Routledge and Kegan Paul, 1966, I, pp. 99-100.

[8] *Crossings to another world: Machiavelli and Others*, «Journal of the History of Ideas», XLV, 1984, pp. 145-151.

[9] P. VILLARI, *Machiavelli e i suoi tempi*, Milan, Hoepli, 1897, pp. 367-371, quoting the text in French on p. 370, note 1.

also seems to misinterpret what Machiavelli says in *Discourses* book II, chapter 5, about whether the world is eternal (as Aristotle believed) or not. Far from doubting it himself, as de Grazia suggests, Machiavelli deftly removes the grounds on which he believes most people might doubt it, lack of evidence, by explaining how such evidence may have come to be destroyed. De Grazia is also wrong to suggest that Machiavelli proposed to enlarge the Great Council in his 1520 *Discursus* by increasing it to a thousand or "at least six hundred citizens", when in fact it originally consisted of over three thousand citizens with sovereign functions which Machiavelli in his 1520 blueprint removed. It was, as I have argued above, more restrictive that it might appear.[10] These are small matters in view of the exciting new-look Machiavelli we have been offered, but they illustrate the dangers as well as the strengths of relying so heavily on the flickering images projected by Machiavelli's *fantasia.*

The combined insights of both Rebhorn and dẹ Grazia prepare us for the subject of Peter Donaldson's *Machiavelli and the Mystery of State.* Here Rebhorn's confidence-man and de Grazia's prince-new are first reflected in Cardinal Pole's 1538-1539 *Apologia*, in which he argues that Henry VIII's claim to be head of state, his desecration of shrines and monasteries and his destruction of his opponents all stemmed from adherence to the secret doctrine of *The Prince*, taught to him by Thomas Cromwell. The doctrine was secret because Cromwell failed to disclose to Henry the source of these ideas: and it already contained an element of paradox and deceit through Machiavelli's claim to have written *The Prince* to hasten the downfall of the Medici (which was reported to Pole by Florentines). In this form it was promoted to the status of an arcane prophetic utterance. In the hands of William Thomas, clerk to the Privy Council, and Bishop Stephen Gardiner, by contrast, Machiavelli's *Prince* and *Discourses* were used not as evidence of anti-Christ at work but to provide practical advice for Henry and Philip of Spain as princes-new. Between 1584 nd 1588 Machiavelli's major writings were printed (in Italian) for the first time in England by John Wolfe, who had studied with the Giunti in Florence in the 1570s and returned to England to specialize in publishing foreign books on the Index under false imprint. The secrecy and equivocation involved in this piratical printing further encouraged the diffu-

---

[10] See *Platonism in fifteenth-century Florence*, p. 239 above.

sion of Machiavellian ideas about the value of flexibility and cunning as republican arcana.

It was in France in the seventeenth century that Machiavelli became associated, through the additional concept of reason of state, with the ideology of sacred kingship – the *arcana imperii*, Donaldson calls it. Jean Bodin was the first to associate him with it in his *Methodus*,[11] but the key pieces in this tradition are Arnold Clapmar's *De arcanis rerumpublicarum* (1605), Gabriel Naudé's *Considérations poltiques sur les coups d'état* (1639), and Louis Machon's *Apologie pour Machiavel*, first written in 1643 (and revised in 1668) at the suggestion of Cardinal Richelieu, who was amazed that everyone writing about politics "attended to this rare spirit [Machiavelli] without one of them ever having had the courage or the heart to defend the indispensable and reasonable maxims of this solid and truthful writer". Adopting a 'sensible' approach to the Bible as well as to classical political writings, Machon's Machiavelli is "a misunderstood Christian moralist", whose ethical principles were nevertheless reserved "for the gods and sovereigns of the earth". The contrast between Donaldson's *arcana imperii* for the prince-new and the cunning, foxy *arcana republicana* aptly represents the difference between de Grazia and Rebhorn: reading all three we are well prepared to understand the changing faces of this still not totally reconcilable figure.

[11] Jean Bodin, *Methodus ad facilem historiarum cognitiarum*, Paris, 1566, English tr. by B. Reynolds, New York, W. W. Norton, 1945.

INDEX OF NAMES

Finito di stampare nel settembre 1992
con i tipi della Tiferno Grafica
di Città di Castello